America's Democracy

America's Democracy

THE IDEAL AND THE REALITY

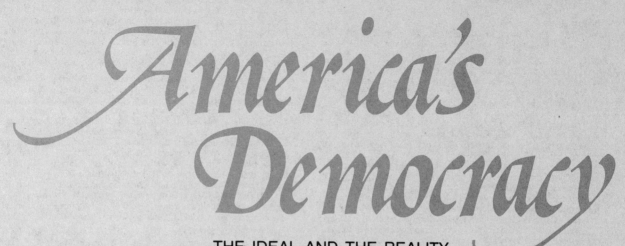

America's Democracy

THE IDEAL AND THE REALITY

Fred R. Harris

University of New Mexico

Scott, Foresman and Company   Glenview, Illinois
Dallas, Texas   Oakland, New Jersey   Palo Alto, California
Tucker, Georgia   London, England

ACKNOWLEDGMENTS

Photographs

Endsheets: "Three Flags" by Jasper Johns. From the collection of Mr. and Mrs. Burton Tremaine, Meriden, Connecticut.

Part 1: pp. 2–3: The Bettmann Archive; p. 4: Martin A. Levick/Black Star; p. 7: Reproduced from the Collections of the Library of Congress; p. 8 (left): The Bettmann Archive; p. 8. (right): Brown Brothers; p. 10 (left): Reproduced from the Collections of the Library of Congress; p. 10 (right): The Bettmann Archive; p. 14: Historical Pictures Service, Inc.; p. 18 (top): The Bettmann Archive; p. 18 (center, bottom): Historical Pictures Service, Inc.; p. 20: Historical Pictures Service, Inc.; p. 23: Elinor S. Beckwith/Taurus Photos; p. 26: Historical Pictures Service, Inc.; p. 32 (top): The Bettmann Archive; p. 32 (bottom): Historical pictures Service, Inc.; p. 35: Historical Pictures Service, Inc., p. 40 (top left, top right, bottom right): The Bettmann Archive; p. 40 (bottom left): Historical Pictures Service, Inc.; p. 44 (all): Historical Pictures Service, Inc.; p. 53: Jean-Pierre Laffont/Sygma; p. 59: The Bettmann Archive; p. 63: Owen Franken/Sygma; p. 64: Reproduced from the Collections of the Library of Congress; p. 68: Gerhard E. Gscheidle/Peter Arnold; p. 70: David Margolin/Black Star; p. 75: Ted Cowell/Black Star; p. 80: Photograph by Dorothea Lange. War Relocation Authority in the National Archives; p. 81: UPI; p. 91: Martin A. Levick/Black Star.

Part 2: pp. 98–99: James H. Karalos/Peter Arnold; p. 100: UPI; p. 106: Elliot Erwitt/Magnum; p. 109: UPI; p. 111: Wide World Photos; p. 118: Ellis Herwig/Stock, Boston; p. 123: George Ballis/Black Star; p. 128: Frank Johnston/Black Star; p. 131 (top): Brown Brothers; p. 131 (bottom): Martin A. Levick/Black Star; p. 136 (top left): Michael D. Sullivan; p. 136 (top right): Martin A. Levick/Black Star; p. 136 (bottom left): UPI; p. 138: Photograph by Byron. The Byron Collection. Museum of the City of New York; p. 140 (left): Brown Brothers; p. 140 (right): Historical Pictures Service, Inc.; p. 147: Gerhard E. Gscheidle/Peter Arnold; p. 155: Arthur Grace/Stock, Boston; p. 165: TVA.

Part 3: pp. 168–169: Eric Kroll/Taurus Photos; p. 170: Michael D. Sullivan; p. 176: Paul D. Hain; p. 178: Richard Kalvar/Magnum Photos; p. 180: Michael D. Sullivan; p. 185: Sybil Shelton/Peter Arnold; p. 187: Burk Uzzle/Magnum Photos; p. 188: © 1980 Children's Television Workshop, "Ernie" and "Bert" © 1980 Muppets, Inc. p. 191: Carl Weese/Rapho-Photo Researchers; p. 196: UPI; p. 200: Jan Lukas/Rapho-Photo Researchers; p. 209: Martin A. Levick/Black Star; p. 210: UPI; p. 217: Michael C. Hayman/Photo Researchers; p. 220: D. Dietz/Stock, Boston; p. 223: Arthur Grace/Sygma; p. 227: Mark Godfrey/Magnum Photos; p. 230: Michael D. Sullivan; p. 234: UPI; p. 247: Ken Hawkins/Sygma; p. 256 (left): Jean-Pierre Laffont/Sygma; p. 256 (right): Henri Bureau/Sygma; p. 266: Jean-Pierre Laffont/Sygma;

p. 279: Daniel S. Brody/Stock, Boston; p. 281: © Joel Gordon 1978; p. 294: Richard Kalvar/Magnum Photos; p. 295: Michael Loyd Carlebach/Nancy Palmer Photo Agency; p. 300: J. Berndt/Stock, Boston; p. 303: Bruce Roberts/Rapho-Photo Researchers; p. 309: Bob Adelman/Magnum Photos; p. 311: Jeff Albertson/Stock, Boston; p. 315: Photographs by Jon Naar and Random House, Inc. from *Design for a Limited Planet*, Ballantine, 1976; p. 316: Michael D. Sullivan.

Part 4: pp. 326–327: Peter Southwick/Stock, Boston; p. 328: Alex Webb/Magnum Photos; p. 339: Michael D. Sullivan; p. 354: Ellis Herwig/Stock, Boston; p. 361 (top left): Mark Godfrey/Magnum Photos; p. 361 (top right, bottom): Dennis Brack/Black Star; p. 374: Dennis Brack/Black Star; p. 383: UPI; p. 388: Dirck Halstead/Time-Sygma; p. 390: Adam Scull/Black Star; p. 392: Dennis Brack/Black Star; p. 408: Dennis Brack/Black Star; p. 422: Arthur Grace/Stock, Boston; p. 426: Arthur Grace/Sygma; p. 433: UPI; p. 441: Martin A. Levick/Black Star; p. 443: D.B. Owen/Black Star; p. 459: Flip Shulke/Black Star; p. 464: John J. Lopinot/Black Star; p. 469: Jan Lukas/Photo Researchers; p. 478: Peter Southwick/Stock, Boston; p. 481: Owen Franken/Stock, Boston; p. 492: Michael D. Sullivan; p. 495: Chris Maynard/Stock, Boston; p. 498: UPI; p. 502: (top) Bill Grimes/Black Star; p. 502 (bottom): Peter Southwick/Stock, Boston.

Part 5 pp. 506–507: Owen Franken/Stock, Boston; p. 508: UPI; p. 512: James Vaughan/Black Star; p. 514: UPI; p. 518: UPI; p. 520: Ginger Chih/Peter Arnold; p. 521: UPI; p. 528: UPI; p. 528 (right): Arthur Grace/Sygma; p. 533 (top left): Ted Rozumalski/Black Star; p. 533 (bottom right): Andrew Schneider/Black Star; p. 536: Diego Goldberg/Sygma; p. 539: Daniel S. Brody/Stock, Boston; p. 541: Michael Crummett/Black Star; p. 550: Arthur Grace/Sygma; p. 552: UPI; p. 565: T. Korody/Sygma; p. 572 (top, bottom left) UPI; p. 572 (bottom right): Dennis Brack/Black Star; p. 574 (left): Courtesy of the Hoover Institution, Stanford University; p. 574 (right): Wide World Photos; p. 584: Sipa Press/Black Star; p. 590: Austerlitz/Magnum Photos; p. 594: UPI; p. 598: Dennis Brack/Black Star; p. 604: D.B. Owen/Black Star; p. 610: Mark Godfrey/Magnum Photos; p. 618: Sipa Press/Black Star.

Part 6: pp. 620–621: "Three Flags" by Jasper Johns. From the Collection of Mr. and Mrs. Burton Tremaine, Meriden, Connecticut.

Maps, Charts, and Tables

Part 2. From Figure 6–1, Burns, Peltason, Cronin, *Government by the People*, National Edition, © 1978, p. 133, 10th ed. Reprinted by permission of Prentice-Hall, Inc., Englewood Cliffs, New Jersey.
   "The 500 Largest Industrial Corporations (ranked by sales)," from *Fortune 500* p. 270, May 7, 1979, Time Inc. From "Number of Corporate Mergers and Acquistions," *Law Enforcement/Judiciary-2*, pp. 482–485. © March 17, 1979, Congressional Quarterly, Inc.

Part 3. From Sidney Verba and Norman H. Nie, "Citizen Participation: How Much? How Widespread?," p. 31 and "The Participation Input," pp. 98–100, *Participation in America: Political Democracy and Social Equality.* Copyright 1972, Sidney Verba and Norman H. Nie. From Edgar Litt, "Civic Education, Community Norms, and Political Indoctrination," *American Sociological Review, No. 1, Vol. 28,* Table 2, p. 72. Copyright 1963, Journal of the American Sociological Association. From M. Kent Jennings and Richard G. Niemi, "The influence of families and schools," *The Political Character of Adolescence,* p. 39. © 1974 by Princeton University Press. Table 2.1, in adapted form. Wolfinger, Shapiro, Greenstein, *Dynamics of American Politics,* © 1976, p. 96. Reprinted by permission of Prentice-Hall, Inc., Englewood Cliffs, New Jersey. From Dean Jaros, et al., "The malevolent leader: political socialization in an American sub-culture," *The American Political Science Review, No. 62,* pp. 564–575. Copyright 1968, The American Political Science Association. From Kenneth P. Langton and M. Kent Jennings, "Political socialization and the High School civics curriculum in the United States," *The American Political Science Review,* pp. 852–67. Copyright 1968, The American Political Science Association. From Mark R. Levy and Michael S. Kramer, "Methodological Note," *The Ethnic Factor,* p. 225. © 1972, 1973, The Institute of American Research, Inc. Reprinted by permission of Simon and Schuster, a Division of Gulf and Western Corporation.
   From "Candidates, congress, and constituents," Series 70, No. 7, Report 5. CBS News Poll. From Burns W. Roper, "Public Perception of Television and Other Mass Media: A Twenty-Year Review, 1959–1978," p. 3. Reprinted by permission of The Roper Organization,

Library of Congress Cataloging in Publication Data

Harris, Fred R. 1930-
   America's democracy.

   Includes bibliographies and index.
   1. United States—Politics and government.
I. Title.
JK274.H22   320.9′73   79-22626
ISBN 0-673-15162-X

Preface

I was once involved in a spirited discussion in Moscow with Georgi Arbatov, the Soviet Union's principal "Americanologist." He took me to task for what he charged were serious political and economic failings in the American system. I probably know more about the failings (and the strengths) of our system than he does, but didn't feel it was my proper role as a U.S. senator to travel around the world at taxpayers' expense to criticize my home country. So, partly to change the subject, I said, "You have me at a disadvantage, Mr. Arbatov. American scholars are not allowed to study the ways economic and political decisions are made in the Kremlin. Ours, on the other hand, is an *open* system, which you can and do study freely."

Arbatov paused only briefly. "That is no disadvantage to you," he said. "We study your system, and we still don't understand it!"

Growing up in the American political system, studying our country's history, and perhaps taking a government or civics course in high school, most of us probably feel that we know how American government works. At first glance, especially to one raised in it, the American system seems neatly organized and simple. But, as Arbatov's comment indicated, that first impression is deceptive. In some ways, the American political system is like the English language. It was discovered during World War II that people who learn to speak only 800 English words can express every thought imaginable. But if people want to go further and learn to *read* and *write* English, they soon find that the language is a labyrinth of complexity. A student new to English learns, for example, that it is strange but true that "the train slowed *up*" means the same thing as "the train slowed *down*." A person who wants to go past the *forms* of American government and learn how things really work—and how to influence policy-making—is faced with similar complexity.

As a result of my experience teaching introductory American government courses, I have undertaken to write *America's Democracy* with five goals in mind. First, I want students to have a textbook that is engaging and easily read. No nuance of complex ideas is left out or glazed over, but the emphasis is on communicating nuances and complexities in understandable, useable form.

Second, this is a book of fundamentals; the principles, forms, and issues of the American political system are clearly and fully stated, and attention is given to the historical context of their origin and development.

Third, the fundamentals are tied in with current political actors and events to indicate their immediacy and relevance for our lives today.

Fourth, *America's Democracy* recognizes that a person who learns "how" government policy is made—how a bill goes through Congress, for example—should also have an opportunity to learn "why" policy turns out the way it does.

Finally, this book emphasizes political participation and the value of such participation, both for society and for individual participants. The ways and means of political participation are given special attention.

In line with these goals, *America's Democracy* has certain unique features. In addition to the usual chapters found in American government textbooks, there are separate chapters on political socialization and on the tensions in the relationship between capitalism and democracy. There is a separate chapter on *direct* citizen participation through such nonelectoral vehicles as boycotts, tenants' organizations, and cooperatives. A section is devoted to the policy-making process, with special chapters on selected policy areas as illustrations. "Viewpoint" inserts on particular subjects appear within the chapters; they are separated from the main text and intended to spark thought and discussion. There are "how to" mini-manual inserts in fields ranging from how to conduct a vote canvass to how to file a civil rights complaint. There is a comprehensive discussion of modern democratic theory, which is centered around the question of whether more participation is desirable, and a chapter on methods for increasing participation. Finally, at the end of the book, the Declaration of Independence and the Constitution are printed in full.

To aid students in the use of the book, a *Study Guide* prepared by Professor Thomas E. Scism of the University of North Carolina at Asheville is available. This study guide includes an outline of each chapter, gives special emphasis to key terms and concepts, and contains fill-in-the-blank study questions. Professor Scism has also prepared a highly useful *Instructor's Manual* to assist those who teach from *America's Democracy*.

No book of this scope can be produced without the help of a great many people. A number of political scientists reviewed all or part of the book. Their names are listed on another page. I am grateful for their helpful suggestions and criticisms. I also appreciate very much the help I received from two outstanding student research assistants, Judith Bova and Michael Davis. My wife, LaDonna, was, as usual, an inspiration.

The people at Scott, Foresman and Company were a joy to work with. Bruce Borland helped to develop the book and its concepts. Robert Johnson was the superb political science editor who guided my work from start to finish. Charley Schaff did a first-rate job as copy editor. Lucy Lesiak's creative design and Sandy Schneider's picture editing resulted in a truly attractive text. Others—such as Jim Bradford, Jennifer Toms, and John

Armstrong—have contributed much to making this a book that we hope students will want to read and study—and keep.

I like today's students. I have seen them in every setting and in schools all over the country. They are serious and concerned about their futures. Sometimes I worry about the increased pressures on them to acquire "credentials" for whatever they are going to do next—get a job or enter a graduate or professional school. I dedicate this book to students and say to them: I hope that with the help of *America's Democracy*, the introductory American government course will turn out to be not only a useful credential for you but also an interesting and enlightening experience as well.

FRED R. HARRIS
Albuquerque, New Mexico

Postscript: At the end of the book, there is an evaluation form that I hope you will use. You can mail it to me without any postage to let me know what you think about the book and how it can be improved.

F.R.H.

Overview

Contents

America's Democracy:

The Ideal

Ideals, or standards of perfection, and *reality* are not simple concepts. Indeed, explaining what "reality" is has been the main preoccupation of philosophers throughout human history. But for our purposes, we can put these concepts in terms that anyone who has ever planted a seed will understand. The *ideal* is the picture on the front of the seed packet—the cluster of full, colorful marigolds, say, or the perfect, uniform pods of green beans—and *reality* is what sprouts and grows. They may or may not be the same.

In Part 1, we examine American political ideals, primarily from the standpoint of the people who first planted them. Even the seeds of these ideals were not always perfect, and they were not always intended to be. We will see that the seeds have been changed or improved since they were planted.

In Chapter 1, we consider the implications of the Declaration of Independence. In Chapter 2, we discuss the origins and meaning of the U.S. Constitution. In Chapter 3, we examine the Bill of Rights.

These chapters demonstrate that the American ideals of citizen participation in government and protection of human rights are well established, because of both historical inheritance and modern belief. We will begin to see that there is a dynamic tension between those ideals, on one hand, and our institutions and practices, on the other.

1 The Declaration of Independence

What Does America Stand For?

Soon after Jimmy Carter was sworn in as the thirty-ninth President of the United States in January 1977, he began to declare America's strong support for human rights throughout the world.[1] He admitted that America itself did not have a perfect record on human rights, but he announced that he would seriously consider reducing or eliminating aid to foreign countries that dealt unfairly or inhumanely with their own citizens.[2] At the same time, President Carter wrote a widely publicized letter of encouragement to Andrei Sakharov, a dissident within the Soviet Union, and he warmly and publicly received another, Vladimir Bukovsky, as a visitor in the White House.

President Carter's campaign in support of human rights around the world received widespread approval, as illustrated by this demonstration protesting the trial of a Soviet dissident.

Soviet leaders in Moscow took vigorous and vocal exception to these actions. Although the Soviet Union, together with thirty-four other nations, had signed the Helsinki Agreement in 1975—committing it to the recognition of human rights—Soviet officials argued that human rights within the Soviet Union were an internal matter that Carter had no business interfering with. One Soviet journalist in Washington criticized the United States for not including economic rights in our definition of human rights. He declared that in the Soviet Union, by contrast, the right to a job and the right to health care were considered to be human rights.

Some Americans also criticized Carter's statements, arguing that the statements might damage détente (lessening of tensions) with the

Soviet Union and might slow down progress toward an agreement with the Russians to limit military arms.[3] Other Americans, who thought that the U.S. itself had a long way to go to achieve complete and equal rights for all citizens, felt that Carter was being hypocritical.

President Carter was not to be swayed, however. As he put it, America has a "historical birthright" to champion human rights throughout the world.[4] He was saying, in essence, that the ideals expressed in the American Declaration of Independence of July 4, 1776, are universal and that all people have a right to strive for them. Indeed, throughout American history the Declaration has stood as the basic statement of the ideals upon which this nation rests. In 1863, as our country was being torn apart by the Civil War, Lincoln's Gettysburg Address referred to the Declaration, not to the Constitution, as the source of the ideal of "government of the people, by the people, for the people."

It was in support of these ideals—human rights and government by the people—that the signers of the Declaration pledged to each other ". . . our lives, our Fortunes, and our sacred Honor." But what do these ideals mean? Where did they come from? What do they have to do with us today?

THE AMERICAN REVOLUTION

During the century and a half following the first settlement at Jamestown (1607), the British colonies in America developed a considerable degree of local autonomy and self-government, partly because they were three thousand miles across a treacherous ocean from their British homeland. Colonial assemblies assumed the power to decide for themselves whether to provide funds to pay for government functions within the colonies. According to the research of three noted American historians, "Nowhere else in the world at the time did so large a proportion of the people take an active interest in public affairs."[5] American colonial merchants, shippers, wealthy planters, family farmers, artisans, trappers and traders, and land speculators—and their employees and slaves—developed an increasingly robust colonial economy and system of commerce.

Until the mid-1700s, the relationship between the American

---

[1]*Time* (February 21, 1977).

[2]*Weekly Compilation of Presidential Documents,* 13, no. 14 (General Services Administration, April 4, 1977): 473.

[3]*Time* (February 21, 1977; March 7, 1977; March 28, 1977).

[4]Speech by President Carter to United Nations, March 17, 1977, *Weekly Compilation of Presidential Documents,* 13, no. 12 (General Services Administration, March 21, 1977): 401.

[5]T. Harry Williams, Richard N. Current, and Frank Freidel, *A History of the United States to 1877,* 3rd ed. (New York: Alfred A. Knopf, 1969), p. 125.

colonies and Britain was a relatively easy and mutually beneficial one. Each needed the assistance of the other to counter the French Canadian threat to the British-backed colonial interests, such as the land and fur trade in the Ohio Valley. Thus, the Whig party in the British Parliament, led by William Pitt the Elder, was willing to accord the American colonies a large measure of autonomy, or self-rule, and the colonies were willing to give Britain their loyalty.

This easy relationship was to change dramatically because of two watershed events: the French and Indian War (1754–1763) and the advent of George III to the throne of England in 1760.

The French and Indian War resulted in the defeat of France in America. This defeat weakened the bond of military interdependence between the American colonies and the British homeland by eliminating their chief opponent.[6] Another result of the French and Indian War was that the British government wound up with a very large war debt.

In the middle of these war years, George III became king of England. Although he was a constitutional monarch, limited in authority by the powers of Parliament, George III was also a shrewd politician who intended to rule as well as to reign. "His method of dominating parliament was not particularly subtle: he bought the necessary numbers by handing out sinecures to those who would do his will."[7] He began to undercut the power of the Whigs, and he replaced Pitt with George Grenville, a prime minister more to his liking.

The first act of George III during the Grenville ministry was the Proclamation of 1763, a royal decree closing *Western* America to settlement. Its purpose was to stop the dilution of the concentrated colonial market through westward emigration and to maintain the British monopoly on land speculation. The Sugar Act of 1764 meant new taxes to be paid by the colonists, and it provided for more effective enforcement than previous tax laws had. The Currency Act of the same year forbade the colonial assemblies from issuing any new paper money and required them to pay off and redeem the old. This law protected British merchants from having to accept payment in low-value, inflated currency. The Mutiny Act of 1765 compelled the colonists to help pay for the British troops that were now to be permanently stationed in the colonies. And the infamous Stamp Act, also of that same year, required the colonists to pay a tax on local legal documents, pamphlets, newspapers—and playing cards and dice!

Just as George III and Prime Minister Grenville had hoped, the colonies began to pay off handsomely. British revenues from the colonies increased tenfold over what they had been prior to 1763.

---

[6]E. James Ferguson, *The American Revolution* (Homewood, Illinois: Dorsey Press, 1974), p. 67.

[7]Clarence B. Carson, *The Rebirth of Liberty* (New Rochelle, N.Y.: Arlington House, 1973), p. 77.

The king probably expected some grumbling from the colonies, but he could never have imagined the heated resistance these arbitrary acts would actually engender. The king and his prime minister thought of the American colonies as children who had neither the means nor the desire to flaunt parental authority when, in fact, the colonies were more like young adults. There was indeed a storm of colonial protest, some of it violent. But in 1765, most of the colonists were still protesting as members of the British family. They were not yet ready to leave home.

The Virginia House of Burgesses, inflamed by the oratory of Patrick Henry (whose defiant words against Britain were called treason by some of his listeners), argued that the colonies could be taxed only by their own elected representatives. In 1765, nine colonies sent delegates to the Stamp Act Congress in New York and agreed to petition the king and the Parliament against taxation except by their provincial assemblies. This idea of "no taxation without representation" was probably a fairly novel one to most Englishmen at the time, since only one in twenty-five of them could vote for members of Parliament. Ireland and whole British boroughs were represented in Parliament by people whom the local citizens had not elected.

A colonial boycott, led by merchants in a number of American seaports, caused the British Parliament to repeal the Stamp Act. But the Parliament then adopted in its place the Declaratory Act, which claimed complete legislative jurisdiction over the colonies.

When New York refused to comply with the Mutiny Act, Parliament passed a law suspending the New York assembly altogether. A new law then imposed taxes on the importation into the colonies of a number of important items, including lead, paint, and tea. Renewed colonial protest produced another boycott of British goods. There were disorders in Boston, one of which became known in colonial propaganda as the "Boston Massacre." In the famous "Boston Tea Party," British tea, which was purposely priced lower than that of colonial merchants and bore the hated tax, was taken from a warehouse by Bostonians dressed as "Mohawks" and dumped in the bay.

More British repression followed. Parliament passed what were called the Coercive Acts which, among other things, closed Boston harbor and sought to reduce the right of the Massachusetts colony to govern itself. Throughout the colonies, "committees of correspondence" were formed as leaders began to decide upon the kind of concerted action that they felt should be taken. The First Continental Congress was finally called together in Philadelphia in September 1774. It drew up a list of grievances to be put before King George by petition. The delegates agreed upon a united economic boycott of Britain. They also took steps to prepare for military defense. And they agreed to meet again.

The lines were drawn—more irrevocably than some wanted. By

Opposition to the Stamp Act, requiring payment of a tax on written documents, led to defiant outbursts throughout the colonies. In Boston, enraged colonists burned papers bearing the hated "tax stamps."

the time British troops had marched to Lexington and Concord on April 19, 1775, and exchanged shots with a group of "minutemen," the American Revolution could not be stopped, even by belated British attempts at conciliation. It started as an effort by the colonists to secure the rights to which they felt themselves entitled as *British*

COMMON SENSE;

ADDRESSED TO THE

INHABITANTS

OF

A M E R I C A,

On the following interesting

S U B J E C T S.

I. Of the Origin and Design of Government in general, with concise Remarks on the English Constitution.

II. Of Monarchy and Hereditary Succession.

III. Thoughts on the present State of American Affairs.

IV. Of the present Ability of America, with some miscellaneous Reflections.

A NEW EDITION, with several Additions in the Body of the Work. To which is added an APPENDIX; together with an Address to the People called QUAKERS.

N B. The New Addition here given increases the Work upward of one Third.

Man knows no Master save creating HEAVEN,
Or those whom Choice and common Good ordain.
THOMSON.

PHILADELPHIA PRINTED.

And sold by W. and T. BRADFORD.

As the British response to colonial protests became more repressive, opposition grew more hardened. By January 1776, when Thomas Paine published *Common Sense,* the colonies had moved beyond opposing "taxation without representation." Paine's arguments against the monarchy and his call for outright rebellion reflected the developing mood among many colonists.

citizens. But, as wars have a way of doing, violence and killing in the Revolutionary War rapidly escalated until the offenses committed by both sides had grown so onerous that the revolutionary leaders could not turn back from a complete break.[8] January 1776 saw the publication of Thomas Paine's pamphlet, *Common Sense,* an inflammatory call to outright rebellion. It was eagerly received and acted upon by thousands of colonists.

THE DECLARATION OF AMERICAN IDEALS

When the Second Continental Congress met in Philadelphia and on July 2, 1776, appointed a committee to draft a Declaration of Independence, they wanted the strongest possible argument for a decision that had already been made. It had been more than a year since the Battle of Lexington and Concord and "the shot heard 'round the world." The war against Great Britain was well under way.

The American colonies had a much smaller population and much

---

[8]Williams, Current, and Freidel, *A History of the United States to 1877,* p. 125.

Not everyone in the colonies supported the Revolutionary War. A sizable minority remained loyal to King George, despite great personal risks. Who were the loyalists? What was their role during the war?

The Declaration of Independence divided those who hoped to solve the problem of imperial order by evolution from those who insisted on revolution. By calling into existence a new nation it made loyalty to King George treason; and in most colonies patriot committees went about forcing everyone, on pain of imprisonment and confiscation of property, to take an oath of allegiance to the United States. Thus it gave to the loyalists or tories the unpleasant alternative of submission or flight.

There were loyalists in every colony and in every walk of life. In New York, New Jersey, and Georgia they probably comprised a majority of the population. Although it is impossible to ascertain their number, the fact that some 80,000 loyalists left the country during the war or after, and that everyone admitted these to be a minority of the party, gives some index of their strength. Most loyalists took the required oaths and paid taxes, while praying for the defeat of the American cause, simply because they had no place to go. As late as 1830 there were old ladies in New York and Portsmouth, N.H., who quietly celebrated the king's birthday, but drew curtains and closed shutters on the Fourth of July.

The American Revolution was a civil rather than a class war, with tories and whigs [patriots] finding support in all classes. Outside Virginia and Maryland, most of the great landowners were tory, although many remained passive during the war to save their property. Yet the loyalists also won the allegiance of many back-country farmers in New York and the Carolinas. Officials went tory as a matter of course; so, too, most of the Anglican clergy, whose church prescribed loyalty to one's lawful sovereign as a Christian duty. The merchants in the North, except in Boston and the smaller New England seaports, were pretty evenly divided; and many lawyers remained faithful to the Crown. In general the older, conservative, established, well-to-do people were inclined to oppose revolution, but there were countless exceptions. . . . Many families were divided. Gouverneur Morris's mother was a tory; so too was Benjamin Franklin's son, the royalist governor of New Jersey.

Although most of the prominent leaders of the Revolution were gentlemen, they could not carry their entire class into a revolution which involved not only separation from the mother country but the stability of society. . . . When the conservatives realized that liberty could be won only by opening the floodgates to democracy, many drew back in alarm. . . .

VIEWPOINT

The Loyalists

The loyalist minority played a variety of roles in the war. Some did very effective fighting for the king. New York furnished more soldiers to George III than to George Washington. Loyalist marauders quartered in New York City frequently harried the shores of Long Island, and tory 'partisans,' often allied with Indians, committed atrocities on civilians of the other side. But for the most part the loyalists were good people of respectable principles. . . . [T]he difference between success and failure, more than that of right and wrong, explains the . . . 'verdict of history'. . . .

SOURCE: Samuel Eliot Morison, Henry Steele Commager, and William E. Leuchtenberg, *A Concise History of the American Republic* (New York: Oxford University Press, 1977), pp. 81–82.

less wealth than Britain. The American leaders wanted desperately to put forward the most persuasive and stirring arguments for their independence decision not only to rally the colonists at home, but also to sway world opinion in their favor. The colonists hoped that countries sympathetic to the American cause would offer loans and assistance. The American Revolutionary leaders ceased to speak of their rights as Englishmen: they wanted a declaration of their rights

Thomas Jefferson and his draft of the preamble to the Declaration of Independence.

as human beings. That was the task which the Continental Congress delegated to the drafting committee, whose members included Benjamin Franklin, John Adams, and Thomas Jefferson, among others.

Jefferson, a tall, intellectual Virginia planter with piercing blue eyes and an inquiring mind, wrote the first draft of the Declaration. The other members of the drafting committee requested him to do so because he had a "felicity of expression," an ability to word things well. Jefferson did not, of course, discover the words of the Declaration of Independence engraved in stone. He did not copy them, either. He said that he "turned to neither book nor pamphlet" as he wrote. Nor was it his intention "to find out new principles, or new arguments, never before thought of." Instead, when Jefferson sat down at his private desk, looking very human indeed without the formal, white wig covering his red hair, he sought to harmonize the "sentiments of the day," to produce an "expression of the American mind." He wanted "to place before mankind the common sense of the subject, in terms so plain and firm as to command their assent."[9]

What was this "common sense" Jefferson sought to express? What were these "sentiments" he sought to harmonize? Three principles or ideals are stated in the Declaration of Independence. They relate to *human rights, political participation,* and *limited government.*

The First Ideal: Human Rights

We hold these truths to be self-evident, that all men are created equal, that they are endowed by their Creator with certain unalienable Rights, that among these are Life, Liberty, and the pursuit of Happiness.

With these simple yet powerful words, Jefferson expressed the theory of *natural rights.* Natural or inherent rights are those every person is said to be born with. They are not acquired; rather, they are an integral part of being human. The Declaration's statement concerning human rights consists of two parts: an assertion that all "men" are created equal; and an assertion that all "men" have certain "unalienable" rights, which are then enumerated.

Equal rights. It is clear that by "equal" the Declaration did not mean that people are the same because Jefferson recognized, as all of us do today, that people are different. The equality in the Declaration meant the right to be *treated* equally under the law. It meant that everyone is born with certain rights and that these rights are precisely the same, or equal, for all.

Modern readers of the Declaration note at once that its assertion of equal rights announced a kind of white gentleman's club. First of all, the use of the word "men" is grating. Women were left out. In 1776—and, of course, for almost 150 years thereafter—the prevailing view was that women were not created equal, or at least not equal enough to be allowed to vote. Neither black people nor American Indians were accorded equality by most of the delegates to the Continental Congress or by any of the colonies. The great majority of colonial black people were held in slavery. Many white colonists were not treated equally, either. Those who owned no property (some were bound to others in indentured servitude for a fixed time) could not vote because the colonies typically required *property ownership* as a qualification for voting.[10]

Jefferson must have realized that his sweeping statement that "all

---

[9]Carl L. Becker, *The Declaration of Independence* (New York: Vintage Books, 1958), p. 25.

[10]For a discussion of contemporary criticism of the Declaration of Independence on the grounds that it left out women, blacks, and unpropertied people, see Herbert Aptheker, *The American Revolution,* Part II of *A History of the American People* (New York: International Publishers, 1960), pp. 100–110.

men are created equal" was at least inconsistent with slavery. We know that during his life he was tormented by the discrepancy between his views on equality and his practice of inequality as a slaveholder.[11] Jefferson's original draft of the Declaration of Independence called the slave trade a crime against liberty, but this section was deleted from the final draft by the Continental Congress.[12] American unwillingness to resolve this particular conflict between noble ideals and shabby practice was to cost millions of Americans, black and white, dearly in lives and money.

Unalienable rights. The Declaration asserted that those "men" who were created equal possessed certain "unalienable" rights (today we would say "inalienable"). This statement meant that certain human rights are so basic that they cannot be sold, given away, or justly taken away. The ancient Greek philosopher Aristotle, on whose writings so much of Western political thought is based, maintained that every "man" is born with the right of "liberty" and the right to "live as he likes."[13]

Jefferson was a student of Aristotle's philosophy. He was also greatly influenced by the English philosopher John Locke (1632–1704). As a matter of fact, Locke's views were so well known in the colonies and were so well accepted among American revolutionary leaders that Jefferson could properly regard them as just "common sense."[14]

In his *Second Treatise on Civil Government* (1689), Locke asserted that all "men" in their natural state are free and equal; they are born that way.[15] He argued that since they are created by the same "Maker," they are all the Maker's property; thus, any offense by one such creature against the "life, health, liberty, or possessions" of another is an offense against the Creator. To Locke, then, the human rights of life, liberty, and property were God-given or natural rights. They were therefore inalienable; no government had the right to take them away.

But writings on natural rights predated Locke. In the colonies, outspoken colonial New England preachers, such as Roger Williams (1603–1684), did much to popularize the doctrine.[16] Williams got into trouble in Puritan Massachusetts for advocating religious freedom as

---

[11]See John Chester Miller, *Thomas Jefferson and Slavery* (New York: The Free Press, 1977).

[12]Becker, *The Declaration of Independence*, p. 147.

[13]Aristotle did not recognize women as equal to men and regarded slavery as a natural institution. See Aristotle, *Politics*, Book v, Chapter 9 (Oxford: Clarendon Press, 1961), p. 234.

[14]See Alpheus T. Mason and Richard H. Leach, *In Quest of Freedom: American Political Thought and Practice*, 2nd ed. (Englewood Cliffs, N.J.: Prentice-Hall, 1973), p. 51.

[15]John Locke, *Two Treatises of Government*, Peter Laslett, ed. (New York: Cambridge University Press, 1965), p. 309.

[16]Mason and Leach, *In Quest of Freedom*, pp. 27–35.

a natural human right and for condemning grants of land to colonists as "unjust usurpations" of the property rights of the American Indians. He then *bought* some land from the Naragansett Indians and founded the colony of Rhode Island. Throughout the colonies, even in Massachusetts, the power of religious rule began to lose its force little by little; the ideas of human equality and natural rights gradually came to be generally accepted.

One way to understand the theory of inalienable rights better is to consider how it might have applied to Robinson Crusoe and his island.[17] When Crusoe was alone on the island, he was completely free and independent, subject to no other person. That condition, Locke would have said, is the natural state of man. But if twenty additional people had moved to Crusoe's island and had begun to build their own split-level huts and a downtown restaurant, they and Crusoe might have agreed among themselves to give up *some* of their freedoms for their presumed mutual benefit. (For example, they might have put up a sign in the restaurant, saying "No shoes, no shirts, no service.") But according to Locke, the village council they might have formed could not have justly attempted to abridge or limit the inalienable rights of Crusoe and the villagers—the right to think and speak as they liked, for example— *even if a majority of the villagers believed that such action was necessary for the common good.*

Do you see a philosophical problem here? It is, of course, the potential conflict between inalienable rights and majority rule. What if a majority decided to ban free speech? Nearly a century after the Declaration was written, John Stuart Mill (1806–1873) addressed this issue in *Utilitarianism* and *On Liberty*.[18] The right of free speech, he wrote, like other fundamental rights, is not absolute or God-given but results from its *utility*, its ability to work for the happiness of the greatest number. Mill thought that right and wrong should be determined according to this principle. He said that a majority should not take away the fundamental right of a dissenting minority to free speech, for example, because a majority can make the most satisfactory decisions for its *own* welfare only when it can hear and consider all views. To limit free speech would tend to diminish the

WHY STUDY DEAD PHILOSOPHERS ANYWAY? (or even live ones?)

Practical men, who believe themselves exempt from any intellectual influences, are usually the slave of some defunct economist. Madmen in authority, who hear voices in the air, are distilling their frenzy from some academic scribbler of a few years back. I am sure that the power of vested interests is vastly exaggerated compared with the gradual encroachment of ideas.

SOURCE: John Maynard Keynes, *The General Theory of Employment, Interest and Money* (New York: Harcourt, Brace and Company, 1936), pp. 383–84.

---

[17]Adapted from Charles M. Wiltse, *The Jeffersonian Tradition in America* (New York: Hill and Wang, 1960), p. 74.

[18]See John Stuart Mill, *On Liberty* (New York: The Liberal Arts Press, 1956); and G. L. Williams, *John Stuart Mill on Politics and Society* (Sussex, England: The Harvester Press Ltd., 1976), p. 116.

quality of the majority's own decisions. The modern theory of fundamental human rights is much like Mill's, but it says that such rights should not be allowed to be abridged by the majority except when there is a clear showing of danger to the society. The frequently cited example of a person shouting "fire" in a crowded theater when there is no fire aptly illustrates this principle. That person should not be permitted to exercise the absolute right of free speech because of the injury likely to result when the crowd tries to exit the theater rapidly.

While stating their belief in fundamental human rights and justifying this belief on the basis of Locke's theories, Jefferson and the other leaders of the American Revolution were also adopting what they knew to be the customary or generally accepted rights of English citizens. The colonists felt themselves to be inheritors of the English *common law* (laws based on court decisions and custom rather than legislation); of the thirteenth-century Magna Carta, which limited the monarch's power; and of the seventeenth-century protections contained in the English Habeas Corpus Act and Bill of Rights. But by asserting that these rights were gifts from the "creator," the colonists were saying that human rights are not concessions from kings or governments. They were putting their case before the world in the loftiest possible terms.

"Life, liberty, and the pursuit of happiness." In enumerating these inalienable rights in the Declaration of Independence, Jefferson changed Locke's "life, liberty and property" to "life, liberty, and the pursuit of happiness." It is remarkable that the delegates to the Continental Congress, all propertied men, accepted this change. But they probably understood that the right to pursue happiness also included the right to enjoy one's property without unjust interference; there was no need, therefore, to spell out the right of property separately. Jefferson may have held a somewhat different view, however; when the French statesman Lafayette later submitted to Jefferson his own Declaration of the Rights of Man, Jefferson put brackets around the words "right of property," distinguishing this right from others.[19] Jefferson certainly believed that a person should be able to own private property (as opposed to all property being owned in common by all the members of society); he owned a large amount of property himself. But he may have felt that private ownership of property was not a natural right but a matter that might be agreed upon by the members of a society. If so, this interpretation would have been a departure from Locke's views about property. It would not have been a denial of the right of private ownership of property, but it would have placed it on a somewhat less "sacred" plane.[20]

John Locke, the English philosopher whose writings on the origins and practice of government greatly influenced political thought in the colonies.

[19]Wiltse, *The Jeffersonian Tradition in America*, p. 74. See also L. F. Parrington, *Main Currents in American Thought* (New York: Harcourt and Brace, 1930).

[20]Saul K. Padover, *The Complete Jefferson* (New York: Duell, Sloan and Pierce, 1943), p. 1015.

As he stated in his *Second Treatise on Civil Government*, Locke arrived at his position concerning the natural right of property by asserting that everyone has a property right in his or her own person. Therefore, each person has a property right to whatever he or she removes from nature and mixes his or her labor with—land cleared and plowed, or the lumber from timber, for example. Interestingly, Locke included in the right of property not only the product of a person's *own* labor, but also that which resulted from the labor of a person's beasts or servants. One person might acquire or store up more property than another in the form of land, personal possessions, or money; and according to Locke, this inequality of property was protected by the rights to life, liberty, and property.

Philosophers have disputed whether human equality and fundamental human rights are natural or God-given, utilitarian, customary, or derived from some other source. Regardless of the origin of these rights, the fact remains that a belief in these rights is a vital part of what is meant by the "American way of life."[21]

The Second Ideal: Political Participation

. . . to secure these rights, Governments are instituted among men, deriving their just powers from the consent of the governed.

If all people are created equal and have inalienable rights to life, liberty, and the pursuit of happiness, it follows logically that they should be self-governing and not subject to the will of others except with their own "consent." Otherwise, how could equality for all really exist? Some would be rulers and others would be ruled. This reasoning was the basis for the Declaration's statement of the ideal of *political participation*.

Politics is the process by which individuals and groups seek to secure and preserve their share of power or authority. It deals with the questions of "who gets what, when and how."[22] The Declaration adopted the idea that all "men" should have an equal opportunity to take part in that process and thus to influence the decisions that affect their lives. That is what is meant by political participation.

There is "politics" in the PTA and in the workplace, but the kind of political participation dealt with in the Declaration and studied most by political scientists has to do with *government*, the individuals, institutions, and processes that officially and enforceably divide and distribute power and authority. We are all affected by politics, whether we know it or not. The price of gasoline or hamburger meat, the level of tuition or taxes, and the availability of student loans or money to buy a house are all determined wholly or partly by political decisions.

---

[21]Samuel P. Huntington, "Paradigms of American Politics: Beyond the One, the Two and the Many," *Political Science Quarterly,* 89, no. 1 (Spring 1974): 19–20.

[22]Harold Lasswell, *Politics: Who Gets What, When, How?* (New York: McGraw-Hill, 1936).

The ideal of political participation—the right to take part in or influence such decisions—is an old one. Jefferson and many of the other early American leaders were as familiar with the historical development of this ideal as carpenters are with their tools. They had studied the Greek and Roman philosophers as well as the writings of John Locke. Locke wrote that governments are based upon a social compact, or *social contract*—an implied agreement *by* all citizens *with*

In any war, people fight for a variety of reasons, including the powerful pull of patriotism and the pressures of community opinion. In an interview held years after the Revolutionary War, one old veteran said that he had fought for the right of self-government.

"Why did you? . . . My histories tell me that you men of the Revolution took up arms against intolerable oppressions."

"What were they? Oppressions? I didn't feel them."

"What, were you not oppressed by the Stamp Act?"

"I never saw one of those stamps. . . . I am certain I never paid a penny for one of them."

"Well, what about the tea tax?"

"Tea tax, I never drank a drop of the stuff. The boys threw it all overboard."

"Then, I suppose, you had been reading Harrington, or Sidney and Locke, about the eternal principles of liberty?"

"Never heard of 'em."

"Well, then, what was the matter, what did you mean in going into the fight?"

"Young man, what we meant in going for those red-coats, was this: we always had governed ourselves and we always meant to. They didn't mean we should."

SOURCE: Interview in 1837 with Captain Levi Preston of Danver, Massachusetts, quoted in Charles Warren, *The Making of the Constitution* (Boston: Little, Brown and Company, 1928) p. 4.

VIEWPOINT

Why Did Americans Fight in the Revolutionary War?

all citizens—in which individuals consent to give up a portion of their liberties, rights, or powers for the common good of all. Thus, government is a result of voluntary agreement or consent.

According to Locke, the union or community formed by this social contract would produce a single authority or will in place of the multiple wills of the individual citizens. Locke could have said that this community will, or single authority, could come about only when individual citizens were in *unanimous* agreement on a given subject. Instead, Locke said that the community will, and thus the actions of government, should be decided by vote of the *majority*, one more than half. Locke felt that it was necessary to allow majority rule because it was the only system that would work. It would be next to impossible, he thought, to secure the consent of every individual; unless majority rule was allowed, the community would either be unable to act or unable to hold together. To Locke, then, consent of the governed meant "consent to be governed by the majority" (subject to the inalienable rights of the individual citizens).[23]

Though Locke was the leading political theorist read by the colonial leaders, the seeds of political participation were planted early in America by a number of religious leaders. Grounded in the teachings of John Calvin, the Puritans who came to America believed that God's law was supreme and that it was contained in the Bible as interpreted by the clergy. They believed that a *theocracy*, the rule of God administered by His representatives, was the best form of government and that there should therefore be no separation of church and state.

From its beginnings, however, Puritan practice in America included some seeds of democracy: the idea that local church communities were based on "covenant" or contract, giving people a free choice to join or not join; the idea that local church communities, or congregations, should be free to govern themselves, not subject to central church authority; and the idea that governments should have limited authority. There were religious dissenters, too, who took these concepts and used them to argue for democracy, not theocracy. Roger Williams, for example, argued against government-enforced conformity to religious dogma because, he said, government should be based upon a social contract, and religious liberty is a natural right that the social contract must respect. Williams went on to found the colony of Rhode Island on the democratic principles that he espoused.

Thomas Hooker (1586–1647) was another colonial nonconformist preacher. In 1639 he helped draft the Fundamental Orders of Connecticut, under which the newly formed colony was governed for many years. The Orders were based upon the right of the people, regardless of religious beliefs, to elect their own government officials and to *hold them accountable* to act for the common good. While Williams and Hooker were considered dissenters in their day from generally held views about government and were primarily religious thinkers, another colonial clergyman, John Wise (1652–1725) of Massachusetts, later refined and simplified the doctrines of natural rights and democratic government in ways that eventually gained for them wide *political* application. By the time of the American Revolution, the idea of political participation had become a part of the "common sense" that Jefferson spelled out and the Continental Congress adopted in the Declaration of Independence.[24]

Some colonial leaders, such as Roger Williams, John Wise, Patrick Henry, and Thomas Paine, spoke out freely in favor of "democracy"—meaning literally, "rule of the people." But for most others, democracy in its purest sense meant "*direct* rule of the people" and suggested a kind of anarchic and unstable mob rule that they felt was

---

[23]Locke, *Two Treatises of Government*, p. 375.
[24]Mason and Leach, *In Quest of Freedom*, p. 31.

neither possible nor desirable. Most colonial leaders preferred the word *republic*, by which they meant, in its strictest sense, *representative* government.[25] But the word was intended to mean more, too. "For let it be agreed," Jefferson wrote, "that a government is republican in proportion as every member composing it has an equal voice in the direction of its concerns (not indeed in person, which would be impracticable beyond the limits of a city, or small township, but,) by representatives chosen by himself, and responsible to him at short periods. . . ."[26]

The "truths" expressed by Jefferson in the Declaration were not merely philosophical ideas. Colonial religious leaders, including (left to right) Roger Williams, Thomas Hooker, and Jonathan Mayhew, contributed to the general acceptance of the idea of "natural rights," both in theory and in practice. The colonists' experience in self-government, beginning with the first settlement at Jamestown, Virginia (1607), also made King George III's acts a century and a half later even more difficult to accept.

By "republic," then, Jefferson meant a government that was democratic in the sense that the people were supreme, but republican in the sense that the people should govern themselves through representatives.

But there was an additional element in the original American definition of republic. Jefferson wrote that the colonial leaders had at first ". . . imagined everything republican which was not monarchy" but that they had later come to the "mother principle," the idea that "governments are republican only in proportion as they embody *the will of their people,* and execute it" (emphasis added).[27]

At the time of the Declaration of Independence, the extent of political participation (who should participate, in which decisions) and the forms of political participation (passive consent, voting) were not spelled out. But from the beginning America has been grounded on the ideal of political participation, which involves two essential elements: first, that citizens should have the right to select their governmental leaders; and second, that governmental policies and practices should reflect the will of the community (while protecting human rights).

---

[25]See generally Saul K. Padover, *The Meaning of Democracy* (New York: Frederick A. Praeger, 1963).

[26]Jefferson to Samuel Kercheval, July 12, 1816, contained in Padover, *The Complete Jefferson*, p. 288.

[27]Jefferson to Kercheval, July 12, 1816.

. . . whenever any Form of Government becomes destructive of these ends, it is the Right of the People to alter or abolish it, and to institute new Government, laying its foundation on such principles and organizing its powers in such form, as to them shall seem most likely to effect their Safety and Happiness.

John Locke wrote that when people enter into a social contract to form a government, the powers they give to that government are limited. The government should not act "arbitrarily" or in violation of "promulgated standing law," which itself should be based upon the common "good of the people."[28] Locke did not think that the people had a duty to support a government not based upon consent. But what about a government, supported by a majority, which transgresses the rights of a minority? That was a harder case for him. He recognized the right of individual resistance to unjust governmental action and, believing that the *threat* of revolution would hold governments in check, did not expect revolution to occur very often. Revolution might come, he thought, when the actions of elected representatives were so grossly unjust as to destroy the very trust between citizens and their government, which is the product of the social contract. When there was no earthly appeal for the peaceful resolution of the grievance, then, he said, "God in heaven is judge."[29]

In the American colonies, this doctrine of the right of resistance was honed to a fine edge both in theory and in practice. Again, it was a free-thinking preacher who had first begun to popularize this revolutionary idea. Jonathan Mayhew (1720–1766) preached that rulers have "no authority from God to do mischief" and that ". . . no government is to be submitted to, at the expense of that which is the sole end of government,—the common good and the safety of society." Mayhew said, "the people know for what end they set up and maintain their governors; and they are the proper judges when they execute their trust as they ought to do it." In other words, government officials, chosen by the people, have a fiduciary or "trust" responsibility to the people, just like the duty of a modern bank or trust company which manages the investments of one of its customers. In the latter case, the bank cannot do anything it pleases with the customer's money; it can only act in accordance with established law and the wishes of the customer. So it is with government, Mayhew would have maintained, and when government abuses its trust ". . . to such a degree that neither the law of reason, nor religion . . ." requires obedience or submission, the people can take back their consent and place it elsewhere, just as a bank

---

[28]Locke, *Two Treatises of Government*, p. 375.
[29]Locke, *Two Treatises of Government*, p. 476.

customer can take back his or her money and put it in the hands of another trustee.

As we saw earlier, the Declaration of Independence was a political document, written to justify a course of action that had already been agreed upon. It emphasized strongly the doctrine of limited government, especially to explain that the central reason for the revolt of the colonies was that King George's government had overstepped its rightful powers. Much of the Declaration was devoted to listing specific instances of this usurpation.

In the Declaration, the signers were saying that citizens have a right—indeed, a duty—to rebel against an oppressive and unrepresentative government. Since the purpose of government is to protect basic human rights, and since a government's existence and power come only from the consent of its citizens, it follows that the people can change the form of their government if it violates these principles. Some colonial leaders may later have come to the view that this revolutionary language was too sweeping and too much of a continuing encouragement to popular unrest. But not its author, Thomas Jefferson. Eleven years later, in 1787, following Shays' Rebellion over debtors' rights, Jefferson stated, "The late rebellion in Massachusetts has given more alarm than it should have done. Calculate that one rebellion in thirteen States in the course of eleven years, is but one for each State in a century and a half. No country should be so long without one."[30] Whether or not other colonial leaders agreed with this doctrine of the value of insurrection, they certainly agreed that a government created by consent has limited powers.

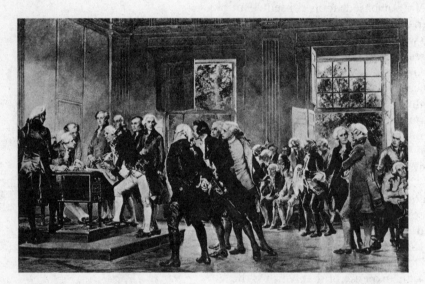

Delegates to the Second Continental Congress sign the Declaration of Independence, August 2, 1776. On July 2, Richard Henry Lee of Virginia had submitted and the Congress had adopted a resolution calling for independence, and on July 4 the formal Declaration was adopted. Though a treasonous document from the British point of view, the Declaration's statement of truths upon which government should be based has inspired political thought and action ever since.

THE AMERICAN PROMISE

What does America stand for? At a bare minimum, it stands for human rights, political participation, and limited government. That is a lot to stand for. And a key element is the ideal of participation. Who knows better what is best for the people than the people

---

[30]Jefferson to James Madison, March 15, 1789, contained in Saul K. Padover, *The Complete Jefferson*, p. 122.

themselves? Who is better able to protect their human rights? Who is better able to keep government in line?

It is true that the Declaration of Independence did not include *all* citizens, nor was it self-executing (immediately effective) for those it did include. But in its sweeping language the Declaration constituted, as Peter Gay has written, a kind of "promissory note."[31]

When a person goes to a bank to borrow money, the bank requires the borrower to sign a promissory note, which states something like the following: "Within thirty days, I promise to pay the bank $10 with interest." Similarly, the Declaration might be said to state: "In the future, the United States of America (to be formed) promises to recognize for every adult citizen (male and female, white and nonwhite, propertied and unpropertied) full human rights and full political participation."

Throughout the years since they were written, the words of the Declaration of Independence have been used over and over again by countless groups and individuals, here and elsewhere, as the foundation of their claims to human rights and participation.[32] "It cannot be long ignored or repudiated," Vernon L. Parrington wrote about the Declaration, "for sooner or later it returns to plague the council of practical politics. It is constantly breaking out in fresh revolt . . . ."[33]

The Declaration of Independence stated a set of political ideals. It did not attempt to establish a government to carry them out. That practical task was taken up in the writing of the U.S. Constitution.

ADDITIONAL SOURCES

Bailyn, Bernard. *The Ideological Origins of the American Revolution.* Harvard University Press, 1967.*
———. *The Origins of American Politics.* Random House, 1970.*
Becker,Carl. *The Declaration of Independence.* Random House, 1942.*
Boorstin, Daniel J. *The Americans: The Colonial Experience.* Random House, 1958.*
Catton, Bruce, and William B. Catton. *The Bold and Magnificent Dream.* Doubleday, 1978.
Locke, John. *Two Treatises of Government* (available in many editions).*
Schlesinger, Arthur M. *The Birth of the Nation.* Knopf, 1968.
Smith, Page. *A New Age Now Begins: A People's History of the American Revolution.* McGraw-Hill, 1976.
Wills, Garry. *Inventing America: Jefferson's Declaration of Independence.* Doubleday, 1978.
*Available in paperback.

---

[31]Peter Gay, "America the Paradoxical," in *Virginia Law Review,* 72 (June 1976): 856.
[32]See Phillip S. Foner, *We, The Other People* (Urbana, Illinois: University of Illinois Press, 1976).
[33]Vernon L. Parrington, *Main Currents in American Thought,* Vol. 3 (New York: Harcourt Brace Jovanovich, 1930), p. 285.

2 The Constitution
Blueprint for a Government

In a few short years, from 1776 to 1783, the American colonies had accomplished a great deal. Not only had they proclaimed their devotion to the ideals of human rights, political participation, and limited government, but they had also fought and won a war for independence from Great Britain, a rich and powerful nation with a colonial empire. With the end of the Revolutionary War, the leaders of the newly independent nation were able to turn their attention more intensively to the task of building a government.

Governments are based upon rules or guidelines that determine how a government is organized and what powers it has. The rules matter because they define the relationship among the people in a society; they determine what each person is entitled to expect from the others and from the government. And no rules matter more than those embodied in a *constitution*, the fundamental and supreme law of a society.

James Madison, one of the principal movers behind America's Constitution, noted a fundamental difference between everyday laws and constitutions. While simple laws are made by governments, he said, constitutions are special kinds of laws that are made by the people. Thus, governments can change laws, but constitutions should only be subject to change by the people.

Great Britain's constitution is mostly unwritten. It is a well-recognized body of various declarations, statutes, practices, and precedents. The Constitution of the United States, on the other hand, is a written document. The signed original is literally enshrined in the National Archives in Washington, D.C., where it can be viewed by visitors during its business hours. Each night, however, the Constitution, together with the Declaration of Independence and other especially honored American documents, is silently and mechanically put away in a closely guarded and impenetrable vault.

Just because a constitution is a written document does not necessarily mean that it will be followed and enforced. Some so-called republics in the world today have written constitutions that have not proved to be reliable guarantees against illegal takeovers and rule by force in those countries. If a nation's constitution is to be really effective in restraining government officials and protecting citizen rights, it must enjoy general respect and support from the citizens of the country. Ours does. It is the oldest living written constitution in the world. In 1987, the United States Constitution will have been in existence for 200 years.

Visitors at the National Archives in Washington, D.C., look at the original copies of the Declaration, the Constitution, and other treasured documents.

The 1976 Supreme Court case, *Buckley* v. *Valeo*,[1] provides a recent example of how the U.S. Constitution works as the fundamental law of the land. In this case, the Court found that part of a law passed by Congress was *unconstitutional*—in violation of the Constitution—and therefore invalid. The law had given Congress the power to name members to a new Federal Election Commission, instead of following the usual practice of establishing the qualifications and duties of its members and then leaving the actual nomination of the members to the discretion of the President. The Court said that the act was unconstitutional because it violated Article II, Section 2 of the Constitution. That provision gives the President, not the Congress, the power (by and with the advice and consent of the Senate) to appoint such "officers" of the national government.

In giving their reasons for the decision, the members of the Court turned, as they often do in written opinions, to the original *intent* of those who framed our Constitution. The Court cited James Madison's support for the "well-known maxim that the legislative, executive and judicial departments ought to be separate and distinct."[2] In the *Buckley* case, the Court was attempting to preserve

---

[1] *Buckley* v. *Valeo*, 96 S. Ct. 612 (1976).
[2] *Buckley* v. *Valeo*, p. 683.

this doctrine of *separation of powers,* or division of governmental duties and authority among the three branches of our national government. The judicial branch (represented by the Supreme Court) declared an act of the legislative branch (Congress) invalid and unenforceable because it infringed upon the powers of the executive branch (represented by the President).

Separation of powers was a well-established concept by the time of the *Buckley* case. But it had not just sprung up out of thin air. Nor had the Supreme Court. Both the concept and the Court were derived from the U.S. Constitution.

Like the Declaration of Independence, the Constitution was fashioned by men, although an almost entirely different set of men from those who produced the Declaration. As one authority wrote:

> *The constitutional movement . . . represented a reaction against some of the democratic values and assumptions of the Revolutionary period. Ironically, the same political philosopher, John Locke, provided some of the major ideas for both. But whereas the earlier period espoused Locke's concepts of majority rule and legislative supremacy, the Founding Fathers rather stressed his concern with property rights and his recognition of executive prerogatives. Thus, different aspects of Locke's philosophy were borrowed for dealing with different conditions in the two periods of national development.*[3]

Our Constitution grew out of a peculiar set of historical circumstances and events in America. We can better understand the Constitution by learning more about those circumstances and events.

A SENSE OF NATIONHOOD

Today, we sometimes hear speakers refer to "*these* United States of America," instead of "*the* United States of America." This plural treatment of the proper name of the national government is heard most often in the South, a section of the country where white leaders were at one time especially devoted to the doctrine of "states' rights." Of course, we are a nation made up of separate, united states, but we are also *one* nation, which is properly called *the* United States of America.

The complex concept of state governments within a national government, which is called *federalism,* was not an easy one for our founders to work out, as we shall see. But it would not have developed at all without a feeling of nationhood in America. For 150 years, those who lived in America had thought of themselves as being English colonists who lived in the Massachusetts colony, the Georgia

---

[3]Richard Watson, *Promise and Performance of American Democracy* (N.Y: Wiley, 1972), p. 72.

colony, or one of the others. Little by little, they began to think of themselves as Americans. In the French and Indian Wars, Americans began to recognize certain goals common to the whole country. After 1763, the acts of George III caused the colonists to increasingly recognize their common interests in opposing the king's measures. By the early 1770s, there was "a distinct American political community."[4]

Even before 1776, the American colonies had acted in concert by sending representatives to foreign countries to negotiate trade and commerce agreements. Then news of the signing of the Declaration of Independence brought out cheering crowds in places like Philadelphia and Boston and helped draw people together in the oneness of their cause. There was a war to be won.

It has been estimated that only about 40 percent of colonial Americans supported the Revolutionary War, while 10 percent opposed it and 50 percent did not care much one way or the other.[5] (The patriots, of course, had the most influence on events.) When approximately 100,000 of those who remained loyal to Great Britain soon left the country, voluntarily or forcibly, the influence of the patriots increased further.[6]

Nevertheless, America was still a long way from being one nation. George Washington, Commander in Chief of the American army, was continuously exasperated by the failure of the states to give adequate support to the war effort. Fortunately, France saw that helping the colonies and thereby weakening Great Britain was in its national interest. So did Spain and the Netherlands. All gave financial help; France's aid alone amounted to $62 million and its loans to $6 million. France's naval forces and ground troops also proved to be vitally important in the remaining years of the war.

Even after the war was won and the Articles of Confederation were ratified by all the new states, most Americans still thought of their government as *these* United States of America. While in England for commercial negotiations in 1784, John Adams was confronted with the question from English officials, who wondered whether he was there to speak for one nation or thirteen. Yet John Jay later wrote that—with the obvious exception of American Indians and black people, who were sadly left out of Jay's consideration—America was "one connected country" composed of "one united people—a people descended from the same ancestors, speaking the same language, professing the same religion, attached to the same principles of government, very similar in their manners and customs."[7] These were important ingredients for nationhood.

---

[4]Richard L. Merritt, *Symbols of American Community 1735–1775* (New Haven, Connecticut: Yale University Press, 1966), p. 126.

[5]Samuel Eliot Morison, *The Oxford History of the American People* (New York: Oxford University Press, 1965), p. 236.

[6]Unless otherwise indicated, the history of the Revolutionary War is drawn from T. Harry Williams, Richard N. Current, and Frank Freidel, *A History of the United States to 1877,* 3rd ed. (New York: Alfred A. Knopf, 1969).

[7]*Federalist,* no. 2.

EXPERIENCE IN GOVERNING

A person who throws off one coat in the dead of winter because of dissatisfaction with the fit must soon find another one or perish in the cold. That fear was what had worried Americans like John Dickinson about throwing off the British government and going all the way for independence, instead of striving for reform within the British system. What would replace England's central authority? Would the thirteen British colonies, now becoming independent states, split up in chaos?

The Articles of Confederation

A bitter and costly war was raging, but the Second Continental Congress still had no clear mandate about how to represent the national interest.

Nevertheless, the Congress did act. Earlier, it had named George Washington as Commander in Chief of the Continental army and had begun to raise money and troops and establish relations with foreign governments. Even before the Declaration of Independence was signed, the Congress had appointed a committee headed by John Dickinson to draft a constitution for the "United colonies." Dickinson had gone along with the decision in favor of independence but advocated a strong national government for America to replace the central authority of Britain.[8] However, the same distrust of central authority that had caused the colonies to rebel in the first place made them reject Dickinson's plan. As historian Samuel E. Morison has written, this spirit of liberty in the colonies would have proved fatal to their independence without the assistance from France and the strong leadership of George Washington.[9]

The Second Continental Congress continued to function throughout the Revolutionary War, though it had no clear legal mandate. By 1781 the Articles of Confederation had been fully and finally approved, and the new Confederation government came into being in time to conclude the war and negotiate the Treaty of Paris (1783).

Shortly after the Congress adopted the Declaration of Independence, it proceeded to consider the drafting committee's recommendation of a "league of friendship and perpetual union" among the states. It was not until a year later that the Congress approved the "Articles of Confederation" and submitted them to the states for ratification. But since *every* state was required to ratify the Articles

[8]Alpheus Thomas Mason and Richard H. Leach, *In Quest of Freedom: American Political Thought and Practice,* 2nd ed. (Englewood Cliffs, New Jersey: Prentice-Hall, 1973), p. 56.
[9]Morison, *The Oxford History of the American People,* p. 226.

before they could go into effect, the Congress operated during most of the Revolutionary War without a written constitution because Maryland was a lone holdout on ratification until 1781. Even without written authority, however, the Congress continued to negotiate with foreign governments, raise and support troops, and borrow and print money.

The Articles of Confederation were different from the Declaration of Independence in two important respects.[10] First, the Articles were intended to be a constitution for a government, while the Declaration was intended to be a statement of principles and grievances. Second, the Declaration dealt with the rights of individuals, while the Articles dealt with states.

Under the Articles, each state continued to be *sovereign,* a supreme and independent government, except for the powers that were *expressly* delegated to the "United States, in Congress assembled." Each state was represented in Congress by from two to seven delegates selected by the state legislature, but each state's delegation could cast only one vote in Congress, regardless of the population of the state. The states paid the salaries of their own delegates and could recall them at will. The Congress could not regulate commerce between the states, could not draft soldiers for the army, and could levy but not enforce collection of taxes. In many ways the Congress was like the present United Nations, which must depend upon member contributions to defray its expenses and rely upon the voluntary provision of troops from willing countries to make up UN peacekeeping forces from time to time.

Yet the Articles of Confederation provided for more than a kind of United Nations. They provided the beginnings of a much tighter national arrangement, and they constituted an important transition between revolution and nationhood. For example, the "free inhabitants" of one state, when present in another state, were required to be accorded the same "privileges and immunities" as the citizens of that state enjoyed. Each state had to give "full faith and credit" to the laws and court orders of another. Without the approval of Congress, a state could not make treaties or even establish diplomatic relations with a foreign government; that power was expressly delegated to Congress. And states could not enter into treaties with each other, unless with the specific, advance consent of Congress.

The authors of the Articles considered certain governmental functions to be national in character; they did not believe that these functions could be performed adequately by the separate states. Congress was given the power ". . . to decide on peace and war, conduct foreign affairs, settle disputes between the states, regulate

---

[10]In regard to the Articles of Confederation and the Continental Congress, see E. C. Burnett, *The Continental Congress* (New York: The Macmillan Company, 1941); and Lynn Montross, *The Reluctant Rebels: The Story of the Continental Congress 1774–1789* (New York: Harper, 1950).

the Indian trade, maintain post offices, make appropriations, borrow money, emit bills of credit, build a navy, requisition [that is, ask for] soldiers . . ." But the Articles also limited the power of the national government. The delegations of nine states had to agree before Congress could exercise these powers. No national court system was established to enforce the acts of Congress or the treaties it entered into; enforcement was left to the state courts.

There was no separate executive department under the Articles of Confederation. However, the Articles did contain a provision for Congress to choose its own President—a president of the Congress, not of the United States. America had fourteen such presidents, some for very brief periods, before George Washington became our first real chief executive.[11] Nevertheless, a kind of embryonic executive department began to grow up out of necessity. The Articles provided for a "Committee of the States," made up of one delegate from each of the thirteen states, to function as a kind of executive committee when the Congress was not in full session. Separate committees were set up to handle the various tasks of government, such as finance and foreign affairs, and a "Secretary" was appointed for each of these committees. With time, these committees might eventually have developed into formal cabinet ministries like those in the parliamentary system in Britain, where the executive cabinet, including the prime minister, comes from the legislative body. But this was not to be. Difficult events—and the feeling on the part of some leaders that the Congress was too weak to deal with them— prevented this system from evolving gradually in America. The Articles of Confederation were eventually replaced, not improved.

The New States

The thirteen state governments that took the place of the old colonial governments were much like the earlier governments in form, but much different in operation.[12] In the new state governments, there were still three branches: executive, legislative, and judicial. Every state except Pennsylvania continued to have a governor, but the governors were elected, unlike most colonial governors, who had been appointed by the king or his representative. Further, the new state governors did not have a complete veto power over legislative acts as so many of the royal governors had. In only three of the new states did the governor have even a partial veto.

In all of the state governments except Pennsylvania and Georgia, the state legislatures were bicameral—that is, made up of two houses.

---

[11]For an interesting article on this subject, see Richard B. Morris, "The Men Who Were Presidents Before Washington," *Smithsonian* (January 1978), p. 92.

[12]In regard to the state governments after the Revolution, see Allan Nevins, *The American States During and After the Revolution* (New York: The Macmillan Company, 1924).

Georgia and Pennsylvania had unicameral, or one-house legislatures. The old colonial Governor's Council was retained in most of the states in the form of an elected Senate. The colonial judiciary, or court system, remained virtually intact in all of the states.

The states adopted written constitutions, and nearly all of these documents contained a bill of rights. Listing specific human rights that governments had to respect was an important innovation in the state constitutions. These lists of rights grew directly out of the colonists' experience with the British government during the pre–Revolutionary War period.

But the principal feature of the new state governments was the power given to the elected legislatures. In five states, the legislature itself appointed most state officials. In three, they selected the judges of the courts. In six states, the legislatures could even amend the state constitutions without a vote of the people. The revolutionary distrust of centralized executive authority had molded the new state governments. Madison and others were to come to the view that the state governments had gone too far toward democracy by giving too much power to the legislatures.

What about human rights and citizen participation in the new states? In only one state, New Jersey, were women allowed to vote, but their right to vote was soon suspended even there.[13] The importation of slaves was prohibited in all the states except Georgia and South Carolina. Several southern states enacted laws encouraging the case-by-case, voluntary freeing of slaves. The Massachusetts Supreme Court ruled slavery unconstitutional, and Pennsylvania adopted a law for the gradual emancipation of slaves. Most states began to recognize the fundamental right of religious freedom. Although property ownership was still commonly required as a condition for voting in all the states, the property ownership requirements were so low that they represented only a very limited barrier. A greater amount of property ownership, however, was required for holding public office.[14]

Americans had enjoyed a considerable degree of democracy before the Revolution, greater than Europeans were to achieve for many years to come. There was even more democracy after the Revolution. Some began to feel there was perhaps *too much* democracy.

The War and Its Aftermath

In October 1777, just before a hard winter at Valley Forge, American troops won an important victory at Saratoga, New York. This news, traveling only by ship, finally reached England and France in

---

[13]Kirk Harold Porter, *A History of Suffrage in the United States* (Chicago: The University of Chicago Press, 1918), p. 136.

[14]Robert A. Dahl, *Democracy in the United States: Promise and Performance* (Chicago: Rand McNally, 1976), p. 70.

December. The American victory had dramatic impact in the capitals of both countries. In London, Lord North decided to offer peace to America on the basis of home rule within the empire. If the offer had been communicated and accepted, America might have matured as an independent country along the lines later followed by Canada and Australia.

But what happened in Paris as a result of the news of the Saratoga victory was to short-circuit Lord North's peace decision. Benjamin Franklin and other Americans had been in France for some time, trying to work out a formal treaty of alliance. There was no question of France's support for American independence, but the French foreign minister did not want to act openly against Britain without the concurrence of Spain or without more tangible assurance that the Americans would be successful. Benjamin Franklin, wise and adept at the art of diplomacy, turned the hard fact of the American victory at Saratoga and the provocative rumor of a British peace offer into a persuasive argument and achieved a formal treaty with France.

Even with the open assistance of French troops and money, the war dragged on, and the outcome remained in doubt. It was not until October 1781 that Washington defeated Cornwallis' British army at Yorktown with the aid of a French expeditionary force and a French fleet. Seven thousand British troops surrendered. The war was over. Two years later, the final peace treaty was agreed upon.

For the Second Continental Congress and the thirteen American states, peace was in some ways as hard as war. Debts were the main problem. Congress, the states, and individual citizens had all borrowed money. In addition, Americans owed money to British citizens for debts incurred before the war. British claims for confiscations of loyalist property during the war also had to be paid.

In the year of the peace treaty, 1783, the Congress owed $34 million to domestic creditors. A few years later, it owed another $10 million to foreign creditors. Congressional leaders attempted to secure approval for the levying of an impost, a national tax, but not enough states would agree to give the Congress this power. The national government did remarkably well under the circumstances, but the fact that its capital had to be moved in 1783 from Princeton, to Annapolis, to Trenton, and then later to New York, indicated the low status of the government. The Congress had trouble negotiating adequate trade treaties because of the manifest weakness of the American national government in enforcing the agreements at home. Throughout America, there was no uniform currency. States had issued their own cheap paper money, and the money issued by the Congress had become so inflated in value that there was little demand for it by merchants or bankers in America or abroad. Unable to collect taxes and already greatly in debt, Congress found it increasingly difficult to borrow money except at exorbitant interest rates. To make matters worse, Britain refused to move its troops out of the Great Lakes region, as called for in the peace treaty. The British justified this action by stating that America was violating the peace treaty by failing to make the states pay pre–Revolutionary War debts to British citizens and compensate the loyalists for confiscations of their property. The actual reason for the troop concentrations was to protect British trade with the Indian tribes.

Some of the state legislatures had literally become more democratic than the law allowed. Some intervened in individual disputes between citizens, overturning court decisions. Some acted to prevent creditors from collecting from their debtors. As more and more paper money rolled off the state presses in a blur of printers' ink, the currencies became more and more inflated. A few states revised their constitutions to curb the powers of the legislatures. But these restrictions were not enough to suit revolutionary leaders like Washington, who also felt that the war had been won without the proper and timely support of the states. This lack of state support, he said, would have caused "the dissolution of any army less patient, less virtuous, and less persevering than that which I have had the honor to command." Washington began to fear that the sacrifices of the war might come to nothing. Others shared his concerns. John Jay wrote, "What a triumph for the advocates of despotism to find that we are incapable of governing ourselves, and that systems founded on the basis of equal liberty are merely ideal and fallacious! Would to God that wise measures be taken in time to avert the consequences we have but too much reason to apprehend."[15]

THE CONSTITUTIONAL CONVENTION

During and immediately following the Revolutionary War, events and circumstances were indeed conspiring against continuation of the national government in America under the Articles. But a simple, deterministic view of history—in which one set of events inevitably leads to another, as one receding ocean wave gives birth to its successor—ignores the power of human actors to shape or guide events and change the course of history.

Between 1776 and 1787, several American leaders helped alter the course of American history by shaping such documents and events as the Declaration, the Revolutionary War, and the Constitutional Convention. Without the intellect and advocacy of Thomas Jefferson, the Declaration might have been a far less influential and important statement of universal principles of government. But for the efforts and ideas of James Madison, the U.S. Constitution might have been a far different document, and our national government— or governments, because we could have been several nations instead

---

[15]Charles Warren, *The Making of the Constitution* (Boston: Little, Brown and Company, 1928), p. 18.

Alexander Hamilton (top) and James Madison were two of the leading proponents of a convention to replace the Articles of Confederation with a new constitution that would strengthen the powers of the central government.

of just one—might have been much different. Without popular and dependable George Washington, who could have held together America's ragged, underfinanced, and ill-supported Revolutionary armed forces? Similarly, the Constitutional Convention that gathered in Philadelphia in 1787 might never have occurred except for the persuasive arguments of Washington's young war aide from New York, Alexander Hamilton. Finally, John Adams' influential treatise on the new state constitutions proved to be an important model for the document which emerged from the Convention in Philadelphia.

But of all of these political leaders, none had more to do with turning ideas into action than Alexander Hamilton and James Madison. Alexander Hamilton had the face of an aristocrat and the bearing of one as well.[16] He was slender, of medium height, and a "dynamo of nervous energy." His hair was reddish-brown, and there was a haughtiness sometimes apparent in the gaze of his deep blue eyes. This lawyer-legislator was too arrogant and vain to be popular, but he knew where he was going and where he wanted the new country of America to go, and he often carried others along with him. Hamilton was not an aristocrat by birth—far from it. He had been born in the West Indies and had grown up in hard-scrabble circumstances in an unhappy home. Young Hamilton came to America to make his way, and soon did. Perhaps it was Hamilton's own background of poverty and his hard struggle to rise in life that caused him to have a rather low opinion of human nature and the ordinary person. This attitude (shared by many of our founders) colored Hamilton's views as to what sort of national government America should have.[17]

Equally important in the evolution of Hamilton's views was his experience during the war as Washington's aide de camp. After the decisive victory at Yorktown in 1781, Hamilton resigned from the army and returned to New York to devote his time and considerable energies to the idea of replacing the Congress with a strong national government featuring a strong chief executive. During the war he had been highly critical of the weakness of the Congress in supplying the army's needs. He used the doctrine of "implied powers" to argue that the Congress should have simply assumed whatever undefined powers that were needed to prosecute the war successfully and "to preserve the republic from harm."[18]

Hamilton understood finance as few people in America did. He wanted a strong national government established to improve the credit of the new country. He also felt that the government should

[16]Jesse Hendrick Burton, *A Biography of the Constitution* (Boston: Little, Brown and Company, 1941), p. 24; and David Smith, *The Convention and the Constitution* (New York: St. Martin's Press, 1965), p. 96.

[17]For an interesting treatment of Hamilton's background and attitudes, see James Thomas Flexner, *The Young Hamilton* (Boston: Little, Brown and Company, 1978).

[18]Mason and Leach, *In Quest of Freedom*, p. 57.

"fund" the national debt, or provide for the reliable and regular payment of the interest on the debt by national taxation. This policy would make the government's bonds a secure and attractive investment and thus lure rich people to support the government because they would have a vested interest, a real stake, in the stability and continuation of the new government.

Hamilton was a "nationalist." In other words, he believed that there must be a sovereign and "solid coercive union" that could unite the states, regulate trade, and provide for a national army. Otherwise, he feared, the states might "cut each other's throats" and the new nation might come to a "speedy and violent end."[19]

James Madison, too, was a nationalist. A Virginia planter, small of stature, friendly but somewhat shy, Madison was said to be "always dressed in black." His speaking style was quiet and logical, without ringing phrases or emotional rhetoric. But Madison was a deep thinker, a political theorist and scholar of highest quality. His careful notes are our principal source of information concerning the debates in the Constitutional Convention.[20]

Madison shared Jefferson's alarm about the loosely checked powers of the state legislatures. Concentration of power in the same hands "is precisely the definition of despotic government," Jefferson wrote. Such a concentration of power was still despotic, even if it was exercised by "a plurality of hands, and not by a single one." An "elective despotism," he said, was "not the government we fought for. . . ."[21] Madison and Jefferson agreed that governmental powers ought to be separated and that each of the separated powers should check and balance the other. These concepts had their origin in the writings of Aristotle and Cicero. They had been popularized before the Revolutionary War by the Baron de Montesquieu (1689–1755), a French lawyer and jurist. He had written in *The Spirit of the Laws* (1748) that the executive, legislative, and judicial powers in a government should be kept separate and distinct. "There would be an end of everything," he argued, "were the same man, or the same body, whether of the nobles or of the people, to exercise those three powers, that of enacting laws [legislative], that of executing public resolutions [executive], and of trying the causes of individuals [judicial]."[22]

Madison agreed with Jefferson's belief that democracy could be threatened by the tyranny of a few, in an aristocracy, and by the tyranny of the many, through an unchecked majority in a democracy. Jefferson thought that the Virginia government in particular had gone too far toward excessive power in the state legislature, giving

[19]Mason and Leach, *In Quest of Freedom*, p. 59.

[20]Burton, *A Biography of the Constitution*, p. 27; and Smith, *The Convention and the Constitution*, p. 94.

[21]Mason and Leach, *In Quest of Freedom*, p. 62

[22]Charles M. Sherover, *The Development of the Democratic Idea* (New York: New American Library, 1974), p. 182.

too much influence to the majority. He advocated a Virginia constitutional convention to write a new state constitution that would embody the principles of government he espoused and that could not be changed by the legislature.[23]

Madison also shared John Adams' concern about the persecution of minorities by majorities throughout history. Madison was later to write that people are naturally divided into "different interests and factions," " . . . creditors or debtors—rich or poor—husbandmen, merchants or manufacturers—members of different religious sects— followers of different political leaders—inhabitants of different districts—owners of different kinds of property, etc., etc. . . ."[24] He believed that if any one of these became a majority with unrestrained power, it might violate the rights of minorities. A national government characterized by "separation of powers" and "checks and balances" would neutralize this harmful tendency of the majority, Madison thought. He favored a strong national government, too, because he felt that the great size of the whole country—the great distances and the diversity of the population—as opposed to the smaller size of the states, would prevent one group or faction from getting together and forming an oppressive majority.

At the urging of James Madison,[25] the state of Virginia called upon the other twelve states to send delegates to a conference in Annapolis in the fall of 1786 to discuss trade and commerce issues. Only five states responded. The conference broke up almost before it had started, but not before Alexander Hamilton, a delegate from New York, secured agreement to call another meeting of the states in Philadelphia with a much broader purpose: " . . . to take into consideration the situation of the United States, to devise such further provisions as shall appear to them necessary to render the Constitution of the Federal Government adequate to the exigencies of the Union."

A great many of the Revolutionary leaders were quite satisfied with the loose and weak governmental arrangement under the Articles of Confederation. They opposed a strong national government. Others saw no urgency for strengthening the central government. Then in the winter of 1786, a group of Massachusetts farmers who could not make their mortgage payments joined an uprising under the leadership of a Revolutionary War captain, Daniel Shays, and stormed a courthouse to stop the lawyers and judges from foreclosing the mortgages. Alarm spread throughout the states that

---

[23]The discussion of the Constitutional Convention is based in part on Max Farrand, *The Framing of the Constitution of the United States* (New Haven: Yale University Press, 1930); James Madison, *Notes of Debates in the Federal Convention of 1787* (Athens, Ohio: Ohio University Press, 1966); and Warren, *The Making of the Constitution.*

[24]James Madison, *The Federalist,* no. 10.

[25]Homer Hackett, *The Constitutional History of the U.S., 1776–1826* (N.Y.: Macmillan, 1939), pp. 196–97.

anarchy (an absence of government) and an end to property rights might be imminent unless something was done to curb the disorders and the disregard of law and property evidenced by Shays' Rebellion. Others feared that the state of Massachusetts would be unable to restore order alone. Historian Samuel Morison has written that "when Massachusetts appealed to the Confederation for help, Congress was unable to do a thing. That was the final argument to sway many Americans in favor of a stronger federal government."[26]

George Washington had been elected a delegate to the Philadelphia meeting but had not planned to go. But General Henry Knox, who commanded the militia that put down the rebellion in Massachusetts, wrote Washington that the rebellion was a fearful attack on private property. "Their creed is that the property of the United States has been protected from confiscation of Britain by the joint exertions of all, and therefore ought to be the common property of all," he stated. "Our government must be braced, changed, or altered to secure our lives and property."[27] Washington, who had long supported Hamilton's advocacy of a strong central government, did not by any means share Jefferson's view that a rebellion every now and then had a salutary effect on government and helped keep it in line. Washington decided to go to Philadelphia after all. "There are combustibles in every State which a spark might set fire to," Washington wrote. "I feel infinitely more than I can express for the disorders which have arisen. Good God!"[28]

After seven of the states had already elected delegates to the Constitutional Convention, which was to meet in Philadelphia in May 1787, and after it was clear that the Convention would indeed be held, the Congress passed a resolution approving it. But it attempted to restrict the Convention to the "sole and express purpose of revising the Articles of Confederation."

Rhode Island did not elect delegates. The other twelve states elected seventy-four, of which only fifty-five ever participated in the Convention. Several of these were not present during large portions of the proceedings. Only thirty-nine of the delegates eventually signed the finished document; some of those who had been most active in its preparation refused to do so.

Only eight of the signers of the Declaration of Independence were also delegates to the Constitutional Convention. (It is interesting to note also that only four of these men finally signed the Constitution.) Washington and Benjamin Franklin were among the best known of the Revolutionary leaders present at the Convention. Washington, fifty-five years old, was unanimously chosen to chair the proceedings. Franklin, at eighty-one the oldest delegate, was a philosopher and

Shays' Rebellion in the winter of 1786 convinced many political leaders of the need for a strong central government. Discontent among farmers in Massachusetts reached the point of armed insurrection during the depression following the Revolutionary War, when high land taxes and heavy mortgage payments threatened many farmers with foreclosure of their mortgages and with imprisonment for nonpayment of their debts.

[26]Morison, *The Oxford History of the American People,* p. 304.

[27]Warren, *The Making of the Constitution,* p. 31; and Mason and Leach, *In Quest of Freedom,* p. 68.

[28]Quoted in Williams, Current, and Freidel, *A History of the United States to 1877,* p. 181.

Many people, especially those who owned no property or who were in debt, were not as happy with political and economic conditions following the Revolutionary War as some wealthier Americans were. In an address to the people of Hampshire County (Massachusetts), Daniel Gray, chairman of a committee of rebels protesting the plight of debtors, explained the reasons behind the 1786 riots led by Daniel Shays. Thomas Grover, a Massachusetts citizen, listed a number of grievances and goals in a letter to the Hampshire Herald.

Daniel Gray

We have thought proper to inform you of some of the principal causes of the late risings of the people. . . .

1. The present expensive mode of collecting debts, which by reason of the great scarcity of cash will of necessity fill our jails with unhappy debtors, and thereby a reputable body of people [will be] rendered incapable of being serviceable either to themselves or the community.

2. The monies raised by impost and excise being appropriated to discharge the interest of governmental securities, and not the foreign debt, when these securities are not subject to taxation.

3. A suspension of the writ of habeas corpus, by which those persons who have stepped forth to assert and maintain the rights of the people are liable to be taken . . . to the most distant part of the commonwealth, and thereby subjected to an unjust punishment.

4. The unlimited power granted to justices of the peace, and sheriffs, deputy sheriffs, and constables by the Riot Act, [exempting them from] prosecution thereof; when perhaps [they are] wholly actuated from a principle of revenge, hatred, and envy.

Furthermore, be assured that this body, now at arms, despise the idea of being instigated by British emissaries, which is so strenuously propagated by the enemies of our liberties; and also wish the most proper and speedy measures may be taken to discharge both our foreign and domestic debt.

Thomas Grover

. . . upon the desire of the people now at arms, I take this method to publish to the world of mankind in general, particularly the people of this Commonwealth, some of the principal grievances we complain of and of which we are now seeking redress, . . . which we hope, will soon take place; and if so, our brethren in this Commonwealth that do not see with us as yet shall find we shall be as peaceable as they be.

done, we verily believe, nay, positively know, it would save this Commonwealth thousands of pounds.

4. Let the lands belonging to this Commonwealth, at the eastward, be sold at the best advantage to pay the remainder of our domestic debt.

5. Let the monies arising from impost and excise be appropriated to discharge the foreign debt.

6. Let that act passed by the General Court last June by a small majority of only seven, called the Supplementary Act, . . . be repealed.

7. The total abolition of the Inferior Court of Common Pleas and General Sessions of the Peace.

8. Deputy sheriffs totally set aside as a useless set of officers in the community; and constables, who are really necessary, be empowered to do the duty, by which means a large swarm of lawyers will be banished

VIEWPOINT
The Causes of Shays' Rebellion

In the first place, I must refer you to a draft of grievances drawn up by a committee of the people, now at arms, under the signature of Daniel Gray, chairman, which is heartily approved of; some others also are here added, . . .

1. The General Court, [capitol] must be removed out of the town of Boston.

2. A revision of the constitution is absolutely necessary.

3. All kinds of governmental securities, now on interest, . . . have been bought of the original owners for 2s. . . . and the highest for 6s. 8d. on the pound, and have received more interest than the principal cost [paid by] the speculator who purchased them—that if justice was

from their wonted haunts, who have been more damage to the people at large, especially the common farmers, than the savage beasts of prey.

To this I boldly sign my proper name, as a hearty wellwisher to the real rights of the people.

SOURCE: George Minot, *History of the Insurrections in the Year 1786 and the Rebellion Consequent Thereon*, 2nd ed. (Boston: 1810). Reprinted in *The Annals of America* (Chicago: Encyclopaedia Britannica, 1968).

statesman of world reknown. He was witty and likable; as ambassador to France during the Revolution, Franklin had made a great hit with the French. Because of Franklin's age, his speeches had to be read to the Convention by James Wilson, but they were listened to attentively, as was his counsel, although on most issues Franklin was willing to accord more power to ordinary people than were most delegates.

A number of the delegates were fairly young. In a sense they represented a new generation after the signers of the Declaration. Madison was thirty-six, Hamilton thirty. A majority of the active delegates were college graduates.

Much has been written about the motivations of the delegates.[29] When they wrote the Constitution, were they thinking about their country's interests or about their own? Well, probably both, but most of the delegates would probably not have recognized any difference between the two. Early historians agreed with Jefferson that the delegates were "an assembly of demigods" who built a stable national democracy out of economic and political chaos following the "critical period" of the 1780s. Later historians were more realistic, and they also asserted that the economic and political conditions of the times were not as bad as they had been painted.

Then, in 1913, Charles Beard's *An Economic Interpretation of the Constitution of the United States* was published.[30] For many years thereafter, it was the most influential and controversial book about the motivations of the delegates. Beard cast the struggle over the Constitution as a "deep-seated conflict between a popular party based on paper money and agrarian interests and a conservative party centered in towns and resting on financial, mercantile, and personal property interests generally." This view is no longer credited by most historians as being justified by the facts. For one thing, there were people from Beard's two groups on both sides of the question of adopting the Constitution. Most historians would say, too, that Beard's assertion that the Constitution was "an economic document drawn with superb skill by men whose property interests were immediately at stake" is an oversimplified and unwarranted generalization.

There is no doubt that the delegates—lawyers, land owners, speculators, former officers in the armed forces, government bondholders, merchants, and commercial people—were the products of their own backgrounds as owners and defenders of property, whether land or personal possessions. They certainly intended the right of property to be protected against any unchecked majority. But,

---

[29]For a brief survey of the literature on this subject, see Gordon S. Wood, ed., *The Confederation and the Constitution; Critical Issues* (Boston: Little, Brown and Company, 1973).

[30]Charles A. Beard, *An Economic Interpretation of the Constitution of the United States* (New York: The Macmillan Company, 1913).

according to Robert E. Brown, "practically everyone [in the country] was interested in the protection of property."[31] The delegates also had clear philosophical ideas about the best form of government, and these ideas had considerable influence on their thoughts and acts.

The Congress had directed the Philadelphia Convention to confine its work to proposing revisions in the Articles of Confederation, which would have required approval by all thirteen of the state legislatures. However, the delegates soon chose a vastly more sweeping undertaking: they decided to write a new constitution. They agreed to submit it to popularly elected state conventions for ratification, not to the state legislatures, as had been done with the Articles. Thus, the delegates had to be mindful of what the voters would accept. In addition, the delegates decided that the new constitution would go into effect when only nine of the thirteen states had approved it.

They were able to adopt these provisions partly because a number of men who could have been counted on to oppose them—men such as Richard Henry Lee, who had made the motion for independence in the Second Continental Congress, and Patrick Henry, whose oratory had helped win Americans to the Revolutionary cause—were not present. Henry had refused to be a delegate because, he said, "I smelt a rat." Both Henry and Lee later opposed ratification of the Constitution, but by then it was too late.

The delegates had little trouble agreeing that the national government should be *republican* in form, deriving its powers "from the great body of the people," with provision that "the persons administering it [the government] be appointed, either directly or indirectly, by the people," as Madison later put it. But many of the other issues that the convention was confronted with were much more divisive and controversial, and these issues threatened to make a strong union impossible.

The Issues

Gathering at the Philadelphia State House—now called Independence Hall—the delegates decided to keep their meetings closed and secret to facilitate free debate and compromise. They soon agreed to a highly important motion, designated the Fourth Virginia Resolve, which stated that "a *national* government ought to be established consisting of a *supreme* legislative, executive, and judiciary." This motion meant that whatever new government they later decided to establish would deal with people—not just with states, as the Articles of Confederation did. It also meant that there would be a separation of powers within the new national government.

---

[31]Robert E. Brown, *We the People: The Economic Origins of the Constitution* (Chicago: University of Chicago Press, 1958), p. vii.

Other issues were more difficult to settle. Philadelphia's humid weather grew hotter and more uncomfortable as the spring of 1787 lengthened into summer. And the debate inside the State House became more heated, too. How could the power of a strong national government be reconciled with the jealously guarded sovereignty of the states? How could the small states be assured that the more populous states, such as Virginia, would not run over them? How could the powers of the legislative branch be kept within some reasonable bounds? How could the interests of the various classes of people be assured representation in the national government? What was to be done about slavery, which the southern states wanted to continue without interference?

The Virginia plan: A strong union. James Madison came to the convention having studied and prepared, as if for a college examination. With his guidance, the Virginia delegation caucused and agreed upon a series of resolutions outlining the kind of new government they favored. Soon after the convention opened, the Virginia Plan (as we now call it) was presented to the convention by the chairperson of the Virginia delegation, Virginia Governor Edmund Randolph. The plan called for a two-house "National Legislature"; members of one house would be elected by the people of each state, and members of the other house would be elected by the first house from a list of people nominated by each state legislature. This national legislature would be able to deal directly with people, not just states. It would have the power to "legislate in all cases to which the separate states are incompetent"; the legislature itself would apparently decide when this was true. Finally, it would be able to veto any state laws that, in its opinion, violated the national constitution.

There would be a single "National Executive," chosen by the national legislature. There would be a "National Judiciary," which would also be chosen by the national legislature and would serve during "good behavior," that is, probably for life. What if the national legislature passed a law that violated the national constitution? A "Council of Revision," made up of the national executive and judges from the national judiciary, could examine and reject such a law.

A crucial question soon arose: How many members would each state have in the national legislature? According to the plan, representation would depend upon how many people lived in the state or how much the state contributed to the national government—tests highly favorable to Virginia, which was both a wealthy state and the most populous state.

The New Jersey plan: A revised confederation. Delegates from the small states—Delaware, Connecticut, and New Jersey—caucused and came up with an alternative to the Virginia Plan. The New Jersey Plan, as we call it, was presented to the convention by William

Paterson, who had served as New Jersey's Attorney General. Under this plan, a revision of the Articles, "the United States in Congress" would be strengthened, but the individual states would remain the most important units of government. Congress would have the power to tax and to regulate foreign and interstate commerce. It would continue to be a unicameral legislature, just as it was in the Articles; delegates would continue to be elected by the state legislatures, not by the people.

How many votes should each state have in the Congress? Just the same as under the Articles: one for each state. What about an executive department and a judicial department, not provided for in the Articles? There would be a plural "Federal Executive," chosen by Congress. There would be a "Federal Judiciary," chosen by the federal executive, not by Congress, with the judges to serve during good behavior. But a majority of the state governors could have Congress remove the federal executive. Although the New Jersey Plan provided that the national constitution, treaties, and laws would be the "supreme law" of the states, it allowed some flexibility to the state courts in recognizing and enforcing this supreme law.

Those backing the New Jersey Plan had an important practical argument on their side. The Virginia Plan, which would give the three large states of Virginia, Massachusetts, and Pennsylvania the power to control the national government if they acted together, would have little chance of ever going into effect because the plan would first have to be referred to the states for ratification, and the small states would surely block it.

Leading figures during the Constitutional Convention (clockwise from top left): Benjamin Franklin; John Jay, coauthor with Hamilton and Madison of *The Federalist Papers;* John Adams, who later was elected as the second President of the United States; and William Paterson.

Hamilton's plan: A British model. Alexander Hamilton felt that the states were too much under popular control, dominated by the "avarice, ambition, and interest which govern most people." He thought that the states should be abolished altogether and replaced by one national government, as in Britain. However, he did not seriously advocate this idea because he feared that it would "shock the public opinion." Instead, he proposed to make the states dependent, administrative units of the national government by reducing their power. "The people are turbulent and changing; they seldom judge or determine right," Hamilton declared. He conceded that the people should be represented in one house of the national legislature on the basis of universal white male suffrage (incidentally, with no property ownership requirement for voting, as Madison and others favored). But he proposed to restrain and check this house by having a coequal Senate, chosen for life, like the British House of Lords, and an "elected monarchy," also chosen for life.

Well! No wonder the delegates, who had so lately supported the Revolution against just that sort of government, gave scant consideration to Hamilton's plan. However, it may have had some effect in causing the convention eventually to tilt a little more toward a strong union and a little less toward a loose confederation.

The Connecticut Compromise: Federation.   A basic issue was thus posed for the convention by June 15: Would there be national sovereignty and *consolidation,* or state sovereignty and *confederation?* The solution was that *neither* alternative would be chosen. Instead, a middle ground was adopted. The delegates decided upon a *federation,* a government with mixed and overlapping national and state sovereignty. As Madison had foreseen, the key to breaking the stalemate on the sovereignty issue turned out to be the matter of how many votes each state should have in the national legislature.

The delegates had agreed earlier that the national legislature should be bicameral, although Franklin and others had advocated a one-house legislative body. Then, on June 29, Dr. William Samuel Johnson of Connecticut suggested the germ of an idea that was later refined and presented to the convention by a special committee. This plan came to be called the Connecticut Compromise, or the Great Compromise. Dr. Johnson asserted that the states should be thought of in two ways: as districts, or simple geographical areas in which individual Americans lived; and as political societies, units of government. In the national legislature, he said, ". . . the two ideas embraced on different sides [of the debate], instead of being opposed to each other, ought to be combined; that in *one* branch the *people,* ought to be represented; in the *other,* the States." The Connecticut Compromise was adopted on July 16 but only after protracted argument. The vote of the states was 5-4-1.

Madison found the idea of equal representation for each state in the Senate as a check against representation of population in the House of Representatives an abhorrent notion, which struck at the very heart of the idea of a national government. He was not mollified by the provision in the Compromise that only the popularly elected body, the House, could originate taxation measures. James Wilson and others were equally vehement in their opposition to the Compromise. "Can we forget for whom we are forming a government?" Wilson asked. "Is it for *men,* or for the imaginary beings called States?" Wilson and Madison felt that the principle involved was a far more important one than the small-state-versus-large-state controversy. For them, the issue involved the very foundation of the government, which they declared ought to rest upon suffrage, or voting by people, rather than upon consent by the states. Therefore, representation in *both* houses should be based on population. Even after the Compromise had been adopted, opponents could still not bring themselves to accept it until they became convinced at last that there would be no Constitution without it.

In regard to slavery and export trade, the southern states were able to get a large measure of what they wanted, both in the Connecticut Compromise and in the decisions made thereafter. They could count three-fifths of their slaves for purposes of representation in the House of Representatives; slave importations could not be prohibited by the national government for at least twenty years; and slaves could not be taxed more than $10 a head. In addition, the southern export trade was protected by a provision that the Congress could not tax exports at all and by a requirement that no treaty made by the national government with a foreign country would become effective until it had been ratified by a two-thirds vote of the Senate.

THE FIGHT FOR RATIFICATION

We the people of the United States, in Order to form a more perfect Union, establish Justice, insure domestic Tranquility, provide for the common defence, promote the general Welfare, and secure the Blessing of Liberty to ourselves and our Posterity, do ordain and establish this Constitution for the United States of America.

These are the words of the *Preamble* of the United States Constitution, the introductory section of the document that the delegates finally signed on September 17, 1787—109 days after they had first convened. Governeur Morris of Pennsylvania, a member of a Committee on Style, was largely responsible for the final wording of the Constitution.

No delegate was completely happy with the result. Some thought it went too far toward a strong union; others felt it did not go far enough. But most of the delegates decided that the final product was one which had the best chance of actually being ratified by the states. Benjamin Franklin verbalized this sentiment when he said, "Thus, I consent, Sir, to this Constitution, because I expect no better, and because I am not sure, that it is not the best . . ." Franklin's final speech, read by Wilson, urged the delegates to put aside their doubts and differences and sign the Constitution. And all those present, except Edmund Randolph and George Mason of Virginia and Elbridge Gerry of Massachusetts, rose and went forward to place their signatures on the finished document.

The Constitution was finished. The delegates had no way of knowing at that time whether the new government would ever come into existence. But many felt that the new Constitution was the only hope for the avoidance of additional violence and bloodshed in America. Now it was up to the states to decide whether to adopt it. Congress submitted the document to the states for ratification in special state conventions.

No sooner had the delegates left the Constitutional Convention than the debate on their work began to rage throughout the country. Proponents of the Constitution had the advantage. The question of ratification asked for only a simple "yes" or "no" in each convention. Those who favored ratification had something to sell. Those who opposed the Constitution were agreed on no plan to offer in its place. In politics, it is sometimes said, "You can't beat something with nothing." And this lack of a clear alternative was a serious problem for the opponents of the Constitution.

They had another problem, too. Proponents of the Constitution chose the best name for themselves: "Federalists." They chose this name because they knew that one of the most serious objections to the Constitution would be that it sought to establish a *consolidated* national government at the expense of state powers. Under the pen name Publius, James Madison, Alexander Hamilton, and John Jay wrote a series of newspaper articles in New York, *The Federalist Papers,*[32] which carefully stated the political philosophy and arguments of the Federalists. The opponents of the Constitution had no popular name by which to call themselves. The Federalists called them "Antifederalists."

A very serious argument made against the Constitution was that it contained no Bill of Rights. Indeed, Jefferson and others who supported ratification of the Constitution raised this objection themselves.[33] To overcome this criticism, Madison decided to propose a Bill of Rights in the first Congress; these rights were adopted as the first ten amendments to the Constitution.

George Mason of Virginia, who had refused to sign the Constitu-

THE CONSTITUTION: RISING SUN OF A NEW NATION?

When their work was finished, many of the delegates to the Constitutional Convention of 1787 were not quite sure how it would all turn out. But James Madison reported that Benjamin Franklin ended the convention on a note of optimism.

"Whilst the last members were signing it," Madison wrote in his notes, "Doctr. Franklin looking towards the President's chair, at the back of which a rising sun happened to be painted, observed to a few members near him, that painters had found it difficult to distinguish in their art a rising from a setting sun. 'I have,' said he, 'often and often in the course of this session, and the vicissitudes of my hopes and fears as to its issue, looked at that behind the President, without being able to tell whether it was rising or setting; but now at length I have the happiness to know that it is a rising and not a setting sun.'"

SOURCE: James Madison, *Notes of Debates in the Federal Convention of 1787*, p. 659.

---

[32]Later published in book form as *The Federalist*.

[33]For a discussion of the struggle over ratification, see Robert A. Rutland, *The Ordeal of the Constitution* (Norman, Oklahoma: Univeristy of Oklahoma Press, 1965).

Anti-Federalists raised a number of serious objections to the proposed Constitution; most are contained in the following "Address and Reasons of Dissent," written by anti-Federalists in Pennsylvania after the state became the second to ratify in December 1787.

Our objections are comprised under three general heads of dissent, viz.:

We dissent, first, because it is the opinion of the most celebrated writers on government, and confirmed by uniform experience, that a very extensive territory cannot be governed

VIEWPOINT

Against the Constitution

on the principles of freedom otherwise than by a confederation of republics, possessing all the powers of internal government but united in the management of their general and foreign concerns. . . .

We dissent, secondly, because the powers vested in Congress by this Constitution must necessarily annihilate and absorb the legislative, executive, and judicial powers of the several states, and produce from their ruins one consolidated government, which from the nature of things will be *an ironbanded despotism,* as nothing short of the supremacy of despotic sway could connect and govern these United States under one government.

We dissent, thirdly, because if it were practicable to govern so extensive a territory as these United States include, on the plan of a consolidated government, consistent with the principles of liberty and the happiness of the people, yet the construction of this Constitution is not calculated to attain the object; for independent of the nature of the case, it would of itself necessarily produce a despotism, and that not by the usual gradations but with the celerity that has hitherto only attended revolutions effected by the sword.

To establish the truth of this position, a

Leading opponents of the Constitution: Luther Martin (top left) of Maryland; Patrick Henry (top right) and Richard Henry Lee (middle left) of Virginia; Elbridge Gerry (middle right) and Sam Adams (bottom) of Massachusetts.

cursory investigation of the principles and form of this Constitution will suffice.

The first consideration . . . is the omission of a *Bill of Rights* ascertaining and fundamentally establishing those unalienable and personal rights of men, without the full, free, and secure enjoyment of which there can be no liberty, . . .

. . . the legislature under this Constitution . . . is deficient in every essential quality of a just and safe representation.

. . . the sense and views of [the] . . . people, diffused over so extensive a territory, comprising such various climates, products, habits, interests, and opinions, cannot be collected in so small a body; and, besides, it is not a fair and equal representation of the people even in proportion to its number, for the smallest state has as much weight in the Senate as the largest; and from the smallness of the number to be chosen for both branches of the legislature, and from the mode of election and appointment, which is under the control of Congress, and from the nature of the thing, men of the most elevated rank in life will alone be chosen. The other orders in the society, such as farmers, traders, and mechanics, who all ought to have a competent number of their best-informed men in the legislature, shall be totally unrepresented.

The next consideration that the Constitution presents is the undue and dangerous mixture of the powers of government; the same body possessing legislative, executive, and judicial powers. The Senate is a constituent branch of the legislature; it has judicial power in judging on impeachments; and, in this case, unites in some measure the characters of judge and party, as all the principal officers are appointed by the President General, with the concurrence of the Senate, and, therefore, they derive their offices in part from the Senate. This may bias the judgments of the senators and tend to screen great delinquents from punishment.

And the Senate has, moreover, various and great executive powers, viz., in concurrence with the President General, they form treaties with foreign nations that may control and abrogate the constitutions and laws of the several states. Indeed, there is no power,

privilege, or liberty of the state governments, or of the people, but what may be affected by virtue of this power. For all treaties made by them are to be the "supreme law of the land; anything in the constitution or laws of any state, to the contrary notwithstanding."

The power of direct taxation applies to every individual, as Congress, under this government, is expressly vested with the authority of laying a capitation or poll tax upon every person to any amount. This is a tax that, however oppressive in its nature and unequal in its operation, is certain as to its produce and simple in its collection; it cannot be evaded like the objects of imposts or excise, and will be paid, because all that a man has will he give for his head. This tax is so congenial to the nature of despotism that it has ever been a favorite under such governments. . . .

. . . that strongest of all checks upon the conduct of administration, *responsibility to the people*, will not exist in this government.

The permanency of the appointments of senators and representatives, and the control the Congress have over their election, will place them independent of the sentiments and resentment of the people, and the administration having a greater interest in the government than in the community, there will be no consideration to restrain them from oppression and tyranny. . . .

If the people part with a responsible representation in the legislature, founded upon fair, certain, and frequent elections, they have nothing left they can call their own. Miserable is the lot of that people whose every concern depends on the will and pleasure of their rulers. . . . in short, the system of despotism will soon be completed.

SOURCE: *Pennslyvania Packet* and *Daily Advertiser* (December 18, 1787). Reprinted in *The Annals of America* (Chicago: Encyclopaedia Britannica, 1968).

Ratification of the Constitution

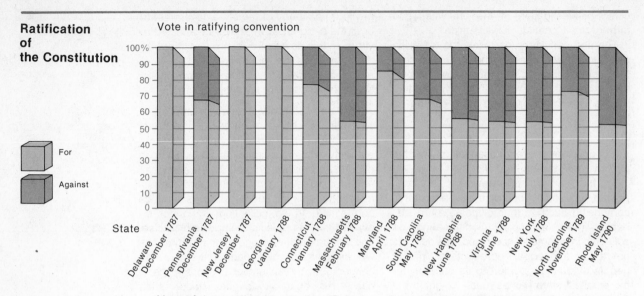

Vote in ratifying convention

For

Against

State

Delaware December 1787 · Pennsylvania December 1787 · New Jersey December 1787 · Georgia January 1788 · Connecticut January 1788 · Massachusetts February 1788 · Maryland April 1788 · South Carolina May 1788 · New Hampshire June 1788 · Virginia June 1788 · New York July 1788 · North Carolina November 1789 · Rhode Island May 1790

Most of the small states, such as Delaware, New Jersey, and Georgia, quickly ratified the Constitution. Two conventions were necessary in New Hampshire—the ninth state to ratify, enabling the document to take effect. Without New York and Virginia, however, the new government would have had little hope of survival; and the votes in both states were narrow victories for ratification. In Virginia, the vote was 89–79; in New York, 30–27. Both North Carolina and Rhode Island finally ratified the document only after a bill of rights was added.

tion in Philadelphia, was a leader against its ratification in Virginia, and his words were quoted in other states. Mason warned that the Presidency might become a monarchy or aristocracy. He feared, too, that Congress would use the *necessary and proper clause*—the phrase in the Constitution, "to make all Laws which shall be necessary and proper . . ."—to expand its powers unduly. He did not like the fact that Congress could enact laws by a simple majority vote, and he objected to the prohibition in the Constitution against interference with the slave trade for twenty years. Finally, he asserted that the Constitution's lack of a Bill of Rights was a fatal flaw.

Richard Henry Lee, Patrick Henry, Luther Martin of Maryland, and Samuel Adams of Massachusetts were other leaders against ratification. Lee argued that the Constitution served only two extreme groups, one "composed of the little insurgents, men in debt, who want no law, and who want a share of the property of others," and the other made up of "a few, but more dangerous men" who "avariciously grasp at all power and property." He said that the first group had brought about the Constitutional Convention and the second group had dominated it. Lee claimed that the Constitution was not fair to "the men of middling property, men not in debt on the one hand, and men, on the other, content with republican governments, and not aiming at immense fortunes, offices and powers."

Despite these arguments, five of the necessary states ratified the

Constitution within five months after the Constitutional Convention had adjourned, and four more approved it within six months thereafter. The old Congress was dissolved, the new government was established, and President George Washington was sworn in on April 30, 1789. The ratification fight in many of the states, however, was a bitter one. North Carolina did not come into the Union until nearly nine months after Washington's inauguration. Rhode Island, which had not even sent delegates to the Constitutional Convention, finally ratified the Constitution in May 1790. At last there could be a national flag with thirteen stars, which truly represented all the united states and which symbolized a single United States of America.

**Sentiment
For and Against
the Constitution**

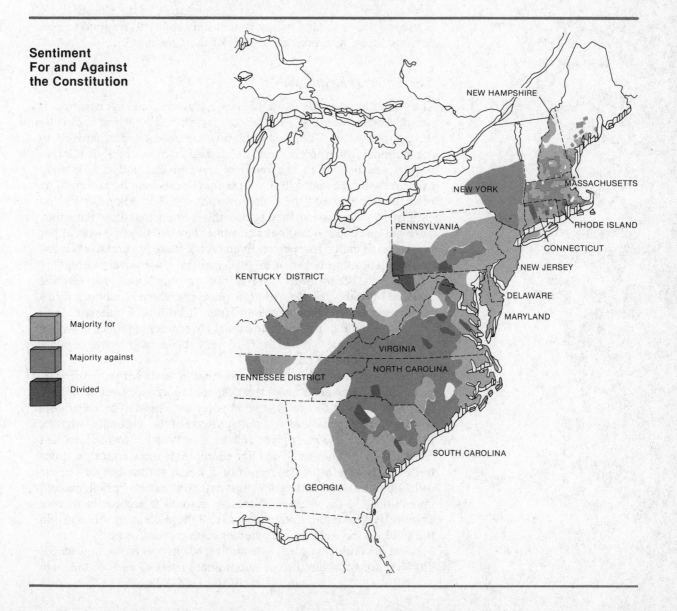

Majority for

Majority against

Divided

THE CONSTITUTION

The governmental system established by the U.S. Constitution divides power between the national government and the states, and among the three branches within the national government itself. Our government is also an evolving system; it has changed with time. It is, indeed, based upon a written Constitution, but the way the governmental system operates today cannot always be traced back to the exact wording of the original document. This is because the Congress, the President, and the Supreme Court have usually followed a "broad construction" approach, or an expansive view of the powers granted to these bodies by the Constitution, rather than the "strict construction" approach, or literal interpretation of the Constitution. Some see this flexibility in our system, this ability to respond to new circumstances, as a positive feature of the Constitution.

The Federal Principle

The government of the United States is truly national in character. It can deal with the people of the country directly, not just indirectly through the states. That is, certain powers are granted exclusively to the national government and are denied to the states. But other powers are denied to the national government and are retained exclusively by the states. Still others overlap and can be exercised by both the national and the state governments. The delegates had no pattern to go by when they sewed this system together. And they were not quite sure what they had when they had finished with it, but it came to be called *federalism*. Even today, there is a creative tension in the relationship between the national and state governments.

Under the Constitution, states are the *basic units* for electing national officials. The Constitution *guarantees* them republican forms of government, equal representation in the U.S. Senate, and protection and defense by the national government in times of war or domestic violence. A state may levy taxes and may regulate commerce within its boundaries.

There are a number of powers that a state *cannot* exercise, including the power to make treaties, coin money or issue their own currency, impair contracts, tax imports or exports, or enter into compacts with each other without approval of the national Congress. In addition, a state *must* give "full faith and credit" to the laws and court orders of another state. For example, it must honor an order from another state for the return of a stolen automobile or for the collection of a debt. Each state must extend the same "privileges and immunities" to the citizens of another state as it accords to its own citizens. For example, a state must tax all those doing business within the state on the same basis, whether state citizens or not.

Local governments, such as counties, towns and cities, and school districts, are considered to be subordinate parts of each of the state governments. These local governments derive their powers and existence from their parent governments, the states, and are bound by the same constitutional provisions that apply to the states.

The Constitution did not address the question of whether a state could undo its decision to ratify the Constitution and *secede* from the union. A bloody Civil War nearly seventy-five years later finally settled that question in the negative, once and for all.

The wording of the Constitution is very concise, and a lot of meaning is packed into its seemingly simple phrases.[34] Sometimes the meaning is not clear. The Constitution is considered a *living document* because its meaning has been interpreted and reinterpreted over the years in the light of changed conditions. As a result of this process, the federal government now has far greater powers, as compared with the states, than any of the delegates to the Constitutional Convention of 1787 would probably have ever imagined.

The doctrine of *implied powers* has been one important basis for these enlarged federal powers. It was first recognized by the U.S. Supreme Court in the 1819 case of *McCulloch* v. *Maryland*.[35] This case arose when the state of Maryland attempted to levy a state tax on a branch of the national bank, which had been created by Congress at the suggestion of Alexander Hamilton, Secretary of the Treasury in President Washington's government.

In the *McCulloch* case, the Supreme Court declared Maryland's tax unconstitutional. The reasoning of the opinion, written by Chief Justice John Marshall, went this way. First, Marshall stated in the opinion that Congress has the "implied power" to establish a bank because of the necessary and proper clause in Article I, Section 8 of the U.S. Constitution. Second, Chief Justice Marshall referred in the opinion to the *supremacy clause* which holds that a constitutional law passed by Congress is superior to a state law that conflicts with it. Such a state law becomes unconstitutional. Lastly, Marshall's opinion declared that since "the power to tax is the power to destroy," any attempt by a state to levy a tax on an agency or institution properly created by the national government is unconstitutional and invalid.

Chief Justice Marshall reached this conclusion despite the fact that the Tenth Amendment to the Constitution had by then been adopted. This amendment states, "The powers not delegated to the United States by the Constitution, nor prohibited by it to the states, are reserved to the States respectively, or to the people." Marshall pointed out that the Articles of Confederation had reserved to the states all powers not "expressly" delegated to the Congress, but that the word "expressly" had been left out of the Tenth Amendment. Thus, the federal government had certain "implied" powers that were not directly spelled out in the Constitution.

---

[34]A full copy of the Constitution is printed at the back of this book. You will see that it can be quickly and easily read.

[35]17 U.S. 316 (1819).

Neither Thomas Jefferson nor James Madison believed that the federal government should have implied powers. They were both strict constructionists. For this reason, they had vigorously opposed Hamilton's plan for a national bank, and they were equally outraged by Chief Justice Marshall's broad construction of the Constitution. However, as President, Jefferson made an exception to this view when he decided to consummate the Louisiana Purchase, despite the fact that he could not find such power specifically authorized in the Constitution. But even though President Richard Nixon revived the doctrine of strict construction when nominating members of the Supreme Court, it has not been a dominant approach to constitutional interpretation.

The *commerce clause*, contained in Article I, Section 8 of the Constitution, gives Congress exclusive power to regulate commerce "among the several states." Its broad interpretation by the Supreme Court has greatly enhanced the powers of the national government.[36] Similarly, national powers have also been enhanced by a broad interpretation of the *welfare clause,* a paragraph in the same article and section which states that Congress has the power to provide for the "general welfare of the United States."

The commerce clause also gives Congress the exclusive power to regulate commerce "with the Indian tribes." Early Supreme Court opinions written by Chief Justice Marshall held that American Indian tribes are "domestic dependent nations" and that their members have a "unique relationship" with the federal government.[37] American Indians are therefore different from other American minorities. Though not the same as states, tribal governments are political entities that are an integral part of the federal system. State governments do not have jurisdiction over Indian reservations or the citizens of them, except when a state has been delegated that power by the federal government.

In addition to its exclusive power to regulate commerce among the states and with Indian tribes, the federal government has certain "enumerated" (stated) ones including sole authority to wage war, make peace, conclude treaties, and provide for the common defense. It also has been held that the federal government has the "inherent" power, whether it is spelled out in the Constitution or not, to do what needs to be done in the field of foreign relations, such as appointing ambassadors and setting up embassies.[38]

The states and the federal government share some powers, such as the power to tax. A person who works as a truck driver in New Mexico, say, pays both a federal income tax, which was established by

---

[36]See *Steward Machine Co.* v. *Davis,* 301 U.S. 548 (1937); and *National Labor Relations Board* v. *Jones & Laughlin Steel Corp.,* 301 U.S. 1 (1937).

[37]*Cherokee Nation* v. *Georgia,* 30 U.S. 1 (1831); *Worcester* v. *Georgia,* 31 U.S. 315 (1832).

[38]*United States* v. *Curtiss-Wright Export Corp.,* 299 U.S. 304 (1936).

the Sixteenth Amendment in 1913, and a New Mexico state income tax. Spending is now shared, too; under a program called "revenue sharing" the federal government collects taxes and gives some of the money to state and local governments to spend. Administration of a number of modern programs is also shared. For example, the Congress adopted and partially funded a national interstate highway program, but state governments had to put up a portion of the costs, and state highway departments supervise the actual construction and maintenance of the highways. There are a number of similar programs, such as welfare assistance, health care, and unemployment compensation.

Federalism is a complex and overlapping system of government. It diffuses, or scatters, the powers of government. In some ways, this makes it easier for individual citizens to participate in the making of decisions, because some of the decisions are close to home. It makes effective participation more difficult, however, in cases that involve overall national policy but require the decision to be made separately in each of the fifty states.

The federal system also provides multiple points at which powerful interests can block action. That is one reason why social activists, those seeking government action on such social problems as health, education, and unemployment, have in modern times focused their efforts on the national government, rather than dividing them in many separate state efforts.

Separation of Powers and Checks and Balances

Just as power is fragmented between the states and the federal government, it is also divided among the different parts of the federal government itself. The executive branch, the legislative branch, and the judicial branch exercise powers that are largely separate and distinct. Congress is the legislative branch. It makes laws. The President is supposed to execute, or carry out, the laws. And the courts interpret the laws—saying exactly what they mean—if there is a dispute.

In many instances, all three branches must agree on a decision, or at least acquiesce in it, before the decision can go into effect. No person can be drafted into the armed forces of the country, for example, unless Congress enacts a draft law, the President signs it, and (if a proper federal court suit is brought by a citizen to stop enforcement of the law) the Supreme Court or some lower federal court rules the new law valid.

But there is not a strict and rigid separation of powers; the powers of the three branches overlap. The separation and the overlapping of powers is called *checks and balances*. The presidential veto is a good example. If the President disagrees with a bill passed by Congress, he can veto (reject) it. In that case, the bill cannot become law unless it is again passed by both houses of Congress, but this time it must be passed by a two-thirds vote of the House of Representatives and Senate to become law. There are many other examples of checks and balances in the Constitution.

The Congress. The Constitutional Convention devoted most of its time to the provisions in Article I of the Constitution. This article established the Congress and set forth its powers. Not only did the framers divide the executive, legislative, and judicial powers, they also subdivided the legislative powers by making the Congress bicameral. There are two coequal houses. No bill can become law unless it is passed by both.

The Congress has jurisdiction over taxing and spending. It creates the laws of the country, and it has the power to regulate interstate and foreign commerce and commerce with the Indian tribes. In practice, a large part of this lawmaking and regulatory power is delegated by Congress to government agencies or regulatory bodies. For example, when Congress passed new laws in regard to the environment, it established the Environmental Protection Agency and granted that agency the discretion to issue regulations to fill in the details of the new rules and procedures. These regulations have the same effect as a law passed by Congress itself.

The Constitution purposely gives Congress, not the President, the power to "declare war." But the Constitution also states that the President is the Commander in Chief of the armed forces. Through the years, Presidents have used this provision to dominate the process of initiating and waging war. In 1973, however, Congress passed the War Powers Act, which attempts to return more of the war power back to the Congress.

The role of Congress is, of course, primarily a legislative role, but Congress also "checks and balances" the power of both the judicial and executive branches. Congress has the authority to decide how many Supreme Court justices there are and how many and what kind of "inferior" federal courts are established. It determines the budgets for the courts and the salaries of the justices and judges. The Senate must approve judicial appointees before they can take office.

Congressional laws established most of the present officers, agencies, and departments of the executive branch of the government, and Congress provides for their budgets and salaries. This power to oversee the executive departments—to scrutinize how the laws are carried out and how the money is spent—is another important check in the system. The principal executive officers of the federal government cannot be appointed by the President without the consent of the Senate, nor can the President enter into a binding treaty with a foreign government without the ratification of the treaty by a two-thirds vote in the Senate.

Another way in which Congress is able to check and balance the power of the executive department is impeachment. What if a federal

justice or judge, or an officer of the government, or even the President of the United States commits treason, bribery, or "other high crimes and misdemeanors"? Such an official can be *impeached* (formally accused) by a majority vote in the House of Representatives and tried in the Senate. If two-thirds of the senators present and voting vote to convict, the official is removed from office. When a President is being tried in the Senate, the chief justice of the Supreme Court presides. Only one President, Andrew Johnson, has ever been tried on impeachment charges, and the vote on that occasion fell one short of the number required for conviction. The House Judiciary Committee recommended that President Richard M. Nixon be impeached for transgressions in connection with the Watergate burglary of the offices of the Democratic National Committee and the ensuing cover-up. Nixon resigned the Presidency before a full session of the House could vote on the impeachment issue.

The House of Representatives. The House is sometimes called the lower house or chamber of the Congress, and the Senate is sometimes called the upper house. (Since House members and senators have equal powers in respect to the passage of a law, House members object to these designations.)

A person must be twenty-five years of age and a U.S. citizen to be elected a member of the House of Representatives. There is no property ownership requirement and no religious test for this or any other national office. There is no limit on how many times a person can be elected to the House of Representatives, and many now make it a career.

The Constitutional Convention decided to leave to the states the question of who could vote in the election of House members. The Constitution stated that all persons who were eligible in each state to vote for members of that state's most numerous legislative house could also vote in the election of a member of the U.S. House of Representatives from that state. Later laws and constitutional amendments established certain federal standards for voting.

To ensure that the House of Representatives would represent the popular will, the framers limited the term of office for members to two years. The idea was that members should frequently have to go back to the people for approval. The entire membership of the House of Representatives, which now numbers four hundred thirty-five, is up for election every two years. If all of the voters in America wanted to end the federal income tax, they would have to wait a maximum of only two years before they could try to elect candidates for the House of Representatives who would pledge to vote to repeal that tax.

Any measure having to do with taxes *must* originate in the House, not the Senate. All other bills may be originated in either house. This power to originate "revenue raising measures," which was a part of the Connecticut Compromise, was a concession to those who opposed the idea of each state having the same number of members in the Senate. It allowed the house representing the popular will to decide first about taxes. This provision has been customarily interpreted by the House and Senate as applying to *any* tax bill, whether it raises or lowers taxes, and also to appropriations bills, which deal with spending. But a bill that goes to the Senate after being passed by the House may be amended in the Senate. So, a senator who wants to raise or lower social security taxes, for example, can simply wait until a tax bill comes to the Senate from the House and if a majority of the Senate agrees, he or she can attach the social security measure to the House bill as an amendment. Of course, the amended bill must then go back to the House for approval of the change, but in effect, a revenue-raising measure can be originated in the Senate by this method.

The House has another power that it does not share with the Senate. If no presidential candidate receives a majority vote in the Electoral College (discussed later in this chapter), the election must be decided in the House of Representatives.

The Senate.   Senators and House members receive exactly the same salaries, and their duties are roughly the same, except that senators represent whole states while House members represent districts. A senator must be a citizen of the United States and at least thirty years of age. There are no limits on how long a senator may serve.

The framers of the Constitution wanted to insulate the Senate from control by a popular majority. Thus, the Constitution guarantees every state two senators, regardless of the state's population; the present Senate, then, has one hundred members. All senators are elected for six-year terms, and only one-third of the Senate is elected each two years. It is quite possible, therefore, that a measure—such as a bill to end the federal tax—could be blocked in the Senate even if a majority of the people in the country wanted the measure adopted.

That is what the framers of the Constitution intended. They anticipated that senators would be drawn from the "better element" of society—the educated, wealthy class of people. Senators, they felt, should not have to test the political winds on each issue but could vote according to their own judgment and conscience. To further assure that senators would be insulated from majority control and to make clear that senators would represent states, the Constitution required senators to be selected by state legislatures. This provision was changed to direct popular elections in 1913 as a result of the Seventeenth Amendment to the Constitution.

It might reasonably be anticipated (as the framers certainly expected) that the House would always be more "liberal" and the Senate more "conservative" on legislation dealing with property, taxes, spending, and social issues. But that has not always proved to be true in modern times. For various reasons, the liberal-conservative pendulum has swung back and forth between the two houses. One reason is that a new political trend in the country—conservative or liberal—would probably be more quickly reflected in the House because the Senate is shielded from this immediate kind of shift. Also, since senators are elected by the entire population of a state, it is less likely that a "new majority" will emerge there overnight.

The Senate possesses two exclusive powers. Only the Senate has the power of *ratification*, the authority to approve or reject treaties, and the power of *confirmation*, the authority to approve or reject presidential appointees.

The President.   Every fourth year in January, generally on a frosty, cold day, the newly elected President of the United States stands on a specially built platform on the east steps of the Capitol in Washington and takes the oath of office. The person taking the oath must be at least thirty-five years of age and must have been born in the United States. The Twenty-second Amendment (1951) states that no person may be elected to this office more than twice, and only once if serving out an earlier unfinished term of more than two years. The Vice-President, also sworn in at the same time, serves as presiding officer of the Senate and succeeds to the Presidency in the event of the death or disability of the President.

The framers of the Constitution intended to insulate the Presidency from immediate popular control, just as they did with the Senate. The technique they adopted was the Electoral College. The Constitution provides that each state shall choose as many electors as the state has senators and representatives combined. Today, they are popularly elected in each state. These electors meet in the states and cast their votes for President and Vice-President, who run as a team. Thus, in a presidential election, voters are really voting for electors who are pledged to a specific President/Vice-President slate.

The results of the electors' votes in each state are certified to the president of the U.S. Senate, who opens the certificates in the presence of a joint session of the Senate and House and announces the results. Until the Twelfth Amendment was adopted in 1804, the presidential candidate receiving the highest number of votes (if a majority) became President, and the candidate receiving the next highest number became Vice-President. The Amendment was passed to prevent a President from being saddled with an opposing presidential candidate as Vice-President.

Candidates who receive a majority of the electoral vote for President and Vice-President are declared elected. If no candidate for President receives a majority of the votes of the electors, the election is then decided from a list of the three highest candidates by a majority vote in the House of Representatives, each state casting only one block vote. If no candidate for Vice-President receives a majority of the electoral votes, the election is decided from among the two highest candidates by a majority vote in the Senate, each state again having an equal vote.

The Electoral College is one of the most controversial features of our Constitution.[39] Opponents of this institution criticize the unit rule, or the "winner-take-all" practice by which *all* of a state's electoral votes are cast for the candidate who receives the greatest number of popular votes in that state. To change this practice, critics have suggested a constitutional amendment that would provide a proportional split of a state's electoral votes among candidates. According to this proposal, each candidate would receive electoral votes in the same proportion as the state's popular vote was split among them. An alternative reform suggestion would allow the unit rule to be used only by districts within a state, not on a statewide basis.

Another criticism of the Electoral College involves the so-called faithless elector. Nothing in the Constitution prevents an elector from casting his or her vote for a candidate other than the one most favored by the voters in the elector's state. Indeed, some electors have occasionally done just that. This problem could, of course, be solved by an amendment to the U.S. Constitution. Some states have attempted to bind their electors by state law.

More serious criticism of the Electoral College is that it violates the principle of "one person, one vote" because the votes of citizens in the large states and in the smallest states have more weight than the votes of citizens in the middle-sized states. The bias in the system in favor of the smallest states results from the fact that each state, no matter how small, gets one elector for each of its two U.S. senators. The bias in favor of the large states—especially for minority-block voters within these states—results from the winner-take-all practice. For example, a candidate will give much more attention to large

[39]For criticisms and defenses of the Electoral College, see Alexander Bickel, *Reform and Continuity* (N.Y.: Harper and Row, 1971); John Yunker and Lawrence Longley, *The Electoral College: Its Biases Newly Measured for the 1960s and 1970s* (Beverly Hills: Sage, 1976); and Judith Best, *The Case Against Direct Election of the President* (Ithaca: Cornell Univ. Press, 1971).

states such as New York or California, because picking up 50,000 additional popular votes there—if that puts the candidate out front in that state—means far more in Electoral College votes than gaining the support of 50,000 additional voters in a state such as Oklahoma.

The most serious criticism of the Electoral College is that it is quite possible for a candidate who does not receive the highest number of popular votes nationwide to become President nevertheless through a majority vote in the Electoral College. This is the "runner-up candidate" problem. Many observers feel that such a President would not be considered "legitimate" by a sufficient percentage of Americans and that such a President's leadership would thereby be dangerously weakened and undermined.

Supporters of the present system have argued that it favors a strong two-party system, which they like. A major reform or abolition of the system, they insist, would give rise to a number of new parties, fragmenting our political system. Other observers claim that our system has remained stable over the years precisely because we have not replaced our constitutional institutions, and they suggest that we should not do so in the case of the Electoral College either.

The most fundamental reform which has been suggested concerning the Electoral College is that it be abolished altogether and replaced with a direct popular election of the President. U.S. Senator Birch Bayh (D., Indiana), backed by an American Bar Association committee report, has been the principal proponent of such a constitutional amendment. So far, however, it has failed to gain sufficient support in the U.S. Congress—in 1979, for example, the proposal gained only fifty-one votes in the Senate, much less than the required two-thirds vote.

Despite the continuation of the Electoral College, which filters the popular will for President through state units, those who hold this office assume the role of *national leader*. This is an informal role, not specifically mentioned in the Constitution, but it is a vitally important one. Presidents Andrew Jackson and Franklin Roosevelt were especially responsible for the growth of this aspect of the office; they

The Electoral College and the "Runner-up Candidate" Problem

In 1976, if 5559 voters in Ohio and 3687 voters in Hawaii had voted for Ford rather than Carter, Ford would have won the popular votes—and therefore the electoral votes—in both states. Ford's Electoral College votes would have made him President, although his popular vote total nationwide still would have trailed Carter's by 1.7 million votes.

Actual Votes		Carter	Ford
popular vote:	Ohio	2,011,621 (48.9%)	2,000,505 (48.6%)
	Hawaii	147,375 (51.3%)	140,003 (48.7%)
	national total	40,828,657 (50.6%)	39,145,520 (48.4%)
electoral vote:	Ohio	25	—
	Hawaii	4	—
	national total	297	241*

*One of Ford's electors voted for Ronald Reagan

Hypothetical Votes		Carter	Ford
popular vote:	Ohio	2,006,062 (48.8%)	2,006,064 (48.8%)
	Hawaii	143,688 (50.0%)	143,690 (50.0%)
	national total	40,819,411 (50.5%)	39,154,766 (48.5%)
electoral vote:	Ohio	—	25
	Hawaii	—	4
	national total	268	270*

*Assuming that all of Ford's electors voted for Ford

developed its potential for influencing and implementing national public opinion and the popular will.

The founding fathers did not mention political parties in the Constitution. They expected each state to select electors from the "better element" who would then vote for President and Vice-President without regard for political parties. The candidates would do no campaigning, just as present-day candidates for grade-school class offices are not supposed to campaign or even vote for themselves. At the time, no one doubted that George Washington would be the first President. But after his two terms, the Electoral College system never worked the same way again. Serious differences of opinion arose concerning what the new government could and should do. Factions developed, and then parties. Today, a President is a *party leader,* campaigning vigorously for the office as the nominee of a political party convention. Electors now generally cast their electoral votes almost automatically for the presidential candidate who receives the highest number of popular votes in the state's general election.

The Constitution does state that the President "shall take Care that the Laws be faithfully executed, and shall Commission all the officers of the United States." The President, then, is the *chief executive* of the federal government, the officer whose duty it is to carry out the laws passed by Congress. The President names the principal cabinet officials and other executive officers. The President is also *commander in chief* of the armed forces and the nation's *chief diplomat* in dealing with foreign governments.

In addition to executive power, the President was given authority to "check and balance" legislative power by using the veto, as we have seen, and by calling special sessions of the Congress. The President is also required by the Constitution to give the Congress "information concerning the State of the Union, and recommend to their Consideration such Measures as he shall judge necessary and expedient. . . ." This last function of the President now has been formalized into an annual message, which is followed by numerous other presidential recommendations in regard to the federal budget and new legislation. Thus, particularly since the administration of Franklin Roosevelt, the President has assumed a strong role as *chief legislator.* Since President Nixon's involvement with Watergate and his subsequent resignation, however, there has been some attempt by Congress to redress, or repair, the imbalances of power that have developed in favor of the Presidency.

The President also exercises judicial power by appointing (by and with the advice and consent of the Senate) the members of the Supreme Court and the other federal courts. This power can markedly effect judicial decisions. For example, the judicial philosophy of justices appointed by President Franklin Roosevelt resulted in Court decisions that supported the great expansion of the powers and activities of the federal government during his term. Justices added to the Court under President Richard Nixon have restricted somewhat the earlier, more liberal civil rights and civil liberties rulings of the Supreme Court during the 1950s and 1960s.

The Judiciary.   Neither the members of the Supreme Court nor the judges of the federal district courts and the circuit courts of appeal are elected. They are appointed and serve for life. The federal judiciary is, therefore, the branch of our government that is least subject to direct popular control. The Constitution did not make clear who would determine whether actions by the federal government were consistent with the Constitution. All citizens and all states, according to the supremacy clause, are required to obey the laws passed by Congress and the treaties entered into by the federal government, but only *if* these laws and treaties do not violate the U.S. Constitution. The Virginia Plan at the Constitutional Convention had called for a "Council of Revision" to determine constitutionality. This suggestion was rejected, and no other was specifically agreed to in its place.

The landmark case of *Marbury* v. *Madison,*[40] decided in 1803, filled this void in the Constitution. Again, Chief Justice John Marshall wrote the majority opinion, which held for the first time that an act of Congress is invalid if it conflicts with the U.S. Constitution. Marshall based this power of the Supreme Court to rule on the question of constitutionality—which we call *judicial review*—on sections 1 and 2 of Article III of the Constitution. Section 1 states that the "judicial power of the United States, shall be vested in one Supreme Court and in such inferior Courts as the Congress may from time to time establish." Section 2 states that this "judicial power" extends to all cases "arising under this Constitution, the Laws of the United States, and Treaties . . ." Marshall took these provisions to mean that the Supreme Court has the final say on what is, and what is not, constitutional when a proper case is presented to it. The power of judicial review has been recognized ever since, which has led some lawyers to state that "the Constitution means what the Supreme Court says it does."

Since *McCulloch* v. *Maryland,* the Supreme Court has held many acts of state legislatures to be unconstitutional. Except for a number of cases during the first years of President Roosevelt's administration, however, the Supreme Court has used its power to declare congressional acts unconstitutional rather sparingly. Still, whenever this doctrine is applied, the Supreme Court can, in effect, make important political decisions without the direct participation of the people of the country. However, the people participate indirectly through the elections of the President and senators. For example, one of the issues in the 1968 presidential election contest between Hubert H. Humphrey and Richard M. Nixon involved the type of person each candidate would nominate for membership on the Supreme Court.

John Marshall, fourth chief justice of the U.S. Supreme Court (1801-1835). His opinions in the *Marbury* and *McCulloch* cases established the key position of the Supreme Court in the federal government.

---

[40]*Marbury* v. *Madison,* 1 Cranch 137 (1803).

Amending the Constitution

Any part of the Constitution may be altered by amendment, but no state can be deprived of its equal vote in the Senate. It is noteworthy, however, that only twenty-six constitutional amendments have ever been adopted, and these include the Bill of Rights, the first ten amendments. Amendments have precisely the same weight and effect as the original, unchanged portions of the Constitution.

Amendments become a part of the Constitution in a two-step process: proposal and ratification. This process is set forth in Article V of the Constitution.

An amendment to the Constitution (or a completely new constitution) may be proposed either by a two-thirds vote in both the House and Senate or by a new constitutional convention called by the Congress on the application of two-thirds of the state legislatures. All of the amendments adopted to date were proposed by a two-thirds vote of the Congress. No new constitutional convention has ever been held. From time to time, a number of unsuccessful, one-issue movements, such as the antiabortion group called Americans for a Constitutional Convention, have advocated a new constitutional convention.[41] The most noteworthy effort so far may be the movement to balance the federal budget. By mid-1979, twenty-eight states—only six short of the required two-thirds majority—had petitioned Congress for a convention to propose a balanced-budget amendment. Some scholars have themselves suggested a wholesale revision of the Constitution to make it more democratic and efficient, but these efforts and ideas have not generated widespread support.[42]

Once an amendment (or a new constitution) has been proposed, it may be *ratified* in one of two ways decided upon by Congress: by approval of three-fourths of the state legislatures; or by approval of three-fourths of the ratification conventions called for that purpose in each of the states. The state convention method has been used only once (in the ratification of the Twenty-first Amendment in 1933 for the repeal of Prohibition).

Amending the Constitution

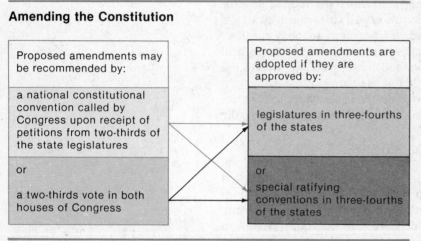

Proposed amendments may be recommended by:

a national constitutional convention called by Congress upon receipt of petitions from two-thirds of the state legislatures

or

a two-thirds vote in both houses of Congress

Proposed amendments are adopted if they are approved by:

legislatures in three-fourths of the states

or

special ratifying conventions in three-fourths of the states

---

[41]See Lisa Cronin Wohl, "Are We 25 Votes Away from Losing the Bill of Rights?" *Ms. Magazine* (February 1978), p. 46.

[42]See Leland D. Baldwin, *Reframing the Constitution* (Santa Barbara, California: American Bibliographical Center/Clio Press, 1972); Henry Hazlitt, *A New Constitution Now* (New Rochelle, New York: Arlington House, 1974); and Rexford Guy Tugwell, *Model for a New Constitution* (Santa Barbara, California: Center for the Study of Democratic Institutions, 1970).

What can we say about the Constitution as it affects political participation, that key ideal expressed in the Declaration of Independence? Thomas Jefferson's idea of democracy—or republicanism, as he would have termed it—called for the election of government officials by the people and for governmental decisions that reflect the popular will. The democracy envisioned by the writer of the Declaration was, then, both a process and a result. How well was that ideal expressed in the Constitution?

The right of the people to elect the President and members of Congress was prescribed (process); judges and civil servants are not directly elected. The Constitution protects the majority against the concentration of power in a few hands (result). But the Constitution also shields governmental decisions from the day-to-day control of a popular majority. Thus, the Constitution was meant to restrict the majority as well as to protect it. The legitimacy of our government and the power and authority that it exercises are quite clearly based upon popular sovereignty, the ultimate supremacy of the people. But this supremacy—over elections and policy—can sometimes only be expressed indirectly and over a wide interval of space and time.

One key factor that explains the long life of the Constitution is the definite and orderly, though far from easy, manner in which the fundamental law of America may be amended when a sufficient number of Americans become dissatisfied and seek a change. The Constitution has not been altered often, but almost as soon as it went into effect, it was amended to spell out the protection of certain basic human rights. The origins and history of the first ten amendments—the Bill of Rights—are the subject of Chapter 3.

ADDITIONAL SOURCES

Beard, Charles. *An Economic Interpretation of the Constitution of the United States.* Macmillan, 1935; originally published in 1913.*

Brown, Robert E. *Charles Beard and the Constitution.* Norton, 1965.*

Hamilton, Alexander; James Madison; and John Jay. *The Federalist* (available in many editions).*

Jensen, Merrill. *The Articles of Confederation,* 2nd ed. University of Wisconsin Press, 1959;* and *The New Nation.* Random House, 1965.*

Mason, Alpheus T., ed. *The States' Rights Debate: Antifederalism and the Constitution,* 2nd ed. Oxford University Press, 1972.*

Riker, William. *Federalism: Origin, Operation, Significance.* Little, Brown, 1964.*

Rossiter, Clinton. *1787: The Grand Convention.* Macmillan, 1966.

Smith, Page. *The Constitution: A Documentary and Narrative History.* Morrow, 1978.

Wood, Gordon S. *The Creation of the American Republic, 1776–1787.* University of North Carolina Press, 1970.*

*Available in paperback.

3 The Bill of Rights
Improving the Blueprint

In 1978, the American Nazi party applied for a permit to stage a demonstration in Skokie, Illinois. The American Nazi party is a small anti-Semitic group that likes to wear uniforms modeled on those of the original Nazi party in Hitler's Germany. Skokie is a largely Jewish suburb of Chicago in which many of the survivors of the Nazi holocaust now live.[1]

Suppose your mother, uncle, or brother had died in the Nazi ovens. Would you think that the American Nazi party should be allowed to march in your hometown? The American Jewish Congress, the Anti-Defamation League, and the town of Skokie went to court to stop the demonstration.

Suppose we change the date and the names and places involved. Suppose the organization involved is not the American Nazi party but the Southern Christian Leadership Conference (SCLC), the largely black organization formed to work for the civil rights of black people in America and headed by Dr. Martin Luther King, Jr. Suppose the date is not 1978 but 1955, and the town is not Skokie, Illinois, but Montgomery, Alabama, a southern city controlled by white supremacists. Suppose you are black and your mother has been ordered to sit in the back seat of the local city bus. Would you think that black people should be allowed to march to protest such treatment? Even though most of the white people in the city would find such a demonstration offensive?

---

[1] For contemporary views on both sides of the Skokie case, see *America* (June 17, 1978), pp. 475–76; *The Nation* (September 23, 1978), pp. 258, 275, 276; *The New Republic* (April 23, 1978), pp. 5, 6, 8; *National Review* (May 12, 1978), pp. 588–93.

In the Skokie case, the American Civil Liberties Union (ACLU) went to court to defend the right of the American Nazi party to demonstrate peacefully, however repugnant their views. The ACLU pointed out that the American Bill of Rights protects "symbolic" freedom of speech—which is what a demonstration is—whether or not the majority agrees with the views expressed. This view was upheld in the federal courts (although the American Nazi party finally moved their demonstration from Skokie to a park in Chicago).

Should the outcome of such a case depend upon the popularity of the views involved? Should we leave it up to a majority in each community to decide who can demonstrate, and for what causes? The first Congress of the United States sought to answer these kinds of questions by adding the Bill of Rights to our original Constitution.

Many early American leaders shared Alexander Hamilton's belief that there was no need to include a bill of rights in the Constitution. In *Federalist* 84, Hamilton wrote that a bill of rights might be necessary to restrict a king, but not a government established by the people; such a government, he argued, possesses only the powers given to it by the people. "Why, for instance, should it be said that the liberty of the press shall not be restrained, when no power is given by which restrictions may be imposed?" Adding a bill of rights to the Constitution would even be dangerous, Hamilton said; placing restrictions on powers that had not been granted to the government in the first place might give the government a "pretext to claim more than were granted." (Later on, of course, Hamilton was to be a strong advocate of the "implied powers" of the national government. But here he was making a political argument in favor of adopting the Constitution.) Another part of Hamilton's argument against a bill of rights was that the Constitution already included sufficient limitations on the federal government. It protected the right of *habeas corpus* and prohibited *ex post facto* laws, *bills of attainder*, and titles of nobility.[2]

Hamilton's opposition to a bill of rights was not shared by most American leaders. As noted earlier, Jefferson supported the Constitution but felt the document was seriously deficient because it did not contain a bill of rights. As he wrote to James Madison from Paris, "A bill of rights is what the people are entitled to against every form of government on earth. . . ."[3]

Those who opposed ratification of the Constitution because it contained no bill of rights lost the battle, of course, but they carried the day on their main argument. By the time the Constitution was

Do Nazis have the right of free speech? The attempt by the American Nazi party to march in Skokie, Illinois, on July 4, 1978, raised difficult moral and constitutional questions for many people.

---

[2] *Habeas corpus* is a safeguard against illegal detention; it is a court order requiring that a prisoner be brought before a court to determine the legality of the detention or imprisonment. An *ex post facto* law is a retroactive criminal law which attempts to make something a crime or increase the punishment for it after the offense has already been committed. A *bill of attainder* is a legislative attempt to punish particular individuals without a trial.

[3] Saul K. Padover, *The Complete Jefferson* (New York: Duell, Sloan & Pearce, Inc., 1943), p. 121.

finally ratified in the last states, it was generally understood that it would be amended immediately after it went into effect to provide a specific list of protected rights.

One of the first acts of the first Congress was to adopt and send to the states for approval twelve proposed "human rights" amendments. The states approved ten of the amendments, known as the Bill of Rights.

During the first session of Congress, James Madison (who had been elected to the U.S. House of Representatives from Virginia) introduced a series of proposals for amending the Constitution.[4] Hearkening back to the Declaration of Independence, he said that it was necessary to make clear that the new U.S. government would not attempt to transgress the rights of persons and property, which had been declared "unalienable" by the Declaration. The states ratified ten of twelve proposed amendments approved by Congress. They became the first ten amendments to the Constitution, commonly called the Bill of Rights.

The first eight amendments place certain restrictions on the national government. They restrict the government from interfering with rights that are deemed especially important for the proper functioning of a democracy; they guarantee certain personal freedoms; and they provide specific protections for people whom the government accuses of committing a crime.

The Ninth and Tenth Amendments are different from the others. The Ninth Amendment affirms that the other amendments do not constitute an exclusive list of all fundamental rights. It states: "The enumeration in the Constitution, of certain rights, shall not be construed to deny or disparage others retained by the people." The Tenth Amendment declares that the states or the people retain all the powers which have not been delegated to the national government and which are not prohibited to the states by the U.S. Constitution; it was the basis for the long and bitter argument over "states' rights."

---

[4] Edward Dumbauld, *The Bill of Rights* (Norman, Oklahoma: University of Oklahoma Press, 1957), p. 33.

THE DEMOCRATIC FREEDOMS

Certain freedoms are deemed necessary to the proper functioning of a democracy. These are the freedoms of speech and press, the right to petition the government and to peaceably assemble, and the freedom of association and dissent. These freedoms come from the Bill of Rights, particularly the First Amendment, which states: "Congress shall make no law respecting an establishment of religion, or prohibiting the free exercise thereof; or abridging the freedom of speech, or of the press; or the right of the people peaceably to assemble, and to petition the government for the redress of grievances."

We noted in Chapter 1 that there is a tension between human rights, including civil liberties, and majority rule. Polls show that many Americans, sometimes a majority, are what might be called "freedom, but" Americans. They may say, in effect, "Yes, I'm for freedom of speech, *but* I don't believe Communists ought to be able to speak against our form of government." Or, "Yes, I'm for freedom of assembly, *but* I don't believe the American Nazi party ought to be able to march through Skokie, Illinois, where a large number of Jewish Americans live." Yet the Bill of Rights was intended to *protect* these democratic freedoms and other rights against majority rule. To understand this concept better, we can think about the analogy of economic competition in the marketplace. Suppose that there was only one place in town to buy meat and that a majority of the townspeople liked the person who owned the meat market. In such a situation, it is likely that the market's customers, including the majority who liked the market owner, would not be able to buy meat of as high a quality for as low a price as they would if they had a choice among competing meat markets. A famous Supreme Court Justice, Oliver Wendell Holmes, once wrote that a democratic society needs similar competition in ideas. "When men have realized that time has upset many fighting faiths," he wrote, "they may come to believe . . . that the ultimate good desired is better reached by free trade in ideas—that the best test of truth is the power of the thought to get itself accepted in the competition of the market . . ."[5] That is, how can people be sure their opinions are right unless they hear wrong opinion? How can wrong opinions, which do not even serve the interests of those who hold them, be changed, unless right opinions can be heard?

Suppression of the democratic rights can also be dangerous for a democracy. "When the channels of opinion and of peaceful persuasion are corrupted or clogged," Justice Robert H. Jackson has written, "political correctives can no longer be relied on, and the democratic system is threatened at its most vital point."[6] There is a

---

[5] William Cohen and John Kaplan, *Bill of Rights* (Mineola, New York: The Foundation Press, 1976), p. 55.

[6] Robert H. Jackson, *The Supreme Court in the American System of Government* (Cambridge, Mass.: Harvard University Press, 1955).

connection between the democratic rights, such as freedom of speech, and nonviolent change. If people can change things peacefully, they may be less likely to resort to force and violence. Thus, a democratic society—and the majority within it—has a vital stake in protecting the democratic rights, whether or not the majority approves of all that is done and said.

Freedom of Speech

What a person thinks or believes is his or her own business. Government cannot restrict freedom of belief or thought. But what if a person *says* what he or she thinks?

An individual's speech may or may not be the public's business, depending upon what is said, where it is said, and for what purpose. Just as there is a distinction between thought and speech, there is also a distinction between speech and action. Clearly, the government can restrict certain types of action, such as rioting. But should it be able to restrict mere talk about rioting? "No one pretends that actions should be as free as opinions," wrote the nineteenth-century English philosopher John Stuart Mill in his essay *On Liberty*. "On the contrary, even opinions lose their immunity when the circumstances in which they are expressed are such as to constitute a positive instigation to some mischievous act." Mill went on to say that a mere statement, such as "corn dealers are starvers of the poor," should ordinarily be freely allowed. But such a statement, he said, might properly incur punishment if "delivered orally to an excited mob assembled before the house of a corn-dealer."[7]

This issue reveals another tension in our system—the tension between liberty and order. Americans have the right of free speech. The American government has the power and duty to maintain public order. Neither the individual right nor the governmental power is absolute. Thus, there must be a way to balance the two. This process has largely taken place in the courts.

But judicial rules about balancing are not clearly defined, and the courts exercise much discretion in applying them in particular cases. The earliest rule, called the *clear and present danger* doctrine, was first announced in a decision by Justice Holmes. With later modification, it held that speech or other expression cannot be restricted unless the words used and the circumstances in which they are used create a clear and present danger that substantive evil will result before there is time for full discussion.[8]

Some justices have considered this rule to be too lenient; one Supreme Court decision held that speech or other expression can be restricted if it has even a *dangerous tendency* to bring about a substantive evil. On the other hand, several justices—but not a

---

[7] John Stuart Mill, *On Liberty* (New York: Bobbs-Merrill Co., Inc., 1947).
[8] *Schenck* v. *United States*, 249 U.S. 47 (1919).

majority of the Supreme Court—have felt that the clear and present danger rule is too strict and allows too much limitation on speech. They hold to the *preferred position* rule, a doctrine which holds that First Amendment liberties should be preferred over other provisions of the Constitution because they are almost absolute rights. Therefore, any attempt to restrict these liberties is presumed to be unconstitutional unless it can be shown that the restriction is absolutely necessary to prevent very imminent and serious evils.

In recent cases, *balancing* has become the rule for speech that advocates violence or violation of the law. In such cases, the Supreme Court balances, or weighs, the interests of the government in keeping order and the interests of the individual in exercising First Amendment freedoms. Much depends upon the facts of the particular case before the Supreme Court, the composition of the Court at that time, whether the case arises in peacetime or wartime, and what the public mood is. The Supreme Court has used the balancing rule to decide that it is constitutional to punish a person for urging resistance to the draft or to the war effort, or for advocating the violent overthrow of the government.

It can be generally said, however, that legislation which attempts to restrict First Amendment freedoms of expression must not be vague or any broader than necessary to accomplish a legitimate and very important governmental purpose. The Supreme Court has looked with special skepticism at governmental attempts through laws, enforcement, or lower court decisions to impose *prior restraint* on expression—to prevent it from being uttered or printed—rather than punishing it afterward.

Suppose a speaker's words are likely to evoke such a hostile reaction from a crowd that the speaker may be attacked if allowed to continue. Should the police be permitted to stop the speaker, or should their duty be to protect the speaker from the crowd? The Supreme Court has gone both ways on this issue, but the basic question seems to be how dangerous the situation is. In one case, the Supreme Court upheld the arrest of a speaker who, the Court found, "gave the impression he was endeavoring to arouse the Negro people against the whites," because his words constituted an incitement to a riot that the two police officers involved probably could not have quelled.[9] In another case, the Court reversed the conviction of parading black protesters because the number of police officers present and the relatively calm mood of the onlookers made a breach of the peace seem unlikely.[10]

The Court has viewed certain conduct as "symbolic speech." As we saw earlier, the American Nazi party's attempt to demonstrate in Skokie falls in this category. The Court has ruled that peaceful picketing for a lawful purpose by black protesters or by a labor union

---

[9] *Feiner* v. *New York*, 340 U.S. 315 (1951).
[10] *Edwards* v. *South Carolina*, 372 U.S. 229 (1963).

is a form of constitutionally protected speech. In addition, the Court has held that wearing a black armband to school to protest the Viet Nam War and flying an American flag upside down with a peace symbol on it for the same purpose are both within the bounds of the First Amendment. But burning a draft card has usually been viewed not as speech but as "conduct" which can be punished.

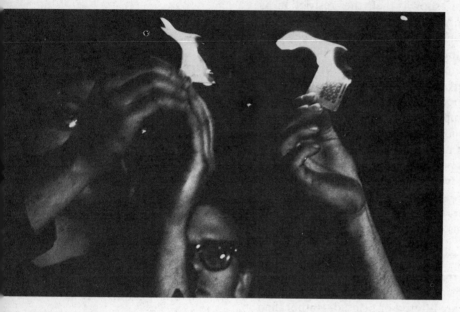

Supreme Court decisions have expanded the First Amendment's protection of free speech to include "symbolic speech" as well, such as picketing or wearing black armbands in school. Where does "speech" end and "conduct" begin? During the 1960s the Court refused to grant First Amendment protections to anti–Vietnam War protestors who burned their draft cards to show opposition to the war.

Spending money for political purposes has been held to be a form of speech. In its rulings on this issue, however, the Supreme Court has distinguished between contributions and spending. Congress may limit the size of people's contributions to the campaign of a political candidate. But it cannot limit their independent, noncollusive spending on behalf of a candidate because that would infringe upon their freedom of speech. In the same case, the Court held that it is unconstitutional for Congress to attempt to limit what a candidate who does not receive direct federal campaign subsidies may spend on his or her own campaign. This ruling favors rich candidates.[11] A business corporation also has a modified right of free speech. A corporation cannot be limited in what it may spend to affect the outcome of a citizen's vote on an issue, although its contributions to an individual candidate's campaign can be.[12]

Another interesting class of speech cases involves "fighting words," or abusive language that would be likely to evoke a violent response from the person to whom the words are directed. The Supreme Court has held that the use of fighting words, such as

---

[11] *Buckley* v. *Valeo*, 965 S. Ct. 612 (1976).
[12] *First National Bank of Boston* v. *Francis X. Belloti*, U.S. Law Week, 46, no. 41 (April 26, 1978).

"damned racketeer" or "damned fascist," can be restricted or punished by law when they are directed at a specific person.[13]

Thus, the Court has not interpreted the wording of the First Amendment to mean exactly what it says. The First Amendment provides that Congress can make *no* law restricting freedom of speech, but Court rulings have changed this to mean that Congress (and the state legislatures) can make *some* laws restricting this freedom, as long as they follow certain strict rules for balancing the interests of the government and the public against the interests of the individual.

Freedom of the Press

The general rules of law that apply to freedom of speech also apply to freedom of the press. Both are constitutionally important forms of expression. But special questions concerning freedom of the press have been raised. They deserve special attention because so much of our communication today involves the mass media.

The law treats commercial advertising differently from editorial comment or news reporting. Commercial advertising can be more strictly regulated, or even prohibited in some cases (as with cigarette advertising on television), without violation of freedom of the press. Fraudulent advertising, of course, is not protected by the First Amendment.

The publication of false and injurious statements about a person, which is called *libel*, can be the subject of a civil suit for damages. It can also result in punishment under criminal law. Freedom of the press does not give anyone the right to libel another person. But in recent years, court rulings have severely limited the possibility of recovering damages for libel, and criminal prosecutions for libel are rarely brought anymore. The current rule is that a public official or public figure cannot recover damages for libel unless it can be shown that the published statements in question were knowingly false or were published with a reckless disregard for the truth.[14] Private persons can recover damages for untrue and injurious statements by showing that the publisher *should have known* the statements were false and that *actual* injury resulted from the publication.[15] Thus, court decisions have placed more emphasis on protecting freedom of the press than on the possible harm that libel may do to a particular person. If damages could be recovered every time a false statement was published about a person—even though no proof existed that the publisher knew or should have known that the statement was false—freedom of the press and freedom of discussion might be stifled.

---

[13] *Chaplinsky* v. *New Hampshire*, 315 U.S. 568 (1942).
[14] *New York Times* v. *Sullivan*, 376 U.S. 254 (1964).
[15] *Gertz* v. *Robert Welch Inc.*, 418 U.S. 323 (1974).

Does the First Amendment give a person the right to publish, sell, distribute, or transport *obscene materials*? What is obscenity? One Supreme Court Justice once said that he could not actually define obscenity or hard-core pornography, "but I know it when I see it."[16] That statement is about as close as the Supreme Court has come to a working definition. Ironically, it is very much like the cliché, "I don't know much about art, but I know what I like." What is pornography, and what is art? What is legitimate entertainment? And what difference does it make? In 1970, the Commission on Obscenity and Pornography declared that it could not be shown that either the public or the adults involved suffered any harm from viewing pornographic films, photographs, books, magazines, and other materials. The Commission recommended the repeal of anti-pornography laws applicable to consenting adults. Reacting politically, the U.S. Senate voted overwhelmingly to repudiate this finding and recommendation of the Commission. President Nixon took the same position.

Does the First Amendment prohibition of laws regulating freedom of the press include pornography? The Supreme Court has said it is not protected, and many citizens feel it should not be. Still, the Court has found it difficult to define what "obscenity" is.

The Supreme Court of the United States has continued to hold that obscenity is not protected by the First Amendment. But the definition of obscenity is still a matter of considerable confusion. The accepted doctrine once was that a film, book, or other work was obscene if it was "utterly without redeeming social value."[17] The Court later abandoned that standard, adopting a two-part test in its place, and this is the present law. A work is obscene if, first, it lacks serious literary, artistic, political, or scientific value and, second, if it appeals to a "prurient interest in sex" according to local community standards.[18] The Court said that the people of Maine or Mississippi should not be bound by some national definition of obscenity, which would make them subject to the standards of Las Vegas or New York City. The justices were trying to avoid the clumsy and embarrassing task of having to personally view or read every allegedly obscene work and make a decision about it. But no sooner had the Court announced this "community standards" doctrine than it overturned a local court

---

[16] *Jacobellis* v. *Ohio*, 387 U.S. 184 (1974).
[17] *Memoirs* v. *Massachusetts*, 383 U.S. 413 (1966).
[18] *Miller* v. *California*, 413 U.S. 15 (1973).

decision that had allowed Jacksonville, Florida, to block the showing of the movie, *Carnal Knowledge*.[19] The following year, 1975, the Court ruled that Chattanooga, Tennessee, could not ban the musical, *Hair*.[20]

The Supreme Court has held that the standards applied to the sale of pornography to minors can be tougher than those applied to adults, but even these standards must not be too vague. In another decision, the Court ruled that the law cannot restrict the right of a person to view pornography privately. (This finding caused one dissenting justice to remark wryly that under these circumstances, the viewer would have to produce the pornography in the same private home where it was to be viewed, since the law prohibits buying or transporting it.)[21]

The debate goes on. For consenting adults, is there any harm in viewing or reading pornography? If so, is the harm to the individual or to society substantial enough to warrant government interference to restrict First Amendment freedoms? Who should decide what obscenity is? Is it possible to define obscenity specifically enough to allow prospective publishers to determine in advance whether the material will constitute a violation of the law? These questions have not been fully settled.

The conflict between the First Amendment right ensuring freedom of the press and the Sixth Amendment right guaranteeing an accused person a fair trial has been called a "civil libertarian's nightmare." Which should take precedence?

In England, there are more restrictions on the right of the press to report news about a trial than there are in the United States. Still, the U.S. Supreme Court has reversed convictions and ordered new trials in cases in which excessive publicity before or during a trial has made a fair and impartial jury trial impossible. In one case, the Court found that the trial had been turned into a "Roman holiday" when press helicopters were allowed to whir overhead as the jury visited the murder site.[22] In another decision, it reversed a conviction because the defendant's videotaped confession had been played to an audience of thousands on a local television station.[23] The question in these cases is whether the local atmosphere and news reporting are likely to prejudice the jury against the defendant.

The American Bar Association has proposed some voluntary guidelines to regulate comments and news releases by prosecutors, lawyers, law enforcement officials, and judges. But in 1976, the U.S. Supreme Court held that a trial judge's "gag order" prohibiting the press from reporting certain lurid evidence in a pretrial hearing was an unconstitutional prior restraint of freedom of the press. Chief

Drawing by Herbert Goldberg; © 1972 The New Yorker Magazine, Inc.

"If it turns me on, it's smut."

---

[19] *Jenkins* v. *Georgia*, 418 U.S. 153 (1974).
[20] *Southeastern Promotions, Ltd.* v. *Conrad*, 420 U.S. 546 (1975).
[21] *Stanley* v. *Georgia*, 394 U.S. 557 (1969).
[22] *Sheppard* v. *Maxwell*, 384 U.S. 333 (1966).

Justice Warren Burger, who wrote the opinion in this case, declared that "prior restraints on speech and publication are the most serious and the least tolerable infringement on First Amendment rights." He said that judges should use other means to protect the right of an accused person to a fair trial—such as isolating the jury from news reports, moving the trial to another location, or postponing the trial—without infringing the freedom of the press.[24]

Standards regarding the use of cameras in the courtroom are more restrictive than those applying to the "writing press." A defendant is entitled to a "public" trial, but judges usually do not allow either still or moving pictures of a trial. In one recent case, the Supreme Court unanimously reversed the conviction of a person whose trial had been televised without his consent because the Court found that the act of televising the trial had changed the way the judge, the prosecutor, and the jury acted, making a fair trial impossible. Four of the justices in that case declared that televising a trial would always prevent a fair trial, whether that could be specifically proved in each case or not.[25]

Freedom of the press to report the news does not necessarily mean that the press has the right of *freedom of information*, the right to get the news. Justice Potter Stewart has said, "There is no constitutional right to have access to particular government information, or to require openness from the bureaucracy." He also believes that the government has no constitutional duty to furnish information to journalists that is not available to members of the general public.[26]

Under executive orders issued by the President, certain information is regularly "classified" as secret—and therefore unavailable to the press—on the grounds that its publication would threaten the country's national security. In the Pentagon papers case, however, the Court prohibited the government from stopping the *Washington Post* and the *New York Times* from publishing classified information concerning the Viet Nam War that they had received from a Pentagon employee, Daniel Ellsberg. Freedom of the press, they argued, did not allow the government to exercise prior restraint on the publication of this classified information.[27] This case did not decide whether Ellsberg could be punished for releasing the information. The separate criminal case against him was thrown out of court because the Nixon administration grossly violated Ellsberg's rights by authorizing an illegal break-in at the office of Ellsberg's psychiatrist. Neither did it settle the question of whether these newspapers could be prosecuted *after* publication of the information, but the government did not pursue this possibility.

In 1974, the U.S. Congress strengthened the 1966 Freedom of

---

[23] *Irvin* v. *Dowd*, 336 U.S. 717 (1961).
[24] *Nebraska Press Association* v. *Stuart*, 427 U.S. 539 (1976).
[25] *Estes* v. *Texas*, 381 U.S. 532 (1965).
[26] Potter Stewart, "Or of the Press," *Hastings Law Journal*, 26: 633–34.
[27] *New York Times Company* v. *United States*, 403 U.S. 713 (1971).

How to . . .

Get Your Files from the Government

The Freedom of Information Act (FOIA) gives you the right to secure files that the government may have on you. These are kept by federal agencies that conduct surveillance on American citizens and others residing here (including the FBI, CIA, IRS, Justice, Defense, Secret Service, and the Civil Service Commission). In "How to Get Your Personal File" (a booklet which you can request copies of), the American Civil Liberties Union explains what the law says and how it works. As the booklet points out, to get your files you begin with a letter to the relevant agency.

Most agencies now require that you notarize your signature on the request letter to ensure that you are who you say you are. Charges for the record search have ranged from $10 to $50, although some agencies generally waive the charges.

If your request is denied, you can appeal by writing to the person named in the denial letter; if you intend to go to court if your appeal is denied, you should indicate this in your appeal letter. Under the FOIA, your appeal must be answered within twenty working days. If your appeal is denied, you can file suit in the federal district court in your area, in the District of Columbia, or where the records are kept. At this point, it is advisable to seek legal counsel.

Though the FOIA deals with national security surveillance files, the Privacy Bill gives citizens access to general governmental records and the Buckley Amendment gives students access to their school files. For information on these procedures, see *Privacy Report,* March 1975 (ACLU Foundation). For additional information on FOIA, you may request the following pamphlets: *The New Freedom of Information Act and National Security Information* (Center for National Security Studies and ACLU Foundation); *The FOIA: What it is and How to use it* (Freedom of Information Clearinghouse); and *Your Right to Government Information/How to Use the FOIA* (ACLU). For specific information or assistance, contact the ACLU office in your area or:

Freedom of Information Project
122 Maryland Avenue, N.E.
Washington, D.C. 20002
(202) 544-5380

National Staff Counsel
American Civil Liberties Union
22 E. 40th Street
New York, N.Y. 10016
(212) 725-1222

Note: An FOIA request will result in a search by the agency for files it may keep on you; if there is a file, your request will be added to it. If there is no file, one will be opened in the agency's freedom of information section.

```
                                                    Your address
                                                    Your phone number
                                                    Date

      Director
      Federal Bureau of Investigation
      10th and Pennsylvania Avenue, N.W.
      Washington, D.C. 20535

      Dear Sir:

          This is a request under the Freedom of Information Act as amend-
      ed (5 U.S.C. §552).
          I write to request a copy of all files in the Federal Bureau of
      Investigation indexed or maintained under my name and all documents
      returnable by a search for documents containing my name.  To assist
      you in your search, I have indicated my social security number and
      date and place of birth below my signature.
          As you know, the amended Act provides that if some parts of a
      file are exempt from release that "reasonably segregable" portions
      shall be provided.  I therefore request that, if you determine that
      some portions of the requested information are exempt, you provide me
      immediately with a copy of the remainder of the file.  I, of course,
      reserve my right to appeal any such decisions.
          If you determine that some or all of the requested information
      is exempt from release, I would appreciate your advising me as to which
      exemption(s) you believe covers the information which you are
      not releasing.
          I am prepared to pay costs specified in your regulations for
      locating the requested files and reproducing them.
          As you know, the amended Act permits you to reduce or waive the
      fees if that "is in the public interest because furnishing the infor-
      mation can be considered as primarily benefiting the public."  I be-
      lieve that this request plainly fits that category and ask you to
      waive any fees.
          If you have any questions regarding this request, please telephone me
      at the above number.
          As provided for in the amended Act, I will expect to receive a
      reply within ten working days.

                                                    Sincerely yours,

                                                    Name
                                                    Social Security Number
                                                    Date of Birth
                                                    Place of Birth

      (Write -- "Attention:  Freedom of Information Act Unit" on envelope)
```

Information Act. This new law requires federal agencies to furnish information to journalists and others who ask for it unless the information involves national security or personnel files. Under this legislation, a person who has been denied information on national security grounds can have a court review the material to determine whether the secrecy is really justified. Today, the law also allows a person to learn what information a federal agency may have in its files concerning that person. Congressional reforms have now opened up most committee meetings to the press and the public, and many states have enacted "sunshine laws," which require open meetings of public agencies and bodies.

Some Presidents have asserted an "executive privilege" to withhold certain information in order to protect national security and the confidentiality of advice given to them in private. This claim is subject to review by the courts, as President Nixon found out when he tried to use executive privilege to withhold information contained on tapes that criminal prosecutors in the Watergate case were seeking. The Supreme Court ruled in that case that President Nixon could not refuse to turn over the information, but it did recognize that in certain circumstances a claim of executive privilege might be upheld.[28]

Reporters have claimed that they will not be able to get information unless they are afforded the right of "protection of news sources." If a grand jury, court, or legislative committee can force them to reveal the identities of their news sources and the information given them, they fear that some news sources will become unavailable. But a recent Supreme Court decision limited journalists' rights to protect their sources. It held that a Kentucky journalist could not refuse to appear before a grand jury and testify about the identity of individuals he had seen using marijuana while he was preparing a story on drug usage; that a Massachusetts reporter could not refuse to appear before a grand jury and testify as to what he had observed inside a Black Panther party headquarters to which he had been given access by promising to report only concerning an anticipated police raid which never occurred; and that a *New York Times* reporter could not refuse to appear before a California grand jury that was seeking further information concerning stories he had written about Black Panther activities in Oakland. "Until now," the Court said, "the only testimonial privilege for unofficial witnesses that is rooted in the Federal Constitution is the Fifth Amendment privilege against compelled self-incrimination. We are asked to create another by interpreting the First Amendment to grant newsmen a testimonial privilege that other citizens do not enjoy. This we decline to do."[29]

Some states have adopted "shield" laws, which allow reporters to

---

[28] *United States* v. *Nixon*, 418 U.S. 683 (1974).
[29] *Branzburg* v. *Hayes*, 408 U.S. 665 (1972).

protect their sources. The case of the Kentucky reporter and the marijuana investigation involved such a law, but that did not stop the Court from upholding the order requiring him to appear before a grand jury. Congress has not adopted a shield law, and the constitutionality of such *state* laws was put in question by a recent New Jersey case. In the fall of 1978, a *New York Times* reporter, Myron Farber, went to jail for forty days, and his newspaper paid fines totalling $285,000 for refusing to turn over certain investigative evidence to a New Jersey court. Farber had used this material to write a series of stories in the *Times* that led to the indictment of a doctor for allegedly killing three of his patients through poisoning. New Jersey had a shield law, but the New Jersey Supreme Court (in a five-to-four decision) struck it down. The New Jersey court claimed that the law was in conflict with the Sixth Amendment to the U.S. Constitution, which guarantees a fair trial for a person accused of a crime. Without giving any reasons, the U.S. Supreme Court thereafter refused to accept an appeal in the case, making the New Jersey Supreme Court decision the final word in that particular instance.[30]

Myron Farber, a *New York Times* reporter who refused to identify the source of an article about the defendant in a murder trial, spent forty days in jail for contempt of court. After the defendant was acquitted, Farber was released. Journalists argue that sources will be unwilling to speak out if their names may become public; but courts have generally held that defendants must have access to all relevant information if they are to receive fair trials.

A 1978 U.S. Supreme Court case involving the *Stanford Daily*, Stanford University's student newspaper, presented another situation in which freedom of the press conflicted with the government's power to investigate and prosecute crimes. The Court upheld the right of police officers to enter the *Daily*'s offices and seize photographs for use in the prosecution of alleged crimes stemming from a local demonstration.[31] After having first sided with the police in this case, President Carter's Justice Department later recommended that Congress enact new legislation to protect newspapers and other media against such searches and seizures.

In 1979, the Court ruled in the *Herbert* case that journalists are not protected by the First Amendment from having to reveal what their

[30] For discussions of the *Farber* case, see *New York Review of Books* (October 26, 1978), pp. 34–36; and *Time* (December 11, 1978), p. 68.

[31] For a discussion of the *Stanford Daily* case, see *New York* (June 19, 1978), p. 10; and *America* (June 17, 1978), p. 476.

editorial process is in preparing a story. If journalists are sued for libel by a public figure, as they were in the *Herbert* case, the journalists must divulge what their thoughts and attitudes were about the allegedly libelous story while they were preparing or writing it.

Freedom of the press applies to radio and television stations as well as to newspapers. But does this freedom mean that Americans must have equal access to the press? No, that is not what it means. Critics complain that freedom of the press actually means "freedom *for* the press," freedom only for those who own the press to use it. This is particularly important because media ownership is increasingly concentrated in a relatively small number of companies. There are limits, but rather high ones, on how many radio stations or television stations one person or corporation may own. The same corporation or individual can control both a newspaper and a television station in the same market. There are no limits on how many newspapers an individual or company can own, and some chains own great numbers of them. Because we are a mass media society, the ownership of a radio or television station or a newspaper can potentially carry with it considerable power over the flow of ideas and the formation of public opinion.

Since the federal government grants monopolies for the use of specific radio frequencies and television channels to particular companies and individuals, the government can constitutionally regulate them. This regulatory power is exercised through the Federal Communications Commission (FCC). Failure to abide by the law and FCC regulations can subject a broadcaster to a loss of license. An "equal time" law requires a broadcaster to sell equal advertising to competing political candidates, but it does not protect the candidate who cannot afford to buy equal time. This law favors the incumbent, who is usually more well known than his or her

"And now Bob Ferguson, with an analysis of our reporting staff's 'state of mind' during the preparation of tonight's news."

opponent, since broadcasters may choose to sell limited or even no campaign advertising in a particular race. The "fairness doctrine" requires broadcasters to present both sides of public issues, even if this sometimes means giving free time for that purpose. But the broadcaster can largely decide who will be allowed to present the opposing view. And little has been done to assure that the most important issues will be given at least some exposure. Special FCC rules require broadcasters to allow a "right of reply" to people who wish to present responsible views opposing a station's editorial comment or to those who want to respond to criticisms made against them on the air. Still, an individual has no enforceable right of general access to radio and television stations—no right to go on the air to talk about the pros and cons of the neutron bomb, say, or to have that or any other issue discussed by others.

There is even less right of access to the print media (newspapers and magazines). It has been argued that without such access—or at least as much access as the law requires for radio and television—the government is allowing private censorship of the flow of ideas, which violates the spirit of the First Amendment as much as does public censorship. What do freedom of speech and freedom of the press really mean when the most influential communication occurs in the mass media, and lack of money may mean lack of access? Current law does not guarantee equal access in the print media. If you are a political candidate who is attacked by a newspaper, you have no right to use free space to make a reply. A Florida law requiring such a right of reply in a newspaper has been held unconstitutional. Nor does a newspaper have to sell you advertising space to allow you to express your side of a public question. The Supreme Court has said, "A responsible press is an undoubtedly desirable goal, but press responsibility is not mandated by the Constitution and like many other virtues it cannot be legislated."[32] Limited or non-existent access for the general public to the mass media has caused some people to call public demonstrations the "poor people's newspapers." For groups who do not have enough money to use television or newspapers, a dramatic demonstration calculated to gain the attention of the mass media may be the only means to get across their message to a large audience.

Freedom of Assembly and Petition

Dick Gregory was one of the first black comedians in America to reach a nationwide audience and gain a national following by pointing out the foibles of whites instead of blacks. By the 1960s he was successful, rich, and famous. But when four little black girls were killed by a bomb in Birmingham in 1963, Gregory gave up much of his comfort to become an activist against racism in the United States.

---

[32] *Miami Herald Publishing Company* v. *Tornillo*, 418 U.S. 241 (1974).

One afternoon during the summer of 1965, Gregory led a group of demonstrators to Grant Park in his hometown of Chicago to demand the ouster of the Chicago Superintendent of Schools for failing to desegregate Chicago's public schools. Calling the city hall the "snake pit" and Mayor Richard Daley "the snake," the eighty-five demonstrators marched five miles to the mayor's residence and began parading around the block, chanting and singing, while approximately 180 police officers watched. A thousand or more hostile onlookers gathered to heckle and throw rocks and eggs at the demonstrators, some shouting epithets such as "get out of here, niggers—go back where you belong or we'll get you out of here." At 8:30 that evening, the marchers stopped their singing and chanting and paraded quietly. At 9:30 P.M., the police officer in charge asked the demonstrators to disperse because, he said, the situation was becoming riotous. When the marching nevertheless continued, Gregory and thirty-nine others were arrested and were eventually convicted for "disorderly conduct."[33]

What do you think? Should Gregory and the demonstrators have been arrested and their peaceful assembly dispersed? Should the hostile onlookers, many of whom were not peaceful, have been arrested and their assembly dispersed? Should neither group have been arrested and dispersed—and disorder risked?

The Supreme Court of the United States reversed the conviction of Gregory and his group of marchers. The Court's majority opinion emphasized the fact that the demonstrators had been convicted of disorderly conduct when they had in fact been orderly. A much earlier Supreme Court opinion had held that the right to petition the government and to peaceably assemble were as "fundamental" as the freedoms of speech and press.[34] But later decisions distinguished between freedom of expression and freedom of assembly, ruling that picketing and demonstrating could be regulated like other conduct.[35] In the Gregory case, it was clear that the Court might have ruled otherwise if the demonstrators had been convicted under a narrowly drawn ordinance such as a law prohibiting parading after a certain time of day.

The freedoms of petition and assembly generally do not include the right to use private property without the consent of the owner (unless the property has been dedicated to public use, as are streets of a company-owned town and, for some purposes, shopping center parking lots). Demonstrators cannot take over public streets or public buildings and prevent people from using them without governmental permission. Government can reasonably regulate the time and place of parades. And, as noted earlier, there is no constitutional protection for incitement to riot or to use force or violence against people or property.

---

[33] *Gregory* v. *Chicago*, 394 U.S. 111 (1969).
[34] *De Jonge* v. *Oregon*, 299 U.S. 353 (1937).
[35] *Bell* v. *Maryland*, 378 U.S. 343 (1964).

The conviction of Dr. Martin Luther King, Jr., and others for parading in Birmingham without a permit was upheld by the Supreme Court.[36] The Court has also upheld laws prohibiting a demonstration near a courthouse for the purpose of influencing the outcome of a trial. It has also prevented demonstrations from occurring so near to a school as to disrupt the teaching process.[37] On the other hand, the Court held unconstitutional an ordinance which made it a crime for three or more persons to gather on a sidewalk, and to annoy passersby. Such an ordinance left too much discretion to the police officer, the Court said.[38]

We are confronted again with the tension between order and liberty. No longer are demonstrations used only by civil rights and antiwar groups. Other groups—consumers protesting beef prices, protesting truckers slowing down highway traffic, and angry farmers turning loose goats and pigs on the Capitol lawn—have adopted this method as their own.

Where does peaceful petitioning and assembling end and unlawful assembly and disorder begin? The fact that a number of the relevant Supreme Court cases have been decided by five-to-four decisions leaves some uncertainty. In addition, there is always the threat that law enforcement officials will come down too hard on the side of order, as they did when the Nixon administration illegally ordered the arrest of thousands of antiwar demonstrators in Washington, D.C., in 1970. This threat is particularly disturbing because court appeals take a long time and are not always feasible because they are so expensive.

Freedom of Association and Dissent

The freedom to differ or dissent from the established or popular view and the freedom to organize and to associate with others to advocate one's views are not specifically stated anywhere in the Constitution or in the Bill of Rights. But these freedoms have been held to be "an inseparable aspect of the 'liberty'" guaranteed by the Constitution.[39]

Justice Holmes once stated, the Constitution protects not only popular beliefs or ideas, but also unpopular ones.[40] Despite these avowed principles, the federal government has made numerous attempts to suppress unpopular ideas. The Bill of Rights had scarcely become a part of the Constitution before Congress had passed the Alien and Sedition Acts (1798). Among other things, the acts prohibited "malicious writing" against the government. One American was actually convicted for accusing President John Adams of grasping for power and having "an unbounded thirst for ridiculous

---

[36] *Walker* v. *Birmingham*, 388 U.S. 307 (1967).
[37] *Cox* v. *Louisiana*, 379 U.S. 559 (1965).
[38] *Coates* v. *Cincinnati*, 402 U.S. 611 (1971).
[39] *NAACP* v. *Alabama*, 356 U.S. 449 (1958).
[40] Dissenting in *United States* v. *Schwimmer*, 279 U.S. 644 (1929).

pomp, foolish adulation and selfish avarice." These acts were repealed during Jefferson's administration. During the Civil War, President Lincoln suspended the right of habeas corpus and caused people who were suspected of disloyalty to the Union to be put in jail without a trial. The Supreme Court eventually ruled Lincoln's action unconstitutional, but not until after the damage had been done. During World War I, Congress passed the Sedition Act, making it a crime to use "disloyal, profane, scurrilous, or abusive language" about the American government or the Constitution, and it outlawed the use of language which was likely to bring the government, the Constitution, the flag, or the uniforms of the military services into disrepute. States passed similar laws. During and after the war, many people went to jail for merely criticizing American laws or governmental conduct.

During World War II, an executive order issued by President Roosevelt forced Japanese Americans living on the West coast to be relocated in internment camps further inland simply because they were Japanese. Although the American government had no proof at all that the individuals involved posed any threat to national security, the Supreme Court upheld this order.[41] In the 1950s, the McCarran Act authorized a similar kind of preventive detention during wartime for people who might reasonably be expected to become spies or saboteurs. Congress finally repealed this provision in 1971.

Congress and the Supreme Court have had considerable trouble trying to decide how to deal with the American Communist party. Should an organization be allowed to exist if it advocates the overthrow of the government by force and violence? At various times in America the answer has been no. During the 1950s and 1960s, however, the Warren Court narrowly restricted the government's power to limit such association and dissent.

The Smith Act, adopted in 1940, at the beginning of World War II, made it a crime to teach, advocate, or encourage the violent overthrow of the government or to knowingly belong to an organization that did. After the war, ten members of the Communist party were convicted under this act. The Supreme Court upheld their convictions. Although those who agreed with the majority opinion could not agree on the exact reasoning behind the ruling, it seemed to be a variation of the balancing test. Thus, the Court approved an act prohibiting membership in an organization that advocated or encouraged the violent overthrow of the government, even though the danger of that result actually occurring was not shown to be imminent.[42]

Well, what is the problem with that? There are several problems. Should it be a crime for someone just to think and talk about the destruction of the government by force when there is no proof that the person intends to incite someone to violence and no proof that

A grandfather and his grandsons await their relocation orders in Hayward, California, 1942. Commenting on the relocation and internment camps for Japanese Americans during World War II, Ray Lyman Wilbur, Chancellor of Stanford University, wrote, "Whenever and wherever the constitutional guarantees are violated in the treatment of a minority . . . the whole fabric of American government is weakened. . . . The test of America is the security of its minority groups."

---

[41] *Korematsu* v. *U.S.*, 323 U.S. 214 (1944).
[42] *Dennis* v. *United States*, 341 U.S. 494 (1951).

violence is likely to occur as a result? Should a professor who sincerely believes in the teachings of Karl Marx and the inevitability of revolution, but who has no intention of trying to bring about such a revolution, be convicted of a crime for talking about it? Should someone be convicted for belonging to an organization that does have such intent, even though he or she personally does not? And if some organizations can be outlawed and their members punished, can we define "subversive" to restrict only the "bad" organizations and not the "good" ones? These questions have plagued the Supreme Court over the years.

The major Supreme Court cases dealing with freedom of association and dissent have been called the "Red" cases and the "Black" cases. The Red cases tested the constitutionality of anticommunist federal and state laws and orders during the McCarthy era, the period from the late 1940s through the early 1950s. During this time, congressional committees led by the late Senator Joseph McCarthy of Wisconsin and Richard M. Nixon (then a senator from California) made political capital by exposing and censuring members of the Communist party or "Communist-front" organizations and "fellow travelers," people who were said to sympathize with Communist causes. In 1947, President Truman issued an order barring federal employment to anyone who belonged to any organization that the attorney general had designated as "fascist, communist or subversive." In 1950, Congress passed the McCarran Act, which required the Communist party, as well as "Communist-action" and "Communist-front" organizations, to register with the government and suffer certain disabilities or penalties.

The Black cases tested the constitutionality of state laws designed to harass the National Association for the Advancement of Colored People (NAACP), intimidate its members and supporters, and inhibit the organization's civil rights activities. Southern segregationists thought the NAACP was as subversive as the Communist party because it sought to destroy what they called the "Southern Way of Life." It was not easy for the Supreme Court to hold such state laws unconstitutional while upholding federal restrictions on the Communist party and related organizations. In 1957, the Supreme Court changed its position in regard to the Smith Act. In that year, the Court ruled in the *Yates*[43] case that a person could not be convicted of

During the Army-McCarthy hearings (1954), Senator Joseph McCarthy used a map to show locations of Communist party organizations and "fellow travelers." Army chief-counsel Joseph N. Welch (seated) had just denounced McCarthy as a "cruelly reckless character assassin" after McCarthy claimed that one of Welch's law partners had affiliations with a "Communist Front"—the National Lawyer's Guild, which the House Un-American Activities Committee had listed as a "subversive" organization. McCarthy's hearings—which eventually led to his censure by the Senate—were intended to investigate whether "communist-sympathizers" had infiltrated high levels of the Army.

---

[43] *Yates* v. *United States*, 354 U.S. 298 (1957).

a crime for mere membership in the Communist party; the person had to be an active member who personally intended to bring about the overthrow of the government by force. Although the Court did not say so directly, this decision virtually nullified the Smith Act. It also strengthened the freedom of association and dissent in America and made it possible for the Court's decisions in regard to the Communist party and the NAACP to be more consistent with each other.

The following year, the Supreme Court ruled unconstitutional an attempt by the state of Alabama to require the NAACP to disclose its membership lists. The Court said that if the identity of NAACP members were disclosed, individual members would probably be subjected to reprisals and coercion. As a result, the organization would have difficulty keeping members and pursuing its lawful objectives. The Court said that Alabama had not shown sufficient justification for so inhibiting NAACP's work.[44] In 1960, the Supreme Court struck down a similar attempt by the city of Little Rock, Arkansas, to require disclosure of NAACP membership lists, saying that such a law could prevail only if the city government showed a compelling interest for such an encroachment of liberty.[45]

After deciding these Black cases against the government, the Supreme Court reached the opposite result in another Red case in 1961. In a five-to-four decision, the Court sustained a federal order requiring the Communist party to register and disclose *its* membership list. The Court said that the government's right to "self-preservation" in this instance was important enough to permit such a restriction on liberty.[46] Four years later, as fears of the "red menace" began to fade, the Court held that an individual member of the Communist party could not be forced to register because this would violate the Fifth Amendment protection against self-incrimination.[47] Soon afterward, a federal circuit court of appeals ruled that the party itself could claim the Fifth Amendment privilege for its members and refuse to disclose their names.[48]

In 1970, the Court let stand a federal court of appeals decision that barred a person from being subjected to criminal or other penalties merely for belonging to an organization that advocates the violent overthrow of the government, unless it could be proved that the person involved shared those intentions.[49] In the same year, the federal government also abandoned the requirement that federal employees must swear that they are not members of a fascist, communist, or subversive organization. (They must still take an oath

---

[44] *NAACP* v. *Alabama*, 356 U.S. 449 (1958).
[45] *Bates* v. *Little Rock*, 361 U.S. 516 (1960).
[46] *Konigsberg* v. *State Bar of California*, 366 U.S. 36 (1961).
[47] *Albertson* v. *Subversive Activities Control Board*, 382 U.S. 70 (1965).
[48] *Communist Party* v. *United States*, 384 F. 2d 957 (D.C. Cir. 1967).
[49] *Boorda* v. *Subversive Activities Control Board*, 421 F. 2d 1142 (D.C. Cir. 1969), cert. denied, 90 S. Ct. 1365 (1970).

to support and defend the Constitution, however.) Today, the Communist party fields candidates for public office.

In its recent decisions, then, the Supreme Court has severely restricted the power of state and federal governments to limit the freedoms of association and dissent. But it has done so largely without expressly overruling earlier decisions that limited these basic democratic freedoms. It is clear that the mood of the country has played some part in the Court's decisions at any given time.

THE PERSONAL FREEDOMS

Americans have the right to freedom of religion, the right to own private property, and the right to privacy. These rights, like the democratic freedoms, are grounded in the Bill of Rights and in judicial interpretations of these first ten amendments to our Constitution.

Religion and Conscience

A basic tenet of the American system is that there should be no government interference with a person's religious beliefs. There should be, as Thomas Jefferson put it, a "wall of separation between church and state." The Constitution prohibits any religious test for holding national office, and the First Amendment provides that "Congress shall make no law respecting an establishment of religion, or prohibiting the free exercise thereof."

There are two parts to the First Amendment declaration concerning freedom of religion. First, there can be no "establishment" of religion by government. Second, there can be no government prohibition of the "free exercise" of religion. These seem to be fairly simple principles. And in most cases they are. But there are difficult questions which cannot be easily answered. What if the establishment clause and the free exercise clause come into conflict with each other? For example, what if government grants a special exemption from the law—the draft law, say—for people who have religious scruples against war? Would that constitute a kind of establishment of religion? What if government forces a person to do something— submit to a vaccination, say—which violates the person's religious beliefs? Would that constitute interference with the free exercise of religion? A number of Supreme Court cases, especially since the 1940s, have explored these and similar questions, and the trend has been toward expanding the concept of religious freedom.

Establishment. The First Amendment prohibits the government from establishing a religion. This means that government laws and acts must be for a secular, nonreligious purpose; they must neither promote nor restrict religion; and they must not actively involve or entangle the government in religious activity.[50]

Yet there has always been a certain amount of commingling of religious and governmental activity in the United States. The U.S. House of Representatives and the U.S. Senate, for example, open each session with a prayer. James Madison privately thought this practice was unconstitutional, but as a member of Congress he never publicly objected to it. The pledge of allegiance to the flag contains the words "under God." American coins carry the phrase "In God We Trust." In court, witnesses often put their hand on a Bible while swearing to testify truthfully. Even in the U.S. Supreme Court, which has a special duty to protect religious liberty, each session opens with the words, "God save the United States and this honorable Court." These practices are apparently too inconsequential to require curbing them.

But what if a school board or state legislature prescribes the Lord's Prayer or some other prayer to be said by schoolchildren or requires a reading from the Bible or some other religious exercise? The Supreme Court has ruled that these governmental actions are unconstitutional violations of the prohibition against the establishment of religion. It makes no difference if the prayer recommended by a state government agency is a "nondenominational" one; the Court has declared that "it is no part of the business of government to compose official prayers for any group of Americans to recite."[51] The ruling applies even when students are excused from the religious activity upon written request.

The so-called "school prayer cases"[52] caused an enormous outburst of complaints against the Supreme Court. Serious but unsuccessful attempts were made to amend the Constitution to allow "voluntary" prayer in the public schools. But the decisions continue to stand. The Supreme Court has also ruled that a state cannot prohibit the teaching of evolution in the schools.[53]

Despite these rulings, prayers are still regularly said and Christian holidays such as Christmas and Easter are still regularly observed in public schools throughout the United States. Since many American schoolchildren come from Jewish and other non-Christian families or from atheistic, humanistic, or other nonreligious families, many public schools continue to be, in a sense, the parochial schools of the majority. Those who might bring lawsuits to challenge these practices are not sufficiently upset, do not want to stand up publicly against strong majority pressure, or do not feel economically able to do so.

What if government funds are used in the operation of parochial or church-run schools or hospitals? The law on this question is not fully

---

[50] *Engel* v. *Vitale*, 370 U.S. 421 (1962).

[51] *Abington School District* v. *Schempp* and *Murray* v. *Curlett*, 374 U.S. 333 (1890).

[52] *Abington* v. *Schempp* and *Murray* v. *Curlett*.

[53] *Epperson* v. *Arkansas*, 393 U.S. 97 (1968).

settled. But the answer depends in large measure on what type of institution is involved and the purpose for which the funds are spent.

The Supreme Court has been fairly lenient in allowing the use of tax money for church-run hospitals and colleges, but it has been much more strict about public funds being used in elementary and secondary schools. The rationale for this difference apparently is that there is much less likelihood of religious indoctrination at public expense in colleges and hospitals as long as the money is not used specifically for religious training or religious buildings. No Supreme Court case has yet considered the question of whether Catholic hospitals that have received federal aid may refuse to allow contraception or abortion.

In regard to elementary and secondary parochial schools, the rule is that government may aid the student in certain ways but not the school itself. There are a large but declining number of parochial schools in America, and most of them are Catholic. Supporters of these schools say that if they are forced to close because of mounting financial problems, their large number of students—over three million—will become an additional burden on the public school system. They have pressed hard for state and federal financial assistance. Opponents of aid to parochial schools argue that this assistance would violate the prohibition against the establishment of religion because taxpayers would be forced to help support schools in which religion is taught.

In 1930, the Supreme Court announced the "child benefit" doctrine in a ruling that allowed the state of Louisiana to provide nonreligious textbooks for students of both public and parochial schools. The Court permitted this form of government aid because it was going to the "children of the state" and not to the private schools as such.[54] The same theory was used to justify President Lyndon Johnson's federal-aid-to-education program, which was adopted by the Congress in 1964. With particular emphasis on low-income areas, this measure provided various kinds of assistance for both private- and public-school students.

The Supreme Court has upheld the use of public funds for students in parochial schools for bus fares and field trips, for speech and hearing services, and for guidance and counseling services away from the parochial school campus.[55] But the use of tax funds in parochial schools for tuition, for teacher's salaries, for instructional materials and equipment, and for the maintenance and repair of school equipment and facilities has been held to be unconstitutional aid to sectarian or religious education.[56]

May a state or city exempt property that is used exclusively for

---

[54] *Cochran* v. *Louisiana State Board of Education*, 281 U.S. 370 (1930).
[55] *Board of Education* v. *Allen*, 393 U.S. 236 (1968).
[56] *Lemon* v. *Kurtzman*; *Committee for Public Education* v. *Nyquist*; *Levitt* v. *Committee for Public Education*, 413 U.S. 472 (1973).

religious purposes from taxation? The answer is yes—even though this practice means that other property may be taxed more heavily than it would otherwise be, and even though the tax-exempt property benefits from government services such as police and fire protection. This tax exemption has been upheld because it singles out no *particular* religion for favorable treatment and because this type of exemption has been allowed in all the states without challenge for most of the nation's history.[57]

Free exercise. Americans have a right to believe in and affiliate with any religion they please. They also have the right *not* to believe in or affiliate with *any* religion. A person cannot be required to swear to a belief in God in order to get a job or hold public office.

A person *can* be required to abide by a "valid secular law"—that is, a proper, nonreligious law that applies to everyone—even though such a law may violate the person's religious beliefs. But what is a valid secular law? The test, again, is a type of balancing. The courts attempt to measure whether the government's interest in making and enforcing the law is sufficiently strong to override the individual's right to religious freedom.

It was once a fundamental religious belief of Latter Day Saints in the United States—the Mormons—that God had ordained the practice of polygamy, which allows a man to be married to more than one woman. Then state and federal laws were passed to prohibit the practice, and Mormons went to court in the late 1800s to fight these laws, which they argued were unconstitutional restrictions on their freedom of religion. Were they right? The court said that the laws did indeed restrict religious freedom but that the restrictions were justified in this instance because the free exercise of religion would interfere with the government's right to protect public morals through proper laws.[58] Similarly, the Court has upheld laws that require vaccination of children on the basis that the government's interest in protecting public health is paramount to conflicting religious beliefs.[59]

But the government cannot legally compel a person to salute the American flag, and parents may not be forced to enroll their children in public schools instead of parochial schools. Two famous "flag salute cases" were decided in 1940 and 1943. Both involved a local public school requirement that all students salute the American flag. Members of the Jehovah's Witnesses sect would not allow their children to comply, believing that saluting the flag constituted a violation of God's commandment against worshipping graven images. In the first case, the Supreme Court surprisingly upheld the flag salute requirement, declaring that the interest of the government in

---

[57] *Waltz* v. *Tax Commission* (1976).
[58] *Reynolds* v. *U.S.*, 98 U.S. 145 (1878).
[59] *Jacobsen* v. *Massachusetts*, 197 U.S. 11 (1905).

promoting national unity and loyalty took precedence over religious belief in this instance.[60] After some important changes in Supreme Court membership, the Court reversed itself three years later. In a decision based both on freedom of speech and freedom of religion, the Court acknowledged that the government has an interest in promoting national unity and loyalty but said that it cannot do so on a compulsory basis because freedom of speech and conscience include the right not to speak or make a symbolic expression. That is the present law.[61]

Can a Jewish merchant, who worships on Saturday, be forced to close his store on Sunday? Can a Seventh Day Adventist, whose sabbath is also Saturday, be forced to work on that day or lose her job? The answer to the first question is yes and to the second question, no. The Supreme Court decisions in these two cases are somewhat conflicting, but the conflict cannot be explained by changes in the Court membership. The Court was probably swayed by the peculiar facts of each case.

In the first decision, the Court noted that Sunday closing laws are passed for a secular, non-religious reason: to give merchants one day of rest without fear that their competitors will stay open. The Court knew that there were thousands of such state and local laws and ordinances, which would have been invalidated if the decision had gone the other way. Furthermore, the Court observed that merchants could still practice their religious beliefs despite the Sunday closing requirement.[62]

In the second case, the Seventh Day Adventist had worked for the same firm for thirty-five years without having to work on Saturday. Then the company rules were changed to require all shifts to work on that day, causing her to have to choose between her religion and her livelihood. The Court was simply not willing to approve such a forced choice.[63]

The Supreme Court has consistently upheld the power of Congress to exempt conscientious objectors—those who, because of religious beliefs or training, are opposed to participating in war—from the military draft. The Court has sidestepped the question of whether this amounts to establishment of religion. Present law does not require that a conscientious objector declare a belief in a Supreme Being. And the Supreme Court has now defined "religious" in such a broad way as to exempt from the draft those whose deeply held "moral and ethical" beliefs cause them to oppose all war. But a person who opposes a particular war, such as the Viet Nam war, but who is not opposed to all wars cannot claim a draft exemption on the grounds of conscience.[64]

---

[60] *Minersville School District* v. *Goblitis*, 310 U.S. 586 (1940).
[61] *West Virginia Board of Education* v. *Barnette*, 319 U.S. 624 (1943).
[62] *Sunday Law Cases*, 366 U.S. 420 (1961).
[63] *Sherbert* v. *Verner*, 374 U.S. 398 (1963).
[64] *Gillette* v. *United States*, 301 U.S. 437 (1971).

Property

The Bill of Rights limits the government to both fair purposes and fair procedures when dealing with a person's life, liberty, and property. This does not mean that a person's liberty may not be taken away and the person confined in prison, nor that a person's life may not be taken by execution of a sentence of death, nor that a person's property may not be confiscated by the government. All of these things may be done—are done—by the government in America. But they must only be done for a reasonable purpose and in a reasonable way.

The writers of our Constitution believed in the right of a person to make binding contracts and to own private property. Article I, Section 10 of the Constitution prohibits a state from passing a law "impairing the obligation of contracts." In the Fifth Amendment the right of private property was spelled out more plainly: "No person shall be . . . deprived of life, liberty, or property, without due process of law; nor shall private property be taken for public use, without just compensation."

Federal and state governments have the power of "eminent domain." State governments also enable local governments and public utilities, such as the gas, telephone, and electricity companies, to use this same power. Eminent domain means that private property may be taken for public use. For example, a person's private property may be taken for a dam, a part of it may be used for a highway, or a telephone line may be built across it. But this power cannot be exercised arbitrarily. It must be for a *reasonable and necessary purpose*. At every stage, the government must follow *fair procedures* to assure the property owner the right to be heard fully. Finally, there must be *just compensation*; that is, the property owner must be paid what the property is worth. If the property owner demands it, the value will be determined in court.

Suppose you own an acre of land on the edge of town, and you decide to build a high-rise apartment on it, but the county zoning board tells you that only one-family dwellings will be allowed. Suppose you correctly calculate that this zoning ruling has cost you $20,000. Does the county government have to pay you for this loss?

Consider another situation. Suppose you own a meat-packing plant and you are planning to sell it for $60,000. Before you can make the sale, Congress passes a new inspection law that will require you to spend a great deal of money to improve your plant's standards. Now you can only get $30,000 for your unimproved plant. Does the government owe you the difference?

Suppose you mow lawns for a living, and you have a written contract with your one employee to pay the employee $2.00 an hour. On this basis, your profit amounts to $6,000 a year. Then the state legislature raises the minimum wage to $3.00 an hour, cutting your annual profit by a fourth. Has your property been taken without just compensation?

Suppose your occupation is plumbing, and you have been fairly successful at it. Then a state agency issues new licensing requirements that prevent you from continuing your work until you have taken additional training and passed an examination. Does someone have to pay you your full wages while you are off work?

The answer in all four instances is no. But there was a time when the answers might have been different. In an early case, the Supreme Court held that the right to liberty included "the right of the individual to contract" and the right of a person "to engage in the common occupations of life."[65] On that basis, a conservative Supreme Court issued numerous rulings against government interference with business property and contracts. But the membership of the Court began to change in the mid-1930s and the times changed. Today, it is a well-established principle of law that these rights are conditional. State and federal governments may regulate occupations and business practices, limit contractual provisions, and restrict property use so long as the purpose and the process are reasonable and fair.[66]

Privacy

The Fourth Amendment states that "the right of the people to be secure in their persons, houses, papers, and effects, against unreasonable searches and seizures, shall not be violated, and no warrant shall issue, but upon probable cause, supported by Oath or affirmation, and particularly describing the place to be searched, or the persons or things to be seized."

A warrant for an arrest is an order issued by a judge or magistrate that authorizes law officers to take a person into custody. It is issued after law officers produce enough evidence to show "probable cause" that the person has committed a crime. Most arrests are made without a warrant. This is permissible when a police officer has probable cause to believe that a crime has been or is about to be committed. But the person arrested must be taken before a judge or magistrate at once and probable cause for the arrest must be shown. In hot pursuit, a police officer may follow a person into the person's home and make an arrest without a warrant.

A judge may dismiss a criminal case if the defendant can show that he or she was illegally arrested. The victim of an illegal arrest may also secure damages. For example, antiwar demonstrators who had been unlawfully arrested in Washington, D.C., in 1970 on orders of President Nixon's Attorney General, John Mitchell, were awarded civil damages totalling $12 million in 1975.

A person's home and body are protected against unreasonable searches. Generally, a search warrant must be obtained from a magistrate or judge before a search can be conducted. It must specify

---

[65] *Lockner* v. *New York*, 198 U.S. 45 (1905).
[66] See *West Coast Hotel* v. *Parrish*, 300 U.S. 379 (1937).

the place to be searched and the articles to be seized. The Warren Court (headed by Chief Justice Earl Warren) issued a number of decisions that broadened protection against unreasonable searches. More recently the Burger Court (headed by Chief Justice Warren Burger) has swung the pendulum back the other way, causing Justice Powell to say that the law on searches and seizures is "a vast twilight zone" and that the Supreme Court's decisions are not noted for predictability.[67]

Today, the police do not need a warrant to "stop and frisk" a person who is believed to be armed and dangerous.[68] If they find other evidence of a crime while looking for weapons, they may go ahead and make a full search.[69] In addition, no warrant is necessary for officers to search an individual and the immediate area that he or she controls while they are in the process of making an arrest or when they have probable cause to make an arrest.[70] They may also do so at border crossings.[71] A person's automobile may be searched without a warrant if the police have probable cause to believe that it is being used to commit a crime or if evidence of crime is in plain view.[72] Police may search an individual's home or hotel room without a warrant under "exigent circumstances"—situations in which the police have reason to believe that a crime has been committed and that the evidence will be destroyed or removed if time is taken to get a warrant.[73] Warrantless searches may also be made when a person voluntarily consents, even though not told of the right of refusal.[74]

What can be done if these rules are violated? In federal courts, the judge may exclude the use of illegally obtained evidence against a defendant.[75] Both the Federal Bureau of Investigation (FBI) and the Central Intelligence Agency (CIA) have recently admitted, under pressure, that in the past they engaged in illegal searches and seizures without warrants. Some efforts have been made to prevent such breaches in the future.

The Supreme Court originally took the view that electronic wiretapping and bugging were not illegal unless a trespass or breaking and entering had been committed to place the tap or bug.[76] But this decision was reversed in 1968. The law now is that a conversation is a tangible thing that must not be illegally seized.[77] The Omnibus Crime Control and Safe Streets Act, passed by Congress in 1968, restricts the use of wiretapping and bugging by state and federal officials. At

---

[67] Concurring in *Schneckloth* v. *Bustamonte*, 412 U.S. 218 (1973); and quoting from Justice Harlan in *Ker* v. *California*, 374 U.S. 23 (1963).

[68] *Terry* v. *Ohio*, 392 U.S. 1 (1968).

[69] *United States* v. *Edwards*, 415 U.S. 800 (1974).

[70] *Chimel* v. *California*, 395 U.S. 752 (1969).

[71] *Almeida-Sanchez* v. *United States*, 413 U.S. 266 (1973).

[72] *Carroll* v. *United States*, 267 U.S. 132 (1925).

[73] *United States* v. *Watson*, 423 U.S. 411 (1976).

[74] *Schneckloth* v. *Bustmonte* (1973); *United States* v. *Matlock*, 415 U.S. 164 (1974).

[75] *Mapp* v. *Ohio*, 367 U.S. 643 (1961).

[76] *Olmstead* v. *United States*, 277 U.S. 438 (1928).

[77] *Katz* v. *United States*, 389 U.S. 347 (1967).

the federal level, warrantless electronic surveillance may be done only in national security cases involving a foreign power, not in "domestic security" cases.[78] In all other cases, the government must first get a warrant from a federal judge. State authorities must also secure a warrant from a state judge prior to conducting electronic surveillance, except in emergency situations involving conspiracies which threaten national security. There was widespread illegal wiretapping and bugging of news reporters, White House aides, and members of radical groups during the Nixon administration. In 1978, President Carter's Attorney General, Griffin Bell, brought criminal actions against former high-level officials of the FBI for authorizing illegal electronic surveillance.

The Supreme Court has recently ruled that the Bill of Rights includes an implicit right of privacy over the use of one's own body. Using this interpretation, the Court has declared that laws against the sale and use of contraceptives are unconstitutional.[79] Lower federal courts have challenged state laws that bar employment or levy criminal penalties for private homosexual acts between consenting adults.[80]

The landmark case in this broader field of privacy occurred in 1973, when the Supreme Court, in effect, struck down the laws of forty-six states prohibiting a woman's right to an abortion during the first three months of her pregnancy.[81] The Catholic Church and others have vigorously opposed this decision and have advocated an amendment to the U.S. Constitution to nullify its authority. Efforts for such an amendment have been unsuccessful so far, but opponents of the Court's abortion decision have been able to get Congress to pass laws prohibiting the use of federal funds for abortions for women receiving welfare assistance.

RIGHTS OF THE ACCUSED

The essential characteristics of liberty in any society are the restraints on how government may treat a person accused of a crime. In America, there are many such restraints. From time to time, particularly when a horrible crime is involved, there are public complaints that the hands of police officers are tied, that judges are too lenient, that juries are confused, that "slick lawyers" can get a guilty person acquitted. These complaints are not without justification. But safeguards are meant to protect the innocent while

The developing concept of the right to privacy was boosted by the Supreme Court's 1973 decision holding that, within certain strict limits, a woman's right to have an abortion was a matter to be decided by the woman and her doctor, not by the government. In this and other cases, the Court has held that the right of privacy is implied in the Bill of Rights.

---

[78] *United States* v. *United States District Court*, 407 U.S. 297 (1972); *United States* v. *Giordano*, 416 U.S. 505 (1974).

[79] *Griswold* v. *Connecticut*, 381 U.S. 479, 1965.

[80] See *In re Kimball*, 33 N.Y. 2d 586, 301 N.E. 2d 436 (1973); *Morton* v. *Macy*, 417 F. 2d 1161 (D.C. Cir. 1969); *People* v. *Roberts*, 256 Cal. App. 2d 488, 64 Cal. Rptr. 70 (1967).

[81] *Roe* v. *Wade*, 410 U.S. 113 (1973).

punishing the guilty. Court decisions upholding these safeguards are sometimes highly unpopular because, as Justice Frankfurter stated, the cases generally involve "not very nice people." Our system of justice is founded upon the idea that nice people can only be protected when not very nice people are also protected. Who is to say which people are not very nice? Too often it is the person despised for unpopular views, or the poor person, or the minority person who most needs the law's protection. Unfortunately, the law sometimes provides little or no protection in such cases.

THE MIRANDA CARD

The Supreme Court's rulings in the Miranda *case and others require police officers to advise people of their rights when arresting them. In order to comply with these decisions, police officers now read suspects their rights from "Miranda cards":*

ADVISE OF RIGHTS

1. I am charging you with _____.
2. Before we ask you any questions, you must understand your rights.
3. You have the right to remain silent.
4. Anything you say can be used against you in Court.
5. You have the right to talk to a lawyer for advice before we ask you any questions and to have him with you during the questioning.
6. If you cannot afford a lawyer, one will be appointed for you before any questioning if you wish.
7. If you decide to answer questions now without a lawyer present, you will still have the right to stop answering at any time until you talk to a lawyer.
8. Do you understand what I have told you?

A person accused of a crime in America is entitled to *due process*. The law books are bulging with cases that seek to define this Fifth Amendment phrase. Procedural due process requires fundamental fairness at every stage of the proceeding, notice of what is happening or is going to happen, and the full right to be heard. Procedural due process must also be observed in a number of other situations, such as student disciplinary[82] and juvenile hearings.[83] Substantive due process requires that the purpose of a criminal or other statute must be reasonable. For example, a mentally ill person who is not dangerous may not be confined involuntarily.[84]

The accused person has the *right to be informed* of the right to remain silent and the right to counsel.[85] This requirement is based on the controversial five-to-four *Miranda* decision. The Warren Court's decision overturned the conviction of Ernesto A. Miranda for kidnaping and raping an eighteen-year-old woman because Miranda had confessed without having been advised of his right to remain silent and his right to a lawyer, and without having been told that anything he said might be used against him. There were numerous complaints that this decision would unduly restrict the police and would "open the jails." But police officers soon began to carry cards from which they read the necessary words to people they arrested, and the requirement of the *Miranda* case did not prove to be difficult to follow. Although the Burger Court has upheld the basic principles of the *Miranda* case, it has seriously narrowed its application in

---

[82] *Goss* v. *Lopez*, 419 U.S. 565 (1975).
[83] *In re Gault*, 387 U.S. 1 (1967).
[84] *O'Connor* v. *Donaldson*, 422 U.S. 563 (1975).
[85] *Miranda* v. *Arizona*, 384 U.S. 436 (1966).

certain instances. For example, it has allowed a confession to be used after only a partial statement by the police of the defendant's rights.[86]

Arraignment—the process in which a defendant is taken before a judge or magistrate and charged with a crime—must occur soon after arrest. Otherwise, defendants can secure their release with a writ of habeas corpus.

The Sixth Amendment guarantees the defendant the right of *counsel* at every stage of the proceedings. The court must in most cases supply a lawyer without charge to the defendant if the defendant cannot afford to hire one.[87]

The accused person is entitled to *bail*. This provision allows the defendant to be released from custody if money or other property is given as security that the defendant will show up for trial. Under the Eighth Amendment, bail must not be "excessive," or out of proportion to the seriousness of the offense and the likelihood that the accused person may fail to appear. Bail may be denied in capital offenses (crimes punishable by death) if the defendant is not likely to show up for trial. By the same token, an accused person may be released without bail if the judge decides that the person can be trusted to appear.

According to the Fifth Amendment, a person cannot be tried on federal charges of capital or other serious crimes unless there has first been a *grand jury indictment*. The Sixth Amendment provides that an accused person must be fully *informed of the charge* before trial in order to prepare a defense.

The Sixth Amendment also guarantees a defendant a *speedy and public trial*. If an accused person is not brought to trial within a reasonable time, the charge actually may be dismissed. But the defendant may ask, and often does, for some postponement. Because of crowded trial dockets and the uncertainty of the outcome in a trial, prosecutors frequently enter into *plea bargaining*. In this process, the defendant, with court approval, agrees to a conviction on a lesser charge or is given a reduced sentence in return for a plea of guilty.

For serious crimes, which in the federal courts are those punishable by six months in prison or a $500 fine, the defendant is entitled to a *jury trial*.[88] In federal criminal cases, there must be twelve jurors,

WHAT TO DO IF YOU ARE ARRESTED

The Bill of Rights provides a number of important protections for those who are accused of crimes. The American Indian Law Center at the University of New Mexico has issued a card which gives advice on these rights:

When questioned by the police, stop if ordered to do so. Show driver's license or identification. Police have the right to search you for weapons.

If you are arrested, do not fight. Police can use force if you resist.

You should be told of your rights. (See the "Miranda card" reprinted in this chapter.)

If you are taken to the police station, you have a right to make a telephone call and to be released until your trial if you can pay bail.

Do not plead guilty until you see a lawyer.

---

[86] *Michigan* v. *Tucker*, 417 U.S. 433 (1974).
[87] *Gideon* v. *Wainwright*, 372 U.S. 335 (1963).
[88] *Duncan* v. *Louisiana*, 391 U.S. 145 (1968).

selected from a list that is representative of the local community—not discriminating against black jurors,[89] for example—and all twelve jurors must agree in order to convict the defendant.[90] Under the Sixth Amendment, defendants also have the right to have the judge *compel witnesses* to testify in the defendant's behalf and the right to *confront and cross-examine witnesses* for the prosecution.

Americans have a carefully protected *right against self-incrimination*. An old fundamental principle of English and American law, this right arose to prevent force or coercion from being used by the authorities to exact confessions. In America the exercise of this right is sometimes called "taking the Fifth," because the right against self-incrimination is one of the several rights enumerated in

Must human rights only relate to political and legal rights? What does freedom of speech mean to an Appalachian carpenter out of work? Or a Harlem mother whose electricity has been turned off?

President Franklin D. Roosevelt proposed a *second* bill of rights, which included the right to a job, to an education, and to adequate housing, food, and medical care. More recently, U.S. Senator Edward M. Kennedy (D., Mass.) has spoken of health care as a "right" of Americans and has advocated a national health insurance plan. The Humphrey-Hawkins bill, in its original form, would have made the right to a job a legally enforceable right; the government would have been required to supply the job if there were none available in the private sector.

Daniel Webster tied these kinds of questions to the fate of democracy. "A great equality of condition," he said, "is the true basis, most certainly, of popular government."

Is a certain amount of inequality necessary to give people incentives? If so, how much inequality is enough? How much is too much? To what degree should the government intervene to bring about the "equality of condition" that Webster spoke of as necessary to the survival of democratic government? These are the unanswered questions of the American experiment.

VIEWPOINT

Should Human Rights Include Economic Rights?

the Fifth Amendment to the Constitution. People testifying before congressional committees sometimes use this privilege. In court, this safeguard means that people charged with crimes have the right to remain silent; they are not required to claim the right publicly unless already voluntarily testifying on some matters. A federal judge must instruct the jury that they are not to draw any conclusions from a defendant's failure to testify. People charged with crimes are also protected by a *presumption of innocence*. Finally, the government has the burden of proving guilt beyond a reasonable doubt, a stricter standard than that used in civil cases.

---

[89] *Peters* v. *Kiff*, 407 U.S. 493 (1972); *Taylor* v. *Louisiana*, 419 U.S. 522 (1972).
[90] *Maxwell* v. *Dow*, 176 U.S. 581 (1900).

The Fifth Amendment gives a convicted person a *right against double jeopardy*. That is, a defendant cannot be tried twice for the same offense. But it is not double jeopardy to try and convict a person in both a state court and a federal court when the same offense—possession of narcotics, say—is a crime under both state and federal law.[91]

After conviction, defendants have a *right of appeal*. Under the Eighth Amendment they also have a *right to be protected from cruel and unusual punishment*. Cruel and unusual punishment can include a sentence that is too severe for the crime committed,[92] intolerable prison conditions,[93] or in some instances, the death penalty. In 1972, the Burger Court issued a highly controversial five-to-four decision which held that the unpredictable way capital punishment was imposed in state trials was unconstitutional because it amounted to cruel and unusual punishment.[94] Prior to this decision, poor and minority people found guilty of crimes received the death sentence more often than other defendants. The Court did not hold that capital punishment always constitutes cruel and unusual punishment, even though many people oppose it on such humane grounds. Instead, it ruled that the uneven and inconsistent application of this extreme penalty was unconstitutional. After this ruling, most of the states passed new capital punishment laws to eliminate the earlier unpredictability of such sentences. For example, state laws that make the death penalty mandatory in cases involving the murder of a law enforcement officer have been upheld by the Supreme Court.[95]

CIVIL LIBERTIES, THE STATES, AND INDIAN TRIBES

The Bill of Rights was an addition to the *federal* Constitution; it was intended to restrict what the *federal* government could do. But does it also restrict what the states can do?

In 1833, the Supreme Court declared that the Bill of Rights did *not* operate as a restraint on states. The Court held that a state was not bound by the provision in the Fifth Amendment which declares that private property may not be taken for public use without just compensation.[96] States were, of course, bound by any similar provisions in their own state constitutions, but the state courts were sometimes not as vigorous in applying the provisions in state constitutions as the U.S. Supreme Court was in applying the Bill of Rights in the U.S. Constitution.

---

[91] *Bartkus* v. *Illinois*, 359 U.S. 121 (1959).
[92] *Coker* v. *Georgia*, 53 L. Ed. 2d 982 (1977).
[93] *Estelle* v. *Gamble*, 429 U.S. 97 (1972).
[94] *Furman* v. *Georgia*, 408 U.S. 238 (1972).
[95] *Woodson* v. *North Carolina*, 428 U.S. 289 (1976); *Gregg* v. *Georgia*, 428 U.S. 153 (1976).
[96] *Barron* v. *Baltimore*, F. Peters 243 (1833).

The original Bill of Rights declared that the national government could not deprive citizens of certain rights or freedoms. Now, because of the Civil War Amendments, state governments cannot do most of those same things, either.

Following the Civil War, the Thirteenth, Fourteenth, and Fifteenth Amendments were proposed by Congress and ratified by the states. These amendments were intended to abolish slavery and establish the equal rights of the former slaves, but their effect is far broader than that. The Fourteenth Amendment provides, among other things, that no state may deprive any person of life, liberty, or property without due process of law. But it was not until the 1925 case of *Gitlow* v. *New York*[97] that the Court announced the doctrine of *incorporation*, holding that the freedoms of speech and of the press, as set forth in the U.S. Bill of Rights, were a part of the "liberty" that the Fourteenth Amendment prohibited the states from denying. By the late 1970s, the Supreme Court had held on a case-by-case basis that the Civil War Amendments had, in effect, incorporated most of the provisions of the Bill of Rights, making them apply to state as well as federal actions. The only Bill of Rights safeguards that have not been incorporated are the right to grand jury criminal indictment, the right to trial by jury in civil cases, the right to bear arms, protection against excessive bail and fines, and the right against involuntary quartering of troops in private homes.

Like states, Indian tribes were not bound at first by the Bill of Rights in the U.S. Constitution. (Unlike states, they were not bound by the Civil War Amendments, either.) Some tribal members suffered violations of their rights by their own tribal governments and had no remedy.[98] The Indian Civil Rights Act, passed by Congress in 1968, changed that.

The Act spelled out a kind of bill of rights for Indians and non-Indians on a reservation. The establishment-of-religion clause was left out, though. So, a tribal government can establish a religion, but it cannot restrict religious freedom. The Act also outlawed tribal enactment of ex post facto laws and bills of attainder. Provisions were made in the Act for strengthening tribal codes and courts so that the tribes' own courts could enforce these newly enacted rights. But the law authorized habeas corpus proceedings to be brought in the federal courts when a person was unlawfully detained.

The Supreme Court has held that tribal members must use tribal courts, not federal courts, to bring civil suits for violations of their rights under the act.[99] The Court has also ruled that a non-Indian is not subject to the jurisdiction of a tribal criminal court.[100]

---

[97] *Gitlow* v. *New York*, 268 U.S. 652 (1925).
[98] *Talton* v. *Mayes*, 163 U.S. 376 (1895). See also *Native American Church* v. *Navajo Tribal Council*, 276 F. 2d 131 (10th Cir., 1959); and *Toledo* v. *Pueblo de Jemez*, 119 Fed. Supp. 429 (D.N.M., 1954).
[99] *Santa Clara Pueblo* v. *Martinez*, 98 S. Ct. 1670 (1978).
[100] *Oliphant* v. *Suquamish Indian Tribe*, 98 S. Ct. 1101 (1978).

Some Indians and tribes have viewed this law as a violation of tribal sovereignty. Although major crimes are still tried in the federal courts under an earlier congressional act, the Indian Civil Rights Act has caused notable development and improvement of Indian legal systems.

CONCLUSION

The Declaration of Independence set forth certain ideals, including those involving fundamental human rights. The Constitution established a government. The Bill of Rights sought to serve as a bridge between the two functions: it declared certain ideals to be human rights and established them as restraints on government.

The Bill of Rights—including the democratic freedoms, the personal freedoms, and the rights of the accused—was adopted with little difficulty. These inalienable rights, or "civil liberties" as we call them today, have been recognized almost from the very first days of our national government. But political equality, or "civil rights," and economic opportunity were not to be recognized so rapidly or easily.

ADDITIONAL SOURCES

Abraham, Henry J., and Grace Doherty. *Civil Rights and Liberties in the United States*, 3rd ed. Oxford University Press, 1977.*

Berns, Walter. *The First Amendment and the Future of American Democracy*. Basic Books, 1976.

Brant, Irving. *The Bill of Rights: Its Origins and Meaning*. Bobbs-Merrill, 1965.*

Dworkin, Ronald. *Taking Rights Seriously*. Harvard University Press, 1977.*

Fellman, David. *The Defendant's Rights Today*. University of Wisconsin Press, 1977.*

Jackson, Robert H. *The Supreme Court in the American System of Government*. Harvard University Press, 1955.*

Krislov, Samuel. *The Supreme Court and Political Freedom*. Free Press, 1968.*

Nagel, Stuart S., ed. *The Rights of the Accused*. Sage, 1972.*

Rucker, Bryce W. *The First Freedom*. Southern Illinois University Press, 1968.*

Smith, James Morton. *Freedom's Fetters: The Alien and Sedition Laws and American Civil Liberties*. Cornell University Press, 1956.*

Sunderland, Lane V. *Obscenity: The Court, the Congress and the Presidential Commission*. American Enterprise Institute for Public Policy Research, 1975.

*Available in paperback edition.

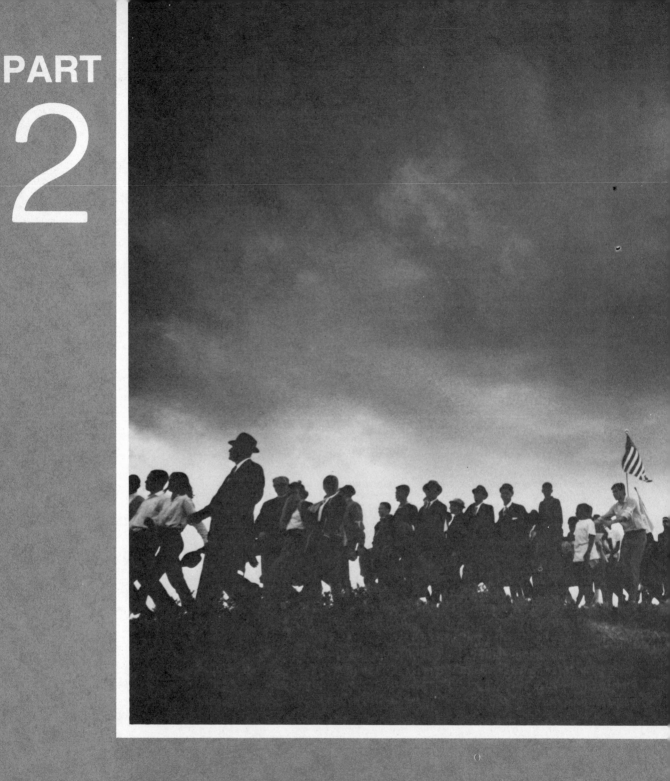

Democracy and Equality

As the Constitutional Convention completed its work in 1787, Benjamin Franklin was stopped by a woman in the streets of Philadelphia. "What manner of government have you given us?" she asked. "A republic, madam," Franklin replied, "if you can keep it."

As important as ideals and constitutions are, they are, after all, only words. The people make those words come to life. The Constitution itself was not perfect, and the Bill of Rights did not protect the liberties of all Americans; but the ideals of human rights, equality, and participation applied to all. Gradually, the people—blacks, women, American Indians, Hispanic Americans, and others—struggled to achieve those rights, to become full and equal participants in American society and politics.

Americans have made great strides toward political and social equality, as we shall see in Chapter 4. But there has been and continues to be a tension between political equality and economic equality, which is the subject of Chapter 5.

4 Civil Rights
The Struggle for Equality

A neatly dressed woman got on a city bus and sat in a seat near the front. It was the kind of thing that happens every day in every city in America. But on this particular day, this seemingly simple act would make history. It signaled the start of a movement that would change America in dramatic ways.

The year was 1955. The city was Montgomery, Alabama. The woman, Rosa Parks, was black. She was in her forties and made her living sewing for other people. She was a gentle and quiet woman. But she was determined, on this day, to be treated fairly. When the driver told her to give up her seat to a white man and move to the back of the bus, as black people were customarily required to do, she refused.

Her refusal sparked a black boycott of the city's buses. No one could know on that day in 1955 that the boycott would be successful—that blacks would be able to ride public buses with dignity. Or that a young black preacher, Dr. Martin Luther King, Jr., would emerge from the boycott as a national civil rights leader who would later receive the Nobel Peace Prize. Or that Congress would eventually pass new laws prohibiting discrimination not only in public transportation and accommodations, but also in voting, housing, jobs, and education.

There was no way that Rosa Parks or anyone else could have

December 1956: Rosa Parks rides in the front of a Montgomery bus after the Supreme Court ruled that segregation in public transportation was unconstitutional.

known on that day that a whole series of movements—among American Indians, Hispanic Americans, women, and others—would develop in the wake of the black civil rights movement. Each would demand payment on the "promissory note" of the Declaration of Independence: full human rights, including full equality, for all Americans.

The Montgomery story and its aftermath constitute a shorthand description of the struggle for civil rights in this country. Advances were often slow, halting, and painful. Many came only with great human cost and after much human suffering. Courageous struggle was frequently the essential catalyst for change. Still, the long view of our history shows a definite expansion of civil rights through Constitutional amendments, court decisions, and new laws. Yet even now, the promissory note of the Declaration of Independence cannot be stamped "paid in full."

CITIZENSHIP AND CIVIL RIGHTS

Framers of the Constitution seem to have assumed that citizenship began at the state level and that people became citizens of the United States as a result of their state citizenship—not the other way around. This concept of citizenship changed with the adoption of the Civil War Amendments: the Thirteenth, Fourteenth, and Fifteenth Amendments to the United States Constitution. The Thirteenth Amendment, ratified in 1865, prohibits slavery. The Fourteenth Amendment, ratified four years later, provides for U.S. citizenship and establishes the rights of citizens and others living in the various states. This amendment, among other things, set aside the U.S. Supreme Court's Dred Scott decision of 1857. In that case, the Court had held that black people were not included—and were never intended to be included—in the meaning of the word *citizens* in the original Constitution.[1] The Fifteenth Amendment, ratified in 1870, deals with the right to vote.

Citizenship

The fundamental law in regard to American citizenship is stated in Section 1 of the Fourteenth Amendment: "All persons born or naturalized in the United States, and subject to the jurisdiction thereof, are citizens of the U.S. and of the state wherein they reside."

Nations use two doctrines to confer citizenship. One is based on where a person was born, the other upon who the person's parents were. The Fourteenth Amendment is based upon where a person is born. This amendment was intended to confer citizenship on former

---

[1] *Dred Scott* v. *Sanford*, 19 How. 393 (1857).

slaves who had been born in the United States. Today, its application is broad enough to include *all* persons born in the United States. They are citizens. In addition, Congress has passed a law which confers citizenship on the basis of blood. It gives American citizenship to children born to American citizens outside the United States.

The Fourteenth Amendment recognized another way to achieve American citizenship: the process of naturalization. This process, governed by congressional laws, applies to people who are not born in the United States and whose parents are not American citizens. It requires a period of residency within the United States, a rudimentary knowledge of English, the successful completion of an examination concerning U.S. history and government, and the taking of an oath to support and defend the United States and to give up all allegiance to a foreign government or power.

Congress has complete control over who can come into the United States and who can become citizens. Until the twentieth century, there was little or no restriction on immigration to the United States. America is indeed a "nation of immigrants," as President Kennedy put it. Yet Congress began to limit immigration in 1925, and the present law still does. Today, only 170,000 immigrants can come to the United States each year from countries outside our hemisphere, and only 120,000 immigrants can enter each year from nations in this hemisphere. No more than 20,000 can come from any one country in a year. Our law does not discriminate today against immigrants on the basis of national origin; earlier laws, however, favored Caucasians. Present law gives preference to relatives of American citizens. Children, spouses, and parents of American citizens are not subject to the annual quota. Preference is also given to people skilled in an art or profession and to political or racial refugees from other countries.

Until 1924, it was not clear whether American Indians were U.S. citizens under the terms of the Fourteenth Amendment. Although they were born here, Indians, in a sense, were not "subject to the jurisdiction" of the United States because most were citizens of separate tribal governments. A special act of Congress in that year, however, granted U.S. citizenship, including the right to vote, to American Indians.

As a result of the Fourteenth Amendment, citizens of the United States are automatically citizens "of the State wherein they reside," and they are entitled to all "the privileges and immunities of citizens of the United States." Among other things, these phrases mean that a state cannot bar the travel of citizens from one state to another, as California unsuccessfully tried to do when it put up entry barriers to the "Okies" in the 1930s.[2] However, the federal government *can* deny the right of citizens to travel to foreign countries.[3]

---

[2]*Edwards* v. *California*, 314 U.S. 160 (1941).
[3]*Zemel* v. *Rusk*, 381 U.S. 1 (1965).

Aliens—people residing in the United States who are not American citizens—are also protected by the U.S. Constitution. For example, neither the federal nor the state government can deny an alien freedom of speech or freedom of religion. Aliens *can* be denied the right to vote; today, in fact, they are not allowed to vote in any state in the country. States have the power to grant aliens the right to vote, and many once did.

There are several million "undocumented" people in the United States. They are often referred to as "illegal aliens." Most of these people have entered the United States from Mexico. Some have been in this country for a number of years. Labor unions want the borders policed more effectively to hold down the numbers of these entrants, who, they fear, are competing for scarce American jobs. President Carter has recommended a new law to Congress, which would allow those who have been in the United States a certain number of years to remain here legally. The bill would also require employers to find out whether prospective employees are legally residing in the United States before hiring them. Many employers and Chicano organizations oppose this legislation. Chicano groups fear people with Spanish surnames would be harassed and discriminated against if this bill became a law.

Voting

The Constitution left the question of voting to the states. That is not true today. Constitutional amendments, congressional acts, and Supreme Court decisions have set national standards for voting in national elections. However, much discretion is still allowed to each state in setting voting qualifications, especially in state elections.

The Fifteenth Amendment, adopted after the Civil War, states: "The right of citizens of the United States shall not be denied or abridged by the United States or by any State, on account of race, color, or previous condition of servitude." Section 2 of the amendment gives Congress the power to enforce the provisions of the amendment by "appropriate legislation." But Congress did not pass effective laws to carry out the intent of the Fifteenth Amendment until almost one hundred years later.

Equal Protection

No sooner had slavery been outlawed by the Thirteenth Amendment than the southern states began to pass what were called Black Codes. These new laws were designed to keep black people in a revised form of slavery. Congress proposed the Fourteenth Amendment in part to reverse the effect of the Black Codes. It states: "No State shall make or enforce any law which shall abridge the privileges or immunities of citizens of the United States; nor shall any State deprive any person of life, liberty, or property, without due process of law; nor deny to any person within its jurisdiction the equal protection of the laws."

What is the meaning of the phrase "equal protection of the laws"? To whom does it apply? Does it mean that every citizen must be treated exactly the same by government?

First, the equal protection clause applies to all citizens, not just to black people. Second, because of the due process clause of the Fifth Amendment, the federal government is also bound by the same restraints that the equal protection clause places on the states. Third, equal protection does not require the government to treat all citizens exactly the same way, but it does require that when one class of persons is treated differently from others, there must be a reasonable connection between the classification of the people involved and the restriction contained in the law. For example, blind people can be prohibited by law from driving cars, but they could not be prohibited from running for public office. The distinction between the two cases, of course, is that there is a reasonable connection between vision and safe driving but not between vision and holding public office. Similarly, the equal protection clause does not prevent governments from passing laws limiting the right of young people below a certain age to vote, drive, buy alcoholic beverages, or marry without parental consent. In each of these cases, the courts presume that some reasonable connection exists between a certain age level and the requisite ability, skill, or judgment to perform these acts.

But there are "constitutionally suspect" classifications and other cases involving "fundamental rights" that the courts view with extra scrutiny and skepticism. In such instances, courts will rule that a restrictive law is unconstitutional unless it is clearly shown that the law embodies a compelling or important public purpose that cannot be accomplished in a less restrictive way.

The fundamental rights that receive such special attention from the courts include voting and freedom of speech, press, and religion. Housing, education, and welfare benefits are not considered fundamental rights in this sense because they are not protected by express or implied guarantees in the U.S. Constitution.

Race is the most "constitutionally suspect" classification. Laws that classify and treat people on the basis of national origin or because they are aliens are also suspect. In addition, classifying people on the basis of poverty can be suspect. For example, the Supreme Court has struck down laws that required people to pay a filing fee in order to run for public office or to get a divorce. The Supreme Court has not yet declared that classifying people on the basis of sex is suspect, although a substantial minority on the Court have said that they think it should be. However, it has held that treating female and male surviving spouses differently in regard to social security and death benefits is an unreasonable classification and therefore unconstitutional. The ratification of the Equal Rights Amendment would make classification on the basis of sex suspect. The doctrine of constitutionally suspect classifications is intended to provide special protection from majority rule—and therefore equal protection of the law—to those classes of people who have suffered special disabilities, discrimination, or political powerlessness. Whether they fall into the constitutionally suspect category, involve fundamental rights, or merely use unreasonable classifications, federal and state laws must not deny equal protection to any person, male or female, black or white, rich or poor, young or old.[4]

THE BLACK CIVIL RIGHTS MOVEMENT

Black people have been in America as long as any group except the American Indians. The first blacks to arrive in Jamestown were indentured servants, as were many of the first whites who came to America. Indentured servants were bound to an employer for a definite period of years. But it did not take long for inherited slavery—a system that classified the children of black slaves as slaves themselves—to become the rule for black people in America. There were black protests and revolts in America beginning in early colonial days and continuing until the Civil War. But they were scattered and ultimately unsuccessful.

The Civil War brought freedom in name only for most black Americans. Although the noxious weed of slavery had been chopped down, the roots of racism still remained. They soon began to sprout again. The emanicipation of the slaves and the ratification of the Civil War amendments did not end racism or its dreadful effects. The Freedman's Bureau was established to assist the newly freed slaves, but an official of this agency reported that the former slaveholders "still have an ingrained feeling that the blacks at large belong to the whites at large." A congressional proposal for federal aid to education, aimed principally at upgrading education for the former slaves, was defeated. So, too, was the idea of providing "forty acres and a mule" for freed slaves. The former slaves therefore had little opportunity to acquire capital—particularly land and the means of working the land—or educational skills. Thus, although the Thirteenth Amendment guaranteed them *legal* freedom, the former slaves were in reality neither free nor equal.

The Era of "Jim Crow"

Soon even the legal freedom of the former slaves was taken away. In state after state in the South, laws were passed and constitutions were changed to disenfranchise—take the vote away from—former slaves. The methods used were poll taxes, literacy tests, restricted party

---

[4]See William Cohen and John Kaplan, *Bill of Rights* (Mineola, New York: The Foundation Press, Inc., 1976); and Robert J. Harris, *The Quest for Equality* (Baton Rouge: Louisiana State University Press, 1960).

primaries, and "grandfather clauses" (allowing the right to vote only to those whose grandfathers had been voters). Whites also frequently used fraud and violence to keep blacks from voting.

The Fourteenth Amendment was adopted to provide full citizenship for blacks. Congress also passed a Civil Rights Act soon afterward to assure black people equal access to hotels, public transportation, and theaters and other places of entertainment. But in the *Civil Rights Cases* of 1883,[5] the U.S. Supreme Court declared

that the Civil Rights Act was unconstitutional because the Fourteenth Amendment constituted a restriction on states, not on individuals or private businesses. Racism sprouted in new and terrible forms and spread through the South like Johnson grass. America had missed its chance. An appalling tragedy was to shadow the lives of millions of black Americans for years and years to come.

Without the right to redress their grievances by voting, betrayed by the highest court in the land, forgotten by Northern politicians, black people rapidly fell victim to all kinds of discrimination and persecution. Rigid segregation reinforced the image of inferiority. Too often it became a self-image for blacks, and a self-fulfilling prophecy for millions of black children. Separate and inferior black schools dulled the mind and consigned millions of black children to a life of poverty and hard manual labor. Horrible lynchings sought to keep the rebellious in line. Those who could help often looked the other way, and many of those who wished to help were powerless.

Throughout the South and the border states, Jim Crow laws were passed to prohibit blacks from using the same public accommodations or conveyances as whites. These state laws required segregated schools, hospitals, prisons, restaurants, bars, hotels and boarding houses, theaters, toilets, railways and streetcars, and waiting rooms. Blacks and whites could not use the same water fountains or ticket windows. They could not mix in fraternal societies or at circuses, parks, racetracks, and sports events. They could not live in the same residential areas. Some communities passed "Sundown Ordinances," which prohibited blacks from staying in town overnight. Blacks and whites could not even be buried in the same cemeteries.

There seemed to be no limit to the logical absurdity of the Jim Crow laws. New Orleans required separate districts for black and

---

[5]*Civil Rights Cases*, 109 U.S. 3 (1883).

white prostitutes. In Oklahoma, blacks and whites could not use the same telephone booths. In North Carolina and Florida, school textbooks used by little black children had to be kept and stored separately from those used by white children. In Birmingham, the races were specifically prohibited from playing dominoes or checkers together.

In the 1896 case of *Plessy* v. *Ferguson*,[6] the U.S. Supreme Court implicitly approved the state Jim Crow laws, holding that "separate but equal" facilities for blacks and whites were not a violation of the Fourteenth Amendment. Homer Adolph Plessy was a black man who lived in Louisiana; like Rosa Parks more than sixty years later in Alabama, he had been arrested for refusing to move to the "colored" section of a public conveyance, in this case a train. The Supreme Court upheld his conviction. "Separate but equal" was the law, but the "equal" part was largely ignored. During President Woodrow Wilson's administration, even the nation's capital, Washington, D.C., became a racially segregated city.[7]

The Modern Era

America fought in World War I to "make the world safe for democracy"; yet discrimination was still the rule at home. The first civil rights victories were to be won in the courts. Two factors were responsible for these advances. First, as Franklin Roosevelt and succeeding Presidents filled vacancies on the Supreme Court, there was a gradual change in the philosophical leanings of Supreme Court justices. Taking office in 1952, President Dwight Eisenhower appointed a liberal Republican governor of California, Earl Warren, to be the chief justice of the Supreme Court.

Second, the change in the Court's makeup came at just the time when black leaders were increasingly sponsoring suits in the courts to challenge racial discrimination. The NAACP led the fight, setting up the Legal Defense Fund for this purpose. Chosen to head the Legal Defense Fund was Thurgood Marshall, a law graduate of Howard University in Washington, D.C., and the grandson of a Maryland slave. Marshall's perseverance and legal scholarship were to make history and were to result in his appointment to the Supreme Court in 1967 as the first black justice.[8] All that was far in the future when the Legal Defense Fund was formed in 1938, but the battle had unmistakably been joined. In 1954, the Supreme Court reversed the holding of the *Plessy* case and ruled that separate public schools were inherently unequal. The landmark case was called *Brown* v. *Board of Education*,[9] although it actually consolidated five similar cases. It

[6]*Plessy* v. *Ferguson*, 163 U.S. 537 (1896).
[7]Fred R. Harris, *Alarms and Hopes* (New York: Harper & Row, 1968), p. 86.
[8]See John P. MacKenzie, "Thurgood Marshall," in Leon Friedman and Fred L. Irael, eds., *The Justices of the United States Supreme Court, 1789–1969*, Vol. 4 (New York: R. R. Bowker Company, 1969), pp. 3063–3108.
[9]*Brown* v. *Board of Education*, 347 U.S. 483 (1954).

principally involved an eight-year-old black girl, Linda Carol Brown, who lived in Topeka, Kansas, where the schools were rigidly segregated. Her father had tried to enroll her in a white public school four blocks from their house, but she had been denied enrollment and required to attend an all-black school twenty-one blocks away. The NAACP Legal Defense Fund came to the assistance of Linda Carol Brown and her father. In a unanimous decision written by Chief Justice Warren, the Supreme Court said that the equal protection of the laws provision of the Fourteenth Amendment did indeed prohibit separate public schools for blacks and whites. The Supreme Court's opinion contained sociological findings as well as legal reasoning. It declared that segregated schooling for black children might "affect their hearts and minds in a way unlikely ever to be undone." In a later case, the Court also ordered desegregation in other public facilities.

It was one thing for the Court to make a ruling, however, and quite another to have it enforced. Throughout the South, white officials girded up for "massive resistance" to the Court decisions. These officials were backed by white citizens' councils. Highway billboards, sponsored by the right-wing John Birch Society, went up throughout the country, demanding the impeachment of Earl Warren. Even President Eisenhower, who had appointed Chief Justice Warren, said privately that the Court had gone too far.

But President Eisenhower felt bound by his constitutional duty to "take care that the laws be faithfully executed." After the Court had ruled in a later version of the same case that its *Brown* decision had to be implemented by the states "with all deliberate speed" and supervised by federal district courts, a major state-federal government confrontation arose in Little Rock, Arkansas, in 1957. The governor of that state, Orval Faubus, a clever and ambitious country politician who catered to the state's white majority, called out the Arkansas National Guard to block integration in Little Rock's Central High School. The lines were clearly drawn. To use one of President Eisenhower's phrases, it was time to "fish or cut bait." Though he did not want to do so, President Eisenhower felt that he had no alternative but to nationalize the Arkansas National Guard and to use it and U.S. Army paratroopers to enforce the Supreme Court decision and force integration of the Little Rock school.

Resistance to the Court's decisions continued throughout the South. President John F. Kennedy sent federal marshals to Oxford, Mississippi, in 1962 to enforce the right of a black student, James Meredith, to attend that state's university, despite the opposition of state officials. President Kennedy also nationalized the Alabama National Guard in 1963 to thwart the attempt of Alabama's governor, George Wallace, to block school integration in that state.

From the time of the Montgomery bus boycott, touched off by the courage of Rosa Parks, the black civil rights movement had increasingly been marked by demonstrations. Blacks were no longer willing to rely solely upon gradual progress in the courts. The Southern Christian Leadership Conference (SCLC), led by Dr. Martin Luther King, Jr., was instrumental in these efforts, which also won notable white support in the North. The Congress of Racial Equality (CORE), headed by James Farmer, and the Student Non-Violent Coordinating Committee (SNCC), led first by John Lewis and later by Stokely Carmichael and H. Rap Brown, were also actively involved in the movement. Lunch-counter sit-ins by young blacks swept southern cities, starting in Greensboro, North Carolina, in 1960. Black and white "freedom riders" tried to ride public buses through the South. Even before the *Brown* decision, the Supreme Court had declared that blacks had the right to use public transportation. What these rides proved, though, was that there was no such right in the South. Freedom riders were brutally beaten. A bus was burned. In Birmingham in 1963, Police Commissioner Eugene "Bull" Connor turned his police loose to wield cattle prods and firehoses on civil rights marchers, and as the marchers sang "We Shall Overcome," he set savage police dogs on them. Dr. King went to jail as a leader of this demonstration.

U.S. Army paratroopers were sent by President Eisenhower to Little Rock to enforce the Supreme Court's ruling that school desegregation had to occur "with all deliberate speed."

The televised brutality of the Birmingham police aroused the sympathies of a great many Americans. To protest the lack of federal action in support of civil rights, black leaders organized a "March on Washington" in September 1963. Nearly a quarter of a million people—blacks and supporting whites—filled the area in front of the Lincoln Memorial in the nation's capital. It was here that Dr. King made his impassioned and inspiring "I Have a Dream" speech, which still brings tears to the eyes of millions of Americans who hear a recording or watch a film of it. "From every mountainside, let freedom ring," he concluded movingly, ". . . to speed up that day when all God's children, black and white men, Jews and Gentiles, Protestants and Catholics, will be able to join hands and sing in the words of that old Negro spiritual, 'Free at last! Free at last! Thank God Almighty, we are free at last!'"

The freedom of which Dr. King spoke so movingly was not to come easily or quickly. Hardly an American city was without black demonstrations that summer. Four little black girls were killed when a bomb exploded in a black church in Birmingham. President Kennedy proposed a sweeping civil rights bill to a Congress that showed no willingness to pass it. Then, in November, 1963, President Kennedy was assassinated in Dallas. His successor, Lyndon B. Johnson, appeared before a joint session of Congress and, in the name of the slain President, called for passage of the civil rights legislation, dramatically invoking the familiar words of the movement's anthem, "We Shall Overcome." After a long filibuster in the Senate, the first one ever broken on a civil rights bill, the Civil Rights Act of 1964 was passed and signed into law.

The new law prohibited racial or religious discrimination in public accommodations, such as hotels, restaurants, and movie houses. The Supreme Court later upheld the power of Congress to legislate concerning such privately owned establishments. The law also prohibited unions and employers from discriminating on the basis of race, color, sex, or religion. It outlawed the use of different standards for whites and blacks who attempted to register to vote. To enforce the act, the previously created Civil Rights Commission was continued, and a new Community Relations Service and Equal Employment Opportunity Commission were created. Finally, the act authorized the government to cut off federal funds for institutions and organizations that violated its provisions.

The following year, the Voting Rights Act was pushed through a suddenly responsive Congress. Federal examiners were appointed to stop discrimination in voter registration in the South. Voter registration drives were mounted among black people. Despite stubborn and sustained white resistance, these efforts were markedly successful.

But the impatience of black people had been growing for years; racial progress and change could hardly come fast enough for them. In many places throughout the South, white people were determined to allow no change at all.

As President Johnson's War on Poverty program began to identify and organize poor people throughout the country in the 1960s, it became clear to everyone that racism was not just a problem confined to the South. After World War II, millions of black people had quickly left the South for what they hoped would be better lives in the large cities of the rest of the country. But what they usually found were poor or nonexistent jobs, segregated slums, and bitter disappointment. In the North and West, where they had already had the right to vote, black people began to say that the new civil rights laws had done almost nothing to improve their lives.

The black civil rights movement and President Johnson's Great Society programs aroused great expectations, many of which were not fulfilled. Some of the President's programs provided increased training for jobs without providing jobs. There was encouragement to organize and get into the system, but often the system did not respond. And the all-white television programs showed that blondes

During the spring of 1963, Dr. Martin Luther King, Jr., and the Southern Christian Leadership Conference led a series of massive, nonviolent marches in Birmingham, Alabama, against segregation in public accommodations. After King was arrested (for disobeying a court order prohibiting a march), eight local clergymen published a statement criticizing the tactics and timing of the demonstrations. King wrote his now-famous response on scrap paper and envelopes, defending his nonviolent methods and attacking the apathy of white churches in the face of injustice. In the excerpt that follows, King addresses the issue of "timing."

Dr. Martin Luther King, Jr., receiving the Nobel Peace Prize in 1964.

We know through painful experience that freedom is never voluntarily given by the oppressor; it must be demanded by the oppressed. Frankly, I have yet to engage in a direct-action campaign that was "well timed" in the view of those who have not suffered unduly from the disease of segregation. For years now I have heard the word "wait!" It rings in the ear of every Negro with piercing familiarity. This "Wait" has almost always meant "Never." We must come to see, with one of our distinguished jurists, that "justice too long delayed is justice denied."

We have waited for more than 340 years for our constitutional and God-given rights. The nations of Asia and Africa are moving with jetlike speed toward gaining political independence, but we still creep at horse-and-buggy pace toward gaining a cup of coffee at a lunch counter. Perhaps it is easy for those who have never felt the stinging darts of segregation to say, "Wait." But when you have seen vicious mobs lynch your mothers and fathers at will and drown your sisters and brothers at whim; when you have seen hate-filled policemen curse, kick and even kill your black brothers and sisters; when you see the vast majority of your twenty million Negro brothers smothering in an airtight cage of poverty in the midst of an affluent society; when you suddenly find your tongue twisted and your speech stammering as you seek to explain to your six-year-old daughter why she can't go to the public amusement park that has just been advertised on television, and see tears welling up in her eyes when she is told that Funtown is closed to colored children, and

see ominous clouds of inferiority beginning to distort her personality by developing an unconscious bitterness toward white people; when you have to concoct an answer for a five-year-old son who is asking: "Daddy, why do white people treat colored people so mean?"; when you take a cross-country drive and find it necessary to sleep night after night in the uncomfortable corners of your automo-

VIEWPOINT
Letter from Birmingham Jail

bile because no motel will accept you; when you are humiliated day in and day out by nagging signs reading "white" and "colored"; when your first name becomes "boy" (however old you are) and your last name becomes "John," and your wife and mother are never given the respected title "Mrs."; when you are harried by day and haunted by night by the fact that you are a Negro, living constantly at tiptoe stance, never quite knowing what to expect next, and are plagued with inner fears and outer resentments; when you are forever fighting a degenerating sense of "nobodiness"—then you will understand why we find it difficult to wait. There comes a time when the cup of endurance runs over, and men are no longer willing to be plunged into the abyss of despair. I hope, sirs, you can understand our legitimate and unavoidable impatience.

had more fun; wonderful white, middle-class families were living happily ever after. Why are *we* on the streets with no jobs? blacks wondered. Why are *we* living in this wretched tenement where the toilet won't flush and the rats bite our babies? Even a little improvement seemed to produce more frustrations than it alleviated, heightening the sense of relative deprivation.

In the summer of 1965, rioting, burning, and looting erupted in Watts, a deprived black area in the city of Los Angeles. Hundreds of people were hurt. Thirty-four were killed. Property damage was in the tens of millions. A citizens commission, headed by John McCone, investigated this disaster. The commission tried to call the nation's attention to the terrible unemployment in Watts, especially among young blacks, and the deplorable health and housing there. Their report said that the lack of privately owned cars and adequate public transportation made it almost impossible for many Watts residents to get to jobs in the white suburbs or elsewhere.

But few Americans read or paid much attention to the McCone Commission report, entitled "Violence in the City—an End or a Beginning?" The Watts riot proved to be a beginning. The next summer, there were disorders in the black sections of Cleveland and Chicago and eighteen other cities. In a march through Mississippi, James Meredith was wounded by a shotgun blast. Young black leaders, such as Stokely Carmichael, began to push the black movement beyond the milder slogan of "Black is Beautiful," designed to improve the self-image of blacks, toward the more aggressive concept of "Black Power." It was time, they said, for black people to organize and *demand* their full rights as Americans.

During the "long, hot summer" of 1967,[10] there were riots in the black sections of Plainfield and Newark, New Jersey; Detroit and Grand Rapids, Michigan; Atlanta, Georgia; Buffalo, New York; Cincinnati, Ohio; Milwaukee, Wisconsin; Tampa, Florida; and Cambridge, Maryland. Twenty-eight other cities had other disorders, and ninety-two had smaller outbreaks of violence. In Newark, twenty-five people were killed; twenty-one were black, and several were women and children. In Detroit, thirty-three blacks and ten whites died.

To determine the causes of the disorders and to find out how to prevent them in the future, President Johnson appointed the National Advisory Commission on Civil Disorders. This committee, which came to be called the Kerner Commission in reference to its chairperson, Otto Kerner, who was then governor of Illinois, declared in its report of March 1968: "What white Americans have never fully understood, but what the Negro can never forget, is that white society is deeply implicated in the ghetto. White institutions created it, white institutions maintain it and white society condones it." Although this statement shocked many whites, it vindicated the views of many blacks. The Commission found that no organized

---

[10]Harris, *Alarms and Hopes*, p. 86.

conspiracy had fomented the riots; instead, they believed that frustration and a sense of powerlessness in the black sections of America's cities had created a situation so volatile that the slightest random incident could spark an explosion.

"Our nation is moving toward two societies, one black, one white—separate and unequal," the Commission Report stated. It called for a "commitment to national action, compassionate, massive and sustained." It recommended such wide-ranging remedies as increased support for civil rights actions, rebuilding the cities, and heavy concentration on jobs for the unemployed.[11] President Johnson refused even to meet with the Commission; among other reasons, he felt that the report seemed to condone violence and that it did not give his administration sufficient credit for its efforts against poverty and racism.

During the controversy created by the Kerner Report, Dr. Martin Luther King, Jr., was killed by an assassin's bullet on April 5, 1968, in Memphis, where he had gone to support the strike of local sanitation workers. Riots broke out again in more than one hundred cities. In Washington, D.C., the riots occurred within blocks of the White House.

Stirred by Dr. King's death and armed with the Kerner Report, Congress passed a bill on April 16, 1968, to end discrimination in the sale or rental of private housing. Equal employment and other civil rights laws were strengthened, and the various federal agencies and departments continued to enforce the new laws.

For the black civil rights movement, the 1970s was a quiet period. White attention shifted first to protests against the country's involvement in the Viet Nam war and then to concerns about the environment. America's interest in civil rights began to wane.

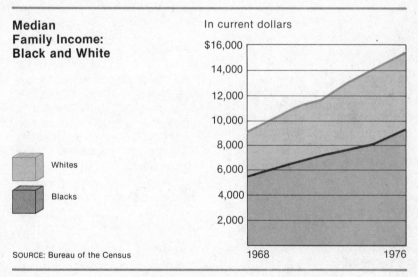

Median Family Income: Black and White

In current dollars

Whites

Blacks

SOURCE: Bureau of the Census

1968   1976

What has happened since the report of the Kerner Commission? By 1976, the median black family income had risen to $9,250 annually—double what it was ten years before. Yet the median annual income of black families was still only 60 percent of the median annual income of white families—$15,500.[12]

Black families earning more than $15,000 per year have increased

[11]*Report of the National Advisory Commission on Civil Disorders* (Washington, D.C.: Government Printing Office, 1968).
[12]*The New York Times* (February 26, 1978).

As a result of the laws and executive orders listed on the opposite page, it is illegal for employers and unions to discriminate on the basis of race, sex, color, religion, age, handicap, or national origin in their hiring, pay, promotion, and firing practices. If you feel you have been discriminated against, what can you do? The

into the matter. However, the more specific you can be, the more likely it is that the Commission will seriously investigate the charge.

The Investigation

If you live in a city or state with a fair-employment practice (FEP) law,

How to...
Fight Job Discrimination

guidelines discussed below are based on Title VII of the Civil Rights Act of 1964, the most sweeping nondiscrimination law (the other laws and orders pertain primarily to firms that receive federal funds).

Filing a Charge

Title VII is enforced by the Equal Employment Opportunity Commission (EEOC); it delegates authority to the office of Civil Rights in the Department of Health, Education, and Welfare when educational institutions are involved. The EEOC is headquartered in Washington and has regional offices throughout the country. To file a complaint, visit an EEOC office and fill out a simple form (called a "charge" form, because you are "charging" the company or union with discrimination). The charge form asks you to "explain what unfair thing was done to you" and "how were other people treated differently." You do *not* have to provide concrete proof; it is the agency's job to investigate the charge. A generalized charge that a company or union discriminates is enough to require the EEOC to look

the EEOC will refer your charge to the relevant city or state agency (as required by Title VII). Only after 60 days can the EEOC begin its own investigation. The EEOC will visit the company or union to talk with people and examine its records, or it will send a questionnaire to be filled out. If discrimination is found, the EEOC will try to settle immediately. If no satisfactory settlement is reached, the EEOC will make a final effort, referred to as "conciliation." If conciliation fails, you will be notified of your "right to sue" and you may take the company or union to court.

The Question of Timing

According to Title VII, if you live in a state with no FEP law, you must file within 180 days of the date you believe you were discriminated against. If your state has an FEP law, you must file within 300 days. (If the discriminatory practice is of a continuing nature, in practice any charge is filed within the time limits.)

If attempts at conciliation have failed, you have only 90 days to file a court complaint. Contact a lawyer at this point.

Note

Your employer or union will be informed of your charge ten days after it is filed. Any retaliation, however, is just as illegal as discrimination itself.

For further information, contact the EEOC or your local or state FEP agencies (check your phone book under the name of your city or state).

Equal Employment Opportunity Commission
1800 G Street, N.W.
Washington, D.C. 20506
Tel: (202) 343-1000

SOURCE: Susan C. Ross, *The Rights of Women* (Sunrise Books/Dutton, 1973), pp. 31–115, and Vilma Martinez Singer, "Employment Discrimination," in Kenneth P. Norwick, ed., *Your Legal Rights* (John Day, 1972), pp. 189–212.

Major Nondiscrimination Laws Pertaining to Employment

Specific nondiscrimination law	Coverage	Federal enforcement agency	Enforcement action
Title VI—Civil Rights Act of 1964	Discrimination on basis of race, color, religion, national origin prohibited in programs receiving federal funds.	Equal Employment Opportunity Commission, delegated to Office for Civil Rights, HEW for educational institutions.	Withholding of federal grants and/or contracts.
Title VII—Civil Rights Act of 1964	Forbids all discrimination in employment because of race, color, religion, sex, or national origin.	Equal Employment Opportunity Commission, delegated to Office of Civil Rights, HEW for educational institutions.	U.S. Attorney General may file suit on behalf of complainant. EEOC generally attempts conciliation and voluntary compliance. EEOC also issues "right to sue" letters for private action in federal district court.
Executive Order 11246, amended by 11375 (to include sex)	Discrimination in employment (hiring, salaries, fringe benefits, etc.) on basis of race, color, religion, national origin, sex prohibited.	Office of Federal Contract Compliance, delegated to Office for Civil Rights of HEW for educational institutions.	Debarment from federal contracts and grants, withdrawal of current federal funds.
Age Discrimination in Employment Act of 1967	Same as Title VII for those persons over 40 and under 65 years of age.	Department of Labor, Wage and Hour Division.	Provides for a civil suit after complainant has filed with Department of Labor.
Vocational Rehabilitation Act of 1975, amended December, 1974	Forbids discrimination against the handicapped under any program or activity receiving federal funds.	Department of HEW.	May result in suspension, termination, or refusal to grant federal funds. Referred to Department of Justice for recommendation for appropriate proceedings in case of a violation or to any applicable state or local law.
Vietnam Era Veterans Readjustment Act of 1974 (Section 2012)	Affirmative Action in employment for Veterans of the Vietnam Era and Disabled Veterans required by all contractors holding contracts in the amount of $10,000 or more.	Department of Labor, Veterans' Employment Service.	Department of Labor may file suit. Debarment from new grants and contracts, cancellation of current funds, and withholding of funds is possible under this act.
Title IX of the Education Amendments of 1972	Forbids discrimination against students, employees, etc., in educational institutions.	HEW, Office of Civil Rights.	Debarment from new awards, cancellation and termination of new, pending, or current federal funds. Also, Department of Justice can sue at HEW's request.

SOURCE: From J. M. Burns, J. W. Peltason, and T. E. Cronin, *Government by the People*, 10th ed. (Prentice-Hall, 1978), p. 133.

from 2 percent of the total to 30 percent. A great many black families have joined the middle class and moved to the suburbs. But millions of black people are still in the ghettos of the central cities. In the North at least, white attitudes have changed on some issues. For example, a poll conducted in 1978 indicated that nine out of ten white people believed that blacks should be able to live wherever they want to, compared to only six out of ten in a poll taken a decade earlier. Yet America's cities are still best described by the title of a scholarly paper on Detroit: "Chocolate City, Vanilla Suburbs."[13]

Federal money has been poured into the cities, but much of it has been used to replace other revenue sources rather than to eliminate the deepest problems. Central city schools have declined in quality in the last decade. Federal programs have not kept pace with housing needs. But the biggest problem in the black ghettos is still unemployment. Black unemployment in the cities in 1978 was 14 percent, twice the rate it was ten years before and twice the 1978 unemployment rate for whites. Among black youths in the ghettos in 1978, the unemployment rate was a crushing 40 to 50 percent.

**Unemployment Rates:
Black and White**

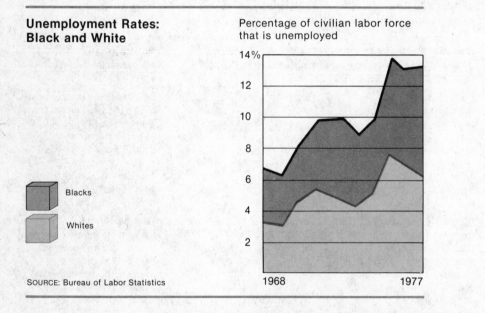

Percentage of civilian labor force
that is unemployed

Blacks

Whites

SOURCE: Bureau of Labor Statistics

Many whites tend to feel that racial problems have been solved. In 1978, a *New York Times* poll showed that whites in the urban North have a far different perception of how things are than do urban northern blacks.[14] Ten years after the Kerner Report, two-thirds of these whites had come to believe that blacks had made a "lot of progress." Only 45 percent of the urban northern blacks agreed, a

[13]*The New York Times* (February 26, 1978).
[14]*The New York Times* (February 26, 1978).

decline from 63 percent ten years earlier. While only 17 percent of the blacks polled felt that white people want to keep blacks down (a decrease from 28 percent in 1968), the percentage of blacks who felt that white people want to see a better break for blacks had also declined from 29 percent to 25 percent during the same period. The number of blacks who felt that whites "just don't care" had increased from 33 percent to 44 percent.

The school busing controversy. No issue involving race has stirred up more controversy among whites and blacks in recent years than court-ordered busing to achieve racial balance in the schools.[15] Busing orders have been handed down in northern as well as southern cities, and white opposition has been just as strong in the North as in the South. The Supreme Court has in effect ruled that the school districts involved have brought the orders on themselves by failing to abide by the law expressed in the *Brown* case. The first such ruling occurred in 1971 in the case of *Swann* v. *Charlotte-Mecklenburg County Board of Education.*[16] By a unanimous vote, the U.S. Supreme Court upheld a finding that schools in Charlotte, North Carolina, were still *officially* segregated on the basis of race. In its opinion, the Court said that busing was "one tool of school desegregation." Thus, it required the school district to take positive action to bring about desegregation, including changing school district lines, busing white children to previously all-black schools, and busing black children to previously all-white schools.

There were angry protests by whites in Charlotte and other cities where similar orders were issued by courts. In Pontiac, Michigan, school buses were firebombed. In Boston, there were sustained disorders. Members of Congress and officials in President Richard Nixon's administration attempted to block the use of any federal funds to pay for busing to achieve racial balance in the schools. In a five-to-four decision concerning Detroit's school system, the Supreme Court, later refused to order "cross-district busing," the transportation of children across city and county lines. The Court held that there was no clear showing that segregation in Detroit's schools was intentional; rather, it appeared to be merely the result of housing patterns—whites in the suburbs, blacks in the central cities. However, the Court did order cross-district busing in Louisville, Kentucky, because it found the schools there to be purposefully segregated.[17]

Busing is a difficult solution for the terrible problem of segregated schools. What if you were a white mother or father who had moved your family to the suburbs to get away from the inferior schools and the fear of crime in the city? How would you feel about having to put

[15]For a definitive study of busing, see Gary Orfield, *Must We Bus?* (Washington, D.C.: The Brookings Institution, 1978).

[16]*Swann* v. *Charlotte-Mecklenburg Board of Education,* 402 U.S. 1 (1971).

[17]*Millikin* v. *Bradley*, 418 U.S. 717 (1974).

Segregated schools existed in the North as well as the South, but it was not until the late 1960s that federal courts ruled that *de facto* segregation in the North (resulting from traditional housing patterns) was as unacceptable as the South's *de jure* ("legal") segregation. When the courts ordered busing to desegregate schools in Boston, Pontiac, Michigan, and other northern cities, violent protests occurred.

your schoolchild on a bus each morning to be driven back to the kind of neighborhood and school you had moved away from? Many white mothers and fathers—some of whom had sympathized with the black civil rights movement—bitterly opposed the busing orders. In some cases, racism was involved in this opposition, too. There was also some class bias against poor people and much concern about the antisocial behavior and increased crime that often go hand in hand with poverty.

What if you were a black mother or father who had known discrimination all your life, and you were worried about the hostility your schoolchild might face from the white students in the school to which your child was to be bused? Some black parents were, indeed, opposed to their children being bused out of their home neighborhoods. Some black leaders said that the notion that black children could only learn while sitting next to white children was degrading to blacks.

But most black leaders spoke out in favor of court-ordered busing to break segregation patterns. How else will black children have a chance to escape from the inferior central city schools, where notably less money is spent per child than in the more affluent suburbs? they asked. How else will white people become interested in upgrading all schools equally, unless white and black children go to the same schools? Supreme Court Justice Thurgood Marshall warned that "unless our children begin to learn together, there is little hope that our people will ever learn to live together."[18]

Although busing continues to be used as a tool of desegregation, the busing controversy has subsided. But a large percentage of American schools continue to be virtually all black or all white, particularly because of housing patterns and the drawing of district lines.

---

[18]*Milliken* v. *Bradley.*

Reverse discrimination.   Some people have argued that government intervention to ensure equal protection to minorities has resulted in discrimination against members of the majority. According to the Supreme Court, however, a federal law giving an employment preference in the U.S. Bureau of Indian Affairs to American Indians does not deny equal protection to non-Indian job applicants. In addition, the Court has ordered a classification of public-school children by race in places where it considers that method necessary to achieve racial balance and reverse years of racial segregation. What about classifications giving preferences to minorities in admissions to graduate or professional schools? That was a question the Supreme Court sought to decide in 1978 in the *Bakke* case.[19] One side argued that giving preference to minorities violates the right of nonminority people to equal protection of the laws. The other side argued that minorities cannot obtain equal protection of the laws unless their rights and needs are given extra attention to compensate for the country's neglect and denial of these rights for so long. In two separate five-to-four opinions, the U.S. Supreme Court ruled that a university could not establish a quota system with an established percentage of new admissions reserved for minorities, but that race is properly *one* of the factors that may be considered in admissions policy.

The issue of reverse discrimination in the use of quotas favoring minorities arose again in the case of *Kaiser Aluminum Co.* v. *Weber* (1979). In a five-to-two decision written by Justice Brennan, the Court interpreted the Civil Rights Act of 1964 to mean that in a private industry, a *voluntary* agreement between a company and a union could legally establish a quota system for selecting participants for a special training program leading to newly created jobs.

Racial discrimination is by no means an American invention. It exists in many other parts of the world as well. But the special "American dilemma" (as it was described by the Swedish sociologist Gunnar Myrdal in his famous study by that title)[20] is that our society stands for equality and democracy but has too often practiced discrimination and racism. America *has* made unmistakable progress, particularly in regard to knocking down legal barriers of discrimination against black people. Still, the United States has a long way to go in its effort to eliminate the separate and unequal nature of our society that the Kerner Commission spoke of. Concerned black and white leaders today increasingly concentrate on economic equality for black people. They have found that legal and political equality—while basically important—are not in themselves sufficient to eradicate the causes and effects of inequality. Interestingly, Dr. King's fateful trip to Memphis in 1968 to support the economic advancement of sanitation workers—black and white—presaged this new focus.

---

[19]*Regents of the University of California* v. *Bakke*, 98 S. Ct. 2733 (1978).
[20]Gunnar Myrdal, *American Dilemma: The Negro Problem in Modern Democracy* (New York: Harper, 1944).

HISPANIC AMERICANS: VIVA LA RAZA!

Black people are not the only group that has been discriminated against in this country. Hispanic Americans—those with Spanish-speaking or Spanish-surnamed backgrounds—have also experienced discrimination. Today, there are twelve million Hispanic Americans.[21] Although they are a diverse group, they are linked together by the heritage of a common language and, particularly within groups, by a similar cultural background.

Nearly a million Hispanic Americans are of Cuban origin. They are relatively recent immigrants, having fled their homeland in the late 1950s when Fidel Castro assumed power. They have settled mostly in Florida. The recent move by non-Cuban business leaders in Miami, Florida, to require that Spanish be taught as a mandatory second language in that city's school system underscores the importance of this group of former Cubans in Miami, where many are active business people.

Over two million Hispanic Americans have come to America from various countries in Central and South America. Many others have come from the Caribbean island of Puerto Rico, which is a common-wealth, or self-governing territory, of the United States. Puerto Ricans are citizens of the United States, and they are represented in the U.S. House of Representatives by a nonvoting resident commis-sioner. Although there is some movement and visiting back and forth, the relative size of the migration from Puerto Rico is shown by the fact that approximately three million people live in Puerto Rico today and some two million people of Puerto Rican origin live in the United States. Most of these immigrants came to the mainland seeking jobs. The jobs they found were often poor ones. Many of those who came faced economic, language, and racial barriers. A majority of them now live in New York City, but there are sizeable Puerto Rican communities in Chicago and Philadelphia. Confronted with such problems as substandard housing and an unemployment rate often twice as high as that for the rest of the country, Americans of Puerto Rican origin have in recent years strengthened the internal ties of cultural pride within their own communities and have turned to political and social action, focusing on such issues as bilingual education, jobs, and the elimination of discrimination.

The majority of Hispanic Americans—over seven million—have their roots in Mexico.[22] These are the Mexican Americans, or "Chicanos," as a great many members of this community, especially the younger and more active ones, prefer to call themselves. The

---

[21]For Hispanic American population numbers and a general discussion, see *Time* (October 16, 1978), p. 48.

[22]Except as otherwise indicated, material in this section is taken from F. Chris Garcia, Rudolph O. de la Garza, *The Chicano Political Experience* (North Scituate, Massachusetts: Duxbury Press, 1977), p. 68.

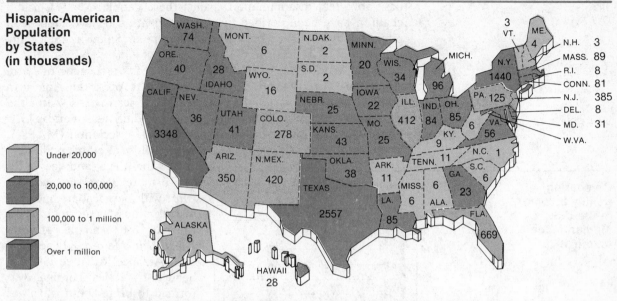

Hispanic-American Population by States (in thousands)

WASH. 74
MONT. 6
N.DAK. 2
MINN. 20
MICH. 96
VT. 3
ME. 4
N.H. 3
MASS. 89
N.Y. 1440
R.I. 8
CONN. 81
N.J. 385
DEL. 8
MD. 31
W.VA.

ORE. 40
IDAHO 28
WYO. 16
S.D. 2
WIS. 34
IOWA 22
ILL. 412
IND. 84
OH. 85
PA. 125
VA. 56

CALIF. 3348
NEV. 36
UTAH 41
COLO. 278
NEBR. 25
MO. 25
KY. 9
N.C. 1

ARIZ. 350
N.MEX. 420
KANS. 43
OKLA. 38
ARK. 11
TENN. 11
GA. 23
S.C. 6

TEXAS 2557
MISS. 6
ALA. 6
FLA. 669

LA. 85

ALASKA 6

HAWAII 28

Under 20,000
20,000 to 100,000
100,000 to 1 million
Over 1 million

SOURCE: U.S. Bureau of the Census, Department of Commerce, 1976. (Excludes the approximately 7 million illegal aliens.)

term *Chicano* once had a derogatory connotation when used by Anglos, or non-Hispanic Americans. In the 1960s, however, the word Chicano and the spirit of *Chicanismo* became a badge of pride as the more aggressive and militant leaders of the *Movimiento* (the movement) for "Brown Power" among *La Raza* (literally, the race) helped produce a resurgence of cultural nationalism among Mexican Americans.

Most Chicanos live in five southwestern states: California and Texas, where they constitute about 10 percent of the total population of each state; and New Mexico, Arizona, and Colorado, where they also make up a sizable, but slightly smaller, proportion of the population. Many of them are descendants of people who first came to those areas in the 1500s and 1600s, long before they became a part of the United States. They were the earliest people to live there except for the American Indians. Many are descendants of a wave of Mexican immigrants in the early 1900s. Still others came into the United States from Mexico in the 1950s and 1960s as a part of the legal "bracero" program to provide cheap farm workers. Although nobody knows exactly how many "indocumentados" (undocumented people) in recent years have illegally entered the United States from Mexico and stayed on permanently, their number is thought to be several million.

A diverse group, Chicanos nevertheless have a great deal in common. Their language is obviously a strong tie, as is their historical relationship with Mexico and their relative proximity to its borders. But the language and ties to Mexico have also frequently been the basis for great discrimination against these people. Many Chicano children have been derided by other students and have even been punished by their teachers when they spoke Spanish, their only language.

Before World War II, organizations such as the League of Latin American Citizens (LULAC) were formed to press the American political system to respond to Mexican American needs. After the war, new organizations came into being, including the American G.I. Forum and the Mexican American Political Association (MAPA). These, too, have worked in the field of traditional ethnic politics.

Comparing Family Income in the U.S. Median Income, March 1978

In thousands of dollars

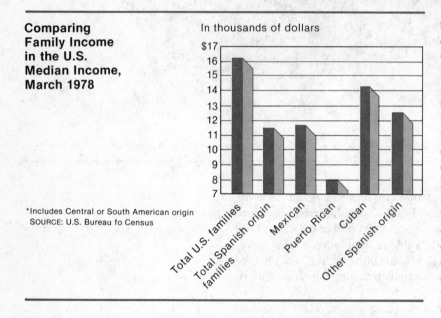

*Includes Central or South American origin
SOURCE: U.S. Bureau fo Census

But the 1960s and the 1970s saw a more aggressive *movimiento*, with new leaders and new organizations. In northern New Mexico, for example, *Alianza Federal de Mercedes* (The Federal Alliance of Free States), headed by Reies Tijerina, was formed to bring about what was called a *reconquista* (reconquest) of the lands that he and his followers claimed had been illegally and fraudulently taken away from their forebears, in violation of the provisions of the Treaty of Guadalupe Hidalgo, which ended America's war with Mexico in 1848. Alianza has been unsuccessful to date in its land claims and in its attempts to seize federal lands. Although the group at one time stormed a local courthouse, causing Tijerina to serve a prison term, they seem to be putting more emphasis now on working through the courts and the political system.

Many Chicanos live in cities. In Denver, as in a number of other cities, new Chicano centers and other supportive organizations have sprung up. Rodolfo "Corky" Gonzales helped form Denver's *La Cruzado Para La Justicia* (Crusade for Justice). "Everybody in the barrios [the Mexican American neighborhoods] is a nationalist, you see, whether he admits it to himself or not," Gonzales has said. "It doesn't matter if he's middle class, a vendido, a sell-out or what his politics may be. He'll come back home, to La Raza, to his heart, if we will build centers of nationalism for him."[23]

An especially hard-pressed Chicano group are the low-paid workers who do the back-breaking labor of America's farm fields and groves. Frequently moving from place to place as the available work

---

[23]See F. Garcia, ed., *La Causa Politica* (University of Notre Dame Press, 1974).

César Chávez, leader of the effort to unionize farm laborers and migrant workers in California. During *la huelga,* "the great strike" when the United Farm Workers union was being organized, Chávez explained that "the business of convincing a man is the business of spending time with him."

moves with the seasons, these people have received little payment on America's promise of decent pay, health, education, and housing. César Chávez used trade union tactics to attack these problems, organizing these workers into the United Farm Workers of California. After years of struggle, strikes and boycotts, and jurisdictional disputes with the Teamsters Union, the United Farm Workers has gained the right to bargain collectively with California growers as a labor union.

In southern Texas, particularly around Chrystal City, Chicanos have secured political control of several local communities. Jose Angel Gutierrez has been a leader in the *La Raza Unida* party, the third-party vehicle for this successful political action. Chrystal City, Texas, is surrounded by spinach fields, largely owned by Del Monte corporation. The central feature of the town used to be a giant statue of the spinach-eating cartoon character, Popeye. He was not exactly a cultural hero for the Chicanos who worked in the spinach fields and constituted a majority in the Anglo-run town. After La Raza Unida's candidates were elected to run the local government, one of the first things they did was to get rid of the Popeye statue.

Following large-scale rioting in 1970 in the Chicano area known as East Los Angeles, the U.S. Cabinet Committee on Opportunities for Spanish Speaking People was created to coordinate the federal government's efforts to provide bilingual education and to eliminate discrimination. Today, Edward R. Roybal of California chairs a five-member Hispanic Caucus in the U.S. House of Representatives. (He is, incidentally, the only Chicano member of California's forty-three-member delegation.) Two states, New Mexico and Arizona, elected Hispanic state governors in the late 1970s.

Still, there is a long way to go before Chicanos as a group will achieve true equality. The U.S. Civil Rights Commission reported in

1977 that Hispanic unemployment was still 1.6 times higher than among whites, that the average income of Hispanic families was less than two thirds of that for white families, and that bilingual, bicultural education—considered a "critical component of equal educational opportunity"—was "hampered by generally weak political support and widespread confusion and debate over its basic philosophy." But the newly gained identity and potential political power among Hispanic Americans will ensure continued efforts to achieve full equality.

AMERICAN INDIANS

About one million people living in the United States are American Indians or Alaskan Natives. Nearly half now live away from their traditional reservation areas, mostly in the cities. For example, there are probably more American Indians living in the city of Los Angeles alone than in any other area of the United States except the Navajo Reservation.

Who is an American Indian? It depends upon who is asking. When the U.S. Census Bureau is asking, it is purely a matter of self-identification by the person who is being asked to check the appropriate box. For certain governmental service agencies, such as the U.S. Indian Public Health Service, the answer depends upon "blood quantum," or Indian ancestry. Generally, one-fourth Indian blood is required. The adoption of this standard may be one of the reasons why Indians are often annoyed by non-Indians who ask, "How much Indian are you?" Similar questions—such as "How much Chicano are you?" or "How much Negro blood do you have?"—would almost never be asked of members of other ethnic groups. Most American Indians would prefer to say that a person is an Indian if that person thinks of himself or herself as an Indian and is so recognized by his or her own tribe.

There are more than three hundred Indian tribes in America. Most have greatly different histories, customs, and traditions and mutually unintelligible languages. "Can you speak Indian?" is a question that is unanswerable in that form. The question should be "Do you speak Comanche?" or "Do you speak Sioux?" or "Do you speak Navajo?" Many of the Indian languages are as different from each other as Chinese is from Russian.

Yet in recent years a strong and highly important movement based upon a renewed pride in "Indianness" has developed among American Indians. How did this movement come about with so many differences among the various tribes? It was not easy.

Unlike other American ethnic groups, Indians have tribal governments, which serve as political units of government. This form of organization gives them *dual citizenship*—the citizenship most Americans have as U.S. citizens (including the state citizenship that

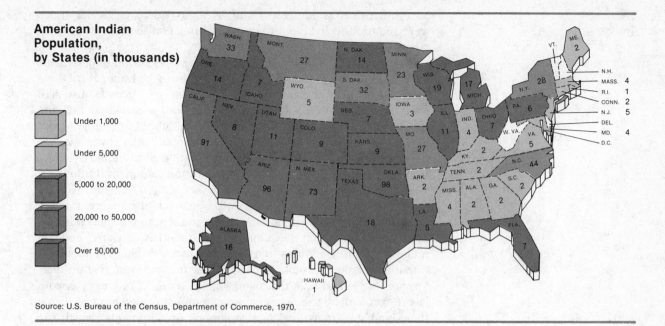

American Indian Population, by States (in thousands)

Under 1,000
Under 5,000
5,000 to 20,000
20,000 to 50,000
Over 50,000

WASH. 33
MONT. 27
N. DAK. 14
MINN. 23
VT.
ME. 2
ORE. 14
IDAHO 7
WYO. 5
S. DAK. 32
WIS. 19
MICH. 17
N.Y. 28
N.H.
MASS. 4
R.I. 1
CONN. 2
CALIF. 91
NEV. 8
UTAH 11
COLO. 9
NEB. 7
IOWA 3
ILL. 11
IND. 4
OHIO 7
PA. 6
N.J. 5
DEL.
MD. 4
D.C.
ARIZ. 96
N. MEX. 73
KANS. 9
MO. 27
KY. 2
W. VA. 2
VA. 5
N.C. 44
TEXAS
OKLA. 98
ARK. 2
TENN. 2
S.C. 2
GA. 2
MISS. 4
ALA. 2
LA. 5
18
FLA. 7
ALASKA 16
HAWAII 1

Source: U.S. Bureau of the Census, Department of Commerce, 1970.

goes with it) and the citizenship in the tribe to which they belong. They also have *dual entitlement*. According to this doctrine, Indians are entitled not only to the services and privileges that other American citizens have, but also to special consideration of their health, education, and other needs because they are Indians. Contrary to what some believe, however, American Indians do not receive a regular individual payment from the federal treasury.[24]

Government policy toward American Indians has gone through several stages. The first European (and American) policy was one of conquest and even extermination. European diseases were often more devastating than military weapons in their effect on the Indians. Isolated on this continent, Indians had built up no immunities to diseases such as diphtheria, flu, smallpox, and typhoid, which were introduced by European carriers. These diseases sometimes wiped out more than half of the members of a tribe at one time. These deaths often caused serious political disorganization and broke down cultural cohesion.

At first, the United States government dealt with Indian tribes on the same legal basis with which it dealt with foreign governments. But it soon asserted the power to restrict the sovereignty of tribes, primarily because of the right of conquest. This assertion has been upheld by the U.S. Supreme Court. The U.S. Constitution gave the federal government, not the states, the exclusive power to regulate trade with the Indian tribes. From time to time, the federal

---

[24]See Lynn and Kirke Kickingbird, *Indians and the U.S. Government* (Washington, D.C.: Institute for the Development of Indian Law, 1977).

government set aside "reservations," areas where particular tribes were required to live, and relocated them when the federal government thought it advisable to do so.

In federal Indian policy, 1871 to 1928 was the period of *allotments and assimilation.*[25] During this time, the government tried to "assimilate" the Indians by forcing them to become just like everybody else. When Captain R. H. Pratt was named the first superintendent of Carlisle Indian Boarding School in Pennsylvania, he expressed a view that was generally accepted in the government at that time. Regarding the military adage that "a good Indian is a dead Indian," Captain Pratt said, "I agree with the sentiment, but only in this: that all the Indian there is in the race should be dead. Kill the Indian in him and save the man." Indian children were forcibly separated from their families and tribes and sent to boarding schools. They were taught that they could not be "good Americans" and still retain their old traditions, language, customs, religions, and songs. Christian missionaries also preached that Indians must give up their "pagan" ways and take the "white man's road." Congress passed a law to force many tribes to give up communal ownership and divide their land into individual land holdings, or allotments, which the owners could then sell with government approval. The policy further impoverished Indians. Between 1887 and 1934, the amount of Indian-owned land in the United States decreased from 138 million acres to only 48 million acres.

The federal government's Indian policy between 1928 and 1945 was called *reorganization.* The individual allotment of tribal lands was stopped. Congress passed a law to encourage the strengthening of tribal governments. Led by a forward-looking Commissioner of Indian Affairs, John Collier, the government reaffirmed its "trust" responsibility to Indians and tribes, its obligation to assist them toward political self-government and economic self-sufficiency. The Bureau of Indian Affairs, a division of the U.S. Department of the Interior, was the primary agency responsible for carrying out this trust.

But, by 1945, the pendulum had swung back the other way again. The *termination* period, which lasted until 1961, began with the report of the Hoover Commission, a special federal committee headed by former President Herbert Hoover. The commission's purpose was to suggest ways to streamline the organization of the federal government. One of their recommendations was the "complete integration" of American Indians into American society. Their suggestions, however, went beyond the old assimilation doctrine. This time whole tribes were to be assimilated at once—terminated as recognized tribes. For example, Congress passed a law ending the status of the Mennominees in Wisconsin as a tribe. Their reservation

---

[25]Except as otherwise indicated, material in this section is taken from David H. Getches, et al., *Federal Indian Law: Cases and Materials* (St. Paul: West Publishing Company, 1979).

legally became a county in that state. Although the government had shortchanged them for years on skills and education, the Mennominees suddenly had to raise their own taxes, run their own schools, and provide other services. They had to perform these activities even though many tribe members possessed inferior educational backgrounds, and even though the tax base was woefully small. The tribe cut timber and sold land to keep the fragile and failing county government alive. The Mennominees somehow survived as a people, but a number of tribes similarly hit by the termination process disappeared as tribes forever. During this period, President Dwight Eisenhower's administration started a program to "relocate" individual Indians to the cities. Families were often thrown into unfamiliar urban settings with little preparation and support. A large percentage of these families soon returned to the reservations. But many stayed in the cities and established Indian centers, where they could begin to reach out to each other.

In 1970, President Richard Nixon responded to tribal lobbying and called for an end to forced termination of tribes and, with congressional support, inaugurated a period of *self-determination*. The idea behind this new shift in policy was that Indians are here to stay and that Indians (and other groups) make a significant contribution to American society. By adopting this policy, the government was saying in effect that no minority group should be required to "melt" into the rest of the population because all Americans do not have to look alike, speak alike, or worship alike to be "good Americans." Thus, government policy recognized that individual and national strength could result from people taking pride in their own heritage and finding support from their own ethnic group.

The self-determination policy resulted from the fact that American Indians themselves had already been developing a new cohesiveness and pride in Indianness. The self-determination concept had also gained strength because of President Johnson's earlier antipoverty programs. Since American Indians were the poorest Americans, an increasing number of federal agencies had begun to take an interest in them and in the terrible conditions in which so many of them lived.

Should Indians live on reservations or move away? Indians say that each Indian should make this decision for himself or herself, and the law is in agreement with this policy. But Indians believe that they should have full opportunities to reach their potential wherever they live.

As with other minority groups, progress could not come rapidly enough for American Indians. Militant young Indians occupied Alcatraz Island in San Francisco Bay after the federal government had closed the prison there. The Indian protesters unsuccessfully demanded that the government give them the island to use as a cultural center. There were a number of other such attempts to take over public lands in other areas of the country. In 1972, an Indian caravan called the "Trail of Broken Treaties" arrived in Washington,

American Indians camped in front of the White House in 1978 after completing the "Longest Walk." The march, which began in the Southwest and culminated in Washington, D.C., dramatized the Indians' demand for the restoration of their rights to natural resources on Indian lands.

D.C., to demand restoration of all Indian treaty rights. Frustrated in their attempts to negotiate with federal officials, hundreds of protesters took over the Bureau of Indian Affairs building and held it for six days. A few months later, armed members of the American Indian Movement (AIM) and their followers occupied the village of Wounded Knee on the Pine Ridge Sioux Reservation in South Dakota and held it for seventy days. Two Indians were killed and a federal marshal was seriously wounded before the siege ended.

Congress passed the Self-Determination Act of 1975 to allow Indian tribal governments to administer their own federally supported health, housing, welfare, education, and other programs, much as states do. But many officials in the Bureau of Indian Affairs have been slow to implement this act because it could mean a loss of status or even a loss of employment for them. Congress also established the American Indian Policy Review Commission, which issued a lengthy report in 1976. The report advocated strengthening tribal self-government and economic self-sufficiency and called for increased attention to the needs of Indians who live off the reservation. Federal court opinions upheld the status of tribes as governmental units, and the tribes began to improve their own governments, courts, and legal codes.

The National Congress of American Indians (NCAI) continues to be the most representative national voice of American Indians. Americans for Indian Opportunity (AIO) is another organization that has played a key national role in Indian advocacy. It has concentrated especially on assisting Indian tribes to regain control of their own considerable holdings of land, water, oil, gas, coal, uranium, timber, and other natural resources. Indian tribes in the

1970s began to reverse the leasing policy that the Bureau of Indian Affairs had urged them to accept for so long. Under the old policy, the tribes had leased *out* their resources to non-Indians for low cash payments and royalties, but Indians had not been allowed to participate in risks, profits, management, jobs, or responsibility for ecological and other controls.

In the late 1970s, the Indians' assertion of economic and political power, which was recognized by Congress and the courts, produced what came to be called the "white backlash." Members of Congress introduced a rash of bills to abrogate, or end, old treaties with the tribes and to restrict tribal jurisdiction over non-Indians on the reservations.[26] These bills had little chance of passage. But pro-Indian legislation had little chance of passage, either.

At the end of the 1970s, Indians were still at the bottom of all measurements of social and economic status. They had the highest unemployment and the lowest family income. They had the worst housing, health, and education. But they had achieved a new unity. They had a proliferation of new organizations and new leaders to meet their planning, governmental, legal, and other needs. The Indian renaissance was here to stay.

THE WOMEN'S LIBERATION MOVEMENT

While John Adams was in Philadelphia in 1776 helping to draft the Declaration, his wife, Abigail, wrote to him: "I desire that you would Remember the Ladies, and be more generous and favorable to them than your ancestors. Remember all Men would be tyrants if they could. If particular care and attention is not paid to the Ladies, we are determined to foment a Rebellion, and will not hold ourselves bound by any laws in which we have no voice, or Representation." Adams' reply was a kind of pat on the head; he called his wife "saucy" and added, "We know better than to repeal our Masculine system." Indeed, the Declaration proclaimed all *men* to be equal; neither the Constitution nor the Bill of Rights recognized women as free and equal citizens.

Women are not a minority in the United States; they represent 51 percent of the population. Yet they have often been treated as if they were a minority. Throughout American history, they have suffered from discrimination *because* they are women. This form of discrimination is called *sexism*.

One of the most significant developments in America in the 1960s and the 1970s was the reemergence of the women's movement. The word *re-emergence* is used here because the women's movement and the sentiments behind it go back a long way in American history. During the 1830s, women who were active in the movement to

---

[26]*The New Leader* (April 10, 1978), pp 17–18.

abolish slavery began to realize and call attention to their own lack of equality. They were not even allowed to speak at these meetings because they were women. The women's movement took organized form during the 1880s, as part of the general stirring of philosophical thought about human rights.

Today, it is common to think of this earlier women's movement as only a suffrage movement, to secure the right to vote. However, it represented far more than that alone. It is true that these early feminists objected to having to submit to laws that they could not participate in passing. But they also objected to unequal pay for the same work, lack of educational, occupational, and professional opportunity, lack of equality in the courts and in property rights, and subjection to a different moral code. In the Declaration of Sentiments (which was modeled on the Declaration of Independence) of the Women's Rights Convention in 1848 at Seneca Falls, New York, feminists protested the subjugation of their lives to the will of men who, they declared, sought to destroy the confidence of women in their own powers, lessen their self-respect, and make them "willing to lead a dependent and abject life."

Little by little, this earlier movement was converted into a single-issue movement. Partly to gain respectability, the movement focused its efforts on securing the vote for women. The movement suffered a major disappointment after the Civil War, when the Fifteenth Amendment granted black *men*—but not women, black or white—the right to vote. During the centennial celebration of the signing of the Declaration, Susan B. Anthony, one of the leading suffragists, pointed out that ". . . the women of this nation, in 1876, have greater cause for discontent, rebellion, and revolution than the men of 1776." Slowly, however, progress was made. In 1890, women were granted the right to vote in the new state of Wyoming, which was seeking women to help fill its sparsely populated land. By 1917, eight other states had followed suit. By then, of course, America was involved in World War I. Renewing their efforts, women convinced President Woodrow Wilson to support the Nineteenth Amendment. It was approved by Congress and ratified by the states in 1920. Judith Hole and Ellen Levine have written that when this goal was finally achieved, "so much energy had been expended . . . that the woman's movement virtually collapsed from exhaustion."[27]

The women's movement did not die. Many people, especially women, saw quite clearly that even though women could vote, inequalities between women and men persisted in America. From their earliest years, American children continued to learn from family and schools that men and women were expected to assume very different roles in life. For example, young children learned that it was acceptable for boys, but not girls, to aspire to become lawyers and

---

[27]Judith Hole and Ellen Levine, *Rebirth of Feminism* (New York: Quadrangle Books, 1971).

(Above): Suffragettes march in New York City in support of the proposed Nineteenth Amendment, giving women the right to vote. (Left): Sixty years later, the rejuvenated women's movement won congressional approval of an amendment that would extend full constitutional rights and protections to women.

doctors. Girls were encouraged to become housewives and mothers only or, if they hoped to work outside the home, to become secretaries and nurses.

The civil rights, student, and antiwar movements of the 1950s and 1960s produced large numbers of young women activists. Like the women in the earlier abolitionist movement, they began to call attention to their own inequality in America. By the late 1970s, they had helped to establish what came to be known as the Women's Liberation Movement.

Responding to increased lobbying by women, President John F. Kennedy created a Commission on the Status of Women in 1961. The Commission's report deplored the fact that women continued to be second-class citizens in America, and it led to the establishment of similar commissions at the state level and a national advisory council. The Equal Pay Act was passed in 1963.

In 1966, Betty Friedan, author of *The Feminine Mystique*,[28] led a movement to form the first important national feminist organization in America since Susan B. Anthony's National Woman Suffrage Association. The new organization was called the National Organization for Women (NOW). It continues to be a vocal and visible force in America on such issues as equal employment opportunity for women, full legal equality, and the rights of lesbians.

In 1967, pressured by NOW, President Johnson formally prohibited sex discrimination in federal employment and by those doing business with the federal government. President Nixon extended this order and also applied it to the military. The 1964 Civil Rights Act was also amended to include sex as a prohibited ground of discrimination in private employment.

In 1969, President Nixon set up another presidential task force on the status of women. It found that women had not achieved equality. In higher education, for example, less than 12 percent of the doctoral degrees that were awarded that year in the United States went to women. Only 8 percent of the medical students were women. Less than 6 percent of the law students were women.[29]

In 1972, Congress proposed the Equal Rights Amendment (ERA) by a two-thirds vote in each house, as required by the Constitution, and referred it to the states with March 1979 set as the deadline for ratification. (As was discussed in Chapter 2, three fourths of the states must ratify an amendment before it can become part of the Constitution.)

The Equal Rights Amendment had first been proposed in the Congress nearly fifty years before it was finally approved by the two houses. It states: "Equality of rights under the law shall not be denied

---

[28]Betty Friedan, *The Feminine Mystique* (New York: Dell Publishing Company, 1974).

[29]National Commission of the Observance of International Women's Year, *To Form a More Perfect Union* (Washington, D.C.: U.S. Government Printing Office, 1976).

or abridged by the United States or by any state on account of sex." The words seem fairly plain, but they have caused many conflicting arguments. For example, opponents do not want women to become subject to a military draft, if the draft should be reinstated. Supporters, however, argue that women with children to care for could be given special exemptions and that some women could be given special kinds of military jobs. Opponents fear that divorced women would lose their rights to alimony and child support if the amendment passed. Supporters, on the other hand, believe that marriage partners should be equal; they advocate equal child-rearing responsibilities for men and women and insist that alimony and child support should be given on the basis of the financial capabilities of each partner, regardless of sex. In addition, they point out that only 14 percent of all divorced women are granted alimony and only 44 percent are awarded child support. In each case, less than half of these women actually receive such payments regularly.

The National Women's Political Caucus was formed in 1972 to elect more women to public office, to lobby the political parties and the government for action on issues important to women, and to press for ratification of the Equal Rights Amendment. In 1973, the U.S. Supreme Court held that a woman has a right to an abortion during the first three months of pregnancy and that no state can interfere with this right. Men and women organized themselves in "Right to Life" groups to seek (unsuccessfully) a constitutional amendment to overturn this decision and to lobby Congress (successfully) to prohibit federal welfare funds from being used for this purpose. Supporters of the Supreme Court decision countered with "Right to Choose" campaigns.

By 1978, momentum toward ratification of ERA had slowed. Although thirty-five of the necessary thirty-eight states (three-fourths) had ratified the amendment, efforts to secure approval in three more states ran into organized opposition from some church groups, housewives, and male state legislators. Some state constitutions already contained equal rights provisions for women, and in these states important progress toward equality had occurred without the dire consequences that opponents had predicted.[30] Yet strong, effective opposition to the amendment continued. As the ERA ratification deadline neared, feminist leaders and organizations banded together in a lobbying effort that pushed through Congress a three-year extension of the ratification period.[31] Once again, the fight shifted back to the state legislatures.

ERA became the focal point for a national debate about the changing roles of women in American society. A poll taken in 1975 for the National Commission on the Observance of the International

[30]*Time* (March 26, 1979), p. 25; Jane O'Reilly, "The Bogus Fear of ERA," *The Nation* (July 15, 1978), pp. 45–47.

[31]*The New Yorker* (October 23, 1978), pp. 32–33.

Women's Year showed that 42 percent of American women over eighteen were working outside the home, 31 percent of them full-time. In 28 percent of American families, both husband and wife were working. A large majority of these women said that they *had* to work outside the home—because they were single, because they were divorced, widowed, or separated, or because their husband's salary alone was not enough for them to live on.

How women themselves felt about their changing roles depended greatly upon their age. Over three-fourths of the women polled between the ages of eighteen and thirty-four said they favored a lifestyle that combined homemaking with an outside career. Most women under forty-five disagreed with the statement that "it is better for everyone involved if the man is the achiever outside the home and the woman takes care of the home and family." Most women over forty-five agreed with that statement. Fifty-seven percent of all the women polled had positive comments about the women's movement; 28 percent made negative comments. These responses also varied greatly with the age of the women. In the age bracket from eighteen to twenty-four, for example, 66 percent said they favored present efforts for changes, but only 30 percent of those over sixty-five did.[32]

By the late 1970s, most professions and occupations began to open up to women, and there was a dramatic increase in the number of women entering medical and law schools. Still, there was a long way to go. Women comprised two-fifths of the work force in America, but they were performing four-fifths of the clerical jobs. Women had still not achieved equal pay for equal work or equal treatment in regard to promotions.

What about the women's movement? It has had a dramatic effect in America. It has raised the consciousness of millions of American women by increasing their self-esteem and their expectations about themselves. It has caused a lot of men to change their attitudes about themselves and their own roles. Because of the women's movement, many men now realize that women have been unjustly exploited and unreasonably limited in their opportunities. Men can no longer make sexist jokes about women as a group without objections from women. The old jokes portraying women as flighty, disorganized, unable to drive a car correctly, or balance a checkbook are no longer acceptable. Such changes are important. So is the language used in textbooks. All major textbook publishers now have specific guidelines to eliminate sexist words and examples from their books in order to avoid the stereotypes that can limit young people to narrow expectations. Politicians struggle to say "members of Congress" instead of "congressmen." City ordinances refer to "police officers" instead of "policemen." Men in many businesses have become a little more reticent about asking the "girls in the office" to make the

---

[32]National Commission on the Observance of International Women's Year, *To Form a More Perfect Union.*

coffee. Many men feel freer now about showing their emotions and about admitting an interest in activities such as cooking. Today, law enforcement officials are more likely to treat a woman rape victim or a battered wife with sensitivity and concern.

An increasing number of feminists are making it clear, too, that homemaking itself is a very important profession for women *and* men and ought to be recognized as such. Many women who start a sentence with "I'm no women's libber, but . . ." endorse such causes as government assistance for child care, equal educational, professional, and job opportunity, and equal pay for equal work.

Is a woman's place in the home or in Congress? Feminists would say that each woman should be able to decide to do either or both; whatever she decides, the choice should be made freely, and it should give her full opportunity for dignity and personal fulfillment.

CIVIL RIGHTS: THE CONTINUING STRUGGLE

The idea of equality took on new meaning for a number of other groups during the 1960s and 1970s. Ethnic groups such as Italian Americans and Polish Americans organized to put a stop to ethnic slurs against them and to build a group pride in their ethnicity. Gay and lesbian activists were successful in changing laws that had discriminated against people on the basis of their sexual preference. But at the end of the 1970s, some church groups and other organizations, led by such leaders as fundamentalist Christian singer Anita Bryant, were mounting a formidable campaign against equal rights for homosexuals.

Another group with growing strength in America is the elderly. As older Americans have become an increasingly larger percentage of America's total population, they have become increasingly aggressive in demanding their rights. The American Association of Retired Persons and the National Council of Senior Citizens are two groups that have influenced the passage of laws against discrimination in employment on the basis of age and laws providing better health, housing, social security, and other benefits for older people. The Gray Panthers, led by Maggie Kuhn, is a smaller but more militant organization. In the U.S. House of Representatives, Claude Pepper of Florida has been successful in securing passage of laws prohibiting mandatory retirement before age seventy in private employment or at any required age level in federal employment.

In 1971, young people between the ages of eighteen and twenty-one were granted the right to vote when the Twenty-sixth Amendment was ratified by the states. In 1978, Congress sent to the states a proposed Twenty-eighth Amendment that would end discrimination against yet another group of Americans—the citizens of the District of Columbia. A part of no state, the District of Columbia is

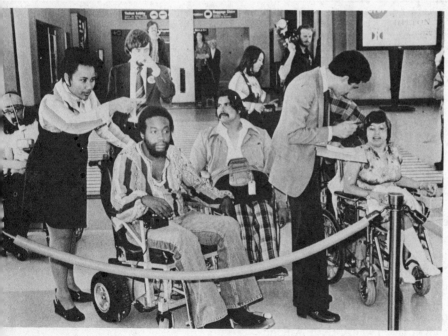

During the 1970s, other groups sought recognition of their right to full equality and an end to discrimination. (Above left): Maggie Kuhn, founder of the militant Gray Panthers, who seek an end to age discrimination. (Left): Twenty-five handicapped persons prepare to fly to Washington to discuss their demands with President Carter. The protesters had occupied HEW offices in San Francisco; they hoped to win Carter's support of legislation outlawing discrimination against the disabled. (Above right): Homosexuals have sought an end to discrimination based on sexual preference. After the movement experienced several setbacks in 1978, when "homosexual rights" ordinances were defeated in several cities, California voters rejected a proposed Constitutional amendment that would have forbidden homosexuals from teaching in California schools.

represented in Congress only by a nonvoting House delegate, much like Puerto Rico. The proposed amendment would give them voting representation in both the House and Senate, just as states have.

Equal rights and full political equality, promised in the Declaration of Independence, are still not realities, but unmistakable advances have been made in modern times. These advances have come largely because people have organized themselves to *demand* equal treatment, not as charity or as a gift, but because that is what they deserve. As legal barriers to equality have fallen, however, some groups have begun to look at economic barriers to equality.

ADDITIONAL SOURCES

Autobiography of Malcolm X. Grove, 1965.*

Banner, Lois W. *Women in Modern America.* Harcourt Brace, 1974.*

Bennet, Lerone, Jr. *What Manner of Man: A Biography of Martin Luther King, Jr.* Pocket Books, 1968.*

Davis, David B. *The Problem of Slavery in an Age of Revolution, 1770–1823.* Cornell University Press, 1975.*

Deloria, Vine, Jr. *Custer Died for Your Sins.* Avon, 1970.*

Dworkin, Ronald. *Taking Rights Seriously.* Harvard University Press, 1977.

Fitzpatrick, Joseph P. *Puerto Rican Americans.* Prentice-Hall, 1971.*

Flexner, Eleanor. *Century of Struggle: The Women's Rights Movement in the United States.* Harvard University Press, 1975.*

Franklin, John Hope. *From Slavery to Freedom: A History of American Negroes,* 4th ed. Random House, 1974.*

Friedan, Betty. *The Feminine Mystique.* Norton, 1963; 2nd ed., 1974.*

Garcia, Chris. *The Chicano Political Experience.* Duxbury, 1977.*

———. *La Causa Politica: A Chicano Politics Reader.* University of Notre Dame Press, 1974.*

Glazer, Nathan. *Affirmative Discrimination.* Basic Books, 1976.*

Gross, Barry R., ed. *Reverse Discrimination.* Prometheus Books, 1977.

Jordan, Winthrop D. *The White Man's Burden: Historical Origins of Racism in the United States.* Oxford University Press, 1974.*

Meier, Matthew S., and Feliciano Rivera. *The Chicanos: A History of Mexican-Americans.* Hill & Wang, 1972.*

Millet, Kate. *Sexual Politics.* Avon, 1973.*

Orfield, Gary. *Must We Bus? Segregated Schools and National Policy.* Brookings, 1978.*

———. *The Reconstruction of Southern Education: The Schools and the 1964 Civil Rights Act.* Wiley, 1969.

Rawls, John. *A Theory of Justice.* Harvard University Press, 1971.*

Sindler, Allan P. *Bakke, DeFunis, and Minority Admissions: The Quest for Equal Opportunity.* Longman, 1978.*

Snyder, C. *Red and Yellow, Black and Brown.* Holt, Rinehart & Winston, 1974.

Washburn, Wilcomb E. *The Indian in America.* Harper & Row, 1975.*

Woodward, C. Vann. *The Strange Career of Jim Crow,* 3rd rev. ed. Oxford University Press, 1974.*

*Available in paperback edition.

5 Capitalism and Democratic Politics

Some political scientists have found it useful to think of politics as a game, with players, rules, rewards, and losses. Although such an analogy can obscure the serious impact of politics on our lives, it is still a useful learning tool. So, for the moment, let us think of politics as a card game, such as poker, bridge, or gin.

Suppose that the rules allow some of the players to receive seven cards while others receive only four. (As we saw in the last chapter, this was precisely the case for women, blacks, and other minorities in the United States for many years.) One's ability to play the game would certainly be limited, to say the least.

Eventually, the rules of the card game are changed, so that if the rules are properly enforced, all players receive the same number of cards. But suppose some of the players do not have enough chips to be able to "ante up" the stakes necessary to enter the game and others have to drop out almost immediately when the betting gets too high. Having all the cards necessary to play the game is of little use if a player doesn't have enough chips to enter or stay in the game.

In fact (to return to reality again), this is a serious problem for America's democracy: the rules require political equality but permit and even protect economic inequality. The result is that political equality can be reduced, and in extreme cases made meaningless, by economic inequality. This is one reason why civil rights leaders of the

Bankers at a dinner given by Harrison G. Fiske, New York City, 1900. Supreme Court Justice Louis Brandeis once wrote, "We can have democracy in this country or we can have great wealth concentrated in the hands of a few, but we can't have both."

1960s came to concentrate on economic rights in the 1970s. As black leader Jesse Jackson and others have pointed out, the legal right to sit at a lunch counter and order a hamburger is of little value to a person who cannot afford to *buy* a hamburger.

The problems of economic inequality, of course, affect whites as well as minorities, men as well as women, the young as well as the old. As we will see in this chapter, the relationship between economics and politics has important implications for America's democracy.

POLITICS AND ECONOMICS

Put in its most basic terms, *political science* is the study of power and authority. Who has power and authority, how did they acquire it, how do they exercise it? *Economics* is the study of the production, distribution, and consumption of goods and services. In particular, it analyzes how government, business, and individuals make costly choices such as deciding to spend money one way rather than another way. But the realms of the two academic disciplines—political science and economics—cannot be so neatly divided; what each seeks to study and explain overlaps with the other. One economist has said, "To put the matter mildly, economists who ignore the politics of economic decision are subject to repeated embarrassment."[1] The matter might be put the other way around as well: Those who study politics cannot ignore the economic influences on political decisions and the economic results of those decisions. Indeed, political science and economics were once parts of the same discipline.

Whether viewed from the perspective of political science or economics, societies are organized according to three basic methods of social control: authority, exchange, and persuasion.[2] These are the ways in which some people control or influence others. *Authority* is exercised by formal organizations—such as corporations, unions, and governments—that have legitimate and accepted power to act for their members or citizens. Through *exchange,* people trade favors or benefits for mutually satisfying purposes. The market system of economics—in which one person earns money, for example, by working to produce automobiles for a corporation—is based upon the concept of exchange. *Persuasion* is the result of instruction or propaganda that influences the attitudes and behaviors of others.

The degree to which a society relies upon one or another method of social control characterizes its "political-economic" system. For example, a "free-market" political economy would operate according to the concept of exchange, which was expressed by Adam Smith in

---

[1]Robert Lekachman, *Economists at Bay* (New York: McGraw-Hill, 1976), p. 6.
[2]Charles E. Lindblom, *Politics and Markets* (New York: Basic Books, 1977).

Wealth of Nations (1776). Smith believed that free exchange was the best way to bring about the good life for the members of any society. If each person were free to pursue his or her own self-interest without interference, he felt, the free exchanges that would result would constitute an "invisible hand" working to society's general benefit. For Smith, free exchange depended upon several factors: competition in industry; an absence of monopoly; the ability of workers to move from job to job with ease; the free flow of capital investments to wherever the opportunities for profit were greatest; and freedom from government regulation and control.

An alternative approach was prescribed by Karl Marx in *Das Kapital* (1867). Marx believed that private ownership of property was a fundamental threat to democratic government because of the

Adam Smith (far left) and Karl Marx, founding theorists of free enterprise and communism, respectively.

political and economic inequities that resulted. He argued that property should be publicly owned. He called for government intervention to abolish or regulate market exchanges. Because of its emphasis on the role of government, this kind of political economy might be called authoritarian.

No existing political economy operates completely according to the theories of either Marx or Smith. And both systems use persuasion. Still, it is instructive to briefly examine the relationship of politics and economics in the political economies that are based primarily on one or the other of these two theories: for Marx's authoritarian model, the Soviet Union, China, and Cuba; and for Smith's free-market model, the United States.

The Authoritarian Model

Today's authoritarian political economies have not abolished all markets. There are three sets of possible markets in a market system. In one set, people offer their energies and assets for money. In another set, consumer markets, people exchange money for the goods and services they desire. In the third set of markets, business enterprises buy and sell from and to each other; retailers buy from wholesalers, and wholesalers buy from manufacturers. Authoritarian systems, such as the communist system in the Soviet Union, have abolished the third set of markets, making it subject to government authority, but they have not abolished the first two sets of markets. Thus, what is produced, whether straw hats or umbrellas, and at what price, as well as where people work and in what numbers, are questions that still largely depend upon some of the marketplace pressures of supply and demand. But authoritarian political economies have generally intervened to prevent substantial unemployment, even if they must put more people to work in a particular plant without increasing the plant's output.

The communist economies have their troubles. For one thing, without reliance upon markets—and supply and demand—it is difficult for government officials to decide upon priorities, such as "whether doctors are generally more important than lawyers, or bicycles more than eggs. . . ."[3] It is difficult, too, for authoritarian political economies to make decisions concerning the allocation of human and other resources. "Suppose, for example, that both truck and aircraft companies need more engineers. To whom should the authority assign available engineers? Perhaps a few to each. But how many to each—should one get more than the other?"[4]

Authoritarian political economies also have trouble ensuring that economic enterprises are run in the most efficient manner and for the most acceptable national purposes. Thus, former Soviet premier Nikita Khrushchev said, "It has become the tradition to produce not beautiful chandeliers to adorn homes, but the heaviest chandeliers possible. This is because the heavier the chandeliers produced, the more a factory gets since its output is calculated in tons."[5] Similar problems of centralized control of enterprises also exist in China and Cuba.

The Free-Market Model

Free-market political economies have certain advantages over the authoritarian system. Markets provide incentives, which encourage efficiency and maximum production. They emphasize resourcefulness and inventiveness rather than the dullness of meeting prescribed goals. And they make economic choices easier: "In a market system, no authority needs to set priorities or come to any other judgment about what is most important to produce. People—consumers, suppliers, businessmen—simply decide whether to buy more or less of any given commodity or service."[6] But America's economic system

---

[3]Lindblom, *Politics and Markets*, p. 69.
[4]Lindblom, *Politics and Markets*, p. 70.
[5]Quoted in Heinz Kohler, *Scarcity Challenged* (New York: Holt, Rinehart and Winston, 1968), p. 507.
[6]Lindblom, *Politics and Markets*, p. 72.

is not completely based upon free exchange. It is still, for the most part, a private enterprise system; that is, most businesses are privately owned. However, there are a number of publicly owned enterprises, such as the Tennessee Valley Authority, a federally owned corporation that produces electricity. Many other companies are publicly owned at the local level. They operate electricity distribution systems, bus systems, and similar enterprises. Moreover, the Amtrak railroad system and many large private defense contractors, which sell most of their output to the federal government, are so heavily subsidized by the federal government and so heavily controlled by federal policy that they are very much like publicly owned enterprises.

No enterprise is truly "free" in America. All are regulated in some way; they must observe rules governing the price they can charge for their products, the wages they can pay their employees, or the standards of product quality and safety that they must meet. Much government regulation of privately owned enterprise in America arose because of inherent problems in the market system. First, left to free-market pressures, business enterprises in the nineteenth and early twentieth century were frequently able to pass along enormous costs to the general public—the costs of polluted air and water; hospitalization and welfare for injured workers; and wage supplements, such as food stamps and public housing, for workers who were not paid enough to fully provide for themselves and their families.

Second, big commercial enterprises also tend to take over little ones or drive them out of business in a free-market system. In their dealings with consumers, these huge business enterprises then tend to become like authoritarian governments; they are no longer subject to the market pressures of supply and demand, and thus they are able to make authoritarian decisions about their operations and the prices and quality of their products.

Third, some national purposes, such as defense and education, which are necessary in any society, may be too costly to achieve through voluntary exchanges only. Thus, they become the province of government.

Fourth, market systems have a kind of built-in insecurity and instability, particularly in regard to employment. It may be good to say that people should be able to move from one job to another with ease, but not everyone has this freedom. For example, an unemployed coalminer who has no other skill and no money for transportation cannot move to some other region of the country. Who can move from one job to another when the national economy is in a recession or depression, when there are simply not enough free-market jobs for all those people who desperately need them? Charles E. Lindblom has written,

In simplest and very rough form, the distinction between what markets can and cannot do is this: for organized social life, people

*need the help of others. In one set of circumstances, what they need
from others they induce by benefits offered. In other circumstances,
what they need will not be willingly provided and must be compelled.
A market system can operate in the first set of circumstances, but not in
the second.*[7]

In America, we have always felt that certain fundamental human
rights should not be subject to the exchange system. Theoretically, in
an exchange between a politician and a citizen, each might benefit. If
the politician paid money for the citizen's vote, the politician would
get another vote toward election to office, and the citizen would gain
monetarily. But such an exchange is prohibited in our system. We do
not allow such rights to be governed by free-market pressures.

Thus, America's political economy is based on exchange, but not
completely free exchange, because markets are in many instances
regulated by government authority. The proper type and extent of
such authoritarian intervention in exchanges have been matters of
continuing debate in America. That debate has focused on two
related issues: the distribution of wealth and income, and the role of
the modern business corporation.

WEALTH AND INCOME IN AMERICA

We noted in Chapter 1 that the framers of America's Constitution
believed in the equal right of citizens to own unequal amounts of
private property. This belief was based upon the ideas of the English
philosopher John Locke. Before the advent of money, Locke wrote,
a person could not hold more property than could be used, for it
would soon spoil from lack of use. But the invention of money, which
"may continue long in a man's possession without decaying," gave
rise to a kind of general consent to "disproportionate and unequal
possession of the earth."[8]

Today we tend to think of the right to private ownership of
property as a freedom *from* government. In fact, however, property
rights are a part of the system of authority; they are established and
protected *by* government.[9] The founders of the United States clearly
recognized this. In *Federalist* 10, James Madison wrote that the
fragmentation of powers in our system of government was specifically
designed to control (among other things) "the rage for . . . an equal
division of property, or any other improper or wicked project."

In America today, there is a great disparity in wealth and income
between the rich and the poor. Wealth is simply what a person owns,

---

[7]Lindblom, *Politics and Markets,* p. 89.
  [8]Quoted in Alpheus T. Mason and Richard H. Leach, *In Quest of Freedom*
(Englewood Cliffs, N.J.; Prentice-Hall, 1973), p. 9.
  [9]See Lindblom, *Politics and Markets,* p. 8.

and some Americans own a great deal more than others. As a group, the wealthiest 10 percent of America's population controls 56 percent of the nation's total wealth. The poorest 10 percent has negative wealth; that is, their debts outstrip their ownership of property.[10] The wealthiest 20 percent of America's households owns more than three fourths of all personal wealth in the country; the poorest 20 percent owns two tenths of one percent of the wealth.[11] More than half of all adult Americans own assets worth less than $3,000—usually houses or cars, which produce no income. By contrast, Americans who have assets totaling more than $1 million make up only one thousandth of 1 percent of our country's population. The wealthiest 1 percent of our people owns eight times as much as the entire bottom half of the population.[12]

Wealthy people are able to earn investment income in addition to or in place of wage income. Since there is such a great disparity in the distribution of wealth in America, it should be no surprise to find that there is also a great disparity in the income earned by Americans. The top 20 percent of the population in 1975 earned 41.1 percent of the total income, while the lowest 20 percent earned only 5.4 percent.[13] There has been little change in this income distribution since the end of World War II. But the absolute difference in dollars between the incomes of the rich and the poor has more than doubled since 1947. Five percent of the population earns $30,000 a year or more; 2 percent has after-tax incomes in excess of $50,000.[14] On the other hand, nearly 12 percent of our population earned less in 1976 than the "poverty-level income"—$5,815 per year—defined by the government.[15] The combined income of the highest 20 percent of our families was more than that earned by the lowest 60 percent.[16]

We can get a graphic idea of what levels of income America's people earn by thinking of them as marchers in an hour-long parade, with the heights of the various marchers in direct proportion to their earned income.[17] First come the "matchstick people," no taller than a kitchen match. These are the unemployed people and the part-time employees, particularly young people and women. Then come the "munchkins," the little people. Some of them are old; others are young wage earners just beginning their careers. Before the last of

---

[10]See *Business Week* (August 5, 1972); and *The Progressive* (July 1977), p. 11.

[11]Office of Management and Budget, *Social Indicators,* 1973 (Washington, D.C.: U.S. Government Printing Office, 1973), p. 182.

[12]Lekachman, *Economists at Bay,* p. 57.

[13]U.S. Bureau of the Census, *Current Population Reports,* Series P-60, no. 105 (Washington, D.C.: U.S. Government Printing Office, 1976), p. 406.

[14]See Arthur Okun, *Equality and Efficiency: The Big Trade-Off* (Washington, D.C.: Brookings Institution, 1975), p. 68.

[15]U.S. Bureau of the Census, *Statistical Abstract of the United States, 1977* (Washington, D.C.: U.S. Government Printing Office, 1977).

[16]*Stat. Abstract of the U.S., 1977.*

[17]This illustration is adapted from Jan Pen, *Income Distribution: Facts, Theories, Policies* (New York: Praeger, 1971), pp. 48–53.

Selected characteristics	Number below poverty level	Poverty rate
All persons	24,720,000	11.6
White	16,416,000	9.1
Black	7,726,000	31.3
Spanish origin	2,700,000	22.4
Under 65 years	21,543,000	11.3
65 years and older	3,177,000	14.1
North and West	14,471,000	10.0
South	10,249,000	14.8
Inside metropolitan areas	14,859,000	10.4
Inside central cities	9,203,000	15.4
Outside central cities	5,657,000	6.8
Outside metropolitan areas	9,861,000	13.9
All families	5,311,000	9.3
Husband-wife	2,524,000	5.3
Male householder, no wife present	177,000	11.1
Female householder, no husband present	2,610,000	31.7
All unrelated individuals	5,216,000	22.6
Male	1,796,000	18.0
Female	3,419,000	26.1

*As of March, 1978
SOURCE: U. S. Bureau of the Census, Department of Commerce, *Current Population Reports, Current Income* (March 1979), Series P-60, no. 119.

the munchkins pass by, the parade has lasted thirty minutes and is therefore already one-half over.

Then come the "cornstalks," who are the size of normal human beings. This group is composed of workers who belong to unions, government employees, schoolteachers, firefighters, police officers, enlisted military personnel, clerks, bank tellers, and those in the professions who are at the lower end of professional income scales.

The last quarter, or fifteen minutes, of the parade begins as the "telephone poles" start to march by. These paraders are four to six *yards* tall. They are the middle-class Americans—airline pilots, school principals, college professors, a few lawyers, and the senior civil servants.

In the last minute of the parade come the "jolly green giants," who are nearly all white, middle-aged, and male. They are the highest-paid lawyers, doctors, bank and corporate executives, and the celebrities in sports and entertainment. They are about twelve yards tall!

Finally, in the last second of the march come the "king kongs," who are as tall as skyscrapers. They represent the extremely small number of Americans of great wealth.

Adam Smith believed that the invisible hand—the operation of innumerable exchanges on the basis of individual self-interest—would produce an overall side effect of better lives for all. Today, the philosophy of the economists in the "Chicago school" of economics (represented most notably by Milton Friedman) is much like the Adam Smith doctrine. They maintain that the free workings of the market and "equality of opportunity" will produce the best economy and society.[18] Even some more liberal economists argue that a certain disparity in wealth and income is necessary for economic purposes: to provide an incentive to encourage work, investment, and production.[19] The question, then, is: How much disparity is enough? Is there a point beyond which the extremes between the rich and the poor become too great for a democracy to tolerate? The French philosopher Jean Jacques Rousseau argued that if the extremes become too great, the stability on which government depends is threatened.[20] The effects of extreme wealth and income disparities should at least be considered in attempting to answer those questions.

Pat Oliphant. Courtesy Washington Star.

"You, sir, are applying for welfare! I, sir, wish to receive temporary government assistance to overcome setbacks I have suffered in the dog-eat-dog arena of the marketplace!"

F. Scott Fitzgerald once said to Ernest Hemingway, "The rich are different from you and me." Hemingway responded, "Yes, they have more money." The rich *do* have more money, but they have more than that, too. Being affluent in America, being a telephone pole or a jolly green giant or a king kong, means more than just having money. It means that one has access to the things money can buy, such as good nutrition, good health services, and good housing. It also means having a far better chance of passing on one's privileged economic status to one's children because the affluent are more able to afford such things as a first-class education for them.

The power of the wealthy is more than just a power to buy things. The wealthy are also able to contribute to the campaigns of politicians who sit on important committees that make decisions

[18]See, for example, Milton Friedman, *Capitalism and Freedom* (Chicago: University of Chicago Press, 1962).
[19]See Arthur Okun, *Equality and Efficiency,* p. 66.
[20]Quoted in Charles M. Sherover, *The Development of the Democratic Idea* (New York: New American Library, 1974), p. 228.

affecting banking or business interests.[21] In addition, wealth enables people to forego wage income for six or twelve or twenty-four months while they run for office. In short, money means political power. Florida orange growers, for example, have influenced both federal and state politics:

> *Florida orange growers recently lobbied in Washington in an effort to prevent the federal government from giving farm workers emergency unemployment compensation of $65 a week. Control over land and money has given these few growers disproportionate power in Florida and national politics . . . they [have] used their economic leverage to prevent Florida educational television stations from showing a documentary about the conditions in which farm workers live and work. Economic power is cultural and political power, and in Florida it is used to keep farm workers, who must struggle for $80 or $90 a week in the best of times, in dehumanizing jobs.*[22]

Those who are not affluent in America—the 40 percent of our families who are struggling just to make ends meet—are often trapped in a seemingly permanent economic bind. Struggling to secure adequate nutrition, health services, and housing, they find it extremely difficult to provide a first-class education for their children, which would give them an opportunity to make better lives for themselves. These families are especially hard hit during periods of high inflation, high unemployment, and depression. They often live in an environment of insecurity and fear because of the higher crime rates in their neighborhoods.

A sharecropper's family. "The Other America"—the poor who live in the midst of affluence—was invisible to most Americans until Michael Harrington's book by that title was published in 1962. Despite a major governmental commitment to end poverty in America, in 1976 nearly 25 million Americans lived on less than the government-defined "poverty-level income" of $5,815 per year.

There are also "hidden injuries of class," as Sennett and Cobb's important book by that title has shown.[23] People are not born with the same amount of property, of course, nor with true equality of opportunity. They are sometimes unable to get jobs because of changed technology or national economic policies, over which they

---

[21]Michael Parenti, *Democracy for the Few* (New York: St. Martin's Press, 1974), p. 184.

[22]"The Gap in Wealth and Income," *The Progressive* (July 1977), p. 11.

[23]Richard Sennett and Jonathan Cobb, *The Hidden Injuries of Class* (New York: Random House, Vintage Books, 1973).

have no immediate control. Yet many poor people tend to internalize these problems, feeling in a sense that there must be something wrong with them. This psychological crippling frequently helps to keep poor people and their children where they are.

Class is a persistent and difficult problem in America, as serious as discrimination on the basis of race and sex. Like discrimination, it is a problem that cannot be solved by the exchange system alone; government authority and persuasion are necessary. But the catch-22 of our system, the irony of democracy,[24] is that those who most need the intervention of government to protect and improve their lives are the least influential politically, while those who least need government intervention are the most politically powerful. Disparity in wealth and income produces a disparity in political influence, and the disparity in influence perpetuates—and may even increase—the disparity in wealth and income.

The American political system has never really come to grips with this "paradox," as Charles Beard called it.[25] Neither has it fully addressed the role of large business corporations in our political economy.

MODERN BUSINESS CORPORATIONS

When America was founded, most personal wealth was in the form of land. Our founders never envisioned that the most powerful form of wealth in America would come to be stock ownership in giant corporations.

A corporation is a form of business organization that allows people to avoid personal liability for the debts of the enterprise. While an individual in business is personally liable for his or her business debts, a corporation's debts are payable only by the corporation, not by its owners personally. So, the primary reason why people form business corporations is to insulate themselves from personal financial responsibility. Second, corporations provide an easy way for a number of people to join together in an enterprise, thus bringing in a larger amount of capital without requiring the investors to be involved in the day-to-day activities of the enterprise. Third, the corporate form of business organization allows enterprises to exist perpetually, long after their owners or managers die.

Business corporations were almost unknown in the colonial period. By 1800, only 335 business corporations had been chartered—mostly banks, insurance companies, water companies, and companies established to build roads, canals, or bridges.[26] But, as the number of

---

[24]Thomas R. Dye and L. Harmon Zeigler, *The Irony of Democracy,* 3rd ed. (North Scituate, Mass.: Duxbury Press, 1975).

[25]See Charles A. Beard, *The Economic Basis of Politics* (New York: Vintage Books, 1960).

[26]Lawrence Friedman, *A History of American Law* (New York: Simon and Schuster, 1973), p. 66.

corporations began to grow, people became concerned about their perpetual life, their potential size and power, and the fact that they were not limited by the ethical concerns that might restrict an individual person. "Corporations did not die and had no ultimate size. There were no natural limits to their life or their greed. Corporations . . . would concentrate the worst urges of whole groups of men; the economic power of a corporation would not be tempered by the mentality of any one man, or by considerations of family or morality."[27]

Despite the fears expressed about corporations, early challenges to their legitimacy were turned aside by the U.S. Supreme Court, which held that business corporations were lawful vehicles for promoting economic growth and protecting property interests.[28] As Robert A. Dahl has written, "By an extraordinary ideological sleight of hand, the corporation took on the legitimacy of the farmer's home, tools and land and what he produced out of his land, labor, ingenuity, anguish, planning, forebearance, sacrifice, risk and hope." The idea of relative autonomy for the farmer, in the farmer's relationship with the government, was transferred to the corporation.[29]

Not all corporations that started as small businesses stayed that way. The same problem exists for us today. In the late 1800s, mergers (the joining of two corporations to form a larger one) and acquisitions (the buying of one corporation by another) caused 301 corporations to disappear each year. Several large corporations today date from that period, including American Tobacco, U.S. Steel, International Harvester, Anaconda Copper, and DuPont. This early merger and acquisition fever resulted from a principal motivation of any corporation: the desire to eliminate competition.[30] In the 1920s and the 1960s, there were other feverish periods of big corporations gobbling up little corporations. This activity increased the size, wealth, and market control of the new corporate giants. In 1947, the two hundred largest manufacturing corporations in the United States owned over 40 percent of all manufacturing assets in the country; by 1968, the two hundred largest manufacturing corporations owned over 60 percent of all manufacturing assets, primarily because of mergers.[31]

When a board member of one company sits on the board of directors of another company, an "interlocking directorate" is formed. Interlocking directorates can restrict competition. For example, members of a bank board of directors may serve on the boards of two or more oil companies.[32]

---

[27]Friedman, *A History of American Law,* p. 171.

[28]Friedman, *A History of American Law,* p. 174.

[29]Robert A. Dahl, "On Removing Certain Impediments to Democracy in the United States," *Political Science Quarterly,* 92, no. 1 (Spring 1977): 8.

[30]See John Blair, *Economic Concentration* (New York: Harcourt Brace Jovanovich, 1972), pp. 257–64.

[31]Blair, *Economic Concentration,* pp. 306–7.

[32]See John M. Blair, *The Control of Oil* (New York: Pantheon Books, 1976), p. 145.

**Number
of Corporate Mergers
and Acquisitions
(Valued at $100 million
or more)**

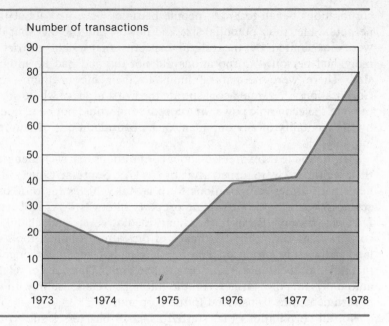

Number of transactions

*A director, whether direct or indirect, of two competing corpora-
tions cannot in good conscience recommend that either shall undertake
a type of competition which is likely to injure the other. . . . A director
on the board of an oil company and a financial institution would find it
hard in good conscience to encourage his bank to finance expansion by
competitors of his oil company thereby jeopardizing its prosperity. Nor
can he in good conscience encourage the oil company to obtain its
credit through other channels.*[33]

The "vertical integration" of a corporation occurs when it becomes
involved, usually through mergers and acquisitions, in all three levels
of business activity—production, refining or processing, and marketing. This is a big problem in the oil and gas industry, as well as in the
food industry. What it means is that a company buys from itself and
sells to itself; thus, the arms-length dealings on which competitive
pricing and other practices are supposed to be based are often
lacking.

The "horizontal integration" of a company occurs when it becomes
involved in enterprises whose products would normally compete
with each other. For example, most companies in the oil industry are
not only involved in oil and gas, but also in what would otherwise be
competing energy sources, particularly coal and uranium.

Finally, there has been a great increase in recent years in
"conglomerates"—corporations composed of several companies.

[33]Stanley H. Ruttenberg and Associates, *The American Oil Industry—A Failure of
Antitrust Policy* (Washington, D.C.: 1974), pp. 78–79.

These companies may not be related; for example, a steel company and a tire company may be part of the same conglomerate. Through their sheer size and economic power, conglomerates can restrict competition.[34] It is estimated that 200 conglomerates control more than 63 percent of all food and tobacco processing sales in America.

The Sherman Antitrust Act of 1890 was aimed at enforcing commercial and industrial competition in America. It outlawed monopoly and "restraints on trade." However, the act has been used mostly against outright price-fixing. It has not been aggressively employed by the Justice Department and other federal agencies to break up large, noncompetitive companies into smaller, more competitive ones. In addition, federal agencies have not consistently attempted to prevent corporate mergers and acquisitions that restrict competition.[35]

The federal government's failure to vigorously enforce antitrust laws—which were designed to prevent noncompetitive market control—caused columnist Art Buchwald to write a satirical story in 1978 about an imaginary merger between the last two giant corpora-

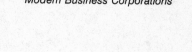

tions in America: Samson Securities, which operated west of the Mississippi River; and the Delilah Company, which operated east of the Mississippi. In Buchwald's column, the timid Antitrust Division of the U.S. Justice Department solemnly announces: "While we find drawbacks to only one company being left in the United States, we feel the advantages to the public far outweigh the disadvantages. Therefore, we're making an exception in this case and allowing Samson and Delilah to merge. I would like to announce that the Samson and Delilah Company is now negotiating at the White House with the President to buy the United States. The Justice Department will naturally study this merger to see if it violates any of our strong anti-trust laws."[36]

There are more than one and a half million business corporations in America today, but they vary widely in size and power. The top 500 American industrial corporations in 1974 sold goods and services

Vertical and horizontal integration—resulting in control of production, refining, and marketing, as well as control of competing energy sources (coal, uranium, and so on)—make the oil companies extremely powerful, both economically and politically.

---

[34]See William F. Mueller, "The Control of Agricultural Processing and Distribution," *Journal of Agricultural Economics* (December 1978).

[35]See Blair, *Economic Concentration,* pp. 555–620.

[36]Art Buchwald, quoted in Ralph Nader, ed., *The Consumer and Corporate Accountability* (New York: Harcourt Brace Jovanovich, 1973), p. 1–2.

The 20 Largest Industrial Corporations (U.S., 1978)

'78	Rank '77	Company	Sales	World Rank ('77)
1	1	General Motors (Detroit)	$63,221,100,000	1
2	2	Exxon (New York)	60,334,527,000	2
3	3	Ford Motor Company (Dearborn, Mich.)	42,784,100,000	4
4	4	Mobil (New York)	34,736,045,000	5
5	5	Texaco (White Plains, N.Y.)	28,607,521,000	6
6	6	Standard Oil of California (San Francisco)	23,232,413,000	9
7	7	International Business Machines (Armonk, N.Y.)	21,076,089,000	10
8	9	General Electric (Fairfield, Conn.)	19,653,800,000	12
9	8	Gulf Oil (Pittsburgh)	18,069,000,000	11
10	10	Chrysler (Highland Park, Mich.)	16,340,700,000	13
11	11	International Tel. & Tel. (New York)	15,261,178,000	15
12	12	Standard Oil (Indiana) (Chicago)	14,961,489,000	16
13	13	Atlantic Richfield (Los Angeles)	12,298,403,000	18
14	14	Shell Oil (Houston)	11,062,883,000	23
15	15	U.S. Steel (Pittsburgh)	11,049,500,000	27
16	16	E. I. DuPont de Nemours (Wilmington, Del.)	10,584,200,000	29
17	18	Western Electric (New York)	9,521,835,000	41
18	17	Continental Oil (Stamford, Conn.)	9,455,241,000	33
19	19	Tenneco (Houston)	8,762,000,000	45
20	20	Proctor & Gamble (Cincinnati)	8,099,687,000	46

SOURCE: *Fortune* (May 7, 1979), p. 270, and (August 14, 1978), p. 184.

worth $844 billion—more than half the nation's gross national product (the total value of goods and services produced in America). Of these major corporations, 203 sold $1 billion worth of goods each, twenty-four sold at least $5 billion worth of goods each, and eleven sold at least $10 billion worth each.[37] The oil industry in particular is dominated by giant corporations. For example, Exxon is so mammoth that, even if it sold its refining and retail operations and kept only its oil exploration operations, it would still be the largest private business corporation in the world.[38]

Is "bigness" bad? Corporate bigness creates serious problems for a democracy in its uses of economic and political power. Further, in many basic industries in America, bigness has meant loss of efficiency. For example, a private management consulting firm testifying before a committee of the U.S. Congress described U.S. Steel Company as follows:

[It is] a big sprawling inert giant, whose production operations were inadequately coordinated; suffering from a lack of a long-run planning agency; relying on an antiquated system of cost accounting; with an inadequate knowledge of the costs or of the relative profitability of the many thousands of items it sold; with production and cost standards

---

[37]Lekachman, *Economists at Bay,* p. 161.
[38]Blair, *The Control of Oil,* p. 38.

generally below those considered everyday practice in other industries; with inadequate knowledge of its domestic markets and no clear appreciation of its opportunities in foreign markets; with less efficient production capabilities than its rivals had; slow in introducing new processes and new products.[39]

The steel industry and some other American industries have become inefficient because they have not had to hustle to keep up with American competition and because the federal government has often protected them from foreign competition by imposing tariffs and import quotas. This inefficiency has caused American jobs to be exported, in effect, to other countries. For example, the Japanese and Italian steel companies have been able to increase their share of the American market because their factories are more modern and efficient than those of their American counterparts. As a result, American steel companies hire fewer workers.

If bigness is often inefficient, how can huge corporations survive? In part, they survive because bigness also means power. Modern business corporations are engaged in all three of the basic methods of social control: authority, exchange, and persuasion. They use these methods for both economic and political power.

Economic Power

In many sectors of American industry today, Adam Smith's "invisible hand"—which was supposed to produce the best products at the best price and thereby produce the good life for people in a free market—has become a kind of "invisible fist" of market control.[40] Because of bigness in industry, prices are often "administered," or set, rather than determined by free market competition.

Corporations exercise authority. They are governments, in a sense, just as the states of Massachusetts and New Mexico, the city of Detroit, and the nation of Venezuela are. The activities of large corporations, like those of powerful governments, can do the following:

. . . cause death, injury, disease, and severe physical pain, e.g., by decisions resulting in pollution, poor design, inadequate quality control, plant safety, and working conditions;

. . . impose severe deprivations of income, well-being, and effective personal freedom, e.g., by decisions on hiring and firing, employment discrimination, and plant location;

. . . exercise influence, power, control, and even coercion over employees, consumers, suppliers, and others, e.g., by manipulating

[39]*Hearings before the Subcommittee on the Study of Monopoly Power,* U.S., 81st Cong., 2d. sess., 1950, p. 967.

[40]This phrase comes from Roger Sherman, *The Economics of Industry* (Boston: Little, Brown and Company, 1974), p. 63.

expectations of rewards and deprivations, by advertising, propaganda, promotions, and demotions, not to mention possible illegal practices.[41]

But who controls them? For the most part, a corporation's employees do not participate in the election of the officers or directors of the corporation. Consumers—those who buy the corporation's products—have no direct vote in corporate decision-making processes. With rare exceptions, only those who own or control stock in a private business corporation in America have a direct say in what the corporation decides to do. Although large numbers of Americans own *some* stock, most corporate stock is owned by a very few people. One percent of the families in America own over 80 percent of all the publicly held stock in this country.[42] Stock ownership entitles shareholders to vote on a kind of "one dollar, one vote" basis, not "one person, one vote."

Theoretically, a corporation's stockholders exercise ultimate control over its activities in annual meetings like this one held by General Electric. Owners of stock vote on motions proposed by a corporation's board of directors—motions which usually pass with little difficulty. Rules governing motions from the floor are strict, and such proposals are rarely approved.

Theoretically, consumers are free actors in the marketplace; they should be able to participate indirectly in corporate decisions by buying or refusing to buy a corporation's products. But because of limited competition, corporations make many price, quality, and other economic decisions with limited regard for the market. Thus, the power of consumers has been greatly curtailed in many American industries.

---

[41]Robert A. Dahl, "Governing the Giant Corporation," in Ralph Nader and Mark J. Green, eds., *Corporate Power in America* (New York: Grossman Publishers, 1973), p. 11.
[42]See Robert Heilbroner, *The Future as History* (New York: Harper and Row, 1959), p. 125; and Ferdinand Lundberg, *The Rich and the Super Rich* (New York: Bantam Books, 1969).

Almost 40 percent of the market activity in America takes place under largely noncompetitive conditions. Approximately two thirds of the manufacturing output in America is in industries in which four or fewer firms account for at least 50 percent of sales, and one third comes from industries in which four or less firms account for at least 70 percent of sales.[43] These industries are called "oligopolies," or shared monopolies. They include such basic American industries as steel, oil and gas, and automobiles. They may not set prices by actual agreement, which would clearly be against the law, but they often do the same thing indirectly. One authority describes these noncompetitive conditions in this way:

If each seeks his maximum profit rationally and intelligently, he will realize that when there are only two or a few sellers his own move has a considerable effect upon his competitors, and that this makes it idle to suppose that they will accept without retaliation the losses that he forces upon them. Since the result of a cut by anyone is inevitably to decrease his own profit, no one will cut, and although the sellers are independent, the equilibrium result is the same as though there were a monopolistic agreement among them.[44]

What are the economic effects of this lack of competition? For one thing, it means higher prices. Adam Smith said that

. . . the price of monopoly is, upon every occasion, the highest which can be got. The natural price, or the price of free competition, on the contrary is the lowest which can be taken, not upon every occasion indeed, but for any considerable time taken together. The one is upon every occasion the highest which can be squeezed out of the buyers, of which, it is supposed, they will consent to give; the other is the lowest which the sellers can commonly afford to take, and at the same time continue their business.[45]

The Federal Trade Commission has estimated that prices in America would fall by 25 percent or more if business competition really existed in America, particularly in the automobile, steel, oil and gas, copper, aluminum container, chemical, detergent, canned soups, and cereals industries.[46]

In addition to higher prices, lack of competition usually means that there is no stimulus for companies to produce goods of the highest quality. Instead, noncompetitive industries tend to spend great amounts on advertising to differentiate the image of their products, although they are not really different in price or quality from those manufactured or produced by others.[47] Quality often suffers in such a

---

[43]See William G. Shepard, *Market Power and Economic Welfare; An Introduction* (New York: Random House, 1979); and Blair, *Economic Concentration*, p. 3.

[44]Blair, *Economic Concentration*, p. 5.

[45]Adam Smith, *The Wealth of Nations*, Book 1, Chapter 7.

[46]See Nader, *The Consumer and Corporate Responsibility*, p. 9.

[47]Charles E. Mueller, "Monopoly," in Nader, ed., *The Consumer and Corporate Accountability*, pp. 321–22.

Industrial Concentration

The following table shows the percentage of the market shared by the four largest firms in each industrial grouping. Economists consider an industry to be concentrated if a few large firms dominate sales and production.

Industry	4-firm market-share	Industry	4-firm market-share
Razor blades and razors	98%	Cereal preparations	87%
Locomotives and parts	98	Chocolate and cocoa products	85
Flat glass	96	Sanitary paper products	85
Aircraft propellers and parts	96	Pressed and blown glass	85
Primary aluminum	95	Engine electrical equip.	85
Aircraft engines and parts	95	Glass containers	80
Electron tubes, receiving	95	Cement	80
Sewing machines	95	Brick and structural tile	80
Safes and vaults	95	Gypsum products	80
Motor vehicles and parts	94	Blast furnaces and steel mills	80
Telephone and telegraph appar.	94	Primary copper	80
Electric lamps	93	Aluminum rolling and drawing	80
Soaps and other detergents	90	Photographic equipment	80
Pharmaceutical preparations	90	Household laundry equipment	79
Metal cans	90	Typewriters	79
Computing and related machines	90	Household vacuum cleaners	78
Steam engines and turbines	90	Flour, blended and prepared	75
Aircraft	90	Pulp mills	75
Hard surface floor coverings	89	Internal combustion engines	75
Cathode ray picture tubes	89	Household refrigerators	72
Chewing gum	88	Industrial gases	72
Primary batteries	88	Explosives	72
Carbon and graphite products	88		

SOURCE: Figures are from a study by William G. Shepard, University of Michigan, printed in Charles E. Mueller, "Monopoly," *The Washington Monthly*, April 1971; reprinted in Nader (ed.), *The Consumer and Corporate Accountability* (Harcourt Brace Jovanovich, 1973).

situation. The automobile industry, for example, is characterized by a kind of planned obsolescence. The automakers put out new, seemingly different models each year, even though this policy involves wasteful tooling changes and consumer costs.[48]

But high industry profits from high prices are not necessarily channeled into research efforts aimed at producing better goods. On the contrary, noncompetitive industries tend to resist innovation and they tend to block the people in small businesses who come up with so many of the new developments.[49] Thus, the steel industry "spends only 0.7 percent of its revenues on research and, in technological progressiveness, the giants which dominate this industry lag behind their smaller domestic rivals as well as their small foreign competitors."[50] The lack of innovation in many American industries, coupled

[48]Lawrence J. White, "The Automobile," in Walter Adams, ed., *The Structure of American Industry,* 5th ed. (New York: Macmillan Publishing Company, 1977), p. 192.

[49]See Nader, ed., *The Consumer and Corporate Accountability,* p. 9.

[50]Walter Adams, quoted in Morton Mintz and Jerry S. Cohen, *America Inc.,* (New York: The Dial Press, 1971).

with the lack of competition in quality and price, has reduced America's ability to compete with foreign companies. It has added to the unemployment problem in the United States and to America's balance-of-trade deficit, the amount by which imports exceed exports. Instead of putting higher profits into research, companies in noncompetitive industries often use them to acquire greater control in an industry, thereby perpetuating and increasing the industry's lack of competition.[51]

Bigness in industries, particularly in conglomerates, also can greatly reduce the bargaining power of a trade union. In their negotiations with big industries, trade unions often have difficulty securing what they consider to be just wages and good working conditions. According to one union official, "If the outfit we bargain with provides only 20 percent of the conglomerate's profit, our strike doesn't hurt them that much."[52]

Finally, concentration of market power in American industries can often thwart government efforts to manage the economy by raising or lowering taxes, expenditures, or interest rates. If the government increases taxes or interest rates to curb consumer demand and slow down inflation, a company in a noncompetitive industry can often raise the unit price of its product in order to compensate for decreased sales volume. This is one of the reasons why in recent years Americans have encountered "stag-flation"—high inflation and high unemployment at the same time.[53] Thus, prices in noncompetitive industries in America may go up rather than down even when demand falls.

Corporations engage in persuasion. They exercise authority, just as surely as governments do. They are also engaged in exchange. Theoretically, a consumer should be able to participate in corporate decisions by buying or refusing to buy a corporation's products—as a free actor in the marketplace. But lack of competition in many American industries thwarts the exchange process.

Political Power

Corporations transform their economic power into political power in America in several ways. The most obvious way is through campaign contributions. Corporations quite regularly solicit campaign contributions from officers and stockholders to help elect or reelect their friends or to defeat those who vote against them.[54]

---

[51]See Mueller, "The Control of Agricultural Processing and Distribution," p. 7.

[52]Union official quoted in Adams, ed., *The Structure of American Industry,* p. 450.

[53]See Michael H. Best and William E. Connolly, *The Politicized Economy* (Lexington, Mass.: D. C. Heath and Company, 1976), pp. 50–52; and Walter Adams, "Public Policy in a Free Enterprise Economy," in Adams, ed., *The Structure of American Industry,* p. 488.

[54]Parenti, *Democracy for the Few,* p. 184.

A federal campaign reform law passed in 1974 allows corporations to form political action committees (PACs). PACs can raise money from individual corporate executives and stockholders and use these funds to contribute up to $5,000 to each candidate of their choice. From 1974 to 1978, the number of these corporate PACs grew from 89 to 776.[55] They contributed approximately $8 million to congressional candidates in the 1978 election alone. Most of this money went to incumbents. One spokesperson for the U.S. Chamber of Commerce has called the PAC method of contributions "a clean means of business involvement in politics." Another corporate executive has said, "It's just as much a civic responsibility as helping the Heart Fund."

But others see this form of corporate campaign financing as a serious threat to democracy. "We are heading for a time when PACs, particularly corporate PACs, will be the dominant force in financing Senate and House campaigns," an official of Common Cause has said. U.S. Senator Edward Kennedy of Massachusetts has stated, "They are multiplying like rabbits, and they are doing their best to buy every Senator, every Representative, and every issue in sight."

The "politics and money cycle" was never more candidly explained than when U.S. Senator Boies Penrose of Pennsylvania told a business group at the turn of the century, "I believe in a division of labor. You send us to Congress; we pass the laws under . . . which you make money; . . . and out of your profits you further contribute to our campaign funds to send us back again to pass more laws to enable you to make more money."[56]

Economic power also translates into political power through corporate advertising and promotion. Corporations use persuasion not only to sell their products, but also to sell their political philosophy. In any city, local corporate executives, such as the president of the electric utility company, are most active in civic and community projects, such as the annual United Fund drive. This goodwill creates political influence in the community. In addition, American corporations spend millions and millions of dollars for TV, radio, and newspaper advertisements on public questions. Mobil Oil Company, for example, spends millions on advertisements to urge the general public to accept Mobil's side of pending public issues.

Advertising on public questions does not just end with company advertising. Spearheaded by the U.S. Chamber of Commerce, a number of giant corporations provide "educational" materials for public school children, either directly or through tax-exempt foundations which they have established. Some of the companies involved are Houston Natural Gas, Gulf Oil Foundation (Texas), California Gas Company, Pacific Gas and Electric (California), General

---

[55] *Time* (December 18, 1978), p. 27.
[56] Quoted in Fred R. Harris, "The Politics of Corporate Power," Nader and Green, eds., *Corporate Power in America,* p. 26.

Telephone (Florida), United Jersey Bank, and the Georgia Bank Association.[57] These instructional materials, of course, espouse the corporate view of the American economic system. Here is a common theme: "'A market feedback system'—that's what our economy is sometimes called. Whenever price or supply get out of line the system will automatically correct itself—and become balanced. That is—if it is *left alone!*" Corporations have also been establishing "chairs of free enterprise" at universities and colleges. Twenty of them are in existence now, and twenty more are planned.

One economist has characterized the U.S. Chamber of Commerce "educational" aids as follows:

> *The portrait is of an American economy which even Irving Kristol and Milton Friedman might reject as a trifle mythological. No monopolies (except for trade unions). No oligopolies. No conscientious attempts by advertisers to manipulate the customers. No whisper of a hint that among interest groups, organized business—not least the Chamber of Commerce—is far stronger than organized labor. . . . No intimation that the only reason why business, kicking and screaming all the way, is reluctantly taking some belated action on air and water pollution is congressional statute and executive enforcement. As one might expect, the Chamber of Commerce is at its most tendentious on the topic of government and its excesses. The incidence of sheer falsehood jumps sharply upward. It is simply not true, for example, that "the major contributing factor to inflation is the United States government and its fiscal policy." It is no truer that unions have a larger role than their employers in promoting inflation. Unions press for higher wages. Helpless corporations pay them and then reluctantly raise their prices to cover new costs. A likely tale.[58]*

In 1978, the U.S. Supreme Court held that it is unconstitutional for a state to prohibit a corporation from advertising on a public question that will be decided by the voters (although a state can prohibit corporate contributions to the campaigns of political candidates).[59] This recent decision, based upon the idea that corporations are entitled to a form of freedom of speech, will make it easier for corporations to influence public policy through advertising.

Corporations turn their economic power into political power in another way. Their financial resources give them access to the courts. Corporations can often keep antitrust or other such actions against them tied up in the courts for years. Those without comparable financial resources may not have as much access to America's judicial system.

---

[57]See Matthew Lyon, "And Now the Word From Our Sponsor," *The Texas Observer* (November 3, 1978), pp. 2–9.

[58]Robert Lekachman, "The Chamber's Tall Tales," *The Texas Observer* (November 3, 1978), pp. 6–7.

[59]Slip opinion, *First National Bank of Boston v. Bellotti*, U.S. Supreme Court, 1978.

In addition, economic power translates into political power through *lobbying*. This term refers to the efforts of people who are hired to influence legislative and executive policy making in federal and state governments. Corporations typically have highly skilled lobbyists in Washington to make sure that their financial interests are protected. Companies such as Exxon deduct the costs of lobbying for tax purposes, but an *individual,* public-spirited citizen who goes to Washington or calls long distance to talk a home-state senator into voting a certain way cannot deduct such expenses.[60]

Finally, economic power may become political power through what is called the "revolving door"—the job interchange between industry and government. A young lawyer just out of school, may first secure a job with a federal regulatory agency. With experience, he or she can then move into a middle-level job in a law firm or in the industry that the agency was supposed to regulate. From there, the lawyer can move to a higher-level position in the regulatory agency and then move back to a top position in a law firm or in the private industry. These job interchanges have been called a "sub-government." One observer has stated, "People in this sub-government typically spend their lives moving from one organization to another in the sub-government. People who pursue the course of protecting the public interest are rarely admitted to this club."[61]

One example of the revolving door method of industry influence over public policy involves the former Chairman of the Federal Communications Commission, Richard E. Wyley. In 1978, he was appointed a trustee of the broadcasting group that distributes industry campaign contributions to political candidates. The former chairman had also become a member of the law firm that counseled broadcasters about problems involving toy advertising during children's television programs. "It is obvious that Mr. Wyley, as chairman of the FCC, was responsible for the failure of the commission to respond to the needs of the child audience," a spokesperson for a children's television group declared. "It would appear that this fee to his law firm is part of his reward [from] a grateful industry."[62]

For what ends do corporations use political power? They use it to secure tax policies that are favorable to business. They lobby for tariffs and import quotas that protect them from foreign competition. In addition, they try to secure relaxed environmental and safety standards, direct federal subsidies, and government regulation that favors business and impedes competition. Finally, they use their political influence to discourage the government from enforcing federal antitrust laws (principally the Sherman Act, mentioned earlier in the chapter).

---

[60]See James Deakin, *The Lobbyist* (Washington, D.C.: Public Affairs Press, 1966).

[61]Nicholas Johnson, quoted in Mintz and Cohen, *America, Inc.,* p. 178.

[62]*The New York Times* (February 12, 1978), p. 29.

As various kinds of large business corporations developed in America, the federal government began to regulate their activities in order to protect the "public interest." But government intervention has only been modestly effective, largely because corporations have been able to translate their economic power into political power. In other words, General Motors is not only powerful in the automobile market; it is also powerful in government circles in Washington.

Thus, the concentration of economic power can seriously limit the right of consumers to participate in economic decisions that affect their lives—to help determine the price of a box of detergent, say—because of a lack of real competition on price or product, or effective regulation of them. The translation of corporate economic power into political power can also restrict the right of individual citizens to participate effectively in the political decisions their government makes.

CONTROLLING ECONOMIC POWER

Americans believe in political equality and in private ownership of property. As we have seen, these traditional beliefs—political equality and the right of unequal property ownership, which has caused great economic inequality—often clash in American life. There are, therefore, built-in tensions between capitalism and democratic politics in our country. To reduce these tensions, or at least to keep them within acceptable bounds, the government has attempted to (1) achieve a fairer distribution of wealth and income; (2) reduce corporate economic power; and (3) restrict economic power from becoming political power.

Fairer Distribution of Wealth and Income

Many Americans do not realize that the redistribution of wealth and income—and power—is a central reason for the existence of government. Thus, the ratification of the Sixteenth Amendment in 1913 allowed Congress to enact an income tax system that is supposed to be based upon ability to pay. In addition, the federal government has adopted numerous social welfare programs, such as those dealing with housing and food stamps, that are supposed to be based upon need. Although the income tax system has been reformed in recent years to reduce the tax burden on low-income Americans, very little progress has been made toward the elimination of "loopholes." Loopholes are clauses in tax laws that give special benefits to certain industries and wealthy taxpayers. Tax reform was a major campaign pledge of President Jimmy Carter, but he has given only limited support to this idea since becoming President.

Unemployment has been a persistent problem in America in recent years. Ever since the days of the Great Depression, the federal government has from time to time attempted to increase employment through such means as special summer employment programs for young people and public works projects. But no federal action in regard to jobs has been nearly as comprehensive as the program President Carter endorsed while he was campaigning in 1976. This specific proposal would have provided for government-guaranteed full employment. It was embodied in a bill introduced by the late Senator Hubert H. Humphrey of Minnesota and Representative Gus Hawkins of California that would have made the right to a job an enforceable *civil* right. The bill would have required the federal government to adopt taxing and spending policies that would stimulate the economy by increasing consumer demand and thus greatly increase the number of private jobs. The bill would also have required the federal government to set up federal employment programs and to serve as the "employer of last resort" when private jobs were not available for all those who desired them.

President Carter relaxed his support of this measure after coming into office. Some members of Congress opposed it, too, because they said it would require too much government intervention in the economy and too much increased federal spending. So, the Humphrey-Hawkins bill was amended to become merely a statement of goals rather than a specific program. In this emasculated form, it was passed by Congress in 1978. There is still considerable agitation, however, for a government program of full employment.

The present federal welfare system allocates federal matching funds to states (and some cities) to provide a minimum income for those who cannot work (blind, aged, and disabled people and dependent children). In some instances, it also provides money for those who cannot find work. The system is not uniform from state to state. In many states, it is criticized because the amounts paid are not sufficient to provide the barest necessities of health, housing, nutrition, and clothing. To replace the present welfare system, some advocate a federally funded national system that would be uniformly applied throughout the country. This system would guarantee a minimum income for people who cannot work or who cannot find work, plus an income supplement for those who do not make enough money from working to provide the necessities for themselves and their families. President Richard Nixon proposed a modified version of this welfare reform, but abandoned it because both liberals and conservatives opposed it. Liberals thought it was not fair enough, and conservatives said it would cost too much money and might reduce incentives for working. Advocates of this uniform "income mainte-nance" system suggest that present programs for poor people should be eliminated and replaced by an overall monthly money payment.

In recent years, organized labor has led the fight for regular increases in the federal minimum wage that private employers are required to pay their employees. They argue that corporate employ-ers should have to pay the *real* costs of employment, rather than paying a substandard wage and having the public assume part of their workers' living costs through food stamps, Medicaid, public housing, and similar supplementary federal assistance. Organized labor has also led the movement to reform federal labor laws by making it easier for employees to form unions. This reform would increase the ability of workers to unite and themselves secure adequate compensation for their work.

Reduction in Corporate Economic Power

Calling business corporations in America "disproportionately powerful," Charles E. Lindblom writes that "the large private corporation fits oddly into democratic theory. Indeed, it does not fit."[63] Whether it fits or not, the corporation has to deal with the federal government's attempts to reduce corporate economic power. These government actions fall into three categories: enforced competition, regulation, and public ownership.

As we saw earlier, the Sherman Antitrust Act provides the basis for government enforcement of business competition. Supporters of this approach call for more vigorous federal enforcement of antitrust laws and less government willingness to approve corporation mergers and acquisition. Some advocate legislation to break up vertical integration in the oil industry. They argue that an oil company should be allowed to engage in production, refining, or marketing, but not all three. Similar legislation has been proposed to break up horizontal integration in the energy field. These proposals would not permit an oil company, for example, to produce oil and gas and also coal. Some senators have also advocated legislation to automatically break up giant corporations that gain a controlling percentage of sales in an industry, unless the corporation could prove that its large size was necessary to produce its products at the lowest possible consumer costs.[64]

Another proposed reform calls for the federal government to form or buy control in selected individual companies in noncompetitive industries and use them to stimulate greater competition. Thus, Senator Adlai Stevenson of Illinois, backed by the Consumer Federation of America, has urged the creation of a public oil and gas corporation that would develop energy resources on federal lands and compete with privately owned companies.

---

[63]Lindblom, *Politics and Markets,* p. 356.

[64]In regard to these suggestions for increased competition, see Walter Adams, "The Anti-Trust Alternative," in Nader and Green, eds., *Corporate Power in America,* pp. 130–137; William G. Shepherd, "Public Enterprise," in Nader and Green, eds., *Corporate Power in America,* pp. 235–255; Walter Adams, "Public Policy in a Free Enterprise Economy," in Adams, ed., *The Structure of American Industry,* pp. 482–514; Willard F. Mueller, "Antitrust in a Planned Economy: An Anachronism or an Essential Complement?" *Journal of Economic Issues,* 9, no. 2 (June 1975): 159–179; and Willard F. Mueller, "The Need for Vigorous Antitrust Enforcement," *Antitrust and Macroeconomics Review,* 3, no. 1 (1978): 83–96.

Ever since the Interstate Commerce Commission was created in 1887 to regulate the railroads (which had a virtual monopoly on transportation), the federal government has been deeply involved in the regulation of American business and industry. As a means for improving federal regulation of corporations, Ralph Nader has proposed a new federal law that would require large corporations to be chartered by the federal government, rather than being chartered separately in each of the states where they do business. Nader's proposal would place restrictions on the exercise of corporate economic power. For example, it would require competitive pricing and better working environments as conditions for continuing to do business as a corporation.[65] There has also been a strong movement (thus far unsuccessful) to create a federal consumer protection agency to serve as a watchdog on federal regulatory agencies and as an advocate of consumer interests within the government.

The right of individual citizens to bring "class actions" in the courts against noncompetitive or price-fixing corporations has also helped to regulate them. Class actions can be brought by a person for himself or herself and for "all other persons similarly situated." They are feared by industry because they provide a way for an individual citizen, whether powerful in government circles or not, to enforce restrictions on corporate economic power. If such a self-starting citizen wins the case, he or she is awarded money damages (which must be divided on some basis with others similarly situated), attorney's fees, and court costs. Although legislation has been sought in recent years to increase the opportunities for class actions, court decisions have tended to restrict them.[66]

The federal government has also tried to use public ownership of certain enterprises as a means of reducing corporate economic power in America. Public ownership has taken a variety of forms: cooperatives, such as those that operate electricty distribution systems; municipal ownership of such enterprises as mass transit systems; and federal ownership of competitive businessses, such as the Tennessee Valley Authority. Some people advocate increased or even total public ownership of American business enterprises. Under these circumstances, they say, corporations would exercise their economic power in ways compatible with the public interest. Not everyone agrees with this view, however. Political scientist Robert Dahl writes:

That the form of ownership does not, per se, determine how an economic enterprise will be governed is confirmed by the similarities resulting from radical variations in the form of ownership. Highly hierarchical, authoritarian government of firms has existed under the

---

[65]See Ralph Nader, "The Case for Federal Chartering," in Nader, ed., *The Consumer and Corporate Accountability*, pp. 351–66.

[66]For information concerning improved regulation of corporations, see Mark V. Nadel, *Corporations and Political Accountability* (Lexington, Mass.: D.C. Heath & Company, 1976), pp. 229–59.

extremes of private and public ownership. The old liberal conception of a privately owned enterprise consisting of freely contracting parties operating essentially without hierarchy and power relationships was virtually all myth. The factory was typically a kind of despotism until trade unions began to make inroads on the powers of management. Yet socialists who hoped that hierarchy would vanish if ownership were transferred to the state, or to a disembodied entity called the people, were profoundly disillusioned to discover that, far from ushering in industrial democracy, government ownership merely preserved or even strengthened hierarchical authority. The bosses' names and faces may have changed; their power remained the same, or increased. Probably in no industrial country, it appears, is the domination of management so great and the influence of workers so slight as in the economic enterprises in the Soviet Union.[67]

Thus a number of people have criticized the Tennessee Valley Authority for not being sufficiently responsive to the public interest and to the interests of the people who live in the region where TVA is located. Even with public ownership, steps must be taken to preserve public participation in the control of enterprises.

Worker ownership, a modified form of public ownership, also exists in America. For example, Consumers United Group, Inc., a

Norris Dam, built on the Clinch River from 1933 to 1936, is one of 31 dams owned or operated by the Tennessee Valley Authority (TVA) in the Tennessee River basin. Financed by congressional appropriations, by limited bond issues, and by sale of surplus hydroelectric and stream-generated power, the TVA is responsible for integrated planning and development for the entire region. The fact that its headquarters are in the region, rather than in Washington, makes it unique among federal agencies. While some critics maintain that TVA is not as interested in the "public interest" as a public utility should be, others decry the TVA as being "socialistic."

[67]Dahl, "Governing the Giant Corporation," in Nader and Green, *Corporate Power in America*, pp. 17–18.

$60 million insurance company in Washington, D.C., and the GAF Corporation, an asbestos company in Vermont, are owned by workers.[68]

Restrictions on Economic Power Becoming Political Power

"We all have our burdens to bear."

The most obvious way in which economic power translates into political power is through the financing of political campaigns. A number of efforts have been made to reform this system. The most notable is the Campaign Reform Act, enacted in 1974. This Act severely restricted the contributions and campaign expenditures of candidates for President and for the U.S. House and Senate. It also provided for federal financing in presidential campaigns. A presidential candidate of a qualified party who can show broad enough support—by raising at least $5,000 in each of at least twenty states, counting no more than $250 per contributor—will receive matching funds up to $5 million prior to the nominating conventions. After receiving their party's presidential nomination, candidates are entitled to have their entire general election campaigns financed by the federal treasury. This law thus allows a presidential candidate who is not backed by rich people or giant corporations to be nominated and elected. Although the Senate has twice approved a bill to extend such public financing to congressional campaigns, the House has so far refused, thereby leaving intact the present system which favors incumbents and those supported by special-interest money. Michigan and Wisconsin have provided for systems of public financing for candidates for their state offices, but most states have not followed suit.

CONCLUSION

The paradox of democracy—the tension between capitalism and democratic politics—continues to trouble us. As Charles Beard put it, "The device of universal suffrage does not destroy economic classes or economic inequalities. It ignores them."[69]

Americans believe that all people should be able to participate in the decisions that govern their lives. Through the years, we have removed most of the legal barriers to participation in the political process. But we have not yet come to grips with the inherent problems of participation in our economic system. Greater economic participation by Americans and less corporate economic power in American politics will require a knowledgeable, concerned, and persistently active American citizenry.

---

[68]See Daniel Zwerdling, "Work Place Democracy: A Strategy for Survival," *The Progressive* (August 1978), pp. 16–24.

[69]Beard, *Economic Basis of Politics,* p. 69.

ADDITIONAL SOURCES

Avineri, Shlomo. *The Social and Political Thought of Karl Marx.* Cambridge University Press, 1971.*

Barber, Richard J. *The American Corporation: Its Power, Its Money, Its Politics.* Dutton, 1970.

Barnet, Richard J. and Ronald E. Muller. *Global Reach: The Power of the Multinational Corporations.* Simon & Schuster, 1975.*

Berg, Ivar. *The Business of America.* Harcourt Brace Jovanovich, 1968.

Cobb, Jonathan, and Richard Sennett. *The Hidden Injuries of Class.* Random House, 1973.*

Domhoff, G. William. *The Powers That Be: The State and Ruling Class in Corporate America.* Random House, 1979.*

————. *Who Rules America?* Prentice-Hall, 1967.*

Edwards, Richard C., Michael Reich, and Thomas E. Weisskopf, eds. *The Capitalist System,* 2nd ed. Prentice-Hall, 1978.*

Friedman, Milton. *Capitalism and Freedom.* University of Chicago Press, 1962.*

Galbraith, John Kenneth. *Economics and the Public Purpose.* Houghton Mifflin, 1973.*

————. *The New Industrial State,* 3rd rev. ed. Signet, 1978.*

Hamilton, Richard F. *Class and Politics in the United States.* Wiley, 1972.*

Harrington, Michael. *The Twilight of Capitalism.* Simon & Schuster, 1977.*

Kolko, Gabriel. *Wealth and Power in America.* Praeger, 1962.*

Lekachman, Robert. *Economists at Bay.* McGraw-Hill, 1975.*

Lindblom, Charles. *Politics and Markets.* Basic Books, 1977.

McConnell, Grant. *Private Power and American Democracy.* Vintage, 1970.*

Mintz, Morton, and Jerry Cohen. *America, Inc.* Dell, 1972.*

Pechman, Joseph A., and Benjamin A. Okner. *Who Bears the Tax Burden?* Brookings, 1974.*

Smith, Adam. *The Wealth of Nations.* Penguin, 1970.*

Tucker, Robert, ed. *The Marx-Engels Reader.* Norton, 1971.

Vogel, David. *Lobbying the Corporation: Citizen Challenges to Business Authority.* Basic Books, 1979.

*Available in paperback edition.

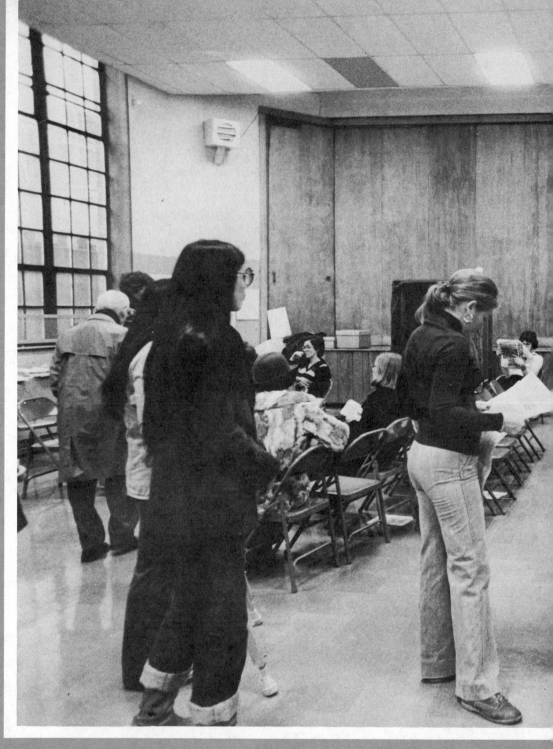

Democratic Citizenship

The ideals of human rights and equality are of fundamental importance in American government and politics. So, too, are the rules according to which the political system operates. But in a democratic society—in a government based upon the consent of the governed—political participation is also fundamentally important.

How do we as Americans learn about how the political system works and what our role is as democratic citizens? Or how do we fail to learn those things? How do Americans feel about their political institutions and about specific political issues? What difference does it make how we feel and what our opinions are? How do democratic citizens transform their opinions into action? These are the questions addressed in Part 3.

We first consider political socialization, which has to do with how, what, and when we learn about the political system. We also discuss the formation and expression of individual attitudes and public opinion, and explore various kinds of active participation in politics through interest groups, political parties, and elections. Finally, we survey some of the "extra-political" means that Americans have used to become involved in decisions that affect their lives. This Part, then, deals with how a person becomes—or may become—a democratic citizen.

6 Political Socialization

Learning About Politics

A second-grade student says, "I like America; we are the best country." A fourth-grader says, "I'm a Democrat." A fifth-grader says, "The President helps people and is the boss of everything."

As these examples indicate, the political learning process begins at a very early age. But none of us is born with political attitudes or beliefs. Nor are we born political participants. Rather, our political ideas and behaviors are learned through the process of *political socialization*. The term *socialization* generally refers to how we learn or acquire our society's norms, traditions, and values; in other words, it deals with how we internalize, or accept as our own, certain cultural patterns.[1] The term *political socialization*, therefore, refers to the process of learning about political ideas, about our political system and how it operates, and about our roles as democratic citizens.[2]

Although there is some truth in the biblical saying, "As the twig is bent, so grows the tree," it does not completely explain the political socialization process. The result of political socialization is never completely predictable. The process is complex and not fully understood; a variety of "agents"—including our families, schools, peers, the media, and political events and experiences themselves—affect the way we learn about politics. Further, political socialization continues throughout our lives.

The reasons why some Americans participate in politics and others do not, why some people are liberal and others are conservative, why some are Democrats and others Republicans, and why some are revolutionaries and others conformists—all have to do with political socialization. These are all individual effects of the process, but they have important implications for society as a whole, too.

[1] Melvin De Fleur, William D'Antonio, and Lois De Fleur, *Sociology: Human Society*, 2nd ed. (Glenview, Ill.: Scott, Foresman, 1976), p. 146.

[2] Gabriel A. Almond, "A Functional Approach to Comparative Politics," in Gabriel A. Almond and James S. Coleman, eds., *The Politics of Developing Areas* (Princeton, N.J.: Princeton University Press, 1960), p. 27.

The famous sociologist Talcott Parsons once compared each new generation to a "horde of barbarians" invading the civilized world. In effect, socialization civilizes these "barbarians." It prepares them for participation in the life of the society. It teaches them how to interact with others and lets them know which social identities and relationships are available to them (or expected of them).[3] Socialization also "tames" the "barbarians." It teaches them to suppress or to redirect "antisocial" tendencies. A person learns, in other words, that certain desires for immediate pleasure or gratification should be checked or directed into other activities that serve the long-range interests of the individual and of society.[4] Finally, through political "enculturation," the "barbarians" acquire certain political outlooks and orientations.[5]

Political socialization, then, affects the individual and the society as a whole. If young people are taught to believe that everyone should vote, for example, one kind of society will result. A quite different society may be produced if most young people are raised to believe that voting is a waste of time.

The American political system has been relatively stable. It has existed for nearly two hundred years in its present form, with very few changes in the Constitution. America still has a bicameral Congress: one house is elected on the basis of population and the other on the basis of equal representation for each of the states. America still has a federal system, with shared sovereignty between the federal and state levels. This stability exists despite the fact that the things that are valued in America—wealth, income, power, influence, and prestige—are unevenly shared.

How can we explain the stability of our system—or of any system—when society's values are unevenly shared? If the tax system places a relatively heavier burden on wage earners than it does on rich people, why do wage earners continue to support the system? Why do the losers in a hotly contested American election nevertheless support the government, which is headed by the winning candidate? These serious questions are major concerns of political scientists who study socialization.

There are two theories that attempt to answer these questions. One is called *systems theory*; the other is *hegemonic theory*.

---

[3]See George Herbert Mead, *Mind, Self and Society* (Chicago: University of Chicago Press, 1934); and Robert A. Levine, *Culture, Behavior and Personality* (Chicago: Aldine Publishing Co., 1973).

[4] See Ruth Benedict, *Patterns of Culture* (Boston: Houghton, Mifflin Co., 1934); and Robert D. Hess and Judith V. Torney, *The Development of Political Attitudes in Children* (Chicago: Aldine Publishing Co., 1967); Fred I. Greenstein, *Children and Politics* (New Haven: Yale University Press, 1965).

[5]See, for example, Abram Kardiner and Ralph Linton, *The Individual and His Society* (New Haven: Yale University Press, 1939); and Jay W. M. Whiting and I. L. Child, *Child Training and Personality: A Cross-Cultural Study* (New Haven: Yale University Press, 1963).

The characteristics of a "good citizen" are defined differently in different political cultures. "The Ideal Soviet Citizen" is adapted from G. Hollander, Soviet Political Indoctri-

VIEWPOINT
The Ideal Citizen

nation (Praeger, 1972). "Characteristics of a Good Democratic Citizen" was developed by a committee of the National Council for the Social Studies in 1950, based on a lengthy survey of American leaders from all walks of life.

The Ideal Soviet Citizen

1. A lover of labor, a willing and enthusiastic contributor to the material growth of the economy.
2. Totally politicized, implying:
   a. continual subjection of the individual will to that of the Party leadership at any given time;
   b. subordination of all personal emotions, needs, values, comforts, and interests to centrally determined goals;
   c. uncritical and enthusiastic acceptance of all Party pronouncements and orders.
3. Always an activist, participating in civic activities, demonstrations, agitation sessions, and so on; in this way a strong sense of social duty is translated into reality.
4. Politically literate, using a firm grasp of ideology to guide actions and attitudes.
5. Unspontaneous and self-disciplined. . . .
6. Vigilant against not only one's own "inner enemies," the emotions, but also against others as enemies.
7. Conscious of a sense of solidarity with workers in all countries, and particularly with those in Socialist countries.
8. Patriotic.
9. Collectivist, anti-individualistic, and anti-egoist.
10. Virtuous in ways which are not political in themselves, but which may be politically derived; honest, sober, modest, courageous, and so forth; and manifests a total lack of snobbishness, arrogance, or desire to exploit one's fellow man. . . .
11. Atheistic, having no need for religion of any kind.

The Good Democratic Citizen

1. Believes in equality of opportunity for all people.
2. Values, respects, and defends basic human rights and privileges guaranteed by the U.S. Constitution.
3. Respects and upholds the law and its agencies.
4. Understands and accepts the . . . democratic principles as guides in evaluating his own behavior and the policies and practices of other persons and groups, and judges his own behavior and the behavior of others by them.
5. Understands that, in the long run, people will govern themselves better than any self-appointed group would govern them.
6. Puts the general welfare above his own whenever a choice between them is necessary.
7. Feels that he has inherited an unfinished experiment in self-government which it is his duty and privilege to carry on.

Systems theory, developed principally by David Easton and Jack Dennis,[6] holds that the stability of a system is the result of a "generational" process of political socialization; political orientations are passed on from older people to younger people. According to Easton and Dennis, politically socialized people can give two kinds of support to a political system: specific support and diffuse support. *Specific support* is the allegiance people give to a system because the system actually delivers what they want. The following two statements are examples of specific support: "I am for my senator, because the senator helped me with my Social Security claim"; "I am a Republican because the Republican party believes in cutting taxes."

---

[6]See David Easton, *A Framework for Political Analysis* (Englewood Cliffs, N.J.: Prentice-Hall, 1965); David Easton, *A Systems Analysis of Political Life* (New York: Wiley, 1965); and David Easton and Jack Dennis, *Children in the Political System: Origins of Political Legitimacy* (New York: McGraw-Hill, 1969).

8. Exercises his right to vote.
9. Accepts civic responsiblilties and discharges them to the best of his ability.
10. Knows [the] technics of social action (e.g. how to win support for desirable legislation) and can cooperate with others in achieving such action.
11. Accepts the basic idea that in a democracy the majority has the right to make decisions under the Constitution.
12. Assumes a personal responsibility to contribute toward a well-informed climate of opinion on current social, economic, and political problems or issues.
13. Realizes the necessary connection of education with democracy.
14. Respects property rights, meets his obligations in contracts, and obeys regulations governing the use of property.
15. Supports fair business practices and fair relations between employers and employees.
16. Assumes a personal responsibility for the wise use of natural resources.
17. Accepts responsibility for the maintenance and improvement of a competitive economic system assisted and regulated when necessary by governmental action.
18. Knows in general how other economic systems operate, including their political and social consequences.
19. Knows about, critically evaluates, and supports promising efforts to prevent war, but stands ready to defend his country against tyranny and aggression.
20. Is deeply aware of the interdependence of people and realizes that a good life can be attained only by the organized cooperation of millions of people all over the world.
21. Understands cultures and ways of life other than his own.
22. Cultivates qualities of character and personality that have a high value in his culture.
23. Is a responsible family member and assumes his full responsibilities for maintaining the civic standards of his neighborhood and community.
24. Recognizes taxes as payment for community services and pays them promptly

Diffuse support, which we are most interested in here, is the allegiance people give to a system *even though they are not at the moment pleased with the operation of the system*. Many people continue to pay taxes, for example, even though they think taxes are too high or are unfairly levied. Many people fought in the Vietnam War, although they did not agree with the war policy. These people probably said something like this: "Once our flag is committed, we have to support it," a variation of an older patriotic statement, "my country, right or wrong."

According to Easton and Dennis, diffuse support is the glue that holds our system together. It is passed on from one generation to another. "Children who begin to develop positive feelings toward the political authorities will tend to grow into adults who will be less easily disenchanted with the system than those children who early acquire negative, hostile sentiments."[7]

---

[7]Easton and Dennis, *Children in the Political System*, pp. 106–107.

Diffuse support is the result of four processes of political socialization that occur during childhood. "Politicization" occurs first. It is the process of becoming aware of the presence of an authority outside, and more powerful than, the family. For example, a child's observation of a police officer giving a parent a speeding ticket is a politicizing experience. "Personalization" occurs when the child begins to associate this outside authority with particular people, notably the President of the United States. Through "idealization," a child comes to view the President or a police officer as protective, helpful, and good. This positive sentiment toward individual figures of authority eventually becomes transformed through "institutionalization" into a positive feeling toward the overall system of government itself.

Peoples' feelings toward the government vary, depending upon how the system responds to their specific needs and desires. But Easton and Dennis maintain that the underlying and continuing diffuse support for the system results from early political socialization. Thus, a general feeling of national loyalty and patriotism keeps the harsh, rough edges of citizens' disagreements with the government within reasonable limits. Systems theory explains political socialization, then, primarily as a generational process in which diffuse support is passed on from older to younger people.

According to hegemonic theory, political socialization occurs between a dominant, ruling group and a dominated or governed group.[8] ("Hegemony" means dominant influence or authority.) For example, Marxists describe the dominant-dominated relationship on the basis of class. They view the ruling group as the owners, or capitalists, and the dominated group as the workers, or proletariat. Elite theorists see the dominant-dominated relationship as one between leaders, or elites, on one hand, and the governed masses on the other.

In any case, hegemonic theory views political socialization as a process in which the dominant group—and the government, which it controls—uses propaganda and censorship to further its own interests. Propaganda includes the use of political ceremonies, the flag, national heroes, school textbooks, and other means to express views that keep the dominant group in power. Censorship is the screening of information and ideas that are not in the interests of the dominant group. Marxists would say that the dominated group has a "false consciousness"; it supports the dominant class even though it is not in its interests to do so.

Both systems theory and hegemonic theory attempt to explain how conflict is reduced and confined within limits in a society. But whether one subscribes to one view or the other it is important to

---

[8]See Mario B. Machado, "Political Socialization in Authoritarian Systems: The Case of Brazil" (Ph.D. Dissertation, University of Illinois, 1975).

remember that political socialization tends to maintain the *status quo*.[9]

Political socialization, as noted earlier, is almost infinitely variable. No two individuals are alike in personality or predisposition. No government can completely control the socialization process because, as we shall see, the agents of socialization are numerous, and because each of us reacts uniquely to whatever we are exposed to. Thus, even if what is taught in school were rigidly controlled, for example, some political socialization from other agents would still continue. But exactly how does political socialization occur? What do we learn about politics, and when do we learn it?

WHAT DO WE LEARN AND WHEN DO WE LEARN IT?

In the political socialization process, what we learn is related to when we learn it. We can divide the process into three principal time periods: childhood, adolescence, and adulthood.

Childhood

It is remarkable how much political socialization takes place during childhood. Children acquire a considerable reservoir of emotionally based political outlooks and orientations that are largely favorable toward political authorities and the system. Even very young American children proudly identify themselves as Americans. This early *national loyalty* or patriotism is much like a religious feeling.[10] In one study, children were asked which of a number of flags they liked best. While most kindergarten children chose a merchant flag of Siam (now Thailand), apparently because the flag had a white elephant on it, first-graders preferred the American flag, identifying it with being American.[11]

Identification with a *political party* also comes at a surprisingly early age. One study found that over half of the children in one second-grade class said, "I am a Democrat," or, "I am a Republican."[12] Another study found the same result from interviews with fourth-graders, even though these children could not identify any leader of the party to which they claimed allegiance.[13]

[9]For a discussion of these two theories, see Richard E. Dawson, Kenneth Prewitt, and Karen S. Dawson, *Political Socialization*, 2nd ed. (Boston: Little, Brown and Co., 1977), pp.13–33.

[10]David Easton and Robert D. Hess, "A Child's Political World," *Midwest Journal of Political Science*, 6 (1962): 231–32.

[11]Edwin D. Lawson, "Development of Patriotism in Children—A Second Look," *The Journal of Psychology*, 55 (1963): 279–86.

[12]Easton and Hess, "A Child's Political World," p. 245.

[13]Fred Greenstein, *Children in Politics* (New Haven: Yale University Press, 1965), p. 241.

Young children are able to identify themselves with *social groups*. They have a sense of what social class they belong to, what race, and what religion.[14] In addition, they begin to distinguish between groups. Thus a young child learns that some people are white and some are not, that some are Catholics, some Jews, some Protestants, and that some people are rich and others are not. And children begin to think of themselves as members of one or another of these groups.

A young child also begins to develop orientations toward *political authorities and roles*. Most children have positive feelings concerning the President of the United States. Responding to a question about what the President does, an eight-year-old told researchers Easton and Dennis, "He runs the country, he decides the decisions he should try and get out of, and he goes to meetings and he tries to make peace and things like that. . . . Well, he's just about the boss of everything."[15] Children idealize the President as a trustworthy and benevolent person. Sixty percent of the second-graders in one study agreed with the statement that the President was "the best person in the world."[16]

Such early positive feelings toward the President are not based upon specific information. In one study, 96 percent of the fourth-graders were able to identify the President by name, but only 73 percent were able to give reasonably accurate responses concerning the duties of the President.[17]

Why are children's views of

I LIKE TO LIVE IN AMERICA

I like to live in America because you're free. What I meen is you can do what you want. You dont have to go to a certain church. Infact you dont even have to goto church. And in some other countries you have to plan ahead; like you would have to write in a year ahead and ask if you could go. Some countries dont have forests. And some countries dont have tv. And some countries have school on saturday etc.   Paul Hain

(Feb '78)

[14]See David Sears, "Political Socialization," in Fred Greenstein and Nelson Polsby, eds., *Handbook of Political Science*, Vol. 2 (Reading, Mass.: Addison-Wesley, 1975), pp. 118–19.

[15]David Easton and Jack Dennis, *Children in the Political System* (New York: McGraw-Hill, 1965), p. 145.

[16]Robert D. Hess and David Easton, "The Child's Image of the President," *Public Opinion Quarterly*, 24 (1960): 632–44.

[17]Fred Greenstein, "The Benevolent Leader: Children's Images of Political Authority," *American Political Science Review*, 54 (1960): 937.

	Response	Knox County	Chicago-area*
1. View of how hard the President works compared with most men.	Harder	35%	77%
	As hard	24	21
	Less hard	41	3
2. View of the honesty of the President compared with most men.	More honest	23%	57%
	As honest	50	42
	Less honest	27	1
3. View of the President's liking for people as compared with most men.	Likes most everybody	50%	61%
	Likes as many as most	28	37
	Doesn't like as many	22	2
4. View of the President's knowledge compared with most men.	Knows more	45%	82%
	Knows about the same	33	16
	Knows less	22	2
5. View of the President as a person.	Best in world	6%	11%
	A good person	68	82
	Not a good person	26	8

*Chicago-area data are from Hess and Easton, "The Child's Opinion of the President," *Public Opinion Quarterly* (1960).

NOTE: The children in the survey ranged from fifth-graders through eighth-graders.

SOURCE: Dean Jaros, Herbert Hirsch, and Frederic J. Fleron, Jr., "The Malevolent Leader: Political Socialization in an American Subculture," *American Political Science Review*, 62 (1968): 564–75.

political figures, such as the President, so idealized? One probable reason is that parents attempt to "sugar-coat" political explanations and shield children from the less attractive aspects of politics, even if the parents themselves are politically cynical.[18] Another reason may be that children screen out information which does not fit their benevolent view of the adult world. As one researcher suggests, they are almost continuously exposed to idealized adult roles such as "Our Friend the Farmer" and "How the Policeman Helps Us."[19] Others have suggested that children may have idealized views of political figures because they tend to project their good feelings toward their parents onto other authority figures.[20]

However, positive attitudes toward political figures are apparently culture-bound. A study comparing the attitudes of Appalachian

---

[18]Easton and Hess, "A Child's Political World," pp. 229–46.

[19]Greenstein, *Children and Politics* (New Haven: Yale University) p. 46.

[20] Harold D. Lasswell, *Power and Personality* (New York: Norton, 1948), pp. 156–57.

schoolchildren in Knox County, Kentucky, with the attitudes of the middle-class, urban children in Chicago concluded, "Children in the relatively poor, rural Appalachian region . . . are dramatically less favorably inclined toward political objects than are their counterparts in other portions of the nation."[21] In the Appalachian subculture, childrens' attitudes toward politics were more affected by their parents' cynicism than by their positive feelings toward their parents as authority figures.

Adolescence

When children reach adolescence, there is a marked change in their political orientations and outlooks. Prior to adolescence, "the child's sense of the political order is erratic and incomplete—a curious array of sentiments and dogmas, personalized ideas, randomly remembered names and party labels, half-understood platitudes. By the

By mid to late adolescence, in addition to having greater political knowledge, students begin to be more interested in politics and may begin to participate.

time adolescence has come to an end, the child's mind, much of the time, moves easily within and among the categories of political discourse."[22] The political attitudes of adolescents are more sophisticated. They are based less on emotion and more on knowledge. For example, while 60 percent of the second-graders in one study agreed with the statement that the President was "the best person in the world," only 2 percent of the eighth-graders chose that most favorable assessment.[23]

School and the media give adolescents increased exposure to

---

[21]Dean Jaros, Herbert Hirsch, and Frederic J. Fleron, Jr., "The Malevolent Leader: Political Socialization in an American Subculture," *American Political Science Review*, 62 (1968): 575.

[22]Joseph Adelson and Robert P. O'Neil, "Growth of Political Ideas in Adolescence: The Sense of Community," *Journal of Personality and Social Psychology*, 4, no. 3 (1966): 295–306.

[23]Hess and Easton, "The Child's Opinion of the President," pp. 632–44.

politics, which results in increased political knowledge. In fact, the political knowledge of older adolescents closely approximates that of young adults (measured roughly by the ability to name public officials).[24] By late adolescence (ages 15–18), young people have become more familiar with the general concepts of equality, human rights, and representation, in addition to specific political knowledge.[25] Further, as they approach voting age, young people become more interested in political events, and some begin to participate.[26]

Adulthood

Early socialization experiences continue to "significantly affect an individual's basic personality predispositions," and may affect political behavior.[27] As we pointed out earlier, some theorists believe that one of the main reasons for the stability of the American political system is the political obedience that young people learn during their early political socialization.

But political socialization occurs throughout a person's life, as we also noted earlier. For example, while the party loyalty that young people acquire is likely to continue through adulthood, people do change their party affiliations. Surveys indicate that 38 percent of eighteen-year-olds consider themselves to be "independents."[28]

People develop strong political orientations and outlooks around the age of thirty, as they assume the roles of taxpayers, parents, and community members.[29] The onset of old age and retirement may be another critical period of political socialization for adults. In addition, occupations, peers, the media, and political events and experiences continue to affect our political beliefs and behaviors throughout adulthood.

Political Information of Adolescents and Young Adults

	Percentage Who Know the Name of Each Official		
	13-year-olds	17-year-olds	Young Adults
President	94%	98%	98%
Vice-President	60	79	87
Secretary of State	2	9	16
Secretary of Defense	6	16	24
Speaker of the House of Representatives	2	25	32
Senate Majority Leader	4	14	23
At least one Senator from own State	16	44	57
U.S. Representative from own district	11	35	39

SOURCE: *National Assessment of Educational Progress*, Report 2: Citizenship: National Results—Partial (Denver and Ann Arbor, 1970), p. 37.

---

[24]*National Assessment of Educational Progress*, Report 2: Citizenship: National Results—Partial (Denver and Ann Arbor, July 1970), p. 37.

[25]Joseph Addison, "The Political Imagination of the Young Adolescent," in Jerome Kagan and Robert Coles, eds., *12 to 16 Early Adolescence* (New York: Norton, 1971).

[26]See Herbert H. Hyman, *Political Socialization* (New York: Free Press, 1959), pp. 51–68.

[27]Gabriel A. Almond and Sidney Verba, *The Civic Culture* (Princeton: Princeton University Press, 1963), p. 324.

[28]Paul Abramson, *Generational Change in American Politics* (Lexington, Mass.: Lexington Books, 1975), p. 53.

[29]Henry Valen and Daniel Katz, *Political Parties in Norway* (Oslo: Universitets-Forlaget, 1964), pp. 211–12.

HOW DO WE LEARN?

Our political orientations and outlooks may develop directly or indirectly, formally or informally, consciously or unconsciously. We learn about politics and about our role in the political system from families, schools, peers, the media, and from political events and experiences themselves.

Family

One of the most influential agents of political socialization is the family, particularly if the parents agree on and discuss political matters. Since the family generally determines what schools children will attend and what religious and other groups children are exposed to, it affects their political socialization indirectly as well.

The family particularly influences the way a child views ethnic, religious, racial, and other groups. It also has an important impact on children's feelings toward political authority and on their willingness

The family is the first social environment where political socialization occurs.

	Parents			
	Democrats	Independents	Republicans	Total
Democrats	32.6%	7.0%	3.4%	43.0%
Independents	13.2	12.7	9.7	35.7
Republicans	3.6	4.1	13.6	21.3
total	49.4	23.9	26.7	

SOURCE: After Table 2.1 in M. Kent Jennings and Richard G. Niemi, *The Political Character of Adolescence* (Princeton University Press, 1974), p. 39.

to comply with the rules, and it affects their identification with a particular party. Indeed, 59 percent of the students in one study identified with the same party as their parents. However, the family does not have as much influence on how a child feels about particular issues as it does in respect to political parties and political leaders.[30]

Whether or not a child grows up to be a political participant has much to do with the way the child's family functions and with the family's attitudes toward participation. American families are more egalitarian than European families; they tend to encourage independence and participation in family decision making. A child raised in such an American family is likely to develop a greater interest in and aptitude toward political participation later on.[31] It is interesting to note that student protestors of the 1960s tended to come from families that had an interest in politics. Indications are that these "activist" students came from liberal families and that their activism did not represent a rebellion against their parents but an attempt to live up to the politically active traditions of their families.[32]

Children who are raised in a lower-income home or who are members of a minority group are likely to be socialized differently. One study, for example, has shown that these children generally learn to accept authority more than do children from upper-income homes.[33]

---

[30]Dawson, Prewitt, and Dawson, *Political Socialization*, p. 48; Robert Weissberg, *Political Learning, Political Choice and Democratic Citizenship* (Englewood Cliffs. N.J.: Prentice-Hall, 1974), pp. 151–53; Angus Campbell, Gerald Gurin, Warren Miller, *The Voter Decides* (Evanston, Ill.: Row, Peterson, 1954), p. 99; and M. Kent Jennings and Richard G. Niemi, *Political Character of Adolescence* (Princeton: Princeton University Press, 1974), p. 78.

[31]See Richard M. Merelman, "The Development of Political Ideology: A Framework for the Analysis of Political Socialization," *American Political Science Review*, 63 (September 1969); and Kenneth Prewitt, *The Recruitment of Politicians* (Indianapolis: Bobbs-Merrill, 1970).

[32]See Kenneth Keniston, *Young Radicals* (New York: Harcourt, Brace and World, 1968); Richard Flacks, "The Liberated Generation: An Exploration of the Roots of Students Protests," *Journal of Social Issues*, 23 (1967): 52–75; and Kenneth Keniston, "You Have to Grow Up in Scarsdale to Know How Bad Things Really Are," *New York Times Magazine* (April 27, 1965).

[33]Greenstein, *Children and Politics*, pp. 155–56.

Schools

In some countries, such as the Soviet Union, political socialization in the schools is so purposeful and so formal that it can be called "political education."[34] Some political education also occurs in American schools. American children are taught to salute and pledge allegiance to the flag; to sing the "Star Spangled Banner"; to respect the history and traditions of our government; and to prefer the American form of government over all others. In one study, a second-grade student reportedly said, "Well, I wouldn't like to be an Englishman because I wouldn't like to talk their way, and I'd rather be an American because they have better toys, because they have better things, better stores, and better beds and blankets, and they have better play guns, and better boots, and mittens and coats, and better schools and teachers."[35] Children also learn to obey the political rules of majority control, partly through participation in traditional school elections. Even first-graders and second-graders strongly accept the idea that the losers in an election should lose gracefully and should support the winner.[36]

American schools teach in indirect ways as well. The teacher is an authority figure who is supposed to be obeyed. There are rituals that encourage consensus, and there is a general norm that rewards competitiveness in students. Students may also learn informally through extracurricular activities and organizations and through the school's general attitude toward participation. If students are allowed to take part in discussions and to participate in decision making, they are more likely to participate politically as adults.[37] But it has been found that civics courses in American schools emphasize obedience and conformity rather than active participation in politics.[38]

What students learn about politics from school may depend upon what economic class or racial group their school primarily serves. A jarring study by Edgar Litt found a great difference in political orientations taught in working-class, middle-class, and upper-class schools. Children in upper-class schools were socialized to become leaders, to see politics realistically as a process of conflict for power, and to understand that one can and should participate in politics. Middle-class schools put major emphasis on citizen responsibility rather than on the way political decisions are made. Working-class schools taught a mechanical, bland, and impersonal view of government. Worst of all, they did not encourage, or train their students for, political participation.[39]

The Relationship Between Civics Curriculum and Good Citizenship Attitudes Among Black and White Students

	Number of Civics Courses	
	0	1+
Blacks stressing:		
Loyalty	51%	75%
Participation	49	25
Whites stressing:		
Loyalty	46	39
Participation	54	61

SOURCE: Kenneth P. Langton and M. Kent Jennings, "Political Socialization and the High School Civics Curriculum in the United States," *American Political Science Review*, 62 (1968): pp. 852–67.

[34]See Merle Fainsod, *How Russia is Ruled* (Cambridge, Mass.: Harvard University Press, 1963).
[35]Hess and Torney, *The Development of Political Attitudes*, p. 32.
[36]Easton and Hess, "A Child's Political World," p. 236.
[37]Almond and Verba, *The Civic Culture*.
[38]Hess and Torney, *The Development of Political Attitudes*, pp. 126, 248.
[39]Edgar Litt, "Civic Education, Community Norms and Political Indoctrination," *American Sociological Review*, 28 (1963): 69–75.

Content Analysis of Civics Textbooks Used in Three Communities*

Political Dimension	Alpha*	Beta*	Gamma*
Emphasis on democratic creed	56%	52%	47%
Chauvinistic references to American political institutions	3	6	2
Emphasis on political activity, citizen's duty, efficacy	17	13	5
Emphasis on political process, politicians, and power	11	2	1
Emphasis on group conflict-resolving political function	10	1	2
Other	3	26	43

*Alpha was the upper-middle class community; Beta the lower-middle class community; and Gamma the working-class community. Percentages indicate the dominant emphasis in random samples of paragraphs from civics textbooks in use in the communities.

SOURCE: Edgar Litt, "Civic Education, Community Norms, and Political Indoctrination," *American Sociological Review*, 28 (1963): 69–75.

Chris Garcia has found that when Chicano children enter school they are not much different from their Anglo peers in their attitudes about politics and participation. But that attitudinal gulf eventually widens for Chicano children from lower-income and Spanish-speaking families. Older Chicano students are less motivated to participate in elections and feel more futility about politics in general. This finding reflects the negative influence of the school system itself or negative experiences the Chicano students have while attending school.[40] Researchers Langton and Jennings also discovered that exposure to civics courses has different effects for black and white students.

In his autobiography, the late militant black leader Malcolm X related an experience he had with his school guidance counselor. It parallels the experiences that many other minority children have had. When Malcolm X told his guidance counselor that he wanted to be a lawyer, he was told that that was not a "realistic goal." The counselor said, "You need to think about something you *can* be. You're good with your hands—making things. Everybody admires your carpentry shop work. Why don't you plan on carpentry? People like you as a person—you'd get all kinds of work."[41]

Still, most American students are taught idealized versions of our history and our political system. Indeed, some experts have argued that one of the principal reasons for the student protests of the 1960s was a sudden realization by young people that the "America is perfect" lesson they had been taught in the schools was not altogether true. Robert Hess has said that many students of the 1960s were

[40]See F. Chris Garcia, *Political Socialization of Chicano Children* (New York: Praeger Publishers, 1973), pp. 108–133.

[41]Malcolm X, *Autobiography of Malcolm X* (New York: Ballantine Books, 1965), p. 36.

What is the role of the schools in preparing citizens to participate in America's democracy? How well have they done—and how might they do better? These questions are addressed by Daniel Zwerdling, an advocate of "democracy at work":

Whenever workers join together to take part in decision-making, they inevitably confront a painful obstacle: even citizens in the United States have never learned how to work

VIEWPOINT
Education for Democracy

together and make decisions together, in an egalitarian, cooperative and democratic way. In fact, some researchers point out, the nation's schools teach citizens precisely the opposite: how to function obediently like cogs in a machine, and take orders from an infallible boss.

To most people raised on the rhetoric of democracy, it's shocking to think the schools might be training students to submit to a dictatorship. But self-management researchers—such as Jaroslav Vanek of Cornell University, and staff members of California's Center for Economic Studies—have shown convincingly why this is true.

From the first day in class to high school graduation, teachers bark the orders and students all obey. Teachers are the infallible experts: they tell the students what's important to learn, and what's not important, what to read and what to ignore. Students are encouraged to memorize isolated facts—what was the date of that Civil War battle?—but not to think creatively in broad concepts and patterns, which are more difficult to measure and grade. Teachers and their textbooks are infallible; students who challenge and question are not encouraged to be creative, but sent to the principal's office and punished.

The schools don't teach students to work cooperatively in groups but to work individually, on their own: students who try to solve test problems together are branded as "cheaters" and suspended or expelled. And students

quickly learn that the way to get ahead is to compete: they aren't evaluated by how much they have matured or grown, but by how they did in comparison with their peers. Students learn rapidly that people are *not* equal, and they get A's—or get flunked—to prove it.

Many educational critics argue that these kinds of traits in the schools are *accidental* byproducts of the school bureaucracy. The schools have lost sight of their purpose, these critics say, which is to prepare students for the democratic society outside. But researchers like Vanek and the staff at the Center for Economic Studies argue that the schools are doing their job: "One of the important functions of school is the preparation of the young for the world of work," the Center writes, "and it is the role of the school to prepare young people to accept the realities" of work.

Those realities, of course, are the typical American workplace, where workers are cogs in a machine and management barks the commands, where some workers get promoted and well paid while others are left behind. "The result," the Center says, "is that much of the alienation, boredom and other aspects of schools that we often think are unintended byproducts of 'mindlessness' . . . actually serve a function in conditioning workers to accept the boredom and alienation that seem to characterize a very high proportion of jobs."

What kind of school would prepare citizens for a democratic workplace? Teachers wouldn't be "experts" but resource people—people with experience and knowledge to share, but fallible people, just the same. Students would be encouraged to forget useless facts and to concentrate on patterns of consciousness instead—to think critically, to question, to challenge. Students would not be compared to others on the basis of standardized tests, but encouraged to work at their own pace and grow within themselves. And far from being encouraged to compete against fellow students, they would be taught to cooperate, and help each other. No one would get special rewards while other students were left behind—all would learn that each person is a unique individual with unique weaknesses and strengths.

SOURCE: Daniel Zwerdling, *Democracy at Work* (Association for Self-Management, 1978), back cover.

First-graders salute the flag.

disillusioned when they found that America's laws were not always fair or that justice did not always prevail. "The increasing volume of protest reflects the new realism," he wrote at that time. "Young people no longer find either government actions or social and economic reality congruent with the national ideology and rhetoric of morality."[42]

It is clear that schools have direct and indirect socializing effects on American young people. But there are significant differences in the lessons they teach, and these differences largely depend upon economic class and race.

Peers

Even as children, we tend to associate with people of similar ages and interests. Our *peers*, as they are called, have a great impact on each of us. According to Jean Piaget, a child psychologist, children do not fully develop morally unless they interact with peers.[43] There is some evidence that people who belong to few or no groups feel powerless toward politics; these people are less likely to participate politically.[44]

Some scholars believe that the peer group is becoming *the* most important agent of socialization as family and community influences weaken.[45] This is apparently less true in Europe, where the control of

[42]Robert D. Hess, "Political Socialization in the Schools," *Harvard Educational Review*, 38, no. 3 (Summer 1968).

[43]Jean Piaget, *The Moral Judgment of the Child* (London: Rutledge and Kegan Paul, 1932).

[44]See Almond and Verba, *The Civic Culture*; and Joel E. Aberbach, "Alienation and Political Behavior," *American Political Science Review*, 63 (March 1969): pp. 86–91; and Lester W. Milbrath and M. L. Goel, *Political Participation* (Chicago: Rand McNally, 1977), p. 77.

[45]See David Riesman, Reuel Denny, and Nathan Glazer, *The Lonely Crowd* (New Haven: Yale University Press, 1950).

the family continues to be strong even after young people have entered college.[46]

It is not difficult to understand the influence of peer groups in the political socialization process. They can offer acceptance and approval. They help an individual to establish his or her own self-image: "I must be a likeable person, because John seems to think so," or "I must be clever, because Mary laughed at my story."[47]

Some peer groups—such as the Soviet youth organizations, the Young Pioneers and the Komsomol—may pass along the prevailing political culture.[48] Government leaders may use youth peer groups to attack more conservative elements in the society, as was done with the "Red Guard" in China during the "Great Cultural Revolution of the 1960s."[49] In the United States, youth groups have not generally been so effective in consciously carrying out government aims or in teaching compliance to authority. (However, it cannot be denied that such groups as Boy Scouts and Girl Scouts, 4-H, and Junior Achievement, and others like them, reinforce politically relevant attitudes.)

As we have noted, merely belonging to a voluntary group may increase the likelihood that a person will participate in politics. This may be true not so much because the group actively teaches the idea of political participation, but because people who belong to groups often learn certain participatory skills, which they can also apply to political participation.[50] Even members of a nonpolitical organization are likely to feel more competent than those who belong to no organization. This is as true for adults as it is for young people. Adults who are allowed to participate in group decisions at work feel more able to participate politically outside the job.[51]

Peer groups can have an important impact on changing a person's political outlooks and political orientations. These changes are most likely to occur when a person passes from one stage of life to another. Peers increase their influence, as compared to parents and teachers, during a person's adolescence.[52] One famous study at Bennington College during the 1930s showed that students became considerably more "liberal" during their four years at Bennington as a result of their new peer relationships with other students and with faculty. A follow-up study found that this change in political viewpoint persisted

---

[46]David C. McClelland et al., "Obligation to Self and Society in the United States and Germany," *Journal of Abnormal and Social Psychology*, 56 (1958): 245–55.

[47]See George Herbert Mead, *Mind, Self and Society* (Chicago: Chicago University Press, 1934).

[48]See Merle Fainsod, *How Russia is Ruled* (Cambridge, Mass.: Harvard University Press, 1963), p. 293.

[49]See Robert J. Lifton, *Revolutionary Immortality* (New York: Random House, 1968), pp. 31–41.

[50]See Hess and Torney, *The Development of Political Attitudes in Children*.

[51]Almond and Verba, *The Civic Culture*, pp. 294–97.

[52]See James S. Coleman, *The Adolescent Society* (New York: The Free Press, 1961).

for at least twenty-five years thereafter.[53] Other scholars disagree about the lasting effects of college socialization and the influence of college attendance.[54] But there is little doubt that college peers have greater impact on political attitudes than does curriculum.[55]

Advocates of greater mass political participation would do well to encourage an expansion of the opportunities for interaction among young people of varied economic backgrounds. One study has shown that young people from working-class families who associate with upper-class youth are more positive about voting and political rights for minorities and more willing to question those in political authority.[56]

Social mobility may change one's peers and peer groups, and different peers, in turn, may have an impact on political orientations and outlooks. Studies indicate that when a person moves upward in the social scale, there is a tendency to adopt the views of the new peer group. Those who move downward on the social scale, however, continue to hold their former views. Similar studies show that a change in geographical location can also affect one's political outlooks and orientations by changing one's peer groups.[57] Similarly, entering a new occupation or profession provides a specialized set of new peers, who can alter political outlooks and orientations.[58] This finding probably explains why women who work outside the home usually become more politically active than those who do not.[59]

Peer groups provide important reinforcement of political attitudes throughout a person's life.

[53]Theodore M. Newcomb, "Attitude Development as a Function of Reference Groups: The Bennington Study," in Eleanor S. Maccoby *et al.*, eds., *Readings in Social Psychology*, 3rd ed. (New York: Holt, Rinehart and Winston, 1958), pp. 266–67; and Theodore M. Newcomb *et al.*, *Persistance and Change: Bennington College and Its Students After Twenty-five Years* (New York: John Wiley and Sons, 1967), pp. 39–40.

[54]See H. T. Reynolds, *Politics and the Common Man* (Homewood, Illinois: Dorsey Press, 1974), pp. 69–70.

[55]See Theodore M. Newcomb and Everett K. Wilson, *College Peer Groups* (Chicago: Aldine Publishing Company, 1966).

[56]See Kenneth P. Langton, *Political Socialization* (New York: Oxford University Press, 1969).

[57]See Herbert H. Hyman, *Political Socialization* (Glencoe, Illinois: The Free Press, 1959), pp. 109–111, 111–115.

[58]M. Kent Jennings and Harmon Ziegler, "Political Expressivism Among High School Teachers: The Intersection of Community and Occupational Values," in Roberta S. Sigel, *Learning About Politics* (New York: Random House, 1970).

[59]See Kristi Anderson, "Working Women and Participation, 1952–1972," *American Journal of Political Science*, 19 (August 1975): 439–55.

Media

Most Americans today could not say, as humorist Will Rogers once said, "All I know is what I read in the newspapers." Nor would it be correct for someone to say, "All I know is what I see on television." Nevertheless, American society is characterized by mass communications, and the media have an important impact on each of us. The major function of the media—television, newspapers, radio, and magazines—is to inform the public about newsworthy events. This function is particularly relevant to the development of public opinion, which will be discussed in the following chapter. Here we will focus on the socializing effects of the media in general and television in particular.

During the past twenty-five years, television has become increasingly important. Nearly every American family now has access to at least one television set—an instant "window on the world" that is unmatched by any other medium in terms of its immediacy and pervasiveness. A dramatic event can be viewed live and in color by millions of people. Even entertainment shows attract huge numbers of viewers. It has been estimated that young people between the ages of three and sixteen spend more time watching television than in school.[60]

The socializing effects of television have recently been investigated, but few firm conclusions have been drawn. It has been shown that exposure to violent TV shows may cause children to become less sensitive about violence and less willing to assist a victim of violence.[61] One important government study pointed to the portrayal of "middle-class life" on TV as a cause of dissatisfaction among poor and deprived people.[62] Thus, some "unintended" socialization occurs from watching television, and this may have important implications for the development of political outlooks and orientations.

TV can also be used for deliberate socialization. The example of programs like *Sesame Street* stand out, particularly in their ability to teach specific educational skills.[63] It is intriguing to note that, in one study of *Sesame Street*, the children who gained the most from viewing the program were previously low-scoring, Spanish-speaking children. These results have important implications for the teaching of the forms and rewards of political participation. But the potential of television or any of the media for deliberate socialization (and

Ernie and Bert, two of the leading Muppet characters created by Jim Henson for public television's "Sesame Street." Nearly 9 million pre-schoolers watch the show, which combines education and entertainment.

[60]See Wilbur Schramm, *Television and the Lives of Our Children* (Stanford, California: Stanford University Press, 1961), p. 30.

[61]See Victor B. Cline, ed., *Where Do You Draw the Line?: An Exploration into Media Violence, Pornography, and Censorship* (Utah: Brigham Young University Press, 1974).

[62]See *Report of the President's National Advisory Commission on Civil Disorders* (Washington, D.C.: Government Printing Office, 1968).

[63]Samuel Ball and Gerry Bogatz, *The First Year of Sesame Street: An Evaluation* (Princeton, N.J.: Educational Testing Services, 1970).

even for unintended socializing effects) is limited. The media are not "all-powerful," as we will see in the next chapter; but they do have important socializing effects on all of us. These effects merit continued research.

Political Events and Experiences

Political socialization never really ends. We are constantly exposed to new ideas, new events, and new experiences, all of which can change our political orientations and outlooks.[64] This is especially true of dramatic events, such as the Depression of the 1930s, the unrest of the 1960s, the Vietnam War, and most recently, Watergate. For example, Watergate increased children's negative attitudes toward the President of the United States; older children in particular had more negative feelings than younger children.[65] The effects of Watergate and other serious problems of the 1970s can be seen in the results of a study done in 1974. Sixty-three percent of the adults surveyed said they believed that government could be trusted "only some or none of the time"; ten years earlier, only 22 percent had felt that way.[66] Thus, because of political events and their own political experiences, adult Americans today are cynical about politics and government. Adults with low socioeconomic status are more cynical than those with high status.[67] Citizens with high socioeconomic status are more active in politics, and activists tend to have greater confidence in democratic procedures.[68]

IMPLICATIONS OF POLITICAL SOCIALIZATION

What do Americans believe? From time to time, efforts have been made to measure and report American attitudes in regard to democratic values, the American political system, political ideology, and political participation. In principle, almost all Americans show *support for the democratic values*, such as freedom of speech and the right of periodic elections. But when these principles are put to specific tests—when the question is whether an atheist or a commu-

---

[64]See Frank J. Sorauf, *Party Politics in America*, 3rd ed. (Boston: Little Brown and Co., 1976).

[65]See Dawson, Prewitt and Dawson, *Political Socialization*, p. 63–68.

[66]Survey Research Center for National Election Studies, "Decrease in Governmental Trust and Responsiveness: 1964–1974."

[67]Dawson, Prewitt, and Dawson, *Political Socialization*, p. 201.

[68]See Robert McCloskey, "Consensus and Ideology in American Politics," *American Political Science Review*, 58 (1964): 361–62; and Key, *Public Opinion and American Democracy*, pp. 536–38.

nist should be allowed to speak publicly, for example—Americans sometimes show less support for the democratic values.[69]

Some people have argued that elite groups, such as community leaders, are more supportive of democratic values.[70] But this assertion is disputed; it has been pointed out that even such elites as U.S. Supreme Court justices have sometimes expressed support for limitations on the freedoms of speech and press when they thought such freedoms might constitute a threat to American society.[71] In any event, studies indicate that support for freedom of speech seems to increase with educational level.[72] Regardless of educational level, people may temporarily express "antidemocratic" attitudes, as they did during the McCarthy era in the 1950s when many Americans believed that communists should not be allowed to speak on college campuses, but their behavior is more democratic than their attitudes.[73] This finding could indicate that some of the attitudes that people express do not reflect deeply held beliefs. It could also mean that an overall belief in democratic values, even in principle, serves as a greater constraint on behavior than on momentary verbal expressions of attitudes.

While Americans have apparently always had a healthy suspicion of authority, they have nevertheless expressed *support for the political system*. A study done in 1963 showed that 85 percent of the people in America were proud of America's political institutions; but only 46 percent of the people in Great Britain and 7 percent in Germany said that they were proud of their political institutions.[74] When asked what they were most proud of about their country, Americans were twice as likely to mention the political aspects of American society: the Constitution, political freedom, and democracy.

In the 1960s and 1970s, there was a marked decline in the percentage of Americans who were satisfied with the way our government is run and with their own ability to have some effect on government policies.[75] For example, while only 18 percent of the

---

[69]McCloskey, "Consensus and Ideology in American Politics," p. 366; James W. Prothro and Charles M. Grigg, "Fundamental Principles of Democracy: Bases of Agreement and Disagreement," *Journal of Politics*, 22 (Spring 1960): 276–94; Louis Harris, *The Anguish of Change* (New York: Norton, 1973), p. 278; James W. Prothro and Charles M. Grigg, "Fundamental Principles of Democracy: Bases of Agreement and Disagreement, *Journal of Politics*, 22 (1966): 276–94; and Samuel A. Stouffer, *Communism, Conformity and Civil Liberties* (Garden City, New York: Doubleday, 1955), pp. 29–42.

[70]See Stouffer, *Communism, Conformity and Civil Liberties*.

[71]See Robert W. Jackman, "Political Elites, Publics and Support for Democratic Principles," *Journal of Politics*, 34 (1972): 361–82; and Lance Bennett, "Public Opinion: Problems of Discrimination and Inference," in Susan Welch and John Comer, eds., *Public Opinion*, pp. 117–31.

[72]National Opinion Research Center, General Social Survey, "Education and Support for Freedom of Speech," 1972.

[73]Prothro and Grigg, "Fundamental Principles of Democracy," p. 294.

[74]Almond and Verba, *The Civic Culture*.

[75]Arthur H. Miller, Thad A. Brown, and Aldin S. Raine, "Social Conflict and Political Estrangement," paper presented at the Midwest Political Science Association meeting, Chicago, Illinois, May 3–5, 1973. See also Everett Carll Ladd, Jr., "What the Voters Really Want," *Fortune* (December 18, 1978), pp. 40–48.

Americans interviewed in 1958 agreed with the statement that "government is run for the benefit of the few," that percentage had increased to 67 percent by 1973.[76] Although 72 percent of the Americans interviewed in 1960 agreed with the statement that "people have some say about what the government does," that percentage had dropped to 49 percent by 1973.[77] Yet Americans seem to differentiate clearly between their general support for the political system and their feelings about the way the government is actually run. In a 1972 study, 86 percent of the Americans interviewed still agreed with the statement, "I am proud of many things about our form of government," instead of the statement, "I can't find much about our form of government to be proud of"; only 15 percent of them said that they felt a "big change" was needed in our form of government.[78]

In *political ideology*, Americans are more liberal than conservative. But this statement needs some explanation and further discussion. For one thing, there is the problem of how to define "liberal" and "conservative." Americans use these labels for themselves rather readily.[79] When people in one study were asked to locate themselves on a scale from "extremely liberal" on one end to "extremely conservative" on the other, 26.3 percent identified themselves as being either extremely conservative, conservative, or slightly conservative; 18.7 percent called themselves

Support for the political system has been a strong characteristic of Americans' political attitudes, regardless of the level of satisfaction people feel about "how the system is operating" at any particular time.

extremely liberal, liberal, or slightly liberal; 27 percent identified themselves as moderate.[80] Yet, despite the fact that the number of conservatives was greater than the number of liberals according to this study, more Americans favor social welfare programs than oppose them.[81] This has caused some authorities to say that Americans are "ideologically" conservative but "operationally" liberal. Americans support government programs in the fields of education, health, housing, unemployment, and poverty. When they

---

[76]Survey Research Center, Institute for Social Research, University of Michigan, 1958–1972; National Opinion Research Center, University of Chicago, 1973.

[77]Survey Research Center, University of Michigan, 1973.

[78]Jack Citrin, "The Political Relevance of Trust in Government," *American Political Science Review*, 68 (September 1974): 975

[79]See *Gallup Opinion Index* (December 1970), p. 7.

[80]National Election Study, University of Michigan Center for Political Studies, 1972.

[81]John G. Stewart, *One Last Chance: The Democratic Party, 1974–1976* (New York: Praeger, 1974), p. 107.

are asked general questions, however—such as whether they believe that "we should rely much more on individual initiative and not so much on governmental welfare programs"—they turn out to be conservative in principle.[82]

Political scientist Everett Carll Ladd, Jr., writes:

> *The American people have not become more conservative in their attitudes toward government. Indeed, the movement of opinion over the past decade or two is better described as liberal than conservative. Americans have become more demanding of governmental services, thus more liberal in the New Deal sense. On 'social issues,' too, we see a liberal drift. There has been a fairly dramatic growth of the pro–civil liberties and pro–civil rights positions; and there has been an erosion of many of the older codes of personal comportment, governing a range of such matters as premarital sex, abortion, and the use of marijuana. . . . Americans remain* institutional conservatives *and* operational liberals. *They want to conserve the basic institutional arrangements of their society—especially the constitutional order and the way the economy is organized—and they strongly back extensions of liberal social and economic programs.*[83]

WHAT'S RIGHT? WHO'S LEFT?

The problem of using standard labels like *liberal* or *conservative* is that liberalism/conservatism is not a simple, one-dimensional continuum. In fact, there is a series of distinct dimensions, and an individual may occupy quite different positions, relative to the general public, on each of them—"liberal," say, on domestic economic policy, "centrist" in foreign affairs, "conservative" on some cultural and lifestyle issues. It is perfectly possible—one is tempted to say *likely*—for a person to be moving in opposite directions at the same time.

For example, a 1976 *Washington Post* survey of leaders of the women's movement predictably found them well to the left on most social issues. Yet a deep respect for individual merit often pulled them perceptibly rightward. Thus 64 percent "strongly" disagreed that government should limit the amount of money a person is allowed to earn.

Similarly, U.S. professors feel strongly that there should be some sort of income "floor" for the disadvantaged; most tend to support preferential hiring for minorities. But 85 percent reject, in principle, government efforts to achieve equality of results instead of equality of opportunity.

In short, terms like liberal and conservative are *ideological* categories, but large numbers of people do not hold views that are as coherently packaged as the term *ideology* implies.

SOURCE: Everett Carll Ladd, Jr. "What the Polls Tell Us," *The Wilson Quarterly* (Spring 1979), p. 75.

According to Ladd, Americans' votes to cut taxes through such proposals as Proposition 13 in California show that they feel anxiety and frustration about soaring prices and taxes. At the same time, 67 percent of the American people favor a national health insurance program; 85 percent feel that the government should in some way help people to get low-cost medical care; 77 percent believe that the government should assure a job to everyone who wants to work; and 61 percent favor government-imposed wage and price controls.[84]

Warren E. Miller, Director of the University of Michigan Center for Political Studies, says that liberals outnumbered conservatives by a three-to-one ratio in 1978 and that "the twenty to thirty-five age group is an extraordinarily liberal group." According to Miller, President Ford overestimated the strength of conservatives in the

---

[82]Lloyd A. Free and Hadley Cantril, *The Political Beliefs of Americans* (New Brunswick, N. J.: Rutgers University Press, 1967), p. 13.
[83]Ladd, "What the Voters Really Want," p. 41.
[84]Ladd, "What the Voters Really Want," p. 44.

Percentage of Citizens Engaging in Twelve Different Acts of Political Participation

Type of political participation	Percentage
1. Report regularly voting in Presidential elections	72
2. Report always voting in local elections	47
3. Active in at least one organization involved in community problems	32
4. Have worked with others in trying to solve some community problems	30
5. Have attempted to persuade others to vote as they were	28
6. Have ever actively worked for a party or candidates during an election	26
7. Have ever contacted a local government official about some issue or problem	20
8. Have attended at least one political meeting or rally in last three years	19
9. Have ever contacted a state or national government official about some issue or problem	18
10. Have ever formed a group or organization to attempt to solve some local community problem	14
11. Have ever given money to a party or candidate during an election campaign	13
12. Presently a member of a political club or organization	8

SOURCE: Sidney Verba and Norman Nie, *Participation in America* (New York: Harper and Row, 1972), p. 31.

1976 election. "Conservatives are getting more attention these days because they're making the most noise," Miller claims.[85]

Until recently, political scientists maintained that elites were more ideologically consistent in their political beliefs than was the general public.[86] But in the last several years, that view has been increasingly challenged, and studies indicate that elites are no more organized along ideological lines in their consideration of political issues than are the masses.[87] In any event, it is clear that American public opinion in recent years has drifted toward the liberal end of the scale on a number of social and economic issues and that American voters are giving increasing weight to issues in making their voting decisions.[88]

Finally, how do Americans feel about *political participation*? On a theoretical level, both students and adults mention some form of active participation in political affairs as being a key characteristic of "a good citizen."[89] But political participation may be affected by people's feelings of "political efficacy," that is, the degree to which people believe that being politically active can "make a difference." According to Jennings and Niemi, "Feelings of political efficacy rise rapidly and continuously in the elementary grades. They level off about the time of high school and remain at a fairly constant level into the middle adult years. A decline in efficacy then sets in, although it is most noticeable among the better-educated. . . ."[90] One striking

---

[85]Quoted in A UPI story published in the *Chicago Sun Times* (January 18, 1978).

[86]See, for example, Phillip E. Converse, "The Nature of Belief Systems in Mass Publics," in David Apter, ed., *Ideology and Discontent* (New York: Macmillan Publishing Co., 1964).

[87]See Norman R. Luttbeg, "The Structure of Beliefs Among Leaders and the Public," *Public Opinion Quarterly*, 32, no. 3 (1968).

[88]Norman H. Nie, Sidney Verba, and John R. Petrocik, *The Changing American Voter* (Cambridge, Mass.: Harvard University Press, 1976), p. 348.

[89]Jennings and Niemi, *Political Character of Adolescence*, p. 121.

[90]Jennings and Niemi, *Political Character of Adolescence*, p. 281.

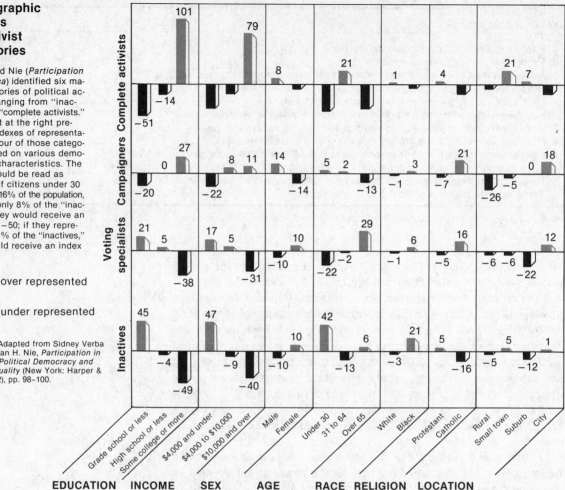

Demographic Profiles of Activist Categories

Verba and Nie (*Participation in America*) identified six major categories of political activism, ranging from "inactives" to "complete activists." The chart at the right presents "indexes of representation" in four of those categories, based on various demographic characteristics. The chart should be read as follows: If citizens under 30 represent 16% of the population, say, but only 8% of the "inactives," they would receive an index of −50; if they represented 24% of the "inactives," they would receive an index of +50.

◨ over represented

◼ under represented

SOURCE: Adapted from Sidney Verba and Norman H. Nie, *Participation in America: Political Democracy and Social Equality* (New York: Harper & Row, 1972), pp. 98–100.

Complete activists — *Campaigners* — *Voting specialists* — *Inactives*

EDUCATION: Grade school or less · High school or less · Some college or more
INCOME: $4,000 and under · $4,000 to $10,000 · $10,000 and over
SEX: Male · Female
AGE: Under 30 · 31 to 64 · Over 65
RACE: White · Black
RELIGION: Protestant · Catholic
LOCATION: Rural · Small town · Suburb · City

difference between voters and nonvoters is that nonvoters tend to feel that more serious changes are necessary to address the country's problems than are possible through electoral politics.[91]

Another indirect indication of how people feel about participation is their actual behavior. According to Verba and Nie, voting is the only form of political activity that more than one third of American citizens say they have performed. The differences in participation among various groups of Americans are pronounced. White high-school graduates are more likely to participate in political campaign activities than whites with less education, and white college graduates are even more likely to be active in campaigns. When whites and blacks who are not high-school graduates are compared, the whites

---

[91]*New York Times*/CBS News Poll, *New York Times* (November 16, 1976).

are more likely to engage in campaign activities; but whites and blacks with some college education are about equal. Generally, lower-income groups and minorities are less likely to be socialized to an understanding of the political process and a desire to participate in it.[92]

Thus, Americans support the democratic values, such as freedom of speech and democratic elections. They believe in the American political system, although they have become increasingly disenchanted with the way it operates. They are generally and increasingly liberal on social and economic questions. Finally, Americans' attitudes toward political participation vary according to income level and level of education.

CONCLUSION

None of us is born with political orientations and outlooks. We gain them as a result of political socialization, which begins at an early age and continues throughout our lives. Family, school, peers, the media, and political events and experiences may affect our beliefs about politics, the political system, and political participation. Americans from upper-class backgrounds often receive a different kind of socialization than Americans from lower-class backgrounds. Therefore, if political participation is to be increased, the economic and social status of minorities and people with low incomes must improve; and the public must take a greater interest in the socialization and education of all Americans to the norms of human rights and participation.

ADDITIONAL SOURCES

Almond, Gabriel A., and Sidney Verba. *The Civic Culture*. Princeton University Press, 1963.*

Barber, James David. *Citizen Politics*. Markham, 1969.*

Easton, David, and Jack Dennis. *Children in the Political System*. McGraw-Hill, 1969.

Greenberg, Edward S., ed. *Political Socialization*. Atherton, 1970.*

Hyman, Herbert H. *Political Socialization*. Free Press, 1969.*

Jennings, M. Kent, and Richard G. Niemi. *The Political Character of Adolescence*. Princeton University Press, 1974.

Lane, Robert E. *Political Life*. Free Press, 1969.*

Sigel, Roberta, ed. *Learning About Politics*. Random House, 1970.

Verba, Sidney, and Norman H. Nie. *Participation in America: Political Democracy and Social Equality*. Harper & Row, 1972.*

*Available in paperback edition.

---

[92]Sidney Verba and Norman H. Nie, *Participation in America: Political Democracy and Social Equality* (New York: Harper and Row, 1972), pp. 30, 98–100.

7 Public Opinion
What We Think About Politics

In 1978, opponents of the Equal Rights Amendment urged state legislators to defeat the proposed amendment because, they argued, "the people are against it." At the same time, ERA supporters, pointing to public opinion polls that showed a majority in favor of the proposed amendment, urged legislators to ratify it.

During the same year, the Soviet Union became increasingly active in the affairs of several African nations. President Carter warned the Soviets that "American public opinion" might turn against the policy of détente between the U.S. and the Soviet Union unless they reduced their involvement. He thus indicated that, whatever his own wishes, he might not be able to proceed with normalization of relations if public opinion opposed it.

At the same time, the President concluded negotiations for a new Panama Canal treaty and recommended it to the U.S. Sen-

President Jimmy Carter at a town meeting in Clinton, Massachusetts. Carter attended several such meetings, a traditional forum in which citizens express their opinions on public issues.

ate for ratification, even though public opinion polls showed that a majority of Americans opposed it. In this instance, President Carter was willing to go against public opinion. In the end, public opinion swung around to the President's position, and the Senate approved the new treaty.

These examples indicate some of the difficulties involved in talking about public opinion. Is there a single, identifiable "public opinion," for instance? Or are there "public opinions," as the debate over ERA suggests? Does public opinion guide public policy, as President Carter implied to the Soviets? Or do public officials try to influence public opinion, as Carter seemed to do with the Panama Canal Treaty? These are a few of the questions we will address in this chapter.

WHAT IS PUBLIC OPINION?

Put simply, *public opinion* is a verbal or written expression of individual attitudes on public issues. If people believe that handguns should be registered, for example, but make no effort to make that belief known, there is nothing we can point to as public opinion concerning handgun registration. If, however, people express their beliefs, and most of them support the idea of handgun registration, we can say that public opinion favors registration.

Sometimes there may not be one "public opinion" on a particular issue. When President Carter increased the amount of foreign beef that could be imported into the United States, saying that this action was necessary to hold down beef prices, most people may not have had an opinion one way or another. But some people certainly did have immediate opinions about the President's action. Cattle raisers strongly opposed it because it would hold down the price they would receive for their product. Some consumer groups supported the President's action because they hoped that it would lower the price consumers would have to pay for beef. Each of these groups constituted what is called a *special public*—a collection of citizens who are intensely interested in and aware of specific issues. The opinions of special publics are important to politicians because they vocalize their opinions and actively support them.

What do members of Congress mean when they say, "Public opinion in my district is strongly in favor of (or opposed to)" a certain issue? Perhaps they have recently returned from a trip to their districts, taken during one of Congress's periodic recesses, which enable members to return home and find out what their constituents are thinking (and do a little campaigning). Would the members have talked with *every* adult in their districts? Certainly not. Would they have talked to a representative sample of the people in their districts?[1] Probably not. They would have probably consulted with the special publics: business leaders, labor union officials, party or political activists, and others. They might also have had a sprinkling of contacts with ordinary people, received some letters from constituents, or read copies of local newspapers with editorials on the issue. None of this could be called a scientific sampling of opinion, although members of Congress may sometimes rely upon public opinion polls, which we will discuss later in this chapter.

---

[1] *A representative sample* is a small number chosen from a larger group, which exactly duplicates the characteristics of the whole group. This subject is discussed later in the chapter.

There are three main characteristics of public opinion.[2] One characteristic is *direction*, which indicates how an individual person stands on a particular issue or question. Direction in public opinion can be broken down in much more detail than simple "yes" or "no" answers. If the question is, "Should there be a tax cut?" public opinion could be gauged from the absolute "no" on one end of the scale to the plain "yes" on the other, with variations in between on how much the tax cut should be and who should get it. Another example is the question, "What is your political ideology?" At the far left would be those who think of themselves as radical, and at the far right, those who might be characterized as reactionary. In between would be liberals and conservatives, and in the middle, moderates. Direction, then, is a characteristic of public opinion that locates individual opinion on a scale between two extremes.

TWO VIEWS OF "PUBLIC OPINION"

In *Public Opinion* (Harcourt, 1922; Free Press, 1965) Walter Lippmann wrote that "public opinions" are the pictures people have "of themselves, of others, of their needs, purposes, and relationships." But pictures "which are acted upon by groups of people, or by individuals also acting in the name of groups, are Public Opinion with capital letters."

Writing in 1886, George Carslake Thompson cautioned, "It must be remembered that 'public opinion,' 'the will of the nation,' and phrases of that kind are really nothing but metaphors, for thought and will are attributes of a single mind, and 'the public' or 'the nation' are aggregates of many minds."

Another characteristic of public opinion is *intensity*. A member of Congress who knows that most people in his or her home district would say they are opposed to the Panama Canal Treaty would be unable to assess the meaning of that measurement of public opinion without also knowing how intensely people feel one way or another. Some opinion is not strongly held and will not be reflected in behavior such as voting. Public officials cannot often be sure they know what a majority of their constituents wants. Thus, they frequently conform to the opinions of those who feel intensely enough about an issue to express or demonstrate active support or opposition on the issue.

A third characteristic of public opinion is *stability*. Some opinions, such as support for a particular political party, seem to be fairly stable.[3] Stability is difficult to assess, however, because measurements of public opinion give us only an overall view of public opinion. We cannot always tell if there have been any shifts within those overall percentages. And individual opinions do seem to

---

[2]B. Berelson and M. Janowitz, eds., *Reader in Public Opinion and Communication*, 2nd rev. ed. (New York: Free Press, 1966).

[3]Angus Campbell et al., *The American Voter* (New York: John Wiley and Sons, 1964), p. 91.

change quite a bit from time to time.[4] We know, too, that there can be shifts in majority opinion on particular issues, as there was in regard to the Panama Canal Treaty. American public opinion has shifted on other issues, too, such as whether the People's Republic of China should be admitted to the United Nations.[5]

THE DEVELOPMENT OF PUBLIC OPINION

The source of the information that a person receives and the way the message is communicated have an important effect on the formation of public opinion. So, too, do the preconceptions of the recipient and the social setting.

First, consider the sources of information, particularly person-to-person communications, media messages, and statements by government and government officials. *Person-to-person* communications are more persuasive and are more likely to engender an opinion in a recipient or change the recipient's opinion than media communications are.[6] There are a number of reasons for this. First, personal contacts are usually "nonpurposive"—that is, not "sales pitches"—and they usually do not create the "sales resistance," which media contacts sometimes do. Second, person-to-person contacts have greater flexibility. The speaker can tailor the message to fit the individual and the individual's reaction. Third, in personal communication, there is a kind of "reward" system, in which the recipient of the message or information receives expressions of personal approval in return for various kinds of reactions. Fourth, there is usually more trust in a person-to-person exchange. Finally, there is usually more emotional involvement in person-to-person communication than in presentations by the media.

Nevertheless, the *media*, especially television, do influence public opinion. Exposure to the media increases political discussion, and political discussion tends to increase exposure to the media.[7] In addition, the media can to some extent set the agenda for political discussion and political campaigns. What subjects the media choose to question and to report about can, therefore, affect public opinion by emphasizing some issues over others.[8] In setting the agenda for

---

[4]See Phillip E. Converse, "Attitudes and Non-Attitudes: Continuation of a Dialogue," in Edward R. Tufte, ed., *Quantitative Analysis of Social Problems* (Reading, Mass.: Addison-Wesley, 1970).

[5]Hazel Erskine, "The Polls: Red China and the U.N." *Public Opinion Quarterly*, 35 (1971): 125–37.

[6]See Paul F. Lazarsfeld, Bernard R. Berelson, and Hazel Gaudet, *The People's Choice: How the Voter Makes Up His Mind in a Presidential Campaign* (New York: Columbia University Press, 1944); and Elihu Katz and Paul F. Lazarsfeld, *Personal Influence: The Part Played by People in the Flow of Mass Communications* (New York: Free Press, 1955).

[7]Robert E. Lane, *Political Life: Why People Get Involved in Politics* (New York: Free Press, 1959), pp. 275–98.

[8]Maxwell E. McCombs and Donald L. Shaw, "The Agenda-Setting Function of Mass Media," *Public Opinion Quarterly*, 36 (1972): 176–87.

political campaigns, for example, the media tend to emphasize the conduct of campaigns—the so-called horse-race aspect of campaigns—rather than the substantive issues.[9]

The news media are also very important sources of information upon which public opinion can be based, as we have seen with the shift of public opinion on the Panama Canal Treaty, the resignation of President Nixon, and the admission of the People's Republic of China to the United Nations.

Although there is a conservative bias to newspaper editorial pages (which, incidentally, only a small percentage of people read), newspapers, television, and radio nevertheless tend to give balanced news reports on particular issues and campaigns. But television networks seem to present similar *types* of stories. By leaving out the class or ethnic origin of social conflicts and social problems, they lessen the likelihood of political opinion forming along those lines.[10]

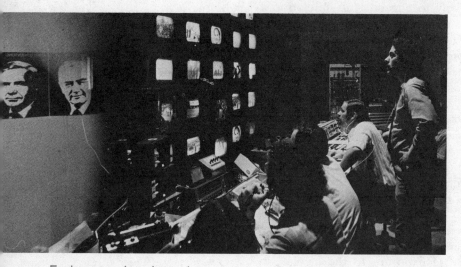

Engineers and producers in a television network's control booth sit before a bank of camera monitors. What the media choose to cover and how they cover it can be an important contributor to the development of public opinion.

We must also consider the impact of *government and government officials* on public opinion. The government may improperly attempt to mislead the public, as in the Watergate case. It may attempt to censor, and it may try to propagandize. The U.S. military establishment and some other government agencies spend a considerable amount of money on public relations efforts to affect American public opinion.

Government can affect public opinion in the United States by helping to shape what people think are "proper" beliefs, what they think the "facts" are, and what their "expectations" of the future are.[11] The government, for example, can provide cues as to which nations are our enemies and which are our friends. It can also influence public opinion by deciding what or how much information to release. Government officials, such as former Secretary of State Henry Kissinger, very often "leak" certain information to the press in order to influence public opinion on a particular issue, such as the Vietnam War.

It is important to note, however, that neither government efforts to influence public opinion nor media messages (including news reports

---

[9]Robert L. Stevenson et al., "Untwisting the News Twister: A Replication of Efron's Study," *Journalism Quarterly*, 60 (1973): 211-19.

[10]For a discussion of media bias, see Susan Welch and John Comer, eds., *Public Opinion* (Palo Alto, Calif.: Mayfield Publishing Co., 1975), pp. 277–89.

[11]Murray Edelman, *Politics as Symbolic Action: Mass Arousal and Quiescence* (Chicago: Markham Publishing, 1971).

Public Opinion on Policy Before and After Presidential Pronouncements on Television

Date	Presidential Action	Poll Results
July 26, 1963	Kennedy announces nuclear test ban treaty	Before: 73 percent favored After: 81 percent favored
Aug. 18, 1963	Kennedy appeals for tax cut from Congress	Before: 62 percent favored After: 66 percent favored
May 2, 1965	Johnson tells of Gulf of Tonkin incident and explains his Vietnam policy	Before: 42 percent positive on LBJ Vietnam policy After: 72 percent positive on LBJ Vietnam policy
Jan. 31, 1966	Johnson announces resumption of bombing of N. Vietnam	Before: 61 percent favored bombing resumption After: 73 percent favored bombing resumption
March 1968	Johnson announces end to bombing of N. Vietnam	Before: 40 percent favored After: 64 percent favored
June 7, 1968	Johnson endorses stronger gun control legislation	Before: 71 percent favored After: 81 percent favored
May 14, 1969	Nixon announces phased troop withdrawals from Vietnam	Before: 49 percent favored phased withdrawals After: 67 percent favored phased withdrawals
April 30, 1970	Nixon announces invasion of Cambodia	Before: 7 percent favored invasion of Cambodia After: 50 percent favored invasion of Cambodia
June 1971	Nixon announces 90 day price and wages freeze	Before: 50 percent approved of "freeze" After: 68 percent approved of "freeze"

SOURCE: "Public Service Time for the Legislative Branch," Hearings Before the Communications Subcommittee of the Committee on Commerce, 91st Congress, second session, pp. 20–21. June 1971 data are reported in *Gallup Opinion Index*, August 1971.

and paid advertising) can propagandize everyone to accept the views that propagandizers wish to inculcate. The reason for this is that the effect of the mass media depends upon the preconceptions and the social setting of the intended receiver of the media message.

An intended receiver's *preconceptions* may produce a "selective exposure" to the message. A person uninterested in politics and candidates may simply ignore political news and advertising. In addition, just as Republicans do not generally attend Democratic rallies, they may also skip over newspaper advertisements and television commercials concerning Democratic candidates.[12] People are, of course, sometimes exposed to messages that contradict what they already believe.[13] But the basic influence of the mass media is to reinforce, or strengthen, the orientations and outlooks that the receiver already possesses.[14] V. O. Key, Jr., has said that ". . . the major influence of the media upon political attitudes is by and large a reinforcement of the *status quo*."[15] In other words, during a political campaign, people tend to pay attention to the speeches of the candidates they already support.[16]

Major Sources of News, 1959–1976

Source*	1959	1967	1976
Television	51%	64%	64%
Newspapers	57	55	49
Radio	34	28	19
Magazines	8	7	7
Don't know, etc.	1	2	—

*Figures may add to more than 100% because of multiple responses.

SOURCE: Burns W. Roper, *"Trends in Attitude Toward Television and other Media: An Eighteen-year Review,"* A Report by the Roper Organization, Inc. (May, 1977), p. 3.

---

[12]See Joseph T. Klapper, *The Effects of Mass Communication* (Glencoe, Illinois: The Free Press, 1960), pp. 19–21.

[13]William J. McGuire, "The Nature of Attitudes and Attitude Change," in Lindsey Gardner and Elliott Aronson, eds., *The Handbook of Social Psychology*, 2nd ed., vol. 3 (Reading, Mass.: Addison-Wesley Publishing Co., 1969), pp. 218–21.

[14]Klapper, *The Effects of Mass Communication*, p. 15.

[15]V. O. Key, Jr., *Public Opinion and American Democracy* (New York: Knopf, 1961), p. 396.

[16]Dawson, Prewitt, and Dawson, *Political Socialization*, p. 197.

The receiver's preconceptions about a media message may also produce "selective perception and retention." Preconceptions can cause the receiver to distort or forget a message. In one interesting study of selective perception and retention, a white person was shown a picture of a white man holding a razor and having an argument with a black man. The first person was then asked to pass along this "rumor" or "gossip" to another person who had not seen the picture, and the gossip was then passed on to a series of others. In more than half of the cases in which this experiment was conducted, those telling the gossip reversed the roles of the attacker and the victim to make it a report about a picture of a *black man* holding a razor and having an argument with a white man.[17] Through selective perception, then, individuals may use propaganda for their own purpose, not for the purpose of the propagandist.[18]

The *social setting* of the receiver of a media message can significantly influence the message's effect on the receiver in two ways. First, if the message does not conform to the clearly stated views of a closely knit group to which the receiver belongs, the receiver is likely to reject it.[19] In one study, several small groups were shown three unequal lines and asked to determine which one was the same length as a fourth line. In each group, however, all the members except one had been coached by the researcher to give an incorrect answer. One third of those who had not been coached changed their correct answer to the incorrect answer of the majority.[20]

BECOMING AN OPINION LEADER

An essential part of any successful political campaign is convincing those who are already committed to the candidate that they have great influence, greater than they realize. Some of this convincing can be done person-to-person. "You are an opinion molder," we would tell our supporters over and over in countless meetings and coffees during the U.S. Senate campaign. "Most people do not have an opinion in this campaign yet, or if they do, they are too unsure of themselves to express it. They are afraid their candidate can't win, and they don't want to appear ridiculous. You *do* have an opinion, and if you're not afraid to express it—if you're not afraid to say, 'I know Fred Harris; he's the best man in this race; and he's going to win'—you'll make that prediction come to pass."

SOURCE: Fred R. Harris, *Potomac Fever* (Norton, 1977), p.34.

Second, the social setting of the receiver can influence the message's effect on the receiver through the "two-step flow of communications." Studies indicate that *opinion leaders*—people who tend to be more avid listeners or readers of the media, at least in matters that interest them—become an important part of the effect of the media message. They receive the message and then pass it along to others who are less avid readers or listeners. Thus, media influence is substantially the result of two steps: the media message is first

---

[17]Quoted in Ralph K. White, *Nobody Wanted War: Misperception in Vietnam and Other Wars* (Garden City, N.Y.: Doubleday and Co., 1970), pp. 262–64.

[18]Joseph Trenaman and Denis McQuail, *Television and the Political Image* (London: Methuen and Co., 1961), pp. 152–53.

[19]See Dorwin Cartwright and Alvin Zander, eds., *Group Dynamics*, 2nd ed. (New York: Harper and Row, 1960).

[20]Solomon E. Asch, "Effects of Group Pressure Upon the Modification and Distortion of Judgments," in Cartwright and Zander, eds., *Group Dynamics*, p. 191.

received by opinion leaders (who may be different for each matter or issue involved) and then relayed to others. These opinion leaders may become filters. About half of the people who learned about the assassination of President Kennedy did so directly from news reports in the media; but the other half received this news indirectly, through person-to-person reports from those who had heard the news directly.[21]

THE STRUCTURE OF PUBLIC OPINION

As we have seen, the process of forming (or failing to form) opinions about public issues is a very complicated matter. The individual, private attitudes that become a part of public opinion when they are publicly expressed are based upon a variety of factors. We know that the agents of political socialization—family, school, peers, the media, and political events and experiences—influence the formation and structure of public opinion. Similarly, public opinion is influenced by the information we receive, our preconceptions, and the social setting when we receive it. As we would expect from our discussion of political socialization, some groups have more influence on the way we receive and digest information than others. They are called *primary groups*: family, peers, and peer groups. Related groups can also be important in the formation of opinion, depending upon how closely we identify with them. They include class status, occupation, age, the region of the country where one lives, race, religion or ethnic group, and political party.

If people are asked a question having to do with economic self-interest, their responses will probably be influenced by their class status. Thus, when the Michigan Survey Research Center asked people to react to the statement, "The government should see to it that people can get doctors and hospital care at low cost," considerably more than half of those whose annual family income was under $6000 agreed with that statement, while slightly less than 42 percent of those whose annual family income was more than $20,000 agreed.[22] However, people do not always act or vote exactly on the basis of their economic self-interest because they may not know where their economic interests lie or because other issues—war and peace or law and order, for example—may seem more important to them at the moment. But three fourths of all Americans can identify the socioeconomic class they fit into.[23] Class identification affects the way people feel about some political issues, such as guaranteed employment.[24]

---

[21]Paul F. Lazarsfeld, Bernard Berelson, and Hazel Gaudet, *The People's Choice*, 3rd ed. (New York: Columbia University Press, 1968).

[22]Michigan Survey Research Center, 1968, quoted in Bernard C. Hennessy, *Public Opinion* (North Scituate, Mass.: Duxbury Press, 1975), p. 214.

[23]Campbell, et al., *The American Voter*, pp. 102, 106–7.

[24]Richard Centers, *The Psychology of Social Classes* (Princeton: Princeton University Press, 1949).

Similarly, one's occupation or profession can be an important factor in the formation of political opinions. For example, a poll in late 1977 showed that Americans' occupations affected their thoughts about energy problems. Only 31 percent of all household heads who were polled agreed with the statement that "the energy crisis is extremely serious," while 54 percent of all business executives and 65 percent of all government officials surveyed agreed with that statement.[25]

Age can also have an impact on the formation of opinion. In the poll discussed above, the respondents were also asked who they would be most likely to believe if there was a sudden new energy problem. Sixty percent of the people under thirty-five said they would be most likely to believe "environmentalists"; only 22 percent of them responded "government," and 18 percent answered "business." But for respondents thirty-five years of age or older, only 35 percent said they would be most likely to believe "environmentalists"; 33 percent said "government," and 32 percent responded "business."[26] As we pointed out in Chapter 4, older and younger women have widely different opinions about women's liberation issues and efforts.

Where we live can be important. In the past, there were greater regional differences in American opinion than there are today. Opinion in the South was particularly distinct. It was more conservative, especially on racial issues. In recent years, regional differences in American public opinion have declined, although the South still remains more conservative on racial equality.[27] The election of a Southerner, Jimmy Carter, to the Presidency in 1976 was widely hailed as concrete political evidence that regional differences in American public opinion have declined. The increased movement of people from one region of the country to another may have helped to blur the differences in regional opinion. The availability of national television programming in all parts of the country may also have played a part.

People who live in the central cities tend to be more liberal on political issues than people who live in rural areas or suburbs. This difference, however, may be partly a result of the socialization and filtering influences of the groups or groupings where they live.

Race, religion, or ethnicity can influence our opinions. This is partly a result of historical factors. Catholics, for example, first came to the United States in large numbers at a time when the Democratic party was more willing than the Republican party to act on social and economic needs. In some ways, these Catholics were as much a minority group as a religious group because of discrimination against them. Signs saying "No Irish Need Apply" were a common sight in

---

[25]Marketing Concepts Incorporated Poll for *U.S. News and World Report* (October-December 1977), quoted in *Public Opinion* (May-June 1978), p. 27.

[26]Marketing Concepts Poll, in *Public Opinion* (May-June 1978), p. 27.

[27]See Robert S. Erikson and Norman R. Luttbeg, *American Public Opinion: Its Origins, Content, and Impact* (New York: John Wiley, 1973).

places like Boston in the early 1900s.[28] The same might also be said about many American Jews, who have a group memory of discrimination against them in this country and genocide abroad.[29] Because of their history, members of racial, religious, or ethnic groups may continue to maintain distinctive political opinions even after they have become fairly well integrated into the larger society and have made substantial gains in education, income, and status.[30] Thus, Catholics tend to be more liberal than Protestants today. Jews tend to be more liberal than Catholics, even though Jews enjoy a much higher socioeconomic status than Protestants and even though Catholics have now more than caught up with Protestants in socioeconomic status.[31]

Religious beliefs themselves can affect opinion aside from the hangover effect of minority status. The fact that people are members, especially if they are practicing members, of a particular religious faith can have considerable influence on how they feel about a particular issue, such as abortion or pornography.

As we might expect, black voters in America generally support action on social and economic issues. As we noted in Chapter 4, their perception of the amount of progress that is being made on racial matters differs from that of whites. In 1978, 70 percent of the urban white people interviewed in a poll said that they believed a lot of progress had been made toward eliminating racial discrimination in America. Only 47 percent of the blacks who were interviewed agreed, a marked drop in black optimism from a poll taken in 1968.[32]

The ethnicity of other groups can also influence their political opinions. Despite a similarity in socioeconomic status, the descendants of recent immigrants to the United States are decidedly more liberal than those whose ancestors have been here for a longer period. This result is related also to the religion, geographic location, and urban residency of these groups.

Party identification also influences political opinions. To some degree, party identification overlaps with the other factors we have been discussing. For example, Catholics, Jews, black people, relatively recent immigrants to the United States, working-class people, people of lower socioeconomic status, and urban residents are likely to be Democrats. Protestants, rural and suburban dwellers, and people with upper middle- and upper-income levels are more likely to be Republicans.

---

[28]See Andrew M. Greeley, "Political Attitudes Among American White Ethnics," *Public Opinion Quarterly*, 36 (Summer 1972): 213–21.

[29]See Lawrence E. Fuchs, *The Political Behavior of American Jews* (New York: Free Press, 1956); and Lawrence E. Fuchs, "American Jews and the Presidential Vote," in Fuchs, ed., *American Ethnic Politics* (New York: Harper and Row, 1968), pp. 142–62.

[30]See Michael Parenti, "Ethnic Politics and the Persistence of Ethnic Identification," *American Political Science Review*, 61 (1967): 717-26.

[31]See Lloyd Free and Hadley Cantril, *The Political Beliefs of Americans* (Rutgers: Rutgers University Press, 1968).

[32]CBS-New York Times Survey, *New York Times* (February 26, 1978).

Party identification is a fairly stable factor in a person's life. It can be an important filter through which people receive information and form opinions. However, the party apparatus itself does not necessarily furnish the information to the individual. If the Democratic party is identified with national health insurance, for example, and a person calls himself or herself a Democrat, party identification alone may tend to cause the person to be favorable toward national health insurance. We will discuss this more in Chapter 9.

THE MEASUREMENT OF PUBLIC OPINION

We often see statements like the following in newspapers: "The candidate's speech was interrupted twenty-two times by applause." Or, we may hear a television commentator say, "The President's motorcade had to slow to a crawl because of thousands of enthusiastic spectators who surged into the streets." These examples involve rough attempts to measure and report one aspect of public opinion—crowd support.

Such indications of crowd support often involve manipulation. People on a candidate's or official's staff who do "advance" work—make advance arrangements—go to great pains to turn out large and enthusiastic crowds, to indicate strong and widespread popular support for their employers. For that reason, reporters, especially national reporters who follow presidential campaigns, tend to be wary of manufactured crowds and crowd response.

There are more accurate ways to measure public support for a candidate or a President—or to measure public opinion generally—than by estimating the size of a crowd or by counting the number of times crowd members applaud during a speech.[33] How do people in public office gauge public opinion? Very often, they do so in a most informal and unscientific way. Public officials usually cannot afford to pay for scientific public opinion polls conducted on a regular basis. So, most of them use the "ear-to-the-ground" approach; they attempt to get a general "sense" of public

The Polls—How They've Changed!

In the 1787 Massachusetts gubernatorial election John Hancock, the Revolutionary War hero, defeated the incumbent Governor James Bowdoin, the suppressor of Shays' Rebellion. Shortly after the election, a Boston newspaper published the following analysis of the vote:

	For Mr. B	For Mr. H
Usurers	28	0
Speculators in Publick Securities	576	0
Stockholders and directors of the M-tts B-k	81	0
Persons under British influence	17	0
Merchants, tradesmen, and other worthy members of society	21	448
Friends to the Revolution	0	327
Wizards	1	0

SOURCE: Mark R. Levy and Michael S. Kramer, *The Ethnic Factor* (Institute of American Research/Simon and Schuster, 1972), p. 225.

---

[33]For a general discussion of the measurement of public opinion, see Welch and Comer, eds., *Public Opinion*, pp. 351–409; and Hennessy, *Public Opinion*, pp. 37–129.

opinion from their mail, from telephone conversations, and from personal visits to their home states or districts. This method of measuring public opinion, however, is far from accurate.

Another approach used to measure public opinion, begun by some American newspapers in the 1800s, is the "straw poll," but this, too, is an unscientific method. The straw poll uses written ballots or personal interviews to ask questions of people who have not been randomly selected by a scientific process. For example, a Cleveland newspaper might send a reporter out on a downtown street to ask the first three hundred people that he or she encounters, "Who is your choice in next Tuesday's election for mayor?" This type of poll would obviously be weighted in favor of the opinions of the people who happened to be in downtown Cleveland on that day and at the time and would give no weight to the opinion of those who were at home or in other areas of the city. Thus, straw polls can be as unsatisfactory as the "ear-to-the-ground" method for measuring public opinion.

In the 1930s, a number of people became interested in *scientific polling*. They began to develop a methodology that could produce reliable measurements of public opinion. The American Institute of Public Opinion was formed in 1933 to promote and improve scientific polling. Today many reputable private organizations regularly conduct public opinion polls for newspapers and television. Other respected public opinion research groups are affiliated with various universities, and a number of reliable commercial firms do polling for candidates and other clients. These pollsters seek to base their measurement of public opinion upon scientific methods and mathematical probabilities.

A scientific poll is an attempt to sample the opinion of a particular population, or *universe*. Are we interested in the views of the students in Political Science 200? Do we want to know what adults in New York City think about a particular candidate? Or are we interested in the opinions of farmers in the state of Iowa?

If the universe is small enough—the fifty students who are enrolled in Political Science 200, say—the public opinion of the universe can be measured by interviewing each member of it. Usually, though, the universe is too large to allow the questioning of every member. In that case, the measurement of public opinion depends upon securing a *representative sample*. Representative sampling involves two questions: Who will be interviewed? How will they be interviewed? Random sampling, or probability sampling, is the method most often chosen in scientific polling to determine who will be interviewed. *Random sampling* involves interviewing a randomly selected number of people within a particular geographical area. In a random sample, a pollster tries to select interviewees in such a way that each member of the universe has an equal chance of being chosen for an interview. Federal census tracts (units used in taking the national census) are frequently the basic geographical unit within which scientific pollsters sample opinons. The census provides information about the characteristics of the people who live in a particular census tract. For example, it includes statistics on race, income, and average age.

An alternative to sampling is the *quota method*. This approach involves interviewing a certain number of people from various ethnic, religious, age, sex, and other groups. But the quota method is not as reliable as random sampling because it leaves too much discretion to the interviewer to choose which people will be interviewed within each quota.

Sample size is an important consideration in scientific polling. People are usually surprised to find that a sample can be representative even though it is relatively small. For the whole United States—about 220,000,000 people—a properly selected random sample of only 1500 persons will produce accurate responses (results that can be duplicated) within three percentage points 95 percent of the time. To reduce this sampling error of 3 percent to 1 percent, it would be necessary to increase the size of the sample from 1500 persons to 9500 persons.

The method that pollsters use to conduct interviews can affect the accuracy of the responses they receive. The most reliable method is the face-to-face interview. An interviewer using this method can evalute the person being interviewed and can ask immediate follow-up questions if the truthfulness or intensity of the opinion expressed is in doubt. In addition, it is much more difficult for a person to evade a question when it is asked face-to-face. A telephone interview is generally less reliable than a face-to-face interview, but is usually more reliable than a poll conducted by mail.

In scientific polling, the wording of questions is highly important. Scientific pollsters attempt to word questions in a way that will not indicate a bias, or desired answer. Value-laden words must be left out or used very carefully. For example, suppose we wanted to measure American support for the Bill of Rights protection against self-incrimination. The wording of the question could make a great difference in the result obtained. One way to ask the question might be: "Do you believe that a person charged with murder should be able to thwart lawful authority by stubbornly refusing to answer a single question concerning the crime?" The wording of the question and the use of such value-laden words as "thwart lawful authority" and "stubbornly refuse" would bias this question in favor of a negative answer. Another way of asking the same question might be: "Do you agree with the hard-won sacred Bill of Rights protection against self-incrimination, which was adopted to prevent torture and the third degree?" This question also includes a number of value-laden words, such as "sacred," and it would be biased in favor of an affirmative answer. A neutral way to ask the question might simply be: "Do you believe that a person charged with a crime should have the right to remain silent?" These are fairly simple examples, but they illustrate that the way a question is asked may tend to elicit a particular kind of response. Thus, scientific pollsters must be very careful about the wording of questions.

The type of answers allowed in a poll can help to gauge the intensity of the feelings of a person being interviewed. If a poll has asked only for a "yes" or "no" answer to the question, "Do you favor quotas to aid minority hiring?" it will be impossible for a person to tell from the poll results how strongly the respondent feels about the issue. If, on the other hand, the people being interviewed are given a choice between "strongly opposed" or "strongly in favor," with several gradations in between as well as a "no opinion" option, it will be possible to tell much more about the intensity of the respondents' opinions.

Scientific polling also requires careful selection of the interviewer. Even when the poll questions have been carefully prepared to avoid bias and value-laden words, bias may occur in the poll because of the interviewer's tone of voice or mannerisms.

A scientific poll, then, is based on a representative sample of a particular universe. Pollsters must give special attention to random sampling (including the decisions concerning who will be interviewed and how the interview will be conducted), sample size, question wording, and the selection and training of the person who will do the polling interview.

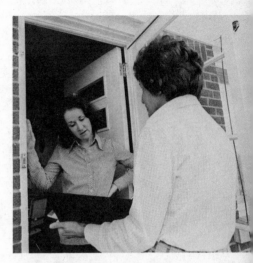

Random sampling, sample size, question wording, and selection and training of interviewers are important considerations in scientific polling.

Evaluating Poll Results

How can the results of even a carefully conducted scientific poll be evaluated? For example, what do people mean by answering "don't know" or "undecided"? Are they really undecided, or do they not care one way or the other? What the pollster does with these kinds of responses—whether they are allocated to one side or another of an issue, whether they are left out of the poll results altogether, or whether they are simply listed in an "undecided" column—is important in understanding the meaning of the poll results. Critics say that polls tend to underestimate the number of the undecideds because the nature of the polling process itself forces people to give answers to questions about which they may not have formed opinions.

Careful pollsters design several ways of asking the same question to determine whether the respondent understands the question, has an interest in it, and has an opinion about it. These procedures allow pollsters to make certain judgments about an answer of "undecided" or "don't know." For example, suppose a poll shows that 30 percent of those interviewed favor one candidate, 30 percent favor another, and 40 percent say they are "undecided." In this instance, the "undecideds" hold the key to an accurate appraisal of public opinion in the race. By other questioning, the pollster might be able to discover whether or not the "undecideds" are actually leaning toward one candidate or another and whether they will go to the polls and vote.

How reliable are the polls? The best are fairly reliable. For example, polls have shown remarkable consistency in interview responses on a variety of issues through the years.[34] However, polls taken during a political campaign purport to gauge opinion only at the time the poll is taken; thus, they do not necessarily predict the eventual election results. Regarding presidential campaigns, Elmo Roper, a well-known pollster, states, "[I am] dismayed at the weight given to preconvention polls which are in my opinion little more than a name-familiarity game, but which are often accepted as gospel evidence of the ability to win in November."[35]

Polls taken during presidential campaigns are well known to the public. These polls have been notably accurate over the years, with two major exceptions. In 1936, *Literary Digest* mistakenly predicted that Republican presidential candidate Alfred Landon would decisively triumph over President Franklin D. Roosevelt. *Literary Digest* based this prediction on mail replies from nearly two and one-half million Americans. Polling by mail is especially subject to error, primarily because the results are based only upon the response of those who decide to reply. But the main trouble with the *Literary Digest* poll of 1936 was that the magazine had mailed its questionnaire to names on a list of Americans who had telephones and automobiles, an unrepresentative list in the 1930s, when many Americans had neither.

After the biggest political upset in modern history, President Truman showed off the early edition of a Chicago newspaper proclaiming Thomas E. Dewey to be the victor on the basis of late poll results and early election returns.

Another spectacular failure in the polls took place in the 1948 presidential race between Thomas E. Dewey, the Republican candidate, and President Harry S. Truman. Although there was apparently a late shift in the undecided vote to Truman,[36] the major pollsters had mistakenly decided very early that Dewey would win. They repeated that prediction in their final forecast, much to their later embarrassment. Since the Truman-Dewey race of 1948, national pollsters have improved their methods and have become more cautious in their predictions.[37] In six presidential and congressional elec-

[34]John E. Mueller, *War, Presidents and Public Opinion* (New York: John Wiley, 1973), pp. 4–7.
[35]Elmo Roper, "Polls and Sampling," *Saturday Review* (October 8, 1960), p. 58.
[36]See Welch and Comer, eds., *Public Opinion*, p. 358.
[37]See Harold Mendelsohn and Irving Crespi, *Polls, Television, and the New Politics* (Chandler Publishing Co., 1970).

tions from 1950 to 1960, the Gallup Poll averaged an error of less than 1 percent. In the 1964 presidential election, the Gallup Poll's error was 2.6 percent; in 1968, 0.4 percent; and in 1972, it was 0.2 percent.[38] In 1976, both the Gallup Poll and the Louis Harris Poll declared that the presidential campaign of Jimmy Carter and President Gerald Ford was too close to call. Each assigned 46 percent of the vote to Jimmy Carter, and each stated that an unusually large number of people were still undecided during the last days of the campaign. Jimmy Carter won the election with 51 percent of the vote, precisely as the Roper Poll had predicted.

Polls and Campaigns

Every presidential campaign since 1960 has placed considerable emphasis on polling for determining campaign strategy and tactics. Jimmy Carter, for example, relied heavily on the findings and conclusions of his pollster, Pat Caddell. Caddell had gained a national reputation for polling accuracy four years earlier when he had done the polling in George McGovern's unsuccessful 1972 presidential campaign. Carter was so impressed by Caddell's ability to gauge public opinion during the 1976 campaign that he continued to rely upon Caddell even after becoming President. Polling is now used in most gubernatorial and senatorial campaigns.

Some people have expressed concern about the effect of publishing poll results during a campaign. They argue that the publication of the results of a public opinion poll may itself affect public opinion and may alter voting behavior in a political campaign. Political candidates are usually especially upset by the announcement of poll results showing them behind their opponents.

Some political observers claim that the publication of polls during a political campaign can create a "bandwagon effect," which influences voters to vote for the candidate who appears to be winning. Interestingly, other people fear that the publication of polls before an election may cause an "underdog effect," which occurs when voter sympathy causes them to vote for the candidate who is behind. Both concerns seem to be groundless. Joseph Klapper, a former professor and now director of social research for CBS, states:

> *There is generally about a 1% bandwagon effect and 1% underdog effect, and they cancel each other out. People tend to make their voting decisions, not because of what the polls say but because of how their family and friends and close associates vote or because of their social background, their party affiliation or their feelings on the issues and the personalities of the candidates. In fact, most studies show that people very often aren't even aware of what the polls show.[39]*

---

[38] See Hennessy, *Public Opinion*, pp. 103–4.
[39] David Shaw, "Political Polls: How to Avoid the Distortions," *Los Angeles Times* (January 3, 1975).

Although the publication of opinion polls during a campaign may not have a direct effect on the voters, published poll results certainly can have an *indirect* influence.[40] A candidate who is running well in the polls will have a much better chance of raising campaign funds and securing campaign volunteers than will a candidate who is running poorly in the polls. Polls can also affect the morale of campaign staff and volunteers, lessening or increasing their enthusiasm and productivity. In addition, campaign strategy can be influenced by the polls. Presidential candidates, for example, may decide to bypass states where poll results are unfavorable to them and campaign instead in states where the polls are favorable. Polls may have the ultimate effect on campaign strategy: a bad poll may cause a person to decide not to run at all or may cause an active candidate to withdraw.

Polls have an additional indirect effect because they are taken seriously by the press, which sometimes makes them become almost self-fulfilling prophecies. One candidate in a Massachusetts race complained that polls showing him behind his opponent "made it impossible . . . to run a good campaign." He said that the polls had killed morale and had caused contributions to his campaign to decrease dramatically. "In my race," he continued, "every time I went into a new town to talk to the local newspaper, they'd wave the Boston Globe poll at me and say I didn't have a chance." Pat Caddell, the pollster for Democratic presidential candidates George McGovern in 1972 and Jimmy Carter in 1976, has said that the effect of polls on the press is especially significant in California, a key state in presidential campaigns. "I've never seen a press corps—especially TV—so geared to polling as they are in California," Caddell says. "It becomes a chicken-and-egg syndrome. If the polls say you aren't a major candidate, you can't get good coverage. But if you don't get the coverage, you can't become a major candidate."[41]

If polls do indirectly affect election results, what should be done about them? U.S. Representative Lucien N. Nedzi of Michigan has proposed a federal law that would require certain information about how and when an opinion poll is taken to be published along with any publication of the poll results.[42] But critics of the Nedzi bill have raised two serious objections to it. First, they say it would be difficult to define "opinion poll" by law in a way that would not include mere "impressionistic reporting." If a television interviewer talked with a few people in the streets and then on that basis made a statement on the evening news something like this: "It is my opinion, based upon some interviews, that Minnesotans are opposed to the school bond

---

[40]Shaw, "Political Polls: How to Avoid the Distortions"; and Welch and Comer, eds., *Public Opinion*, p. 359.

[41]See Shaw, "Political Polls: How to Avoid the Distortions."

[42]For hearings on the Nedzi bill see *Public Opinion Polls; Hearings before the Subcommittee on Library and Memorials of the Committee on House Administration*, September 19–21 and October 5, 1972 (Washington D.C.: U.S. Government Printing Office, 1973).

issue," would that be an "opinion poll" subject to regulation? Second, critics of regulation claim that regulation of polls by law would violate the First Amendment freedoms of speech and press. They argue that anyone should be allowed to measure public opinion and say whatever he or she thinks public opinion is, even if the measurement is inaccurate.

Two other approaches for regulating polls are based upon voluntary compliance rather than regulation by law. The public interest group Common Cause regularly suggests that whenever candidates in any race release any part of an opinion poll that they have privately taken, they should release the entire poll to give the public a better chance to evaluate it. The American Association for Public Opinion Research has recommended that pollsters voluntarily comply with the basic requirements of the Nedzi bill when they release poll results. This organization of pollsters suggests that the minimum requirements of disclosure should include the identity of the poll sponsor; the exact wording of the questions asked; a definition of the poll sample; the sample size; the allowance for sampling error; the interviewing methodology (whether by mail, telephone, street corners, or door-to-door); the timing of the interviewing in regard to relevant events (for example, was it before or after the President's speech on Africa?); and the results that are based on parts of the sample rather than on the total sample (for example, whether only likely voters were included).[43]

THE ROLE OF PUBLIC OPINION IN A DEMOCRACY

The writers of the *Federalist* declared that "all government rests on opinion." Much earlier, Niccolò Machiavelli had written that public opinion is important even for the government of a nondemocratic state. He said that a ruler "who has the masses hostile to him can never make sure of them, and the more cruelty he employs the feebler will his authority become; so that his best remedy is to try and secure the good will of the people."[44] In the United States, where the government is based upon consent of the governed, public opinion is even more important. James Bryce, a perceptive English observer of the American scene in the late nineteenth century, wrote that "public opinion stands out in the United States as the great source of power, the master of servants who tremble before it."[45] V. O. Key, Jr., defined public opinion as "those opinions held by private persons

---

[43]American Association of Public Opinion Research, "Standards for Reporting Public Opinion Polls," (September 27, 1968).

[44]Niccolò Machiavelli, *The Discourses* (New York: Random House, Modern Library Edition, 1940), p. 162.

[45]James Bryce, *The American Commonwealth,* Vol. 1 (Putnam, Capricorn Books, 1959), p. 296.

which governments find it prudent to heed."[46] But how exactly does government "rest on opinion"? To what degree must a government "heed public opinion"?

All public officials pay attention to public opinion, whether they gauge it by the ear-to-the-ground method or by some kind of polling. While in office, President Lyndon Johnson carried reports of recent polls in his coat pocket, so that he could use them to convince recalcitrant members of Congress on a particular issue or to impress reporters. (Acknowledging criticism about this habit, President Johnson once kiddingly remarked that Patrick Henry had conducted a poll before delivering his famous "Give-me-liberty-or-give-me-death" speech and that the results were 46 percent for, 29 percent against, and the rest "didn't know.")[47] Johnson stopped referring to the polls when they began to show that the public no longer supported his policies. His realization that public opinion had turned against him and his handling of the Vietnam War played a part in his decision not to seek reelection.

How much does—or should—public opinion control the day-to-day decisions of public officials? This is not an easy question to answer. At election time, of course, public opinion can be freely expressed and directly felt. But what about between elections?

The question raises the issue of the proper responsibility of elected public officials. Should officials lead or follow the public? Should they sometimes lead and sometimes follow? These questions have plagued political scientists for a long time. Most Americans today feel—as the writers of our Constitution felt—some ambivalence about these questions. Hanna F. Pitkin has written that American public opinion is fairly evenly divided on the issue of whether representatives should follow public opinion or rely on their own judgement.[48]

Congressional and Public Opinion on Five Policy Issues, 1970

	Public	U.S. House Members	U.S. Senators
Percent favoring speeding up our withdrawal from Vietnam	27	30	45
Percent wanting to place less emphasis on military weapons programs	30	37	45
Percent approving at least 1600 dollars for a family of four or more	48	65	76
Percent saying government should go further to improve black conditions	53	58	76
Percent denying that Supreme Court gives too much consideration to rights of people suspected of crimes	29	36	56

Note: Questions for members of Congress and the public were similar but not identical.
SOURCE: "Candidates, Congress, and Constituents," CBS News Poll, Series 70, No. 7, Report 5.

A citizen might on one occasion say about a particular office-holder, "The Mayor is just a damned politician, thinking only about what will get the most votes, instead of what's right"; on another occasion he or she might remark, "The governor had better do what

---

[46]Key, Jr., *Public Opinion and American Democracy*.

[47]Leo Bogart, *Silent Politics: Polls and the Awareness of Public Opinion* (New York: John Wiley and Sons, 1972), p. 4.

[48]Hanna F. Pitkin, *The Concept of Representation* (Berkeley: Univ. of California Press, 1967), p. 149. See also Hadley Cantril, *Public Opinion, 1935–1946* (Princeton: Princeton Univ. Press, 1951), p. 133.

the people want on this issue; we elected him, and we can throw him out." In one instance, the person wants a public official to do what is "right," regardless of public opinion; in the other, he or she wants the public official to follow public opinion without deviation. (The decision to adopt one of these views may sometimes depend upon whether the politician's position is "right"—if it represents our side—or "wrong"—if it's against us!)

Should government policy reflect the will of the majority in a democracy? Jefferson said it should. We would all probably agree. Yet we would probably also agree with the well-known statement, "A politician thinks about the next election, while a statesman thinks about the next generation." Consider the point of view expressed by John F. Kennedy in his Pulitzer prize–winning book, *Profiles in Courage*, written before he became President. The book celebrated several famous members of the United States Senate as American political heroes precisely because, at crucial times in their careers, they stood up *against* what they knew to be the majority opinion of their constituents and voted according to their consciences instead.

Public opinion in a democracy must *in some way* be reflected in government policy and in the decisions made by public officials. How should this "reflection" be accomplished? The answer to that question depends on one's view of the representative role.[49] Some think of representatives, or public officials, as "delegates." According to this view, representatives should do exactly what a majority of their constituents wants on any particular issue, regardless of their own conscience. Others argue that representatives should act as "trustees." Advocates of this view believe that representatives should consult the wishes of their constituents and then make a decision based on what they feel is in the best interests of their constituents, regardless of majority opinion. While some representatives may think of themselves as trustees and others may consider themselves to be delegates, some see their role as a mixture of the two. Many representatives probably act as trustees on some occasions and as delegates on others, depending upon the issue.

There are several problems with the delegate concept of representation. First, it is not always possible to find out what a majority wants. Public opinion polls, for example, have been criticized for not always asking questions in an unbiased way; for not measuring the intensity of feeling on a particular issue; and for sometimes changing what they are trying to measure by asking people to answer questions on issues about which they may not have formed an opinion. In addition, critics argue that public opinion polls are conservative, or biased on the side of the *status quo*, because they indicate reactions to past events and do not predict future reactions.[50]

---

[49]For a discussion of the trustee and delegate role of representatives, see John C. Wahlke, Heinz Eulau, William Buchanan, and LeRoy C. Ferguson, *The Legislative System: Explorations in Legislative Behavior* (New York: Wiley, 1962), pp. 272, 276.

[50]See, for example, Michael Wheeler, *Lies, Damn Lies and Statistics* (New York: Liveright, 1976).

If there are problems in gauging public opinion by polls, other methods are even more unreliable. Members of Congress often send out mail questionnaires to voters, but those who respond may constitute an unrepresentative group of constituents. Unsolicited mail on public issues also tends to be unrepresentative.[51] In addition, the community leaders that representatives consult in order to sound out "grass-roots opinion" may be unrepresentative because of their higher socioeconomic status. These leaders may not know the opinions of others in their own communities.[52] Thus, representatives frequently are not well informed about the opinion of their constituents.[53]

A second criticism of the delegate concept of representation is that a majority of people may not always know what they want. Consider an issue that arose in 1968 and 1969: the debate about whether to build an Anti-Ballistic Missile system (ABM).[54] The issue was a highly complex one, and it involved classified information. The United States Senate debated the issue in one of its rare secret sessions.

A 1969 Gallup poll showed that only 69 percent of the American people had even heard or read about the ABM program. Only 40 percent had an opinion about it: 25 percent were in favor and 15 percent were opposed. A Harris poll at the same time showed that 47 percent approved the building of the ABM, while 26 percent disapproved, and 27 percent were not sure. In the Harris poll, a majority agreed with the statement that it is "better to be overprepared," but a majority also agreed with the view that the money which would be used for the ABM could better be used for education, health, and other needs. President Nixon, who favored the ABM, used a poll of his own, which showed that 84 percent of the American people supported the ABM and that only 8 percent believed that the system was not needed.

If you had been a senator sitting in the closed session, listening to detailed and complex debate on the issue, how would you have decided to vote? Most senators probably voted according to their own judgment. (Incidentally, there was a tie vote in the Senate on this issue, and the Vice-President broke the tie in favor of the ABM.) On issues that do not involve classified information, the public has a much better opportunity to be informed and therefore to know what they want done. But the public may not always have sufficient information even on nonclassified matters, especially the hundreds of

---

[51]See Phillip E. Converse, "The Nature of Belief Systems in Mass Publics," in David Apter, ed., *Ideology and Discontent* (New York: Free Press, 1964); and Sidney Verba and Richard A. Brody, "Participation, Policy Preferences and the War in Vietnam," *Public Opinion Quarterly*, 34 (1970): 325–32.

[52]Roberta Sigel and H. Paul Friesema, "Urban Community Leaders' Knowledge of Public Opinion," *Western Political Quarterly*, 18 (1965): 881–95.

[53]Warren Miller and Donald Stokes, "Constituency Influence in Congress," *American Political Science Review*, 57 (1963): 45–46.

[54]For a discussion of the polls on this issue, see Bogart, *Silent Politics: Polls and the Awareness of Public Opinion*, pp. 10–13.

less important issues that must be decided by public officials on a day-to-day basis.

Third, critics of the delegate concept of representation argue that leaders have a responsibility to lead. Leaders, they insist, should use their best judgment, vote according to their consciences, and then try to persuade a majority of their constituents to their view. Edmund Burke, the conservative eighteenth-century British writer and politician, said that a representative should give great weight to the wishes and opinions of constituents and should "sacrifice his repose, his pleasure, his satisfaction, to theirs—and above all, ever, and in all cases, to prefer their interests to his own. But," Burke added, "his unbiased opinion, his mature judgment, his enlightened conscience he ought not to sacrifice to you, to any man, or to any set of men living. . . . Your representative owes you, not his industry alone, but his judgment; and he betrays, instead of serving you, if he sacrifices it to your opinion."[55]

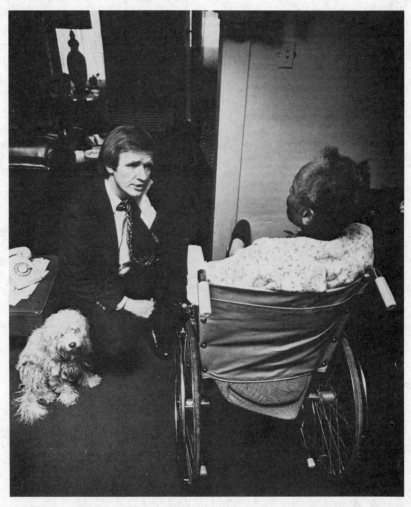

U.S. Senator Donald Riegle talks with a constituent. In a democracy, are public officials "delegates" or "trustees"—or some mixture of both?

Burke thus believed in the trustee concept of representation. He thought that the constituent-representative relationship was very much like the client-lawyer relationship. When a client hires a lawyer, the client is not entitled to demand that the lawyer violate the law or do something unethical, even though the client is paying the lawyer's fee. Nor is the client entitled to tell the lawyer exactly how the legal matter or lawsuit should be handled, since the lawyer's job is to give sound advice and counsel based upon special knowledge and skill. The safeguard for the dissatisfied client is the ability to discharge the lawyer. Burke would say that a constituent has the same right to turn a representative out of office. (In fact, Burke himself was not reelected by his

---

[55]Ross J. S. Hoffman and Paul Levack, eds., *Burke's Politics: Selected Writings and Speeches of Edmund Burke on Reform, Revolution and War* (New York: Knopf, 1949), p. 115.

constituents after he gave his famous speech on the duty of a representative.)

Some advocates of the trustee concept of representation would argue further that a representative has a duty to lead because there may not be any public opinion at all on an issue until the elected representative takes action. According to social philosopher Jacques Ellul, "The government cannot postpone actions and decisions until vague images and myths eventually coalesce into opinion. In the present world of politics, action must at all times be the forerunner of opinion. Even where public opinion is already formed, it can be disastrous to follow it."[56] President Johnson's Secretary of State, Dean Rusk, once made a similar argument:

We cannot test public opinion until the President and the leaders of the country have gone to the public to explain what is required and have asked them for support for the necessary action. I doubt, for example, that three months before the leadership began to talk about what came to be the Marshall Plan,[57] any public opinion expert would have said that the country would have accepted such proposals.[58]

In practice, then, public opinion often is a reaction to decisions made by public officials or to government actions. But there is a "feedback" process in addition to the pattern of government action and public opinion reaction. Government may act, public opinion may react, and then government may revise its action. Each particular issue may give rise to a somewhat different process.

Are the delegate and trustee concepts contradictory, or is it possible that *together* they make up what we call representation? In her influential book, *The Concept of Representation*, Hanna F. Pitkin concludes:

Representing . . . means acting in the interest of the represented, in a manner responsive to them. The representative must act independently; he must be the one who acts. The represented must also be . . . capable of independent action and judgment, not merely taken care of. And, despite the resulting potential for conflict between representative and represented about what is to be done, that conflict must not normally take place. The representative must act in such a way that there is no conflict, or if it occurs an explanation is called for. He must not be found persistently at odds with the wishes of the represented without good reason in terms of their interest, without a good explanation of why their wishes are not in accord with their interest.[59]

---

[56] Jacques Ellul, *Propaganda* (New York: Knopf, 1965), p. 124.

[57] The Marshall Plan, a plan for American assistance to European nations following World War II, was named for former U.S. Army General George C. Marshall. He helped conceive and administer the plan as President Harry Truman's secretary of state.

[58] Dean Rusk, "A Fresh Look at the Formulation of Foreign Policy," *U.S. Department of State Bulletin*, 44 (March 1961), p. 398.

[59] Pitkin, *The Concept of Representation*, pp. 209–10.

CONCLUSION

Although it is not always possible to explain exactly what its role is, public opinion plays an important part in the formation of public policy in America. The effect of public opinion depends on what information the public has upon which to base an opinion. The impact of public opinion on public officials may also depend upon its intensity. Though a large majority of Americans apparently favor the abolition of the Electoral College, for example, Congress has not acted on this issue, presumably because public opinion on it lacks intensity. On the other hand, President Johnson did not run for reelection in 1968 after public opinion turned against him and his policies. Opinion that is intensely held—even by special publics, which may not represent the majority view—can be more influential than vaguely held opinions among the general public. But citizens are not limited to verbal or written expressions in making their opinions known. They may also act through organized groups; they can become involved with political parties; and they may speak with special authority in the voting booth.

ADDITIONAL SOURCES

Bogart, Leo. *Silent Polls: Polls and the Awareness of Public Opinion.* Wiley, 1972.*

Gallup, George, ed. *The Gallup Poll: 1937–71*, 3 vols. Random House, 1972.

———, ed. *The Gallup Poll: 1972–77.* Scholarly Research, Inc., 1978.

Key, V. O., Jr. *Public Opinion and American Democracy.* Philadelphia Book Co., 1961.

Lippmann, Walter. *Public Opinion.* Free Press, 1965.*

Nie, Norman H., Sidney Verba, and John Petrocik. *The Changing American Voter.* Harvard University Press, 1976.*

Pitkin, Hanna. *The Concept of Representation.* University of California Press, 1967.*

"Public Opinion." *The Wilson Quarterly.* Spring 1979.

Verba, Sidney, and Norman H. Nie. *Participation in America.* Harper & Row, 1972.*

Weissberg, Robert. *Public Opinion and Popular Government.* Prentice-Hall, 1976.*

*Available in paperback edition.

8 Interest Groups
Organizing for Influence

A lobbyist—a representative of an interest group—meets with a legislator to express his group's position on an issue.

An ambitious young Washington lawyer who represents an association of chemical companies is having lunch with a former classmate who now works in the Environmental Protection Agency (EPA). "My people are getting awfully jumpy about what kind of regulations are going to be issued under the new pesticide legislation," the lawyer says to the EPA staff member.

"I can imagine," she responds. "We're coming out with the final regs next Thursday. There's no secret about it, but we haven't broadcast it because the director doesn't want to be bothered with having everybody on his neck. I can tell you, though, that the regs are going to be pretty tough on pesticides. Of the three plans, the director is going to go for the toughest one."

"Who has the final say?"

"The director's handling this one himself."

After lunch, the young lawyer catches a cab up to the New Senate Office Building on Capitol Hill. "What greedy scheme have you come to lobby me about, now?" the senator asks jokingly as the young lawyer is shown into his office. "You've bought my secretary by bringing her chocolates nearly every time you come up here. You've got my administrative assistant addicted to those fine Cuban cigars you dole out to him one by one, and because of the one-thousand-dollar contribution you made to my last campaign, you think you own me." The senator says all this with mock outrage. He and the lawyer know each other well. They have an easy, friendly relationship.

"What I need, senator, is a call from you down to the director of EPA to ask him to go for the less harsh Plan One regulations on pesticides, instead of the unreasonable Plan Three regulations. He's going to come out with the regulations next Thursday, and they're going to kill the chemical industry unless we can do something."

"I wish you'd come in here sometime with something I could help you on," the senator says. "You know damned well that my environmentalist convictions won't let me help you on this one."

"Well, at least you gave me some of your time," the young lawyer says amicably. "One of these days, you're bound to do something good for me. Anyway, I'll file a report with my people about our conversation, telling them that you can't help us, of course, and I'll get a good fee just for having access to Mr. Environment himself."

Next, the young lawyer goes over to the Old Senate Office Building. When he finds that the senator he wanted to see there is too busy to see him immediately, he speaks with the senator's administrative assistant instead. "All right, I'll make a call down there in the senator's name, and I'll have him sign a letter to the EPA director," the assistant says. "As you know, the senator is a farmer himself, and he's got little use for these red-hot environmentalists who want to save every grasshopper."

Back at his office, the young lawyer places two long-distance calls. One is to the president of his association, who heads a chemical company that manufactures pesticides. "This would be a good time for you to call your friend on the White House staff," he tells the official. "Tough regs are about to come out unless the EPA director gets a stern call from higher up." The other call is to a chemical plant manager in the home state of the senator who is known as "Mr. Environment." The young lawyer tells the plant manager, "The senator and I get along awfully well, but he's gone haywire again. I know he likes you, and I know he wants to protect those jobs in his home state. A call from you right now and also from the business agent of your plant's union, if you can swing that, might push him over the line and get him to help us quietly on this one."

This narrative account is, of course, fictional. But it accurately portrays how interest groups make their influence felt in the government policy-making process.

There are three principal characteristics of an *interest group*.[1] First, an interest group is organized. It is not just a categorical grouping, such as all black people or all women in the United States. Second, an interest group is an organization of shared attitudes. Members of the group may not agree on everything, but they do agree on the issue or issues upon which the organization is based. Third, an interest group acts through or upon government institutions. Defined in this way, interest groups might also be called "pressure groups" or "lobbies."

There are two major differences between an interest group and a political party. First, the principal purpose of a political party is to contest elections, which may be only one of several purposes of an interest group. Second, the names of a party's candidates appear on voting ballots under the party label. Interest groups, on the other

---

[1]See David B. Truman, *The Governmental Process* (New York: Knopf, 1951), p. 37.

hand, do not have their own organizational name or label on the ballot, although they may support or oppose candidates for election.

Interest groups are an important and influential part of the political process. Therefore, we need to know more about their role in the political system, whose interests they advance, how they operate, and the extent of their power.

INTEREST GROUPS IN AMERICA

James Madison worried about "factions"—which were more or less equivalent to what we call interest groups—and their possible effects on the new government that he had helped to form. In *Federalist* 10 he wrote: "By a faction, I understand a number of citizens whether amounting to a majority or a minority of the whole, who are united and actuated by some common impulse of passion, or of interest, adverse to the rights of other citizens, or to the permanent and aggregate interests of the community." He went on to say that "the most common and durable source of factions has been the various and unequal distribution of property." Although Madison deplored the existence of factions (interest groups), he felt that they were "sown in the nature of man" because unequal distribution of property resulted from the "diversity of human faculties." To guard against the excesses and evils of interest groups, Madison helped to design a governmental system in which power was fragmented between the states and the federal government and, within the federal government, among the executive, legislative, and judicial branches.

Functions of Interest Groups

Many people today continue to think of interest groups as an evil influence on government policy, however inevitable the formation and activity of such groups may be. Others view interest groups as a good and necessary part of the democratic process. They point to four positive functions that interest groups perform.

First, proponents of interest groups say that they serve as links between the people and the policy-makers, as "transmission belts" between individual needs and government institutions.[2] According to this theory, the activity of interests groups helps the government identify opinions that it must respond to.

Second, interest groups may increase political participation. They inform their members of recent or pending government decisions, explain how members can influence such decisions, and encourage them to use this influence. As we noted in Chapter 4, experience in

[2]Harmon Ziegler and Michael A. Baer, *Lobbying: Interaction and Influence in American State Legislatures* (Belmont, California: Wadsworth, 1969), pp. 2–3.

any kind of organization may produce skills that can be used in political participation. Membership in interest groups further encourages political participation by increasing a person's sense of competence (knowing how to use the system) and sense of efficacy (feeling that the system can be made to respond).

Third, advocates argue that interest groups supplement official representation. For example, individuals may not feel either competent or efficacious in their efforts to affect a federal agency's regulations. As members of an interest group, however, they may be able to influence such government policy-making. Thus, people who are unable to go to Washington and testify before a congressional committee on pending legislation may nevertheless be represented in the legislative process through an interest group. Further, because political representation in America is based on geographic units, interest groups can also supplement official representation by representing issues and interests that extend beyond state and district lines.

The role of interest groups in America's political system is a subject of some controversy. Do they expand the potential for citizen participation? Or do they mostly represent the interests of a minority?

Finally, supporters of interest groups claim that they serve as an important means of resolving conflicts in our society. Some even argue that policy is the product of the competition and compromises among interest groups, with the government simply giving its approval to decisions that have already been reached outside the government.[3] This theory of how democracy works is called *pluralism*.

Criticisms of Interest Groups

Pluralism and interest groups have been criticized on several counts. First, all interests in America are not equally represented by interest groups. Although 62 percent of the American people say that they belong to an organization, only 40 percent are *active* in an organization, and only 31 percent belong to an organization in which political discussion takes place.[4] Eight percent belong to political groups, such as Democratic or Republican clubs, or to political action groups, such as voters' leagues.

---

[3]Earl Latham, *The Group Basis of Policy* (New York: Octagon Press, 1952), p. 35.

[4]Material regarding participation in America is taken from Sidney Verba and Norman H. Nie, *Participation in America* (New York: Harper and Row, 1972).

Members of these kinds of organizations tend to have attained higher levels of education than nonmembers, and educational levels are largely products of income levels. Fifty-nine percent of Americans who have attended college are active in at least one organization, while only 43 percent of the high-school graduates and 27 percent of those who did not graduate from high school are active. Minorities and people of lower socioeconomic status are less likely than businesspeople and more affluent Americans to be members of interest groups. E. E. Schattschneider has written that the "pressure system" of interest groups is "skewed, loaded and unbalanced" in favor of a small fraction of Americans.[5]

A second criticism of interest groups is that leaders, or elites, dominate the organizations themselves, a practice that has been called the "iron law of oligarchy."[6] (Oligarchy is the rule of the few rather than the many.) Critics claim that the groups tend to be dominated by an active minority, who conduct the affairs of the organization and make decisions concerning policy. This is not only true of interest groups that lobby for their own economic interests; it also holds for "citizens' lobbies," such as Common Cause and Ralph Nader's fund-raising organization, Public Citizen. Public Citizen makes it clear when it solicits funds by mail that members will not receive reports on the organization's activities. Common Cause does send out questionnaires on issues to its members, but only about 10 percent actually respond, leaving most of the policy-making to the more active members and to the organization's professional staff.[7]

Interest groups are not always able to speak for all their members. In fact, on certain issues, broad-based groups sometimes take positions with which some members disagree.

A third criticism of interest groups is that they are not really accountable to anyone, except their members (and not always to them). In this respect, interest groups are not as responsible to the general public as are elected public officials, who must account for their actions, at least at election time.

Finally, critics of interest groups argue that competition and compromise among various groups do not necessarily result in coherent government policy. Instead, it often produces only government stalemate and inaction. Theodore J. Lowi has criticized interest groups—and pluralism—on this basis: "Government that is formless in action and amoral in intention (i.e., *ad hoc*) is government that can neither plan nor achieve justice."[8]

---

[5]E. E. Schattshneider, *The Semisovereign People* (New York: Holt, Rinehart and Winston, 1960), p. 35.

[6]See Robert Michaels, *Political Parties: A Sociological Study of the Oligarchical Tendencies of Modern Democracy,* Eden and Cedar Paul, trans. (New York: The Free Press, 1966).

[7]Theodore Jacqueney, "Common Cause," *National Journal Reports* (September 1, 1973), pp. 1294–1304.

[8]Theodore J. Lowi, *The End of Liberalism: Ideology, Policy and the Crisis of Public Authority* (New York: Norton, 1969), p. x.

Supporters of the interest group-pluralism model of democratic government view politics as a process that is very similar to the adversary relationships in a lawsuit, in which all of the interests are represented (not by lawyers, of course, but by interest groups). Critics point out that some of the lawyers (interest groups) are more skilled and more influential in the use of the system than others are. Some of the lawyers are not really controlled by those whom they are supposed to represent. Moreover, some of the interests are not even represented. Finally, the compromises worked out among the contending lawyers may result in no action at all or may result in action that is not in the public interest.

TYPES OF INTEREST GROUPS

Interest groups operate even in authoritarian societies, including the Soviet Union.[9] Historically, they have been especially active in America. "Americans of all ages, all conditions, and all dispositions constantly form associations," wrote Alexis de Tocqueville in the 1830s. "They have not only commercial and manufacturing companies, in which all take part, but associations of a thousand other kinds,—religious, moral, serious, futile, extensive or restricted, enormous or diminutive."[10]

Tocqueville said that Americans successfully used associations more than any other people in the world. One influential study found that Tocqueville's statement is still true.[11] According to the study, 56 percent of Americans said that they would form an informal group in order to protest an unjust law, compared to only 34 percent in Great Britain, 13 percent in Germany, and 7 percent in Italy. Although the number of Americans who *say* they would form a group to protest an unjust law may be considerably higher than those who actually *do* form or join such groups, interest groups are very numerous in this country. In 1968, there were nearly eleven thousand such *national* organizations.[12]

Why are people so willing to join groups? There are a variety of reasons. Some people join groups because of their interest in particular political causes or issues. Others do it to further their economic interests. People also become members of groups for social reasons, or for companionship. Peer pressure may cause others to join groups. In some communities, for example, people may say, "Everyone who is anyone belongs to the Chamber of Commerce."

[9]See Joel J. Schwartz and William R. Keech, "Group Influence and the Policy Process in the Soviet Union," *American Political Science Review,* 62 (September 1968): 840–51.

[10]Alexis de Tocqueville, *Democracy in America,* Vol. 2, Henry Reeve, trans. (New York: Schocken Books, 1961), p. 128.

[11]See Gabriel A. Almond and Sidney Verba, *The Civic Culture: Political Attitudes and Democracy in Five Nations* (Princeton, New Jersey: Princeton University Press, 1963).

[12]See Verba and Nie, *Participation in America.*

Finally, some do it because they have to. If labor and management at a particular plant agree to maintain a "union shop," for example, the workers in the plant will be required to join the union (unless state law prohibits this).

Interest groups can be divided into two general categories: special-interest groups, and public-interest groups. If the membership of a group is exclusive—open only to veterans or only to doctors, for example—it is called a *special-interest* group. Organizations whose membership is open to anyone who wants to join are called public-interest groups. Anyone can join Common Cause, for instance, by paying a $15 membership fee. But these are not totally satisfactory definitions. Even David Cohen, the president of Common Cause, has had difficulty distinguishing between special-interest groups and public-interest groups. "We are *a* citizens' lobby, *a* public-interest group. The difference between 'a' and 'the' is very important. We don't define 'the public interest' in the sense that one group represents it while others don't."[13] Another authority has said that it would be more accurate to call such consumer and citizen organizations "citizens' lobbies," rather than public-interest groups.[14] In any event, it is generally understood that a public-interest group is one which represents the interests of the general public, as opposed to special economic, professional, ethnic, or other narrow interests.

Public-Interest Groups

The term *public-interest group* is well understood in Washington, D.C. It refers to an organization that represents broad, diffuse, noncommercial interests. In the past, such groups were usually liberal, but conservatives have been forming public-interest groups recently, too. Unlike such groups as the NAACP, the American Medical Association, Americans for Democratic Action, and the United Auto Workers, public-interest groups are organized around roles that all Americans share—as consumers, citizens, taxpayers, breathers of the air, and drinkers of the water. Common Cause, with 250,000 members; Ralph Nader's Public Citizen, with 65,000 members; the Sierra Club and the League of Women Voters, each with about 200,000 members; and smaller groups, such as Friends of the Earth and the Environmental Defense Fund, are all public-interest groups. The increased strength of these groups has produced new challenges to governmental authority and has provided new avenues for citizen involvement in the policy-making process.

Common Cause was formed in 1970 under the leadership of a former secretary of Health, Education and Welfare, John Gardner. Although it initially received some "seed" money from wealthy

---

[13]Congressional Quarterly, *Weekly Report* (May 15, 1976), p. 1197.
[14]See Peter H. Schuck, "Public Interest Groups and the Policy Process," *Public Administration Review,* 37 (March 1977): 132–140.

donors, it now depends upon membership dues to fund its operations. Common Cause maintains a rather large and highly professional staff in its Washington headquarters. It concentrates on "process" issues. That is, Common Cause has lobbied for open meetings in the Congress and in the executive branch of the government, for financial disclosure by public officials, for reform of campaign financing, and for reform of lobbying regulations. State chapters of Common Cause are involved in similar process issues at the state level.

Probably the best-known public-interest group activities are those associated with Ralph Nader. He became famous in the late 1960s after criticizing the unsafe features of one of General Motors' cars. GM hired a private detective to try to find information that would discredit him. GM was unsuccessful, and their efforts were exposed. Nader became a front-page personality. He sued General Motors for damages, and collected. But consumer advocacy was just the first of Nader's activities. Since then, he has formed organizations that have studied and criticized Congress and numerous federal agencies; brought public-interest lawsuits; and lobbied Congress for new consumer and environmental protection laws. Nader's operations were initially funded by the proceeds from his lawsuit against General Motors. Today they are financed by lecture and other fees that he receives and by contributions from individuals who are solicited by mail. Local Nader-affiliated Public Interest Research Groups, which are active on consumer and environmental issues, are often financed by a portion of student activity fees on some campuses.

Ralph Nader—"Mr. Public Citizen"—has been a leading spokesman for "the public interest" since the late 1960s.

Public-interest groups are usually at a considerable disadvantage in comparison to special-interest groups. The financing of public-interest groups is typically very precarious because it is difficult to organize people and keep them interested enough to pay dues. In addition, public-interest organizations, which hope to receive contributions from foundations and donors who want to deduct their contributions for tax purposes, cannot devote a substantial part of their efforts to influencing legislation.

The relatively low salaries that many public-interest groups pay their staffs creates another disadvantage. There is a high turnover of staff. Public-interest groups, therefore, must rely principally upon young staff members who may move on to more remunerative jobs after short stays. Some observers maintain that President Carter has appointed so many former public-interest group activists to government positions that he has unintentionally but measurably weakened the influence of public-interest groups.

A number of suggestions have been made to correct the imbalance of power between public-interest groups and special-interest groups. Ralph Nader has suggested that taxpayers should be allowed to allocate a small portion of their taxes to one or another public-interest group, just as students allocate student activity fees to public-interest research groups on college campuses. Others have suggested a change in federal income tax laws and regulations that would eliminate a business corporation's present tax deduction for lobbying expenses, which gives them an advantage over individual citizens and public-interest groups. But little support has been generated for either suggestion so far.

Another important proposal calls for the creation of a consumer protection agency in the federal government. The proposed agency would take over part of the present work of public-interest groups and would represent consumer and citizen interests before federal agencies and commissions. Despite a finding by a Senate committee that industry predominates in proceedings before federal agencies, often with little or no consumer participation, Congress killed this proposal again in 1978 after very heavy pressure from business and industrial groups.[15]

Public-interest groups are less powerful than special-interest groups. But they are not without resources of power. On a number of occasions they have been highly successful. Their main problem is that it is difficult to sustain sufficient intensity of consumer interest in day-to-day government decisions. On the other hand, the chemical and the oil and gas industries—two special-interest groups—are always aware of and intensely interested in any government policy or action that may affect them.

Special-Interest Groups

Special-interest groups include business, labor, professional, ethnic, and other issue-oriented organizations. The most numerous and influential are business groups. There are nearly three thousand trade and business associations in the United States. Two national organizations, the U.S. Chamber of Commerce and the National Association of Manufacturers, are umbrella organizations for many businesses and industries. But many other associations—from the Grocery Manufacturers of America to the American Petroleum Institute—represent more narrow interests.

The American Petroleum Institute represents the big oil companies, seven of which are among the twenty largest corporations in America. The oil industry is an enormously powerful special-interest group. It has enjoyed very large profits in recent years. Some of these profits have been converted into political influence, particularly through campaign contributions. (However, the only legal means to do this are through individual contributions by corporate officials or by corporate political action committees.) Many oil companies spend huge sums of money on "public relations" activities and advertisements. In addition, the government has come to depend upon the oil companies for information about how much oil, gas, and other energy resources exist in America and in the rest of the world. In

---

[15]See Mark Green, "Why the Consumer Bill Went Down," *The Nation* (February 25, 1978), pp. 198–201.

government policy-making, information is power; special-interest groups often have the information decision-makers need.

Professional organizations are also influential special-interest groups in America. They include such organizations as the American Bar Association (ABA) and the American Medical Association (AMA). The ABA is a professional organization for lawyers. The government regularly requests it to submit reports and recommendations concerning presidential nominees for judicial positions throughout the country. The ABA also makes recommendations regarding codification and reform of the laws in special fields, such as criminal and commercial law.

The American Medical Association wields considerable power on health-care issues, particularly those that threaten the independence and income of medical doctors. The AMA is well financed, both by membership dues and by paid advertising in its national magazine. It can mobilize its members rapidly and effectively. For years, the AMA worked with the American Dental Association, other health professional organizations, and the insurance industry to block the passage of Medicare, a system of health insurance for older Americans. It still opposes the adoption of a national health insurance system for all Americans. Its political action committee collects and dispenses money to assist political candidates who favor the AMA's position on this and other issues.

Another influential professional organization is the National Education Association (NEA), which has nearly seven hundred staff members in its national headquarters in Washington, D.C. NEA represents the schoolteachers of America. It works to improve their salaries and working conditions and supports legislation designed to improve the American educational system. Like many other special-interest groups, NEA has become directly active in political campaigns since 1972.

On economic and most civil rights issues, organized labor is the most important and influential liberal group in America. For one thing, there are many unionized workers in the United States. For another, their national organizations, particularly the American Federation of Labor-Congress of Industrial Organizations (AFL-CIO), have excellent research staffs and can support their arguments with reliable information.

Organized labor is not as powerful and influential as it might be because it is fragmented into several national organizations. The AFL-CIO was formed in 1955 by the merger of two rival labor organizations: the AFL, which represented crafts (such as carpenters, plumbers, and welders); and the CIO, which represented industry-wide unions (such as those of the steelworkers and automobile workers). Marked differences still exist in the political outlook of union leaders in the two halves of the AFL-CIO; AFL leaders tend to be more conservative than CIO leaders.

In addition, three major national unions are not members of the

AFL-CIO. The United Mine Workers is not affiliated with the AFL-CIO, primarily because of the desires of their fiery founder, John L. Lewis. The Teamsters Union was purged from the AFL-CIO because of corruption among its highest leaders. A charismatic liberal unionist, Walter Reuther, head of the United Auto Workers, led his union out of the AFL-CIO a number of years ago because he and the AFL-CIO's tough old president, George Meany, disagreed on issues. Thus, labor organizations often work together on important issues, but because of their fragmentation, no single voice can speak for the interests of organized working people.

Still, George Meany—aided by his hand-picked heir apparent, Lane Kirkland—presides over an organization of working people that has great influence on government policy. The AFL-CIO's support is central to legislative success on economic issues such as tax reform and full employment; on social issues like health, housing, and education; and on civil rights issues. But on some issues, particularly international questions, the AFL-CIO is conservative. Its leaders favor restrictions on free trade and foreign imports. They take a hard line concerning America's relationship with the Soviet Union. Their support of the Vietnam War separated them for a while from many of their traditional liberal allies. And on civil rights, although the AFL-CIO has been a leader in the battle to eliminate racial discrimination, they have upheld the seniority rights of union workers when these rights have been threatened by affirmative action on behalf of minorities.

Senator Ted Kennedy and AFL-CIO President George Meany have an after-dinner chat. Representing the interests of a large constituency and having a "war-chest" of potential campaign contributions gives groups like the AFL-CIO access to governmental officials.

Labor organizations have separate political arms. The AFL-CIO arm is the Committee on Political Education (COPE). These political committees raise money from union members and use it in political campaigns.

Ethnic organizations are also influential special-interest groups. The National Association for the Advancement of Colored People (NAACP) maintains an active national office. The Urban League and similar organizations serve the interests of black people. American Indian organizations—particularly the National Congress of American Indians, the National Tribal Chairman's Association, and Americans for Indian Opportunity—take stands on issues of importance to the Indian community, and their views influence legislation and policies in this field.

Other issue-oriented organizations abound in Washington. One of the most powerful is the National Rifle Association (NRA), which works to kill any legislation or government policy that might restrict or regulate the ownership and use of guns. NRA members have intense feelings about gun issues, and they are not timid about expressing them.

Interest groups are as varied as the questions and the issues confronted by government. They can be large or small, influential or relatively inconsequential, permanent fixtures of American politics or single-issue organizations that spring up and die. It is impossible to understand how the American political system works without understanding their role. They are almost an unofficial part of the government.

INTEREST-GROUP TACTICS

Our account at the beginning of this chapter of the young Washington lawyer representing an association of chemical companies illustrates three tactics that interest groups use: lobbying, political campaign activity, and grass-roots pressure. Interest groups also employ two other important tactics: litigation and mass propaganda. Some interest groups rely on certain tactics more heavily than on others. Other interest groups use them all at one time or another.

Litigation

Activist citizens are frequently frustrated by the American political system's fragmentation of power. Favorable action by only one branch of the federal government does not necessarily guarantee success. But this very fragmentation of power can also serve the interests of activist citizens. When one branch will not act, citizens may turn to another, as black people, led by the NAACP, did in the 1950s. For a long time, Congress would not act on civil rights legislation. Southerners were very powerful, and in the Senate, they conducted a *filibuster*. This term means "talking a bill to death," or preventing it from coming to a vote. A filibuster can only be stopped by a three fifths vote of the Senate. The NAACP turned to the courts—with great success. As the Supreme Court said, "For such a group, association for litigation may be the most effective form of political association."[16]

Particularly because of Ralph Nader's efforts, litigation—the process of bringing lawsuits—has become a frequently used and highly effective tactic for public-interest groups. They have filed suits to protest utility rate increases and have brought court actions against federal agencies. In addition, public-interest groups also participate

---

[16]*N.A.A.C.P.* v. *Button,* 371 U.S. 415 (1963).

in lawsuits by filing briefs as an *amicus curiae,* or "friend of the court." These are legal arguments submitted on behalf of claimants they support. *Class actions*—lawsuits brought by individuals for themselves and "others similarly situated"—are sometimes financed by public-interest groups. Class actions seek to recover damages and attorneys' fees for corporate wrongdoing, such as pricefixing.

Litigation offers a way to protect citizen and consumer rights, independent of Congress or the executive department. It is a kind of self-help procedure. The development of "public interest law" has been called one of the most innovative challenges to public administration.[17]

But litigation is not just a tactic used by public-interest groups. More and more special interests are forming tax-exempt foundations to fight government regulations and environmental reform in the courts. There were eight such special-interest legal foundations in 1978.[18] One official of one of these new legal foundations said, "We felt somebody had to be there in court to give the other side"; a spokesperson for the Center for Law and the Public Interest responded that public-interest law is supposed to represent the unrepresented, and corporate interests are already overrepresented in the courts.

Mass Propaganda

Interest groups with money can mount public relations and advertising campaigns to affect public opinion, which in turn, will affect public officials.[19] Individual corporations buy paid advertising on public issues. Sometimes a company and its labor union purchase advertising to explain their sides of a labor dispute. Most large corporations send their officials before public audiences to expound views that are favorable to the companies' interests. Such blatant appeals to public opinion are less effective than advertisements in which the special interests are not identified. For example, companies that make and use bottles and cans may advertise through a "screen" organization, telling people not to litter and urging them to pick up bottles and cans. The implication is that there would be no need for legislation prohibiting no-return bottles and cans if people voluntarily refrained from littering.

Interest groups also spend large sums of money on public relations (or "PR" as it is sometimes called) to secure favorable media coverage or comment. The source of public-relations campaigns may not always be revealed, and the public may not realize that they are receiving biased information. For example, the Business Roundtable, which was formed by 157 business corporations and organizations,

---

[17]Schuck, "Public Interest Groups and the Policy Process," pp. 132–140.
[18]*The New York Times* (February 12, 1978), p. 1.
[19]V. O. Key, Jr., *Politics, Parties and Pressure Groups,* 5th ed. (New York: Crowell, 1964).

hired the North American Precis Syndicate in 1977 to prepare and mail out "canned" editorials and cartoons opposing the creation of a new consumer protection agency.[20] The 3800 newspapers that received these prepared materials—and their readers—had no way of knowing that the source was highly biased. The materials appeared approximately 2000 times throughout the country. Ten different newspapers used identical editorials opposed to the consumer protection agency bill.

While Congress was considering the consumer protection agency bill, the U.S. Chamber of Commerce used an opinion poll, which it had commissioned in 1975, to try to convince members of Congress to block the creation of the agency. The Chamber of Commerce stated that their poll revealed that "81 percent of Americans are opposed to a new consumer agency." The Library of Congress, however, declared that the poll was biased and unfair because the question asked by interviewers had been improperly worded. Senator Charles Percy of Illinois also denounced the poll, saying that "the dissemination of useless poll information does nothing to help the image of American business, which is at an all-time low."[21]

Advertising and other forms of mass communication designed to influence public opinion are very expensive. Thus, it is not surprising that public-interest groups are generally less able to use mass propaganda as a tactic than are special-interest groups. As a result, public-interest groups sometimes turn to protests and demonstrations to dramatize their demands, build support for their organizations and aims, and secure free media coverage.

Grass-Roots Pressure

In the example at the beginning of the chapter, the young Washington lawyer who represented a chemical company association asked an official of a chemical company in the senator's home state to call the senator and to try to get the plant's union business agent to do the same. That is one kind of grass-roots pressure. It may also take the form of mail or telegram campaigns in which group members flood their representative's office with appeals to take a certain position on an issue. These appeals sometimes contain veiled or outright threats that the representative will not be reelected if he or she opposes the group's position. A telephone conversation with a public official or a key assistant is even more effective than a letter or telegram. A personal conversation is perhaps most effective.

Many interest groups arrange to have constituents from the member's home state or district talk to the member in Washington. This method can be very effective; it demonstrates intensity of feeling, and it can furnish persuasive information (particularly if the information ties the issue in question to the well-being of citizens in

[20]Green, "Why the Consumer Bill Went Down," pp. 198–201.
[21]Green, "Why the Consumer Bill Went Down," pp. 198–99.

Opponents of abortion have effectively used grass-roots pressure, including mass demonstrations, to make sure their representatives know where they stand on the issue.

the member's home district or state). Personal lobbying of this kind is even more successful when it is applied to members of Congress while they are visiting their electoral districts. For one thing, it is often easier to see members of Congress personally while they are at home than while they are in Washington. And a visit to the member's local offices may have greater impact because many constituents feel more confident on their home ground than they do in unfamiliar Washington surroundings.

Grass-roots pressure may be combined with mass propaganda, particularly on a controversial issue like abortion or busing. A senator or representative may come home to find two or three hundred people waiting to present their views on an issue, and such demonstrations are usually well covered by the media.

National representatives of interest groups—hired employees or retained lawyers—may believe that their influence on government policy-makers stems from their gifts of persuasion, and they may also try to give this impression to the interest groups that pay them. But influencing policy-makers is not so much a matter of the persuasiveness of an interest group's representative as it is the result of other tactics, including grass-roots pressure. Although the interest group representative usually orchestrates these tactics, numbers generally count more, especially with elected officials. That is, the number of people who express their views to their elected official, coupled with the intensity of those views, matter more than an interest group representative's lobbying. They may translate into actual or potential votes and campaign contributions. For example, supporters of the consumer protection agency bill in 1978 felt that one of the main reasons why they lost the congressional vote on that issue was that local Chamber of Commerce voices were more frequently heard by members of Congress than were the voices of consumers. "You win or lose in the districts, not in Washington," one member of Congress told consumer advocates.[22]

[22]Green, "Why the Consumer Bill Went Down," pp. 198–99.

Political Campaign Activity

When a candidate for Congress who *already* supports labor reform legislation is elected to office, the AFL-CIO's work to secure that member's vote on such legislation is already nine-tenths done. When a senator who supports the deregulation of natural gas is reelected, the oil industry, which favors deregulation, does not have to worry about that vote when the matter comes before the Senate. It is not surprising, therefore, that one of the principal tactics of interest groups is political campaign activity designed to elect their friends and defeat their enemies.

For one thing, political campaigns require large sums of money. The more powerful the office, the more money it takes to run. California political figure Jesse Unruh once said that "money is the mother's milk of politics." Political campaigns depend upon contributions, and those contributions often come from special-interest groups and their members. Campaign contributions allow interest groups to secure influence with elected public officials through legal means. Corporations are prohibited by law from using corporate funds for campaign contributions, and labor unions are prohibited by law from using regular union funds for that purpose. But both business corporations and labor unions can set up separate political action committees (PACs) and solicit *voluntary* funds for political campaigns. Labor unions contribute large sums of money to political campaigns through these "voluntary" contributions. Corporations may legally ask their officers and employees to make "voluntary" contributions to political campaigns as well. In both instances, of course, pressure may be applied to secure the contributions.

Contributions to Congressional Campaigns by Political Action Committees (PAC), 1976

Business PACs*	Incumbents	$4,715,950	Republicans	$4,083,757
	Challengers	1,159,568	Democrats	2,849,167
	Open Seats	1,057,406		$6,932,924
		$6,932,924		
Labor PACs**	Incumbents	$5,108,747	Republicans	$ 279,090
	Challengers	1,676,861	Democrats	7,788,174
	Open Seats	1,281,656		$8,067,264
		$8,067,264		

*Total includes corporate PACs and business-related trade association PACs.
**Total includes contributions by the National Education Association.
SOURCE: Common Cause; reprinted in *Electing Congress* (Washington, D.C.: Congressional Quarterly, Inc., 1978).

In 1974, Congress passed a law limiting campaign contributions in national campaigns, requiring candidates to disclose contributions and expenditures, and providing for the public financing of presidential campaigns. Presidential candidates can now secure federal matching funds prior to the nominating conventions if, through their own fund-raising, they show sufficiently widespread support throughout the country. Once the parties have nominated their candidates, the presidential campaigns (of the two major parties at least) are almost completely financed out of the federal treasury. The idea behind this legislation is to decrease the political influence that special-interest groups may secure through campaign contributions.

The 1974 reform legislation, however, did not provide for public financing of House or Senate campaigns. (This was due primarily to the opposition of House members who feared that they would have to face a well-financed opponent every two years.) Neither did the new law restrict the formation of PACs. It did prohibit presidential nominees who accept federal financing from receiving individual contributions in the general election campaign. As a result, special-interest contributors turned their major attention—and increased money—to congressional campaigns. The number of PACs, most related to business and the professions, increased from 608 in 1975 to 1828 in 1978. Special-interest contributions to congressional campaigns in 1976 were nearly double what they had been in 1975.[23] In 1978, congressional campaign donations by special-interest groups were even higher; they totaled $33.1 million.

Contributors often feel that they have the right to ask for special favors from the public officials to whose campaigns they have contributed. President Carter, who had received campaign donations of $23,000 directly from maritime unions and, reportedly, another $200,000 in personal campaign donations from union officials, endorsed the maritime unions' bill in 1977. The bill contained a provision requiring almost 10 percent of imported oil to be shipped on U.S. tankers. Carter took this position against the strong advice of his economic, defense, and foreign-policy advisers. The maritime unions also contributed almost $500,000 dollars to 215 members of Congress in the 1976 campaign.[24] As a rule, campaign contributors do not demand a pledge of support when they donate money. But they do not have to. The message usually gets across anyway. Two members of Congress, whose votes were critical on the consumer protection agency bill in 1978, said that for the first time they had received between $20,000 and $40,000 for their reelection campaigns from small business groups that were opposed to the bill.[25]

The implicit threat of using money against an incumbent senator or representative can have a strong negative influence. Incumbents do not like to have to face the possibility of hard reelection campaigns. This is especially true of members of the House of Representatives, all of whom come up for reelection each two years. When a wealthy interest group supports one side of a controversial issue, money may have an effect on how members vote, even if no money actually changes hands. If a member votes "wrong," the interest group might finance a serious opponent in an upcoming election. Thus, the implied threat of money being used against an incumbent and the implied offer of a financial contribution to the incumbent may both affect decision-making.

Federal law prevents corporations from using regular operating funds to contribute to a candidate's campaign for federal office.

[23]*Congressional Quarterly, Weekly Report* (April 16, 1977), p. 710.
[24]*Chicago Sun-Times* (October 3, 1977, and October 18, 1977).
[25]Green, "Why the Consumer Bill Went Down," p. 200.

Federal laws also prohibit labor unions from spending "treasury funds"—money that members have not voluntarily donated for political candidates—on campaign contributions of any kind. In the past, there were many violations of these laws. For example, President Nixon received over three quarters of a million dollars in illegal corporate funds for his 1972 reelection campaign. Corporations usually "laundered" this illegal corporate money by giving extra "bonuses" to their officers and then requiring them to make campaign contributions from this extra money. Federal laws have been tightened to prevent such abuses in the future.

Campaign contributions are not the only ways in which interest groups can assist in political campaigns. They can mobilize their own members to vote. They can furnish campaign volunteers to answer phones and mail and especially to do door-to-door campaigning. In fact, an interest group with little money can offset the monetary contributions of opposing interest groups by providing volunteer workers. Both are important in a campaign.

Just as labor unions and corporations are prohibited from using operating funds to make campaign contributions, they are also prohibited from making "in kind" contributions. This term refers to the practice of using officers or employees to engage in political campaigning during working hours. But labor unions may use treasury funds to send campaign materials and information to their own members. Similarly, corporations may seek to influence the votes of their own officers and employees.

Both corporations and labor unions have used their employees illegally in campaigns in the past; they have gone beyond permitted internal campaigning. Corporations and unions have also made illegal payments to printers and advertising agencies for campaign services, making these contributions look like normal corporate or union expenditures. Such practices have, however, come under more severe scrutiny in recent years.

People who run for office obviously want to get elected. Presumably, most have convictions on major issues. But to get elected and to get reelected, candidates must have money and workers. So, political campaign activity is a central tactic of interest groups.

See how they run

Lobbying

Interest-group representatives and others who sought to influence state legislatures used to congregate in the lobbies, just off the floors of the legislative chambers. They came to be called "lobbyists," and their activity, "lobbying." Lobbying is an effort to influence the decisions of governmental policy-makers at the state or federal level, in either the executive or legislative branch.[26]

Our political system's fragmentation of power encourages the

---

[26]Lester Milbrath, *The Washington Lobbyists* (Chicago: Rand-McNally, 1963).

formation of interest groups. Power fragmentation produces "pressure points" in the decision-making process. These are places where influence can be wielded most effectively, especially to block action. Consider a hypothetical example. Suppose a pesticide bill is first introduced in the House of Representatives. It will go to a subcommittee (pressure point), which must act upon it before the bill goes to the full committee (pressure point) for final action. Then the bill will go to the floor of the House of Representatives for a vote (pressure point). Thereafter, the bill must go to the Senate, where it will again be considered first by a subcommittee (pressure point), and later by the full committee (pressure point). It will then go to the floor of the Senate for a vote (pressure point). If there are differences between the House and Senate versions, the bill must next go to a conference committee (pressure point) and the compromise worked out there must again be voted on in both the House (pressure point) and Senate (pressure point). After the bill has been agreed to in identical form by both the House and Senate, it will go to the President for his approval or disapproval (pressure point).

This first pesticide legislation is only the "authorization" bill. Before the new program can be put into effect, there must be an appropriation of money to pay for it. An appropriations bill for this purpose will be introduced in the House of Representatives, considered in a subcommittee (pressure point), in the full committee (pressure point), and in the full House (pressure point). It will thereafter be considered in a Senate subcommittee (pressure point), in the full committee (pressure point), and in the full Senate (pressure point). Any differences between the two bills will be worked out again by a conference committee (pressure point), submitted for final vote in the House (pressure point) and Senate (pressure point), and sent to the President for approval or disapproval (pressure point).

The issue will still not be settled! The President (pressure point) may have to appoint new officials, who must be confirmed by the Senate (pressure point) before they can administer the new pesticide program. Also, most legislation leaves many details to be filled in by regulations, which must be issued by those who will administer the new program (pressure point). Most regulations must be interpreted on a day-to-day basis by lower-level employees (pressure point). Finally, those who are charged with violations of the law are entitled to hearings (pressure point).

A fragmented system of power protects against a strong minority or a runaway majority. But it also results in a highly complicated system, which ordinary citizens may find confusing and difficult to influence. Hence, fragmentation of power is an important cause of the formation and influence of interest groups in America.

Interest groups may seek to influence public policy decisions in a variety of ways. They may try to ensure that people who are sympathetic to their interests are appointed to administer programs

Whether you are a private citizen seeking to make your opinion known to your senator, representative, or other national, state, or local official, or a registered lobbyist working for an interest group, you need to know the "informal rules."

1. *Be pleasant and nonoffensive.* Since decision-makers must meet with many people every day, it eases their burden considerably if these associations are pleasant.

2. *Convince the official that it is important to listen. . . .* Since elected officials are nearly always concerned with constituent interests, a demonstration of constituent interest is one of the best ways to insure attention.

3. *Be well prepared and well informed. . . .* Officials require lobbyists to be knowledgeable because they need information and want something in return for the time and attention they give.

4. *Be personally convinced. . . .* Advocacy is also reported to be generally more successful if it is well balanced. Many lobbyists deliberately present arguments on the other side. They do this partly to suggest fair-mindedness, but mainly to strengthen their own side. . . . the lobbyist who presents both sides leaves the official with the impression that he has looked at all sides of the question and then arrived at his conclusion.

5. *Be succinct, well organized, and direct. . . .* The challenge to the lobbyist is to communicate the greatest amount of relevant information in the shortest possible time. Presentations should not only be short but simple, well organized, and direct.

6. *Use the soft sell. . . .* Some lobbyists make the mistake of pushing their case too hard. . . . This is fool-hardy in the atmosphere of compromise that inevitably prevails in legislative decision-making.

How to...
Lobby Government Officials

7. *Leave a short written summary of the case.* Most officials prefer to have something in writing to relieve them of the necessity of taking notes and to ensure correctness of information and interpretation.

SOURCE: Lester Milbrath, *The Washington Lobbyists* (Rand McNally, 1963), pp. 220-26.

that are important to them. They may quietly but effectively get involved in the election of officers of the House and Senate. They often use their influence to block new legislation; people with power are usually satisfied with the status quo. In addition, interest groups may promote legislation or other government policies or propose new ideas.

Access is a very important resource for an interest group. A person who makes a campaign contribution will often say something like this: "I don't want any special promise from you; all I want is the right to come and talk to you when I need to." This seemingly modest request may in fact be significant. For example, one large stockholder in an American airline, who had contributed $200,000 to President Nixon's reelection campaign in 1972, later talked to the President on the phone and asked him not to object to the airline's proposed merger with another line. The stockholder claimed that there was no connection between his campaign contribution and this lobbying. But it is important to note that most Americans would not have been able to get the President of the United States on the telephone or to lobby the President so directly in favor of their own interests. Access is power.

The lobbying influence of an interest group depends on several factors. The interest group's ability to use grass-roots pressure, mass propaganda, and political campaign activity, of course, is essential to its lobbying effectiveness. But other things make a difference, too. *Size* can be very important. The AFL-CIO, for example, can mobilize its large constituency on labor legislation. Size is not as effective, however, on issues that interest-group members do not feel very intensely about.

Therefore, the *intensity* of the interest-group opinion is also very important. Even a relatively small group can be effective if its members are intensely committed to its goals. One of the reasons why the National Rifle Association is so powerful is that its members are vigorously and bitterly opposed to any form of gun control.

The National Rifle Association example also illustrates another factor in interest-group influence—*narrow focus*. An interest group that speaks only on limited issues of special concern to its members will be more influential. The National Association of Manufacturers, for example, could not lobby effectively about free trade because there is no agreement among its members on this issue.

Geography can be a factor in the effectiveness of interest groups. Some interest groups, such as importers, are so concentrated in specific geographical areas that they wield little influence with most members of Congress who have few importers in their home states or districts. On the other hand, when the Coca Cola Company and other soft-drink bottlers were seeking legislation to overturn an antitrust court order, they mobilized bottlers in every congressional district in

copyright 1979 by Herblock in The Washington Post.

"I only fire blanks but they jump anyhow."

The following is excerpted from a speech by Senator Edward M. Kennedy (D., Mass.) given in 1979 at Lake Superior State College in Sault Ste. Marie, Michigan:

Representative government on Capitol Hill is in the worst shape I have seen it in my 16 years in the Senate.

The heart of the problem is that the Senate and the House are awash in a sea of special-interest campaign contributions and special-interest lobbying.

As Mark Twain once said, "We have the best Congress money can buy." And the problem is worse today than Tom Sawyer or Huckleberry Finn could possibly have imagined.

At the end of 1974, there were already 516 organizations called "PACs"—political action committees—on file with the Federal Election Commission. These are groups that register in order to be able to contribute to candidates for federal office. By 1978, that number had more than tripled to 1,709. Corporations this year have been creating political action committees at the rate of one a day.

They are multiplying like rabbits, and they're doing their best to buy every senator, every representative and every issue in sight.

The numbers tell the story:

•In the 1972 congressional election, campaign contributions by special-interest political action committees totaled $8.5 million.

•In 1974, the total climbed to $12.5 million.

•In 1976, it was $22.5 million.

•By mid-July, 1978, these special-interest groups already had contributed $11 million—and they had an additional $27 million in cash on hand.

Let me give you a specific example of the problem. The House Commerce Committee this year voted 22 to 21 to kill the important hospital cost-containment measure that would have placed modest ceilings on rates at which hospital charges are growing. One of the best opportunities we have had in many years to halt the soaring inflation in the cost of health care was defeated by a single vote.

Of those 22 congressmen who voted to kill the measure, 19 had received a total of $85,000 in campaign contributions from the American Medical Assn. in the last three years, an average of almost $4,500 each. And on the crucial vote, they voted with the AMA to kill the measure.

There is a very simple and obvious answer to these abuses: Take elections off the auction block and allow candidates to pay for their campaigns with public funds. We already pay for presidential elections through public financing. And that is how we ought to start paying for elections to the Senate and to the House of Representatives, if there is to be any real hope of making our democracy work the way it should.

We in Congress are elected to represent all the people of our states, not just those rich or powerful enough to pay for our campaigns and to hire lobbyists to hold megaphones constantly at our ears.

VIEWPOINT

The Best Congress Money Can Buy?

America and made sure that each member of the House and Senate was lobbied by people from his or her own home district.

The *moral strength* demonstrated by an interest group can also contribute to its influence. Although black people are a minority in America, they have in recent years caused the removal of legal barriers to equality, partly because of their appeal to the consciences of Americans. Similarly, there are only one million American Indians, but they have considerable influence on government policies relating to their specific interests. Their disproportionately large influence can be attributed in part to the moral obligation that many Americans feel our society owes to Indians to redress past wrongs.

The possession of needed *information,* as mentioned earlier, enhances an interest group's influence. The relationship between a lobbyist and a policy-maker is not always a one-way street. The lobbyist may achieve something from the relationship: the policy-maker's support for the interest group's position. But the policy-maker may also get something from the relationship: reliable information. Some interest groups are better equipped to do first-rate research on issues than are others. Some are better known than others for furnishing reliable information. Information is used by policy-makers in making decisions; it is also used to justify positions that they have already taken. The AFL-CIO staff in Washington is particularly professional and qualified in this regard, and they use their reliable information and research to advantage.[27]

Attempts are sometimes made to purchase influence outright, as evidenced by Korean businessman Tongsun Park's payments to some members of Congress. In response to recent corruption scandals, however, new laws have been adopted to provide stricter sets of ethics for public officials, both executive and legislative, including stricter rules concerning the receipt and disclosure of outside income. Common Cause has been particularly active in support of this legislation at both the national and state levels.

LIMITS ON INTEREST-GROUP POWER

Interest groups are important but not all-powerful. Events, the actions of leaders, the influence of the media, and the effects of the law all limit the power of interest groups.

The combined impact of the first two of these factors can be seen from a consideration of the first years of President Lyndon Johnson's administration. After Johnson took office following President John F. Kennedy's assassination, Congress adopted a number of new laws

---

[27]See Lewis Anthony Dexter, *How Organizations Are Represented in Washington* (Indianapolis: Bobbs-Merrill, 1969).

which had been gathering dust in the legislative hoppers for years. This flurry of legislative activity was partly due to the national mood of sympathy for the slain President's recommendations, especially his civil rights proposals. But it was also due to Johnson's consummate skill, as a former Senate majority leader, in getting Congress to follow his leadership. For example, President Kennedy had taken one element—health care for the elderly—of the national health insurance program recommended by President Harry S. Truman a dozen years earlier—and had recommended it to the Congress in 1961 in the form of Medicare. But medical, insurance, and other interest groups that opposed Medicare had successfully blocked its passage. These same groups still fought the proposal after Johnson became President, just as they had when Kennedy was President. Yet Johnson was able to get Medicare enacted.

Leaders' influence does not always depend upon interest groups. They may use interest groups to secure approval for their policies, and they can also check the power of interest groups. Events, such as the accident in 1979 at the Three Mile Island nuclear plant in Pennsylvania, can also limit the power of interest groups by producing a powerful change in public opinion. The mass media can serve as an important check on interest groups, too. These are the findings of James Wilson, who writes:

Organized groups can rarely accomplish unaided such changes in opinion or such redefinition of what constitutes legitimate public action; instead, these changes are the result of dramatic or critical events (a depression, a war, a national scandal), extraordinary political leadership, the rise of new political elites, and the accumulated impact of ideas via the mass media of communications. [28]

Like interest groups, the mass media in the United States constitute almost an unofficial arm of the government. They serve as a check on government, as well as on interest groups. The press often produces and publishes evidence of official wrongdoing and corrupt dealings between officials and interest groups. That is why Common Cause and other political reformers have lobbied so strongly for such reforms as open meetings of all public agencies and bodies and full disclosure of financial information by public officials. Such openness allows the press to exercise its watchdog function and to alert the general public to procedures and policies that are not in their interests.

Interest groups often enjoy their greatest influence when their activities are shielded from public view. When congressional committees could regularly meet behind closed doors to make final decisions on proposed legislation, the power of interest groups was enhanced.

---

[28] James Q. Wilson, *Political Organizations* (New York: Basic Books, 1973), p. 330.

In tax legislation, for example, a slight change in wording arrived at in a secret session could mean millions of dollars in gains or losses for businesses and other taxpayers. Now that most such committee meetings have been opened to the public and to the press, it is much more difficult for members of Congress and representatives of interest groups to strike private deals that favor special interests but not the general interests of all citizens.

Finally, the power of interest groups can be limited and regulated by law. But at the national level, the existing law regulating lobbying (first adopted in 1946) has little effect. This law only requires interest groups to register with the House and Senate if lobbying is their "principal purpose." Further the Supreme Court has held that grass-roots lobbying is not covered by the act.[29] Most of the interest groups that lobby in connection with economic interests—business, labor, and professional organizations—were not formed for the primary purpose of lobbying. A labor union is formed primarily to negotiate contracts with management. Trade and professional associations and chambers of commerce are formed primarily to provide largely nonpolitical services to their members. Many interest groups, then, take the position that lobbying is not their principal purpose, so they do not register at all. Virtually all interest groups take advantage of the exemption in the reporting requirements concerning grass-roots lobbying, which is always a large part of any major interest group's activities.

In many ways, the present federal law regulating lobbying is a joke. For example, the American Petroleum Institute reported having spent only $121,276 for lobbying in 1973; the AFL-CIO said it spent only $240,800; and the American Medical Association reported lobbying expenditures of only $114,859—all ridiculously low figures.[30] By contrast, Common Cause, voluntarily complying with the stricter reporting requirements it advocates, reported lobbying expenditures of nearly $1,000,000.

In 1978, many special-interest groups and some public-interest groups joined forces to block or weaken rigorous new laws designed to regulate lobbying at the federal level. The proposed legislation, which was passed by the House of Representatives, was an attempt to strike a proper balance "between individual citizen's right to petition their government and the public's right to know what organizations are doing to pressure Congress," said a representative of Common Cause, which backed the bill.[31] An even more stringent bill, passed by the Senate in 1976, died in the House.

The 1978 House bill would avoid the "principal purpose" loophole in the existing law by requiring any organization that spends more

---

[29]See *United States* v. *Harriss,* 347 U.S. 612 (1954).

[30]Congressional Quarterly Service, *The Washington Lobby,* 2nd ed. (Washington, D.C.: Congressional Quarterly, 1974), p. 38.

[31]*Congressional Quarterly* (April 29, 1978), p. 1027.

than 1 percent of its total budget on lobbying to register. It would also require a lobbying group to report the names of those from which it had received more than $3,000 a year in dues or contributions, and it would mandate full disclosure of grass-roots lobbying efforts. Some special-interest groups opposed these provisions because they do not want such public scrutiny of their lobbying activities. Some opponents claimed that organizations, like individuals, are entitled to the right of privacy, which they said the House bill would abridge. Some public-interest groups like the American Civil Liberties Union argued that the bill would allow "unprecedented surveillance of political activities" by the government.

New laws regulating lobbying are necessary if there is to be any regulation at all. The old law is unenforceable. Only four cases have ever been prosecuted under it. Congress is faced with the alternative of continuing an unenforceable and ineffective law or adopting a new law that will give the general public a fairly accurate picture of the activities and influence of interest groups in the American political system.

CONCLUSION

The First Amendment safeguards the rights of Americans to organize and to petition their government. Participation in interest groups is an important way for citizens to exercise those rights. The fragmentation of power in our governmental system—designed to prevent the concentration of political power in too few hands and to restrict majority control—is one reason why there are so many interest groups in this country. Complicated modern problems are another reason. As a Senate committee report noted, "The increasing complexity of modern life, and the consequent increase in the role of government in the lives of all Americans, have caused the pressure groups to play a more important part in our government than was anticipated a hundred years ago."[32]

The influence of interest groups is probably neither as benign nor as powerful as their pluralist supporters claim. But their influence in our system is probably not as evil as their detractors say it is, either. Interest groups are a perennial plant in the American political garden. Although they perform important functions in our political system, there are legitimate criticisms of them and their activities. Foremost is the fact that not all interests are represented by interest groups, and those that are do not have equal influence.

Both special-interest groups and public-interest groups use a variety of tactics to achieve their goals. There are limits on their

---

[32]*1957 Report of the Senate Special Committee to Investigate Political Activities, Lobbying, and Campaign Contributions,* quoted in The Congressional Quarterly Service, *The Washington Lobby,* p. 2.

power. But because of the increase in their activities in recent years and because of the growing influence of money in the political process, legislators have proposed new restrictions on interest-group activities. These include campaign financing reforms and more stringent disclosure requirements for lobbyists.

The American political system is complex. But those who participate in the system as members of interest groups are more likely to cause the system to respond to their needs than those who do not.

ADDITIONAL SOURCES

Berle, Adolph A. *Power.* Harcourt Brace Jovanovich, 1969.

Berry, Jeffrey, *Lobbying for the People: The Political Behavior of Public Interest Groups.* Princeton University Press, 1977.*

Galbraith, John Kenneth. *The New Industrial State,* 3rd rev. ed. Houghton-Mifflin, 1978.

Greenwald, Carol S. *Group Power: Lobbying and Public Policy.* Praeger, 1977.*

Key, V.O., Jr. *Politics, Parties, and Pressure Groups,* 5th ed. Harper & Row, 1964.

Milbrath, Lester W. *The Washington Lobbyists.* Rand-McNally, 1963.

Ornstein, Norman J., and Shirley Elder. *Interest Groups, Lobbying, and Policymaking.* Congressional Quarterly, 1978.*

Salisbury, Robert H. *Interest Groups: Who They Are and How They Influence.* National Journal, 1977.*

Schattschneider, E.E. *The Semisovereign People.* Holt, Rinehart, Winston, 1960.

Truman, David. *The Governmental Process: Political Interests and Public Opinion,* 2nd ed. Knopf, 1951.*

*Available in paperback.

9 Political Parties
Organizing for Political Power

Suppose someone asks, "Will the Democratic party support national health insurance?" There is no single, easy answer to that question. Before it can be answered at all, we must have some additional information from the questioner. We would have to inquire, "What do you mean by 'the Democratic party'?" In 1979, we would also have had to ask, "Do you mean the Democrat who is now in the White House, President Carter? Do you mean the majority leader of the U.S. Senate, Robert Byrd (D., W. Va.)? Are you referring to the speaker of the U.S. House of Representatives, Thomas P. O'Neill (D., Mass.)? Do you mean Senator Russell Long (D., La.), the chairperson of the U.S. Senate Finance Committee, which has jurisdiction over health insurance? Or Representative Al Ullman (D., Wash.), the chairperson of the House Ways and Means Committee, which has similar jurisdiction in the House? Are you referring to all the Democratic members of the House and Senate? Or do you mean the chairperson of the Democratic National Committee, John White? All the members of the Democratic National Committee? All the chairpersons of the Democratic state committees? A majority of those Americans who call themselves Democrats?"

Democratic party leaders (in foreground, left to right): Senate Majority Leader Robert Byrd, Vice-President Walter Mondale, President Jimmy Carter, and Speaker of the House Tip O'Neill.

These are by no means all the questions one might ask in order to find out what "the Democratic party" is. Each of these members of "the Democratic party" may have different opinions on national health insurance (and on other issues). The same is true for "the Republican party."

The first thing to understand about American political parties is that they do not exist, at least not in the European sense or in the way many Americans believe. In the United States, there is no such thing as *the* Democratic party or *the* Republican party for all purposes. The federal principle of shared sovereignty between the state and federal governments means that each party has a national organization and separate state and local organizations as well. The separation of powers in our government is paralleled by a separation within the parties. A political party does not have a single position on issues for all the branches in either the federal government or a state government. In America, then, there is a *fragmentation* of political parties, which parallels the fragmentation of power within our political system. By contrast, power in European governmental systems is usually less fragmented, and there is less fragmentation within their political parties, which are usually centralized.

American political parties are different from European parties in three other respects. First, American political parties are characterized by *membership by self-identification*. Membership in an American political party, for example, is nothing like membership in the Conservative party of Great Britain. A person might say, "I am a Republican," even though he or she might never have attended a precinct meeting or any other party gathering, might never have paid any party dues, might never have taken part in a political campaign, and might have voted only infrequently. Such a person may register as a Republican in order to vote in a primary election, which nominates the party candidates, but that registration requires no approval by a Republican party organization. Similarly, people can change their party registration without securing party approval. Thus, American political parties have no control over who may become members.

Second, most American elections are characterized by *uncontrolled party nominations*. In the early 1900s, the Progressive Movement worked for a number of electoral reforms in America. Among the reforms that were adopted was the direct primary election, a method of nominating party candidates. In a direct primary election, the voters of the party, rather than a caucus of party leaders or a convention of party delegates, decide which candidate will be nominated. Even in states which still have party conventions for selecting or endorsing party nominees for state offices, unsuccessful candidates can get their names on the primary election ballot by securing enough signatures on a petition. This procedure thus allows candidates to circumvent the will of the party organization. Presidential nominees are selected in national conventions, but a large number of the delegates at such conventions are elected in state primaries or have been instructed in advance, based on the popular state vote, to support a certain candidate at the national convention.

Third, the American parties are characterized by a *lack of party discipline*. That is, an elected official's political party cannot effectively require the official to vote in accordance with the party platform. In Great Britain, on the other hand, a prime minister who does not act in accordance with the wishes of a majority of the prime minister's party members in the House of Commons cannot continue in office. In addition, members of the British House of Commons who do not vote in accordance with their party platform face the possibility of being refused the party's nomination at the next election because the party organization controls the nominations. In the United States, of course, members of Congress who vote against a plank in their party platform can nevertheless be renominated by going directly to the people in a primary election.

What, then, do we mean by *political parties* in America? Each of our two major political parties—the Democratic party and the Republican party—is a group that seeks to elect people to governmental offices under a specific label.[1] (At the national level, minor parties may only be nominally electoral. They seek to influence government policy, but they have little hope of controlling it.) This simple definition of a major political party obscures several factors, however. American political parties exist in three "guises": as the "party-in-the-electorate"; as the formal party organization; and as the "party-in-government."[2] When we speak of the Democratic party or the Republican party, we must be specific and indicate which of these characteristics of American political parties we have in mind.

THE PARTY-IN-THE-ELECTORATE

When someone says, "I am a Republican," that person is a part of the Republican party-in-the-electorate. The *party-in-the-electorate* is made up of people who call themselves by one or another party label. As we saw in Chapter 6, party identification begins at an early age and has a lasting effect.

The Two-Party System

America has a two-party system, consisting of the Democrats and the Republicans. By contrast, in thirty other countries with competing political parties, only eight had two-party systems in 1966; the rest

---

[1] Leon D. Epstein, *Political Parties in Western Democracies* (New York: Praeger, 1967), p. 9.

[2] See Frank J. Sorauf, *Party Politics in America,* 3rd ed. (Boston, Mass.: Little, Brown, 1976), pp. 9–12.

had multiparty systems.[3] Our two-party system has been an enduring feature of our society. With few exceptions, the two major parties together have accounted for about 90 percent of the total popular vote since the early 1800s.[4]

George Washington warned against the effects of political parties, and John Adams declared that there was nothing he dreaded as much as the division of the country into "two great parties."[5] Yet there has been a *historical dualism* in American politics ever since the early 1800s.[6] At that time, supporters of Alexander Hamilton, on one hand, and Thomas Jefferson, on the other, formed the beginnings of the first modern political parties in America: the Federalists and the Democratic-Republicans, respectively. The Democratic-Republican party, a coalition of farmers, laborers, and slaveowners, was slowly transformed into the Democratic party. During the mid-1800s, when the Whig party developed in opposition to the Democrats, the formal party structures that exist today—national nominating conventions and national and state committees—were organized. The Republican party—the forerunner of the present party—was founded in 1854; it included not only financiers, industrialists, and merchants, but also workers, farmers, and newly freed blacks. Except for Grover Cleveland's two terms as President (1884–88 and 1892–96), the Republicans dominated the Presidency from 1860 until 1912. Not until 1932, when Herbert Hoover was defeated by Franklin Roosevelt, were the Democrats able to put together a lasting national coalition. The party alignments that resulted from President Roosevelt's New Deal continued to characterize the two major parties, at least until the late 1960s and early 1970s. In 1976, Jimmy Carter was able to put together the "traditional" Democratic coalition. It soon began to fall apart, however, as some of its members, notably black people and other minorities and members of organized labor, grew dissatisfied with some of his policies.

In part, then, our two-party system endures because it has always been that way; we have always had two major political parties. But our electoral system has also favored the continuation of a two-party alignment in America because of the legal and structural barriers that have prevented the rise of minor parties. The election laws of most states make it very difficult for new or minor parties to get on the ballot.[7] The American electoral structure is based upon single-member districts, with winner-take-all victories on a plurality basis. This means that there can generally be only one winner from each

[3]Robert A. Dahl, *Political Oppositions in Western Democracies* (New Haven, Connecticut: Yale University Press, 1966), p. 333.

[4]Allen P. Sindler, *Political Parties in the United States* (New York: St. Martin's Press, 1966), p. 15.

[5]Wilfred E. Bindley, *American Political Parties* (New York: Knopf, 1963), p. 19.

[6]See Clinton Rossiter, *Parties and Politics in America* (Ithaca, N.Y.: Cornell University Press, 1960).

[7]Jim McClellan and David E. Anderson, "The Bipartisan Ballot Monopoly," *The Progressive* (March 1975), pp. 18–21.

district; the votes of those who supported the loser or losers are "lost." Some other democracies have electoral structures that award percentages of membership in their parliaments (which are like our Congress) to political parties on the basis of their share of the total vote. In such countries, if a party or its candidates receive 30 percent of the total vote, the party will have 30 percent of the elected parliamentary members, even though the party did not "win" the election in the American sense.

By contrast, it is theoretically possible in the United States for the Republican party, say, to elect every member of the U.S. House of Representatives, even if the Republican candidates for the House receive only a combined total of 50.1 percent of the national vote, and the Democrats receive 49.9 percent. This improbable but possible result would occur if the Republican candidate in every congressional district received at least one more vote than any other candidate in that district. This example illustrates how the American electoral structure discourages minor parties; a party must have substantial strength at the polls in order to gain any political office at all.

The American method of electing Presidents also discourages minor parties in America. In parliamentary democracies, such as France, Italy, and Great Britain, the parliament elects the prime minister from its own membership. Except in Great Britain, where there have historically been two major parties, governments are usually elected by a coalition of two or more parties because no one party has a majority of the parliamentary members by itself. In those countries, a minor party, though not able to gain majority control of the parliament and the government, may nevertheless have influence. It may even be awarded a cabinet position in return for its support of the majority coalition. No such opportunity for coalition politics and minor party influence readily exists in American political practice. Although the Electoral College, in the first instance, and the U.S. House of Representatives, if no majority emerges in the Electoral College, could serve as the mechanism for coalition selection of the American President, this has not been done in modern times.

Still, we do not completely understand why our system is a

Significant Minor Parties in Presidential Elections, 1880–1976*

Year	Candidate	Party	Popular Vote	Per-centage	Electoral Vote
1880	James B. Weaver	*Greenback-Labor*	308,578	*3.4%*	0
1888	Clinton B. Fisk	*Prohibition*	249,506	*2.2%*	0
1892	James B. Weaver	*People's (Populist)*	1,029,846	*8.5%*	22
	John Bidwell	*Prohibition*	264,133	*2.2%*	0
1904	Eugene V. Debs	*Socialist*	402,283	*3.0%*	0
1908	Eugene V. Debs	*Socialist*	420,793	*2.8%*	0
1912	Theodore Roosevelt	*Progressive*	4,118,571	*17.1%*	88
	Eugene V. Debs	*Socialist*	900,672	*6.0%*	0
1916	A. L. Benson	*Socialist*	585,113	*3.2%*	0
1920	Eugene V. Debs	*Socialist*	919,799	*3.4%*	0
1924	Robert M. LaFollette	*Progressive*	4,831,289	*17.1%*	13
1932	Norman Thomas	*Socialist*	881,951	*2.2%*	0
1936	William Lemke	*Union Party*	882,479	*2.0%*	0
1948	J. Strom Thurmond	*States' Rights*	1,169,063	*2.4%*	39
	Henry Wallace	*Progressive*	1,157,172	*2.4%*	0
1968	George Wallace	*American Independent*	9,906,141	*13.5%*	46

*Includes candidates receiving 2% or more of the popular vote.
SOURCE: U.S. Bureau of the Census, *Historical Statistics of the United States.*

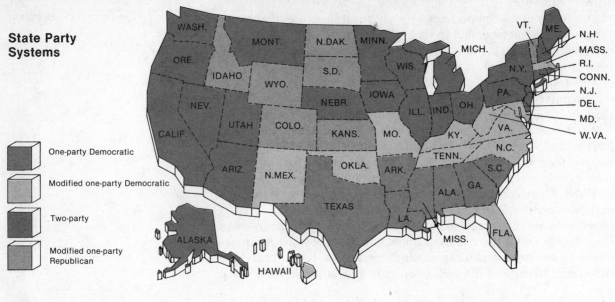

State Party Systems

Legend:
- One-party Democratic
- Modified one-party Democratic
- Two-party
- Modified one-party Republican

SOURCE: Herbert Jacob and Kenneth Vines, eds., *Politics in the American States*, 3rd ed. (Boston: Little, Brown, 1976), p. 62.

two-party system and most other parliamentary democracies are not.[8] As noted earlier, there are historical forces at work; America may have a two-party system because it has almost always been that way, and people do not change their party loyalties or their party systems very readily. Most Americans say they like the two-party system.[9]

Some states and congressional districts have been characterized as "one-party" areas. For a long time, it was possible to speak of the "solid South" as completely Democratic. But the elections of the 1960s and the 1970s saw a number of southern states switch to the Republican party in presidential races. Jimmy Carter's campaign in 1976 brought most of the South back into the Democratic fold in that election, partly because he was a Southerner. Although a single party may still be dominant in some localities, the trend now is toward greater competition between the two major parties throughout all parts of the country.[10]

Despite the two-party nature of our political system, minor parties, sometimes called third parties, have always been present in the American system. Some have been based upon an ideology, such as the Socialist Workers party and the Libertarian party. Others, like

---

[8]See Walter Dean Burnham, "Party Systems and the Political Process," in William Nesbitt Chambers and Walter Dean Burnham, *The American Party Systems*, 3rd ed. (New York: Oxford University Press, 1975), pp. 289–304.

[9]Aaron B. Wildavsky, "A Methodological Critique of Duverger's Political Parties," *Journal of Politics*, 21 (May 1959): 303–18.

[10]See Jack Dennis, "Trends in Public Support for the American Party System," *British Journal of Political Science*, 5 (1974).

Theodore Roosevelt's Progressive party of 1912 and George Wallace's American Independent party of 1968, have been organized around individuals. Several minor parties, such as the Prohibition party, have also been organized around particular issues. Many of these parties have lasted for a long time, although they have had little influence. Others have lasted only a short time. Most have been more like interest groups than parties, seeking to influence public opinion and government policy rather than to win elections. Minor parties were organized by black people in the 1960s to contest the racist "regular" Democratic parties of the South; they achieved considerable influence in the national Democratic party. They became the recognized Democratic party in some states and in others, they were eventually merged into the regular party. The Raza Unida party, organized by Chicanos in California, Texas, and other southwestern states, is trying to become a permanent and influential third party in those states. In New York, the Liberal party has sometimes been able to wield the balance of electoral power by endorsing candidates of one or the other of the major parties.

Nationally, minor parties have enjoyed little electoral success and have not been able to show consistent and continuing strength. High points for minor parties in American history were the 8.5 percent of the national vote achieved by the People's party, also known as the Populist party, in 1892; the 17.1 percent of the national vote won by Theodore Roosevelt's Progressive party, also known as the Bull Moose party, in 1912; the 17.1 percent of the national vote garnered by Robert M. La Follette's Progressive party of 1924; and the 13.5 percent of the vote received by George Wallace's American Independent party in 1968. Minor parties have sometimes served the important purpose of raising and popularizing issues, but one of the main reasons why they have not enjoyed electoral success is that the major parties have frequently adopted the issues of the minor parties. For example, after the 1892 election, the Democratic party adopted some of the central themes of the Populist party. In fact, the Democratic nominee for President in 1896, William Jennings Bryan, ran on joint tickets with Populist candidates in a number of states.

Party Identification Trends

During the period from 1952 to 1972, the percentage of Americans who called themselves either Democrats or Republicans declined, and the percentage who called themselves Independents increased. From 1972 to 1978, the percentages showed a decline for the Democrats, and the Republicans, and a slight gain for the Independents. In 1978, 39 percent of the American people identified themselves as Democrats, 37 percent said they were Independents, and 20 percent called themselves Republicans.[11] Thus, neither of the two major parties by itself constitutes a national majority.

---

[11]Survey Research Center of the University of Michigan (1978).

Perhaps even more significant than the overall percentages are the findings concerning intensity of party identification. From 1952 to 1972, the percentage of Americans who said they were "strong" Republicans or "strong" Democrats dropped sharply. For the Republicans the figure decreased from 13 to 10 percent; for the Democrats, from 22 to 15 percent.[12]

Thus, we have seen a *declining party loyalty* in the American electorate in recent years. The increase in "ticket splitting," which occurs when a voter votes for the candidates of different parties in different races during the same election, also indicates this trend. For example, a voter might vote for the Republican candidate for Congress and the Democratic candidate for President. In the 1972 election, 69 percent of the Democratic voters, 49 percent of the Republican voters, and 73 percent of the Independent voters split their tickets in the presidential and congressional races.[13]

Party Identification In the United States, 1952–78

	1952	1956	1960	1964	1968	1972	1976	1978
Democrat	47%	44%	46%	51%	45%	40%	40%	39%
Independent*	22	24	23	23	30	34	37	37
Republican	27	29	27	24	24	23	23	20
Apolitical/ Don't know	4	3	4	2	1	3	1	3

*Includes "Independent Democrats" and "Independent Republicans."
SOURCE: University of Michigan Survey Research Center/Center for Political Studies.

Prior to 1950, congressional districts with split results in presidential and congressional races constituted less than 15 percent of all the districts; in 1972, slightly over 44 percent of the congressional districts had split results.[14]

Who are the Independents? The traditional view of political scientists was that Independents were less active politically, less informed, and had less understanding of major political issues and alternatives.[15] In recent years, however, a new type of Independent seems to have emerged. Americans under thirty are more likely to be Independents than are those over thirty. This younger group of Independents has attained a higher educational and socioeconomic level than the older Independents. The new Independents may simply have declined to identify with either major party because they

[12]See Austin Ranney, "Parties in State Politics," in Herbert Jacob and Kenneth Vines, eds., *Politics and the American States* (Boston, Mass.: Little, Brown and Company, 1971); and James Sundquist, *Dynamics of the Party System: Alignment and Re-Alignment of Political Parties in the United States* (Washington, D.C.: The Brookings Institute, 1973).

[13]See Herbert Asher, *Presidential Elections and American Politics: Voters, Candidates and Campaigns Since 1952* (Homewood, Ill.: The Dorsey Press, 1976), p. 68.

[14]Walter Dean Burnham, *Critical Elections and the Mainsprings of American Politics* (New York: Norton, 1970), p. 109; and Walter Dean Burnham, "American Politics in the 1970's: Beyond Party?" in Chambers and Burnham, eds., *The American Party Systems*, p. 321. See also Everett Carll Ladd, Jr. with Charles D. Hadley, *Transformations of the American Party System* (New York: Norton, 1975), p. 296.

[15]For a discussion of this traditional view, see V. O. Key, Jr. with Milton C. Cummings, *The Responsible Electorate* (Cambridge, Mass.: Harvard University Press, 1966).

cannot find any real meaning in the values and activities of the major parties.[16] (But, at least as far as elections are concerned, Independents must still choose between the candidates of the two major parties.)

Not only do Americans identify with the parties less, they also seem to see less value in parties today than they did in the past. Eighty percent of the American people think that it is better to vote for the person than for the party. Less than 4 percent say that political parties have done the "best job" in the last couple of years, compared to Congress, the Supreme Court, and the President. Only 38 percent of the people interviewed in one state, Wisconsin, agreed that party labels should continue to be kept on the ballot.[17]

Although we should not overemphasize the importance of the party label, we should not underestimate its importance either. As Frank J. Sorauf has pointed out, people's party identification "tells us more about their political perceptions and political activities than does any other fact. It is the single most important influence on the political behavior of the American adult."[18] Even in the 1960 presidential campaign between Richard M. Nixon and John F. Kennedy, when Kennedy's Catholicism was an important issue, "Protestant Democrats were more likely to behave as Democrats than as Protestants, and Catholic Republicans were more likely to behave as Republicans than as Catholics."[19]

Since many more people label themselves Democrats than Republicans, party identification is a much more important appeal for the Democratic party and its candidates than for the Republican party and its candidates. Thus, Republican candidates tend to play down their party label. The Republican party tends to campaign nationally on noneconomic issues like law and order, which cut across party lines. And the Republican party tends to nominate especially attractive candidates who can make a nonpartisan appeal to voters. World War II hero Dwight D. Eisenhower was a perfect example. Democrats, on the other hand, tend to emphasize their party label.

The party label is especially important to voters from lower socioeconomic levels and to those with less education. These voters may be less experienced and less actively involved in politics, so they may find the voting choices more confusing than more experienced and active voters. "In this dilemma," one authority has stated, "having the party symbol stamped on certain candidates, certain issue positions, certain interpretations of political reality is a great psychological convenience."[20]

---

[16]See Burnham, *Critical Elections and the Mainsprings of American Politics,* p. 127.

[17]See Dennis, "Trends in Public Support for the American Party System," pp. 200–207.

[18]Sorauf, *Party Politics in America,* p. 168.

[19]Phillip E. Converse, "Religion and Politics: The 1960 Election," in Angus Campbell et al., *Elections and the Political Order* (New York: Wiley, 1966), p. 123.

[20]Donald E. Stokes, "Party Loyalty and the Likelihood of Deviating Elections," in Campbell, et al., *Elections and the Political Order,* pp. 126–27.

For many voters, then, the party label continues to be an important *cue* for voting behavior. Without the cue—when elections are on a nonpartisan basis, for example—Republican candidates and candidates from middle- or high-income areas receive a boost in electoral support.[21]

Are Democrats Different from Republicans?

Democrats and Republicans cannot be categorized into two completely different groups of people. The two groups overlap, just as the type of U.S. senators who belong to one party or another overlaps. Democrats have liberals, such as Edward M. Kennedy of Massachusetts, and conservatives, such as John Stennis of Mississippi, in their party; the Republicans also have moderate liberals like Jacob Javits of New York, and conservatives like Oren Hatch of Utah.

How accurate, then, is the party label as a voting cue? Does it correctly indicate which voting choices are in the voters' best interests? It is usually fairly accurate. If voters know only one thing about the candidates in a particular race—their party affiliation—they have a fairly good chance of choosing a candidate who will be likely to vote on issues the same way they would.

Are Democrats different from Republicans? Delegates at the 1976 Republican Convention (left) and the 1976 Democratic Convention (right) display the party symbols.

[22] Why is this true? We know that people are most likely to acquire party loyalty through the early influence of the family; this is as true for leaders and public officials as it is for average voters. But how do people's parents acquire their party loyalty? And why does a person change from one party to another? We saw in Chapter 6 that socioeconomic status, events, race, religion, and the region of the country where a person lives influence a person's choice of party affiliation. People of lower socioeconomic status are more likely to be Democrats, and those of higher socioeconomic status are more likely to be Republicans. Catholics, Jews, blacks, and other minorities, and

---

[21]See Edward Banfield and James Q. Wilson, *City Politics* (Cambridge: Harvard University Press, 1963), p. 157; and Kenneth Prewitt, *The Recruitment of Political Leaders: A Study of Citizen Politicians* (Indianapolis: Bobbs-Merrill Co., 1971), p. 226.

[22]For a study of the different views held by Democratic and Republican members of Congress, see Congressional Quarterly, *Weekly Report* (October 16, 1970), pp. 2567–69.

urban dwellers are more likely to be Democrats; Protestants and suburban and rural dwellers are more likely to be Republicans. These probabilities apply to candidates and public officials as much as they do to voters.

There is a relationship between people's party loyalty and their feelings about important issues.[23] For example, most Republicans think of themselves as conservatives, while most Democrats consider themselves moderate or liberal.[24] Less than half the people who identify themselves as "strong" Republicans favor government action to provide medical care for American citizens, while 80 percent of the "strong" Democrats do.[25] Only 21 percent of the Republicans favor a government role in guaranteeing jobs. More than half of the Democrats, however, are strongly in favor of such government action.[26]

Party leaders and public officials usually share the views of the voters in their own party, particularly on economic issues. For example, one study showed that delegates to the Republican National Convention identify with "business, free enterprise, and economic conservatism in general," while Democratic delegates are favorable toward "labor and toward government regulation of the economy."[27] In 1976, Democratic party officials ranked the need to reduce unemployment first in importance among political issues and the need to reduce the role of government tenth. Republican party officials, on the other hand, ranked the need to reduce unemployment sixth in importance and the need to reduce the role of government second.[28] These differences were reflected in the 1976 party platforms.[29]

There is also a relationship between party label and elected public officials' votes on issues. Ninety-two percent of the Democratic members of the U.S. House of Representatives in 1975 voted in favor of emergency jobs for the unemployed, for example, while only 13 percent of the Republican members of the House favored this legislation.

In summary, the party-in-the-electorate is made up of individual citizens who identify with a particular political party. A majority of Americans identify with either the Republican or the Democratic

Voters' Opinions of "the Most Important Problem," 1976

	Demo-crats	Repub-licans
Jobs more important	27%	11%
Inflation more important	18	36
Both equally important	53	51
Not sure	2	2

SOURCE: NBC Election News conducted this survey in randomly selected precincts; the data in this table are based on interviews with 6,297 voters who identified themselves as Democrats and 3,712 who identified themselves as Republicans.

[23]See David E. RePass, "Issue Salience and Party Choice," *American Political Science Review* (June 1971), p. 400; and Gerald M. Pomper, "From Confusion to Clarity: Issues and American Voters, 1956-1968," *American Political Science Review* (June 1972) pp. 415–28.

[24]Survey Research Center of the University of Michigan (1972).

[25]Gerald M. Pomper, "Toward a More Responsible Two-Party System? What Again?" *Journal of Politics*, 33 (August 1971): 926.

[26]Survey Research Center of the University of Michigan (1972).

[27]Herbert McClosky, Paul J. Hoffmann, and Rosemary O'Hara, "Issue Conflict and Consensus Among Party Leaders and Followers," *American Political Science Review* (June 1960), pp. 415–26.

[28]Survey by *The Washington Post* and the Harvard University Center for International Affairs, *The Washington Post* (September 27, 1976).

[29]E. Tufte, *Political Control of the Economy* (Princeton, N.J.: Princeton Univ. Press, 1978), p. 75.

party, giving America a two-party system. Minor parties have had little influence on the outcome of national elections. Although the two-party system has endured in America, the strength of party loyalty has declined in recent years, and the percentage of Americans who call themselves Independents has increased. Still, party identification has considerable influence on how a person votes.

As we noted earlier, the political opinions of Republican voters and leaders are generally different from those of Democratic voters and leaders. The Republicans are more likely to be conservative, particularly on economic issues, and the Democrats are more likely to be liberal. For those who are less experienced and less involved in politics—especially for minorities and people of lower socioeconomic status—a candidate's party label is an important and fairly accurate cue for voting decisions.

THE FORMAL PARTY ORGANIZATION

A more tangible aspect of parties than the self-identifiers of the party-in-the-electorate is the formal *party organization*. In this regard, parties are like interest groups: both enable people to actively participate in political affairs, and both link the people and their government. Yet parties are also different from interest groups. Their principal aim is to contest elections and unlike interest groups, the party has its label on the ballot. Parties seek to fill governmental positions with people who share their views and who will carry out their program. Thus, an interest group seeks to influence the government, but a political party seeks to control it. And although the U.S. Constitution does not mention them, parties are almost semipublic institutions because state constitutions and statutes define their nature and prescribe their duties.[30]

European political parties are mass membership parties. By contrast, America's parties are cadre parties. A *mass membership party* has many dues-paying members and full-time professional officers. It carries on continuous organizational activity, sponsors educational as well as electoral efforts, and has influence over officials in government. On the other hand, a *cadre party*—the kind that exists in America—has few members and is run by a small number of leaders and activists. It is primarily an electoral organization, active chiefly at election time, and is usually subordinate to party officials in government.[31] Former U.S. Representative Donald Fraser of Minnesota, a member and later chairman of the Democratic Party Commission on Rules and Organization, which was established in 1969, recommended converting the Democratic organization into a dues-paying, mass membership party, but this proposal did not get anywhere.

---

[30]Sorauf, *Party Politics in America*, p. 65.
[31]Sorauf, *Party Politics in America*, p. 65.

Permanent Party Structures

For most of the year, American political party organizations are much like tentframes at a summer camp in the off season. Only during periods of electoral activity are they, so to speak, covered with canvas and made habitable.

Local and state party organizations. The smallest geographical unit of political parties in America is the *precinct*. Theoretically, every precinct in America has a precinct party committee for each of the major parties, and each committee is headed by a precinct chairperson. In reality, a large percentage of the party precincts have no officers at any given time, and there is usually very little activity—rarely even a meeting—at the precinct level. Each county has a *county central committee,* headed by a county chairperson, for each of the major parties. (In the cities, there are usually ward committees. Sometimes, as in New York City, there is a committee and a leader in each state legislative district. The larger cities usually have city-wide party committees.) Each of the major parties has a *state central committee,* directed by state party chairpersons. Many states also have party committees at the congressional district level, between the county and state level.

In most states, the process of selecting these various state and local party committees and officials begins with a meeting in the various precincts. The time and date for the precinct meetings are frequently prescribed by state law. The major national parties now have rules requiring that standards of fairness in the notice, conduct, and openness of these and other party meetings be followed. Some states provide for the election of party officials by the voters in party primary elections, just as candidates are nominated. In others, state party officials are chosen in party conventions. Each succeeding level of the state and local party machinery is more like "a system of layers of organization" than a pyramidal hierarchy.[32] Each level within the party is not necessarily dependent for its election upon the level below.

What do the officers and activists of this party structure do in nonelection years? Most state laws do not address this question. Their duties partly depend upon whether their party is the *in-party*—the party whose leaders hold important elective public office at the moment—or the *out-party*. For example, if the mayor's office in a given city is not occupied by a party member, that party is the out-party. The basic job of out-party officials and activists is to show that the party is still alive between elections. They may have booths at fairs and other gatherings, pass out party literature, issue press releases criticizing public officials of the other party, and conduct registration drives to enroll more of their members as voters. But the extent of this political activity often depends upon the inclinations of

---

[32]V. O. Key, Jr., *Politics, Parties, and Pressure Groups,* 5th ed. (New York: Crowell, 1974), p. 316.

the particular party officials and activists. And all political activity takes money, which state and local out-parties have difficulty raising. Some parties have instituted a system for collecting regular contributions or dues, but this has been only modestly successful. Others hold bake sales and other similar fund-raising events. State parties typically sponsor "Jefferson-Jackson Day" dinners (Democrats) or "Lincoln Day" dinners (Republicans), but the success of these dinners is often limited without the "clout," or persuasiveness, that comes from having a party member in a powerful or influential public office.

A particularly aggressive group of state or local party officials and activists, with money available in the party coffers (and the two go together), can carry on an effective public relations campaign against an incumbent official of the opposite party. They can whittle away at the official's image and political strength through critical press releases issued week after week.

How many party activists are there? Only 9 percent of all Americans in 1972 attended a political meeting, rally, or dinner and only 5 percent worked for a party or candidate.[33] Who are the activists? Increasingly, they are people who get involved because of their strong feelings about issues and ideology.[34] They sometimes cause state and local out-party organizations to sponsor seminars and other meetings on issues.

The in-party—the party with one or more of its own members in important government positions—presumably has more power than the out-party. But this presumption is often unwarranted because the public official, rather than the party organization, actually exercises the power that comes from holding office. In other words, the government official dominates and uses the party organization, rather than the other way around. The in-party, then, is like the male praying mantis who is devoured by his mate. If a party organization is successful in electing one of its own members to a powerful public office, the party organization is often devoured, in effect, by the new public official.

There are still some in-party "machines" in America, principally in the large cities of the Northeast. But the number and power of these machines have declined sharply in modern times. The old in-party machines, headed by "bosses," were powerful because they could control party nominations for public office. Then, through the elected public officials who had been nominated by the party machine, they could exert control over patronage, the power to name people to jobs and appointments. They also gained control of social welfare programs by designating the recipients of food and financial assis-

[33]Survey Research Center, University of Michigan, cited in William H. Flanigan and Nancy H. Zingle, *Political Behavior of the American Electorate*, 3rd ed. (Boston, Mass.: Allyn, Bacon, 1975), p. 155.

[34]See Nelson W. Polsby and Aaron Wildavsky, *Presidential Elections: Strategies of American Electoral Politics*, 4th ed. (New York: Scribners, 1976), pp. 29–34.

tance; and over preferments, by influencing the choice of those who would receive construction, insurance, and other contracts.

Some machine influence still exists. In New York City, for example, many young lawyers take an interest in party activities in order to secure appointments to judgeships. The Democratic machine still exists in Chicago, but it has lost some of its power. In 1979, several years after the death of the machine's former boss, Richard J. Daley, who was both the mayor of Chicago and the chairperson of the Cook County Democratic party, Jane Byrne became the Democratic nominee for mayor over the opposition of the old Daley machine. (The machine members then fell into line and she won the election handily.)

The day of the all-powerful in-party machine has largely passed however. The main reason has been the adoption of the direct primary election, which allows the party in the electorate, rather than the party organization, to nominate party candidates. In addition, the word "machine" has a bad image for most voters because of past abuses. Stricter laws have helped to prevent much of the fraudulent voting, which was one of the machine's main levers of power. Civil service and merit systems have taken many of the old patronage jobs away from parties and the politicians. Many of the jobs that can still be passed out on the basis of political patronage are unattractive because of their low status or low pay or because they require skills that cannot always be met by the politically faithful. Further, federal and state welfare laws now base eligibility for assistance on need rather than on political influence. The increased importance of the mass media, which gives voters their political information directly and permits political candidates to bypass the in-party political machine and go directly to the people, has also played a significant role in the decline of the machine.

Aside from the situation of the in-party machine, the typical in-party organization largely follows the wishes of the dominant state or local government official. At the state level, the governor can generally name the state party chairperson, and the state chairperson serves as a partisan voice and fund-raiser for the governor.

National party organizations.   Each of the major parties is headed by a national chairperson, who is elected by the party's national committee. The Republican National Committee is made up of two committeepersons from each of the state parties. As a result of the reforms of 1972 and 1974, the Democratic party has a written national charter, or constitution, and an expanded national committee with over three hundred members. The Democratic National Committee now includes the chairperson and the next highest ranking officer of the opposite sex from each of the states, two hundred other members apportioned to the states on the same basis as delegates to the national convention, the chairperson and two other members of the Democratic Governors' Conference, the

Democratic leader and one other person from the U.S. Senate and House, the chairperson and two other members of the Democratic Mayors' Conference, the president and two other representatives of the Young Democrats, and up to twenty-five additional members.

A division of each of the national parties into a "presidential wing" and a "congressional wing" parallels the separation of powers in the federal government. The national committee of each of the parties represents the presidential wing. Its outlook is national, and its principal goal is the election or reelection of one of its party members to the Presidency of the United States. The congressional wing of each of the parties is composed of the party leaders, the party caucus, and the campaign committees of the U.S. House and Senate. Nothing requires the congressional wing and the presidential wing of each of the parties to work together. For that matter, nothing requires a party in the House and its counterpart in the Senate to work together. In practice, there is more cooperation between the Republicans in both houses of the Congress and the Republican National Committee than there is among the Democrats.

Like those of the state and local party organizations, the activities of the national committees of each of the major parties vary, depending upon whether the national committee represents an in-party or an out-party. At the national level, the party that has a President in the White House is the in-party. The national committee of the in-party is usually dominated by the President.[35] President Kennedy, for example, named John Bailey to head the Democratic National Committee and made the committee a political arm of the White House. Lyndon Johnson also dominated the Democratic National Committee but relied upon it far less than Kennedy had. Presidents Nixon, Ford, and Carter followed the Kennedy example. By contrast, President Dwight D. Eisenhower was not very interested in party affairs, and he largely ignored the Republican National Committee while he was in office.

A President usually names the chairperson of the national committee of his party, even though the formal rules provide for an election by the committee members. For example, when President Jimmy Carter took office, he named former Maine Governor Kenneth Curtis to run the Democratic National Committee, subject to formal approval by the committee. Then, when President Carter became disenchanted with Curtis, the President named John White of Texas to take his place.

Presidents may use the national committee of their party as a convenient payroll for people who cannot be placed in the government itself. Thus, President Carter's son became an employee of the Democratic National Committee soon after President Carter's inauguration. Since Presidents usually prefer to seem "above politics,"

---

[35]Cornelius Cotter and Bernard Hennessey, *Politics Without Power* (N.Y.: Atherton Press, 1964), p. 81.

they sometimes use the national committee as a partisan voice, particularly to criticize the other party and its officials. In addition, Presidents may use their national party committees to raise funds to defray the expenses of presidential trips and activities that have a political character and to assist in congressional and other campaigns. As a rule, Presidents do not appreciate being advised on issues by the national committees of their party.

When the national committee of one of the major parties represents the out-party (does not have a President in the White House), the national committee has more flexibility in its activities. In this situation, the national committee may choose its own chairperson. For example, following the defeat of President Gerald Ford in 1976, the Republican National Committee elected former U.S. Senator William Brock of Tennessee as its chairperson, despite Ford's recommendation of another candidate for the post. The out-party typically attempts to "rebuild," or improve the party's image and standing. And, like the in-party national committee, it does the necessary detailed work to prepare for the next national convention.

When the Democratic National Committee represents the out-party of the presidential wing, it frequently runs into trouble with the Democratic leaders of the House and Senate when it attempts to speak out on ideology and issues. The Democratic congressional leaders feel that this is their own province. Congressional leaders of both parties generally prefer the national committees of their party to deal only with "nuts and bolts" projects, such as registration, organization, and getting people to vote. For some time, the Democratic National Committee has had a mechanism for speaking out on issues. Prior to the 1972 reforms, there was a Democratic Policy Council, appointed by the chairperson of the Democratic National Committee. The 1972 reforms provided for a convention every two years, even though presidential nominating conventions come only every four years. But the first such off-year convention of the Democratic party, held in 1974, restricted itself to fairly bland issues, much to the satisfaction of Democratic members of Congress and other Democratic officeholders.

Where do the national committees get their money? The Democratic National Committee would like to know. It has been seriously in debt ever since the 1968 presidential campaign. The Democratic National Committee has used nationwide telethons, direct mail solicitation, dinners, and receptions to raise money. The success of these methods has been mixed, but it has improved since the election of Jimmy Carter, a Democrat, to the Presidency. When either party has a President in the White House, fund-raising is easier because contributors may give money to the party organization in the hope of gaining influence with the government.

The Democratic National Committee has a regular program of soliciting contributions by mail. This program, however, has not been highly successful, since Democratic ideologues are much less likely to contribute to the party than they are to candidates whose stands on issues they like.[36] The Republicans have been much more successful over a much longer period of time in their direct mail solicitation of contributions.

The Republican National Committee typically works closely with the Republican campaign committees in the House and the Senate in joint fund-raising efforts. Democrats in the House and Senate, on the other hand, have been less willing to enter into joint fund-raising efforts with the national committee of their party, especially when there is no Democratic President in the White House. The congressional Democrats are usually much more successful than the Democratic National Committee at fund-raising.

Party Organization Functions

Campaigns in America have three phases: prenomination, nomination, and election. In a general election, voters choose one person for each elective office from among the nominees of each of the parties. The candidate with the highest number of votes is declared the winner. The winning candidate is not required to receive a *majority* (one more than half) of all the votes cast. Election is by *plurality* vote only (one more vote than any other candidate).

How does a person become the nominee of a party? *Party nomination* may either be by direct primary election or by convention. The convention method provides for nomination by vote of party delegates who have been selected and convened for that purpose. Presidential nominations are made by national conventions.

The primary election method of nomination gives party voters a choice among competing party candidates. Primary elections are usually decided by plurality vote, although a few states provide for a run-off primary between the two highest party candidates if no one achieves a majority in the first primary. In a "closed" primary, party voters may only choose among candidates of their own party. Republican voters only receive Republican ballots in a closed primary election; they are not allowed to vote on the Democratic nominees for various offices. An "open" primary allows voters— whether registered Republicans, Democrats, or Independents—to choose to vote either in the Democratic primary or the Republican primary. Most states have closed primaries, allowing no crossover voting.

How does a person receive a party nomination? The prenomination procedure in most states requires only the filing of a petition with a requisite number of signatures. In other states, candidates need only appear at the appropriate state or local office and make a written declaration of candidacy. Some states have endorsing conventions, which automatically place on the primary election ballot any candidate who receives a certain minimum percentage of the convention

---

[36]See Richard Reeves, "Nationally, the Democrats Are a Fiction," *The New York Times* (June 1, 1975).

vote. In New Mexico, for example, the figure is 20 percent. (States with endorsing state conventions allow candidates who do not receive a qualifying percentage of the convention vote to be listed on the primary election ballot if they can thereafter secure a specified number of signatures on a petition.) The prenomination procedure for choosing delegates to the national conventions of the parties, where presidential candidates are nominated, may be based upon state conventions or presidential primaries.

National conventions. The party's national convention is the ultimate authority in each of the political parties. The convention decides upon the rules and operation of the party between conventions. It also determines the party's *platform,* a statement of its philosophy and its positions on important issues. In short, the platform represents what the party promises to do if it gains control of the government. Perhaps most important, the convention nominates party candidates for President and Vice-President.

The common view of party platforms is that they do not mean very much, that they are mere "campaign promises," forgotten as soon as the campaign is over. In fact, platforms are important.

Platform "planks"—positions on specific issues—are typically hammered out after special hearings held prior to each party's national convention. This allows for a public airing and testing of opinions, which has some educational value for the general public and for officeholders. The assembled party delegates debate and vote on the planks during the nominating conventions. In part, the platforms set the tone for the general election campaigns because the leading candidates usually exert influence over their content. Platforms also have an effect on government policy. Gerald Pomper has found that there is a difference in the platforms of the national parties and that during the twenty-one-year period from 1944 to 1964, more than 70 percent of the national party pledges were carried out. On economic issues over 84 percent of the pledges were fulfilled.[37]

Because of the importance of national conventions, the delegates are also important. Increasingly, convention delegates are party activists who are committed to a presidential candidate, often because they are in strong agreement with the candidate's position on issues.

For years, no one paid much attention to the question of whether the internal party methods of selecting delegates were democratic. Then, during the 1968 Democratic Convention in Chicago, a confrontation between the "new politics" supporters of Senator Eugene McCarthy of Minnesota and the late Robert F. Kennedy of New York, on one hand, and the "regular" supporters of Vice-President Hubert H. Humphrey, on the other, brought this issue to the foreground.

---

[37] Gerald M. Pomper, *Elections in America: Control and Influence in Democratic Politics* (New York: Dodd, Mead, 1971), p. 178.

The 1976 Republican National Convention in Kansas City, Missouri, where Gerald Ford won the presidential nomination over Ronald Reagan. In addition to nominating party candidates, national conventions establish the party platform and determine party rules and operations.

The Kennedy and McCarthy supporters had gone into the precincts and the primaries to campaign for their candidates and their issues, only to find that undemocratic practices and processes of the Democratic party often shut them out. The party's *unit rule*—which awarded all the delegates from a precinct, county, or even a state to the candidate who received a majority of the votes—often left other candidates with no representation at all at the next level in the process, regardless of how many votes they actually received. "Nonregular" Democrats frequently received insufficient notice of meetings, or meetings were held at a time and place different from that specified in the notice. Local or state rules governing delegate selection were sometimes unwritten and unclear. In many states, the Democratic party made no effort to choose delegations that were representative of women, minorities, and young people. Some state Democratic party organizations in the South systematically discriminated against black people. Several state delegations were hand-picked by Democratic governors or party officials, allowing little or no input from the rank-and-file party members. Other delegates were automatically named because of their positions in the party or in state government; many of them were chosen two years or more before the presidential campaigns had developed.

The fight in the 1968 Democratic Convention over the substantive issues of who would be the party's candidate for President and what the party's position would be on the Vietnam War spotlighted the inequities in the party's processes. There were bitter conflicts over the seating of various delegations and heated debates about rules and procedures. In the streets of Chicago, there were violent clashes between Chicago police and demonstrators protesting America's involvement in the war in Vietnam. The demonstrators' chant, "the whole world's watching," was accurate; the major television networks televised the clashes that occurred in the streets and in the convention hall.

The convention voted to prohibit forever the use of the unit rule at any level in the delegate selection process. It mandated the appointment of interim party committees to "democratize" party rules and the processes for selecting national convention delegates. The reforms adopted during the 1972 Democratic Convention and modified in the 1974 off-year convention and afterwards include affirmative action for the fair representation of women, minorities, and young people, and complete fairness in all procedures.[38]

Some leaders of organized labor and of other interest groups, who had been more powerful under the old system in the Democratic party when delegates were chosen by mayors and governors or were otherwise hand-picked, unsuccessfully opposed the reforms. One AFL-CIO official even declared in the middle of an argument that the 1968 Democratic Convention had been "one of the most democratic I've ever seen."[39] But women had made up only 13 percent of the delegates to the 1968 Democratic Convention; following the reforms, 38 percent of the delegates in 1972 were women, and 34 percent in 1976. The number of black delegates and young delegates, which also increased markedly in 1972, dropped slightly in 1976, but not nearly to the level it had been in conventions prior to the Democratic reforms.[40]

The Republicans did not go as far with their reforms as the Democrats did, but the Republicans had never used the unit rule. The Republican National Committee set up reform studies and adopted general provisions for affirmative action to encourage the participation of minorities and women. Both parties were affected by changes in state laws in response to party reform pressures. Most important was the adoption by a large number of states of the primary election method for selecting delegates to presidential nominating conventions. By 1976, three fourths of all Democratic national convention delegates and more than two thirds of all Republican national convention delegates were selected in such primaries.[41]

Whether delegates to national conventions are selected by state

---

[38]For a history and assessment of Democratic party reforms since 1968, see William Crotty, *Decision for the Democrats* (Baltimore: Johns Hopkins Univ. Press, 1978).

[39]Congressional Quarterly, *Weekly Report* (December 2, 1972), p. 3095.

[40]See Final Report on the Commission on Party Structure and Delegate Selection, *The Party Reformed* (Washington, D.C.: Democratic National Committee, July 7, 1972), pp. 7–8 and *The New York Times,* (July 12, 1976) p. C5.

[41]Everett Carll Ladd, Jr. " 'Reform' Is Wrecking the U.S. Party System," *Fortune* (November 1977), p. 179.

conventions or by state primaries, procedures are now more open to public participation in both parties, especially the Democratic party. Reforms have reduced the prospect that national party conventions will represent "the private domain of the rich, the white and the party regulars," as reform-minded former Senator Harold Hughes said of the Democratic party prior to 1972.[42]   At least one political scientist, however, has argued that the democratization of the Democratic party and the increase in the number of state primaries for both parties have produced convention delegates who are not representative of the rank and file of the parties.[43] But the corollary argument that the old boss-picked delegates were more likely to be representative seems impossible to sustain.

Because of the party reforms and the increased use of the presidential primary elections, the selection of delegates to national party conventions is dominated by the campaigns of presidential hopefuls. Some have argued that the entire process of nominating a party's presidential candidate should be replaced by one nationwide presidential primary.[44] But some critics claim that a single primary election would limit the voters' choice to candidates who were already well known or well financed, or both. Under the present system, Jimmy Carter, who was not very well known nationally, not very well financed, and not supported by national political figures in his party, became an instant nationwide celebrity by doing well in the first state contests. He was then able to amass enough delegates and support to win the nomination and the election. A less extreme suggestion for reforming the present nominating system is to replace the patchwork of state conventions and primaries with several prescribed regional primaries. But this suggestion, too, has not had widespread support. Both proposals would limit even further the formal role of the party organization in the process.

The party in general elections.   Once the party nominees have been chosen, they must then compete against the nominees of the other party or parties in the general election. The role played by the party organization in the general election is usually within the discretion of the principal party nominees. A candidate may merge his or her prenomination campaign organization with that of the party, taking over the party apparatus and naming a new party chairperson. Or, the organizations may remain separate. In this case, the candidate's prenomination organization continues to run the real campaign, leaving very little for the party organization to do. The party organization usually cannot raise the money and recruit the workers necessary for a successful general election campaign by itself; only

---

[42]Congressional Quarterly, *Weekly Report* (March 7, 1969), p. 33.

[43]See Ladd, Jr., " 'Reform' Is Wrecking the U.S. Party System," pp. 177–88.

[44]Judith H. Parris, *The Convention Problem* (Washington, D.C.: The Brookings Institute, 1972), pp. 172–77.

How to...
Get Involved in Party Activities

It is not difficult for any concerned person to become an active participant in party affairs. Political party organizations are always eager to recruit "new blood"—especially during an election campaign. As a rule, campaigns never have enough workers, so any willing worker is likely to be well received. Some pointers for becoming involved in a campaign include:

—Try to join the campaign in its early stages. You'll be able to participate in the full spectrum of campaign activities and build up seniority, too, making it more likely that you will be given tasks of greater responsibility as the campaign continues.

—Be flexible in terms of the tasks you will perform. Even the most menial of tasks is important in a campaign—and you'll establish a reputation as a willing worker.

—Maintain flexibility in your time commitment. "Dabbling" in politics will limit your effectiveness and value.

These guidelines also apply during the quiet periods between elections, when the on-going business of politics takes place. In fact, getting involved in a party organization between elections has some advantages. Fewer people will be active, so your contribution will stand out more visibly; and you'll be able to work more closely with party activists, learning from them in the process. The basic party organizations are at the precinct level, usually headed by elected ward chairpersons, vice-chairpersons, and secretaries. The chairperson appoints precinct captains, who in turn rely upon volunteer block workers, to maintain on-going contacts with the people in their neighborhoods. Most political activists consider block workers to be the most important people at the ward level. They are the "good neighbors" who are concerned about political issues and about their neighbors and who are interested enough to become actively involved. They provide the personal contact between the party organization and the people.

Other tasks must be performed by the party organization between elections, too, and all enable a newcomer to get a foot in the door; serving on a "telephone committee," maintaining an up-to-date filing system of registered voters in the ward or precinct, and so on, may mean greater responsibilities in the future. It's unrealistic to expect that you will have a say in party platforms, campaign issues, or candidate selection until you've performed what may seem to be "menial" tasks. But those tasks are part of what politics is about: keeping in touch with the people. Performing those tasks well can open up a wide range of party activities. All you have to do is get involved.

SOURCE: Adapted from James Brown and Philip M. Seib, *The Art Of Politics* (Alfred Publishing Co., 1976), Ch. 2.

the candidate can do so. Thus, the choice of merging the prenomination organization with the party campaign organization or keeping them separate is usually left to the candidate.

The general practice at the national level is typical of the other levels as well. Immediately following the party's national convention, the national committee holds a meeting to formally elect a new chairperson, who is named by the presidential nominee. Thus, right after the 1968 Democratic Convention, Hubert H. Humphrey chose Lawrence J. O'Brien to head the Democratic National Committee and run the national campaign. Similarly, following the 1972 Democratic Convention, George McGovern chose Jean Westwood as chairperson of the Democratic National Committee. Most presidential candidates prefer to have a separate "citizen's" campaign organization in addition to the one directed by party committees. This second organization makes it easier to attract the support of Independents and members of the other party. Some presidential candidates run campaigns that virtually ignore their party's national committee. When Richard Nixon sought reelection in 1972, his campaign was run by a separate organization, the Committee for the Reelection of the President (which reporters came to call CREEP). Nixon used CREEP because he wanted to make a nonpartisan appeal to all the people, instead of emphasizing that he was a Republican. In addition, he felt that he could get more blind loyalty from this separate organization than he could from the Republican National Committee, which he relegated to a figurehead role in the campaign. The blind loyalty of CREEP officials in performing "dirty tricks" and financing the burglary of the Democratic headquarters in the Watergate Hotel eventually resulted in prison terms for a number of CREEP and government officials and forced Nixon out of office in disgrace.[45]

Following the 1976 Democratic Convention, the party's nominee, Jimmy Carter, decided to retain Democratic chairperson Robert Strauss in his position. The real Carter campaign, however, was directed from Georgia by Carter's prenomination campaign managers, but, of course, without the criminal consequences of the CREEP example.

The Campaign Reform Act passed by Congress in 1974 provides for virtually full federal financing of the general election campaigns of presidential candidates. The money for this purpose, as well as for the prenomination matching funds, comes from an optional one-dollar contribution on individual federal income tax returns. In 1976, this general election financing amounted to over $20 million for each of the candidates of the two major parties. Note that the federal financing of general election campaigns for the Presidency goes not to the national party organizations, but to the candidates. Under the reform law, the national committees of the parties are allowed to

---

[45]See Walter Pincus, "The GOP Money Scandal," *The New Republic* (April 21, 1978), pp. 17–21.

raise funds to finance committee operations during the general election (in 1976, this amounted to approximately $3 million for each of the two major parties). But this money must be raised from private contributions, and the Democrats had a hard time raising it. Present public financing of presidential campaigns, therefore, favors candidates rather than parties.

The party organization role—state, local, or national—in general election campaigns, then, is usually what the principal party candidate at each level wants it to be. Party candidates are usually more concerned about media attention and about financial and other kinds of support from interest groups, volunteers, and individual contributors than they are about the support of the party organization.

THE PARTY-IN-GOVERNMENT

Public officials who hold office under a party label are called the *party-in-government*. The party-in-government exists at the federal, state, and local levels. At all governmental levels, the party-in-government is divided into the executive, legislative, and judicial branches. Within each level and within each branch, the party-in-government is relatively autonomous or independent. In other words, the President of the United States cannot tell a state governor what to do, even though they may belong to the same political party. Likewise, the Republican members of Congress do not have to vote the way a Republican President wants them to vote.

The Executive Wing

At all levels of government, American political parties are "executive-centered."[46] The chief executive office—the Presidency or the governorship, for example—is the center of influence for a number of reasons. First, the chief executive is elected by the total electorate, while the legislative branch is made up of many members, each with provincial constituencies that may have distinct viewpoints and interests. Second, as we indicated in the last section, the chief executive is the leader of the party organization and is usually able to dominate it. Third, the chief executive is the electoral leader. In other words, a popular President who is running for reelection at the head of the ticket can often help to elect legislative members of the President's party, although this "coattail" effect should not be overemphasized.[47] The chief executive is also the symbol of the party. The standings of other officeholders and their chances at the polls may depend to some degree upon the popularity or lack of popularity of the party image as projected by the chief executive.[48] Fourth, through patronage and other means, the chief executive can some-

[46]See Judson L. James, *American Political Parties* (New York: Pegasus, 1969).

[47]See Malcolm Moos, *Politics, Presidents and Coattails* (Baltimore: Johns Hopkins Press, 1952).

[48]See Sorauf, *Party Politics in America,* p. 371.

times offer rewards or impose punishments on party and public officials. State governors have relatively more patronage power than a President does, but Presidents are generally better able to command the attention of the mass media, and thus of the electorate, than state governors are. This gives Presidents indirect influence over national legislators and other party and public officials.

The Legislative Wing

Throughout this chapter, we have discussed some of the differences between American and European political systems in respect to political parties. These differences are evident in the legislative wing of the party-in-government. Nominations for the British House of Commons, for example, are controlled by the British political party organizations. In the United States, nominations for the U.S. Senate and House of Representatives are made by the party-in-the-electorate. Party candidates for the House of Commons are pledged to support their party platform, and the candidates receive important party assistance in general elections. In the United States, nominees for the U.S. House and Senate do not usually depend upon their political parties for crucial election help, and they are not obligated to announce their support for their party platforms. In the British House of Commons, the majority party or a coalition of parties elects the prime minister from the membership of the House of Commons itself. In the United States, of course, the President is not elected by Congress but is chosen in a separate nationwide vote.

If the British "government"—the prime minister and the cabinet—loses a vote in the House of Commons on a serious issue or on a "vote of confidence," the government "falls." When that happens, a new government must be chosen by a new majority in the House of Commons, or new elections for all members of the House of Commons must be called. In the United States, by contrast, the Congress and the President quite often disagree on issues, without such consequences. The only way a President may be removed is by impeachment. American elections for members of Congress are held only at regular, scheduled times, regardless of how much Congress and the President may disagree with each other or how unpopular each may become with the general public.

Thus, there are several reasons why members of the British House of Commons are constrained to support their party. Members depend on their party for renomination. Further, if a member joins in a vote of no confidence against his or her own party's government and thereby helps to cause the government to fall, the member may lose influence and power as the party loses influence and power. If new elections are called, he or she may personally have to risk not being reelected. The American system does not provide for such pressures for party loyalty.

Nevertheless, three important elements of *party cohesion,* or

Support for Presidential Policies in Congress

	1973		1974—Nixon		1974—Ford		1975		1976		1977	
	Dem.	Rep.	Dem.	Rep.	Dem.	Rep.	Dem.	Rep.	Dem.	Rep.	Dem.	Rep.
Support												
Senate	44	66	39	57	39	55	47	68	39	62	70	52
House	47	64	46	65	41	51	38	63	32	63	63	42
Opposition												
Senate	41	20	50	31	47	27	41	22	44	23	21	38
House	37	22	42	27	45	35	51	31	23	27	28	50

NOTE: These scores are based on party identification. The *Congressional Quarterly* analyzes all presidential messages, press conferences, and other public statements to determine what the President does or does not want in the way of legislative action.

SOURCE: *Congressional Quarterly Almanac.*

agreement, exist in Congress. First, there is strong party cohesion in the organization—that is, in the election of officers—of both houses of the Congress. At the beginning of each Congress, the members of each party in each house meet in separate *caucuses* (meetings), or conferences, as the Republicans call them. Each party caucus nominates some of its members to fill official positions in the full legislative body. The Speaker of the House of Representatives and the majority leader in the Senate are official positions filled in effect by the majority party; the minority leader of the House and of the Senate are official positions filled in effect by the minority party. Party nominations for these congressional offices are tantamount to election because the voting in these contests in the full House and Senate is done strictly along party lines. The same is true of the procedure for choosing the chairpersons of the various House and Senate committees. This procedure is a formality; the most senior majority-party member of each committee is almost always chosen. However, House Democrats have in recent years deposed committee chairpersons who opposed the election of the party's presidential nominee or who were grossly unacceptable to most House Democrats.

After a majority in a House or Senate party caucus has decided upon its nominees for legislative officials, all the members of that caucus vote as a bloc when the election takes place in the full House and Senate. Thus, in 1977, even though Representative James Wright of Texas won the nomination for House majority leader by only one vote in the House Democratic caucus, all House Democrats voted as a bloc for Representative Wright when the full House met for the election.

Second, some party cohesion in the Congress often develops from recommendations made by the President. Members of the President's own party tend to vote with the President, but members of the opposition party tend to unite against the President's recommendations. In recent years, party cohesion in both houses of Congress has occurred in only 40 percent of all roll-call votes, but the figure increases to 60 or 70 percent or more when the roll call asks members to support the recommendations of a President of their own party.[49]

Third, party cohesion in Congress frequently occurs on votes that involve labor-management or economic issues. Thus, from 1946 to 1966, Senate Democrats supported the AFL-CIO's position on 72 percent of the votes taken in the Senate, while Senate Republicans supported the AFL-CIO's position only 28 percent of the time.[50] But party cohesion on these issues probably results not so much from party influence as from the similar backgrounds and beliefs that individual members of Congress and their constituents may share. This fact, in turn, probably has something to do with the initial choice of party label that the member of Congress and his or her constituents make.

One might expect party policy committees (established by the Congressional Reorganization Act of 1946) and the congressional campaign committees (established by each party in both houses) to require adherence to party positions. But this is not the case. The policy committees were supposed to develop and present party positions on issues, but they have focused primarily on organizational and procedural cohesion rather than issue-oriented or ideological cohesion. Similarly, the campaign committees, which raise funds to help elect or reelect party members to the House or Senate, make no effort to force candidates to support a party platform. They only require the candidates to pledge that they will vote with their party on organizational matters.

Some state legislatures show more party cohesion on issues than Congress does, and some show less. A state governor usually has more power in dealing with a state legislature than a President does in dealing with Congress, because a governor has more control over patronage and other rewards. Since there are fewer controversial issues at the state level than at the federal level, greater possibilities for cooperation exist between the executive and legislative branches of the party in state government. State legislatures in the urban northeastern states seem to have more party cohesion, partly because of tradition. And more legislative party cohesion occurs in states where there is vigorous electoral competition between the two major parties.

The legislative party-in-government, then, in accordance with the separation-of-powers doctrine, operates with considerable independence from the party in the executive branch. It also operates independently of the party organization. Party cohesion is most apparent on "housekeeping" or organizational matters; on questions involving support for or opposition to the chief executive; and on substantive issues involving labor-management or economic policies. The amount of cohesion is much less than that found among party members in European parliaments.

---

[49]*Congressional Quarterly Almanac*, quoted in Sorauf, *Party Politics*, pp. 355–356.
[50]William J. Keefe and Morriss Ogel, *The American Legislative Process: Congress and the States*, 3rd ed. (Englewood Cliffs, N.J.: Prentice-Hall, 1973), p. 276.

The Judiciary

The judiciary is usually thought to be "above" politics. It might be more correct to say that judicial decisions are not explicitly made on the basis of politics or partisanship. There is a difference. Federal judges, for example, are appointed. The President (a politician) nominates them, and the Senate (all politicians) confirms. In recent years, more than 90 percent of the presidential appointees have come from the President's own party. [51]

In the states, judges are usually elected, sometimes on a nonpartisan basis. Many state judges, however, begin their service when a state governor appoints them to fill a vacancy, and they seldom have serious opposition once they are in office. Party identification plays as much a part in the selection of state judges as it does in the appointment of federal judges.

Judges are expected to be objective; they are not supposed to allow their personal bias to affect their conduct. But studies show that Democratic judges are more likely than Republican judges to decide for the defendant in criminal cases and for claimants in cases involving workmens' compensation, unemployment compensation, and automobile accidents. [52] This party influence on judicial decisions is indirect. Frank J. Sorauf has said:

> *Quite simply, judges of the same party vote together on cases for the same reasons of ideology and outlook that led them to the same political party, or because they have been socialized into the goals and values of the same party. In other words, two judges vote together on an issue of the administrative regulation of utilities because of deep-seated values they share about the relationship of government and the economy. Those same values or perceptions led them some years earlier to join the same political party, or they were developed out of experience in the same political party.* [53]

TOWARD RESPONSIBLE POLITICAL PARTIES?

Should parties be more "responsible"? In other words, should there be some way to require the party-in-government to carry out the party's platform pledges and campaign promises? Should there be more party cohesion within the party-in-government on issues and ideology? Should there be more party discipline, or enforcement of party unity, through political rewards and punishments? More and

[51]See Hugh A. Bone, *American Politics and the Party System,* 4th ed. (New York: McGraw-Hill, 1971), p. 248.

[52]See David W. Adamany, "The Party Variable in Judges' Voting: Conceptual Notes and a Case Study," *American Political Science Review,* 63 (1969): 57–73; and Sheldon Goldman, "Voting Behavior on the United States Courts of Appeals, 1961–1964," *American Political Science Review,* 60 (1966): 374–83.

[53]Sorauf, *Party Politics in America,* p. 380.

more political and party activists are answering yes to these questions. Some agree with Frank J. Sorauf, who writes, "As more and more citizens are attracted to the party organization (and also to the party electorates) for reasons of policy, important intraparty pressure builds for some measure or variety of party responsibility."[54] Some political scientists have taken the same position. "What kind of party is it that, having won control of government, is unable to govern?" E. E. Schattschneider has asked.[55] The American Political Science Association (APSA) in the late 1940s went on record for greater party responsibility. The APSA argued that this would require clearly stated party positions on issues and ideology; the nomination of candidates loyal to the party positions; campaigns conducted on the issues; and action by the party-in-government to carry out the party positions.[56]

Advocates of greater party responsibility say that it would encourage more campaign activity by citizens who feel strongly about particular issues, thus making candidates more responsive to the popular will. They argue that it would also make public officials more accountable for the decisions they make after they are elected.

Objections have been raised to making parties more responsible in America. Some critics claim that party responsibility is not desirable because it would create a "partyocracy," a domination by the party organization of the party-in-government which would reduce the importance of elected public officials. Others argue that greater party responsibility in America is not desirable because it would fragment the American political parties, destroying the present two-party system by upsetting the parties' broad consensus on policies and the broad coalitions within them. The result, they say, would be a number of highly ideological parties. Whether one thinks this objection has merit largely depends on whether one is satisfied with the present two-party system and with present governmental policy on social, economic, and other issues.

Another criticism of greater party responsibility in America is that it is not possible, at least not in the way recommended by the American Political Science Association. Proponents of this view argue, first, that governmental authority in America is fragmented by federalism and the separation of powers and that this necessarily results in fragmented parties. Second, they point out that the direct primary method of nominating candidates has greatly reduced the ability of the party organization to reward or punish its candidates and public officials.

One way to achieve a greater measure of party responsibility in

---

[54]Sorauf, *Party Politics in America,* p. 339.
[55]E. E. Schattschneider, *Party Government* (New York: Holt, Rinehart, and Winston, 1942), p. 132.
[56]Committee on Political Parties of the American Political Science Association, *Toward a More Responsible Two-Party System* (New York: Holt, Rinehart, and Winston, 1950).

America would be to increase the degree of consensus on issues and ideology among the members of the parties-in-the-electorate, the party organizations, and the parties-in-government. The parties have made some progress in this direction, but not nearly enough to overcome the barriers to party responsibility created by governmental fragmentation and the direct party primary.

CONCLUSION

American parties do not exist in the European sense. They are cadre parties, not mass membership parties. Candidates do not usually depend upon them for nomination or election. The party organization has very limited influence over its members in public office.

Party responsibility in America cannot develop to the same extent that it has in Great Britain. The federal system, the separation of powers, and the direct primary election prevent that from happening. It is not likely that the trend toward the declining influence of party organizations will be reversed. But strong party organizations are not necessarily essential for the functioning of democracy. Activists may simply continue to be selective in their support of political candidates and parties, basing their support on the candidate's position on ideology and issues.

But there is an increasing difference between the parties—in all three "guises"—on issues and ideology. There are four principal reasons for this trend. First, party activists are more likely to be ideologues today. As one writer has pointed out, "there is a 'new look' among today's political activists. They are 'respectable,' solid middle-class citizens. The party 'hacks' of fiction, films, and the traditional literature are hard to find among the young, well-educated, affluent and socially acceptable committee men—and women—of the nineteen-sixties."[57] Republican ideological activists tend to be more conservative than other Republicans, and Democratic ideological activists tend to be more liberal than other Democrats.[58]

Second, the views of the parties-in-the-electorate, particularly on economic issues, are increasingly different: the Democrats are more liberal and the Republicans are more conservative.[59] Third, voters perceive a greater difference between the two major political

---

[57]John Fischer, "Please Don't Bite the Politicians," *Harper's* (November 1960), p. 16.

[58]See Everett Carll Ladd and Charles D. Hadley, *Political Parties and Political Issues: Patterns in Differentiation Since the New Deal,* Vol. 1 of Sage Professional Papers in American Politics (Beverly Hills: Sage, 1973); Herbert McClosky, Paul J. Hoffmann, and Rosemary O'Hara, "Issue Conflict and Consensus Among Party Leaders and Followers," *American Political Science Review,* 54 (1960): 406–27; and David Nexon, "Asymmetry in the Political System: Occasional Activists in the Republican and Democratic Parties: 1956–1964," *American Political Science Review,* 65 (1971): 716–30.

[59]Gerald M. Pomper, "From Confusion to Clarity: Issues and American Voters, 1956–1968," *American Political Science Review* 66 (1972): 415–28.

parties,[60] which can serve as a kind of self-fulfilling prophecy. Fourth, the alternatives presented by the two national parties on issues are becoming more distinct.[61]

Although they are in a state of flux, the two major American political parties—in the electorate, in the party organization, and in the government—continue to be important for several reasons. They still furnish an important cue for a great many voters. They are on the ballot in all the states and are semipublic entities. They furnish the organizational focus for Congress and all the state legislatures except Nebraska's, and their national conventions formally decide upon party presidential nominations and platforms.

ADDITIONAL SOURCES

Bernhard, Winfred E., Felice A. Bonadio, and Morton Borden, eds. *Political Parties in American History* (3 vols.). Putnam, 1974.*

Bone, Hugh A. *Party Committees and National Politics,* rev. ed. University of Washington Press, 1968.

Chambers, William N., and Walter Dean Burnham. *The American Party System: Stages of Political Development*, 2nd ed., rev. Oxford University Press, 1975.*

Crotty, William J. *Decision for the Democrats: Reforming the Party Structure.* John Hopkins, 1978.

Hofstadter, Richard. *The Idea of a Party System.* University of California Press, 1969.*

Huckshorn, Robert. *Party Leadership in the States.* University of Massachusetts Press, 1976.

Keech, William R., and Donald R. Matthews. *The Party's Choice: With an Epilogue on the 1976 Nominations.* Brookings, 1977.*

Keefe, William J. *Parties, Politics, and Public Policy in America,* 2nd ed. Dryden, 1976.*

Key, V. O., Jr. *Politics, Parties, and Pressure Groups*, 5th ed. Harper & Row, 1964.

Ladd, Everett Carll, and Charles D. Hadley. *Transformations of the American Party System: Political Coalitions from the New Deal to the 1970s.* Norton, 1978.

Mazmanian, Daniel A. *Third Parties in Presidential Elections.* Brookings, 1974.*

Ranney, Austin. *Curing the Mischiefs of Faction: Party Reform in America.* University of California Press, 1975.*

———. *Participation in American Presidential Nominations: 1976.* American Enterprise Institute, 1977.*

Royko, Mike. *Boss: Richard J. Daley of Chicago.* New American Library, 1971.*

Sorauf, Frank J. *Party Politics in America,* 3rd ed. Little, Brown, 1976.
*Available in paperback.

---

[60]Pomper, "From Confusion to Clarity: Issues and American Voters, 1956–1968," p. 418.

[61]See Pomper, "From Confusion to Clarity: Issues and American Voters, 1956–1968," pp. 415–28; Gerald M. Pomper, *Voters' Choice* (New York:Dodd, Mead, 1975); and Ladd, Jr. and Hadley, "Political Parties and Political Issues: Patterns in Differentiation Since the New Deal."

10 Campaigns and Elections

The People Choose

In the quiet of the polling booth, each voter's decision contributes to the selection of his or her leaders. For all the concern that has been expressed in recent years about campaigns and elections in America, the fact that they occur at all is one important measure of the vitality of America's democracy.

While studying for the American naturalization examination, an immigrant once said to her instructor, "Americans seem to be voting on something about every thirty minutes. How do you keep it all straight?" That is a good question. There are, indeed, numerous opportunities for voting in this country.

At the national level, voters choose among candidates for the Presidency, the Senate, and the House of Representatives. At the state level, voters choose among candidates for the governorship, judgeships, the state legislature, and frequently for positions in the state executive cabinet, such as attorney general or state treasurer. At the local level, there are elections for county and city officials, school board members, and officers of other local units like water districts. Elections are also held on bond issues, constitutional amendments, and legislative questions.

In recent years, a trend toward decreasing voter turnout in American elections has developed. Perhaps the very multiplicity of elections confuses voters and discourages them from voting. As we saw in the last chapter, political parties, which can simplify voting decisions, seem to have lost some of their meaning for Americans.

In order to understand how governmental decisions are made in America and how individual citizens may participate in the decision-making process, it is necessary to know how the electoral system works. Authoritarian systems of government do not have free elections with rival political parties and candidates. America does. Although the United States has a complicated electoral system, the fact that it exists at all has an important impact on citizens' participation in the decisions that govern their lives.

Voting and taking part in political campaigns constitute two basic means of political participation in a democracy. Opportunities for participation exist in local, state, and federal elections; in primary elections, which choose party nominees; and in general elections, in which the party nominees compete against each other for the right to hold public office.

How does the American electoral system work? Who votes—and why? Who are the candidates, and how do they campaign?

THE ELECTORAL SYSTEM

Democratic elections between competing candidates and parties serve several important functions. First, they enable citizens to formally decide who will govern. Second, they increase citizen involvement in government policy-making by engaging more people in debate and discussion of campaign issues, thereby influencing elected public officials. As V. O. Key, Jr., has written, "The wishes and probable actions of a vast number of people at the polls must be taken into consideration in the exercise of public power."[1] Third, elections offer an opportunity for citizens to reaffirm their sense of self-rule and their support for the political system.

Voting Barriers

Voting is a right in America. For years, that right was denied to many. But legal barriers to voting based upon race, sex, age, property, ability to pay a poll tax, residence, and literacy have been removed or greatly reduced. Today, state registration laws constitute the major remaining legal barrier to voting. In most states, a person must register before an election (usually twenty to thirty days) in order to vote. President Carter and others have recommended that citizens be allowed to vote without prior registration, simply by showing proper identification at the polls on election day. The few states that already have such a law have higher rates of voting than states that still require prior registration. Since minorities and people of lower socioeconomic status, who are the least likely groups to vote,[2] are more likely to vote Democratic than Republican when they do vote, Democratic officials have supported proposals to remove registration barriers more than Republican officials have.

The Electoral College

Except for the election of the President, American elections are direct. For example, in a senatorial or gubernatorial election, voters vote for one of the candidates. But they do not vote directly for candidates in a presidential election. Instead, they cast their ballots for groups of presidential *electors,* who are ostensibly pledged to a

---

[1]V. O. Key, Jr., *Politics, Parties, and Pressure Groups*, 5th ed. (New York: Thomas Y. Crowell, 1964), p. 622.

[2]See U.S. Bureau of the Census, "Voting and Registration in the Election of 1978" (Advance report) (Wash., D.C.: U.S. Government Printing Office, 1978).

To be qualified to vote, you must be a U.S. citizen (by birth or naturalization) over the age of 18, and you must be registered to vote. Registration procedures are determined by state law, and therefore differ from state to state. To find out how to register in your state, contact the offices or officials listed below; the procedures described here are for New Mexico.

In New Mexico, there is no residency requirement for registering to vote. However, registration books are closed 42 days before an election; in order to vote in an election, you must register prior to that date. Citizens must register by precinct in the county in which they live. Applications may be made to the county clerk's office or to a qualified registration officer in the county; information can be obtained by contacting the county clerk's office. Absentee registration is available for people temporarily living outside New Mexico or outside their county of residence; contact the county clerk for information. Note: A person registered in another state cannot register in New Mexico without first cancelling the prior registration.

The following information is required in order to complete an affidavit of registration:

- Your given name, middle name or initial, and last name
- Address of residence
- Place and date of birth
- Sex
- Social Security number
- Party affiliation (you may decline to state a party affiliation, but will not be allowed to vote in primary elections)

Applicants must sign the registration form, affirming that all facts listed on the form are true and correct.

Registration is permanent unless the registrant dies; is declared legally insane; is convicted of a felony; fails to vote in two consecutive general elections; or moves to another state.

For information on residency requirements and registration procedures in other states, contact your county clerk's office or (in metropolitan areas) your County Board of Elections (listed in your telephone directory under the name of your county). You may also contact the Secretary of State's office or local branch offices of the Secretary of State.

SOURCE: "Voters' Information Pamphlet for the Citizens of New Mexico," Secretary of State, New Mexico.

How to...

Register to Vote

presidential candidate. Each state has the same number of electors as it has members of the U.S. Senate and House of Representatives combined. After the election, the electors of the winning candidate in each state meet at the state capitol and cast their ballots. All the state's electoral votes are usually cast for the winning candidate. Nothing in the U.S. Constitution, however, bars the so-called faithless elector from casting a vote for any other candidate. As we saw in Chapter 2, the Electoral College has been criticized for this and other reasons,[3] but thus far, proposals for reforming or abolishing the institution have not received sufficient support in Congress.

The Secret Ballot

Americans vote by *secret ballot.* This system, adopted from Australia, is taken for granted today. But there was a time when political parties printed the ballots; the ballot that a citizen chose, marked, and put in the ballot box was often identifiable by a distinctive color, revealing to onlookers how the person had voted. Today, the printing of ballots is a government responsibility, and citizens may mark their ballot in secret.

There are two kinds of general election ballots. The *party-column ballot* allows citizens to vote a "straight ticket" for all the candidates of one party in every race. This can be done by making one mark above or next to a party emblem on the ballot or by pulling one party lever on a voting machine. To "split" a vote, a voter must pull individual levers or mark individual boxes. On most state ballots, the rooster is the emblem of the Democratic party, and the eagle is the emblem of the Republican party. Party officials and candidates regularly urge citizens to vote a straight ticket. The Democratic campaign cry is often something like this: "Stamp the rooster 'til the feathers fly!" Studies indicate that the party-column ballot increases straight ticket voting.[4]

The other type of ballot, the *office-column ballot,* lists candidates according to the office they seek. People who want to vote a straight ticket have to make a separate mark or pull a separate lever for each of the party candidates in each of the races, as do voters who want to split their votes.

THE VOTERS

What if we held an election and nobody showed up? Would that mean that everyone was satisfied? Probably not. Yet for quite some time, the percentage of eligible voters who actually vote in American elections has been decreasing. The United States ranks last among the world's major democracies in terms of voter turnout.[5] Voter

---

[3]See Congressional Quarterly, *Weekly Report* (March 10, 1979), pp. 405–10.
[4]Angus Campbell, Gerald Gurin, and Warren Miller, *The Voter Decides* (Evanston: Row, Peterson, 1954), p. 285.
[5]*Congressional Record* (April 10, 1973), p. 7030.

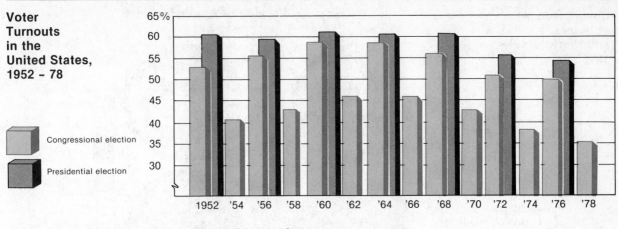

Voter Turnouts in the United States, 1952 – 78

☐ Congressional election

▨ Presidential election

SOURCE: U.S. Bureau of the Census, *Statistical Abstract of the United States*

turnout is lower in state and local elections than in national elections. It is also lower for legislative offices than for chief executive offices. Voter turnout is greater in areas where campaigns between candidates and between parties are more competitive.[6]

Thus, we can expect the largest turnout for any election in America to occur in an intensely competitive campaign by presidential candidates. But even in recent highly competitive presidential campaigns, the percentage of Americans who vote has significantly declined. After a modern high of 62.8 percent in the 1960 election between John F. Kennedy and Richard Nixon, turnout decreased to 60.9 percent in 1968, when Richard Nixon ran against Hubert Humphrey. In the 1972 election between Nixon and George McGovern, it went down to 55.7 percent and dropped to 54.4 percent in 1976, when Gerald Ford ran against Jimmy Carter. Other election turnouts have followed this downward trend; the turnout in the 1978 congressional elections fell to 35.1 percent.[7]

Voters and Nonvoters

One third of all Americans do not vote, join groups or parties, or take part in politics in any way.[8] Eligible voters under thirty-five are less likely to vote than those over thirty-five, and those between the

Comparative voter turnouts, national elections*

Australia, 1972	97%
Italy, 1972	93
W. Germany, 1972	91
Netherlands, 1972	83
France, 1973	82
Canada, 1972	74
Great Britain, 1970	71
United States, 1972	55

*Percentage of eligible voters casting ballots.
SOURCE: *Congressional Record* (April 10, 1973), p. 7030.

[6]This illustrates one reason why reform of voter registration laws may contribute to higher voter turnouts and may decrease voter disillusionment. Most general election campaigns tend to "peak"—to reach a high point in visibility and competitiveness—as election day approaches, rather than 20 to thirty days before the election, when most states require voters to register. As campaigns come to a peak, media coverage increases, which generates greater interest in the election among potential voters. This might encourage people who hadn't planned to vote to do so after all—if they could.

[7]Congressional Quarterly, *Weekly Report* (March 31, 1979), p. 574.

[8]Charles E. Lindblom, *The Policy-Making Process* (Englewood Cliffs, N.J.: Prentice-Hall, 1968), p. 44.

Comparison of Voters and Nonvoters, 1976

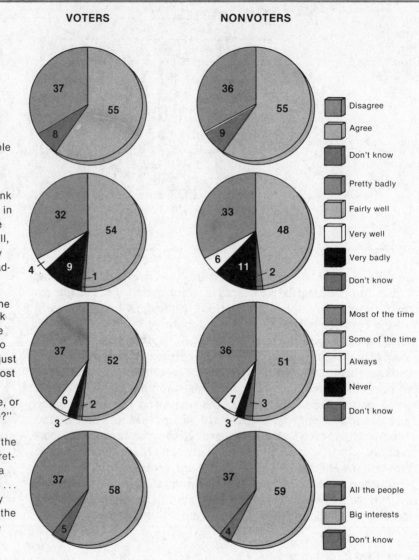

VOTERS **NONVOTERS**

"Public officials don't care much about what people like me think."

"How do you think things are going in the county these days . . . very well, fairly well, pretty badly, or very badly?"

"How much of the time do you think you can trust the government to do what's right . . . just about always, most of the time, only some of the time, or none of the time?"

"Would you say the government is pretty much run for a few big interests . . . or would you say that it is run for the benefit of all the people?"

Disagree
Agree
Don't know

Pretty badly
Fairly well
Very well
Very badly
Don't know

Most of the time
Some of the time
Always
Never
Don't know

All the people
Big interests
Don't know

SOURCE: *New York Times*, (November 16, 1976) Based on New York Times/CBS news poll of 2,042 persons of voting age.

ages of eighteen and twenty are the least likely to vote.[9] People with low incomes, minorities, and those who are not active in organizations are less likely to vote than other Americans.

Why do people fail to vote? Nonvoters may be less informed on political issues. They may feel less politically competent, less able to understand how the system works. They may also feel less politically efficacious, less able to influence the system. Voters and nonvoters are very much alike in their suspicious, cynical, and cautious

---

[9]Walter T. Murphy, Jr., "Student Power in the 1970 Elections: A Preliminary Assessment," *Political Science* (Winter 1971), pp. 27–32.

evaluations of the political system, but nonvoters are distinguished by their general sense of helplessness and indifference.[10] Almost 60 percent of the nonvoters (but only slightly over 40 percent of the voters) agree with the statement, "The country needs more radical change than is possible through the ballot box."[11] Many nonvoters, then, apparently stay away from the polls not because they are satisfied with the way things are, but because they are *dissatisfied* with the way things are and feel that voting will make little difference.

Who does vote? The people who are most likely to vote are white, middle-aged or older, better paid and better educated than the average citizen, and active in a political party or some other organization.[12] In addition, people who have been contacted personally by a party or campaign worker are more likely to take part in campaigns and elections.

Factors in How People Vote

Why do voters vote the way they do? Family, school, and peers have some impact on the kinds of opinions that people develop on public matters and consequently on how they vote. Income level, socioeconomic class, race, religion, and the region of the country where people live also influence voting patterns. The effect of these groups and groupings can vary, of course, with events and with particular candidates. "Cross-cutting issues"—important questions which cut across usual voting patterns—can also alter voting behavior. The Vietnam War was such an issue. Sometimes, race and social issues, such as law and order, welfare, abortion, and marijuana, also can be cross-cutting. The presence of a military hero like Dwight D. Eisenhower on a party ticket can cut across voting lines, too.

Party affiliation is an important factor in a voter's choice in an election. "Few factors are of greater importance for our national elections than the lasting attachment of tens of millions of Americans to one of the parties. These loyalties establish a basic division of electoral strength within which the competition of particular campaigns takes place."[13]

The influence of party affiliation on voting in the 1976 presidential election was greater than in preceding elections. According to Gerald M. Pomper,

One of the most striking characteristics of the 1976 vote is its partisan character. For the first time in a generation, the electorate was sharply divided along lines of party loyalty, with Carter gaining four of every five Democrats, and Ford doing even better among the GOP, winning

[10]*New York Times*/CBS News Poll, *New York Times* (November 16, 1976).

[11]*New York Times*/CBS News Poll.

[12] See Angus Campbell, Philip E. Converse, Warren E. Miller, and Donald E. Stokes, *The American Voter* (New York: Wiley, 1960); Norman H. Nie, Sidney Verba, and John R. Petrocik, *The Changing American Voter* (Cambridge, Mass.: Harvard University Press, 1976); and Warren E. Miller and Teresa E. Levitan, *Leadership and Change* (Cambridge, Mass.: Winthrop, 1976).

[13]Campbell et al., *The American Voter,* p. 121.

almost nine of every ten Republicans. Since there are almost twice as many Democrats as Republicans in the country, the return to partisanship was critical to Carter's victory.[14]

As we saw in Chapter 9, Independents are an important element of the American electorate. Their votes may provide the difference between defeat and victory. Carter was able to split this vote with Ford.

Campaign *issues* have a great effect on how people vote and on which political party they identify with.[15] In the 1976 presidential election Gerald Pomper reported that "the electorate divided clearly along lines of self-described ideology, three-fourths of the liberals casting their ballots for Carter and seven of ten conservatives choosing Ford." There was also a close relationship between votes and income. Carter won the support of two thirds of the voters from the lowest income levels and Ford gained similar support from those with the highest income.[16]

In 1976, the differences between the presidential candidates were blurred on the social issues. The Vietnam War no longer was an issue. Both President Ford and Jimmy Carter opposed busing as a tool for integrating public schools. So, economic issues were of special importance, and this helped the Democrats.[17] The differences in the economic views of the two candidates and their parties were pointed up by the Republican and Democratic platforms. The 1976 Republican platform called inflation the number one problem in America and named government spending as one of its principal causes. It stated:

We believe it is of paramount importance that the American people understand that the number one destroyer of jobs is inflation. We wish to stress that the number one cause of inflation is the government's expansion of the nation's supply of money and credit needed to pay for deficit spending. It is above all else deficit spending by the federal government which erodes the purchasing power of the dollar.

The 1976 Democratic platform, on the other hand, pointed to unemployment as the primary problem in America and affirmed that government action and spending were necessary to reduce it. It stated:

The Democratic Party is committed to the right of all adult Americans willing, able and seeking work to have opportunities for useful jobs, at living wages. To make that commitment meaningful, we pledge ourselves to the support of legislation that will make every responsible effort to reduce adult unemployment to 3 percent within 4 years.

---

[14]Gerald M. Pomper, "The Presidential Election," in Gerald M. Pomper et al., *The Election of 1976* (New York: David McKay Co, 1977), p. 73.

[15]Pomper, *Voters' Choice*, chaps. 8, 9.

[16]Pomper, "The Presidential Election," pp. 74–75.

[17]See Henry A. Plotkin, "Issues in the 1976 Presidential Campaign," in Pomper et al., *The Election of 1976*, pp. 35–53.

Voting decisions do not take place in a vacuum. All these factors interact with each other within the context of a candidate's campaign. Who the candidates are and how they campaign also influence voting decisions.

THE CANDIDATES

Who runs for public office in America? Why do they run? Motivations of candidates probably involve a desire to be of service to others, a love of public attention and acclaim, and an enjoyment of a sense of power, of the ability to have some control over events. Different public officials may represent different ratios of these ingredients.

Sometimes people are "recruited" to run for public office. Friends or interest groups, such as unions or business organizations, may suggest that a person run for office. A party organization—the local committee, the state chairperson, or the campaign committee in one of the houses of Congress, for example—may also do the recruiting.

Probably the largest percentage of candidates are self-starters. Most candidates are actively interested in being elected to public office. (Not all candidates for local offices, however, actively seek election. Some of them run only because of a sense of "civic duty.") The myth of the office seeking the person rather than the person seeking the office is not often translated into reality in American politics. Thus, political reality is different from the norm in fourth-grade school elections, which discourages candidates from campaigning or even voting for themselves. Even Abraham Lincoln, who is often thought of as the epitome of the nonpolitician, actively campaigned for several political offices—including the state legislature, Congress, and the U.S. Senate—before he actively sought election to the Presidency.

Most people who seek and are elected to high public office are white males who have incomes in the upper-middle or high-income brackets, have careers in the professions, own property, or are investors. The more influential the office, the more likely it is that officeholders will have these characteristics. These people are likely to have been socialized from an early age to understand the political system and its rewards. They have the free time to campaign and the money to live on while campaigning. Because they have contact with influential and wealthy people, they can readily build a base of strong support. In addition, they may be able to contribute substantial amounts of money to their own campaigns. Having a "famous name"—as a war hero, astronaut, or as the son of a well-known person—is also an advantage. Thus, those who seek and hold public office (particularly high public office) often come from backgrounds different from those of average American citizens. Some inroads have been made to broaden the base from which public officials come, but more could be done.

THE CAMPAIGN

The phone rings jarringly. For a moment, she cannot remember where the phone is—or even where *she* is. It is still dark outside. But months ago, she started leaving the light on in the bathroom of each motel she stayed in, so that she could quickly get her bearings when, like this morning, she woke up disoriented.

"Yes?" she asks raspingly into the mouthpiece, her voice slightly hoarse from too many speeches.

"Time to get moving, boss," an aide's voice says, adding with an attempt at humor, "If you hadn't wanted to work, you shouldn't have hired out."

She ignores the humor, but she does get moving. She has to. There is an important breakfast meeting this morning with a classroom teachers' group, and she desperately needs their support.

Since she announced her candidacy for governor, a year and a half before the election, she has logged thousands of miles, using virtually every kind of transportation and sleeping in hundreds of strange beds. She has answered the dozen or so usual questions so often that she can now do it by rote. She has delivered "the speech," the basic statement of her campaign, so many times that even her husband, sitting next to her at countless public functions, has to work at looking interested. She has eaten enough tough roast beef and cold peas to deserve a medal for bravery and has consumed enough coffee to cause a rise in world coffee prices.

She has also learned to travel light and dress quickly, so she is ready when the aide knocks on her motel door, just thirty minutes after the wake-up call.

At the breakfast, the eggs are cold and the bacon is greasy, but she eats them anyway while she thinks about what she will say to this group. She's been trying to eat more lately because in the closing weeks of the campaign, she has been losing weight. She has even taken to drinking a milkshake every day to keep her face from looking thin and haggard on television. Her major campaign promise is a cut in property taxes, but she assures the teachers that savings in expenditures will allow for a cost-of-living increase in teachers' salaries.

After the breakfast and an on-the-spot radio interview, she is driven to a shopping center for some handshaking. She is preceded by a sound truck and three campaign aides who pass out literature while "Come meet your next governor" blares out over the loudspeaker. She wonders if shaking hands with prospective voters makes any real difference, but she feels better on this misty morning when a local television crew shows up to film her campaign activity for the evening news. "I love it," she says during the interview. "You get a chance to talk to people personally and find out what's on their minds."

There is a ten o'clock press conference at the local press club. A reporter rides with her to the press conference. He is doing a story about her family life. "But don't you feel bad about having to be

How to . . .

Run for Office

Once you've decided to seek an elected office, what do you do next? The techniques and strategies employed in any campaign—whether local, statewide, or national—are very similar, differing mainly in the emphasis placed on publicity and advertising versus personal contact. An average campaign would include the following:

1. Arrange a meeting of friends and persons who you believe share your ideology and will support your candidacy. Organize a citizens' committee.

2. Prepare a profile of the district, showing partisan registration and ideological commitment to your campaign objectives, as indicated by public opinion polls.

3. Originate a campaign theme and a slogan expressing it. Appoint a campaign manager, secretary, publicity chairman, treasurer or financial chairman, and a chairman to supervise canvassing.

4. Announce your candidacy and campaign program, telling why you think it is needed. Publicize your background and qualifications.

5. Start raising funds and recruiting volunteers. Get organized for action, setting up a speaker's bureau.

6. Open a headquarters as near the center of your district as possible. Equip it with desks, chairs, filing cabinets, phone, etc.

7. Start getting signatures of registered voters to serve as your sponsors in getting your name on the ballot. Also begin getting written endorsements to use in publicity.

8. Begin holding rallies, coffee hours, and other special events to enlist workers and raise campaign funds.

9. Get your campaign literature ready for the printer. Write a biographical sketch and have photographs made with endorsers for publicity use.

10. Use your volunteer and paid workers to encourage registration of voters through door-to-door canvassing and telephone calls. Have canvassers distribute leaflets or campaign folders at homes, meetings, and supermarkets.

11. Follow up with newspaper publicity, display advertising, direct mail, and radio and television commercials, pointing up why your constituents should vote for you.

12. Stage pep rallies, demonstrations, and parades to arouse enthusiasm.

13. Conduct a last-minute round of telephone calls to remind supporters to go to the polls and vote.

14. Arrange to have poll watchers at polling places to guard against vote fraud.

15. Publicly thank all who assisted in your campaign. Send thank-you letters to leading supporters.

SOURCE: William L. Roper, *Winning Politics: A Handbook for Candidates and Campaign Workers* (Chilton Book Co., 1978), pp. 163–64.

away from your children so much?" he asks. It is a question she has fielded a hundred times before. "My husband is very good with them," she says, "and then Betsy, who's eleven, and Henry, who's fourteen, are very much involved in the campaign themselves, and they feel that what we are all doing together is very important."

The press conference goes smoothly. She reads the prepared statement, which explains how much the proposed property tax cut will mean for the average family. She and her staff write many of her press statements long before they are to be used. During the last two weeks of the campaign, she will issue two such statements each day, one in the morning and one in the afternoon. The statements are aimed at making news twice a day—in both the morning and evening newspapers—but the main hope is that one of them will get a minute segment on the nightly television news broadcasts. She knows that television is the key to a successful statewide campaign, and she has planned her campaign accordingly.

At noon, she visits a senior citizens' center, where hot lunches are served to about sixty older people each day. She prefers to call them "older people," and they appreciate her frankness and support.

After lunch, she goes back to her motel room for some urgent fund-raising, the aspect of the campaign that she likes least. But it has to be done. Today, on the way to the motel, she learns that she could lose the right to buy some vital last-week TV advertising spots; they will be offered to other candidates unless she can can come up with $12,000 to pay them before the day ends. At the motel, two wealthy friends are waiting. She has another cup of coffee, pours them a beer, and makes the pitch. "I know you've given more than you should be asked to give," she says sincerely, "but we've just got to raise the money for these spots." She always finds it a little demeaning to ask for money, and she wonders what kinds of implied commitments she may be making. One of the men she is soliciting for an additional contribution is a wholesale beer distributor. The other is an architect. What will they want when she becomes governor?

The two friends write checks for another $1000 each and leave. She talks to seven more prospective contributors on the telephone, as each is dialed in turn by an aide. "Did you see the *Tribune* poll?" she asks. "We're really coming up, but these spots are crucial." With all but $4000 of the needed money raised (which will probably be picked up through an aide's follow-up calls), she changes clothes and heads for a local, low-budget cafe to film the TV spots.

The cafe is crammed with television lights, reflectors, cameras, camera crews, technicians—and spectators anxious to get into the picture. The producer from her advertising agency works at getting everyone—the waiters and customers—to act naturally during the filming. The candidate briefly studies a script, which will take forty-five seconds to recite. With the cafe and its employees and customers as backdrops, she looks into the camera on cue and begins,

"In the closing days of this campaign, ordinary people have increasingly been joining with me in demanding a cut in property taxes . . ."

"Hold it!" the producer says. "We're getting a buzzing on the sound track from the ice machine."

She starts again. "In the closing days of this campaign, ordinary people have increasingly been joining with me in demanding a cut in property taxes . . ."

"Wait a minute," the producer interrupts. "We're getting some kind of funny shadow on her face."

The lights are adjusted, and she begins again—and again and again. A minute spot takes two hours to film.

After filming the TV spot, she hurries to two "coffees" in private homes, one at 4:30 and one at 5:15. Each is in the home of a supporter. She makes a brief opening statement at each coffee, explaining why she wants to be governor and what she hopes to accomplish, and then answers questions. At the end of each session, she asks those who are willing to help with telephoning, canvassing, stuffing envelopes, or other campaign chores to sign a pledge sheet.

Back at the motel, she takes the phone from an aide and responds to a prearranged, live radio interview for fifteen minutes. Her stomach tightens as she begins to think ahead to the last of the day's activities, a televised "debate," or joint appearance, with the other gubernatorial candidates before a League of Women Voters audience. Too tense to eat, she turns down a sandwich and goes over her notes. "Should I be rough with the general or not?" she asks her campaign manager.

Riding back to the motel after the debate, she feels good. She has made points, she feels, with her statement, "The general may want the governorship as a kind of honor to cap off his career, but I want to be governor because I feel deeply about what we ought to be doing for this state's people."

She talks to her husband and one of the children by telephone; the youngest child is already asleep. Her husband is enthusiastic about the debate, and this is a good note to end the day on. But just before she gets into bed, she calls the motel desk. "Would you ring me in the morning at six o'clock?" she says.

This account is fictional, but it accurately depicts life on the campaign trail. With some changes in the facts, it could describe a day in the life of candidate Ella Grasso, who was elected governor of Connecticut in 1973, or of candidate Dixie Lee Ray, who was elected governor of Washington in 1976, or of many other recent gubernatorial candidates. If our fictional candidate was the *incumbent,* the person already in office, rather than a challenger, her campaign would have been somewhat different, as we shall see in the next section. But in all campaigns—for local, state, or national office—canvassing, communications, and financing are important factors.

The Advantage of Incumbency

The incumbent has an advantage in most campaigns. Incumbents can claim experience on the job. They usually can concentrate on the general election without having to worry about primary election challenges. They have "name recognition" with the voters. And they can use their official positions to do favors for the voters, building voter support. They can publicize their accomplishments in office through official newsletters and press releases. Thus, it is not surprising that since 1954, approximately 94 percent of the incumbent members of the U.S. House of Representatives and a little over 84 percent of the incumbent members of the U.S. Senate who have sought reelection have been successful.[18] Incumbency can also have its drawbacks, of course, since voters tend to blame existing problems on those already in office.

The Canvass

Campaigning, of course, affects how people vote, but we do not know exactly how much and in what way. We do know, as noted earlier, that person-to-person contact is the most effective means of changing public opinion and affecting the way people vote. So, candidates and their workers attempt to contact voters personally. *Canvassing* voters has become highly important. It involves sending workers—or in some cases, candidates—door-to-door to talk with voters directly. In a highly efficient canvass, such as those done in all campaigns by major presidential candidates, the workers are given "walking lists" of the names of the people who live in each house on the block they are to canvass. Canvassers are carefully instructed about what to say and do as they go about their work. Careful reports are made on each voter who is to be contacted. Some voters may already support the candidate for whom the canvassing is being done or may be "leaning" toward the candidate. Other voters may be committed to or leaning toward another candidate, or they may be undecided. Follow-up canvasses are later made to further persuade those who were leaning toward the candidate and those who were undecided. On election day, campaign workers make a special effort to get known supporters to the polls.

Opinion leaders are often the conduits through which people receive political information and opinions. Thus, an important part of any campaign is identifying these opinion leaders and persuading them to support the candidate—or turning supporters into opinion leaders. Many people do not have an opinion or do not want to express one. Consequently, a person who does have an opinion and is willing to express it is influential and is by definition an opinion

[18]See *Congressional Quarterly* for appropriate years; and Warren Lee Kostroski, "Party and Incumbency in Post-War Senate Election: Trends, Patterns, and Models," *American Political Science Review,* 67 (December 1973): 1217.

How to...

Canvass for Votes

Canvassing is grass-roots politics at its most basic level: individual citizens going door-to-door to talk with their neighbors about issues and candidates. It is also a special kind of personal face-to-face communication. Most campaigns develop instructions for canvassers, to fit specific situations, but there are certain general guidelines for doing it right:

1. Find out the person's name before knocking on the door, if possible. Next-door neighbors are the best sources of information, but voters' registration lists, names on mailboxes, or telephone directories would also be helpful.

2. Introduce yourself and smile as you explain the purpose of your call.

3. Tell the person briefly about your candidate, his or her program, and why the program is important.

4. Find out if the person is registered. If he or she is of your party and for your candidate, urge the person to register.

5. Don't interfere with family or social affairs. Make your call brief— about five minutes or so.

6. Answer the voter's questions if you can. If you don't know, say so, and offer to find out and send the person an answer.

7. Leave some campaign literature and leave with a smile.

8. Always carry a notebook in which to make a brief record of your visit. Note who would benefit from a return visit, either on election day or in general.

9. Never knock on a stranger's door after 9:30 p.m.

10. Try to call on at least ten homes a day (more or less, depending on the area you are asked to canvass).

SOURCE: Adapted from William L. Roper, *Winning Politics: A Handbook for Candidates and Campaign Workers* (Chilton Book Co., 1978), pp. 136–37. See also Michael Walzer, *Political Action* (Quadrangle Books, 1971).

An important part of campaigning is meeting the people—and even future voters get their share of attention.

leader. Candidates tell their supporters that any of them can become important opinion leaders. The central goals of any political campaign, therefore, are identifying supporters, turning them into opinion leaders, and then giving them reinforcement so that they will continue to be active and enthusiastic.

Campaign Communications

Campaigns use public appearances and rallies, printed materials, billboards, the mass media, and the mail to convey their messages and project their desired images. Newspapers are more effective than television for presenting issues and the qualities of candidates.[19] Much of the television news about campaigns focuses only on the "horse race" aspects—on how the candidates are running. But television news coverage and paid advertising are important because they are the major sources of news for most Americans. Television coverage has made the candidate's "image" more important.

It is probably not true, as some have said, that Abraham Lincoln could never be elected President today because a candidate's "looks" on television are so important to his or her image. "Clearly, images depend on what a candidate represents—his party, his actions, his policies—and just as clearly on how a voter feels about what the candidate represents—his party, past actions, future policies. For almost every voter, a candidate's image depends on these two realistic factors and not on whether he looks good or bad on television."[20] Nevertheless, image is important, and candidates spend much time and money attempting to project a desired image, often hiring consultants to advise them.

This desired image is made up of several elements. One of these is honesty. This standard means more than not lying, cheating, or stealing. To fulfill this part of the image, candidates must also appear open and straightforward on the issues, not evasive; they must be willing to "take a stand." Candidates also want to appear to be "one of us," to convey the impression that they have the same problems and concerns that we do. They want to seem "on our side" on the issues, although they may attempt to avoid taking a stand on the more controversial issues. In addition, it is important for candidates to appear qualified, or competent to handle the duties of the office they seek. This latter element is especially important in a campaign for the presidency, since voters are always concerned not only about the relative knowledge and ability of the candidates, but also about which candidate is the most disciplined, most in command of himself or herself, and thus, best "able to govern."

Some of these elements of candidate image came into play in the

[19]See Thomas Patterson and Robert D. McClure, *The Unseeing Eye: The Myth of Television Power in National Politics* (New York: Putnam, 1976).
[20]Thomas E. Patterson and Robert D. McClure, "Political Campaigns; TV Power is A Myth," *Psychology Today* (July 1976), p. 90.

1976 presidential campaign. The incumbency of President Ford was another factor. The voters had a choice between President Ford, who seemed predictable, stable, experienced, and familiar and Jimmy Carter, who seemed more intelligent, compassionate, and committed to change. "Narrowly the voters chose the greater risks and greater opportunities offered by Carter to the safety and predictability presented by Ford."[21]

For image projection and other purposes, campaigns spend by far the largest part of their advertising budgets on television. TV commercials can help to reinforce beliefs and inform "opinion leaders." They can also help to persuade undecided voters, who can represent the margin of victory in a close race.

Modern campaigns, especially those for the more influential offices, often use paid experts for public relations, advertising, polling, and fund-raising. In some states (California is a prime example), there are political consulting firms that can manage an entire campaign. Many modern campaigns have begun to use "direct mail" increasingly, and mailing lists can be rented for that purpose. Subscription lists to certain magazines and membership lists in certain organizations are two examples. From census information, types of voters and issues may be correlated with census tracts and mailing addresses. Candidates for the California legislature typically send two computer-typed letters addressed to each registered voter in the legislative district. The first letter mentions one or more issues that are likely to be on the mind of the particular voter to whom the letter is mailed. The second letter is usually a reminder to vote, and it usually lists the address of the voter's voting place.

Though person-to-person campaigning is the most effective, TV commercials and shows like "Issues and Answers" and "Face the Nation" enable candidates to project their ideas—and "images"—to millions of people at a time.

Campaign Financing

Money is often the key to a successful election. Candidates do not necessarily have to have as much money as their opponents to get elected, but a successful campaign requires at least enough money to convey the basic message about the campaign, the candidate, and the issues. Campaigns have become very expensive, particularly because of the greater use of television. According to the Federal Election Commission, presidential candidates in 1976 spent a total of $66.9

---

[21]Pomper, "The Presidential Election," pp. 75–76.

Major Provisions for the Regulation of Campaign Financing in Federal Elections

I. Contribution Limits
A. No individual may contribute more than $1000 to any candidate in a primary, runoff, and general election or more than $25,000 to all federal candidates in one year.
B. Candidates for President (including their families) may spend no more than $50,000 of their personal funds on their campaigns, candidates for the U.S. Senate no more than $35,000, candidates for the U.S. House of Representatives no more than $25,000.
C. The political arms of such organizations as the AFL-CIO or the AMA may not donate more than $5000 to any one campaign. There are no limits, however, on their aggregate spending or on the amounts they may contribute to party organizations supporting federal candidates.
D. Contributions *in cash* are limited to $100.

II. Expenditure Limits
A. Candidates are limited to an expenditure of $10 million each in *all* presidential primaries and limited in the amount that can be spent in *each* state presidential primary (no more than twice the amount a candidate for Senate may spend in that state).
B. Presidential candidates in the general election may spend no more than $20 million.
C. Candidates for the U.S. Senate may spend no more than $100,000, or 8 cents per eligible voter (whichever is greater) in primaries and $150,000, or 12 cents per voter (whichever is greater) in general elections, except that certain fund-raising costs (up to 20 percent of the spending limit) may be added to these amounts.
D. Candidates for the U.S. House of Representatives may spend no more than $70,000 in primaries and $70,000 in general elections, except that certain fund-raising costs (up to 20 percent of the spending limit) may be added to these amounts. Including fund-raising outlays, the effective total for House candidates is $84,000 for each election.
E. Expenditures by national party organizations on behalf of each candidate for the House are limited to $10,000, for each Senate candidate to $20,000, or 2 cents per voter (whichever is greater), and for presidential elections to 2 cents per voter. (These expenditures are *in addition* to those allowable for individual candidates.)

III. Public Financing
A. Major party candidates for the presidency qualify for full funding ($20 million) prior to the campaign, the money to be drawn from the federal income-tax dollar checkoff. Candidates may decline to participate in the public funding program and finance their campaigns through private contributions.
B. Minor party and independent candidates qualify for lesser sums, provided their candidates received at least 5 percent of the vote in the previous presidential election. New parties or parties that received less than 5 percent of the vote four years earlier qualify for public financing *after* the election, provided they drew 5 percent of the vote.
C. Matching public funds of up to $5 million are available for presidential primary candidates, provided that they first raise $100,000 in private funds ($5000 in contributions of no more than $250 in each of 20 states). Once that threshold is reached, the candidate receives matching funds up to $250 per contribution. No candidate is eligible for more than 25 percent of the total available funds.
D. Optional public funding of presidential nominating conventions is available for the major parties, with lesser amounts for minor parties.

IV. Disclosure and Reporting
A. Each federal candidate is required to establish a single, overarching campaign committee to report on all contributions and expenditures on behalf of the candidate.
B. Frequent reports on contributions and expenditures are to be filed with the Federal Election Commission.

V. Enforcement
A. Administration of the law is the responsibility of an eight-member, bipartisan Federal Elections Commission. The Commission is empowered to make rules and regulations, to receive campaign reports, to render advisory opinions, to conduct audits and investigations, to subpoena witnesses and information, and to seek civil injunctions through court action.

SOURCE: *Congressional Quarterly, Weekly Report,* 32 (October 12, 1974), pp. 2865–70, and 33 (June 14, 1975), pp. 1239–48.

million in the primaries and $45.9 million in the general election. In the same year, total spending for U.S. Senate and House races amounted to just under $100 million; by the 1978 campaigns this figure had jumped to $150 million. The average House candidate—winners and losers—spent $71,000 in 1976 and $108,000 in 1978. The average Senate candidate spent $600,000 in 1976 and $920,000 in 1978.[22]

Where does the money come from? Candidates use several means to secure campaign contributions. Soliciting friends is one basic way. Soliciting large contributions from people who have special viewpoints or interests is another. Candidates can contribute to their own campaigns, sometimes borrowing the money to do so. Candidates may seek contributions by advertising on television, radio, or in newspapers, but this is generally not very effective unless there is strong enthusiasm for the candidate or intense support for an issue associated with the candidate. In recent years, concerts and personal appearances by entertainers and other famous people have become commonplace in national elections. Direct-mail solicitation of campaign contributions is a very important means of campaign fundraising, but this method requires spending a considerable amount of money in advance. In Senator Jesse Helms' North Carolina reelection campaign in 1978, direct-mail expert Richard Viguerie raised nearly $7 million. About fifty cents of each dollar, however, went to pay for the direct-mail campaign itself.[23]

There are a number of reasons why people contribute to a campaign. Friendship is one. Some people simply enjoy having the opportunity to associate with candidates who are, or may become, famous or powerful. People who hold strong opinions about political issues or ideology are becoming increasingly important campaign contributors. And those who have "axes to grind"—interests to protect or push—give money to secure access and influence.

The people who are the least likely to vote and least likely to run for public office are also the least likely (or able) to contribute money to a campaign. Hence, people with low incomes are at a disadvantage in influencing government, although they would gain the most from government attention in the form of jobs and health care, for example. We say that we believe in the principle of "one person, one vote," but it is clear that the political influence of those with money to contribute to campaigns goes beyond their single vote.

The 1974 Campaign Reform Act contains provisions that are intended to lessen the influence of money. The law limits contributions and expenditures in federal campaigns; requires candidates for federal office to disclose all the financial aspects of their campaigns; and provides a public financing system for presidential campaigns. But especially for congressional campaigns, the reforms have failed to live up to the hopes of those who advocated them. Campaign

---

[22]*New York Times* (January 18, 1979).
[23]Congressional Quarterly, *Weekly Report* (October 28, 1978), p. 3113.

expenditures for the U.S. House and Senate, as well as special-interest contributions in these races, have continued to grow at an alarming rate. Although federal matching funds are provided for the preconvention campaigns of presidential candidates who qualify, and although full federal financing is available for the general election campaigns of the presidential candidates of the two major parties, no system of public financing exists for congressional candidates. Later efforts to pass such legislation have been unsuccessful. In 1977, the Republican leader in the Senate, Howard Baker of Tennessee, was able to forge a cohesive front of Senate Republicans against the bill. He contended that public financing would help Democrats far more than Republicans.[24] The Carter administration and public-interest groups like Common Cause have continued to apply pressure for public financing of congressional campaigns.

The Supreme Court opened two loopholes in the 1974 Campaign Reform Act. First, the Court held that government cannot limit congressional candidates' contributions to their own campaigns. However, the Court did make it clear that if there were public financing for congressional campaigns, candidates who accepted it could be limited in their personal contributions. Second, the Court ruled that the government cannot restrict spending by noncollusive, self-starting supporters—those who give money without prior arrangement with candidates—to further candidates' campaigns. Both loopholes were upheld on the basis of freedom of speech.

The 1974 Campaign Reform Act limits the public financing of party presidential nominees to the candidates of parties that received 5 percent or more of the total vote in the previous general election. So far, this requirement has only been met by the Republican party and the Democratic party. If a minor party's candidate received 5 percent or more of the total vote in a presidential general election, the candidate of the minor party would be reimbursed after the election for campaign expenditures, on the same per-vote basis that applies to the major parties. Thereafter, the presidential candidates of that minor party would be entitled to prior campaign financing as long as the party nominees continued to receive at least 5 percent of the national vote in the general election.

Critics of this provision have said that it discriminates against minor parties and prevents them from developing significant strength in the future. The Supreme Court has rejected this attack. Others have argued that the present general election financing system could actually encourage the growth of minor parties by making one or more of them permanent fixtures in American politics. A minor party with a relatively popular issue or candidate—such as George Wallace, who received over 13 percent of the national vote in 1968—would qualify for public financing and would be less likely to fade out as minor parties have usually done in the past.

---

[24]*Chicago Sun-Times* (August 4, 1977), p. 14.

CONCLUSION

The day before an election, candidates make their last campaign stops, their final speeches, their last appeal for votes, and "press the flesh" for the last time. The frantic pace slows to a halt. On election day the voters speak. After millions of individual voting decisions, one candidate is chosen to fill each elected public office.

Campaigns have been called "democracy's circuses." But free, competitive elections are the hallmark of democratic politics. Although many Americans do not take part in campaigns or even vote in elections, the fact is that they *can* do so. And that is vitally important.

The ability of voters to choose between competing parties and candidates on the basis of ideology and issues has improved. More responsible parties and more issue-oriented (rather than image-oriented) campaigns might encourage more Americans to participate in campaigns and elections. Greater involvement in campaigns and elections would give more Americans—especially minorities and people with low incomes, who are least likely to vote or to run for office—a better opportunity to participate in government policy-making and a better chance to hold public officials accountable.

ADDITIONAL SOURCES

Alexander, Herbert. *Campaign Money: Reform and Reality in the States.* Free Press, 1976.*

———.*Financing Politics: Money, Elections, and Political Reform,* new ed. Congressional Quarterly, 1976.

Burnham, Walter Dean. *Critical Elections and the Mainsprings of American Politics.* Norton, 1971.*

Campbell, Angus, Philip Converse, Warren Miller, and Donald Stokes. *The American Voter.* Wiley, 1960.

Crouse, Timothy. *The Boys on the Bus: Riding with the Campaign Press Corps.* Ballantine, 1976.*

Hadley, Arthur T. *The Empty Polling Booth.* Prentice-Hall, 1978.

Key, V.O., Jr. *The Responsible Electorate: Rationality in Presidential Voting, 1936–1960.* Harvard University Press, 1966.

Ladd, Everett Carl. *Where Have All the Voters Gone? The Fracturing of America's Political Parties.* Norton, 1978.

McGinnis, Joe. *The Selling of the President, 1968.* Popular Books, 1969.*

Miller, Warren, and Teresa Levitan. *Leadership and Change: The New Politics and the American Electorate.* Winthrop, 1976.

Nie, Norman H., Sidney Verba, and John R. Petrocik. *The Changing American Voter.* Harvard University Press, 1976.*

Pomper, Gerald. *The Election of 1976: Reports and Interpretations.* Longman, 1977.*

———.*Elections in America: Control and Influence in Democratic Politics.* Dodd, Mead, 1968.

———*Voters' Choice.* Dodd, Mead, 1975.

Witcover, Jules. *Marathon: The Pursuit of the Presidency, 1972–1976.* New American Library, 1978.*

*Available in paperback.

11 Direct Action
Organizing for Self-Help Efforts

Legal direct action tactics like demonstrations, boycotts, and initiative petitions provide ways for citizens to participate in decisions that affect their lives.

Suppose you lived in a community where month after month the utility company sent out what you were convinced were unjustifiably high electricity bills? What could you do about it? Should you use political action or some other means to address the problem?

Thus far, we have focused on how citizens can become involved in decisions that affect their lives through *political action*. This kind of activity takes place within the political arena and seeks governmental action. For example, you could write, call, or visit your governor or the local public utility commission to urge a roll-back in utility prices. Alternatively, you could campaign and vote for a candidate who supports such a measure, or run for office yourself. Or you could file a lawsuit if you felt a law had been violated.

By contrast, *direct action* consists of self-help efforts by citizens to participate in decisions that affect their lives. But direct action may be political, and to that extent the distinction between direct action and political action is somewhat blurred. Both may seek remedial action, but unlike political activity, direct action may bypass government altogether. The major difference between them involves the tactics that they use.

For example, when the residents of Westwood, California, a town of 2,500 people, became outraged about increases in the electricity rates that California-Pacific Utility Company was charging them, they decided to take direct action. They organized an electricity boycott. All the town's residents turned off their electricity and went for a full week without electric lights, hot water, electric stoves, and television sets. "We figure it's a patriotic move—like the Boston Tea Party," Pauline Asmus, a leader of the boycott, said at the time.[1]

The boycott worked! Service improved, and the rates were

---

[1]Environmental Action Foundation, *The Power Line*, 3, no.9 (April 1978): 1, 5.

substantially reduced. There were side benefits, too. About one year after the boycott, Pauline Asmus said, "We learned that we don't have to be so dependent on electricity—so, we've cut down on luxury appliances, like can openers, electric knives, and coffee makers, and have begun to insulate better—and we also learned that we don't have to be so dependent on 'big brother.' "[2]

Their boycott also led to political action, an important side effect that usually follows direct-action campaigns. The boycott proved to be a politicizing experience for many people; that is, they were exposed to and became more informed about government policy and how it is made. The community had started out to remedy what they felt was an intolerable situation by taking action on their own, without help. But before they were through, they had also secured an investigation and remedial action by the California Public Utility Commission, the state's regulatory agency.

Westwood's boycott was a type of *legal direct action*. Like political action, it is backed by the constitutional guarantees of free speech, press, assembly, and association. Americans have sometimes used *illegal direct action*—in the form of violence or civil disobedience—to get what they want. In this chapter, we will consider both types of direct action.

VIOLENCE AND CIVIL DISOBEDIENCE

The use of violence and civil disobedience to further a cause is clearly a violation of the law. Individual participants, of course, are guaranteed certain constitutional safeguards, such as the right to counsel and the right to a jury if charged with a crime. *Civil disobedience* involves breaking the law in an open, deliberate, nonviolent manner. The people who employ this tactic are willing to suffer the consequences of their acts in order to make a public protest. A sit-in at a lunch counter where service to blacks has been refused is an example of civil disobedience. The people who practice civil disobedience intend that only they will suffer the penalty for their act. By contrast, persons who advocate or practice violence as a tactic intend to cause harm to others—to their person, their property, or both.

Historically, violence has scarred the American political landscape the way meteor showers have pockmarked the surface of the moon. Military conquest of the American Indians was the principal feature of the first settlement of this continent by Europeans. The enslavement of thousand of Africans and their descendants is a shameful, horrifying part of our history. Our country was founded by a war—the American Revolution—and was forcibly held together by another one—the Civil War. We have fought other wars, such as the Vietnam conflict, that are difficult to justify. Political assassinations

---

[2]Pauline Asmus, from a telephone conversation with author, May 30, 1979.

have left terrible stains on our political system. Corporations have violently resisted union organizing, sometimes hiring "thugs," and union members have frequently fought back. One study concluded, "The United States has had the bloodiest and most violent labor history of any industrial nation in the world."[3] Horrible race riots and devastating urban disorders have also occurred in America. One study found that between 1963 and 1968, in terms of the total magnitude of violent civil strife, America ranked first among democratic countries of the world.[4] Civil strife has sometimes resulted in "police violence," or officially condoned overreactions to street violence and provocations.

Violence may be planned or unplanned. Planned violence may be used for propaganda—to call attention to and build support for a cause—or it may be used for revolution—to overthrow the government. The 1975 kidnaping of Patricia Hearst by a few self-styled revolutionaries who called themselves the Symbionese Liberation Army and the scattered bombings in the 1960s by the Weathermen were planned acts of *propaganda violence*. In America, this kind of violence has usually been met with counterviolence by police and has often caused a backlash of public opinion against those who use violent means.

It is hard to imagine how *revolutionary violence* could be successfully employed to overthrow the government of the United States under present conditions. There is no territorial revolutionary enclave here, as Mao Tse-tung had in the Chinese revolution.[5] Nor is there a highly disciplined revolutionary cadre or circumstances which seem to make widespread spontaneous revolt inevitable, as there was in Russia in 1917.

America has experienced much *unplanned violence*. Most modern prison riots and most of the urban disorders of the late 1960s began relatively spontaneously. Formal complaints and grievances were often formulated after the fact.

Why has America's history been so violent? The amount of violence in any society depends, first, on the intensity of the grievances, and second, on the effectiveness of nonviolent remedies. The grievances of a complaining group may become more intense, even when notable progress is being made, if their sense of "relative deprivation" increases. That is, they may become more aware of the gap between their living conditions and those enjoyed by other groups. During the largely spontaneous disorders in the black

---

[3]Phillip Taft and Phillip Ross, "American Labor Violence: Its Causes, Character, and Outcome," in Hugh Davis Graham and Ted Robert Gurr, eds., *Violence in America: Historical and Comparative Perspectives* (New York: New American Library, 1969), p. 281.

[4]See Ted Robert Gurr, "A Comparative Study of Civil Strife," in Graham and Gurr, *Violence in America: Historical and Comparative Perspectives*, p. 549.

[5]See Mao Tse-tung, *Chinese Communist Revolutionary Strategy, 1945–1949* (Princeton: Princeton University Press, 1961); and Mao Tse-tung, *On Guerrilla Warfare* (New York: Frederick Praeger, 1962).

sections of many American cities in the 1960s, for example, living conditions for black people were generally no worse than they had been in the past. Yet black people had become increasingly aware of their relative deprivation. They had come to realize that their living conditions and opportunities were inferior to those of a majority of other Americans. The violence in the black ghettos also came at a time when many black people felt that local police, schools, city administrators, and federal officials were unresponsive to lawful means of redressing the wrongs that they suffered. Thus, stability and security in a democratic society may be associated with widespread participation in decision-making—participation that is readily available and demonstrably effective to redress grievances. An ostensibly democratic society that does not offer its citizens the possibility of effective participation may be asking for trouble.

Civil disobedience is employed as a matter of conscience by people who are opposed to the use of violence as a tactic. They believe that the political system is unjust and, therefore, that political or legal direct action would not be successful. Civil disobedience has had a long history in America. (One might even say that the Revolutionary War was an act of civil disobedience.) Its earliest major advocate and practitioner was Henry David Thoreau, who wrote *Civil Disobedience* (1849). Later, this tactic was used successfully by Mahatma Gandhi to protest British colonial rule in India. In the 1950s and 1960s, Dr. Martin Luther King, Jr., and other civil rights activists used civil disobedience successfully to fight racial discrimination in America.[6]

A lunch counter sit-in during the early 1960s in Charlotte, N.C., where blacks had been refused service. Throughout this period, civil rights activists engaged in various acts of civil disobedience to protest racial discriminaton in the United States.

Civil disobedience has a significant propaganda effect. People perform acts of civil disobedience to call public attention to what they believe are immoral or unconstitutional laws. This tactic has also been used to set up "test cases," which challenge the constitutionality of objectionable laws in court. Thus, people have deliberately provoked an arrest in order to be able to question in court the constitutionality of the act under which the arrest was made. Of course, no one has the "right" to break the law in America, even if the lawbreaker sincerely feels that the law is unjust.

---

[6]See Martin Luther King, Jr., "Letter From Birmingham Jail," in Staughton Lynd, ed., *Nonviolence in America: A Documentary History* (Indianapolis: Bobbs-Merrill, 1966).

In 1846, Henry David Thoreau was jailed for refusing to pay his taxes because of his opposition to slavery and to America's invasion of Mexico. When someone paid his taxes after he had spent one night in jail, Thoreau's hope of publicly dramatizing his position on the issues rested on lectures he presented in Concord. He published Civil Disobedience *in 1849.*

. . . a government in which the majority rule in all cases cannot be based on justice, even as far as men understand it. Can there not be a government in which majorities do not virtually decide right and wrong, but conscience?—in which majorities decide only those questions to which the rule of expediency is applicable? Must the citizen ever for a mo-

VIEWPOINT

From *Civil Disobedience*

ment, or in the least degree, resign his conscience to the legislator? Why has every man a conscience, then? I think that we should be men first, and subjects afterwards. It is not desirable to cultivate a respect for the law, so much as for the right. The only obligation which I have the right to assume is to do at any time what I think right. . . . Law never made men a whit more just; and, by means of their respect for it, even the well-disposed are daily made the agents of injustice. . . .

. . . There are thousands who are *in opinion* opposed to slavery and to the war, who yet in effect do nothing to put an end to them; who, esteeming themselves children of Washington and Franklin, sit down with their hands in their pockets, and say that they know not what to do, and do nothing; . . . . They hesitate, and they regret, and sometimes they petition; but they do nothing in earnest and with effect. . . .

. . . Unjust laws exist: shall we be content to obey them, or shall we endeavor to amend them, and obey them until we have succeeded, or shall we transgress them at once? Men generally, under such a government as this, think that they ought to wait until they have persuaded the majority to alter them. . . .

If the injustice is part of the necessary friction of the machine of government, let it go, let it go: perchance it will wear smooth—certainly the machine will wear out. . . . but if it is of such a nature that it requires you to be the agent of injustice to another, then, I say, break the law. Let your life be a counter friction to stop the machine. What I have to do is to see, at any rate, that I do not lend myself to the wrong which I condemn. . . .

I do not hesitate to say, that those who call themselves Abolitionists should at once effectually withdraw their support, both in person and property, from the government of Massachusetts, and not wait till they constitute a majority of one, before they suffer the right to prevail through them. I think that it is enough if they have God on their side, without waiting for that other one. . . . any man more right than his neighbors constitutes a majority of one already. . . .

Under a government which imprisons any unjustly, the true place for a just man is also a prison. The proper place to-day, the only place which Massachusetts has provided for her freer and less desponding spirits, is in her prisons, to be put out and locked out of the State by her own act, as they have already put themselves out by their principles. . . . If any think that their influence would be lost there, and their voices no longer afflict the ear of the State, that they would not be as an enemy within its walls, they do not know by how much truth is stronger than error, nor how much more eloquently and effectively he can combat injustice who has experienced a little in his own person. Cast your whole vote, not a strip of paper merely, but your whole influence. A minority is powerless while it conforms to the majority; it is not even a minority then; but it is irresistable when it clogs by its whole weight. If the alternative is to keep all just men in prison, or give up war and slavery, the State will not hesitate which to choose. . . .

SOURCE: Excerpted from Henry David Thoreau, *Walden and Civil Disobedience*, Sherman Paul, ed. (Houghton, Mifflin, 1960), pp. 236, 239–40, 242–45.

The main characteristics of civil disobedience, then, are the openness of the act and the willingness of the lawbreaker to suffer the legal consequences of the illegal action. Therefore, someone who decides to practice civil disobedience is confronted with different ethical considerations from someone who decides to use violence, although both are clearly illegal actions.

DIRECT ACTION

In the 1970s, the use of legal direct action increased in America. It was employed more and more as a supplement to political action. When Ralph Nader led a group of activists to a General Motors' stockholders' meeting in 1972 to protest certain practices of that corporation's management, corporate executives undoubtedly felt that the activists were attacking the American system. But Nader and his followers maintained that they were trying to make the system work as it should.

Organizing for Direct Action

Urbanization and population mobility have frequently broken down natural support systems, or "mediating structures," between the people and their government, particularly for minorities and the poor. These mediating structures include extended families, neighborhoods, and voluntary associations.[7] People have often felt that they had nowhere to turn for help, except to overworked and impersonal bureaucrats. Different kinds of legal direct action have helped rebuild these structures, which can help to provide an immediate response to community needs, communicate citizen desires to public officials, and help individual participants overcome their sense of isolation and powerlessness. The federal antipoverty program, which began during President Johnson's administration, encouraged the formation of community-based organizations to administer some federally financed programs at the local level.[8]

Labor unions are among the oldest direct-action organizations in America. They were formed primarily to seek direct action—increased wages and benefits and improved working conditions—from employers. Today they are also very involved in political action. Cooperatives, another type of direct-action organization, have also existed for a long time in America. They received a particular boost through financing measures and other kinds of assistance enacted during President Franklin Roosevelt's administration. Cooperatives are business corporations that are owned by the people they serve. They have no outside investors. Any earnings of the cooperative that

---

[7]See Peter L. Berger and Richard John Neuhaus, *To Empower People; The Role of Mediating Structures in Public Policy* (Washington, D.C.: American Enterprise Institute for Public Policy Research, 1977).

[8]See Frank X. Steggert, *Community Action Groups and City Governments* (Cambridge, Mass.: Ballinger Publishing Co., 1975).

exceed its operating costs are returned to the members or put into service improvement. Cooperatives have been formed in such fields as food production, food marketing, health-care plans, "free schools," electricity distribution, and telephone service.

In recent years, neighborhood and community organizing has increased significantly in America. Although no one knows how to create real neighborhoods or real communities, Americans have been adept at destroying them through thoughtless highway building, urban renewal, and other programs.[9] But all over America, many neighborhoods and communities have organized themselves without waiting for government encouragement or support. For example, thousands of American Indians, who were removed from their reservations and placed in unfamiliar city settings during the 1950s and 1960s as a result of the government's Indian policy, nevertheless were able to find each other (even though they had been deliberately scattered thoughout each metropolitan area) and establish their own Indian centers to provide mutual support and reinforcement.

Gale Ciancotta of Chicago is a leader in National People's Action, a group that promotes community organization. "There aren't many vehicles for blue-collar and marginal people to feel that they can do anything," she has said. "That's what organization does. It gives a sense of control and dignity."[10] In black areas, community control is also an important goal of direct citizen action.[11]

Some community organizations have spotlighted the commercial bank practice of "red-lining," or refusing to make mortgage loans in certain deteriorating neighborhoods. These groups have forced some of the banks to change their practices. Other neighborhood organizations like Fair Share in Massachusetts, a militant and confrontational group, have organized around issues such as street repairs, housing rehabilitation, playgrounds, and schools. Fair Share supports itself mostly through door-to-door solicitations, a method that citizen groups are using more frequently.

Many community organizations use techniques first developed and taught by the late Saul Alinsky, who organized a Chicago stockyards neighborhood, known as "Back-of-the-Yard," in the 1930s. Alinsky believed that confrontation was necessary for two reasons. First, it would get the attention of the people who have the authority to make decisions. Second, it would "radicalize" community members by making them more conscious of the wrongs being done to them and giving them confidence that the wrongs could be righted.[12]

---

[9]See Rachelle B. Warren and Donald R. Warren, *The Neighborhood Organizer's Handbook* (Notre Dame, Indiana: University of Notre Dame Press, 1967), p. 203.

[10]Unless otherwise indicated, quotations and discussions concerning neighborhood organization which follow are from Harry Boyte, "Citizens in Revolt," *The Progressive* (January 1978), pp. 16–19.

[11]See Allan A. Altshuler, "Community Control" in *Participation in Large American Cities* (New York: Pegasus, 1970).

[12]See Saul D. Alinsky, *Reveille for Radicals* (N.Y.: Vintage Books, 1969); and *Rules for Radicals* (N.Y.: Vintage Books, 1971).

How to...
Raise Money

Money is like sex. Everyone thinks about it, but no one is supposed to discuss it in polite company.
—*The Grass Roots Fundraising Book*

For most community self-help organizations, there usually comes a time when money must be talked about—polite company or no. How can you raise "start-up" money, or "keep-going" money if your group's bills start coming due? A source of helpful suggestions and step-by-step procedures is described below.

Every year, many community organizations and activist groups spend a lot of time and energy persuading foundations and rich people to support their endeavors. When money raising of this sort works, it can provide a group with substantial funds and—symbolically at least—it redistributes a tiny fraction of the national income from those who have it to those who need it. But the strategy has its drawbacks. Even if the money can be obtained—and a lot of groups fold up when their elaborate proposals are rejected—it puts an organization at the mercy of its financial backers. It also typically requires a sophisticated fund-raising operation, including staff with the right skills and the right contacts.

A better fund-raising strategy, says Joan Flanagan in *The Grass Roots Fundraising Book,* is for a group to get money from its own constituents and community. How can it do that, especially if the members or neighbors are poor? Flana-

gan's answers will be familiar to anyone who has raised funds for church groups, a charity, or a local Girl Scout troop. Benefits. Bake sales. Bazaars. Dinners (maybe a "Las Vegas Night"). She tells the story of one group in Tennessee that raised $25,000 in two years for a health clinic, most of it from local residents with incomes around $5,000. Their methods: rummage sales, quilt raffles, and turkey dinners.

The Grass Roots Fundraising Book spells out all the details of this kind of money raising: where to write for films to be shown at a benefit, how to put together a book with ads from local businesses (and how to convince businesses to buy the ads), ways by which organizations can establish regular sources of income. And it emphasizes a do-it-yourself approach that confronts the beginner's fears and embarrassments about fundraising and moves on to the organizational benefits self-help fund raising can provide. "When people can raise money," says Flanagan, "they can do anything."

The book is published by the Youth Project, a Washington foundation that raises money from more lucrative sources and then disburses it to activist organizations. (Youth Project grants, usually in the form of seed money or matching contributions, are ordinarily linked to a program of self-sufficiency developed by the recipient group.) The project is also sponsoring a series of 17 workshops on fund raising for local

organizations. These two-day sessions are given by Flanagan and other consultants, and cover both specific techniques and long-range strategies.

The Grass Roots Fundraising Book costs $5.25 a copy ($3.25 each for 50 or more). Write The Youth Project, Grass Roots Fundraising Book, Department WP1, PO Box 988, Hicksville, New York 11802.

SOURCE: *Working Papers for a New Society* (March-April 1978), p. 3.

Organizing for direct action requires several distinct steps, according to The Institute, a group that trains organizers.[13] First, an issue that involves basic human concerns and that has realizable, concrete goals must be identified. Second, the issue must be stated in terms that give it legitimacy in the eyes of the community and the public; such phrases as "it's only fair," or "health care is a right," are often used. Third, the issue must be politicized so that people take sides; organizers must pose the issue in a way that highlights the differences between the powerful and the powerless, the "haves" and the "have-nots."

Organizing goals should be both short and long. Short-range goals are those that the organizers know the group can win; long-range goals involve major changes that would solve fundamental problems. The director of Midwest Academy, another organization formed to train community organizers, says, "While the citizens' groups are going on, it's important that there be a division of labor. It's important for people to organize to address visionary, long-range questions, issues of national policy, the actual redistribution of wealth."

But the results of direct action may involve more than short- and long-range goals. Direct action can also make a difference in the way community members feel about themselves. "People are changing, you know," observes a leader of the United Neighborhood Organization, a Chicano group in East Los Angeles. "You should hear them talk. Sweet old ladies, boy, it's tremendous. There's dignity in the determination of their lives." The Institute's organizational handbook also lists the following broad standards for determining the success of a direct-action campaign: "Did it bring in new people? How many? Did it build primary and secondary leadership? Did it maintain existing leadership and membership? Is the group better known? Did it build stronger ties with your allies? Was it a good use of the organization's resources? Above all, did it build power?"

Strategy and Tactics

First of all, direct-action strategy involves identifying the decision-makers who can resolve the issue. They are called the "targets" of direct-action tactics.[14] Second, potential allies such as churches, unions, and neighborhood groups, must be identified. These groups may be able to help with endorsements, phone calls, workers, marchers, money, and letters to the editor.

Tactics may involve *boycotts*. The electricity boycott organized in Westwood, California, in 1978 and the nationwide consumer boycott of beef in 1973 are two examples. Direct-action campaigns may also use *strikes*, a tactic borrowed from the labor movement. For instance, tenants in housing projects have organized "rent strikes,"

---

[13]Madeleine Adamson, ed., *Actions and Campaigns: Community Organizing Handbook #3* (Little Rock: The Institute, 1969), pp. 3–4.

[14]Adamson, ed., *Actions and Campaigns*, pp. 3–4.

refusing to pay increased rents. *Demonstrations*, another direct-action tactic, can occur in the form of sit-ins, picketing, paying bills in pennies, blocking traffic, marching, candlelight vigils, and holding up placards at busy intersections.

Direct-action strategy and tactics almost always involve using the media. "Awards" may be given to slumlords for "Worst Neighbor of the Year." Well-publicized petitions may be delivered to direct-action targets. Garbage cans may be taken to the mayor's office to dramatize the fact that garbage is not adequately picked up in poor neighborhoods. Thus, propaganda, which is aimed at forcing government or corporations to respond to problems, is often one of the most important goals of a direct-action campaign.

Another direct-action tactic is the *initiative petition*. The "right of initiative" was one of the reforms advocated by the Progressive Movement at the turn of the century. In states where it is used, citizens may make their own laws directly. If a sufficient number of signatures can be secured in support of a legislative question, it can be put on the ballot and decided by a vote of the people. Proposition 13, a proposal to reduce property taxes in California, became the law in 1978 in that way.

Direct citizen action by initiative petition is not limited to tax questions.[15] Some of the initiatives enacted in 1978 were a "sunshine amendment" requiring public disclosures of finances by public officials in Florida; returnable-bottle laws in Michigan and Maine; a local-option fluoridation law in Utah; and a new system for selecting judges in Arizona. In Wisconsin, a judge was forced into a recall election by popular initiative and was voted out of office because, after treating a convicted rapist leniently, he said that the crime was a "normal reaction" to women's lack of "modesty in dress."[16]

One organization, Initiative America, advocates an amendment to the U.S. Constitution that would allow the right of initiative at the federal level upon the petition of 3 percent of the people who voted in the most recent presidential election. Their proposal has gained bipartisan sponsorship in both the U.S. House and Senate. Hearings on the idea have been held in the Senate Subcommittee on Constitutional Amendments, but the full House and Senate have not yet voted on the issue.[17] One of the founders of Initiative America argues that a federal right of initiative is needed to prevent special interests from dominating government policy:

"Right now these groups have an unequal voice in Washington because they can afford to hire full-time lobbyists who know the ropes. But they wouldn't thrive so well in the open. In fact, the major function

---

[15]See Thomas A. Puzzuti, *You Can Fight City Hall and Win* (Los Angeles: Sherbourne Press, 1974).

[16]Michael Nelson, "The Federal Initiative Idea," *The Nation* (February 25, 1978), pp. 210–212.

[17]Nelson, "The Federal Initiative Idea," pp. 210–212. Quotations which follow and further references to the federal initiative proposal are also from this article.

of the initiative is to give citizens a way of busting up the logjams that develop when special interests are able to prevent legislation that a strong majority of people want from getting passed by the legislature."

The federal initiative idea has created considerable controversy. One professor of political science, Peter Bachrach of Temple University, testified against it:

[The federal initiative proposal] incorrectly presupposes that the American people are sane enough to make rational judgments on complex issues. They're not; they haven't had the opportunity to be politically educated. As a result, the people are ignorant and irrational when it comes to the simplest kinds of issues. . . . The issues the elite will present to the masses in initiatives will be 'hate issues'—anti-labor issues, race issues, anti-sex issues and the like."

Bachrach's testimony was contradicted by an official from Washington State, where the right of initiative already exists. According to this official, the initiative issues that had been put on the ballot in Washington involved "substantial questions of public policy . . . seldom the product of a single, special-interest group, and none was frivolous or inconsequential." He said that in 1977, for example, Washington voters approved a repeal of the sales tax on food but voted against repealing a tax increase on gasoline.

One of the sponsors of the federal initiative proposal in the Senate, James Abourezk of South Dakota (who did not seek reelection in 1978), has stated that "in one way or another, the debate about the voter initiative always comes down to whether politicians trust the American people sufficiently to allow citizens the right to vote directly on issues." One of the leaders in Initiative America remarked, "When opponents of the national initiative say that political extremists will dominate, we can point to the states where this hasn't happened. . . . When they say that people can't be trusted, we can point out that more initiatives are defeated than passed. Citizens have used this tool with remarkable restraint." A national poll indicates that Americans favor the federal initiative idea by a two-to-one margin; 74 percent of them say that they would be "more inclined to go to vote if they could vote on issues as well as candidates." In many states they already can.

Basic Human Concerns

Successful organizing for direct action can only be done when the issues involve basic human concerns like food, health, housing, schools, utilities, taxes, the workplace, and consumer interests.

Food.   In the 1970s, increases in taxes and in the cost of living particularly hurt people in low- and middle-income brackets in America. These factors sometimes caused them to reduce their food consumption and in some cases actually caused them to go without meals.[18] The most healthful and basic food items, such as beef, pork, poultry, and fresh fruits and vegetables, rose faster in price than the overall food index.[19]

During the 1970s, farms also got bigger, and the number of family farms decreased. Agribusiness—large corporations engaged in agriculture, food processing, and food marketing—gained greater control over the chain of food production and consumption. There was a corresponding increase in the use of herbicides and pesticides. These developments caused one activist organization, the Exploratory Project for Economic Alternatives, to conclude: "In the coming era of intensified food inflation, shortages, and pollution, the United States can no longer afford a narrowly based policy geared to supporting agribusiness at the expense of family farmers, the environment, and consumers."[20] The group advocates the formation of food production and marketing cooperatives. In additon, it seeks political action to decentralize food production and marketing and to reverse the trend toward bigness in agriculture.

One reason why the number of family-run farms has decreased is that they have not been able to afford high-priced, modern machinery or to exercise much power in the marketplace. Families participating in farm co-ops, however, are able to purchase machinery together, buy supplies in bulk, and pool their products for distribution and marketing, sharing the lowered costs among themselves. A typical co-op consists of a group of people who band together for a specific nonprofit purpose.

Co-ops have also been formed by consumers. Members of food co-ops typically gather "shopping lists" from participating members and purchase meat, vegetables, and other food products in bulk, avoiding "middleman" charges by buying directly from distributors. The members usually take turns performing the various tasks involved. One such co-op, the Food Advisory Service, now serves over 5,000 older people through fifty-three food clubs in a four-county area in and

In many places, consumers have established food co-ops—another form of direct action—to help reduce food bills.

around San Francisco. Members save between 30 and 80 percent on their food bills. The Food Advisory Service has also helped to set up similar programs for older people in three other cities, and it has

---

[18]Joint Economic Committee of the U. S. Congress, *Inflation and the Consumer in 1974* (Washington, D.C.: Government Printing Office, 1974), p. 8.

[19]U. S. Department of Agriculture, *Food Consumption, Prices, Expenditures* (Washington, D.C.: Government Printing Office, December 1974), pp. 69–70.

[20]Joe Belden with Gregg Forte, *Toward a National Food Policy* (Washington, D.C.: Exploratory Project for Economic Alternatives, 1976), p. *iii*.

created a separate, profit-making assembly plant which employs elderly workers.[21]

As we indicated earlier, there is a close connection between direct action and political action. National Land for People, an organization based in California, has engaged in both kinds of action. Believing that small, family farms are best for producing high-quality food at stable, affordable prices, this organization is working to reverse the trend toward bigness in agriculture. It advocates the formation of more food production cooperatives for farmers and stresses the benefits of family farming for America. The group has sponsored successful lawsuits to enforce old federal laws limiting the size of farms that receive water from federally financed irrigation systems.[22] Other organizations have proposed state and federal legislation to increase the number of family-owned farms by prohibiting corporate farming, enacting graduated land taxes, and other means.[23]

Citizens have used different means to improve the production and distribution of the basic necessity of food. At times, they have employed the self-help method of direct action; at other times, they have attempted to influence government policy through political action. Each form of participation tends to complement and strengthen the other.

Health. Citizens have formed group health plans to provide cheaper health care for themselves. They have pressured doctors to write prescriptions using generic drugs, which are usually much cheaper than those with brand names. Through labor unions, citizens have pressed for greater employee control over plant safety requirements. They have used public demonstrations and protests to focus public attention on environmental problems, such as those associated with the construction and operation of nuclear power plants.[24]

Direct action on health matters, as on other issues, has inevitably led to increased political action. Citizens who become concerned about local hospital costs, for example, are likely to begin to ask questions about larger, national problems associated with health-care costs and services. This concern may lead to political action on related issues—such as state antisubstitution laws, which prevent a pharmacist from substituting a cheaper, generic drug for a higher-priced, brand-name drug prescribed by a physician; legislation requiring greater citizen-patient control over local hospitals and other health facilities and agencies; or bills proposing a national system of universal health insurance.

[21]*Aging* (August 1977), pp. 3–5.

[22]See National Land For People, *Newsletter* (1977, 1978).

[23]See Conference on Alternative State and Local Policies, *Ways and Means* (July–August 1978); and Institute for Policy Studies, *National Conference Newsletter* (March 1978).

[24]See Donald K. Ross, *A Public Citizen's Action Manual* (New York: Grossman, 1973), pp. 69–123; in regard to nuclear power plant protests, see *Chicago Sun-Times* (August 8, 1977), p. 11.

Housing. When a landlord fails to meet legal obligations to tenants—by refusing to take care of repairs, for example—tenants sometimes resort to direct action through the formation of tenants' unions. These tenants' unions and other similar organizations may demand greater control over the management of housing projects, which are run by public agencies. They may resist what they feel are unfair rent increases, or they may call for proper heating and other services. Some have resorted to rent strikes to underscore their demands.[25]

Citizens can also take steps to own their own housing. An impressive example of this kind of citizen action is the Housing Development Fund Corporation, a cooperative involving eleven families in Manhattan's Lower East Side.[26] A building at 519 East Eleventh Street had been gutted by fires, leaving eleven apartments and two storefronts to be taken over by junkies and stripped of plumbing and other fixtures. A group of young Puerto Ricans, with no particular skills in building, got together and persuaded the city bureaucracy to turn the building over to them. Then they obtained a reconstruction loan. "We became a co-op because there really wasn't another choice," one of the organizers said. "The only landlords left in this neighborhood are pretty sleazy characters. So we had to rely on ourselves." Using "sweat equity"—the work of the co-op members—as their investment, they rehabilitated the original building and two others. The tenants are now the owners. Several other tenant groups have also been formed in New York and elsewhere for similar self-help projects. Direct action in the field of housing, however, may not always be effective unless government provides funding and other assistance to supplement citizen efforts.

A person who gets involved in a tenants' union or in a cooperative rehabilitation project may soon begin to ask larger policy questions. What causes housing to be abandoned? Why don't public housing projects allow tenants more say in how the projects are run? Why aren't there more funds for "sweat-equity" building and rehabilitation?

Schools. Many parents today complain that their children are not being taught the fundamentals of reading and writing in the public schools. Students often complain that they are not given sufficient individual freedom in the schools, often citing their lack of influence in school decision-making and their lack of control over the pace and manner of the learning process. Parents in poverty areas often feel that teachers' attitudes actually retard learning because they reflect a low regard for the abilities of the students, particularly if the students are members of minority groups and the teachers are not. Many

---

[25]For information on the failure of a rent strike, see Harry Brite, *Why Organizers Fail* (Berkeley, California: University of California Press, 1971).

[26]Community Ownership Organizing Project, *The Public Works* (Fall 1977), pp. 1–4.

VIEWPOINT
"519"

The housing cooperative, 519 East Eleventh Street, on Manhattan's Lower East Side, and some of the tenant shareholders who rehabilitated the building and now own it.

A Manhattan tenement building on East Eleventh Street, in the middle of a ghetto inhabited by a scrambled mix of Blacks, Puerto Ricans, Poles, and Jews, . . . It is a triumph and an anomaly, a humanistic dream that bypassed the city's government bureaucracy, fiscal crisis, and public apathy. The building, number 519, used to be owned by one of the neighborhood's worst slumlords; it was the scene of fifteen fires in one month and was slated for demolition. Today it is owned cooperatively by eleven people, nearly all under thirty-five years of age, who reclaimed it by "sweat equity." 519 East Eleventh Street is Manhattan's showcase prototype of urban homesteading. And it is the first of three more buildings on the block slated for rehabilitation.

"519," as it is now popularly known, is the result of the efforts of a new breed of young political activists working with the ghetto community. "This was not a visionary kind of thing," says Travis Price, one of the building's brain-trust advisors, "it was a last resort, a bare necessity for those who lived here. They had no place to go, they had to make it work; they couldn't afford to move to the suburbs." . . .

The core group formed a corporation and got a municipal loan of $177,000, bought "519" for $1,800, and started a "sweat equity" program, campaigning on street corners to get block residents involved. . . .

"Sweat equity," a term for investing in labor what you can't give in funds to build equity in a place to live, contributed nearly all of the building's installation expenses. The shareholder-tenants—some single and some married, about 60 percent of them Puerto Rican—are the board members of the 519 East Eleventh Street Housing Development Corporation, and also the building's painters, spacklers, floor layers, garbagemen, paralegal professionals, and lobbyists. They paid themselves $3 an hour to work a thirty-two-hour week; one eight-hour day each week, representing each worker's investment in his own apartment, was donated free.

By the time the sweat-equity owners moved into the renovated building, they had worked on it for a year and a half. None had any previous construction experience, although now most are skilled workers and can sell

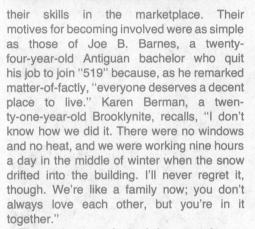

their skills in the marketplace. Their motives for becoming involved were as simple as those of Joe B. Barnes, a twenty-four-year-old Antiguan bachelor who quit his job to join "519" because, as he remarked matter-of-factly, "everyone deserves a decent place to live." Karen Berman, a twenty-one-year-old Brooklynite, recalls, "I don't know how we did it. There were no windows and no heat, and we were working nine hours a day in the middle of winter when the snow drifted into the building. I'll never regret it, though. We're like a family now; you don't always love each other, but you're in it together."

The project transformed the street from a hardcore poverty area, where car stripping was a cottage industry, into a concerned neighborhood. "Eleventh Street between Avenue A and Avenue B was lawless," says Rabbit Nazario (who is now known informally as "the Mayor of the Lower East Side"). "Cars left parked for less than fifteen minutes were broken into and stripped." Junkies accosted pedestrians and hawked 'hot' merchandise. The block is now an ongoing scene of construction activity—three additional tenements are currently under renovation.

Michael Freedberg, the house intellectual, sees the project as seminal in the fight to save the cities. "In the whole history of urban renewal and Model Cities," he says, "the government programs have done nothing to stop the deterioration. What was missing was bringing the people into it, showing them how to do it, giving them an opportunity to accomplish what government money could not. We're doing it here—and I really get off on that." . . .

With the apathy and economic wars fought and almost won, "519" has become a model for other homesteading efforts in poverty areas, particularly where landlords abandon buildings because of escalating maintenance costs. "We have created an energy task force," Travis Price says. "Banks and businesses are coming to us to see what we've done. It's a third-world model for low-income housing programs that others can imitate." Partly as a result of "519"'s success, the federal government has granted $3 million to the newly formed National Center for Appropriate Technology, which sponsors and gives advice to similar urban projects.

But to Santiago Gonzales, thirty-five, married, an actor who hopes to start a community theater when the work on Eleventh Street is finally over, the benefits are more on a gut level. "I love looking down the street and knowing that I helped put it back together. I feel I have a real stake in my community."

SOURCE: Norma Skurka and Jon Naar, *Design for a Limited Planet* (Ballantine Books, 1976), pp. 192–97.

parents—whether majority or minority parents—complain that schools are run by the educational "experts," who allow parents no say in decisions. And teachers frequently claim that rigid administration rules do not give them sufficient leeway in teaching.

These complaints about public education in America raise immediate questions that can best be answered by political action. But in some areas, people have also used direct action to meet these problems. Direct action has most often been used to establish "free schools"—private schools that allow greater community or neighborhood control, more flexibility for teachers, and a better opportunity for students to command the pace and scope of their own education. One report on free schools describes them as follows:

The new schools charge little or no tuition, are frequently held together by spit and string, and run mainly on the energy and excitement of people who have set out to do their own thing. Their variety seems limitless. No two are alike. They range from inner-city

Some parents have used direct action to form free schools—alternative schools that give both parents and students more control over the educational process.

black to suburban and rural white. Some seem to be pastoral escapes from the grip of modern conflict, while others are deliberate experiments in integrated multi-cultural, multi-lingual education. They turn up anywhere—in city storefronts, old barns, former bar racks, abandoned church buildings, and parents' or teachers' homes. They have crazy names like Someday School, Viewpoint Non-School, A Peck of Gold, The New Community, or New Directions—names that for all their diversity reflect the two things most of these schools have in common: the idea of freedom for youngsters and a humane education.[27]

It is said that greater student freedom seems to give parents more faith in their children and involve them more in the educational process. "Now I know that, even though I didn't finish high school, it is possible for me to understand what they are teaching my child," said one New York parent.[28]

Direct action on public-school issues tends to lead to political action, which is based on two themes. First, some people suggest breaking up the "public-school monopoly" and allowing public funding for competing, alternative schools.[29] One plan would give students or their parents a "voucher" that could be spent in any school. Supporters of the plan argue that competitive pressure on schools and educators would increase the general quality of education. But educators and other defenders of public education have strenuously objected to the voucher idea because they view this proposal as a fundamental attack on *public* education. Even without public funding, free schools have served as testing grounds and models for new principles and practices, which can later be used in the public schools. (Of course, some private schools have been established to avoid racial integration, busing, or the integration of socioeconomic classes. But the courts have been used to prevent public funding for these schools.)

Second, political action on public-school issues centers around neighborhood control. In some large cities, where a single school board may control the entire school system, parents often justifiably complain that the mere act of voting for or against a school board member does not give them much control of the school system. They advocate neighborhood control. Some educators argue that such a decentralization of the school systems might reduce the quality of education. In New York City, where many teachers and adminstrators are white and many students are not, educators have expressed fears that neighborhood control will mean loss of employment for them. Nevertheless, progress has been made in New York City and

---

[27]Bonnie Barrett Stretch, "The Rise of the 'Free School'" in Harold W. Sorbel and Arthur E. Salz, *The Radical Papers: Readings in Education* (New York: Harper and Row, 1972), p. 131.

[28]Stretch, "The Rise of the 'Free School,'" p. 137.

[29]See Vernon H. Smith, *Alternative Schools* (Lincoln, Nebraska: Professional Educators Publications, 1974).

elsewhere toward greater neighborhood control of schools. In Washington, D.C., for example, the Adams and Morgan communities now elect their own community school boards.

Advocates of direct action—in regard to the schools and in other fields—frequently complain about what they call "the tyranny of the experts." They say that too many experts—teachers, doctors, and other professionals—feel that they, and they only, have sufficient training and skill to make the decisions in their special field of competence. Many ordinary citizens, on the other hand, resent the idea that "doctor knows best" if it means that patients can have no say in the way health delivery systems work. Many parents feel that parent-teacher activities are often designed to be only "busy work." For example, teachers may ask parents to become involved in a Halloween night at the school, but they do not expect them to get interested in how the school really functions. Direct action and political action offer opportunities for average citizens to share power with the experts. Although expert advice is often needed to help solve modern problems, our system presumes that citizens, armed with adequate advice and information, can and will make the fundamental policy decisions.

Utilities. For most Americans, gas, electricity, and telephones are a necessity. Yet the rates that Americans pay for these utilities have increased enormously in recent years, and no relief is in sight. One electricity company official has said, "In my opinion we will have to have great increases every year for the next decade."[30] The incomes of most Americans have not kept pace with these rapidly increasing utility rates. Citizen concerns about environmental pollution caused by electric utility companies have also increased.

In the 1970s, citizens throughout the country began to organize for both political and direct action against utilities. In some places, there were boycotts because of rising rates. In Chicago, citizens successfully organized massive demonstrations, public debates, and other forms of public protest to force the local utility company to switch to low-sulfur coal and reduce air pollution. This direct citizen action also led to successful political action—a strict new air pollution ordinance adopted by the Chicago City Council.[31] In addition to boycotts and demonstrations to protest rate hikes and air pollution, there have been demonstrations—and civil disobedience—against nuclear power plants and high voltage transmission lines.

Private utilities are different from other privately owned corporations in America. They are "coerced monopolies." That is, they are monopolies protected by law. In some ways, privately owned utility companies resemble governments more than they do corporations in

[30]Environmental Action Foundation, *The Power Line*, 3, no. 9 (April 1978): 1, 5.
[31]Richard Morgan and Sandra Jerabek, *How to Challenge Your Local Electric Utility: A Citizen's Guide to the Power Industry* (Washington, D.C.: The Environmental Action Foundation, 1975) p. 18.

a free-enterprise system. Their "captive" customers and guaranteed territories insulate them from competition. They have the right of eminent domain, the authority to take private property for public use, as long as they follow due process and pay just compensation. Their rates, which are usually established by state government regulatory commissions, are like taxes, since almost no one can avoid paying them. But these charges are not based upon the ability to pay. Instead, utility rates are generally lower for large users and higher for smaller users, including residential customers.[32]

Environmental Action Foundation (EAF), a public-interest group headquartered in Washington, D.C., serves as a clearinghouse for citizens' organizations involved in electric utility issues. EAF opposes laws that allow "promotional" (declining) rates for large users, arguing that such rates "discriminate against small customers and promote the waste of energy by larger users, especially industry."[33] The group is also against "automatic adjustment clauses," which allow electric utility companies to raise their rates automatically every time their fuel costs go up. According to EAF, this practice has been widely abused. One of the group's proposals is to establish "lifeline rates," which would allow every family or individual customer a minimal, "liveable amount of electricity" at a minimun rate. For economic and environmental reasons, EAF opposes the building of any additional nuclear power plants. Finally, it supports measures to stop environmental pollution by electric utilities.[34]

One study prepared by EAF, *Utility Scoreboard*, found that in 1976 consumers were charged approximately $720 million extra in their electric bills because utilities had built too many power plants. During the same period, residential consumers were charged an average of 73 percent more per kilowatt-hour for electricity than industrial consumers.[35]

Many citizens have become concerned about the direction of solar energy development in the United States. Some activists have taken the position that federal subsidies—particularly tax credits—for increasing the use of solar energy should not go to privately owned utilities but go to individual consumers for on-site solar systems.[36] California's Campaign For Economic Democracy has proposed creating a public authority in that state to control development of a new solar industry there.[37]

The ultimate threat that citizens can pose to a utility company, of

[32]Morgan and Jerabek, *How to Challenge Your Local Electric Utility*, p. 85.

[33]See Lee Metcalf and Vic Reinemer, *Overcharge* (New York: David McKay Co., 1967).

[34]Environmental Action Foundation and Movement for Economic Justice, *A Citizen's Position on Electric Rates* (Wash., D.C.: Environmental Action Foundation, 1975).

[35]Environmental Action Foundation, *The Power Line*, 3, no. 7 (1978): 1, 4, 5.

[36]Institute for Policy Studies, *National Conference Newsletter* (November 1977), pp. 3, 5.

[37]Institute for Policy Studies, *National Conference Newsletter* (January 1978), pp. 2, 5.

course, is to take direct action to convert the utility to public ownership. There are more than three thousand public power systems in the United States. They are owned by municipalities, rural electric cooperatives , public utility districts, state authorities, and by federal agencies. They have existed in America as long as electric systems have. Some public systems, like the one in Shawnee, Oklahoma, are small; others, like the one in Los Angeles, California, are large. Public systems sell electricity to one of every four Americans. The rest of the American people receive their electricity from two hundred privately owned utilities.[38] According to a Federal Power Commission report, the privately owned electric systems charged an overall average of 29 percent more for electricity in 1974 than did the public systems, and an average of 37 percent more for residential use.[39]

In the 1970s, citizens in some cities undertook to buy the local, privately owned electric utility. In Berkeley, California, this type of direct action failed in a vote of the people because of a massive counter-campaign by the utility there.[40] In Massena, New York, on the other hand, citizens voted by more than a three-to-two margin for a public takeover of Niagara Mohawk's service to that city.[41]

President Franklin D. Roosevelt believed in the basic role of private ownership in America. But he also felt that when people were dissatisfied with privately owned utilities, they should have the option of public ownership: ". . . where a community, a city, a county, or a district, is not satisfied with the service rendered or the rates charged by the private utility, it has the undeniable right as one of its functions of government . . . to set up . . . its own governmentally owned and operated service. . . ."[42] Arguing that even the *threat* of public takeover could have a good effect on rates, service, and practices, he said:

The very fact that a community can, by vote of the electorate, create a yardstick of its own, will, in most cases, guarantee good service and low rates to its population. I might call the right of the people to own and operate their own utility a 'birch rod in the cupboard, to be taken out and used only when the child gets beyond the point where more scolding does any good.'[43]

Taxes.   If utility charges are *similar* to taxes and are not based upon the ability to pay, taxes *are* taxes. Many of them are not based upon the ability to pay, either. A number of citizen action groups at the

---

[38]Richard Morgan, Tom Riesenberg, and Michael Troutman, *Taking Charge* (Wash., D. C.: Environmental Action Foundation), p. 20.

[39]Morgan, Riesenberg, and Troutman, *Taking Charge,* p. 20.

[40]See Joseph M. Petulla, "How They Hornswaggled Berkeley," *The Nation* (August 13, 1973), pp. 113–116.

[41]See, "More than One Takeover in Massena, N.Y.," *Just Economics* (March 1975).

[42]Judson King, *The Conservation Fight* (Washington, D.C.: Public Affairs Press, 1959), p. 273.

[43]King, *The Conservation Fight,* p. 273.

national and local levels have been formed to bring about fairness in federal, state, and local taxes. One of them, the Tax Reform Research Group, funded by Ralph Nader's Public Citizen, publishes a national newspaper, *People & Taxes*, which keeps local tax groups and activists in touch with what others in the field are doing on tax reform. Many activities of these activist groups are directed toward needed reforms of the federal income tax system, such as "plugging" loopholes which are said to allow wealthier taxpayers and corporations to avoid paying their full tax share.

But, increasingly, local tax groups have focused their attention upon the problem of rapidly increasing local property taxes. In 1977, for example, National Taxpayers United called upon citizens in the North Shore area of Chicago to temporarily refuse to pay their property taxes, some of which had increased by 300 percent in one year. "Why a tax strike? Because we're frustrated," one leader of this organization said. "We need some time, about three months, to work something out with the politicians."[44]

In California, where property taxes were rapidly increasing at a time when the state budget showed a large surplus, direct citizen action took the form of a statewide election on an initiative petition in 1978. This effort—which resulted in the overwhelming adoption of "Proposition 13," as the initiative was called—severely limited property tax rates and spawned similar efforts in other states.

The Workplace. Americans believe in the "work ethic"; most prefer to work. Labor unions and organizations such as the Exploratory Project for Economic Alternatives and Americans for a Working Economy have jointly supported political action to secure federal legislation for guaranteed full employment. They say that government should act as the "employer of last resort." To accomplish this, they advocate using federal funds, if necessary, to pay for jobs in such problem areas as health, education, housing, mass transit, day care, and environmental clean-up.[45]

As noted earlier, labor unions are traditional direct-action organizations. They bargain with management in regard to wages and working conditions, using the threat of a strike or a strike itself to win some or all of their demands. But most American workers are not members of labor unions, and the AFL-CIO is pushing for reforms of the federal Taft-Hartley Act that would prohibit certain antiunion business practices and make it easier for unions to organize workers.[46]

Direct action in regard to jobs can also take the form of pressuring and persuading private businesses and industries to hire and promote more black people. The National Urban League was founded for this

[44]*Chicago Sun-Times* (August 10, 1977), p. 4.
[45]See Gar Alperovitz and Jeff Faux, *An Economic Program for the Coming Decade* (Washington, D.C.: Exploratory Project for Economic Alternatives, 1975); and Americans for a Working Economy, *A Working Economy for Americans* (Washington, D.C.: Americans for a Working Economy, 1977).
[46]See AFL-CIO, *Labor Law Reform Memo*, 2, no.26 (July 24, 1978).

One of the difficulties involved in expanding democracy at work relates to how decisions are made. In most collectives, decisions are reached by "consensus."

Democratic decision-making in a collective is based on one fundamental concept: *all workers take an equal part in making major decisions.*

Living according to this fundamental rule, virtually all collective workers will tell you, is difficult, frustrating, and above all, time consuming. Most collectives use the principle of *consensus.* "This means," according to Vocations for Social Change, "that no decision is finalized until everyone in the group feels comfortable with the decision and is able to implement it without resentment. The skill of coming to genuine consensus decisions is a real and a hard one."

The experiences of numerous collectives suggest that the vital elements of successful collective decision-making include:

Every member of the collective must have equal power. This means that no one person can be allowed to accumulate the special knowledge and authority of a traditional "boss."

Collectives use a variety of techniques to achieve this "equality of power." The most common one is *job rotation.* If every worker learns every job, collective workers say, they can contribute knowledgeably to every decision; no one person will accumulate unique expertise which will allow him or her to wield special authority, as others are forced to sit back in ignorance.

At a collective newspaper in California, according to researcher Rothschild-Whitt, each worker spends 20 hours per week editing, 10 hours writing, and 10 hours in production tasks. At the Stone Soup food collective in Washington, D.C.,

workers rotate jobs as often as every three hours—the same person may work at the cash register in the morning, fish counter at noon and in the stockroom in the evening.

Collectives which have coordinators or managers handling administrative tasks usually rotate that position, too. Stone Soup, for instance, installs a new worker as coordinator every three months.

How to . . .
Achieve Democratic Decisions

Every member of the collective must have an equal opportunity to debate an issue, or voice an opinion before a consensus decision is made.

Collective workers note that if some members of the collective feel afraid of talking in the groups—or if a few members tend to dominate the groups—part of the collective will in effect be cut out of the decision-making process. This weakens the collective's commitment to a decision, and can create resentment and hostility among members of the collective. Some collectives, as a result, have a rule that *every worker in the collective must voice an opinion* at a meeting, before a decision can be made. Other collectives pass rules which prevent any worker from speaking more than once until every other worker has already spoken.

Every member of the collective must be honest and open about his or her feelings—or relationships between the workers will deteriorate, and the collective will be unable to make effective group decisions.

"People's fears can lead to subtle agreements not to talk about certain issues or [not] to deal with certain problems," writes Vocations for Social Change. "This can stifle and then kill a collective."

To encourage collective members to share their emotions honestly, many collectives hold *"criticism-self-criticism"* sessions at the end of every meeting. Members use this time to voice criticisms or complaints about the way they and others have handled the week's work or personal relationships.

Finally, a successful collective requires commitment. Without special commitment, collective workers say, they aren't likely to survive all the frustrations and pains of earning low salaries, laboring long hours, and constantly working out emotional conflicts. "Often the only thing that keeps a collective together throughout its conflicts," writes Vocations for Social Change, "is the conviction that the experiment of collective decision-making has a great inherent value, a value that makes the pain and work worthwhile."

SOURCE: Daniel Zwerdling, *Democracy at Work* (Democracy at Work, 1978), pp. 82–83.

purpose.[47] In Chicago, People United in Support of Humanity (PUSH), headed by Jesse Jackson, uses persuasion, public relations, boycotts, and demonstrations to increase the opportunities for employment that are available to black people in the private sector.

In recent years, more and more direct action campaigns have focused on "workplace democracy." Many jobs are extremely hazardous, and many involve drudgery. The traditional view—which many corporate executives still hold—was that workers should work, managers should manage, and that this "sweat work" and "think work" should not be mixed. But more workers are becoming interested in increasing their share of the management and control of the workplace. That is the goal of one organization in Massachusetts, the Quality of Working Life Center.[48]

Workplace democracy can take several forms. One involves "job enrichment," or "humanization" of jobs. In the General Foods plant near Topeka, Kansas, for example, workers make recommendations on hiring, firing, disciplining, and promoting other workers. They rotate jobs and determine their own work schedules. At this plant, which makes dog food, 70 workers now produce as much dog food as 110 workers did before the change.[49] Similar plans are in effect in a significant number of other American plants, including a Nabisco plant in Houston, the *Minneapolis Star* and *Tribune*, and a body plant owned by General Motors in Michigan. In one plant, Harman International Industries in Bolivar, Tennessee, workers have devised a system that permits employees who meet their eight-hour production quota in less than eight hours to shut down their machines and take off. The workers in the plant have created their own free school with courses ranging from hydraulics to computer language to guitar lessons.

In addition to job enrichment projects, direct action for workplace democracy has resulted in worker or worker-community ownership of several plants. For example, when GAF Corporation decided it was going to close its asbestos mine subsidiary in Vermont and lay off 178 workers, the workers joined with people in the surrounding communities and bought the plant. The same thing happened in Herkimer, New York, when Sperry-Rand was about to shut down a furniture factory there; in South Bend, Indiana, when a lathe factory in that city was about to be closed; and at Puget Sound Plywood in Washington State. Worker-controlled plywood firms are between 25

[47]See Orde Coombs, "Vernon Jordan, The Great Black Hope," *New York* (August 29, 1977), pp. 26–28.

[48]See Massachusetts Quality of Working Life Center, *Newsletter,* 2, no. 7, (November 1977).

[49]Unless otherwise indicated, the references to workplace democracy which follow are based upon Daniel Zwerdling, "Workplace Democracy: A Strategy for Survival," *The Progressive,* (August 1978), pp. 16–24. Also see Paul Dickson, *The Future of the Workplace* (New York: Weybright and Talley, 1975); and Daniel Zwerdling, *Democracy at Work: A Guide to Workplace Ownership, Participation and Self-Management Experiments in the United States and Europe* (Washington, D.C.: Democracy at Work, 1978).

and 60 percent more productive than conventional mills. "It's pretty much like working for yourself—the more you put into it, the more you will get out of it," one plywood worker in a worker-controlled plant said. "It's like my garden at home," remarked another worker. "I sure get a kick out of planting it and taking care of it, and watching it grow."

International Group Plans, a worker-controlled insurance firm that sells insurance packages to such corporations as *McCall's* and *Redbook*, follows the philosophy that citizens should have the same democratic power over their lives in the workplace as they have in their communities and homes. All told, there are sixty-eight firms in America in which workers are at least part owners.

Some union leaders have criticized workplace democracy. Jerry Wurf, president of the American Federation of State, County and Municipal Employees, has said scoffingly, "The concept of workers' control is an exciting one for soapbox oratory in the street and rap sessions in the faculty lounge." Labor unions view worker control as a threat because, in a sense, it puts the workers in conflict with themselves. "If we're taking part *in* management, who in hell will we be fighting *against?*" another union committeeperson has asked.

On the other hand, Paul Blumberg, a sociologist, has pointed out that when the same people are workers and owners, the situation is no different from citizens electing both a school board and a city council, which may clash and negotiate with each other. A bill is pending in Congress to provide federal assistance for "employee or employee-community ownership of concerns which would otherwise close down" and training of workers and community residents for participation in workplace decision-making.

Consumer Interests. In the 1970s, citizens frequently used direct action to protect their interests as consumers. Numerous new organizations—local, state, and national—were formed, and they engaged in a wide range of political action, too.

Citizens took direct action in a number of ways and on many issues.[50] They participated in consumer picketing and distributed leaflets against stores that seemed to be cheating consumers. Citizens made retail comparisons and leaked the results of their surveys to the press. They worked within local savings and loan institutions, another type of cooperative, pressuring them to better serve community interests. They established buyers' action centers and automobile safety and complaint centers to call attention to grievances about automobile defects and repairs. Direct action on behalf of consumer interests often inspired political action; on many issues, citizens became convinced that "there ought to be a law!"

---

[50]See Ross, *A Public Citizen's Action Manual,* pp. 1–69.

CONCLUSION

Particularly in the 1960s and 1970s, Americans organized for legal direct action—self-help efforts to remedy problems. At the same time, many took political action by voting, campaigning, lobbying, and bringing lawsuits. Both are important aspects of citizen participation in America. Each kind of participation—and there is no clear line between them—improves and complements the other. A person who becomes involved in direct action by participating in a beef boycott or picketing a bank to stop "red-lining" of the neighborhood may begin to ask larger questions, which will lead to increased and more effective political participation. Who determines beef prices? Should government regulate prices? Can competition be increased so that prices will be held down naturally? Who regulates the banks? Who owns the banks?

Participation in the decisions that govern one's life may involve more than just traditional political action. Both political action and self-help remedies are important aspects of citizen participation in America, and Americans are showing an increased awareness of this fact.

ADDITIONAL SOURCES

Alinsky, Saul. *Reveille for Radicals*. Random House/Vintage, 1969.*

———. *Rules for Radicals*. Random House/Vintage, 1972.*

Case, John, and Rosemary C. R. Taylor, eds. *Co-ops, Communes, and Collectives: Experiments in Social Change in the 1960s and 1970s.* Pantheon, 1978.*

Cohen, Carl. *Civil Disobedience: Conscience, Tactics, and the Law*. Columbia University Press, 1971.*

Farr, Walter G., et al. *Decentralizing City Government: A Practical Study of a Radical Proposal for New York City*. Irvington, 1972.*

Graham, Hugh D., and Ted R. Gurr, eds. *The History of Violence in America: Historical and Comparative Perspectives*. Praeger, 1969.*

Jacobson, Michael, and Catherine Lerza, eds. *Food for People, Not for Profit: A Source Book on the Food Crisis*. Ballantine, 1975.*

Morris, David, and Karl Hess. *Neighborhood Power: The New Localism*. Beacon Press, 1975.*

Piven, Frances Fox, and Richard A. Cloward. *Poor Peoples' Movements: Why They Succeed, How They Fail*. Pantheon, 1977. (See also Paul Starr's review, "How They Fail," *Working Papers for a New Society*, March-April 1978.)

Thoreau, Henry David. *Walden* and *Civil Disobedience*. New American Library, 1973.*

Warren, Rachelle, and Donald I. Warren. *Neighborhood Organizer's Handbook*. University of Notre Dame Press, 1977.*

Zwerdling, Daniel F. *Democracy at Work*. Democracy at Work, 1978.*

*Available in paperback.

Democratic Government

In Part 4 we turn to the formal institutions that make up America's government: Congress; the Presidency and the executive branch; the courts; and state and local governments. We have touched upon these institutions in previous chapters; their constitutional origins were discussed in Chapter 2 and their roles as "targets" of citizen participation were treated in Part 3. In the chapters that follow, however, we examine how these institutions actually operate today and how their functions have changed since they were established almost two hundred years ago. Underlying our examination are several basic questions: How does government "work"? How democratic is America's government? How responsive are these institutions to the desires, needs, and concerns of American citizens?

12 Congress
The Legislative Branch

Members of Congress—senators and representatives—meet in a joint session to hear an address by President Gerald Ford.

A member of the U.S. House of Representatives or of the Senate would never be so foolish as to say to constituents, "Love me, love the Congress." Why? Because Americans usually like their own senators and representatives, but they tend to have low opinions of Congress as a whole. One reason for this paradox is that Congress is both a collection of individuals and an institution. As citizens, we may expect certain things from our own members in Congress and something different from Congress as an institution. As we will see in

this chapter, these expectations may occasionally conflict. Although we may think our own senator or representative is the "best in Congress," we may applaud candidates who attack the very institution to which they seek election or reelection. In fact, one member of the large class of new members elected in 1974 said, "We ran against Congress, most of us, against its stodginess, its unresponsiveness, its lack of new ideas, its inability to move."[1]

We will begin our discussion of Congress by looking at the individuals who work there. Who are they? How do they get there? How do they perform their jobs? Then we will examine Congress as an institution: its functions and powers, its organization, and its formal procedures.

MEMBERS OF CONGRESS

The United States Congress has 535 members—100 in the Senate and 435 in the House. Any American who has been a citizen for at least nine years and who is at least thirty years old is eligible to serve in the United States Senate. Any American who has been a citizen for at least seven years and is at least twenty-five years old may serve in the United States House of Representatives. But these constitutional qualifications of age and citizenship do not tell the whole story.

Who Are They?

The age and party affiliation of the average member of Congress is not much different from those of the average adult American. The average age of House members in 1979 was forty-nine years, roughly the same as for other adult Americans. The average age of senators was somewhat higher: fifty-three years. Democrats far outnumber Republicans in the House and Senate, as they do in the general population. In 1979, 63 percent of the representatives and 59 percent of the senators were Democrats.

When we consider other factors—particularly sex, race, and socioeconomic status—we find that the membership of the House and Senate is not by any means a mirror reflection of the total population in the United States. Although women constitute more than 50 percent of America's population, there was only one woman, Nancy Landon Kassenbaum (R., Kansas), among the Senate's 100 members in 1979 and only 16 women among the 435 representatives in the House. The total membership of the House and Senate included only 17 blacks, 4 Asian Americans, and 5 Hispanic Americans.[2]

---

[1]Quoted in William Greider and Barry Sussman, "The House Today: A Badly Tattered People's Institution," *Washington Post* (June 29, 1975), pp. A1, A12.

[2]For characteristics of the members of Congress in 1979, see Congressional Quarterly, *Weekly Report* (January 13, 1979), pp. 43–55; and *Weekly Report* (January 20, 1979), pp. 80–81.

Senators and House members usually come from "high-status" occupations.[3] Lawyers predominate, making up slightly more than half the membership of Congress. In 1979, there were 65 lawyers in the Senate and 205 in the House. Each body, too, contains many people with backgrounds in business and banking—29 in the Senate and 127 in the House. Educators also constitute a substantial group in both houses—7 in the Senate and 57 in the House.

More than 90 percent of the congressional legislators claim some religious affiliation, compared to only 60 percent among America's total population. One church executive has said that the higher rate of church identification among senators and representatives is probably due to political considerations. "We haven't reached the point where very many members can list themselves as having no religion and get away with it," she stated.[4] In the past, the percentage of Protestant members of Congress was considerably higher than their percentage of the total population. But the number of Jewish and Catholic House and Senate members has significantly increased in recent years. In 1979, the number of Protestants, Catholics, and Jews in Congress was roughly proportionate to the total number of each group in the country. Among Protestant members of the Congress, however, Episcopalians and Presbyterians were substantially overrepresented.

Senators and representatives are different from average citizens in their educational attainment and, of course, in their experience in political office. More than 90 percent of the members of the Senate have attended college, compared to only 24 percent of the general adult population in America.[5] Most senators have held more than one previous political office.[6] Most senators and representatives have been elected more than once to the office they presently hold. One fifth of the representatives have been elected ten times or more,[7] and the average representative has served ten years.[8]

Members of Congress have to work hard to "stay in touch with people." Their salaries alone put them among the top 1 percent of all Americans in income. The salary of both senators and representatives is $57,500. But congressional salaries are not out of line with the salaries of the President, cabinet members, and corporate executives. The retirement program for senators and representatives is also rather generous but not out of proportion to those of other federal officials and corporate executives. In 1979, seven retiring members of Congress were eligible for the maximum pension of $46,000 a year for

---

[3]R. Davidson, *The Role of the Congressman* (N.Y.: Pegasus, 1969), p. 69.

[4]Mary Cooper, a National Council of Churches official, quoted in Congressional Quarterly, *Weekly Report* (January 20, 1979), p. 80.

[5]William J. Keefe and Morris S. Ogul, *The American Legislative Process* (Englewood Cliffs, N.J.: Prentice-Hall, 1977), p. 117.

[6]Joseph A. Schlesinger, *Ambition and Politics: Political Careers in the United States* (Chicago: Rand McNally and Co., 1966), p. 92.

[7]Charles S. Bullock, III, "House Careerists: Changing Patterns of Longevity and Attrition," *American Political Science Review,* 66, no. 4 (December, 1972): 1296.

[8]Keefe and Ogul, *The American Legislative Process,* p. 127.

life, and five others qualified for annual pensions of $30,000.[9] One of the reasons for enacting the congressional pension plan was to encourage greater turnover in congressional membership through retirement. The pension plan has had some effect on retirement; at the end of 1978, for example, ten senators and thirty-one representatives voluntarily retired.[10] Other perquisites of congressional office—"perks," as they are called—include free plants and flowers for a member's office, free stationery, free postage (called the "franking privilege") for official business, cut-rate life insurance, gymnasium and health facilities, a free medical clinic, special beauty and barber shops, allowances for telephone and telegraph, trips home, official staff and other professional assistance, and free offices in Washington and back home.[11]

As a group, members of Congress tend to vote on the conservative side. Despite the fact that a substantial majority in both houses are Democrats, a loose, informal "conservative coalition" of Republicans and southern Democrats exists.[12] In 1975, this coalition was successful on 60 percent of the votes on which it opposed a majority of northern Democrats,[13] and in 1977, on 68 percent of the votes.[14] First-term House Democrats in 1977 were more conservative than other members of the House.[15]

What do all these statistics mean? What does it mean that senators and representatives are not strictly typical of the average American citizen? If you were a young Hispanic woman, say, with only a grade-school education, you might feel that the interests, outlooks, and opinions of this kind of Congress would differ considerably from your own. And you would probably be right. But must our members of Congress be *exactly* like us in order to represent us? For example, is an educated lawyer unable to represent the interests of working people? Not necessarily, but most Americans would probably feel better if membership in Congress—particularly in regard to race and sex—were more reflective of America's general population. All Americans have a right to wish that high public office in America were more open to a broader cross section of people.

How Do They Get There?

Members of Congress must be elected before they can serve. (People are occasionally appointed, however, to finish the term of a senator

---

[9]Congressional Quarterly, *Weekly Report* (March 11, 1978), p. 636.

[10]Congressional Quarterly, *Weekly Report* (July 1, 1978), p. 1670.

[11]Robert Shrum, "The Imperial Congress," *New Times* (March 18, 1977), pp. 20–34; and *Time* (March 14, 1977).

[12]See John F. Manley, "The Conservative Coalition in Congress," *American Behavioral Scientist,* 17 (November-December, 1973). Also see Congressional Quarterly, *Weekly Report* (April 15, 1978), pp. 911–29.

[13]Congressional Quarterly, *Weekly Report* (January 25, 1975), pp. 189–94.

[14]Congressional Quarterly, *Weekly Report* (January 7, 1978), p. 3.

[15]Congressional Quarterly, *Weekly Report* (January 21, 1978), p. 116.

What does it take to be a good senator? . . it's a serious question, one about which I sometimes sought other opinions. Vice-President Humphrey told me that a good senator knew how to compromise on minor

VIEWPOINT
On Being a Good Senator

matters, but was willing to die, politically, for more serious ones. "The difficulty," he said, "is knowing which is which." Some ideas on the subject were also suggested by my reading. . . .

Among the books I studied was *The Public Philosophy,* by Walter Lippman. . . . Lippmann wrote, and I agreed with him, that a public official represents *"The People"*—that is, "a community of the entire living population, with their predecessors and successors"—and not just "the voters." A good senator must [have] the courage to represent *"The People,"* while hoping to get re-elected by "the voters."

And that's a difficult enterprise. For, as Lippmann wrote, "the general rule is that a democratic politician had better not be right too soon. Very often the penalty is political death. It is much safer to keep in step with the parade of opinion than to try to keep up with the swifter movement of events."

The Senate reception room always fascinated me because it contained the painted portraits of five great former senators—Daniel Webster, John C. Calhoun, Henry Clay, Robert M. La Follette, Sr., and Robert A. Taft. I wondered how and why they had been chosen. . . .

. . . Lyndon Johnson had said that "character" was the common attribute of the five senators. Johnson had emphasized, too, that each of

them had been a master of the Senate and that most of them had been thwarted in other, higher aspirations.

Everett Dirksen had called them crusaders and dedicated men, and he had said that they exemplified moral courage. I, too, decided that courage was their most important shared characteristic. . . .

These were all men of hard, sharp edges. They made enemies, and they were unafraid of controversy. That was one lesson I learned from studying their lives. Another was that they were all human. I think we make a mistake in teaching our children a cherry-tree-myth, spurious kind of history which makes it next to impossible for them to imagine the Father of Our Country ever going to the toilet or taking out his wooden teeth at night. The role-model value of heroic lives is thereby diminished, cheapened. Clay, Calhoun, Webster, La Follette, and Taft were all human. But precisely therein lies their greatness.

Courage in a public official is the resolution to risk standing alone, if need be, before the firing squad of "the voters" in order to serve the perceived higher interests of *"The People."* The possibility of remembrance after death, actual or political, or the comfort of self-assurance in rectitude, or both, is preferred to the present satisfaction of contemporary approval and acclaim. . . .

These *were* men of courage. Henry Clay had said, "If anyone desires to know the leading paramount object of my public life, the preservation of the Union will furnish him with the key." Clay was "the

great compromiser," risking the wrath of both sides to forge three great compromises on the slavery issue . . .

Webster, the eloquent champion of "Liberty and Union, now and forever, one and inseparable," knowing that he would be crucified by his abolitionist supporters, had been largely responsible for the adoption of Clay's 1850 slavery compromise, which delayed secession and the Civil War for another decade. . . .

[Calhoun] . . . was the most notable political thinker ever to sit in the Senate, and he was "the intellectual leader and logician of those defending the rights of a political minority against the dangers of an unchecked majority."

Taft was not afraid to go it alone, against his party and against the majority in the Senate, when he felt principle demanded it—opposing with equal and unavailing fervor, for example, President Truman's military draft of striking railroad workers, as unconstitutional, and the Nuremberg trial of Nazi war criminals, as being unjustified under international law.

La Follette, as Kennedy pointed out, was an isolationist in a time of internationalism, an independent in time of conformity, and a "ceaseless battler for the underprivileged in an age of special privilege."

They were not always perfect; they were human. They were not always "right" by my lights; they were sometimes blind. But they were not afraid to stand up to adverse public opinion . . .

SOURCE: Fred R. Harris, *Potomac Fever* (Norton, 1977), pp. 74–75, 85–87.

or representative who has died or resigned.) In 1978, all members of the House and Senate were either Republicans or Democrats, except Senator Harry F. Byrd, Jr., of Virginia, an Independent. Both senators and representatives are selected by plurality vote in general elections.

The states are the units for electing senators. Both senators from each state must run on a statewide basis. Representatives, on the other hand, are elected from districts. Each state is allotted a number of representatives on the basis of the state's population, but each state has at least one House member. The framers of the U.S. Constitution intended to make the House of Representatives represent the general population. Until the Supreme Court decided *Wesberry* v. *Sanders* in 1964,[16] however, the number of people who lived in different congressional districts varied considerably. The results of a study done prior to Court-ordered reapportionment and redistricting showed that in twenty-one of the forty-two states which had more than one congressional district, the largest district had twice the population as the smallest district. In effect, a vote in the largest district was worth only one-half as much as a vote of a resident in the smallest district.[17] The *Wesberry* case corrected this imbalance by requiring all congressional districts to be approximately equal in population.

The *Wesberry* decision followed an earlier landmark case concerning the state legislatures. In *Baker* v. *Carr,* the Supreme Court held that the courts could decide legislative apportionment matters, which had previously been considered "political," not "justiciable," issues.[18] Chief Justice Earl Warren said that the *Baker* decision was the most important Supreme Court ruling during his tenure.[19] The rule is now "one person, one vote," and all congressional districts today contain approximately 500,000 people.

The state legislatures draw the congressional district lines after each federal decennial census. When a state loses population relative to the national population and to other states, its number of House seats may be reduced. A House member may find that his or her district has been merged with the district of another incumbent. While keeping each district approximately equal in population, state legislatures can still draw boundary lines in a way that favors particular candidates, incumbents, or parties. This practice is called *gerrymandering*.

The Republican National Committee's allocation of $1 million in 1978 as a campaign fund for Republican *state* legislative candidates underscores the importance of congressional redistricting. The Republicans considered these campaigns significant because the

---

[16]*Wesberry* v. *Sanders,* 376 U.S. 1 (1964).

[17]See, Andrew Hacker, *Congressional Districting: The Issue of Representation* (Washington D.C.: The Brookings Institute, 1963), p.2.

[18]*Baker* v. *Carr,* 369 U.S. 186 (1962).

[19]S. Sidney Ulmer, "Earl Warren and the *Brown* Decision," *Journal of Politics,* 33, no. 3 (August, 1971): 689–702.

Democrats controlled so many of the state legislatures, which would vote on congressional redistricting after the 1980 census.[20]

All candidates for the House and the Senate must campaign, and campaigns cost large sums of money. In the 1976 congressional primary and general elections, candidates spent a total of $99 million, a considerable increase from the $74 million spent in 1974. Common Cause found that an increased share of this money came from special-interest groups—business, labor, and others—who donated a record sum of $22.6 million to 1976 congressional candidates, almost twice the $12.6 million they had contributed in 1974.[21] By 1978, the total spent on all congressional campaigns had risen to $150 million. Special-interest contributions rose to more than $35 million.[22]

The campaigns of Republican candidates are usually better financed than those of Democratic candidates. In 1978, following highly successful Republican fund-raising efforts, the Democratic majority on the House Administration Committee approved a bill that would have cut from $30,000 to $10,000 the maximum contribution a political party is allowed to make to a federal candidate. In addition, it would have reduced similar contributions from special-interest groups from $10,000 to $5,000. Republican House members and newspaper editorials lambasted the bill as a blatant attempt to favor the Democratic candidates, and it was defeated on the floor of the House.[23] Partly because of the party polarization in the House as a result of the bill to cut contributions, the House also rejected the idea of public financing for congressional campaigns.[24]

As we saw in Chapter 10, voters, candidates, campaigns, the media, and campaign expenditures all affect the outcome of an election. Two additional factors are of special interest in congressional elections: the Presidency; and the power of incumbency. A "coattails effect" may occur when a popular candidate for the Presidency runs for election at the same time that a member of the same party is campaigning for the U.S. House or Senate. The presidential candidate's popularity supposedly helps the congressional candidate to get elected. But there was little, if any, coattail effect in 1976. Although 292 Democrats were elected or reelected to the House in that year, all but twenty-two of them received a larger share of the vote in their district than did Jimmy Carter, the Democratic candidate for President. The same result occurred in the Senate races; of twenty-one Democrats who were elected or reelected, only one ran behind Carter.[25] Austin Ranney wrote that "candidates didn't ride in on his coattails. They stumbled in over him."[26]

Regardless of the coattail effect—or lack of it—the trend in the

[20]Congressional Quarterly, *Weekly Report* (July 29, 1978), pp. 1933–36.
[21]Congressional Quarterly, *Weekly Report* (January 21, 1978), pp. 118–19.
[22]*New York Times* (January 18, 1979).
[23]Congressional Quarterly, *Weekly Report* (March 25, 1978), p. 752.
[24]Congressional Quarterly, *Weekly Report* (July 22, 1978), p. 1866.
[25]Congressional Quarterly, *Weekly Report* (April 22, 1978), pp. 971–74.
[26]Congressional Quarterly, *Weekly Report* (April 22, 1978), p. 971.

past was that the President's party in Congress lost seats in mid-term elections, two years following the presidential election. This result showed the effect of the Presidency on congressional elections but it may also have been due in part to the lower voter turnout in congressional elections. However, while in the past the presidential party lost an average of thirty-four House seats and four Senate seats in mid-term elections, in recent years this trend has diminished greatly, primarily because of the advantage of congressional incumbency.[27]

More than 90 percent of the incumbent House members who run for reelection are successful.[28] More than 65 percent of the incumbent members of Congress occupy what might be called "safe seats," because they tend to win reelection by more than 60 percent of the general election vote. The number of safe House seats is increasing.[29] The number of safe Senate seats is also growing, except in the southern states, where Republicans have made notable gains since World War II.[30]

Incumbents have several advantages over their opponents in congressional elections. Redistricting after each decennial census helps incumbents, at least in the first election after the new boundary lines are drawn. State legislatures often draw the lines in a way that protects vulnerable incumbents.[31] In addition, incumbents have a public record; they can call attention to particularly popular votes that they have cast. Incumbents are also more recognizable and visible to constituents than their opponents are because of their use of the franking privilege to send out free mail, their public appearances and press releases, and their travel through the district. One member of Congress says:

I have the feeling that the most effective campaigning is done when no election is near. During the interval between elections you have to establish every personal contact you can, and you can accomplish this through your mail as much as you do it by means of anything else. At the end of each session I take all the letters which have been received on legislative matters and write each person telling him how the legislative proposal in which he was interested stands.

Personally, I will speak on any subject. I am not nonpartisan, but I talk on everything whether it deals with politics or not. Generally I speak at non-political meetings. I read 48 weekly newspapers and clip everyone of them myself. Whenever there is a particularly interesting item about anyone, that person gets a note from me. We also keep a complete list of the changes of offices in every organization in our

---

[27]Congressional Quarterly, *Weekly Report* (March 25, 1978), pp. 754–57.

[28]Congressional Quarterly, *Weekly Report* (March 25, 1978), p. 755.

[29]See Albert D. Cover and David R. Mayhew, "Congressional Dynamics and the Decline of Competitive Congressional Elections," in Lawrence Dodd and Bruce Oppenheimer, eds., *Congress Reconsidered* (N.Y.: Praeger, 1977), pp. 54–56.

[30]Cover and Mayhew, "Congressional Dynamics and the Decline of Competitive Congressional Elections," pp. 56–57.

[31]Congressional Quarterly, *Weekly Report* (April 1, 1978), p. 812.

district. Then when I am going into a town I know exactly who I would like to have at the meeting. I learned early that you had to make your way with Democrats as well as Republicans. And you cannot let the matter of elections go until the last minute. I budget 17 trips home each session and somehow I've never managed to go less than 21 times.[32]

Incumbents' advantages of recognition and visibility may also result from holding official hearings in their home states or districts. The late Senator Lee Metcalf of Montana told the *Washington Post* that he could ask Henry M. "Scoop" Jackson, who chaired a committee on which Metcalf served, to allow him to hold official hearings in Montana to help his reelection chances. "I would say, 'Scoop, I'll get some favorable publicity out of this.' That's the best argument that you have for things like this."[33]

Incumbents also have paid staffs and offices. None of the perquisites of office is supposed to be used for political or campaign purposes, but the line between campaigning and the legitimate functions of office is a hard one to draw. "I don't see the out-party able to get in, when incumbents flood their districts with questionnaires and staff," one Republican representative has said. "I think our ability to pick up seats in an off-year election has been blunted."[34] One organization has calculated that the value of being an incumbent in congressional elections—aside from press coverage and the ability to raise campaign funds—was worth over $500,000 in 1977.[35]

Incumbents find it much easier to raise campaign funds, too. In 1976, incumbent members of Congress running for reelection were able to raise an average of $91,000 in campaign contributions, compared with an average of only $50,000 for each of the challengers in those races.[36]

Because of the advantages of incumbency, the Republicans—who are a minority in both houses of Congress—decided to concentrate in the 1978 election on those Senate and House seats where no incumbent was running. This strategy represented a change from 1976, when the Republicans had little success trying to dislodge first-term Democrats who had won their seats by slim margins. "We underestimated the value of incumbency," said one Republican party official.[37] This new strategy may be one reason why the Republicans were able to gain three Senate seats and twelve House seats in the 1978 elections.

The power of congressional incumbency tends to maintain stability and the status quo. It makes sudden or major changes in government policy less likely to occur through election upheavals. One's attitude

---

[32] Quoted in Charles L. Clapp, *The Congressman: His Work As He Sees It* (Washington, D.C.: The Brookings Institution, 1963), p. 332.

[33] *Washington Post* (February 17, 1975).

[34] Congressional Quarterly, *Weekly Report* (March 25, 1978), p. 754.

[35] Americans for Democratic Action study, quoted in Congressional Quarterly, *Weekly Report* (April 22, 1978), p. 754.

[36] Congressional Quarterly, *Weekly Report* (April 22, 1978), p. 754.

[37] Congressional Quarterly, *Weekly Report* (April 1, 1978), p. 809.

toward this trend depends largely upon whether one is satisfied with the way things are. The influence of incumbency may also be permanently establishing the "one and one-half party system" in Congress. Some political observers believe that the Republicans, the minority party in the House and Senate, may find it difficult to win enough seats to become the majority party.[38] (The new Republican strategy of placing greatest emphasis on nonincumbent congressional campaigns, however, may reduce this disadvantage.)

What Are Their Days Like?

The senator awakes before it is quite light outside, dresses quickly, slips out of the house while others are still sleeping, and is soon driving in heavy traffic toward the Capitol Building. On the days when he does not have to attend a breakfast meeting with some group from his home state, as he does today, he can leave home at 8:30 A.M. and get to his office in twenty-five minutes. But at 6:45 A.M. there is heavy traffic into Washington from the suburbs. This morning he will be lucky if he arrives on time for the 7:30 breakfast.

At the Capitol, the senator parks his car in the courtyard of the Russell Building (formerly called the Old Senate Office Building) and walks briskly to a bank of elevators just inside the building's entrance. He pushes the "senators only" button, and the elevator comes at once. "Good morning, senator," a deferential young elevator operator greets him. "What floor, please?" He asks to be taken to the basement. Other people in the elevator were obviously in mid-course toward their destinations on upper floors, but the elevator goes at once to the basement. On the way, the young attendant asks the senator if he wants a trolley. He nods, and the attendant pushes a button on the elevator console, signaling the underground trolley operator that a senator is on the way.

At the basement floor, the senator exits and walks rapidly down the hall toward the subway. Senate employees and others who are arriving for work greet him cordially. "Good morning, senator." "How are you this morning, senator?"

The trolley operator is out of his seat, blocking tourists and others from sitting in the very front trolley bench, which is reserved for senators. "Good morning, senator," he says, holding back the small crowd. As soon as the senator is seated, the trolley operator bounces back into his seat and calls out, "Watch the doors, please." The trolley whirs away, perhaps leaving a number of tourists and others still waiting to get on.

Making the transit from the basement of the office building to the basement of the Capitol Building in four or five minutes, the trolley comes to rest, and the doors are opened. "Have a good day, senator," the operator says. Another attendant sees him. "Good

---

[38]See Cover and Mayhew, "Congressional Dynamics and the Decline of Competitive Congressional Elections," pp. 54–74.

morning, senator," he says, hurriedly pushing a button, which causes an audible ringing of bells. The senator takes an escalator up to a bank of elevators, all of which are waiting with their doors open, attendants outside. "Good morning, senator," they chorus. Tourists nudge each other; "It's a senator," they say to each other. He gets on an elevator by himself. The other people are left standing outside (unless he decides to hold the door and invite them to ride with him).

As he leaves the elevator, the senator is greeted by one of his own staff members. "They have already sat down and started breakfast. Carl is not here yet," the staff member says, referring to the other senator from the state. "You remember that this is the Farmers Union. They are really upset about the President's decision to increase beef imports. So, you will want to mention that you have cosponsored the resolution against it. They will call on you first, because I've told them that you have a committee meeting you've got to get to as soon as you can."

The senator and his staff member enter the breakfast meeting, which is being held in a dining room near the Senate floor. As the senator enters, the group of about twenty farmers from his home state stands immediately and applauds him vigorously. He walks down through the aisles between each of the tables, shaking hands with everyone and speaking to them individually as the applause ends and the visitors begin to seat themselves again. At the head table, he is welcomed by the group president. The senator ignores the cold scrambled eggs and bacon. He talks with the people at the head table and with the people who come up to bring special greetings from his home state or to discuss special, individual problems. Twice he calls over his legislative aide, who is sitting in the back of the room. "Jim," he says, "you remember George, here? He's got a problem with the Soil Conservation Service. I want you to take him back over to our office after breakfast and call over there and make him an appointment to get this thing straightened out."

The president calls the meeting to order. He explains why they have come to Washington about beef imports and then asks each person present to introduce himself or herself. House members from the state then introduce themselves. The administrative assistant of the other senator rises and explains that the senator is "deeply sorry" that other business prevents him from being present. But he assures the group that the senator strongly sympathizes with the Farmers Union position on beef imports. "I hope each one of you will come by the office, because I want to visit with you and see how we can be helpful," the adminstrative assistant concludes. The senator who is present is then introduced. He calls many of the members of the group by their first names and pledges support for their beef imports position. Then, after apologizing for having to leave, he concludes his remarks. His exit draws another standing ovation.

The senator's staff member leaves with him. Two other staff members are waiting outside. Each has a question that must be settled at once. One involves the senator's press release, which will be issued today. It opposes a proposal to add funds to the President's budget for another nuclear carrier. The other question is what to do with a group of mayors who are waiting to see the senator in his office. "Tell them to wait, and after our staff meeting, they can walk with us over to the hearings of the Governmental Affairs Committee," the senator says.

With his aides trailing behind him, the senator now retraces his earlier path. Down the elevator with the deferential attendants. Down the escalator to the waiting trolley and the deferential trolley operator. The ride back to the Russell Building. Then up the elevator with the deferential attendant to the senator's floor.

The senator walks down the hall and into the back door to his office, where his senior staff members are gathering. Some have brief questions or comments. The senator's executive secretary hands him some letters that require his attention. The senator looks at his agenda for the day. As usual, there are conflicting committee meetings. He serves on the Governmental Affairs Committee and the Finance Committee, and both are meeting simultaneously today, as usual, at ten o'clock, ten minutes from now.

It wouldn't be entirely correct to say that a member of Congress is only as good as his or her staff, but such assistants have become increasingly important as the legislative workload has increased in recent years.

As the senator steps into the reception room, the four mayors from his home state rise to greet him. "You remember Mayor Phelps, senator," a staff member prompts him, gesturing toward the nearest visitor. "Sure, how are you, Christine?" the senator says and gives her a hug. After shaking hands with the others, he leads them all down a hall, outside the building, and across the street to the Dirksen Building (formerly called the New Senate Office Building). He pushes a "senators only" button at a bank of elevators, motions his guests in with him, is whisked up to the committee room floor, and then walks down the hall to the hearing room. All along the way, the mayors have been explaining their complaints about the appropriations for revenue sharing, a program that allocates a portion of the taxes collected by the federal government to state and local governments. "Lois," the senator says to one of his staff members who has been striding along with him, "I want you to take them back to the office and go over this in detail. Find out if there isn't some way we can help."

The senator then excuses himself, goes inside the committee room, and walks up to the horseshoe-shaped table, taking a seat at the place with his nameplate in front of it. A staff committee member lays a number of papers in front of him. The committee hearing is already underway, and the director of the General Services Administration is testifying. Several senators who are present outrank the senator in seniority—they have served on the committee longer than he has—and, therefore, they would normally have the first chance to ask the witness questions or make comments. But today the senator speaks up as soon as the witness has completed the written statement. "Mr. Chairman, I apologize for interrupting at this time, out of turn, but we are having mark-up sessions in the Finance Committee on the tax bill. With the chairman's indulgence and the indulgence of the other members of the committee, I wonder if I might be permitted to ask a couple of questions of the witness out of turn, and then be excused?" The committee chairman consults briefly with the ranking minority member of the committee, the most senior member of the minority party, and then gives his consent. It is a common practice. Indeed, both the chairman and the ranking minority member of the Governmental Affairs Committee regularly engage in it themselves when they are attending other committee meetings or hearings. The senator asks the witness two questions, one of which had been written in advance for him by one of his staff members. When the questions have been answered, the senator thanks the witness, thanks the committee chairman, and excuses himself.

Outside the committee room, a staff member is waiting with a lobbyist for the Machinists Union, who wants to talk to the senator about the minimum-wage bill scheduled to be voted on in the full Senate this afternoon. "Can you help us on the amendment to raise the level which the President has recommended?" the lobbyist asks. They walk together toward the elevator and then ride down to the floor where the Finance Committee is meeting. The senator is on the spot on this issue. Some personal friends and his state Chamber of Commerce office have written and called him from home. They complain that the bill would be very harmful to them because it would raise their costs of doing business. The senator is noncommittal, but he feels the pressure. "This is a really big one with our members," the lobbyist says. "I haven't wanted to cause you a lot of trouble or put a lot of pressure on you, but you know how much this means to our members in the aircraft plant in your home state," he continues, subtly applying pressure while denying the desire to do so.

The senator enters the Finance Committee meeting and quickly receives a written agenda from a committee staff member. The meeting is already in progress. One of the senator's own staff members, who has been following the meeting for him, hands him a couple of scribbled notes about the next amendments coming up for committee votes. As the senator takes his seat at the committee table, the staff member whispers an additional report in his ear.

At the head of the table is the committee chairman. To the senator's left are members of the senator's own party who are senior to him. To his right are members of the senator's party who are junior to him. Across the table, also arranged by seniority, are members of the opposing party. Committee staff members and Treasury Department and Internal Revenue Service representatives sit close to the committee members. The large audience in the front of the room is composed primarily of lobbyists for groups that would be affected by the tax bill. Discussions and voting proceed in the committee until a recess is called at noon.

The senator is scheduled to meet for lunch in the Senators Dining Room with some close friends from his home state, who were very active in his last campaign. But as he leaves the Finance Committee room, his executive secretary meets him. She tells him that his wife has called to remind him that today is his daughter's birthday and that he had earlier agreed to take her to lunch at Duke Zeibert's Restaurant. "Get Jim (the senator's administrative assistant) to meet me over at the dining room," the senator says. "Tell him that I'll just barely get to sit down and visit before I'll have to leave, and he can stay on and then give them a tour of the Capitol Building. Maybe Jim can put them up in the Family Gallery in the Senate Chamber this afternoon, so they can watch the vote on the minimum-wage bill."

As she walks to the trolley with him, the executive secretary shows the senator a stack of twenty-five telephone calls that must be answered. He assigns all but seven of them to be answered by various staff members and takes the rest for himself. At the Senators Dining Room, he is greeted cordially by the maitre d'. After seating his own guests, the senator is asked by other senators to come to their tables and meet their guests from home. The senator has been in the news lately and on *Meet the Press,* and it is a matter of courtesy to allow other senators to introduce him to their constituents, who are obviously impressed that their own senators know such a well-known national figure. After a brief conversation at his own table, he excuses himself and hustles out to the car that a staff member has waiting.

Duke Zeibert, the owner, greets the senator at the entrance to the popular restaurant. Famed lawyer Edward Bennett Williams, who has also just arrived, is glad to see the senator, as are a number of other people at various tables. Twice during lunch, out-of-town visitors ask the senator for his autograph. Duke takes a Polaroid picture of him with his daughter and gives it to her as a memento. After lunch, his daughter goes home in a cab, and the senator and his staff member go back to the Hill.

During the few minutes before the Finance Committee reconvenes, the senator returns some of his telephone calls. One of the calls is from the White House; a presidential aide wants to discuss the ratification of a treaty that will soon be debated and voted on in the Senate. "I haven't had too much pressure on this from home, and I believe the treaty ought to be ratified," the senator tells the aide. "You can count on me on this one."

In the Finance Committee, discussions and votes on the tax bill continue, but they are interrupted all afternoon long by votes on the minimum wage bill. When the Senate is about to vote, a buzzer sounds in the committee room and a particular light flashes. The committee then takes a recess to allow senators to go over to the Senate floor.

As the senator enters the Senate chamber from the back door, a Senate staff member who works for the Senate majority party explains to him what the vote is. Not completely sure about the bill or about how he should vote, the senator talks with the manager of the bill, the senator who is handling the bill on the floor. He also discusses it with one of his seatmates, a trusted friend with similar views and outlook. By the time the senator arrives on the floor, the clerk has already called his name; so the senator rises and is recognized at the end of the roll call. He then votes in favor of this amendment. "The Chamber of Commerce is going to be on my neck," he says to his seatmate.

Before the senator can reach the Finance Committee session, a lobbyist for the Interior Department catches him in the reception room and walks with him to the elevator. "The confirmation of the new assistant secretary is coming up next Wednesday," the lobbyist tells the senator. "I will send the nominee around to see you, and, while I don't think he'll have any trouble, we would really like to have you on our side."

Discussions and debates in the committee alternate with roll calls in the Senate throughout the afternoon. When the senator leaves the committee for the Senate floor, he is usually met by staff members who have particular matters to discuss. When he can break away from committee deliberations, he gets to a telephone to try to return calls, the number of which is growing as the day wears on.

At 3:00 P.M., the senator excuses himself from the Finance Committee session to go to a press conference. He announces that he is introducing a new bill, which would establish wage and price controls to hold down inflation. Many reporters from the "writing press" are present, but only one network television camera is there. The senator reads a prepared statement and then answers questions. He tries not to act offended when one of the reporters asks, "Is this the kick-off for your presidential campaign?"

Toward the end of the day, during a lull in Senate voting, the senator goes to the Senate gymnasium for a sauna, a brief swim, and a massage. But the massage is cut short by a roll-call vote, and the senator, still feeling a little sweaty, has to dress quickly and rush over to the Senate floor.

The Senate session runs late. No one knows in advance exactly when it will end for the day, although the majority leader indicates that it will probably go as late as 8:30 P.M. That is a problem for the senator, because he and his wife have agreed to go to a dinner party at the home of Georgetown friends. By 8:00 P.M., the senator is already late for the dinner party. His wife has called the hosts, who are accustomed to such situations. The senator's wife brings his tuxedo to the office, where he changes. On the last several roll calls in the Senate, several senators, each with similar dinner engagements, come to the chamber in formal dress. The senator's wife and his executive secretary await him outside the Senate Chamber following the final vote for the evening. The executive secretary has brought the senator's airline ticket and itinerary for his trip to his home state tomorrow morning—a trip he makes at least two weekends a month. "Have a good evening, Senator," she says as the senator and his wife rush toward their car.

That is what a senator's life is like. Although House members have similar pressures and experiences, they do not serve on as many committees and subcommittees as senators do. They do not have as many staff members, do not receive as much deferential treatment, and rarely run for President of the United States. In addition, House members are not as sought after by the national press and do not make as much "news" or appear as much on national television. On the other hand, they are usually more worried most of the time about whether they will have a serious opponent in the next election which is never more than two years away.

How Are They Expected to Act?

In Congress, as in any large group of people, certain *norms,* or standards of behavior, have developed over the years. These "informal rules, frequently unspoken because they need not be spoken . . . may govern conduct more effectively than any written rule. They prescribe 'how things are done around here.' "[39] If members wish to have influence in the House or Senate, they must show some deference to these norms. When he was Speaker of the House, the late Sam Rayburn regularly told new House members, "If you want to get along, you must go along."

The importance of the old norm of "apprenticeship," which required new members to be seen and not heard, has declined considerably in recent years.[40] One member of Congress described this trend as follows:

---

[39]Barbara Hinckley, *Stability and Change in Congress* (New York: Harper and Row, 1971), p. 59.

[40]In regard to congressional norms, see Randall B. Ripley, *Congress: Process and Policy* (New York: W.W. Norton and Co., 1975), pp. 62–75.

For many years before I became a member of Congress, and even at the time I entered as a member of the freshman class in the 85th Congress, we often heard it said that 'freshmen members of the House should be seen and not heard.' The fact of the matter is that this seemed to be pretty much the way things were until the early 'sixties. Since that time, many new members have aggressively moved forward introducing new programs and legislation which they promptly supported in what appears to be a far more vocal manner than was previously done.[41]

Thus, new members, especially in the Senate, have a good chance today to receive a prestigious committee assignment in their early years in Washington. Most new members do not hesitate to take an active part in congressional activities and speak their minds on issues that are important to them.

The norm of "specialization" continues to be important in the House and Senate. This norm encourages new members to pick out one, or a few, fields of interest, such as military or health issues, and become experts on those subjects. House members are expected to specialize more than senators are.

Another important norm is "cooperation." House and Senate members are expected to be able to "disagree without being disagreeable." Senators and representatives are very courteous with each other in formal House and Senate sessions. This courtesy is more than a matter of rules. Members of Congress are supposed to get along with each other. "Institutional loyalty" is also an important norm in both the House and Senate. Members are expected to speak well of Congress when they are interviewed or make public appearances. At the very least, they are supposed to refrain from derogatory statements about Congress. Further, House members are expected to be loyal to the House, as opposed to the Senate, and Senators are expected to be loyal to the Senate, rather than to the House. Some House members often feel jealousy and antagonism toward senators; representatives sometimes say, not always with justification, that senators "appear on television and work at getting their names in the papers so much that they can't seem to get their business done as rapidly as we do."

The norm of "internal orientation" is closely related to the standard of "institutional loyalty." It refers to the pressure on senators and representatives to be "workhorses," instead of "showhorses," as Lyndon B. Johnson put it when he was Senate majority leader. Some senior members of the House and Senate feel some resentment toward colleagues who receive greater publicity than others. But the norm of "internal orientation" is not nearly as strong as it once was, particularly in the Senate. One Senate observer once said that "the Senate type is, speaking broadly, a man for whom the Institution

---

[41]Herbert B. Asher, "The Changing Status of the Freshman Representative," in Ornstein, *Congress in Change,* pp. 217–18.

is a career in itself, a life in itself, and an end in itself."[42] In recent years, a number of senators, including the late Hubert H. Humphrey of Minnesota, have said that being an effective senator requires not only working within the Senate, but also speaking to a larger national audience, which can influence the Senate.[43] Senate norms are allowing this inside-outside orientation of members more and more.[44]

New House and Senate members are socialized to the congressional norms. They learn from each other and tend to stick together. They also learn from the other members of the congressional delegations from their home states, from fellow congressional committee members, senior colleagues, experienced staff assistants, and reporters.[45]

One of the major functions of Congress as an institution, as we will discuss later in this chapter, is lawmaking. For individual members of Congress, it involves committee work, voting, and debate on the floor of the House or Senate. (Debate is not particularly important, though, since most members have already become familiar with the issues and usually know how they intend to vote by the time the votes are taken.) Voting requires attendance on the floor of the House or Senate when roll calls are taken. Roll-call attendance is slightly higher in nonelection years than in election years. In 1977, a nonelection year, the average member of Congress answered 90 percent of the roll calls, compared to 86 percent in the election year of 1976.[46]

How do members of Congress decide which way to vote? There are inside and outside influences. From the outside, the pressure of public opinion—the influence of constituents—affects their decisions. Some think of themselves as *delegates;* they feel they must vote with the majority opinion in their district or state. "I'm here to represent my district," one member of Congress has said. "This is part of my actual belief as to the function of a congressman. What is good for the majority of my district is good for the country. What snarls up the system is these so-called statesmen-congressmen who vote for what they think is the country's best interest."[47] Others think of themselves as *trustees;* they feel obligated to vote as their judgment and conscience dictate. Most senators and representatives are both delegates and trustees most of the time. "I am sent here as a

[42]William S. White, *Citadel: The Story of the U.S. Senate* (New York: Harper and Row, 1956).

[43]See Nelson W. Polsby, "Goodbye to the Senate's Inner Club," in Norman J. Ornstein, *Congress in Change,* pp. 208–15.

[44]Ralph K. Huitt and Robert L. Peabody, *Congress: Two Decades of Analysis* (New York: Harper and Row, 1969), pp. 159–78.

[45]See Richard F. Fenno, Jr., "The Freshman Congressman: His Views of the House," in Nelson W. Polsby, ed., *Congressional Behavior* (New York: Random House, 1971); and Herbert B. Asher, *Freshman Representatives and the Learning of Voting Cues* (Beverly Hills: Sage, 1973).

[46]Congressional Quarterly, *Weekly Report* (January 7, 1978), pp. 18–20.

[47]Quoted in Lewis Anthony Dexter, "The Representative and His District," in Robert Peabody and Nelson W. Polsby, *New Perspectives on the House of Representatives* (Chicago: Rand McNally, 1969), p. 6.

One of the most common ways constituents try to influence their senators and representatives is through letter-writing. While most members of Congress welcome such expressions of opinion, the sheer volume of mail they receive has increased dramatically. To make sure your letter is thoughtfully considered, be sure it is thoughtfully written. The following tips are suggested by Representative Morris K. Udall (D., Ariz.) and the League of Women Voters:

(newspaper reports or magazine articles, *CQ Guide to Current American Government*, and *Congressional Monitor*, available in most libraries, are the best sources for this information).

- Include pertinent editorials from local papers, if possible.
- Be constructive. If a bill deals with a problem you admit exists, but you believe it takes the wrong approach, explain what you think might be the right approach.
- If you have expert knowledge or

How to...

Write Effective Letters to Legislators

- Write to your own senator or representative. (Letters written to other members will end up on their desks anyway, eventually.)
- Write at the proper time, during committee or subcommittee deliberations or when the bill is being debated on the floor.
- Use your own words and stationery. Avoid using forms or mimeographed letters, which indicate less intense feelings on your part.
- Don't be a "pen pal." Your letters will be taken more seriously if you don't try to instruct your legislator on every issue that comes up.
- Don't demand a commitment before all the facts are in; bills rarely become law without some amendments or changes.
- Identify all bills by title and number

wide experience in a particular area, share it with your legislator. Don't pretend to wield vast political influence.
- Write to your legislator when he or she does something you approve of: A note of appreciation *this* time may give your next letter a more favorable reception.
- Feel free to write if you have a question or problem dealing with procedures of government departments.
- Be brief, and write legibly (better yet, type your letter).
- Be sure to use the proper form of address:

The Honorable John Doe
United States Senate
Washington, D.C. 20510

(Dear Senator Doe:)

The Honorable John Doe
House of Representatives
Washington, D.C. 20515

(Dear Mr./Mrs./Ms./Miss Doe:)

An alternative to a letter is a telegram. Letters are better for explaining your position, but telegrams are attention-getters and can be effective just before a vote as a reminder of your interest—and awareness. By calling Western Union, you can send a fifteen-word "Public Opinion Message" from anywhere in the country for a dollar; it usually will arrive within a day.

SOURCE: *Congressional Quarterly* (November 14, 1962), p. 2283.

representative of 600,000 people," another member of Congress has said. "I try to follow my constituents—to ignore them would be a breach of trust—but I use my judgment often because they are misinformed. I know they would vote as I do if they had the facts that I have."[48]

Some members of the House and Senate feel that their image—the way their constituents view them—is more important than how they vote on issues. "The people back home don't know what's going on. Issues are not most important so far as the average voter is concerned. The image of the candidate plays a much greater role."[49]

Democrats in Congress tend to cast liberal votes and Republicans tend to cast conservative votes because of the opinions they share with the people in their districts.[50] But members do not always know what their constituents want or simply cannot thoroughly consult on a day-to-day basis with them on voting decisions. So, their decisions are often influenced from the inside; they tend to get "cues" from other members of Congress with whom they identify.[51] For example, a senator may ask a colleague while riding over to the Senate chamber for a roll-call vote, "What's this?" The colleague may reply, "It's the Miller amendment," referring to another member of the Senate. "Oh, an easy 'no' vote," the first member might say.

In other words, Senators and House members often get a cue on how to vote by learning who is for and against the question. Cues have special weight when they come from people who are considered experts on the issue involved. In making a voting decision, a member of Congress may also pay attention to the outside influences of interest groups and the President, especially if the President is from the member's own party. Finally, the inside influence of the member's own staff can sometimes be important.[52]

What Motivates Them?

At first, members of Congress did not think of their service in the U.S. House or Senate as a long-term career. As one authority put it, "They fled the Capitol—not yet located in Washington—almost as fast as was humanly possible."[53] Members of Congress went to Washington for a short stay and then returned home to pursue

[48]Charles O. Jones, "The Agriculture Committee and the Problem of Representation," in Peabody and Polsby, *New Perspectives on the House*, p. 168.

[49]Clapp, *The Congressman: His Work As He Sees It*, p. 421.

[50]Louis A. Froman, Jr., *Congressmen and Their Constituencies* (Chicago: Rand McNally, 1963).

[51]Donald Matthews and James Stimson, "Decision-Making by U.S. Representatives, A Preliminary Model" (paper presented at conference on political decision-making, University of Kentucky, 1968).

[52]John W. Kingdon, *Congressmen's Voting Decisions* (New York: Harper and Row, 1973).

[53]H. Douglas Price, "Congress and the Evolution of Legislative 'Professionalism,'" in Norman J. Ornstein, ed., *Congress in Change* (New York: Praeger Publishers, 1975), p. 5.

whatever it was they did the rest of the year. Today, however, there is a high degree of congressional "professionalism." Congressional sessions now continue all year long, and most senators and representatives consider their service in those bodies to be a professional career.

What keeps them going? Members of Congress are motivated by three basic factors: reelection, influence in the House or Senate, and good public policy. "All congressmen probably hold all three goals. But each congressman has his own mixture of priorities and intensities—a mix which may, of course, change over time."[54]

THE CONGRESS AS AN INSTITUTION

The United States Congress is a collection of individuals, but it is also an institution, an entity with a life of its own. The Constitution established it as a coequal branch of the federal government. It has rules, functions, and special ways of going about its work.

Functions and Powers

Congress has specific functions, or particular kinds of work it is supposed to perform. It also has specific powers which enable it to carry out those functions. Americans believe that Congress is supposed to solve national problems. This expectation about Congress results from its four major functions, the four major goals of its action.[55]

The first words of the U.S. Constitution (after the Preamble) concern one of these functions. Article I, Section 1, says: "All legislative Powers herein granted shall be vested in a Congress of the United States, which shall consist of a Senate and House of Representatives." One fundamental congressional task, then, is *lawmaking,* the process of establishing overall national policy. But the lawmaking function is not exclusively performed by Congress. National policy is also made in the executive department and, to a lesser extent, in the judiciary. By applying the law in specific cases and by determining the meaning of constitutional provisions, the courts actually make substantive policy. The Supreme Court's *Brown* decision, which ordered the desegregation of public schools, is one example. Part of the policy-making in the executive department occurs because Congress often delegates a portion of its lawmaking function to that branch. For example, when Congress passes a new law to protect the environment, it may allow the appropriate federal agency or department to fill in the details of the new program by issuing regulations. The executive department may also make policy

---

[54] Richard F. Fenno, Jr., *Congressmen in Committees* (Boston: Little, Brown and Co., 1973), p. 1.

[55] In regard to congressional functions, see Ripley, *Congress; Process and Policy,* pp. 9–19.

when Congress is relatively passive in the development of policy in a particular field. For instance, it sometimes leaves much of the policy-making in foreign affairs to the President.

Beginning with President Franklin D. Roosevelt's administration and continuing through the Presidencies of Lyndon B. Johnson and Richard M. Nixon, the coequal branches of Congress and the executive department became unequal. The presidency attained greater national policy-making power. But Congress reacted to Johnson and Nixon's handling of the Vietnam War and to the Watergate affair during the Nixon administration by reasserting its policy-making function. The pendulum of power thus swung back toward Congress, away from the President.[56]

Soon after Jimmy Carter took office, a conflict developed between his administration and Congress on national policy issues. This conflict was partly due to the inexperience of his White House staff. It was also partly a result of the President's lessened influence with Congress because of his declining standing in national public opinion polls.[57] Although there were substantive differences on issues, too, the conflict between the President and Congress was deeper than these causes alone would indicate. President Carter came into office at a time when Congress was seeking to redress the imbalance in power between itself and the presidency.[58] One political observer has found that Presidents tend to be more powerful during crises and that Congress becomes more assertive in relatively calm periods. "In an era of nuclear weapons, emerging nations, and a potential energy crisis, it is problematical how long the current era of congressional assertiveness can last. If the nation finds itself in the midst of an immediate crisis, demands for presidential action should quickly mount, and the balance begin to swing back to the executive again."[59]

The growing support among senators and representatives for a bill that would give Congress a veto power over almost any regulation issued by a federal agency or commission reflects the current assertiveness of the legislative branch.[60] So far, proponents of this measure have not been able to build enough support to secure its passage. But Congress has already passed 195 pieces of legislation in recent years to give itself, or even one house alone, a legislative veto over specific executive actions, including Federal Election Commission regulations, international arms sales, rules issued by the Office of Education, and presidential executive orders reorganizing federal agencies and departments. The idea of broadening the congressional veto power has been attacked on several grounds. Opponents argue that it would add new and unnecessary burdens to the congressional

© Valtman - Rothco Cartoons

[56]See Harvey C. Mansfield, Sr., ed., *Congress Against the President* (New York: Praeger Publishers, 1975); and Nelson W. Polsby, *Congress and the Presidency,* 3rd ed. (Englewood Cliffs, N.J.: Prentice-Hall, 1976).

[57]Congressional Quarterly, *Weekly Report* (March 4, 1978), pp. 579–86.

[58]Congressional Quarterly, *Weekly Report* (January 28, 1978), pp. 235–77.

[59]Congressional Quarterly, *Weekly Report* (January 28, 1978), p. 237.

[60]Congressional Quarterly, *Weekly Report* (March 4, 1978), pp. 575–76.

workload; that it would give wealthy and powerful special interests a new way to set aside regulations that they dislike; and that it would water down executive action to avoid controversy in the Congress.[61]

The second major function of Congress is *oversight*. That is, Congress serves as a "watch-dog" over the executive department and, to a lesser extent, over the judiciary. It attempts to ensure that these branches of government perform properly and in accordance with congressional laws. For this purpose, the Congress has set up its own official watchdog arm, the General Accounting Office (GAO). In addition, individual members of Congress and the congressional committees carry out the oversight function by questioning officials and conducting investigations and hearings.

Education is a third congressional function. This role involves keeping the general public informed about issues and congressional actions regarding them. But Congress has no central, single way to speak to the nation, such as through a spokesperson or public relations office. The leaders and other members of Congress are free to speak as they please.

The education function of Congress, then, is carried out through an uncoordinated series of announcements by individual members, leaders, and officers, through committee hearings, and through debate. The inability of Congress to speak with a single voice probably contributes to the public's generally low opinion of it. By contrast, a President *can* speak with one voice. But in Congress, senators and representatives engage in conflicting debate and discussion, and Congress often conducts its business in a time-consuming and confusing way. Thus, Congress involves the public in public controversy by making its decisions publicly; the President, on the other hand, has a much greater opportunity to make decisions privately and later announce them publicly.

Finally, Congress performs the function of *representation*. Since this function is carried out by individual members of Congress, it is at any given time the result of a temporary combination of individual views of representation. And, as we saw in Chapter 6 and earlier in this chapter, individuals vary in their view of what representation requires. A delegate feels obligated to follow the "instructions" of constituents. One member of Congress, who shares this view, said, "The most important thing I can do is to represent my people." A trustee, on the other hand, believes in exercising independent judgment on issues. Another member of Congress, who agrees with the trustee concept, said, "The Founding Fathers intended us to exercise our own judgment, not to weigh the mail." Most senators and representatives are sometimes delegates and sometimes trustees, depending upon the importance of the principle involved and the

[61]Mark Green and Frances Zwenig, "The Legislative Veto Is Bad Law," *The Nation* (October 28, 1978), pp. 434–36.

[62]For a discussion of the representative role for members of Congress, see R. Davidson, *The Role of the Congressman* (New York: Pegasus, 1969), pp. 110–42.

intensity of constituent feeling on it.[62]

Although Americans tend to have a low regard for Congress, they usually like *their own* members of Congress.[63] We expect different things from Congress as a whole than we do from our individual senators and representatives.[64] We expect Congress, as an institution, to solve national problems. We expect our own members of Congress, as part of their representation function, to perform constituent service and to articulate our local and individual interests.

Constituent service is often called "casework." It involves helping constituents solve individual problems, complaints, or claims. A veteran who has been turned down for a disability pension may turn to his or her member of Congress as a "court of last resort." A surviving child may ask a senator for help to expedite a Social Security claim. No provision in the laws or in the Constitution requires members of Congress to give this kind of service. But those who want to get reelected render it, and many members view casework as an important way to make government policies humane and workable.

The constituent service expected of an individual legislator in Congress may conflict with the lawmaking function of Congress as an institution. For example, a zealous member of Congress, pressing a particular constituent's claim, may ask for a generous ruling by a federal agency, such as a liberal definition of disability, which, if it were followed in every case, would result in a different national policy than that laid down by Congress as a whole.

The interest articulation expected of senators and representatives requires them to serve as "lawyers" or advocates for the interests of their district or state. This obligation may also conflict with the lawmaking function of Congress as a whole. For example, a member of Congress may feel that he or she must fight to get a dam built back home or to prevent a military base from closing, even though the legislator—and the legislator's constituents—also favor the idea of cutting back on federal expenditures generally.

Congressional Powers

To carry out its intended functions, Congress has certain powers. These powers come from specific provisions in the Constitution and from interpretations of the Constitution by the U.S. Supreme Court.[65]

Only by an act of Congress can money be raised to pay for the

---

[63]For a discussion of this phenomenon, see Richard J. Fenno, Jr., "If, as Ralph Nader Says, Congress Is the Broken Branch, How Come We Love Our Congressmen So Much?" in Norman J. Ornstein, ed., *Congress in Change* (New York: Praeger Publishers, 1975), pp. 277–87.

[64]For a good discussion of these conflicting congressional functions and member duties, see David J. Vogler, *The Politics of Congress,* 2nd ed. (Boston: Allyn and Bacon, 1977), pp. 1–41.

[65]In regard to congressional powers, see Congressional Quarterly, *Powers of Congress* (Washington, D.C.: Congressional Quarterly, 1976).

government's operations and programs; and only by an act of Congress can money be spent by the government. This *fiscal power*—or "power of the purse"—is one of the most important congressional powers. It includes the authority to raise or lower taxes and to decide which individuals or corporations will pay what share of the taxes; to raise money by borrowing; and to decide how much money the federal government will spend and how the money will be spent. In recent years, Congress has raised the national debt limit at regular intervals to finance increased spending by the federal government.

The exercise of the congressional fiscal power has two major effects. First, Congress' taxing, spending, and borrowing policies have an important impact on the economy. For example, Congress can stimulate the economy by cutting individual income taxes, which leaves more of the taxpayers' money in their hands; by spending more, particularly on social programs; or by both decreasing taxes and increasing spending. These policies tend to stimulate consumer demand and result in more jobs for people. On the other hand, Congress can slow down the economy by increasing individual income taxes; by decreasing federal spending; or by both increasing taxes and decreasing spending. These policies tend to lower consumer demand, thereby reducing the number of jobs available. Taxing, spending, and borrowing can also affect the rate of inflation.

The exercise of congressional fiscal power also affects the redistribution of wealth and income. Congressional decisions on taxes and who will pay them, and on spending and who will receive the money, can transfer wealth and income from one group of Americans to another. For example, these policies may cause money to flow from higher income brackets to lower income brackets (and the reverse may also be true sometimes). Article I, Section 8 of the Constitution gives Congress the authority to provide for the "general welfare." Congress has used this power to enact many social programs that seek to redistribute wealth and income on the basis of need.

At the beginning of each congressional session, the President presents to Congress his proposed federal budget, a report containing his recommendations regarding taxes, spending, and borrowing. (The Office of Management and the Budget assists the President by screening the requests and recommendations of the various executive agencies and departments.) Congress gives the President's proposals very serious consideration, since the legislative branch has no simple way of devising a coherent budget of its own. First of all, there are two separate, independent houses of Congress. Within each house, the taxing committee is separate from the spending committee. In the House, the taxing committee is called the Ways and Means Committee, and in the Senate, the Finance Committee. In both houses, appropriations committees have jurisdiction over spending. The appropriations committees are broken down into subcommittees, each with a considerable degree of autonomy. To complicate matters further, no appropriation bill can be passed unless it conforms to an earlier authorization bill, which in turn is handled by a separate standing committee. The fiscal power of the Congress, then, is fragmented between the two houses and among the committees in each house. And, of course, each member of the House and Senate eventually casts separate votes on the fiscal issues.

To synthesize the congressional fiscal process, Congress passed the Budget and Impoundment Control Act in 1974. This act set up new budget committees in the House and Senate and required Congress to vote on a total, overall budget in addition to voting later on the component issues. The act was passed to provide a mechanism that would enable Congress to set the proper level of economic stimulus or restraint, decide on priorities in the goals of federal spending, and better compete with the President in determining fiscal policy. Some conservative members of Congress also hoped that it would help to hold down federal spending. Another purpose of the act was to prevent the President from "impounding" funds, or refusing to spend all the money appropriated by Congress.[66] Although the new budget reform has improved Congress' ability to deal rationally with budget and economic issues, it is still not functioning as well as its supporters had hoped.[67]

Congress also has *foreign policy power*, which involves issues of war and peace. This authority stems from three sources: Congress' control of spending and taxing; Article I, Section 8, of the Constitution, which gives Congress the exclusive power to declare war; and Article II, Section 2, which gives the Senate the power to ratify treaties negotiated by the President and to confirm presidential appointments of ambassadors and other public officials.

Presidential and congressional powers overlap on foreign policy.[68] The Constitution gives Congress the exclusive power to declare war, but in Article II, Section 2, it declares that the President is the commander in chief of the nation's armed forces. President Abraham Lincoln, for example, claimed the power to call up troops at the beginning of the Civil War without waiting for prior legislative authorization. He said, "Are all the laws *but one* to go unexecuted and the government itself go to pieces lest that one be violated?"[69] President Truman sent troops to war in Korea, calling it a "police

---

[66]See John W. Ellwood and James A. Thurber, "The New Congressional Budget Process: The Hows and Whys of House-Senate Differences," in Dodd and Oppenheimer, eds., *Congress Reconsidered,* pp. 163–92.

[67]See Congressional Quarterly, *Weekly Report* (January 21, 1978), p. 103.

[68]In regard to the separation of powers between the President and the Congress in the field of foreign policy, see Edward A. Kolobziej, "Congress and Foreign Policy: The Nixon Years," in Harvey C. Mansfield, Sr., ed., *Congress Against the President,* pp. 167–79; Congressional Quarterly, *Powers of Congress,* pp. 51–108; and Alton Frye, *A Responsible Congress: The Politics of National Security* (New York: McGraw-Hill, 1975).

[69]Edward S. Corwin, *The President: Office and Powers, 1787–1957* (New York: New York University Press, 1957), p. 64.

action," and Presidents Johnson and Nixon justified America's involvement in the Vietnam War—all without any formal declaration of war by Congress.

Power over foreign policy in peacetime is equally fragmented under the Constitution. Although Congress must ratify treaties and confirm appointments before they can become effective, it is the President who negotiates treaties and who nominates people for federal office. At times, Presidents have entered into "executive agreements" with foreign governments—obligating themselves to defend a foreign country, for example—without submitting the agreements to the Senate for ratification as treaties.

In recent years, the Congress has reasserted its foreign policy power. In 1969, the U.S. Senate overwhelmingly adopted a nonbinding "national commitments resolution" declaring that the President could not commit the United States to a foreign obligation unless "affirmative action [had been] taken by the executive and legislative branches of the United States government by means of a treaty, statute or concurrent resolution of both houses of Congress specifically providing for commitment."[70] In other words, the Senate said that the President should not make foreign commitments by himself. In 1973, the Congress passed the War Powers Act over President Nixon's veto. This law recognizes the power of the President to order military action for defense, but it requires the President to terminate any such troop commitment within sixty days unless Congress specifically extends it.

The *commerce power* is set forth in Article I, Section 8, of the Constitution, which states that Congress shall have the power "to regulate Commerce with foreign Nations, and among the several States, and with the Indian Tribes." This clause gives Congress the power to regulate business and industry in the United States and to set up regulatory commissions (such as the Interstate Commerce Commission, the Federal Trade Commission, and the Federal Communications Commission). Congress also has the authority to regulate trade with foreign governments and to provide for tariffs, or taxes, on foreign imports. In addition, Congress has the exclusive power under this clause to legislate concerning Indian tribes.

Much of the work of Congress is carried on in committee and subcommittee hearings and meetings. Here, members of the Senate Foreign Relations Committee receive testimony from witnesses.

---

[70]*Congressional Quarterly Almanac* (1973), p. 177.

Article I, Section 3, of the Constitution establishes the *impeachment power* of Congress. By majority vote, the House of Representatives may *impeach,* or charge, any officer of the executive or judicial branches of the federal government, including the President. If the House votes to impeach, the Senate conducts the trial which requires a two thirds vote of those present and voting for conviction. When the impeachment proceeding involves the President, the Chief Justice of the Supreme Court presides over the trial in the Senate. The articles of impeachment do not need to allege that a crime has been committed. The Constitution provides that an officer may be impeached for treason, bribery, and other "high crimes and misdemeanors." The punishment for conviction in an impeachment proceeding is removal from office.

The House of Representatives has impeached thirteen federal officers. Most were federal judges; one justice of the U.S. Supreme Court and one secretary of state have been impeached. One President, Andrew Johnson, was impeached by the House but acquitted in the Senate trial because the vote for conviction was one less than the required two-thirds majority. Richard Nixon was the first President to resign. He did so after impeachment charges had been voted by the House Judiciary Committee but before there had been a full vote in the U.S. House of Representatives.

Congress' *investigative power* is based upon the broad legislative authority that the Constitution grants to that body. Congress may undertake investigations for a number of reasons. They can be conducted for fact-finding purposes concerning presidential appointees, treaties, and need for new legislation. In connection with its watchdog function, Congress conducts investigations to look into executive department practices. Investigations are also used in impeachment probes, on questions relating to ethics of congressional members, and for informing the public.[71]

The congressional investigation power has sometimes been used to badger witnesses and expose them to public ridicule and disapproval. The late Senator Joseph McCarthy of Wisconsin was particularly criticized for his rough treatment of witnesses during hearings in the Senate Permanent Investigating Subcommittee concerning alleged communist infiltration into the federal government.

The Supreme Court has held in several recent cases that the investigative power of Congress is very broad. In one decision, the Supreme Court declared that "so long as Congress acts in pursuance of its constitutional power, the judiciary lacks authority to intervene on the basis of the motives which spurred the exercise of that power."[72] Congressional investigations in recent years have covered a

---

[71]See Ernest F. Griffith and Francis R. Valeo, *Congress: Its Contemporary Role* (New York: New York University Press, 1975), pp. 113–23; and Congressional Quarterly, *Powers of Congress,* pp. 155–99.

[72]*Barenblatt* v. *United States,* 360 U.S. 109 (1959). See also *Wilkinson* v. *United States,* 365 U.S. 399 (1961); and *Braden* v. *United States,* 365 U.S. 431 (1961).

wide range of matters, such as possible conspiracy behind the assassinations of President John F. Kennedy and Dr. Martin Luther King, Jr., wrongdoing in the General Accounting Office, and the causes of the nuclear plant accident at Three Mile Island.

Congress has made it a crime to refuse to give information to either house of Congress or to an authorized committee.[73] Witnesses before congressional committees may, of course, claim their right against self-incrimination under the Fifth Amendment to the Constitution. But Congress may still compel testimony if, with court approval, it grants a witness full or partial immunity from prosecution.

Most Presidents have claimed the "executive privilege" to withhold certain information from congressional committees. Presidents have justified the use of this privilege by asserting the need for secrecy in diplomatic affairs and the need to shield individuals from unfair publicity. They have also argued that the privilege enables them to receive frank advice from their staff members and associates without making their staff fear that what they say to the President may later be publicly disclosed. One authority has written concerning presidential claims of executive privilege, "This leaves open the possibility that the President may abuse his prerogative, especially in instances where the information would reflect unfavorably on him or his administration of the nation's affairs."[74] Another writer has pointed out that the right of executive privilege is not granted in the Constitution. He sees it as a myth created by a succession of Presidents to suit their own interests. "At bottom, the issue concerns the right of Congress and the people to participate in making the fateful decisions that affect the fortunes of the nation. Claims of presidential power to bar such participation or to withhold the information that is indispensable for intelligent participation undermines this right and saps the very foundation of democratic government."[75]

Nevertheless, some Presidents have claimed the right to withhold information on certain occasions, and there has never been a complete showdown between Congress and the President on this issue (although in *U.S.* v. *Nixon*[76] the Supreme Court forced President Nixon to hand over tapes and records to a district court for use in criminal proceedings). But it is clear that if Congress firmly declares against permitting such withholding of information, it has certain sanctions it can use to enforce its will. For example, Congress could stop funding for any programs about which the President, or the President's appointees, refused to give full information.

The Constitution gives the Senate a *confirmation power*. Although Presidents "nominate" or name cabinet members, ambassadors,

---

[73]See Telford Taylor, *Grand Inquest* (New York: Simon & Schuster, 1955), p. 35.
[74]Taylor, *Grand Inquest*, p. 101.
[75]Raoul Berger, *Executive Privilege* (Cambridge, Mass: Harvard University Press, 1974), p. 1.
[76] *U.S.* v. *Nixon*, 418 U.S. 683 (1974).

Supreme Court justices, judges, and other federal officials, they cannot actually appoint them, according to the Constitution, except "by and with the advice and consent of the senate." The confirmation power of the Senate is not shared by the House of Representatives.

The framers of the Constitution disagreed about how the Senate's confirmation power would work. Alexander Hamilton wrote, "There will, of course, be no exertion of *choice* on the part of the Senate. They may defeat one choice of the Executive and oblige him to make another; but they cannot themselves *choose*—they can only ratify or reject the choice he may have made."[77] John Adams, on the other hand, declared that "faction and distraction are the sure and certain consequences of giving to the Senate a vote on the distribution of offices." He thus foresaw that the Senate would exert pressure to have particular persons appointed to offices.[78]

Hamilton and Adams were both partially right. Most of the President's nominees today are routinely confirmed by the Senate. But the recommendations made by particular senators for the nominations of federal judges, district attorneys, and district marshalls in their home states continue to have a strong influence on appointments. Further, "senatorial courtesy" means that the Senate will not usually confirm a person's appointment to any federal office if the senators from the President's political party, and the state of the nominee, refuse to endorse the confirmation.

Article V of the Constitution provides Congress with an *amending power*. The Constitution specifies two procedures for amending the Constitution, but only one of them has ever been used successfully. The one that has *not* been used provides that Congress will call a constitutional convention to propose amendments to the Constitution upon the application of two thirds of the state legislatures—with ratification of the amendments requiring the approval of three fourths of the states. The amendment does not become law until three fourths of the states approve, or ratify, it. The other amending procedure—which has been used to amend the Constitution twenty-six times—allows Congress to propose amendments by a two thirds vote of the members present and voting in both the House and Senate.[79] Again, ratification requires the approval of three fourths of the states.

The Supreme Court has held that Congress may set a reasonable time limit within which ratification must take place. Congress set seven years as the time limit for the Equal Rights Amendment. But in 1978, when it became clear that the time limit would expire before three fourths of the states ratified the amendment, Congress granted a three-year extension.

---

[77] *Federalist,* no. 66.

[78] Joseph P. Harris, *The Advice and Consent of the Senate: A Study of the Confirmation of Appointments By the United States Senate* (Greenwood Press, 1968), p. 29.

[79] *National Prohibition Cases,* 253 U.S. 350 (1920).

Finally, Congress has an *electing power*. In Article II, Section 1, as amended by the Twelfth Amendment, the Constitution says that if no presidential candidate receives a majority vote in the Electoral College, the House of Representatives will select the President from among the three candidates who receive the highest number of Electoral College votes. (Each state delegation would have one vote.) Similarly, the Senate chooses the Vice-President from the two highest candidates if no candidate receives a majority in the Electoral College.

Thus far, we have discussed what Congress is supposed to do and the powers that enable it to carry out these functions. What in fact Congress does—and how it does it—is substantially influenced by its organization and its formal procedures.

How Is Congress Organized?

Congress is made up 535 individuals with varying backgrounds, motivations, and goals. Since even small goal-oriented groups soon develop organizational structures to help them accomplish their goals, it should not be surprising to learn that the same is true in Congress. Both the U.S. House and Senate are organized chiefly around parties, leaders, committees, and staffs. And all are intertwined with each other.

The parties in Congress. The physical division of the Senate chamber and the House chamber is symbolic of the way the two major political parties contribute to the organization of the two bodies. (We are referring here to the congressional party-in-government, the members of the House and Senate who have been elected under a party label.) Each chamber has a central aisle which runs from the back down to the desk of the presiding officer in front. Looking from the back of the chamber toward the desk of the presiding officer, one sees that all the Democratic members of the House of Representatives sit on the left side of the aisle, and all of the Republican members sit on the right side. Every member of the U.S. House of Representatives was elected as a candidate of one of the two major parties. There are no Socialists, no Independents, and no *Raza Unida* members in the House, for example.

Similarly, looking from the back of the Senate chamber toward the desk of the presiding officer, one sees that all the Republican members of the Senate sit on the right-hand side of the central aisle. All the Democrats sit to the left. All members of the U.S. Senate are either Democrats or Republicans, with the exception of Senator Harry F. Byrd, Jr., of Virginia. Byrd was elected as an Independent, but he chooses to vote with and sit with Senate Democrats. In both bodies, the Democrats are substantially in the majority.

Other physical divisions in Congress are based upon party affiliation. When committees and subcommittees meet or hold hearings, members are seated on the basis of their party affiliation. There are two "cloakrooms," or places for informal discussion, just off the floor of each chamber, which are separately assigned to each party. The "Senators' Private Dining Room" is composed of two separate rooms where senators rigidly segregate themselves by parties.

Each "Congress" lasts two years—a period called the "biennium"—and a "session" is held each year. At the beginning of each Congress, the party caucuses, or conferences, meet to vote on party leaders and to ratify decisions on committee chairpersons and committee membership. But no member who wants to participate in a party caucus needs to pass an ideological test. The member must simply be willing to vote with party members on matters of formal organization. Thus, in the Senate Republican Conference, the House Republican Conference, the Senate Democratic Caucus, and the House Democratic Caucus, a senator or representative achieves membership simply by saying, "I am a Republican," or, "I want to be a member of the Senate Democratic Caucus." Usually, no one asks why.

In 1972, a Senate Democratic reform committee recommended that the Senate Democratic Caucus refuse automatic membership to any senator who had been nominated by a State Democratic party that was not affiliated with the Democratic National Committee or that practiced racial discrimination. This proposal, which was defeated, would have excluded from the Democratic Caucus Senators John Stennis and James Eastland of Mississippi because they had been nominated by a State Democratic party which was not affiliated at that time (since changed) with the national party. Senator Harry F. Byrd, Jr., of Virginia, who had been elected as an Independent, would also have been barred.

The majority party in each chamber selects that body's principal officers and controls the scheduling of legislative business. In addition, the chairperson of each committee and subcommittee is a member of the majority party. The formal party-in-government in the House and Senate usually has its principal impact on procedural issues, rather than on substantive matters, such as influencing members' votes on particular legislative measures.

Yet some party-line voting occurs in both the House and Senate, particularly on measures that involve social and economic issues.[80] "Party-unity voting," which occurs when a majority of voting Democrats oppose a majority of voting Republicans, has increased in recent years.[81] In 1977, for example, Senate and House Republicans voted with their party 70 percent of the time. Senate and House Democrats voted with their party 67 percent of the time.

Party-unity voting in Congress probably stems from four main causes. First, party members tend to have similar backgrounds and

---

[80]See Aage R. Clauson, *How Congressmen Decide* (New York: St. Martin's Press, 1973).

[81]Congressional Quarterly, *Weekly Report* (January 14, 1978), pp. 79–83.

outlooks on issues. Second, party leaders in the House and Senate tend to be active in disseminating information to party members, and they frequently attempt to persuade members to vote with the majority of their party.[82] Third, senators and representatives tend to form their closest friendships with members of their own party. Fourth, congressional members of a President's party tend to vote together to support the President, while opposing party members tend to stick together against the chief executive's proposals.

Thus, although party organizations such as the Democratic National Committee and the Republican National Committee have little influence on party-unity voting in the Congress, there is still an important relationship between party labels and how members organize, behave, and vote.

Congressional leadership. The first order of business of the party caucus at the beginning of each new Congress is the election of officers. The principal leader of the majority party in the Senate becomes the *majority leader* of that body, and the second ranking majority party leader becomes the *majority whip*. The *president pro tempore* of the Senate is also chosen by the majority party, but this office is largely honorary. It is given to the most senior member of the majority party. In the House, the principal leader of the majority party becomes the *speaker of the House,* and the second ranking majority party leader becomes the *majority leader* of that body. In both the House and Senate, the principal leader of the minority party becomes the *minority leader.*

Each party usually reelects its principal leaders, who remain in office from one Congress to another. But in 1965 the Republicans in the House of Representatives chose then-representative Gerald R. Ford, Jr., of Michigan to replace Charles A. Halleck of Indiana, who had served as minority leader for six years. Similarly, in 1969, Senate Democrats replaced their majority whip, Russell Long of Louisiana, with Senator Edward M. Kennedy of Massachusetts. In 1971, they deposed Senator Kennedy and chose Senator Robert Byrd of West Virginia.[83]

The Senate majority leader is the most influential officer of that body. The holder of this office is always recognized by the Senate's presiding officer ahead of any other senator. This custom gives the majority leader a large amount of influence in deciding when measures will be scheduled for debate and voting in the Senate. The majority leader also influences committee assignments and related matters.

In the House of Representatives, the Speaker is an even more powerful official. The Speaker presides over the House, has considerable influence over committee assignments, and exerts pressure on members in regard to substantive issues that come up for vote.

---

[82]Vogler, *The Politics of Congress,* p. 116.
[83]Robert Peabody, *Leadership in Congress* (Boston: Little, Brown, 1976).

Congressional leaders during the 96th Session of Congress. Above left: Speaker of the House, Representative Thomas P. ("Tip") O'Neill (D., Mass.) and House Minority Leader John Rhodes (R., Ariz.) at the podium in the House Chamber; Above: House Majority Leader Jim Wright (D., Texas) confers with White House Congressional Liaison Frank Moore; Left: Senate Minority Leader Howard Baker (R., Tenn.) and Senate Majority Leader Robert Byrd (D., W. Va.).

In the House and Senate, the majority whip and the minority whip serve as a link between the party leadership and membership. They inform members when votes will occur and "count noses" on upcoming votes, reporting them to the party leadership. In the House, the whips and assistant whips also coax members to be present and to vote on substantive issues according to the positions of the party or party leaders.[84] The term *whip*, which is also used in the British House of Commons, comes from the "whipper-in" who kept the hounds together on fox hunts.

Congressional leaders have power and influence for several reasons.[85] First, they know the rules of the body in which they serve, and they know how to use them to their advantage. Second, leaders in both Houses have some control over tangible preferments like committee assignments, foreign trips, and assistance in reelection

[84]Congressional Quarterly, *Weekly Report* (May 27, 1978), pp. 1301–6.
[85]See Ripley, *Congress; Process and Policy*, pp. 134–45.

campaigns; they can also impede or facilitate the flow of legislation in which a member may be interested. They can use psychological preferments; that is, they can let the word get around that a member is a "comer" or is in or out of favor with the leadership. Lastly, they possess more valuable information than the average member does about when decisions will be made, and they dominate the channels of communication.

The power and influence of particular House and Senate leaders also depend upon their personalities and persuasiveness. When he was Senate majority leader, Lyndon B. Johnson was the most powerful Senate leader in modern times. On the other hand, his successor, Mike Mansfield of Montana, saw his job as being more like that of a "shepherd" than a "drover."[86] While Johnson worked at persuading senators to go along with leadership positions on issues, Mansfield believed that individual senators should be allowed to do pretty much what they pleased.

Chairpersons of committees and subcommittees are also among the formal leaders of the House and Senate. Informal leaders include members who are recognized as experts in particular fields, those who build personal followings among their colleagues, and those who are recognized as national leaders. These informal leaders have varying degrees of influence.

The committee system. The basic work of the House and Senate is done through committees, which President Woodrow Wilson called "little legislatures." He wrote that "Congress in session is Congress on exhibition, whilst Congress in its committee rooms is Congress at work."[87]

The most important congressional committees are "standing committees," which are permanent. They handle most of the legislative, appropriations, and investigative work. In 1979, there were fifteen standing committees in the Senate and twenty-two standing committees in the House.[88] Almost all of these standing committees have subcommittees, which have jurisdiction over particular aspects of a full committee's work.

From time to time, the two houses of Congress set up "select committees" or "special committees" to conduct special investigations or to perform other special work. They are not considered permanent committees, although some of them have had relatively long lives. The two houses may collectively establish "joint committees." These groups, such as the Joint Economic Committee, are usually set up to study issues; they rarely have legislative jurisdiction.

One of the perennial suggestions for congressional reform is to

---

[86]See Ornstein, ed., *Congress in Change*, pp. 115–54.

[87]Woodrow Wilson, *Congressional Government*, 15th ed. (Boston: Houghton Mifflin, 1900), pp. 69–79.

[88]For a list of congressional committees and subcommittees, their chairpersons, and members of the ninety-sixth Congress, see Congressional Quarterly, *Weekly Report* (April 14, 1979).

reduce the number of committees and subcommittees in each house, which would mean fewer committee meetings for members.[89] Although both houses have periodically reduced the number of committees and subcommittees,[90] the committees have tended to proliferate again after the reforms.

One authority puts congressional standing committees into three categories.[91] The first is the "power committee," which gives members maximum influence over their colleagues because of the important jurisdiction of the committees. The Appropriations and Finance committees in the Senate, and the Appropriations, Rules, and Ways and Means committees in the House are power committees.

The second category is the "policy committee." These committees are composed of senators and representatives who are more interested in policy goals than in congressional influence or constituent service. In this group are the Foreign Relations, the Energy and the Natural Resources, Human Resources, and the Banking, Housing, and Urban Affairs committees in the Senate, and similar committees in the House.

The third group, "constituency committees," are particularly important because they give members leverage in doing things for their districts or states. This category includes the Public Works and Transportation, the Interior and Insular Affairs, and the Merchant Marine Fisheries committees of the House, and similar committees in the Senate.

Suppose you have just been elected to the United States Senate, and you want to become a member of the powerful Senate Finance Committee. How do you go about getting such a favored committee assignment? Or suppose you have been elected to the House of Representatives, and you would like to be a member of the equally powerful Ways and Means Committee. How do you go about it? Who makes these committee assignments? If you are a Republican in either the House or Senate, you would make contact with the members of your Committee on Committees. They make the initial decisions concerning committee assignments. You would also want to speak with the party leaders in your legislative body. If you are a Democrat, the procedure is similar, but the committees have different names. In the Senate, committee assignments are made by the Senate Democratic Steering Committee; in the House, by the House Democratic Steering and Policy Committee.

Several factors determine who is finally chosen to fill committee vacancies. House and Senate leaders influence the selections. Seniority in the House or Senate can play a part; a senior member generally

[89]See Donald M. Fraser and Iric Nathanson, "Rebuilding the House of Representatives," in Ornstein, ed., *Congress in Change,* pp. 288–94.
[90]See Final Report of the Commission on the Operation of the Senate, *Toward A Modern Senate* (Wash., D.C.: Government Printing Office, 1976); Temporary Select Committee to Study the Senate Committee System, *First Report, With Recommendations* (Wash., D.C.; Government Printing Office, 1976); and *Second Report, With Recommendations* (Wash., D.C.: Government Printing Office, 1977).
[91]See Vogler, *The Politics of Congress,* pp. 141–88.

has a better chance to get a coveted committee assignment than a junior member. The need for regional or geographical balance on a committee may also be taken into account. A desire for ideological balance on a committee may become a factor in assignments. Some strong-willed committee chairpersons "recruit" new members with whom they ideologically agree or who they feel will follow their leadership. Then they urge the appropriate leaders and appointing authority to approve their choices. Special-interest groups may have a behind-the-scenes influence on committee assignments, too.

Once you become a member of the committee, how do you get to be the chairperson of the committee or subcommittee? First, you must be a member of the majority party. Aside from that, it is primarily a matter of seniority on the committee or subcommittee. If you have served longer than any other member of your party on a particular committee, and if you are a member of the majority party, you will almost automatically become the chairperson. The senior minority party member of the committee becomes the ranking minority member. These positions are very important because the chairperson has great flexibility in deciding when hearings will be scheduled and when votes will be taken. The chairperson, too, can largely choose the majority committee staff. The ranking minority member largely chooses the minority staff. In recent years, the influence of individual members of committees and subcommittees over scheduling and choice of staff has increased. In the House, majority members of a subcommittee may vote on the selection of the chairperson.

The final say on the selection of committee chairpersons occurs in the caucus of the majority party in both the House and Senate. The senior member of each committee is usually chosen as the chairperson by the party caucus. In 1975, however, the House Democratic Caucus deposed three committee chairpersons. Since then, committee chairpersons have paid more attention to the caucus, even on substantive issues before the committee.[92] The fact that secret votes can be taken in the caucuses on the selection of chairpersons and ranking minority members means that even though few chairpersons have actually been deposed and even though seniority is still generally followed, the seniority system has been weakened as an automatic method for chossing committee leaders and committee leaders have been made less powerful.

Critics of the seniority system have argued that it primarily rewards people who are simply good politicians in their home states or districts, regardless of their legislative ability. Opponents have also attacked it on the grounds that it keeps people in powerful positions, no matter how old or out of step with the majority they may become.[93] On the other hand, supporters of the seniority system

[92]See Congressional Quarterly, *Weekly Report* (April 15, 1978), pp. 868, 874–76.

[93]For arguments for and against the seniority system, see George Goodwin, Jr., "The Seniority System in Congress," *American Political Science Review,* 53 (June 1959): 412–36.

claim that it provides a relatively noncontroversial way to choose committee leaders, promoting harmony rather than disharmony. They also insist that it tends to select the people who are the most knowledgeable and experienced on matters within the jurisdiction of each committee. If you were a member of the House or Senate, your feelings about the seniority system might depend upon how much seniority you had. The late Senator Robert S. Kerr of Oklahoma said, "When I first came to the Senate, I didn't much care for the seniority system, but the longer I've been here, the better I like it."

Congressional staffs.   Members of Congress have *staffs* to assist them with their work. There is a general staff for the entire Congress, for each house of Congress, and for the majority and minority parties in each house. The Congressional Research Service in the Library of Congress performs a part of the general staff function for the entire Congress. Although it was originally set up to serve Congress, the Library of Congress serves national needs today as well. The Congressional Research Service works only for Senators and House members, who can get answers to their research questions almost overnight. They can find information on issues ranging from how the price of gold has fluctuated in the last ten years to how an increase in price affects the production of natural gas. The General Accounting Office is an accounting and auditing arm of Congress, a part of its general staff. Each House of Congress has a legislative counsel to help with drafting legislation.[94]

Each congressional committee also maintains its own staff. The committee chairperson chooses most of the staff members. Additional staffers are selected by the ranking minority member. Committee staff positions have become more careerist; only the top staff positions change when the committee leadership changes. But this practice still varies from committee to committee. In recent years, committee members and leaders have had increased opportunities to choose at least one committee staff member, but again, this varies by committee.

What do committee staff members do? "Conventionally staff members are loyal to the committee chairman, deferential to the members, moderate in partisanship, and cautious about advocacy," one authority has written. "They are expected to remain outside the spotlight of attention and give credit for their work to the legislators they serve."[95] Their official job is to assist with the committee's legislative and other work. Sometimes, committee staff members also perform political tasks and personal legislative work for the senator or House member who was responsible for their appointment.

The personal staffs of members of the Senate and House answer only to them. A senator's staff is larger and generally more

"Look! One of the senators is briefing his staff."

---

[94]In regard to congressional staff, see Van Der Slik, *American Legislative Processes,* pp. 81–82.

[95]Van Der Slik, *American Legislative Processes,* p. 83.

specialized. Each representative is allotted over $200,000 per year for personal staff, a sum that can largely be used however the House member desires. A representative's staff may include up to eighteen aides. Senators receive an average of more than a half million dollars per year for staff allowance, and a senator's staff members may number as many as fifty.[96] An administrative assistant usually heads the staff of each senator and House member. Most senators and representatives have a press aide and an executive secretary. Most congressional staffs also include one or more legislative assistants, who work on substantive legislative issues, and a number of "caseworkers," who handle constituent services. In addition to their Washington offices, members of Congress have home-state offices, which focus on constituent service and political matters.

The number of congressional staff positions has increased dramatically in recent years. But there has also been a large increase in the congressional workload. For example, from 1971 to 1974, the number of letters received by House members went up from 14 million to 40 million. Senators sent out 190 million letters in 1970, a figure which had doubled by 1975.[97]

The Legislative Process

In the 1970s, the U.S. House and Senate both became more open, more democratic, and less dominated by the South. Still, the processes of the Congress are a labyrinth of complexity.[98]

The passage of a bill through Congress occurs in four stages: the introductory, committee, floor, and conference phases.

The introductory stage. The legislative process begins when a bill is introduced in either the House or Senate. Most bills can begin their life in either house, as long as there is at least one House or Senate sponsor. The principal sponsor of a bill will generally try to secure cosponsors in order to demonstrate that there is larger support for the legislative proposal. Under the terms of the Constitution, "revenue-raising" bills—those having to do with any aspect of taxation—can originate only in the House; and, by custom, the same is true of appropriations bills. The special power of the House to originate taxation and appropriations bills is not very important, however, because the Senate can and does freely amend bills that come to it from the House, sometimes adding wholly new items to them. Thus, the Senate in effect originates such proposals on its own.

[96]See David J. Vogler, *The Politics of Congress,* pp. 128–37; Van Der Slik, *American Legislative Processes,* pp. 84–86; and James Reston, "The Hidden Legislature," *The Washington Star* (January 12, 1979), p. A-7.

[97]Vogler, *The Politics of Congress,* p. 132.

[98]See Norman J. Ornstein, Robert L. Peabody, and David W. Rohde, "The Changing Senate: From the 1950s to the 1970s"; and Lawrence C. Dodd and Bruce R. Oppenheimer, "The House in Transition," in Dodd and Oppenheimer, eds., *Congress Reconsidered,* pp. 3–53.

The introduction of bills not only has a legislative intent, but often a symbolic value as well. By introducing or cosponsoring bills, senators and representatives can demonstrate their position on certain issues to their constituents and others. For example, members of Congress may cosponsor a bill to limit deficit spending by the federal government, even though they know that the measure has no chance of being adopted by Congress. Bills may also be introduced for their "informational" effect; they give a representative or senator a better way to discuss and focus public attention on a particular issue.

The committee stage. After a bill is introduced, it is immediately printed. This gives other members of Congress and other citizens a chance to study its exact wording. The bill is then referred to a committee, usually a standing committee. Since the rules of the House and Senate are rather specific concerning the jurisdiction of committees, it is usually a simple, ministerial matter for the presiding officer in each body (advised by the parliamentarian) to decide which standing committee should receive the newly introduced bill.

Senate and House committees are not required by the rules to take any action at all on a bill that has been referred to them. But procedures exist in both houses for floor votes to force a committee to act on a bill or to release it for full floor action.

A bill is usually referred to a subcommittee for public hearings. These hearings, which are announced in advance, offer a public forum for anyone who has an opinion about a bill and wants to express it to the committee and to the public. Following the public hearings in the subcommittee, there is usually a subcommittee "mark-up" session, where decisions are made concerning amendments and the final wording of the bill. After the mark-up session in the subcommittee, there is a mark-up session in the full committee.

Prior to recent reforms, mark-up sessions in the Senate and House committees were normally closed to the general public and to the press. This procedure allowed members to cast votes in favor of special-interest groups without worrying about full public scrutiny. Committees now regularly hold open mark-up sessions unless—for national security reasons or otherwise—members of the committee publicly vote to close the session. This reform tends to make committees and their members more accountable to the public.

When the bill is "reported," or acted upon by the committee, it is printed again, showing any amendments made in committee. In addition, the committee staff prepares a committee report, which accompanies the bill to the full House or Senate. This report can be highly important. If, later on, for example, a court cannot tell exactly what Congress intended from the words of the bill itself, it may try to discover the "legislative intent" behind the bill by referring to the committee report and the records of hearings and debate.

In the Senate, once a committee has taken final action on a bill, it is

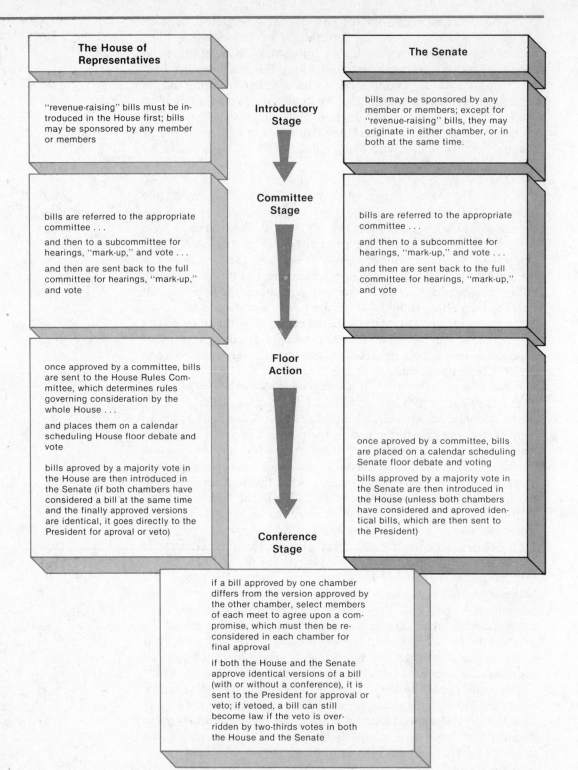

A Bill Becomes Law

The House of Representatives

The Senate

Introductory Stage

"revenue-raising" bills must be introduced in the House first; bills may be sponsored by any member or members

bills may be sponsored by any member or members; except for "revenue-raising" bills, they may originate in either chamber, or in both at the same time.

Committee Stage

bills are referred to the appropriate committee . . .

and then to a subcommittee for hearings, "mark-up," and vote . . .

and then are sent back to the full committee for hearings, "mark-up," and vote

bills are referred to the appropriate committee . . .

and then to a subcommittee for hearings, "mark-up," and vote . . .

and then are sent back to the full committee for hearings, "mark-up," and vote

Floor Action

once approved by a committee, bills are sent to the House Rules Committee, which determines rules governing consideration by the whole House . . .

and places them on a calendar scheduling House floor debate and vote

bills aproved by a majority vote in the House are then introduced in the Senate (if both chambers have considered a bill at the same time and the finally approved versions are identical, it goes directly to the President for aproval or veto)

once aproved by a committee, bills are placed on a calendar scheduling Senate floor debate and voting

bills approved by a majority vote in the Senate are then introduced in the House (unless both chambers have considered and aproved identical bills, which are then sent to the President)

Conference Stage

if a bill approved by one chamber differs from the version approved by the other chamber, select members of each meet to agree upon a compromise, which must then be reconsidered in each chamber for final approval

if both the House and the Senate approve identical versions of a bill (with or without a conference), it is sent to the President for approval or veto; if vetoed, a bill can still become law if the veto is overridden by two-thirds votes in both the House and the Senate

ready for floor action. It is listed on the "calendar," which indicates which bills are ready for full Senate consideration. The Senate leadership and the Senate Democratic Policy Committee consult with the committee chairperson and decide when the bill will be scheduled for consideration and debate in the Senate. In the House, on the other hand, there is an intermediate step between the committee report of a bill and the listing of the bill on the House calendar for consideration. This step involves action by the House Rules Committee, which acts as a "traffic cop" in the House. With 435 members, the House has more restrictive rules and procedures than does the smaller Senate. These include methods for limiting debate and amendments on the floor, and they are largely applied by the Rules Committee.

In the past, a highly conservative and arbitrary House Rules Committee could often determine the outcome of substantive issues by refusing to allow a "rule" at all on a bill. It could prevent the bill from coming to the floor for a vote unless changes were made that suited the wishes of the Rules Committee members. Alternatively, it could establish a "rule" that would not allow any amendments to be considered on the floor, forcing House members to vote either "yes" or "no" on a massive tax measure, for example, without being allowed to vote on separate issues contained in it. Sometimes the

Drawing by Koren: © 1964 The New Yorker Magazine, Inc.

"Next I want to sing a song about the House Rules Committee and how the legislative functions of Congress are tyrannized over by its procedural calendar, dominated in turn by an all-powerful chairman hamstringing the processes of democracy."

committee also established "rules" that limited floor debate on a bill.

The Rules Committee still has these same procedural powers, and most representatives recognize that its functions are necessary. But recent reforms have made the Rules Committee much more responsible to the speaker and to the majority caucus. The speaker now has the power to name Rules Committee members in each congressional session, subject to the approval of the House Democratic Caucus. This is one of the reforms that have made the House more democratic in recent years. It shows how the power of committees and committee chairpersons has been reduced and how the power of the speaker and the majority caucus has increased accordingly.

The floor stage. In the Senate, a bill goes directly from the standing committee to the floor. In the House, a bill makes an intermediate stop in the Rules Committee before going to the floor. Except for tax and appropriations bills, which must be voted on first in the House, floor action on a bill may start first in either legislative chamber. Senators have more power and freedom of action on the floor consideration of a bill than do members of the House. Senate rules are far more liberal, and senators may freely offer and vote upon amendments. Debate is usually unlimited, unless senators unanimously agree on time limits. Senate rules also provide for filibuster, a practice that is not allowed in the House.

A *filibuster*—an attempt to "talk a bill to death"—may be used by senators to prevent a final vote on a bill or other measure. In the Senate, this practice is politely called "extended debate." Senators resort to the filibuster when they are in a minority and want to block the adoption of a bill or other measure by a majority of senators. They justify this minority power by saying that extended debate allows time to educate the general public on an issue and to exert pressure on senators to change their positions. Senators who oppose certain provisions in a bill can also use the filibuster to force the Senate to make changes in it before allowing it to come to vote.

The filibuster has been severely criticized by people who wish to reform Senate procedures. In recent years, the rule has been relaxed. Today, three fifths of the Senate membership can invoke *cloture*—that is, end a filibuster; in the past, the requirement was two thirds of those present and voting. Still, the three-fifths requirement—sixty senators—is rather stiff. The rule thus permits a minority of senators to block a majority in the Senate from passing a measure, even though most American citizens may strongly support it.

The filibuster rule came under its greatest attack when southern senators successfully used it in the 1950s to prevent passage of civil rights legislation. In more recent times, some northern senators have endorsed the rule. They contend that the filibuster protects minority rights against an unchecked majority and slows down hasty and ill-considered action until better reasoning can prevail. In 1978, for example, two liberal senators, James Abourezk of South Dakota and Howard Metzenbaum of Ohio, conducted a lengthy but ultimately unsuccessful filibuster against a bill to deregulate the price of natural gas. On the last night of that session, Abourezk conducted a one-man, "mini-filibuster" on the issue—keeping the House and Senate in session until the early hours of the next morning—before he was finally forced to stop because of a lack of sufficient support.

Passage of a bill in the House or Senate requires a majority vote of those present and voting. Noncontroversial bills, however, are sometimes adopted by unanimous consent, without a formal vote. When the House and Senate pass a bill in exactly the same form, congressional consideration of the measure is complete. It is then sent to the President for approval or disapproval.

The conference stage. If the House and Senate version of the bill differ in any way, each house must appoint conferees for that bill only to meet and resolve their disagreements on the bill. Each set of conferees is honor-bound to support the bill approved by its own house. Each group of conferees votes separately. Before a conference committee report can be adopted, a majority of the House conferees *and* a majority of the Senate conferees must support it.

The purpose of the conference is to make compromises and to arrive at an agreement. But this would not be possible if all the conferees from each house refused to make concessions. After some give and take, a majority of the conferees from each house usually agree on a compromise version of the bill. If no agreement is reached, the bill cannot become law.

Once a conference agreement has been reached, the bill then must go *back* to both the House and Senate for separate votes on the revised version. Either house may turn down the report and ask for an additional conference. When both houses have agreed to the conference version of the bill, it is sent to the President. If the President signs the bill, it becomes law. If the President vetoes the bill, it cannot become law unless the House and Senate again pass the bill, this time by a two thirds vote.

In the Senate, consideration of treaties and presidential appointments is similar to the handling of bills. (Recall that treaties must be sent to the Senate for ratification and that presidential appointments must be sent to the Senate for confirmation.) The introductory stage for treaty ratification and appointment confirmation begins with notification to the Senate. Treaties are always referred to the Senate Foreign Relations Committee. Presidential appointments are referred to the standing committees that have jurisdiction over the particular federal agency or committee or department involved. Hearings and committee meetings are held for final action, which is very similar to the mark-up sessions for committee action on legislation. The treaty or confirmation is then reported to the full

Senate for debate and vote. If the treaty is ratified or the appointment is confirmed, no further action need be taken, since ratification and confirmation powers belong to the Senate, not the House.

CONCLUSION

Some significant reforms have been recently adopted in Congress. The seniority system for choosing committee leaders is not as rigid as it once was. The power of committee chairpersons has been reduced. Committee mark-up sessions are now usually open to the public. The House rules have been made more democratic. The House and Senate have adopted stricter ethical standards regarding public disclosure of personal income and property. They have also placed restrictions on the amount of a member's outside earnings. Attempts have been made to make the budget process more rational. The Senate has recently reorganized and reduced the number of its committees. It has also reduced the number of senators needed to cut off a filibuster.

Are more reforms necessary? Critics of Congress continue to say that it is inefficient. People have made recommendations to streamline congressional machinery and to make it more modern. One suggestion is to hire an administrator in each house, to handle basic management and housekeeping matters.[99] Some critics maintain that there should be greater party responsibility in each house on substantive legislative matters.

Except for joint sessions of the House and Senate, television cameras were not allowed in the House and Senate chambers until recently.[100] In 1979, the House of Representatives began to broadcast its sessions. Proponents of televised House and Senate debates argued that it would force changes in the way the Congress operates and make Congress more efficient and more representative of the public will. They also suggested that television coverage would tend to increase the stature and significance of Congress with the public, particularly on the balance of power between Congress and the President.[101]

One influential political scientist has criticized Congress because it represents narrow, provincial interests and tends to block the national leadership of Presidents. He blames Congress for being the

[99]See U.S. House of Representatives, Report of the Commission on Administrative Review, *Administrative Reorganization and Legislative Management* (Wash., D.C.: Government Printing Office, 1977); and Final Report of the Commission on the Operation of the Senate, *Toward a Modern Senate* (Wash., D.C.: Government Printing Office, 1976).

[100]Congressional Quarterly, *Weekly Report* (January 7, 1978), p. 24.

[101]See Michael J. Robinson, "A Twentieth-Century Medium in a Nineteenth-Century Legislature: The Effects of Television on the American Congress," in Ornstein, ed., *Congress in Change*, pp. 240–61.

"prime *institutional* reason for the lagging social progress of the 1950s and the upheavals of the 1960s."[102]

Despite its fragmentation of power, its inability to act rapidly and decisively, and the doubts about its representative character, the United States Congress still has more power than any other legislature in the world.[103] Some political observers have emphasized that "Congress is the only institution that can stand beside or in opposition to the presidency, when opposition is warranted."[104] This check on presidential power seems particularly important after the Vietnam War years of President Johnson and the Watergate years of President Nixon. According to one writer, "Congress, not the President, is most closely in touch with the people who live beyond the Nation's capital. Our recent experience with two presidents who lost their constituencies and a third who cannot find one helps remind us that Congress remains our most representative institution."[105]

ADDITIONAL SOURCES

Arnold, R. Douglas. *Congress and the Bureaucracy.* Yale University Press, 1979.

Cotton, (Sen.) Norris. *In the Senate: Amidst the Turmoil and Confusion.* Dodd, Mead, 1978.

Drew, Elizabeth. *Senator.* Simon & Schuster, 1979.

Eulau, Heinz, and John Wahlke. *Legislative Politics.* Sage, 1978.

Fenno, Richard F. *Congressmen in Committees.* Little, Brown, 1973.*

Harris, Fred R. *Potomac Fever* (especially Chs. 2,3,4). Norton, 1977.

Keefe, William J., and Morris S. Ogul. *The American Legislative Process: Congress and the States,* 4th ed. Prentice-Hall, 1977.

Kingdon, John W. *Congressmen's Voting Decisions.* Harper & Row, 1973.*

Mayhew, David. *Congress: The Electoral Connection.* Yale, 1974.*

Ogul, Morris S. *Congress Oversees the Bureaucracy: Studies in Legislative Supervision.* University of Pittsburgh Press, 1978.*

Peabody, Robert L. *Leadership in Congress.* Little, Brown, 1976.

Pitkin, Hanna F. *The Concept of Representation.* University of California Press, 1967.*

Polsby, Nelson. *Congress and the Presidency,* 3rd ed. Prentice-Hall, 1976.*

Riegle, Donald. *O Congress.* Doubleday, 1972.

*Available in paperback.

---

[102]James MacGregor Burns, *Uncommon Sense* (New York: Harper and Row, 1972), p. 124; also see James MacGregor Burns, *The Deadlock of Democracy* (Englewood Cliffs, N.J.: Prentice-Hall, 1963).

[103]See Charles O. Jones, "Somebody Must be Trusted; An Essay on Leadership of the U.S. Congress," in Ornstein, ed., *Congress and Change,* p. 275.

[104]Michael J. Robinson, "A Twentieth-Century Medium in a Nineteenth-Century Legislature: The Effects of Television on the American Congress," in Ornstein, ed., *Congress and Change,* p. 259.

[105]Richard F. Fenno, Jr., "Strengthening a Congressional Strength," in Dodd and Oppenheimer, eds., *Congress Reconsidered,* p. 262.

13 The Presidency:
Executive Leadership

Early on a still morning in September 1978, President Jimmy Carter walked briskly across the grounds of Camp David, the presidential retreat in the Coctoctin Mountains of Maryland. He had just left the cabin where Egyptian President Anwar El-Sadat and his aides were staying and was on his way to meet with Israeli Prime Minister Menachem Begin and his aides. For nearly two weeks, the three leaders had been engaged in almost round-the-clock talks to try to preserve the fragile peace prospects that had blossomed in the Middle East after Sadat's historic journey to Israel only ten months earlier.

Negotiations between the two countries had begun to bog down by midsummer, raising again the specter of war in that troubled region. Carter had invited Sadat and Begin to a summit meeting at Camp David. He hoped to resolve the differences between them and to renew the chance for peace.

On March 26, 1979, several months after the Camp David summit meeting, President Carter joined Prime Minister Begin and President Sadat in signing an Egyptian-Israeli peace treaty at the White House.

The Camp David meeting was conducted in utter secrecy. It was closed to the press. No "leaks" of information occurred, and no official reports of the meeting's progress were made. Still, the suspense mounted as the talks continued, despite Carter's efforts prior to the summit to avoid raising expectations that there would be substantive results.

Then on Monday, September 18, the White House requested

prime time access to the three national television networks. After being whisked from Camp David to the White House by helicopter, President Carter and the two foreign leaders made a startling announcement: the summit meeting had produced a "framework for peace." As the three leaders signed the documents, the White House staff, cabinet officials, the Vice-President, and others applauded enthusiastically. Prime Minister Begin then happily embraced the more subdued President Sadat—a stunning picture that United Press International flashed throughout the United States and around the world. Describing the conference, Prime Minister Begin said, "The President of the United States won the day. Peace now celebrates a great victory for the nations of Egypt and Israel and for all mankind."[1]

The next evening, President Carter, President Sadat, and Prime Minister Begin appeared before a joint session of the Congress to further elaborate on the "peace blueprint." This congressional session was televised live, throughout the United States. Millions in the Middle East and elsewhere also viewed it. Senate Republican leader Howard Baker of Tennessee called the summit results "a great victory for President Carter," as well as a "great victory for the world." The Democratic leader in the Senate, Robert Byrd of West Virginia, said the summit was "a great step forward," and added, "President Carter's role was central to the substantial achievements of the summit. He deserves our admiration and a special commendation from all who desire peace in the Middle East."

For several months after the summit, the spirit of Camp David seemed to wane. It appeared that disagreements on details might stymie the peace process. But Israel and Egypt finally agreed on a formal peace treaty. Begin and Sadat came back to Washington to join President Carter, who had been at the center of the negotiations, for a formal treaty-signing ceremony and a gala celebration.

No person in America—and no public official—is able to command as much public attention as the President of the United States. Americans have special and complex feelings about the President.

THE PRESIDENT AND THE PEOPLE

When the queen of England visits the United States, she is honored with the twenty-one gun salute given to heads of state. When the prime minister of England visits America, the welcoming ceremony features only a seventeen gun salute, which is traditional for heads of government. In many foreign countries, such a division of offices— with one person as head of state and another as the head of

---

[1]For more information on the Camp David agreements, see *Time* (October 2, 1978), pp. 8–21; *U.S. News and World Report* (October 2, 1978), pp. 23–29; and *The New York Times* Magazine (January 21, 1979), pp. 20–22, and (January 28, 1979), pp. 32–34.

government—is very common. The head of state is a monarch or a president, and the head of government is a prime minister or premier. In the United States, on the other hand, both positions are combined in one, the President of the United States. The President is both the head of the government, with actual political responsibilities and powers, and the head of state, with ceremonial and symbolic duties.

What difference does it make? As America's symbolic national leader, the President spends much time on ceremonial functions, such as cutting ribbons at dedications and taking pictures with the year's March of Dimes poster child. But even if the President were not the chief of state, those who occupy the office would probably perform such ceremonial functions anyway, because Presidents are politicians. They use these ceremonies—and the press coverage that accompanies them—to enhance their power as national leaders.

Americans tend to identify emotionally with the President. They react with great grief when a President dies in office. For example, many Americans experienced serious physical and emotional distress when President Kennedy was assassinated in 1963.[2] Sidney Verba has called attention to "the intense emotion, the religious observances, and the political-religious symbolism" of American reactions to the assassination of President Kennedy. These reactions, he writes, show that Americans think of the President as "the symbol of the nation."[3] Even the death of President Warren G. Harding, whose national popularity had been declining, caused great national grief.[4]

Because of the symbolic nature of the Presidency, Americans have a great tendency to expect their Presidents to be "superstars." Textbooks on American government perpetuate this belief by referring to the President as the "chief" of everything—chief of state, chief executive, chief diplomat, commander in chief, chief legislator, and chief of party. According to one authority, high expectations force Presidents to make more promises than they can keep and to assume more power than is healthy for the American system.[5]

Another political scientist, Fred Greenstein, has found that the American people think of their political system as a great ship of state, with the President firmly at the helm. Further, the Presidency has important psychological meaning for American citizens. It simplifies their perceptions of government, serves as an outlet for emotional expression, and acts as a symbol of unity. It gives the

---

[2]Paul B. Sheatsley and Jacob J. Feldman, "A National Survey of Public Reactions and Behavior," in Bradley S. Greenberg and Edwin B. Parker, eds., *The Kennedy Assassination and the American Public* (Stanford, California: Stanford University Press, 1965), p. 158.

[3]Sidney Verba, "The Kennedy Assassination and the Nature of Political Commitment," in *The Kennedy Assassination and the American Public*, p. 348.

[4]See F. Russell, *The Shadow of Blooming Grove* (N.Y.: McGraw-Hill, 1968).

[5]Thomas Cronin, "Superman or Textbook President," *Washington Monthly* (October, 1970).

people a vicarious way of taking political action and a sense of social stability.[6]

What Americans expect from their President is not completely clear. Thomas Cronin has pointed out a number of paradoxes in what Americans want their President to be.[7] They apparently want a President to be both tough and gentle. For example, the President is expected to be tough enough to stand up to a foreign adversary but gentle enough to be concerned about less fortunate people in the United States and around the world. They want a President to have strong convictions on issues but to be flexible enough to make compromises when necessary. They expect a President to both lead and listen—to initiate new ideas and new ways of doing things but not to get too far ahead of the American people.

Americans also seem to want their Presidents to be able to inspire the country to high ideals and vigorous action. At the same time, they believe that Presidents should not promise more than they can deliver. Although Americans want their Presidents to be able to work well with Congress and with other officials of the national government, they also expect them to have the courage to stand up for deeply held principles. They want Presidents to be "above politics" but to be political enough to put together a coalition that can govern. They like a President who is ordinary enough to be "one of us," but extraordinary enough to give an uncommon performance. They want a President who can unite the country as a national, rather than just a partisan, figure. They also expect the chief executive to be determined enough to actually lead the country, even though this may cause some division.

Despite these contradictory expectations of the Presidency, Americans tend to "rally round the flag" and support Presidents whenever they take bold action.[8] During the Vietnam War, for example, President Johnson's popularity went up both when he announced a halt in the bombing of North Vietnam and when he announced renewed bombing.[9] Presidents may attempt to use this rallying effect for their own personal ends, as Nixon did when he made his 1972 campaign a "reelect the President" effort.

President Theodore Roosevelt said that America's President is both "a king and a prime minister." He meant that the chief executive is both a real and a symbolic national leader, and in a sense, that is correct. James David Barber maintains that the President is

---

[6]Fred Greenstein, "The Best Known American," in Walter Dean Burnham, ed., *Politics-America* (New York: Van Nostrand, 1973), p. 143.

[7]Thomas Cronin and Rexford G. Tugwell, eds., *The Presidency Reappraised* (New York: Praeger Publishers, 1977), p. 71.

[8]John Mueller, "Presidential Popularity from Truman to Johnson," *American Political Science Review,* 64 (March 1970): 31.

[9]Fred Greenstein, "What the President Means to America: Presidential 'Choice' Between Elections," in James David Barber, ed., *Choosing the President* (Englewood Cliffs, N.J.: Prentice-Hall, 1974), p. 128.

The Presidents and the Polls

From Truman on, presidential "approval curves" (indicating whether people think the President is doing a good job) have been similar. Starting with high approval at the beginning of a term the curves gently slope downward and then slightly upward at the end of a term. Transitory upward "blips" are associated with a kind of rally-'round-the-flag effect, usually after decisive action or following an international crisis. Thus far, President Carter's approval ratings have followed the general pattern.

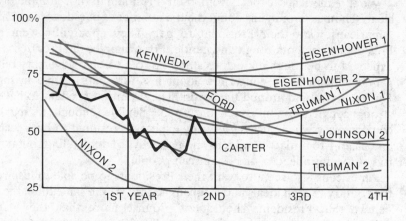

SOURCE: For Truman through Ford: James A. Stinson, "Public Support for American Presidents: A Cyclical Model," *Public Opinion Quarterly* (Spring 1976); for Carter, *Public Opinion* (March-April 1978, November-December 1978). Reprinted from David Gergen and William Schambra, "Pollsters and Polling," *The Wilson Quarterly*, Spring 1979, p. 69.

the "one figure who draws together the people's hopes and fears for the political future. On top of all his routine duties, he has to carry that off—or fail."[10]

Presidents *can* fail, however, and there *are* limits on the influence of the Presidency. The symbolic nature of the Presidency can cause the American people to rapidly turn on the President when events do not turn out the way they think they should. Thus, President Johnson's popularity dropped sharply when he could not successfully conclude the Vietnam War. Similarly, President Nixon's popularity declined when the Watergate scandal could no longer be adequately explained.

Aside from these fluctuations in popular support, Presidents tend to lose popularity and approval throughout their time in office.[11] The paradoxes in American expectations concerning the Presidency may be partly responsible for this trend. It may be partly due to another factor as well. As *Time* magazine has put it:

The once fresh face and crisp, new manner have become as familiar as the local grocer's. What may have been entertaining idiosyncrasies, like Truman's salty language, Eisenhower's chronic golfing and Carter's reflexive grin, can become slightly irritating. No longer larger than life, as on the triumphant eve of inauguration, the mid-term president starts looking all too vulnerably human.[12]

[10]James David Barber, *The Presidential Character: Predicting Performance in the White House* (Englewood Cliffs, N.J.: Prentice-Hall, 1972), p. 4.
[11]Cronin and Tugwell, eds., *The Presidency Reappraised*, pp. 80–81.
[12]*Time* (July 31, 1978), p. 10.

So, as Presidents learn more about their job, their influence, paradoxically, may diminish because of declining public support. President Carter's experience was probably typical. In 1978, two years after his election, he looked back at his first months in office:

I had so much to learn when I first came here. I had to learn the structure of government, the budgeting process. I had to do an enormous amount of background study just to learn where all the nations of the world were and what their major issues might be on a bilateral basis with us.

By 1978, he felt more in command of the job:

I work fewer hours now. I am more relaxed. I am more conversant with the Washington ways. I know much more clearly the strengths and the weaknesses of our own staff, of the cabinet, the Congress, others with whom I have to deal. I think the shortened work day for me is both welcomed and is a sign of an easier approach to the job.[13]

At the time President Carter made this statement, his standing in the polls had slipped to an all-time low. One survey showed that 69 percent of the voters disapproved of the job he was doing.[14]

During the week after the Camp David summit meeting, Carter's approval rating climbed by 16 percent.[15] In the face of continuing energy and economic problems, however, his approval rating soon dropped back down again. By April 1978, Ronald Reagan, a former Republican governor of California, was running even with Carter in the public opinion polls, and Senator Edward Kennedy of Massachusetts was beating him by a margin of 56 to 30 percent.[16]

Political scientists and other observers disagree about the power of the modern Presidency. Some feel that the Presidency has become too "imperial," too powerful.[17] Others argue that the reaction to presidential excesses after the Vietnam and Watergate years has unduly limited presidential authority.[18] In any case, the American Presidency is of central importance in our system. Neither Congress nor the courts can command as much public attention as the President can. According to Thomas E. Cronin, "Whether we like it or not, the vitality of our democracy still depends in large measure on the sensitive interaction of presidential leadership with an understanding public willing to listen and willing to provide support when a president can persuade."[19]

---

[13]*Newsweek* (August 28, 1978), p. 21.

[14]*Time* (August 28, 1978), p. 10.

[15]See *Time* (October 2, 1978), p. 8.

[16]*Time* (April 30, 1979), p. 19.

[17]See, for example, Arthur M. Schlesinger, *The Imperial Presidency* (Boston: Houghton Mifflin Company, 1973).

[18]*Newsweek* (August 28, 1978), p. 15.

[19]Cronin and Tugwell, eds., *The Presidency Reappraised*, p. 70.

THE PRESIDENTIAL OFFICE

Americans are accustomed to news reports that begin, "The White House announced today that . . . ," or "News reports from the Oval Office indicate that . . . " The President's residence and the President's office—both in the same building—seem to have separate identities. At any given time, the Presidency is both an institution and an individual person. The officeholder shapes the office, as we will see later in this chapter. The office—the powers that go with it and the roles that it imposes on the occupant—also shapes the officeholder. A brief examination of the history and development of the Presidency may provide a better understanding of it.

Development of the Modern Presidency

What kind of office did the framers of the Constitution establish when they provided for a "President" to head the new United States of America? It is difficult to say. The framers themselves had some doubts about the nature of the Presidency. There was no office like it in any government in the world at the time.

They had had trouble with kings. They certainly did not want to establish a monarchy in America. Thus, the only news leak that came from the secret meetings of the Constitutional Convention in Philadelphia in 1787 was intended to put an end to a rumor: "Tho' we cannot, affirmatively, tell you what we are doing; we can, negatively, tell you what we are not doing—we never once thought of a king."[20] Yet the delegates' fear of concentrated legislative power was balanced by a similar fear of concentrated executive power. Most of the delegates agreed with Gouverneur Morris, who said that the "Executive Magistrate should be the guardian of the people, even of the lower classes, agst. Legislative tyranny, against the Great & the wealthy who in the course of things will necessarily compose—the Legislative body."[21] Thus, from the beginning, the Presidency was an office with somewhere between "too much" and "not enough" power. One political observer has said:

Not to have an executive that could act would be to have an ineffectual government, but to create an executive that would arouse popular consternation about executive tyranny would be to doom the plan for a new national government. The Founding Fathers had to balance governmental power between these two parameters.[22]

The framers did not spell out in detail the duties and limitations that applied to the President.[23] They failed to clearly define the

---

[20]Carl Van Dorn, *The Great Rehearsal* (New York: Viking Press, 1948), p. 145.

[21]Max Farrand, *The Framing of the Constitution of the United States,* Vol. 2 (New Haven: Yale University Press, 1913), p. 52.

[22]Charles W. Dunn, "The President-Servant to Sun King?" in Charles W. Dunn, ed., *The Future of the American Presidency,* p. 3.

[23]See Edward S. Corwin, *The President: Office and Powers 1787–1957,* 4th ed. (New York: New York University Press, 1957).

Presidency because of their conflicting attitudes toward the chief executive's role and because they were sure that George Washington, a man they trusted, would become the first President under the new Constitution. Article II, Section 1, begins with the words, "The Executive Power shall be vested in a President of the United States of America." The words "Executive Power" are not defined. Yet the framers did make some important decisions concerning the Presidency. First, they decided to have a single executive. A faction at the convention preferred a plural executive; they feared that placing executive power in one person's hands would lead to monarchy. But a majority decided in favor of a "single magistrate, as giving most energy, dispatch, and responsibility to the office." Second, the Convention decided against having the President elected by Congress. This plan had been proposed to make the Presidency an "institution for carrying the will of the legislature into effect." Instead, the framers gave the office of President a separate power base. Finally, they established the outer boundaries of presidential powers.[24] These decisions and boundaries still apply today, of course, but the words of the Constitution regarding the office of President are fairly vague. They leave much to be filled in by actual practice.

Was the President intended to be a kind of elected king or a representative commoner? Nowhere in the Constitution is the answer to that question clearly stated. The first President, George Washington, brought a kind of regal bearing to the office. He resisted becoming an elected king, however, even though some members of the Senate seriously proposed that Washington be addressed as "His Excellency." Jefferson emphasized that the Presidency was not intended to resemble a monarchy. He walked to and from his first inauguration. Jackson further popularized the office, opening the White House to the masses, for example, on the day he was sworn in.

With the administrations of Franklin D. Roosevelt, Eisenhower, Kennedy, Johnson, and Nixon, the Presidency became increasingly "imperial." Nixon, for example, had the White House guards clothed in specially designed "tin soldier" uniforms, a practice he later abandoned in the face of much public joking about such comic-opera presidential pretensions. Presidents Ford and Carter made efforts to tone down the royal aspects of presidential style. Carter reduced the occasions on which "Hail to the Chief"—the only song that belongs exclusively to any national office—would be played. He held "town meetings" at various locations throughout the country, answering audience questions. He appeared on television for "fireside chats" in a sweater, and in his travels around the country, he stayed overnight in private homes.

Whatever the individual styles of Presidents, the Presidency is still held in awe by most Americans. Its powers have been expanded far

Drawing by David Levine. Reprinted with permission from *The New York Review of Books*. Copyright © 1978 NYREV, Inc.

---

[24]For a discussion of the decisions made by the Constitutional Convention concerning the Presidency, see C. Herman Pritchett, "The President's Constitutional Position," in Cronin and Tugwell, eds., *The Presidency Reappraised*, pp. 3–23.

beyond the brief and somewhat vague words of the Constitution. This expansion of presidential powers is due to a number of factors: the actions and outlooks of individual Presidents; the expanded federal role in domestic and economic affairs; the emergence of the United States as a world power in the nuclear age; and a rise in public expectations concerning the Presidency in an era of mass communications.

Individual Presidents have changed the Presidency into an office that requires both national leadership and activism. Andrew Jackson was the first chief executive to transform the Presidency into an office of national leadership. His veto of a bill to recharter the Bank of the United States, which had become especially unpopular in the rural West because it had foreclosed many mortgages during the severe depression of the 1820s, brought him into confrontation with Congress. But it helped to mold the office into one that requires its occupant to execute the will of all the people, not just of the will of the Congress.

Theodore Roosevelt used the Presidency as a "bully pulpit" for rallying the nation. Before he became President, Woodrow Wilson expressed this idea of the President as a leader of the nation: "The nation as a whole has chosen him, and is conscious that it has no other political spokesman. His is the only national voice in affairs. . . . He is the representative of no constituency, but of the whole people."[25] Franklin D. Roosevelt probably asserted the authority of the President to represent the will of the whole nation, instead of the will of Congress, more vigorously than any other chief executive. He vetoed 635 of the bills passed by Congress during his time in office.

With the exception of Eisenhower, modern Presidents have been activists. They have intervened during national crises, claiming that their office gave them the authority to do so. But no President in America's history has stretched the limits of the Constitution as much as Abraham Lincoln did during the extraordinary period of the Civil War. As one authority has written, "It is indeed a striking fact that Lincoln who stands forth in popular conception as a great democrat, the exponent of liberty and of government by the people, was driven by circumstances to the use of more arbitrary power than perhaps any other president has seized."[26] Lincoln believed that his highest duty was to save the Union. Thus, he "carried his executive authority to the extent of freeing the slaves by proclamation, setting up a whole scheme of state-making for the purpose of reconstruction, suspending the *habeas corpus* privilege, proclaiming martial law, enlarging the army and navy beyond the limits fixed by existing law, and spending public money without congressional appropriation." Lincoln recog-

---

[25]Woodrow Wilson, *Constitutional Government in the United States*, quoted in James MacGregor Burns, *Presidential Government* (Boston: Houghton Mifflin, 1965), p. 96.

[26]See James G. Randall, *Constitutional Problems Under Lincoln* (Urbana, Illinois: University of Illinois Press, 1963), pp. 513–522.

nized that most of the steps he took involved powers not usually proper for a President to exercise. Still, the image of the President as activist lingered on after the Civil War crisis.

In modern times, Franklin D. Roosevelt established the pattern for activist Presidents. Coming to office during the Great Depression of the 1930s, when a third of all Americans were out of work, he won "social acceptance of the idea that government should be active and reformist, rather than simply protective of the established order of things."[27] Activist that he was, Roosevelt did not follow established procedures when he was nominated for President. Instead of waiting for several weeks after the 1932 Democratic Convention in Chicago to be formally advised of his nomination, he flew to the Convention and accepted the nomination in person. He was the first presidential nominee to do so. "I pledge you, I pledge myself, to a new deal for the American people," he declared to the cheering Convention delegates.

Franklin D. Roosevelt signing the Social Security Act in 1935. During his administration and afterward, the power of the Presidency increased because of the expanded federal role in domestic and economic affairs.

Roosevelt's New Deal inaugurated the *expanded federal role* in domestic and economic affairs in this country. One authority described Roosevelt's first term as follows:

Headline writers could barely keep pace with lawmakers: ... subsidies to farmers, ... codes for business, relief for unemployed, loans for homeowners, safeguards of "truth in securities," promises of the Tennessee Valley Authority. Amid the Congressional fireworks, some Senators fretted over the long-range implications of this carnival of Presidential initiatives. But Harry Hopkins, who would become Roosevelt's closest counselor, once snapped the retort: "People don't eat 'in the long run.' They eat everyday."[28]

From Roosevelt's time onward, the policy questions that the federal government had to answer became far more complex. Congress became increasingly willing to leave the details of new policies and programs to the various executive agencies and departments over which the President presides.[29] The expanded federal role in domes-

[27]Corwin, *The President*, p. 311.

[28]Emmet John Hughes, "FDR: The Happiest Warrior," *Smithsonian*, 3, no.1, (April 1972): 30–33.

[29]See Raymond Bauer et al., *American Business and Public Policy* (New York: Atherton, 1963).

tic and economic affairs, therefore, has expanded the power of the Presidency.

The Presidency has also gained enormous power as a result of America's *emergence as a world power* in the nuclear age. Following World War II, a "Cold War" developed between the United States and the Soviet Union. Under Truman and Eisenhower, America launched upon a program of "containment of world Communism." Our maintenance of a large standing army, heavy spending for ever more sophisticated weaponry, and the creation of the Central Intelligence Agency paralleled similar actions by the Soviet Union. Our cold-war view of the world and the pursuit of our economic interests caused us to be active in virtually every country on the globe. With some pride, Americans came to think of the President of the United States as the "leader of the free world." They were awed by the fact that it was the President's finger which was on the nuclear button. He could practically blow up the whole world if he decided to. National security and national defense seemed to require the President to be able to act at once in an emergency, without waiting for congressional approval. National security also seemed to dictate extraordinary measures to protect the President from personal harm. Many Americans and many members of Congress came to believe that "the President knows best" and that "only the President has all the information."

These circumstances caused *public expectations* of the President to rise. They also brought a glorification of the Presidency in a mass media era. As a result, Americans have come to expect their President to be an activist national leader. For example, most Americans did not think it especially unusual that President Carter should summon the leaders of two independent foreign nations, Israel and Egypt, to a summit meeting in this country in 1978. They were elated when this meeting, arranged by *our* President, produced a "framework for peace" for that region of the world. On television, they watched the actual signing of that agreement in the White House. As one authority has pointed out, "When George Washington announced his retirement, his words, in print, without any image, took 4 days to reach New York and 10 days to reach outlying regions. When Lyndon Johnson made the same announcement in 1968, he faced an audience of 75 million people."[30] Television news coverage and newspaper reports by the great herd of reporters and photographers who follow the President's every move, have caused the Presidency to seem infinitely larger than life. This media attention has encouraged Americans to feel that a President of the United States can and must intervene to do something about all the problems that each of us faces.

---

[30]William W. Lammers, *Presidential Politics: Patterns and Prospects* (New York: Harper and Row, 1976), p. 49.

It would be correct, in a sense, to say that the President of the United States wears many hats. But this statement gives the impression that the President takes off one hat before putting on another, which is not true. The President usually wears several, or even all, of the hats at the same time. In other words, the chief executive serves in several roles simultaneously.

The President's roles as chief of state, our principal ceremonial official, and as the symbolic leader of the country were examined earlier in the chapter. Presidents are also politicians. Their function as the leader of their political party will be discussed later in this chapter. In the following section, we will consider formal presidential roles and powers that are rooted in the U.S. Constitution: executive manager; policy initiator; chief diplomat; and commander in chief.

Executive Manager

The Constitution makes the President the manager of the executive department, the head of government or chief executive. Article II, Section 3, declares that the President of the United States shall "take care that the Laws be faithfully executed." Among other things, this provision means that the President is our principal law enforcer. The chief executive, then, has the job of seeing that the Constitution, laws passed by Congress, and decisions and orders of the courts are carried out. Congress can enact a civil rights law, for example, or the Supreme Court may interpret the Constitution to require desegregation of the public schools, but the President has the power to order federal marshals to enforce such a law or ruling. The President may also nationalize the National Guard within a state or even call out U.S. Army troops to enforce the law.

Of course, no one person can be responsible for all of the details involved in administering the executive branch. Much of the day-to-day responsibility must be delegated to subordinates. According to Article II, Section 2, of the Constitution, the President has broad appointive powers, enabling him to choose those who will assist in carrying out the law. The principal positions prescribed by the Constitution or by law must be filled "by and with the Advice and Consent of the Senate." The President's personal aides, however, are not subject to Senate confirmation. The power of appointment gives the President preeminence in the executive department.

Immediately after being elected in November, a new President-elect must begin to make plans for taking over the office in January. Today, the law provides special federal funds and other assistance for the transition from one President to another. During this transitional period, a widespread talent search is made. This allows the President to make choices soon after the inauguration about who will serve in

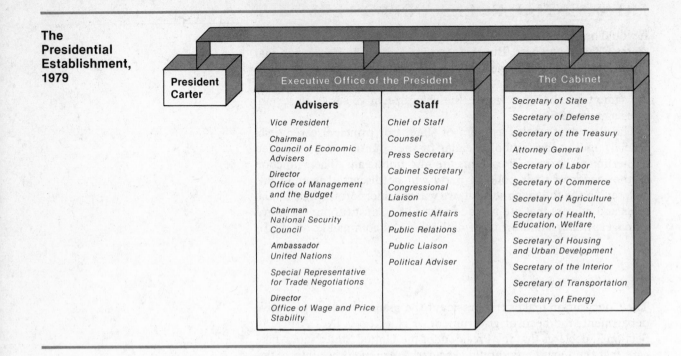

The Presidential Establishment, 1979

President Carter

Executive Office of the President

Advisers	**Staff**
Vice President	Chief of Staff
Chairman Council of Economic Advisers	Counsel
Director Office of Management and the Budget	Press Secretary
Chairman National Security Council	Cabinet Secretary
Ambassador United Nations	Congressional Liaison
Special Representative for Trade Negotiations	Domestic Affairs
Director Office of Wage and Price Stability	Public Relations
	Public Liaison
	Political Adviser

The Cabinet

Secretary of State
Secretary of Defense
Secretary of the Treasury
Attorney General
Secretary of Labor
Secretary of Commerce
Secretary of Agriculture
Secretary of Health, Education, Welfare
Secretary of Housing and Urban Development
Secretary of the Interior
Secretary of Transportation
Secretary of Energy

various appointed positions. In most government agencies and departments, only the principal positions at the top are subject to presidential appointment and removal at will. Most of these must be confirmed by the Senate. The President can also choose—and dismiss—virtually all the White House staff at will. These positions do not require Senate confirmation. But the overwhelming majority of positions in the bureaucracy of the federal government are permanent positions. Thus, the bureaucrats who are already in the executive department when the President is elected continue to serve, unless they are removed for "cause" under a very complicated procedure.

Although the Constitution does not provide for a *cabinet*, all Presidents have used some form of one. Today, the heads of the twelve executive departments make up the cabinet. These cabinet positions range from the secretary of the interior to the secretary of energy to the secretary of state. In addition, other officials are sometimes given cabinet rank; that is, they are allowed to meet with the cabinet at its formal sessions and are given the same deference as cabinet members. For example, President Carter accorded cabinet status to the director of the Office of Management and Budget and the special trade representative. In addition to the cabinet, there are a number of *independent agencies* in the executive department, such as the General Services Administration and the Veterans Administration. They report directly to the President, but they do not have cabinet rank.

The law does not require the cabinet to meet as a group; this is simply a matter of custom.[31] The President alone decides whether to seek and follow the advice of the cabinet as a group. Abraham Lincoln reportedly rejected the counsel of his cabinet on one occasion by announcing, "Seven nays, one aye—the ayes have it."

From time to time, various observers of the Presidency have suggested strengthening the cabinet as an institution. U.S. Representative Morris K. Udall of Arizona, a Democratic candidate for President in 1976, supports such a suggestion:

In my judgment, we are going to have to restore the cabinet and give the president some big men with national reputations who can say "no." . . . And above all, the president is going to have to learn to listen to his cabinet members' advice and give it careful consideration, even if he ultimately rejects their proposals. [32]

In recent years, most Presidents—including Jimmy Carter—have announced their intention to give more power and recognition to the cabinet. With the exception of President Eisenhower, however, they have not kept this pledge.

Presidents have been reluctant to give greater power to the cabinet for several reasons. First, Presidents tend to turn to experts when they seek advice on questions. For example, when a decision must be made on a national security matter, Presidents turn only to those advisers with special experience in that field. Asking each cabinet member—including the secretary of housing and urban development and the secretary of transportation, for example—to comment on a national security matter at a cabinet meeting would be viewed by most Presidents as a waste of time.

Second, Presidents often choose a particular person to fill a cabinet position because of the appointee's independent stature and following. Thus Presidents may feel obliged to appoint a person acceptable to organized labor as secretary of labor and a person acceptable to business as secretary of commerce. They may select a black person, for example, as secretary of housing and urban development and a prominent woman or Italian-American to fill another cabinet position. But Presidents may turn to other advisers, especially White House staff members, for the most influential advice on particular problems. Since Presidents are generally not so worried about how White House staff appointments will look, they give greater consideration to loyalty and expertise when filling these positions.

Third, cabinet officials are likely to develop a certain amount of independence from the White House because of the nature of their positions. For one thing, cabinet officials, unlike White House staff members, can take office only after confirmation by the U.S. Senate.

[31]See Richard F. Fenno, Jr., *The President's Cabinet* (Cambridge, Mass.: Harvard University Press, 1959).
[32]Morris K. Udall, "A Democrat Looks at the Presidency," in Dunn, ed., *The Future of the American Presidency*, p. 244.

They are therefore clearly subject to being called before Senate and House committees from time to time to give account of their stewardship. Also cabinet officials have a dual responsibility—to the President and federal government, on one hand, and to their departments and the constituents of their departments, on the other. According to one authority, the formal responsibilities of a cabinet officer "extend both upward toward the president and downward toward his own department."[33]

Fourth, after their appointment, cabinet officials naturally come to be somewhat removed from day-to-day involvement with the President because of their physical separation from the White House. Cabinet officials have offices in separate buildings, and they must usually go through a "gate keeper," or appointments secretary, on the White House staff to see the President in person or talk to him on the telephone. The physical proximity of the White House staff to the President increases the staff's influence, while the physical distance of cabinet officials from the President limits their influence.

Most modern Presidents, then, have begun their terms by appointing people of stature to cabinet positions. They have announced their intention to give the cabinet officials considerable flexibility in running their own departments, often allowing them to name their own subordinates. But most Presidents have come to feel that cabinet officials and their assistants are not as loyal to them or as supportive of their policies as they should be. These problems do not usually occur with the *Executive Office of the President*, which consists of the White House staff and the heads of certain special offices.

Hamilton Jordan (left), White House chief of staff, and Jody Powell, White House press secretary, confer with President Carter.

Presidents use a number of criteria to choose *White House staff* members. Particularly important are personal loyalty to the President, political effectiveness, and personal compatibility with the President. For this reason, many staff members come from the President's campaign organization. Others may be chosen for their expertise on certain subjects or for dealing with Congress. When choosing White House staff members, Presidents place less emphasis on the public relations effect of such appointments than they do on the choice of cabinet officials. White House staff members help to

---

[33]Fenno, *The President's Cabinet,* p. 218.

schedule the President's time; they give advice on policy matters, public relations, and on dealing with the press. They also act as a conduit between the President, on one hand, and the executive departments and Congress, on the other.

In addition to the White House staff, the Executive Office of the President is made up of several relatively permanent special offices, which are headed by presidential appointees. One of the most important offices is the Council of Economic Advisers. Under the provisions of the 1946 Employment Act, it advises the President on the state of the economy and what should be done concerning it. The Office of Management and Budget is the President's principal agency for managing the vast bureaucracy of the executive department and for preparing and administering the federal budget. The National Security Council coordinates the President's relationship with the various national security agencies and departments, such as the State Department, the Defense Department, and the Central Intelligence Agency. Two other important offices are the Special Representative for Trade Negotiations and the Council on Wage and Price Stability.

The *Vice-President* can be an important assistant to the President, but this largely depends on what the President wants. Vice-presidential nominees are generally chosen soon after the party convention selects its presidential nominee. Party conventions regularly approve the presidential nominee's choice for a running mate. Candidates often make this choice for political reasons. For example, they may use the selection of the vice-presidential nominee to balance out regional, religious, or other factors and thus to add strength to the political support of the presidential nominee in the general election campaign. Sometimes, vice-presidential nominees are chosen simply because they will not *hurt* the ticket.

Modern Presidents have used their Vice-Presidents as partisan voices—to attack the opposition, to speak at party functions around the country, and to sell the President's program to the people. Some Presidents have given governmental duties to their Vice-Presidents as well. In most instances, however, a gap has developed between the offices of the President and the Vice-President. The two staffs have often become estranged. The President cannot fire a Vice-President during the term for which they both were elected, and Presidents and their staffs have been conscious of the fact that they cannot freely give orders to a Vice-President in the same way they can to presidential appointees.

No President has established a closer working relationship with a Vice-President than President Carter has with Vice-President Walter F. Mondale. Carter has used Mondale as an assistant to the President. With his office in the White House—an innovation—Vice-President Mondale is in close physical proximity to President Carter. Another innovation allows Vice-President Mondale to share the services of the President's own staff rather than maintaining a separate one. Carter and Mondale apparently enjoy a considerable

Vice-President Walter Mondale delivering a speech at the 1978 United Nations Conference on Disarmament. Mondale has been an activist Vice-President, serving in effect as a special adviser and assistant to President Carter.

degree of personal compatibility. Since Carter is new to the Washington scene, while Mondale is not (he served as an important senator from Minnesota before becoming Vice-President), Carter has called upon the Vice-President for advice and other assistance on matters ranging from political questions to congressional relations and policy decisions. By contrast, when Truman was Vice-President under Franklin Roosevelt, he was not brought into the high-level councils of government. He was not aware, for example, that the United States had begun development of an atomic bomb until he acceded to the Presidency after Roosevelt's death.

Vice-Presidents, then, have as much or as little authority in the government as Presidents want them to have. Still, the Vice-Presidency is an attractive office for politicians, if for no other reason than that so many of them have held this "understudy" office before becoming President themselves through succession or election.

Presidents often turn to trusted friends for advice and assistance and to members of their own family. President Carter, for example, has often relied upon the counsel of his friend Charles Kirbo. President Kennedy appointed his brother-in-law, Sargent Shriver, to head the Peace Corps and his brother, Robert F. Kennedy, to be Attorney General. President Carter has used his sons and his mother to represent him for various political or official purposes. The President's mother, Lillian Carter, represented the United States at the funeral of Pope John Paul I.

In modern times, a President's spouse has been an important presidential assistant. Since all Presidents to date have been men, the President's spouse has been called the *first lady*. Eleanor Roosevelt set the pattern for modern first ladies, acting as Franklin Roosevelt's liberal conscience and as his political eyes and ears. She spoke out publicly on issues and sometimes disagreed with her husband on issues, such as the internment of Japanese-Americans during World War II.[34] Bess Truman, Mamie Eisenhower, and Pat Nixon were less publicly involved with matters of policy. Jacqueline Kennedy largely confined her public activities to the arts. Lady Bird Johnson, on the other hand, involved herself with a number of public issues, particularly beautification. Betty Ford spoke in favor of the Equal Rights Amendment and became an activist public figure in her own right. President Carter's wife, Rosalynn, has emerged as a trusted adviser to her husband on a wide range of issues. She served as the chairperson of the President's National Commission on Mental Health, and she has represented the President on foreign missions to Latin American countries. One magazine reported:

Mrs. Carter keeps in touch with what goes on beyond her surprisingly bare desk in a small, unpretentious East Wing office. She slips into Cabinet meetings and high-level briefings, like the one held this month

[34]See a photo essay in Mary Klein, ed., *Viewpoints: The Presidency: The Power and Glory* (Minneapolis, Minnesota: Winston Press, 1973), p. 37.

by Vice President Walter Mondale on his return from a Middle East trip. 'I try to stay knowledgeable,' she explains. 'I just try to keep up with what is happening.' Then, in her quiet way, she tells Carter what she thinks. And he listens.[35]

Today, the first lady has her own offices and staff in the East Wing of the White House, and she is expected to perform more than merely social or informal functions.

Policy Initiator

While the basic concept underlying the organization of our national government is a separation of powers between the executive, legislative, and judicial branches, there is also a fusion, or sharing of many of these powers. Although Congress has most of the legislative power, the President and the executive department have the authority to develop regulations to put laws into effect. In this sense, the executive branch has legislative power. (This subject is discussed more thoroughly in Chapter 14.) The President has legislative power, too, because of the influence of the Presidency on congressional action. This influence can be negative or positive. Article I, Section 7, of the Constitution gives the President a *veto power*. When the President vetoes, or rejects, a bill passed by Congress, the measure cannot become law unless it is thereafter approved by a two-thirds vote in both the House and Senate. Since Congress cannot usually muster that kind of a vote, the President's will generally prevails in this kind of a confrontation. A President can often change the nature of proposed legislation and bring about certain compromises by merely threatening veto. In 1978, for example, President Carter said "no" to the Congress on an appropriation for a new nuclear carrier (thereby bolstering his image of a person of convictions). "A veto is a prerogative that a president is given under the Constitution," he said at the time. "It is not an abnormal authority. It is one that should be a routine part of the interrelationship between the White House and Capitol Hill. And it is not only a pleasure to have that authority to make my own leverage more effective, but it is a duty that falls on me."[36]

Carter's veto of nuclear carrier funds was his first on a major bill. It was only the fifth time he had exercised the power during his first nineteen months in office. But his subsequent veto of a public works bill showed that he intended to assert this negative power more frequently in the future.

If the President neither signs nor vetoes a bill within ten working days after Congress has passed it and sent it to him, the bill becomes law without his signature. If, during this ten-day period, Congress adjourns and the President fails to act on the bill, it is killed by a

---

[35]*Time* (July 31, 1978), p. 13.
[36]*Time* (August 28, 1978), p. 10.

pocket veto. Presidents do not have the power of *item veto* which allows some state governors to veto a particular item in a bill passed by a state legislature. Presidents must either accept or reject an entire legislative measure, whether or not they like every item in it.

Another negative legislative power used by Presidents is *impoundment*, the refusal to spend all the money appropriated by Congress. No provision in the Constitution authorizes Presidents to spend money that has not first been appropriated by Congress. But the Constitution is silent on the question of whether a President *must* spend *all* the money that Congress appropriates. No President has ever exercised this power more vigorously than did President Nixon, who refused to spend money appropriated for a number of social welfare programs. His extensive impoundment of funds caused Congress to pass the Congressional Budget and Impoundment Act of 1974, a law that severely curtails this presidential power. If a President delays spending funds appropriated by Congress, Congress may now force the immediate expenditure of such funds through a simple resolution passed by either the House or Senate. A President cannot permanently halt the expenditure of appropriated funds unless both houses of Congress approve this action within forty-five days after the impoundment.[37]

Under the Constitution, Presidents also have *affirmative* legislative powers. Article II, Section 3, states:

He shall from time to time give to the Congress Information of the State of the Union, and recommend to their Consideration such Measures as he shall judge necessary and expedient; he may, on extraordinary Occasions, convene both houses, or either of them, and in case of disagreement between them, with Respect to the time of Adjournment, he may adjourn them to such Time as he shall think proper.

President Carter meeting with congressional leaders. Presidents use persuasion to gain congressional and public support for their legislative proposals.

No President has ever adjourned Congress, but all Presidents now give a state of the Union address at the beginning of each congressional session. They also send a barrage of legislative proposals and recommendations to Congress. The proposed federal budget that Presidents submit to each Congress is particularly important. It sets forth the President's priorities on governmental policies and expenditures. The Constitution, of course, does not require Congress to go along with the President's legislative proposals, recommendations, or assessments of the state of the Union.

---

[37]See Congressional Quarterly, *Powers of Congress,* p. 43.

Some writers have over-emphasized the President's legislative power. According to one authority, "The agency of the Presidential office has been such a master force in shaping public policy that to give a detailed account of it would be equivalent to writing the political history of the United States. From Jackson's time to the present day it may be said that political issues have been decided by executive policy."[38]

But other studies show that many important legislative advances have come not from the President but from Congress.[39] One political observer writes:

From the half-thousand individualists who make up the two houses of Congress the annual harvest of legislative proposals continues uninterrupted. That many of these ideas may be impractical is beside the point. The constant replenishment of the supply is the important thing. . . . From these suggestions come not only the stimulus for positive action but also much of the substance that will eventually become law.[40]

Describing the President's role of chief legislator as a "paper title," a contemporary writer says, "The origins of most of the innovative legislation in the last ten years, or the last century, can be found in Congress."[41] Presidents do have a time disadvantage. They are now limited to two elective terms, while members of Congress usually serve for much greater lengths of time. As a familiar saying in the Congress goes: "Presidents come and go, but the Congress remains."

Still, Presidents have great influence over legislation and congressional action. They have a far greater impact on legislation than any single member of Congress. Presidents derive much of their legislative influence from their access to the American public. Some of it also comes from their ability to speak as the representative of all the people, while casting Congress as susceptible to the special interests. Thus, in 1978 Jimmy Carter said, "The fight against inflation becomes nearly impossible when the pressures of special interest lobbyists are successful. These lobbyists care nothing about the national interest—as long as they get theirs. We will never win the fight against inflation unless we help the Congress to resist these pressures."[42] But attacks on the Congress generate congressional resentment and may help to cause a government stalemate. One such impasse occurred when the House of Representatives turned down

---

[38]Henry Jones Ford, "The Presidency and Congress," in Wildavsky, ed., *The Presidency,* p. 433.

[39]See Lawrence H. Chamberlain, "The President, Congress, and Legislation," *Political Science Quarterly,* 61, no.1 (March 1946): 42–60; and H.C. Gallagher, "The President, Congress, and Legislation," Cronin and Tugwell, eds., *The Presidency Reappraised,* pp. 267–82.

[40]Chamberlain, "The President, Congress, and Legislation," p. 60.

[41]Gallagher, "The President, Congress, and Legislation," p. 281.

[42]*Time* (August 28, 1978), p. 11.

President Carter's gasoline rationing proposal in 1979. Further, the President's ability to sway Congress through public opinion decreases as his national popularity decreases. This, too, was a severe problem for President Carter in 1979, when his job approval rating dropped to 30 percent.[43]

Chief Diplomat

The Constitution established a system of shared power within the federal government for making the nation's foreign policy.[44] Article II, Section 2, of the Constitution gives the President the power to negotiate and sign treaties with foreign countries, but treaties do not go into effect until ratified by a two-thirds vote in the U.S. Senate. Similarly, the President may appoint the secretary of state and U.S. ambassadors to foreign countries, but these officials cannot take office until they have been confirmed by a majority vote in the U.S. Senate. The President may make agreements with foreign nations and take other actions in regard to foreign policy, but such agreements and actions cannot proceed, if they require funds, until such funds have been appropriated by Congress for that purpose.

Yet the President exercises the dominant power in the field of foreign policy. Although the Senate must ratify a treaty before it becomes effective, only the President can negotiate a treaty. The Senate cannot name a secretary of state or a U.S. ambassador. It can only approve or disapprove presidential nominees for these offices and it nearly always approves.

Article II, Section 3, declares that the President "shall receive Ambassadors and other public Ministers." Presidents have used this clause to assert the power to recognize foreign governments and established formal relations with them—without seeking Congressional approval. For example, President Roosevelt recognized the Soviet Union in 1932, and President Truman gave formal recognition to Israel in 1948 without congressional authorization. Similarly, President Carter acted alone to establish formal relations with the People's Republic of China in 1979.

The Supreme Court has upheld the President's *implied* power to enter into "executive agreements" with foreign nations, without necessarily submitting them to the Senate for approval.[45] Since the early 1970s, Congress has increasingly resisted the use of executive agreements in place of treaties. A Senate study found numerous instances of commitments and secret agreements between the U.S. government and foreign nations throughout the 1960s. They involved such countries as Ethiopia, Laos, Thailand, South Korea, and Spain. In 1971, the Congress passed a nonbinding resolution stating that such agreements should be submitted in the future to the Senate for

---

[43]*CBS/New York Times* Poll (June 10, 1979).
[44]Corwin, *The President*, p. 171.
[45]See *United States* v. *Pink*, 315 U.S. 203 (1942).

approval before being put into effect. In addition, the Case Act requires the secretary of state to submit to Congress the final text of any international agreement made by the executive branch within sixty days after it is signed. This legislation, however, does not require congressional approval of these agreements.[46]

One political scientist, Aaron Wildavsky, has written of the "two presidencies": the power of the President in foreign and in domestic policy. He points out that from 1948 to 1964, Presidents secured congressional approval for their domestic policy proposals in only 40 percent of the cases, but "in the realm of foreign policy there . . . [was] not . . . a single major issue on which presidents, when they were serious and determined, have failed."[47] But another political observer, writing more recently, says that the imbalance in foreign-policy power between the President and Congress has been reduced because the Cold War sense of peril has diminished and because Americans' reactions to the Vietnam War have subsided.[48]

In addition to congressional limitations, the President is subject to the broad constraints of public opinion on foreign policy matters. But Presidents can help to shape public opinion, as President Nixon did when he visited the People's Republic of China. According to one writer, "If Congress would strengthen its role, especially when that role appears vital for the proper performance of the country's external relations, it has no choice but to discover some effective means to challenge the president's control of the public mind, a hard chore."[49]

Commander in Chief

Article II, Section 2, of the Constitution provides that "The President shall be Commander in Chief of the Army and Navy of the United States, and of the Militia of the several states, when called into the actual service of the United States." The President appoints and promotes the officers of the armed forces. But the war-making powers are divided between the executive and legislative branches. In Article I, Section 8, the framers gave Congress the power to "provide for the common Defence," declare war, and raise and support armies. Since the Constitutional Convention gave to Congress the power to "declare" war, leaving to the President only the authority to

---

[46]For a discussion of the powers of Congress and the President in regard to foreign policy, see Congressional Quarterly, *Powers of Congress* (Washington, D.C.: Congressional Quarterly, 1976), pp. 58–78.

[47]Aaron Wildavsky, "The Two Presidencies," *Trans-Action* (December 1968), reprinted in *Readings in American Government* (Guilford, Connecticut: Dushkin Publishing, 1975), p. 72.

[48]See Donald A. Peppers, "The Two Presidencies: Eight Years Later," in Aaron Wildavsky, ed., *Perspectives on the Presidency* (Boston: Little, Brown and Company, 1975).

[49]Norman A. Graebner, "Presidential Power and Foreign Affairs," in Dunn, ed., *The Future of the American Presidency*, p. 200.

"make" war, Alexander Hamilton probably expressed the general opinion of the framers when he said that the power of the President as commander in chief "would amount to nothing more than the supreme command and direction of the military and naval forces, as First General and Admiral of the Confederacy."[50] But history has shown that Presidents have used their power as commander in chief in a much more assertive way. America was involved in the Korean War under President Truman and in the Vietnam War under Presidents Kennedy, Johnson, and Nixon, without any formal declaration of war by Congress. The Korean War was called a "conflict." American troops were sent there in response to a United Nations resolution, adopted in the U.N. Security Council while the Soviet Union was boycotting the international organization's meetings. President Kennedy sent troops to Vietnam as military "advisers." President Johnson greatly escalated America's direct involvement in that war after an alleged attack on one of our naval ships led Congress to pass the Tonkin Gulf Resolution, a nonbinding measure that stopped short of a declaration of war. The Tonkin Gulf attack was later shown to have been either entirely fictional or extremely minor in significance.

In both the Korean and the Vietnam wars, Congress could have ended U.S. military involvement at any time, over the President's objection. Congress could have cut off all funds for such wars. They could have adopted a joint resolution prohibiting the further use of American troops. But Congress failed to act on this issue. Congress' inaction caused Arthur Schlesinger, Jr., to write:

If there is an imbalance of powers, if Congress has lost authority clearly conferred by the Constitution, it can only be said that Congress has done little to correct the situation. Its complaints have been eloquent; its practical action has been slight. Its problem has been less lack of power than lack of will to use the power it has—the power of appropriation, the power to regulate the size of the armed forces, the power, through joint resolutions, to shape foreign policy, the power to inform, investigate and censure.[51]

After Schlesinger wrote those words, the Congress did act to redress the imbalance in congressional and presidential war powers. In 1973, Congress passed the War Powers Act over President Nixon's veto. This law requires the President to report to Congress in writing within forty-eight hours after committing any armed forces to foreign combat. It further provides that combat must end within sixty days thereafter, unless it is specifically authorized by Congress.[52] Congress followed up the War Powers Act in 1974 with a law requiring the

---

[50]*Federalist,* no. 69.

[51]Arthur Schlesinger, Jr., "Congress and the Making of American Foreign Policy," in Cronin and Tugwell, eds., *The Presidency Reappraised,* p. 104.

[52]For a discussion of the history and development of the war powers of Congress and the President, see Congressional Quarterly, *Powers of Congress,* pp. 79–98.

Central Intelligence Agency (CIA) to report its covert activities to Congress. In 1976, Congress passed a law reserving for itself the power to veto any foreign arms sales approved by the President that amount to $7 million or more.

Thus far, we have discussed the presidential *office*. But what the Presidency is, or should be, results from both the office and the *officeholder*. Each affects the other, and each is affected by events and by the times.

THE PRESIDENTIAL OFFICEHOLDER

Article II, Section 1 of the Constitution sets forth the qualifications for President. Presidents must be "natural born" U.S. citizens, who have resided in the United States for at least fourteen years and who are at least thirty-five years old. Theoretically, every American boy or girl who meets these qualifications can become President. But few people run for the office, and fewer still are chosen. America has had only thirty-nine Presidents since the Constitution was adopted. Not many Americans during that period would even have been considered presidential possibilities. From 1936 to 1972, for example, only sixty-two Democrats and forty-two Republicans were favored for a presidential nomination by even 1 percent or more of their fellow partisans.[53]

It is possible for a person to become President of the United States without ever having been elected to that office. The Constitution provides that upon the President's death, resignation, or inability to discharge the powers and duties of the office, the Vice-President will assume the office. After the Vice-President, the next officers in line to serve as President are, in order of succession, the speaker of the House and the president pro tempore of the Senate. After that come cabinet officials; precedence is based upon the date when the cabinet position was created. The secretary of state comes first among cabinet officials. The Twenty-Fifth Amendment to the Constitution, adopted in 1967, spelled out the procedures for determining when a President is disabled.

AT YOUR DISPOSAL . . .

Once, as President Lyndon B. Johnson was striding toward the second of three helicopters waiting to whisk him away from the White House lawn, a uniformed Army aide took him by the arm to guide him toward the front helicopter. "This is your helicopter over here, Mr. President," the aide said. Johnson proceeded straight ahead. "They're all my helicopters, boy," he is reported to have said.

Whether it happened just like that or not, it could have, given Johnson's temperament. And there is much truth in the reported Johnson retort. All that the federal government owns and all those who work for the executive department are at the disposal of the President when they are needed for official business. There are cars and drivers, planes and pilots, barbers, photographers, swimming pools, national parks and presidential retreats, cooks, speechwriters, image consultants, pollsters, military strategists, economists, and television experts—and, more importantly, cabinet officials and heads of independent agencies, the White House staff, the Executive Office of the President, and the Vice-President.

---

[53]William R. Keech and Donald R. Matthews, *The Party's Choice* (Washington, D.C.: The Brookings Institution, 1977), p. 222.

Vice-President Lyndon B. Johnson succeeded to the Presidency upon the death of President Kennedy. Vice-President Gerald R. Ford became President after President Nixon resigned. Ford had never been elected Vice-President. Following procedures established by the Twenty-Fifth Amendment, President Nixon had nominated him for the Vice-Presidency when Spiro Agnew resigned from the office after being convicted of income tax evasion charges related to bribery. Ford was required to be confirmed by a majority vote in both houses of Congress. Similarly, after President Ford became President, Nelson Rockefeller became Vice-President through appointment by Ford and confirmation by Congress.

The original Constitution did not specify how long a President could serve. Franklin D. Roosevelt was the only President to serve more than two terms. He was elected four times, although he died soon after being inaugurated for his last term. Vice-President Truman then succeeded to that office. During his administration, in 1951, the Twenty-Second Amendment to the Constitution was ratified. It limits Presidents to two elected terms, or to a maximum of ten years if they succeed to the office without first being elected.

There is a sameness about the age, sex, race, and religion of modern Presidents. President Kennedy was the youngest—forty-three when he took office. The rest ranged in age from fifty-one years at the time of original inauguration (Franklin Roosevelt), to sixty-two (Dwight Eisenhower). From George Washington to Jimmy Carter, all American Presidents have been white men. No woman, no black or other minority person, and no Jew or other non-Christian has ever served as President.

Until John Kennedy's election in 1960, no Catholic had ever been elevated to America's highest political office. It is widely believed that the Catholicism of the 1928 Democratic nominee, Al Smith, was a significant factor in his defeat. After Kennedy confounded the "experts" and broke the Catholic "taboo," however, it has never again been a factor in presidential politics. When Democrat Edmund Muskie of Maine, a Catholic, ran a prominent but unsuccessful campaign for the Democratic presidential nomination in 1972, his religion was never even raised as an issue. (Some observers, therefore, thought it ironic that Senator Muskie stated during his campaign that a presidential ticket featuring a black person as the presidential or vice-presidential candidate could probably not be elected. Because of his prominence, Muskie's statement probably delayed the day when the experts could be confounded on the issue of race, and when this taboo, too, could be set aside.)

Although most Americans live in urban areas, only one modern American President—John Kennedy of Boston—was born and raised in a large city. Lyndon Johnson was from Stonewall, Texas, for example, and Jimmy Carter came from Plains, Georgia.

All modern Presidents except Truman were financially secure when they took office. Some, like Johnson, had accumulated a considerable amount of wealth; others, like Kennedy, had inherited great wealth. But, as William R. Keech and Donald R. Matthews note, Presidents who come from affluent backgrounds are not necessarily more likely to be on the side of the rich than those who come from more modest financial backgrounds.

One of the wealthiest American presidents, Franklin Roosevelt, is considered by some to have been the most radical in recent times. More conservative presidents like Eisenhower and Nixon had more modest backgrounds. In 1964, two rich men from the Southwest ran against one another for the presidency. One was a conservative, the other a liberal who, on his election, proceeded to ram through Congress the most sweeping package of domestic reforms since the New Deal.[54]

Whatever their age, sex, race, religion, financial situation, or where they grew up, all the people who have been elected President of the United States in modern times have sought the office.

The President as Politician

In parliamentary systems of government like Great Britain's, the head of government, the prime minister, is elected by the parliamentary body, the House of Commons, from among its membership. Thus the road to national political leadership is fairly well charted in those systems: one moves up through the ranks of party and parliament. No such well-defined route to America's Presidency exists.

Since Franklin D. Roosevelt's first election in 1932, all Presidents except one have been professional politicians. The one exception was Dwight D. Eisenhower, who gained national attention and fame as an Army general. Four modern Presidents first served as Vice-President: Truman, Nixon, Johnson, and Ford. Four had previously served in the United States Senate: Truman, Kennedy, Johnson, and Nixon. Four had served in the U.S. House of Representatives: Ford, Johnson, Nixon, and Kennedy. Two had been governors: Roosevelt and Carter.

There has been no "draft" of a President since the first days of the Republic, when it *was* generally agreed that George Washington should become our first chief executive. What was true for Abraham Lincoln, the politician, is equally true for Jimmy Carter, the politician. Lincoln was active in politics for years prior to his election as President. David Donald, a well-known historian, has written:

Behind that facade of humble directness and folksy humor, Lincoln was moving steadily toward his object; by 1860 he had maneuvered himself into a position where he controlled the party machinery, platform, and candidates of one of the pivotal states in the Union. A Chicago lawyer who had known Lincoln intimately for three decades

---

[54]Keech and Matthews, *The Party's Choice*, p. 218.

summarized these pre-presidential years: "one great public mistake . . . generally received and acquiesed in, is that he is considered by the people of this country as a frank, guileless, and unsophisticated man. There never was a greater mistake. . . . He handled and moved men remotely as we do pieces upon a chessboard."[55]

This view of Lincoln the politician takes nothing away from him. Democracy cannot operate unless some people participate in its processes enough to stand—and run—for public office.

In order to run for President, a person must have made a "name" for himself or herself, at least regionally, and must have attracted some followers and supporters. A person generally needs to be "mentioned" as a possible contender for the Presidency. Some political observers have facetiously said that there is a "Great Mentioner in the sky," who makes up lists of those who are of presidential timber. Columnists regularly write articles that carry words like the following: "Among those mentioned for President are . . . ."

Being accorded contender status in advance by the "pros" and "pundits" (political columnists) is not nearly as important today for presidential candidates as it once was. The proliferation of party primaries, the reform of the party nomination processes, the adoption of new laws on campaign financing, and the provision of federal preconvention matching funds have reduced the role of the pundits and the pros. Jimmy Carter had little support from national leaders in his party and was given little chance by national political observers. But he won the Democratic nomination for President in 1976 and defeated the incumbent President, Gerald Ford, in the general election. He did this by running much better than expected in the earliest delegate-selection contests. So, today it can be said that the "Great Mentioner" can be *made* to consider candidates as being of presidential timber if the candidates are determined enough and achieve some early campaign successes.

Despite advances in campaign financing laws, presidential candidates must still have some money to run a successful campaign and must still be able to attract skillful and dedicated workers and supporters. The money they need may be their own, or it may come from friends and supporters. Consider this question, for example: what does a presidential candidate live on while campaigning? President Carter used the income from his peanut business. Other candidates, such as Senator Henry M. Jackson of Washington and Representative Morris Udall of Arizona, continued to draw their congressional salaries while campaigning for the Presidency in 1976. Gerald Ford drew his salary as President while campaigning for election to that office.

Although an incumbent President has a number of advantages,

---

[55]David Donald, "A. Lincoln, Politician," in Aaron Wildavsky, ed., *The Presidency* (Boston: Little, Brown and Company, 1969), p. 125.

they are not insuperable, as Gerald Ford's defeat in 1976 shows. From 1936 to the present, all incumbent Presidents, except Gerald Ford, who sought reelection were successful. It should be noted, however, that President Johnson wanted to run for reelection in 1968 but decided not to do so because of great opposition to his Vietnam War policy.[56]

The power base of American Presidents is separate from that of Congress. Presidents are not elected by Congress but by a vote of the people. Because of the Electoral College, of course, voters in each state do not vote *directly* for presidential candidates. They vote for electors, who are pledged to presidential candidates. After the election, the electors meet at the capitol in each state and almost always cast the state's total number of electoral votes for the winning slate—the presidential and vice-presidential candidates who received the highest number of popular votes in the state. The Constitution did not originally provide for a presidential and vice-presidential slate. Instead, the candidate who received the highest number of national electoral votes, if it was a majority, was designated President. The person receiving the second highest total of national electoral votes became the Vice-President, unless there was a tie. The Twelfth Amendment, adopted in 1804, changed these procedures; electors now cast separate ballots for the office of President and the office of Vice-President, and the candidates run as a slate.

Presidents are politicians, even after they take office. Presidents always dominate their national party organization. They generally name its officials and dictate its activities. Even an outgoing President can usually have great influence on the choice of the party's next presidential nominee. (However, this was not true when Nixon was forced to resign or when Johnson was forced to retire. It should also be noted that Eisenhower was not really interested in party politics.)[57]

President Carter's partisan activities exemplify the norm. Carter named the officials of the Democratic National Committee, but he gave the Committee little to do. One critic, political scientist Austin Ranney, says that Carter's only interest in the Democratic party was "in eliminating or softening the rules that make it easy to challenge his re-nomination." Most Presidents, according to Ranney, share this attitude. "Characteristically incumbent presidents have regarded the national committee as their own private property. It can't unroll a roll of toilet paper without the president's permission."[58] Carter has followed the presidential norm, too, by attempting to work closely with the leaders of his party in the U.S. House and Senate and by campaigning in various parts of the country for his party's congressional nominees.

---

[56]See William L. Lammers, *Presidential Politics: Patterns and Prospects* (New York: Harper and Row, 1976), p. 70.

[57]See Richard Neustadt, *Presidential Power* (New York: John Wiley, 1960), p. 166.

[58]Congressional Quarterly, *Weekly Report* (January 14, 1978), pp. 57–58.

But most Presidents also desire to be "above party." President Carter is no exception. He said that one of the most difficult decisions he had to make as a candidate was to be completely loyal to Democratic nominees throughout the country, because such partisan identification was damaging to his campaign.[59] One political observer says that "parties are legal shells needed to get on the ballot and make it easier to get government campaign money; as McGovern showed in 1972 and Nixon in 1968, a person running for the presidency now builds his own political party de novo."[60]

After they are elected, Presidents try to secure congressional approval of their programs, get reelected, and win the approval of history. One writer explains it this way:

Once in office the office is his, and he belongs to the office, not his backers. Only the sustained opposition of the nation as a whole—not the withdrawal of the support of his backers—can bring him down. He is now motivated by his own sense of who he is—a person placed in a historic office who will be judged in retrospect in terms of his ability to radiate the full majesty of that office. The President tries to act as the legitimate spokesman of an entire people.[61]

Presidential Personality

President Woodrow Wilson said, "The President is at liberty, both in law and conscience, to be as big a man as he can."[62] And it is true that one President's administration differs from another's, depending upon the personality of the person who occupies the office.

One of the most important recent attempts to classify Presidents on the basis of personality is the work of political scientist James David Barber.[63] Barber's work, called "psychobiography," also attempts to predict what kind of President a candidate might turn out to be. Critics claim that the categories he establishes for judging presidential character are so broad and imprecise that it is impossible to determine their accuracy. One writer argues that Barber has often "molded data to fit the categories—thus succumbing as others have done to that great psychobiographical temptation."[64] But the same

[59]See Jules Witcover, *Marathon: The Pursuit of the Presidency,* 1972–1976 (New York: Viking, 1977).

[60] Nicholas von Hoffman, "Winner Take Nothing," *The New York Review of Books* (August 4, 1977), pp. 3–4.

[61]F. G. Hutchins, "Presidential Autocracy in America," in Cronin and Tugwell, eds., *The Presidency Reappraised,* p. 137.

[62]Quoted in Emmet John Hughes, "Presidential Style," *Smithsonian,* 2, no.12 (March 1972): 28–36.

[63]See Barber, *The Presidential Character.*

[64]Alan C. Elms, *Personality in Politics* (New York: Harcourt Brace Jovanovich, 1976), p. 118. See also Alexander L. George, "Assessing Presidential Character," *World Politics,* 26 (1974): 234–82; and Erwin C. Hargrove, "Presidential Personality and Revisionist Views of the Presidency," *American Journal of Political Science,* 18 (1973): 819–35.

authority concedes that psychobiography is the most well-developed means of screening presidential candidates and categorizing presidential personality. As long as we are aware of some imprecision in Barber's categories and the fact that events and actors may offset or counteract a President's personality, his classifications may be helpful in judging Presidents and presidential candidates.

Barber first divides Presidents and candidates into those who are active and those who are passive. He makes these classifications on the basis of how much energy they bring to the job. Comparing Johnson with an earlier President, Calvin Coolidge, Barber says:

Lyndon Johnson, clearly one of the most active politicians ever, went about his job like a human cyclone. He spent half the day and night calling up people, shaking hands, working very hard at the job. In contrast—undoubtedly the most striking contrast—is Calvin Coolidge. Calvin Coolidge slept about eleven hours a night, and he still needed a nap in the middle of the day.[65]

Barber then divides Presidents and candidates into those who are positive and those who are negative about presidential duties. He makes these classifications on the basis of whether they enjoy doing what they have to do.

Today-it-was-fun was Franklin Roosevelt's attitude. He had fun being president. He liked dealing with people in that way of his. For contrast, take Herbert Hoover or Andrew Johnson, who was known as the "Grim Presence" in the White House, who practically never smiled. Hoover discouraged the presence of people in the White House. He did not like to see the servants in the hall, so when he walked down the halls the servants would jump into the closets and close the doors, so you had the waiters and waitresses crowding in there with trays. Hoover exuded a sense of suffering, of having a rough time of it rather than enjoying it.[66]

Presidential Personality: Barber's Classifications

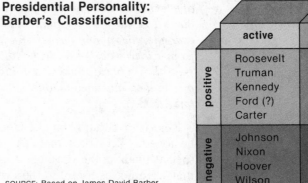

	active	passive
positive	Roosevelt Truman Kennedy Ford (?) Carter	Taft Harding
negative	Johnson Nixon Hoover Wilson	Eisenhower Coolidge

SOURCE: Based on James David Barber, *Presidential Character* (Prentice-Hall, 1972.)

According to Barber, Eisenhower was the only passive-negative personality among modern Presidents. This classification means that

---

[65]James David Barber, "Predicting Presidential Character," in Charles W. Dunn, ed., *The Future of the American Presidency* (Morristown, New Jersey: General Learning Press, 1975), p. 316.

[66]James David Barber, "Predicting Presidential Character," in Dunn, ed., *The Future of the American Presidency*, p. 317.

the President does not bring much energy to the duties of his office and does not really like politics or the chief executive's job. Barber argues that the country is better off when the President is active-positive. Of modern Presidents, Barber would place Franklin Roosevelt, Truman, Kennedy, Ford, and Carter in that category. One writer, using Barber's criteria, disagrees about Ford, calling him a passive-positive: "A nice enough guy . . . good-hearted, really kind of loveable. But not much *drive*."[67] Barber classifies President Carter as an active-positive personality, and Carter has so categorized himself. He has said that Barber's book has heavily influenced him.

Barber believes that the worst kind of personality to have in the White House is the active-negative, a classification he has assigned to both Nixon and Johnson. He feels that this type of active-negative personality tend to be driven but has rigid perspectives and is likely to turn inward and become even more rigid in the face of unfavorable public opinion or other political setbacks. Doris Kearns, who had occasion to observe Johnson's political personality firsthand, has emphasized the impact of Johnson's personality on his Presidency.[68]

Johnson's career also provides further evidence that the basic qualities of a leader do not change when he assumes new and larger responsibilities. It is more a metaphor than an accurate description to say, for example, that a man 'grows' in office. Of course, individuals do learn from experience—some better than others, and some become more skillful. But basic abilities, ambitions grounded on inner needs, modes of conduct, and inclinations of behavior are deeply and permanently imbedded.[69]

Kearns says that from childhood on, Johnson had a great need to be loved. She writes that his personality was also shaped by the special qualities he developed as Senate majority leader, qualities that were not as useful in the Presidency.

He could not lead or inspire the nation by secret deals; he did not understand foreign policy; he could not deal with conflicts taking place in a setting where he could not establish personal detailed knowledge of the problem and the participants; and the same search for control that gave such force and direction to his legislative career caused him now to move toward coercive action and to transform the executive branch into a personal instrument, and a weapon for concealing facts and policies from other branches of government and the people.[70]

When Lyndon Johnson began to come under severe attack because of the Vietnam War, he resented the criticism, turned inward, became

---

[67]See Walt Anderson, "Looking for Mr. Active-Positive," *Human Behavior* (October 1976).

[68]See Doris Kearns, *Lyndon Johnson and the American Dream* (New York: New American Library, 1976).

[69]Doris Kearns, "Lyndon Johnson's Political Personality," in Cronin and Tugwell, *The Presidency Reappraised*, pp. 129–130.

[70]Kearns, "Lyndon Johnson's Political Personality," p. 127.

more rigid in his views, and, to use one of his own phrases, "hunkered down like a heifer in a hailstorm." Public opinion eventually forced him to give up the idea of running for reelection.

Even before Nixon's unconstitutional use of presidential power in the Watergate affair forced him to resign, Barber had classified him as an active-negative character. "The danger is that crisis will be transformed into tragedy. . . . The loss of power to forces beyond his control would constitute a severe threat. That would be a time to go down, if go down one must, in flames."[71] Nixon did isolate himself in the White House, almost from the start, preferring to see only a small number of close aides. When more and more damaging facts began to come out about his authorizing or sanctioning illegal conduct for political reasons, Nixon isolated himself still further, lashing out at his critics, until he finally had to resign.

Presidential personality is only one of the factors that can affect the Presidency, and it cannot be precisely classified. But the personality that a successful presidential candidate brings to the office is an important factor in how presidential powers are exercised and how Presidents perform as leaders.

Presidential Performance

Presidents do shape the office to some extent. As we have seen, their impact on the office is partly a result of presidential personality. But it also stems from other factors. Their view of the Constitutional provisions relating to the office; their image of what a President should be; their relationship with other agencies, officials, and the press; and the way they make decisions all shape the office.

Some Presidents have viewed the Constitution as a limit, others as a license. Louis W. Koenig has classified these presidential types as either mostly "literalists" or "strong." Literalists do not attempt to expand the letter of the Constitution in exercising presidential powers. Strong Presidents give the Constitution a broad interpretation.[72] He writes that literalists tend to be deferential to Congress, make little use of implied presidential powers, exert political pressure sparingly, and do not care much for social innovation. Koenig names Madison, Buchanan, Taft, and (to some degree) Eisenhower as literalists. He classifies Washington, Jackson, Lincoln, Wilson, and the Roosevelts as strong Presidents. Strong Presidents, according to Koenig, flourish in times of crisis and change; they are precedent-makers and precedent-breakers. Although he feels that America needs strong Presidents to meet changing conditions, Koenig recognizes that there is always a danger that they may go beyond what is legal and proper.

Presidents also differ in the type of images they wish to project,

---

[71]Barber, *The Presidential Character,* pp. 441–42.
[72]Louis W. Koenig, *The Chief Executive,* 3rd ed. (New York: Harcourt Brace Jovanovich, 1975), pp. 14–17.

and these images affect presidential performance. Some Presidents have tried to magnify the "dignity" of the office. Others have sought to emphasize its "populistic" aspects.[73] Koenig puts Franklin D. Roosevelt, Eisenhower, and (to a lesser extent) Kennedy in the "dignity" group. Truman's image, however, was "populistic." Carter also cultivated such an image by walking down Pennsylvania Avenue after being inaugurated, and by conducting "town meetings" throughout the country.

How Presidents deal with the great number of agencies, departments, staff members, and other advisers within the executive department, and how they make decisions, depend very much upon their particular dispositions. Some Presidents have encouraged an almost militarylike chain of command, with the President at the top of a pyramidal reporting system. Eisenhower was like this; perhaps because of his military background, he preferred to deal personally with only those questions which could not otherwise be resolved. Nixon also preferred to see and talk with only a small number of his closest White House staff members. His "Chief of Staff," Bob Haldeman, almost terrorized people who wanted to meet with the President. Jimmy Carter originally made a point of not having a White House "Chief of Staff," but increasingly during his tenure, Hamilton Jordan began to perform the functions of the position and was eventually named to it officially. On the other hand, Franklin Roosevelt and Lyndon Johnson wished to be in personal contact with a wide number of government officials and others outside the government at all times. As a result, only they had a clear understanding of everything that was being done or thought in the government. Unlike several recent Presidents, Franklin Roosevelt also encouraged controversy and debate among his advisers as a management tool and as a way of choosing the best alternative among a number of possible options.

How does a President get the necessary information on which to base decisions? Much of it is filtered through the White House staff. Some of it comes to him orally through conversations. Other information comes in the form of written memoranda from staff members and officials. Some Presidents prefer one over the other, but they all have to do a considerable amount of reading. Typical presidential reading involves a lengthy memorandum listing proposals and alternatives, with a one- or two-page summary at the front. Presidents can read the summary, and if necessary, read more of the whole memorandum, noting decisions or instructions on the front and returning it to the appropriate White House staff member or other official. Carter has worked very hard on this aspect of the job, often reading lengthy, detailed memoranda and "working papers" late into the night. According to his former speechwriter, James Fallows, however, Carter tends to involve himself in too many small

---

[73]Koenig, *The Chief Executive*, p. 336.

details of programs and proposals. Fallows says that while Carter has rapidly mastered the details, he has failed to fit them into broad policy themes or goals.[74]

Presidents do not generally have the time to read books or lengthy magazine articles. Some Presidents receive more outside information—beyond what their closest advisers and White House staff members give them—than others. Johnson almost made a fetish of keeping up with news reports. In addition to reading a number of newspapers, he kept an Associated Press and an United Press International Wire service machine in his office. He also had three television sets in his office, which allowed him to see the newscasts on all three networks simultaneously. Presidents maintain that traveling the country for public events gives them a chance to keep from being isolated, but these events are generally more important for their political impact than for their information-gathering aspect.

Security arrangements, heavy duties, and the awesome nature of the office itself tend to insulate Presidents from the ·general public and from ordinary experiences.[75] It is very easy for a President to become isolated from the outside world and to receive only the information and advice that comes through the White House staff.[76] Presidents must also guard against the "chilling effect" that the awesome nature of the Presidency has on those who talk with or give advice to the chief executive. Advisers tend to refrain from being as abrupt or as frank, especially in regard to a disagreement with the President, as they would be in talking with some ordinary person outside the Oval Office. President Johnson's press secretary has said, "Inevitably in a battle between courtiers and advisers, the courtiers will win out. This represents the greatest of all barriers to presidential access to reality."[77] Following the criticisms of the "imperial" Presidency under Nixon and his predecessors, Presidents Ford and Carter made notable attempts to break out of the protective cocoon of the White House.

Presidents cannot lead the country—or persuade Congress and other government officials most effectively—without contact with the general public. Presidents use the mass media for this purpose. On live telecasts, Presidents can speak directly to the nation, bypassing news reporters. Following any televised speech by a President, therefore, television networks generally provide balancing commentary and discussion by reporters and others. President Nixon tried to minimize this "instant analysis." For a while, he was successful in intimidating the networks into curtailing such neutral commentary. Presidents may also attempt to get their message across to the general public, without much debate or discussion, through interviews with

[74]James Fallows, "The Passionless Presidency," *Atlantic Monthly* (May 1979), pp. 33–48.
[75]See George Reedy, *The Twilight of the Presidency* (New York: World, 1970).
[76]See Henry Fairlie, *The Kennedy Promise* (New York: Doubleday, 1973).
[77]Reedy, *The Twilight of the Presidency,* p. 98.

favored or friendly columnists, reporters, and commentators.

In the White House and the executive department, the news "leak" is widely used to further the President's objectives. By this method, the President or some unnamed source may send up a "trial balloon," or attempt to persuade the public to accept one of the administration's policy positions without engaging the executive department in head-on debate on the question at issue. Thus, many news columns and news stories carry reports that often begin with the words: "A high-level administration spokesperson today announced that the administration is considering a new policy concerning. . . ." News reporters regularly agree to this "not-attributable-as-to-source" reporting because they can get a story that they might not otherwise obtain. But many news reporters are increasingly worried about the ethics and the effect of such reporting.

In modern times, Presidents have also used the press conference as a means of informing the public. At these formal functions, which are broadcast live on television and radio, the President answers questions from the press. Some observers have said that the press conference is the only American equivalent of the "question period" to which British prime ministers must submit in regular sessions of the House of Commons. But this analogy probably makes too much of the point. Presidents have an advantage over reporters. For one thing, Presidents can give as long or as short an answer as they wish. They can evade. The President can use a joke or witticism

President Carter answering reporters' questions during a press conference. Presidents use these meetings to inform the public about important issues.

to avoid answering directly or to change the subject. Since the journalist's role prevents reporters from debating with Presidents, the question-and-answer session is a one-sided affair. One authority describes the presidential press conference as follows:

Whether off the record or fully publicized the conference's plainest potential is as a leadership tool for the president. He may choose the conference as a place to lash opponents or push favorites. He may use it as a forum for pronouncements designed to get or test policy support from the nation as a whole. He can try to stimulate the public to pressure Congress. He can stir his own bureaucracy or discuss the citizens and the governments of other nations. When news from opposition headquarters has been getting a lot of space, a president may, by way of the conference, recapture the limelight. He can rely on coverage of the conference to give him at least some attention in even the most unfriendly newspaper. All twentieth-century presidents have used the conference for some of these purposes; most of them have used it for all.[78]

Yet there *is* a useful confrontation between the President and the press in the United States. According to President Johnson's press secretary, George Reedy:

The president and the press have a different job to perform. The president is an advocate who seeks to persuade, while the press has the job of chronicling daily events in a way that will make them understandable to the public. . . . A Democratic society is inconceivable without tension and the objective reporting that democracy requires will always produce tension. I might add that I do not think our country has ever been hurt by a sceptical and rambunctious newspaperman.[79]

While agreeing that a President can always dominate a press conference, reporter David Broder believes that the press conference furnishes an important way of "bypassing the President's staff, and opening the White House and the President to non-programed items."[80]

PRESIDENTIAL POWER: TOO MUCH OR NOT ENOUGH?

In our discussion of the Presidency, we noted that the office has always had somewhere between "too much" and "not enough" power. That position is the result of a conscious decision by the framers of the Constitution. They certainly did not want a monarch, but they did not want an "imperial legislature," either. This tension has existed throughout our history. Since the chief executive's formal powers are somewhat vague, each President has been able, within limits, to do what he wanted—or could—with those powers.

In recent years, some observers have written that Presidents have too much power. They mean that Presidents have misused power and have been too secretive and isolated in their decisions and acts. They claim that Presidents have not been accountable enough to the people and that they have been too dominant in their relationship with the Congress.

[78]Fauneil J. Rinn, "The Presidential Press Conference," in Wildavsky, ed., *The Presidency*, p. 335.

[79]Quoted in James Reston, *The Artillery of the Press* (New York: Harper and Row, 1967), pp. 58–59.

[80]David S. Broder, "The Presidency and the Press," in Dunn, ed., *The Future of the American Presidency*, p. 266.

Others argue that the pendulum has swung too much in the other direction since Vietnam and Watergate, leaving the President with too little power and vulnerable to too many attacks. Former President Ford shares this view. He says that the executive office has changed from an "imperial" to an "imperiled" Presidency whose occupant does not have enough leeway to act.[81]

Public participation is one key criterion by which to judge presidential power. For example, do we really participate sufficiently in the selection of the President? Reforms in campaign financing and in the nomination process have increased popular participation and its effectiveness. Suggested reforms in registration laws would make it possible for a greater number of people to participate in presidential elections.

Do we have enough information about presidential decisions? Recent "freedom of information" trends and laws make it possible for the general public to know more about presidential decisions. These trends increase the opportunity for greater public participation in decision-making.

Is the President held sufficiently accountable? Congressional actions—such as the War Powers Act and the Congressional Budget and Impoundment Act—increase presidential accountability to the public through the vehicle of Congress.

The Twenty-Second Amendment, adopted in 1951, is the only constitutional amendment that limits, rather than expands, the electoral power of the people. This amendment diminishes the choices available to the public by preventing Presidents from running for office more than twice.

Some observers—including President Carter—have suggested that the President should be further removed from public accountability, based upon the President's desire to be reelected. They advocate a constitutional amendment to limit Presidents to one term, but to increase its length from the present four years to six years. But others, like Representative Morris K. Udall of Arizona, consider this idea for placing the President "above politics" as hostile to democracy. Udall says:

I think we should reject the idea that we need a non-political president, or a non-political governor, or a non-political congressman. I think some of the key things Richard Nixon did that history will honor him for were done only because he was facing the 1972 election.

I question whether he would have found a way to end the war in Vietnam or started talking with the Russians and Chinese if he weren't facing an election in 1972. I know he wouldn't have started his economic program in August, 1971, if it weren't for the upcoming election.[82]

[81]Gerald Ford, quoted in editorial, *U.S. News & World Report* (January 15, 1979), p. 88.

[82]Morris K. Udall, "A Democrat Looks at the Presidency," Dunn, ed., *The Future of the American Presidency*, p. 248.

Another writer suggests that the most troublesome concern about the power of the modern American Presidency results from the American mystique of the President as the nation's chief problem-solver and symbolic leader.[83] A number of suggestions have been made to take away some of the aura and the awe-inspiring aspects of the Presidency. They range from proposals for separating the duties of the chief of state from those of the head of the government, to requiring the President to appear at regular intervals before Congress and submit to questions, as the prime minister of Great Britain does.

Structural changes will probably not be made in the Presidency in the foreseeable future. Much, then, depends upon the President's willingness at any given time to reduce or eliminate the imperial trappings of office. President Carter tried to do this by toning down the presidential style of recent years and reducing the size of his staff. Much depends, too, upon the American public's attitude toward the Presidency. Recently the public has shown a renewed determination to hold the President accountable.

Americans today face the same question that the original framers did: How powerful should the President of the United States be? Like the framers, we certainly do not want a king, but we do not want an ineffective weakling, either. Arthur M. Schlesinger, Jr., has said, "The American democracy must discover a middle ground between making the President a Czar and making him a puppet. . . . We need a strong Presidency—but a strong Presidency within the Constitution."[84]

ADDITIONAL SOURCES

Barber, James David. *The Presidential Character: Predicting Performance in the White House*, 2nd ed. Prentice-Hall, 1977.*

Burns, James MacGregor. *Leadership* (esp. Ch. 14). Harper & Row, 1978.

Califano, Joseph A. *A Presidential Nation*. Norton, 1975.

Cronin, Thomas E., and Rexford G. Tugwell, eds. *The Presidency Reappraised*, 2nd ed. Praeger, 1977.*

Hess, Stephen. *Organizing the Presidency*. Brookings Institution, 1976.*

Hughes, Emmet John. *The Living Presidency*. Coward, McCann & Geoghegan, 1973.*

Koenig, Louis W. *The Chief Executive*, 3rd ed. Harcourt Brace Jovanovich, 1975.*

Neustadt, Richard. *Presidential Power*, rev. ed. Wiley, 1976.*

Pious, Richard M. *The American Presidency*. Basic Books, 1979.

*Available in paperback.

---

[83]See Philippa Strum, "A Symbolic Attack on the Imperial Presidency: An American 'Question Time'," in Cronin and Tugwell, eds., *The Presidency Reappraised*, p. 250.

[84]Schlesinger, *The Imperial Presidency*, p. x.

14 The Bureaucracy

The Executive Branch

Official government documents were once bound together with red ribbon. The ribbon was threaded through holes punched in the various pages of a document, and the ends of the ribbon were then sealed together with melted wax to prevent the addition of new pages or the substitution of one page for another. Thus *red tape* came to be associated with excessive formality and mechanical adherence to rules and regulations. There are references in early American literature to a public official who is a "red-tape minister" and complaints about citizens having to spend "all morning at the custom-house, plagued with red-tape."[1] Today, "too much red tape" is still one of the most common complaints about modern bureaucracy.

Bureaucracy is a formally established type of organization with four basic characteristics.[2] The first is *job specialization*. Each employee in a bureaucracy is supposed to perform a certain, specific job. Second, there is a *hierarchy of authority*, or chain of command, within the bureaucracy, moving from the top to the bottom. Third, a bureaucracy has a *system of rules* that defines its operations. Finally, a bureaucracy is characterized by *impersonality*. Employees within the bureaucracy are expected to treat all persons fairly and impartially.

Although these characteristics theoretically provide for the most efficient operation of a bureaucracy, they also give rise to some of the most severe criticisms of the way the system functions. We want government officials to treat all citizens alike, but when we are personally involved, we would appreciate a little special consideration. We expect the bureaucracy to keep within the bounds of the

---

[1] See, "red tape," Oxford English Dictionary.
[2] See Peter M. Blau and Marshall W. Meyer, *Bureaucracy in Modern Society* (New York: Random House, 1971), pp. 9, 58.

law, but we also worry that this can result in unreasonably rigid adherence to the letter of the law, without initiative or innovation.

There seems to be a rising chorus of criticism of bureaucracy from both conservatives and liberals, and from all those in between.[3] Much of this criticism is justified. But some form of organization is necessary to carry out serious and complex tasks. For example, most Americans today would agree that any institution that receives tax funds, such as a hospital or a university, should not practice racial discrimination. Yet the passage of a law is not enough to carry out that policy goal. Somehow, compliance with the law has to be ensured. Historically, bureaucracies have served this function.

Inspectors, hearing officers, and a staff are hired. To make sure that these employees follow the law and act fairly, someone is put in charge, and rules and regulations are developed. And—voilà!—a bureaucracy is born.

Amidst the complaints about governmental bureaucracy, some public misconceptions persist:

1. All bureaucracies are *not* governmental. Each large corporation or private institution also has a large bureaucracy.

2. Most of the governmental bureaucracy exists *not* at the federal level but at the state and local levels. There are fewer than three million federal employees but more than twelve million state and local employees.[4]

3. The federal bureaucracy has *not* recently experienced runaway growth in relation to state and local bureaucracy or to total national population. From 1949 to 1976, the federal bureaucracy grew by about 37 percent, while employment in state and local bureaucracy increased 200 percent. During the same period, there was actually a decline in federal employees as a percentage of total national population. The number of state and local employees for every one thousand Americans increased from about twenty-six to almost fifty-seven, an increase of over 100 percent.

4. Most federal employees do *not* live and work in Washington, D.C. Only about 12 percent do.[5]

5. Most federal employees do *not* work for social welfare agencies. Almost 39 percent of all full-time federal civilian employees work for the Department of Defense. Sixty-eight percent of all federal civilian employees are employed in just three federal agencies: the Department of Defense, the U.S. Postal Service, and the Veterans Administration.[6]

---

[3]See, James Q. Wilson, "The Rise of the Bureaucratic State," *The Public Interest*, 41 (Fall 1975): 7–103.

[4]Except as otherwise indicated, statistics concerning governmental bureaucracy are taken from Advisory Commission on Intergovernmental Relations, *Intergovernmental Perspective* (Fall 1976), p. 9.

[5]Bureau of Manpower Assistance, U.S. Civil Service Commission.

[6]"Special Analysis H," in *Special Analyses, Budget of the United States Government* (Fiscal Year 1977), p. 150.

Number of Government Employees (civilian) 1948-77

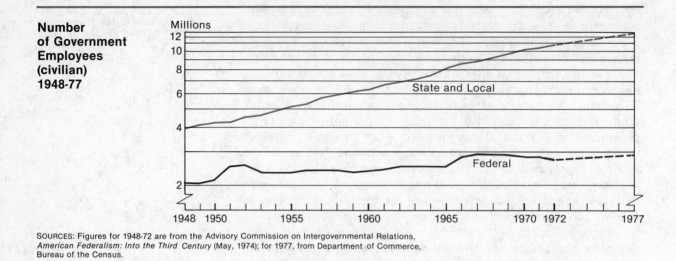

Millions

State and Local

Federal

1948 1950   1955   1960   1965   1970 1972   1977

SOURCES: Figures for 1948-72 are from the Advisory Commission on Intergovernmental Relations, *American Federalism: Into the Third Century* (May, 1974); for 1977, from Department of Commerce, Bureau of the Census.

Still, the number of federal agencies keeps on growing. Once an agency is created, it tends to have virtually an immortal life of its own.[7] In addition, it tends to grow in size, according to "Parkinson's Laws": "Work expands so as to fill the time available for its completion," and "In any public administrative department not actually at war, the staff increase . . . will invariably prove to be between 5.17 percent and 6.56 percent (per year), irrespective of any variation in the amount of work (if any) to be done."[8] Parkinson's humorous observations have been substantiated by serious studies.[9]

THE DEVELOPMENT OF BUREAUCRACY

The Chinese probably developed the first governmental bureaucracy. By 196 B.C., their civil service system required written examinations for career government employees.[10] Five hundred years passed before the British established a civil service system, recruited lifelong government careerists from the upper classes.[11]

[7]See Herbert Kaufman, *Are Government Organizations Immortal?* (Washington, D.C.: Brookings Institutions, 1976), p. 67.

[8]C. Northcote Parkinson, *Parkinson's Law* (Boston: Houghton Mifflin, 1957), p. 2; and C. Northcote Parkinson, *Parkinson's Law and Other Studies in Administration* (Boston: Houghton Mifflin, 1962), p. 2.

[9]See, for example, Anthony Downs, *Inside Bureaucracy* (Boston: Little, Brown and Company, 1967), pp.5–23.

[10]See Phillip H. DuBois, *A History of Psychological Testing* (Boston: Allyn and Bacon, 1970), p. 3; and Joseph Needham, *The Grand Titration: Science and Society in East and West* (Toronto: University of Toronto Press, 1969), p. 27.

[11]See V. Subramanian, "The Relative Status of Specialists and Generalists: An Attempt at a Comparative Historical Explanation," *Public Administration* 46 (August 1968): 334; and J. Donald Kingsley, *Representative Bureaucracy: An Interpretation of the British Civil Service* (Yellow Springs, Ohio: Antioch Press, 1944).

The United States Constitution contains no provisions about the governmental bureaucracy. However, it gives the President the power to "require the opinion of the principal officers in each of the Executive Departments" and to appoint the heads of those departments. One of George Washington's first acts (in 1789) was to ask Congress to establish the departments of State, Treasury, and War and the office of the Attorney General; the Post Office was created in 1792. The entire staff of the first State Department consisted of the secretary, a chief clerk, seven other clerks, and a messenger boy. In 1800, the entire federal government (excluding the military) consisted of only 3,000 bureaucrats.[12] Our earliest Presidents were able to freely appoint federal employees on the basis of political loyalties, friendship, and other considerations.[13] When Andrew Jackson was President, the phrase, "To the victor belongs the spoils," was used to defend his appointment of so many supporters from among the "plain people." Thus, the term *spoils system* came to refer to the practice of appointing federal employees on the basis of political patronage.[14] Abraham Lincoln made greater use of the spoils system than any other President up to that time.[15]

The assassination of President James A. Garfield by a disgruntled officeseeker in 1881 helped to create a public climate for reform. Congress passed a law creating the U.S. Civil Service Commission and establishing a merit system for choosing federal employees.[16] Before becoming President, Theodore Roosevelt served as civil service commissioner. As President, Roosevelt strongly supported the merit system of federal employment. "The merit system of making appointments," he said, "is in its essence as democratic and American as the common school system itself."[17]

In 1939, Congress passed the Hatch Act to prevent federal employees from engaging—or being forced to engage—in political campaign activity although these restrictions do not prevent federal employees from putting bumper stickers on their cars, attending political rallies, wearing campaign buttons, and expressing political opinions). But federal employee union officials and some Democratic politicians today argue that political restrictions on federal civil

[12]Richard L. Schott, *The Bureaucratic State: The Evolution and Scope of the American Federal Bureaucracy* (Morristown: General Learning Press, 1974), pp. 4–5.

[13]See Herbert Kaufman, "The Growth of the Federal Personal System," in Wallace S. Sayre, ed., *The Federal Government Service, the American Assembly* (Englewood Cliffs, N.J.: Prentice-Hall, 1965), pp. 13–16.

[14]See Sidney H. Aronson, *Status and Kinship in the Higher Civil Service: Standards of Selection in the Administrations of John Adams, Thomas Jefferson and Andrew Jackson* (Cambridge, Mass.: Harvard University Press, 1964), pp. 19, 55; and Erik M. Erikson, "The Federal Civil Service Under President Jackson," *Mississippi Valley Historical Review*, 13 (March 1927): 540.

[15]See Franklin Kilpatrick, Milton Cummings, Jr., and Kent Jennings, *The Image of the Federal Service* (Washington, D.C.: Brookings Institution, 1964), p. 33.

[16]See Frederick C. Mosher, *Democracy in the Public Service* (New York: Oxford University Press, 1968), p. 66.

[17]Mosher, *Democracy in the Public Service,* p. 202.

servants should be relaxed to allow greater political freedom. There is much opposition to this proposal. President Ford vetoed such a bill in 1976 because he felt it would turn back the clock in civil service reform and "politicize" the federal civil service.[18]

Today, almost all federal jobs come under the civil service system. For these jobs, appointments must be made on the basis of merit. Only slightly more that 2,000 positions can be filled by presidential appointment, and only about one fourth of these are important.[19]

According to federal law, civil service positions must be filled from among the three applicants who have been rated the highest on the basis of civil service examinations and related criteria. In recent years, The Civil Service Commission has been increasingly criticized as being itself a bureaucracy (which it always has been). Particularly troublesome were the civil service protections that made it difficult to discharge incompetent or even dishonest employees or to reward especially efficient or hard-working employees. President Carter, who had campaigned for changes in the civil service, proposed a reform bill. After a difficult battle in Congress, the bill was passed. The law, called the Civil Service Reform Act of 1978, did not alter the provisions of the Hatch Act, however. Nor did it change the preference in the civil service for armed services veterans, which gives them a special advantage in federal civil service employment. The new act also did not materially alter the present labor-relations law regarding civil service employees. Federal employees can form and join labor unions, but it is still illegal for them to strike.

The new law does provide for a "senior executive service" for employees in the higher grades. This is an attempt to provide a roster of high-level federal managers who can be moved from one agency to another with some ease, who can be fired with less difficulty than under previous laws, and who can be rewarded for special service. The senior executive service, first recommended by the Hoover Commission in 1955, is similar to the top civil service corps in Great Britain. It is intended in part to reduce the development of special relationships between bureaucrats, members of Congress, and interest groups—sometimes called the "cozy triangle." The law's supporters hope that by periodically moving bureaucrats to new agencies, they will also get a fresh perspective on the government's operations.

The new law makes it easier to prove that a federal civil service employee should be discharged for cause, provides special merit pay for meritorious service in the middle-level civil service grades, and stipulates that rudeness to the public can be considered a factor when making decisions on promotions.

Today, federal *bureaucrats*—those who work somewhere in the federal bureaucracy—have become highly important in our daily

---

[18]See Henry Rose, "A Critical Look at the Hatch Act," *Harvard Law Review*, 75 (1962); and John R. Bolton, *The Hatch Act: A Civil Libertarian Defense* (American Enterprise Institute, Washington, D.C., 1976).

[19]*Congressional Quarterly, Weekly Report* (January 3, 1969), p. 15.

lives. Sargent Shriver, who has served in high federal offices through presidential appointment, has said, "To a large extent it is the bureaucrats who make the day-to-day decisions on government action. Certainly, for most citizens, it is they who serve as the major point of contact with government."[20] Political scientists agree: one authority declares that "in the important matters of our public lives we are more involved with public bureaucracy than we are with parties, elections, and legislatures."[21] Today, for example, there is more administrative law, which is issued by bureaucrats, than statutory law, which Congress makes.[22]

These decisions can even determine our right to make a living—and more.

At the federal, state and local levels, administrators can grant or withhold licenses and permits; design and implement programs for schools and colleges; allocate research funds; support cultural efforts; decide who receives a television channel, an air route franchise, a railroad right-of-way, or a snack bar monopoly. Bureaucrats may refuse a person admission to the United States, destroy a farmer's sick cows and chickens, deny a person a pension or ask his or her former employers and neighbors if he or she is 'unfit' for a government job.[23]

STRUCTURE OF THE FEDERAL BUREAUCRACY

The first thing one notices when studying—or trying to deal with—the federal bureaucracy is that it is far from neatly organized.[24] First, while most government agencies in Europe are called "bureaus," Americans call their federal agencies by a wide array of names: department, agency, commission, bureau, authority, board, administration. Whether a federal agency is called by one of these names or another is more a result of happenstance than logic. Second, the federal bureaucracy is not very logically organized by function. No particular reason except tradition can explain why federal dam-building, for example, is done by three different agencies: the Corps of Engineers in the Department of the Army, within the Department of Defense; the Bureau of Reclamation, in the Department of the Interior; and the Soil and Water Conservation Service, in the Department of Agriculture. American Presidents have

Copyright 1980 by Sidney Harris.

---

[20]Quoted in the preface to Harry Kranz, *The Participatory Bureaucracy* (Lexington, Mass.: D.C. Heath, 1976), p. xiii.

[21]Eugene Lewis, *American Politics in a Bureaucratic Age* (Cambridge, Mass.: Winthrop Publishers, 1977), p. 8.

[22]See Dwight Waldo, ed., *Public Administration in a Time of Turbulence* (Scranton, Pennsylvania: Chandler, 1971), pp. 218–19.

[23]Kranz, *The Participatory Bureaucracy*, p. 17.

[24]For a brief discussion of the structure of the federal bureaucracy, see Lewis C. Mainzer, *Political Bureaucracy* (Glenview, Illinois: Scott, Foresman, 1973) pp. 18-24.

tried to reorganize the federal bureaucracy, and Jimmy Carter is no exception. Skeptics doubted that the Carter plan would save money,[25] however, and there was good reason to believe that under the Carter plan, federal programs—like those in the Office of Education—would still have as much confusing overlap after a reorganization as they did before.

The federal bureaucracy can be broken down into three main categories: cabinet departments; independent agencies; and regulatory bodies. Yet there is no great logic or consistency regarding jurisdiction and duties. For example, cabinet departments or agencies within them perform some regulatory functions, and responsibility for other functional areas is shared by cabinet departments, independent agencies, and regulatory bodies.

The twelve *cabinet departments*, as we saw in Chapter 13, are headed by secretaries appointed by the President. (In the Justice Department, the cabinet official is called the attorney general). There is usually a second-in-command position, called the deputy secretary or under secretary. The departments also include a number of assistant secretaries, whose duties are based on a special function (such as the assistant secretary of state for international organizations) or on the clientele they serve (such as the assistant secretary of the interior for Indian affairs).

Within the cabinet departments, there are relatively autonomous bureaus, administrations, and services. Examples include the Coast Guard, the Federal Highway Administration, and the Federal Aviation Administration, in the Department of Commerce; the Federal Bureau of Investigation, within the Department of Justice; and the Corps of Engineers, in the Department of Defense. The Agency for International Development is in the Department of State, and the Internal Revenue Service is within the Treasury Department.

Independent agencies are headed by "directors" or "administrators." They do not go through any cabinet officials but report directly to the President. The functions of these agencies and the roles of their directors and administrators are not easily distinguished from those of cabinet departments and chiefs. However, the agencies do not generally have as much prestige, influence, or breadth of jurisdiction as the cabinet departments.

Some of the independent agencies of the federal government perform "housekeeping" functions. For example, the Civil Service Commission administers the federal merit system, and the General Services Administration manages the government's buildings and other property. Other agencies, like the Veterans Administration and the National Science Foundation, serve particular clients. Still others carry out particular functions, such as the National Aeronautics and Space Administration, the Central Intelligence Agency, and the U.S. Arms Control and Disarmament Agency.

---

[25]Lee Walczak, "Commentary," *Business Week* (August 1, 1977), p. 22.

Some independent federal agencies are organized as government corporations. This form of organization presumably gives them a little more freedom in carrying out their responsibilities and removes them more from the "bureaucratic politics" in other federal agencies and departments. Such federal corporations include the Tennessee Valley Authority, which was established to harness rivers and produce electricity; the U.S. Postal Service; and the Federal Deposit Insurance Corporation, which was set up to insure customer bank deposits against losses.

Federal *regulatory bodies* function partly like legislatures and partly like judges. They issue rules and regulations and hold hearings to enforce them as well as the laws passed by Congress. They are governed by boards and commissions, whose members are appointed from both political parties for staggered terms. These presidential appointments must be confirmed by the U.S. Senate. The regulatory bodies are fairly autonomous agencies; they do not report directly to the President, although they are subject to congressional oversight on overall policy and spending.

Among the federal regulatory bodies are the Interstate Commerce Commission, which regulates railroads, trucks, and pipelines; the Federal Communications Commission, which issues television and radio licenses and regulates licensees; the Securities and Exchange Commission, which oversees the operation of the stock market; the Federal Reserve system, which regulates the monetary supply; the National Labor Relations Board, which oversees labor-management matters; and the Civil Aeronautics Board, which regulates the airlines.

A serious complaint against the federal regulatory bodies is that they frequently become vulnerable to "capture" by interest groups. That is, they are often inclined to protect the interest of groups that they are supposed to regulate. There is justification in this complaint, although the groups that are regulated regularly complain about the oppressive and harassing effects of regulation. Any governmental regulatory body can become captured for a number of reasons. First, groups that are regulated by a particular agency usually attempt to influence political appointments to the agency's board or commission, seeking to secure the appointment of people who are sympathetic to their interests.

Also, there is the *revolving door* phenomenon. This is the back-and-forth career movement between an industry and its governmental regulator. Appointees to regulatory boards or commissions, or to the staffs of such agencies, often come from the groups that they are supposed to regulate. This practice occurs presumably because appointees have the special knowledge or expertise needed for the job. After serving awhile, the appointees often go back into a private business or profession associated with the regulated group. For example, a young lawyer just out of law school who wants to specialize in securities law (which deals with corporate stocks and

VIEWPOINT
Regulation: Pro and Con

Herbert Schmertz
Vice-President, Public Affairs
Mobil Oil Corporation

As an energy company, Mobil has experienced the never-never land of Catch-22 created by excessive government regulation. Consider these examples:

• In resolving electricity-generation needs, the nuclear option stands out as the best and most logical. Nuclear power is totally predictable; one can know exactly how much power will be available from a given facility at a given date. Its safety record is excellent, and there's little environmental disruption. But in spite of these virtues, conflicting and sometimes retroactive regulations have reduced orders for new installations from 44 in 1973 to only three in 1977. I know of none in 1978.

• EPA and other government regulators are making it extremely difficult to construct a new refinery or even expand an existing one. The permit-gathering process can easily take between 18 and 36 months, involving federal, state, and local agencies.

How to untangle the morass? First, the president should appoint a commission of citizens from outside government to review all federal regulations five years old or older. Second, legislation should be enacted to schedule the demise of all regulations and regulatory agencies whose charters have not been periodically renewed by Congress. Third, clear and unbiased "economic impact statements" should be required to spell out the effects on the economy of all new major regulations and legislation. Fourth, new standards of professional competence should be set for service on regulatory commissions. People with firsthand knowledge and experience of the industries involved should not be barred from service precisely because of these qualifications.

Robert Lekachman
Distinguished Professor
of Economics, Lehman College,
City University of New York

If corporate leaders were given to self-doubt or introspection, they might wonder why regulation of business has become so politically popular in a conservative society traditionally friendly to private enterprise. The answer is no mystery. With honorable exceptions, entrepreneurs paid little attention to the health and safety of their employees, the impact of their operations on the environment, the reliability of their products, and the truthfulness of their advertising, until Congress, spurred to action by an indignant public, created the flock of new regulatory agencies.

The size of the bills that have now begun to arrive measures the magnitude of past failures of corporate responsibility. They are, nevertheless, smaller than they seem. Much or even most of the cost represents one-time outlay, not a chronic financial burden.

In the jargon of economics, the new regulations compel businessmen to internalize external costs. This is to say, fewer workers and customers will be damaged by their conditions of work and the defects of products they buy. Their health will be better, their working lives longer, and their medical bills smaller as a result. Like any sensible community aspiring toward a reasonably civilized mode of life, Americans are grasping some of the gains of technical progress in the shape of cleaner air and water, attractive scenery, decent workplaces, and safe consumer goods.

I have more faith in private enterprise than some businessmen appear to possess. I am convinced that our corporations, once they accept this new entrepreneurial challenge, can comply with sensible regulatory requirements, win public support for revision of really unfair regulations, and still profit.

SOURCE: From "The Experts Polled," *Saturday Review* (January 20, 1979), pp. 39–41.

bonds) may seek to get an entry-level job with the Securities Exchange Commission. With experience and widened contacts in industry and government, the lawyer may later secure a position with a stock brokerage firm or with a law firm that handles securities matters. Then, after building a reputation in the private sector, the lawyer may—with political support and help from the securities industry—secure a presidential appointment as a member of the Securities Exchange Commission itself. When the lawyer's term as a commissioner expires, he or she may enter a law firm or a brokerage firm as a full partner. A law passed in 1978 and the regulations issued to implement it forbid ex-officials from attempting to influence their former federal agencies on behalf of a new nongovernmental employer.[26] This act will reduce the effect of the revolving door phenomenon.

Interest-group capture is not only a problem for regulatory bodies. It is common in all bureaucracies. It could be lessened by reducing the amount of federal regulation of industries in which no controlled market exists and competition is possible. The airline industry provides one example. In 1979, for example, the Federal Aviation Administration relaxed some of the federal air carrier regulations to allow more competitive rates and services. Interest-group capture could also be reduced by the appointment of more "consumer-oriented" members to federal regulatory boards and commissions. It has been suggested, too, that one of the main reasons for establishing a new federal consumer protection agency within the executive department would be to provide consumer interests with representation before other federal departments, agencies, and regulatory bodies. Thus far, legislation for a consumer protection agency has not been adopted.

THE BUREAUCRATS

When he was running for President in 1968 and 1972, former Alabama Governor George Wallace delighted audiences by complaining that Washington was dominated by "pointy-headed" intellectuals and bureaucrats. He said that they could not park a bicycle correctly and suggested that their briefcases—which contained nothing anyway, except peanut butter sandwiches—should be thrown into the Potomac River. Others, too, have complained that bureaucrats are "rule-bound, precedent-oriented, paper-shuffling, self-protecting, experiment-resisting, conformity-rewarding, responsibility avoiding, and delay-filled."[27]

The general public's attitude toward bureaucracy is little better. Only a small percentage of Americans believes that bureaucrats are

---

[26]Congressional Quarterly, *Weekly Report* (April 7, 1979), pp. 631–32.
[27]See reference to Harold Laski in Mainzer, *Political Bureaucracy*, p. 2.

Many Americans do not have a positive image of bureaucracy as an institution, but those who have contact with individual bureaucrats, such as at this social security office, tend to be satisfied with their experiences.

creative and idealistic.[28] Less than half of the Americans surveyed in one study believe that bureaucrats are competent, fair, and considerate.[29] It is no wonder, then, that most Americans are not very interested in making federal civil service a career.[30]

Yet the truth is that most bureaucrats want to do a good job. This fact is reflected in the finding that a high percentage of Americans who have had contact with bureaucrats rank their experiences as "satisfactory" or "highly satisfactory."[31] The authors of this study state:

Bureaucrats have had a bad press. The vision is of a petty tyrant who wraps the cloak of office around inadequate shoulders, dominates those below him, and crouches sheepishly before those above him. That image has been with us a long time. . . . It turns out, however, that for all the snickering at the stereotype, Americans like the bureaucrats they deal with pretty well.[32]

Who are the federal bureaucrats? The average federal employee is about forty years old and has worked for the government for a little more than fourteen years, attaining an average salary of 17,000.[33] There are far more white-collar workers in the federal service than blue-collar workers. Federal white-collar workers include approximately 250,000 secretaries and clerks; 90,000 scientists; 13,000 attorneys; 3,000 psychologists; and 3,000 photographers. Blue-collar workers include more than 70,000 equipment operators; 15,000 woodworkers; and 10,000 painters and paperhangers.

Considering *all* federal jobs (from top to bottom), women are considerably underrepresented in relation to their percentage of the total population. Black people and American Indians are slightly overrepresented. Hispanics and Asian Americans are underrepresented.[34]

But the federal bureaucracy is far from a mirror of the general American population in the upper grades, particularly among executives and managers. Minorities and women are severely under-

---

[28]Senate Subcommittee on Intergovernmental Relations, *Confidence and Concern: Citizens View American Government* (Washington, D.C.: Government Printing Office, 1973), p. 306.

[29]Robert I. Kahn, Barbara A. Gutek, Eugenia Barton, and Daniel Katz, "Americans Love Their Bureaucrats," *Psychology Today* (June 1975), p. 70.

[30]See Kilpatrick et al., *The Image of the Federal Service.*

[31]Kahn et al., "Americans Love Their Bureaucrats," p. 70.

[32]Kahn, et al., "Americans Love Their Bureaucrats," p. 76.

[33]U.S. Civil Service Commission, *Federal Civil Work Force Statistics* (1978).

[34]See Kranz, *The Participatory Bureaucracy*, pp. 137–201.

represented. In the upper one third of the federal bureaucracy, minorities and women represent less than five percent of all positions.[35] High-level federal employees are also much more likely to be the children of professionals and businesspeople than members of the general population are.[36]

The people who reach the top level of the federal civil service generally start at the bottom in their agency. They usually stay in the same agency during their entire career, working their way up after twenty years or more of service. Even among politically appointed government positions, more than one third are filled by career bureaucrats who have worked their way up through the ranks of the federal bureaucracy.[37]

What do bureaucrats have to do to get ahead? One of the classic theorists of public administration, Max Weber, said, "The fully developed bureaucratic mechanism compares with other organizations exactly as does the machine with the nonmechanical modes of production."[38] But the truth is that bureaucrats are not machines or automatons. From their own backgrounds, training, and associations, they are likely to develop their own ideas about policy and ideology, which may differ from the opinions of the political authorities in the government.[39] Employees may be promoted as much because they identify with their agency, conform to its norms, and support its ideology, because they exhibit initiative and skill.[40] Too, bureaucrats tend to outlast Presidents. They build up their own networks of contacts, and they influence, and are influenced by, those contacts. Arthur M. Schlesinger, Jr., complained about the federal bureaucracy in the Kennedy Administration: "The permanent government soon developed its own stubborn vested interests in policy and procedure, its own cozy alliances with committees of Congress, its own ties to the press, its own national constituencies. It began to exude the feeling that presidents could come and presidents go, but it went on forever."[41]

HOW BUREAUCRACIES WORK

The federal bureaucracy is a part of the executive branch. But it has been called the "fourth branch of government"—in addition to the executive, legislative, and judicial branches—because of its impor-

---

[35]Kranz, *The Participatory Bureaucracy*, p. 140.

[36]See W. Lloyd Warner et al., *The American Federal Executive* (New Haven: Yale University Press, 1963), p. 12.

[37]See David T. Stanley, Dean E. Mann, Jamison W. Doig, *Men Who Govern* (Washington, D.C.: Brookings Institution, 1967).

[38]H. H. Gerth and C. Wright Mills, eds. and trans., *From Max Weber: Essays in Sociology* (New York: Oxford University Press, 1958), p. 214.

[39]See the report on research by Joel D. Aberbach and Bert A. Rockman in *Human Behavior* (January 1977), pp. 54–55.

[40]See H. R. G. Greaves, *The Civil Service in the Changing State* (London: G. G. Harrap, 1947), pp. 65–66.

[41]Arthur M. Schlesinger, Jr., *A Thousand Days* (Boston, Mass.: Houghton Mifflin, 1965), p. 680.

tance, permanence, and partially independent actions. What does the bureaucracy do?

The classic idea of *public administration*, the study of governmental bureaucracy, was that politics and administration were two distinctly different functions of government. This view held that the President and the Congress, elected by the people, should make policy, and that the bureaucracy, which was not elected, should carry it out. Woodrow Wilson wrote that "administrative questions are not political questions. Although politics sets the tasks for administration, it should not be suffered to manipulate its offices."[42] The basic goal of the "science of administration" was "efficiency."[43] Bureaucracy was to be characterized by "neutral-competence."[44] Thus, according to the ideal model of bureaucracy, bureaucrats were supposed to administer policy, supply expert knowledge to the policy-makers, and provide continuity in government functions. But they were not to be involved in the making of policy; that was to be ideally the responsibility of elected leaders.

Today, most political scientists consider this classic view incorrect and naive.[45] Bureaucracies themselves often act as interest groups, or as parts of interests groups, competing with other bureaucracies and other interest groups for their share of the budget. They also try to protect or expand their "turf" (jurisdiction) and influence the decisions of Congress and the President. President Eisenhower called attention to just such activity when he warned about the rising power of the "military-industrial complex" in his farewell address. The military bureaucracy works closely with interest groups that have a financial stake in military appropriations, the defense contractors, and other people who have economic ties with the military. Many of these groups employ former military officers. Both the military bureaucracy and their related interest groups work closely with the congressional committees that have legislative jurisdiction over the armed forces and defense spending. These relationships form the type of "cozy triangle" discussed earlier. Similar complexes and cozy triangles exist throughout the federal government.

A federal agency that enjoys national public support—as the National Aeronautics and Space Administration (NASA) did during the Kennedy and Johnson administrations—can exercise greater influence over elected policy-makers. Most federal agencies employ a

---

[42]Woodrow Wilson, "The Study of Administration," reprinted in *Political Science Quarterly* (December 1941), pp. 493–95.

[43]Luther Gulick, "Science, Values and Public Administration," in Luther Gulick and L. Urwick, eds., *Papers on the Science of Administration* (New York: Institute of Public Administration, 1937), p. 192.

[44]See Herbert Kaufman, "Emerging Conflict in the Doctrine of Public Administration," *American Political Science Review*, 50 (December 1956), pp. 1057–73.

[45]For a general discussion of the policy-making role of bureaucracy, see Peter Woll, *American Bureaucracy*, 2nd ed. (W. W. Norton, 1977), pp. 6–18.

[46]See David Wise, *The Politics of Lying: Government Deception, Secrecy, and Power* (New York: Random House, 1973), pp. 200–210.

number of people to handle public relations.[46] Although its stated purpose is "public information," public relations in federal agencies is often also aimed at influencing public opinion on matters that are important to the bureaucracy. As long ago as 1971, it was estimated that the executive branch of the government was spending half a billion dollars a year on public relations and public information programs. The Defense Department alone was spending over forty million dollars and employing over forty thousand people for that purpose.[47]

In addition, bureaucracies are involved in policy-making because they exercise legislative, judicial, and executive power. For example, Congress gives the Department of Agriculture authority to issue regulations concerning eligibility for food stamps. The Internal Revenue Service (IRS) holds hearings on individual tax cases and makes judicial determinations. This judicial power has been delegated by Congress to the IRS. In exercising executive power, federal bureaucracies engage in formulating overall executive budgets and long-range plans, and they make decisions concerning the day-to-day operations of large governmental programs and enterprises.

The division of expenditures among competing services and programs involves the most serious policy decisions made in the federal government. Federal bureaucracies share in this decision-making. Bureaucracies tend to be territorial, resisting encroachment on their territory by other agencies. They tend to develop ideologies and enforce them internally through selective recruitment, indoctrination, and promotional rewards. And they also tend to generate and require employee loyalty to the bureau, its territory, and its ideology.[48]

Bureaucratic territoriality, ideology, and loyalty, and the "cozy triangle" are all involved in the budgeting process. Consider a typical agency: the Federal Aviation Administration (FAA) in the Department of Transportation. Each year the administrator of the FAA must prepare the agency's budget for the coming year and present it to the secretary of transportation. Theoretically, the process for budget preparation, presentation, and final approval might occur in the following way: Under the direction of the FAA administrator, members of the staff would prepare a budget for all the agency's activities and services. The budget would be presented to the secretary of transportation, who would approve it with modifications and then forward it to the Office of Management and Budget. After consultations between the Office of Management and Budget and the Department of Transportation, the budget, with further modifications, would be recommended for approval by the President. The President would then approve the overall federal budget to be recommended to Congress, including the budget for the FAA. The

---

[47]J. William Fullbright, *The Pentagon Propaganda Machine* (N.Y.: Vintage Books, 1971), pp. 17, 25–27.

[48]See Anthony Downs, *Inside Bureaucracy* (Boston: Little, Brown, 1967).

appropriate committees in both houses of Congress would hold hearings at which the FAA administrator and other officials would testify in support of the recommended budget. Finally, after more modifications, Congress would pass authorization and appropriation bills to provide for the next year's budget for the FAA. At each level of this theoretical budgetary process, the budget would be approved only when the decision-makers were satisfied that each program and service was fully justified and absolutely essential.

This model of the budgetary process does not exist in reality. For one thing, budget-making tends to be based upon *incrementalism*. That is, government does not conduct a searching examination of current programs and services. Instead, programs and services are gradually changed, and their budgets are gradually increased. President Carter has attempted to offset the effects of incrementalism in two ways. First, he has tried to institute a "zero-based budgeting" system within the federal bureaucracy. This system requires each program and service to be justified anew during each annual budgetary process. It remains to be seen whether this concept will actually reduce incrementalism. Second, in 1978 Carter supported the passage of a new "sunset law" which seeks to terminate the life of agencies at the end of each five-year period unless they are formally authorized again. This new law, however, has not yet been put to a test.

The theoretical model of the federal budgetary process is unrealistic for another reason. The people who prepare budgets know that they will not get all they ask for. The officials who make decisions about budgets presented to them understand that a certain amount of "padding" will be added to a budget in expectation of cuts. In a sense, then, the federal budgetary process is a kind of game: The people who request budgets add some padding and the officials who decide upon budgets attempt to find this padding and eliminate it.

Finally, the theoretical model of the federal budgetary process does not take into account a number of interventions at the various junctures of decision-making. For example, consider the Federal Aviation Administration case again. While the FAA is preparing its budget, aviation industry groups—the clients of the agency—interested members of Congress, and the staff members of relevant

The Director of the Office of Management and the Budget (OMB), James McIntyre (right). Federal agencies submit budget requests annually to OMB, which prepares the overall federal budget for approval by the President.

congressional committees may contact FAA officials and seek to convince them to include certain items and amounts in the agency's budget request. When the secretary of transportation later considers the FAA budget, FAA clients and interested congressional members and staff may similary intervene again. As a matter of fact, the FAA may generate some of this intervention, seeking to indirectly influence the secretary's budgetary decisions. The same interventions may take place when decisions concerning the FAA's budget are made by the Office of Management and Budget (OMB). Theoretically, the administrator and other FAA officials are required to follow (and not go outside) the chain of command. Nevertheless, it is not unusual for such officials to let selected "friendly" members of Congress, client groups, and even "friendly" White House staff members know when their budgets are running into trouble with the OMB. They hope that these friends will intervene to influence the decisions of the OMB. The fight can also be taken up in the White House and in Congress with similar interventions at all of the various decision points there. The federal budgetary process, then, is not a neatly compartmentalized system of decision-making or a neutral, apolitical process.

TOWARD A RESPONSIBLE BUREAUCRACY

Clearly, bureaucracies are engaged in making policy, not just in scientifically, efficiently, and neutrally carrying out the policy made by elected leaders. What difference does this make? The fact that an unelected bureaucracy makes policy raises serious questions about democratic participation. How are citizens to participate in this kind of government decision-making? How can unelected bureaucrats be made fully accountable to the people for their decisions and acts? These are not just problems in democratic theory. Because of the power of the federal bureaucracy, they represent important practical problems.[49] Some authorities even argue that the bureaucracy is the predominant political power in this country, making *most* of the major decisions that affect the lives of Americans.

In a democracy, bureaucracy should be representative in two ways. First, it should be responsive to public demands and reflect the policy views of the public. Second, employment in the bureaucracy should be open to all, without discrimination, and be broadly representative of the total population.

There are a number of safeguards against an unrepresentative bureaucracy, and some of them could stand some strengthening. The

---

[49]See Norton Long, "Bureaucracy and Constitutionalism," *American Political Science Review*, 46 (September 1952): 818; and Carl J. Friedrich, *Man and His Government* (New York: McGraw-Hill, 1963), p. 464.

How to...

Use the Bureaucracy

The word itself—"bureaucracy"—conjures up images of a huge, impersonal maze, unmoveable, unreachable. In fact, however, the agencies that make up the federal bureaucracy were established in part to provide assistance and service to citizens. As a result of pressure from consumer groups, especially Ralph Nader's Public Citizen, many federal agencies have established toll-free "Hotlines" you can use to get information. The agencies, the information and assistance they provide, and their phone numbers are listed below:

Fair Housing and Equal Opportunity Hotline (HUD)
Accepts complaints on discrimination in housing based on race, color, religion, sex, or national origin. Continental U.S.: 800-424-8590; Washington, D.C. only: 755-5490.

Consumer Product Safety Commission
Receives reports on injuries/deaths relating to hazardous manufactured products and assists consumers in evaluating safety of products sold to the public. Continental U.S.: 800-638-2666; Maryland only: 800-492-2937.

Peace Corps/Vista
Provides information about volunteer opportunities within the ACTION agencies which perform foreign and domestic social service functions. Continental U.S.: 800-424-8580; Washington, D.C. only: 254-7346, exts. 26 and 38.

National Flood Insurance Hotline (HUD)
Disseminates information about a program that provides federally subsidized flood insurance in hazardous areas. Continental U.S.: 800-424-8872; Washington, D.C.: 755-9096.

Occupational Safety and Health Administration (OSHA)
Provides information about OSHA; accepts reports from workers about work-related accidents or dangerous working conditions. Check the U.S. Government telephone listing in your phone directory or call toll-free directory assistance (800-555-1212) for the regional OSHA toll-free numbers serving 30 states.

National Runaway Hotline (HEW)
Provides advisory services to runaways and parents on a 24-hour, confidential, free basis. Continental U.S.: 800-621-4000; Illinois only: 800-972-6004.

Operation Peace of Mind (State of Texas)
Confidential 24-hour message relay service accepts calls from runaways and forwards messages to parents. Provides counseling and confidential referral information on medical assistance, shelter, and other counseling services. Continental U.S.: 800-231-6946; Texas only: 800-392-3352.

V.D. Hotline (HEW)	Provides confidential, anonymous, free consultation, information, and referral services on all aspects of sexually transmitted diseases. Continental U.S.: 800-523-1885; Pennsylvania only: 800-462-4966; Philadelphia only: LO7-6969.
National Solar Heating and Cooling Information Center (HUD and Dept. of Energy)	Provides information concerning commercial availability of solar installations for heating and cooling. Continental U.S.: 800-523-2929; Pennsylvania only: 800-462-4983.
Education Grants Hotline (HEW, Office of Education)	Provides general information about the Basic Education Grants program, which offers financial aid for post-high school education to students who qualify on a financial need basis. Continental U.S.: 800-638-6700; for application processing (continental U.S.): 800-553-6350.
Federal Crime Insurance Hotline (HUD)	Provides information about and applications for federal low-cost commercial and residential crime insurance (available in over 20 states and the District of Columbia). Continental U.S.: 800-638-8780; Washington, D.C. only: 652-2637; Maryland only (call collect): 301-652-2637.
Commodity Futures Trading Commission	Answers consumer inquiries concerning commodity futures or commodity options. Disseminates information regarding commodity options and firms which are registered to sell these options. Washington, D.C.: 254-8630; states west of the Mississippi River (except California): 800-227-4428; states east of the Mississippi River and California: 800-424-9838.
Federal Tax Information (IRS)	Provides assistance on tax questions. Check the U.S. Government listing in your phone book or call toll-free directory assistance: 800-555-1212.
National Highway Traffic Safety Administration	Receives reports on auto safety problems; provides information on autos recalled and complaints received about specific makes and models. Continental U.S.: 800-424-9393; Washington, D.C. only: 426-0123.
Interstate Commerce Commission	Accepts complaints about interstate moving of household goods, rail and bus passenger problems, and questions on carrier rates. Also provides information to independent truckers on equipment leasing and ways to enter the independent trucking business. Continental U.S.: 800-424-9312; Washington, D.C. only: 275-7301.
Federal Election Commission	Provides information on fundraising regulations that apply to candidates for federal office; the Public Records Division provides materials for requesting financial records of federal candidates. Continental U.S.: 800-424-9530; Washington, D.C. only: 523-4068.
Veteran's Information (VA)	Provides information to veterans and their dependents about a range of benefits, including GI loans, education, and insurance; disability compensation; medical care and dental treatment; and employment. Check U.S. Government-Veteran's Administration in your local phone directory or call toll-free directory assistance for toll-free number in your state: 800-555-1212.
Cancer Information Service (National Cancer Institute, HEW)	Provides information about all aspects of cancer to the general public, cancer patients, and their families. All calls are confidential. There are local centers in 23 states, others are served by the national office. For Cancer Information Service toll-free number in your area, call toll-free directory assistance (800-555-1212) or call the national office: 800-638-6694; Maryland: 800-492-6600.

competition between *interest groups* can restrain arbitrary bureaucratic decisions and acts. If a bureau becomes too client-oriented, favoring one interest group over another, the unfavored interest groups may object and act to counter bureaucratic excesses. Of course, since most Americans are not represented in interest groups, competition among these groups is far from being a full check on arbitrary bureaucracy.

The *media* also serve as an important restraint on bureaucratic power. They call attention to bureaucratic oppression, waste, dishonesty, and red tape. New federal laws giving the press greater access to bureaucratic decisions through "freedom of information" legislation have increased this power. Other legislation has been introduced in the U.S. Congress to protect federal employees who go to the press and "blow the whistle" on federal wrongdoing or mismanagement.[50] The restraining influence of the media is limited, however, because reporters tend to develop good working relationships with the bureaucrats whose agencies they cover. Moreover, reporters often depend on the bureaucrats for information through press releases and "leaks."

Citizen participation can act as a check on the bureaucracy. It can be expanded by decentralizing and localizing decisions and using citizen advisory groups and public hearings on particular policies. Much of this kind of direct citizen participation, however, is no more than "symbolic participation," serving only to legitimize decisions actually made in the bureaucracy. More actual, rather than advisory, power could be placed in local controlling boards.

Another basic safeguard against unchecked bureaucratic power is *constitutional authority*. This power is exercised by elected public officials in the office of the President and in Congress, and in the judicial power of the courts. The courts, for example, can review and overrule the actions and decisions of bureaucracies. The power of judicial review is limited, however. Only formal orders of federal agencies can be appealed. Further, a person who is aggrieved by a bureaucratic order may not be able to afford the time and expense involved in an appeal.[51]

The power of the American President is very large. It involves the authority to appoint, direct, and remove the people in most of the top positions in the federal agencies. "Today a president may determine the course of antitrust policy during his administration or issue orders to the agencies of government concerned with school desegregation to follow his interpretation of the Constitution and civil rights laws."[52] But presidential authority over the bureaucracy has several limitations: the constitutional provision requiring the Senate to confirm some political appointments; the restrictions on hiring and

---

[50]See *Chicago Sun-Times* (October 21, 1977), p. 20.
[51]See Woll, *American Bureaucracy*, pp. 144–54.
[52]Robert J. Sickels, *Presidential Transactions* (Englewood Cliffs, N.J.: Prentice-Hall, 1974), p. 60.

firing under the civil service system; and the fact that officials in some positions, including all those in the regulatory bodies, are appointed for fixed terms and can only be removed for cause. Still, the chief executive has considerable authority over the bureaucracy, particularly through the budget-making power. And in some areas, the President can demand loyalty from the federal bureaucracy, although many bureaucrats have a considerable amount of independence within the jurisdiction that Congress has assigned them.[53]

Congress created the bureaucracy to perform jobs that Congress could not—or would not—do directly. Thus, Congress has considerable power to keep the bureaucracy in check.[54] It can change a law if it is not being administered to its liking. It can state the law more definitively if it does not approve of a bureaucratic interpretation. In addition, Congress can cut the budget of a bureau with which it disagrees, or abolish an agency or program altogether. And it can pressure the bureaucracy in individual cases through "casework" by senators and representatives.[55]

Congress could reduce the discretion of bureaucrats by specifying the details of laws when they are first passed, leaving little to be filled in by rules and regulations. But this tactic may be impractical because it would drastically expand the already heavy workloads in Congress. Members of Congress may think it impolitic, also, if they do not wish to be associated with the details of a new program or law.

Similarly, Congress could decrease the amount of federal paperwork, which causes a great amount of public complaint, particularly from small businesspeople.[56] But congressional efforts to reduce federal paperwork have not been very successful and have produced a lot of paper and reports themselves. Nevertheless, these reports place the blame for a great deal of government red tape on poorly written legislation.[57]

Finally, bureaucracy could also be made more responsive by making it more representative of the general population through *open employment*. According to a recent federal task force report, past hiring practices and the present policy of promoting from within bureaucracies makes it difficult for women or minorities to move rapidly into upper-level management positions.[58]

Thus, some people have suggested that greater efforts should be made to include a broader range of America's population in the federal bureaucracy. Such openness and representation would aid those groups who are now underrepresented in the federal bureaucracy by increasing their economic status, social prestige, political power, and political participation. It would enable the bureaucracy to

---

[53]See Woll, *American Bureaucracy*, pp. 206–47.

[54]See Woll, *American Bureaucracy*, pp. 155–205.

[55]See Robert L. Lineberry, *American Public Policy* (New York: Harper and Row, 1977), pp. 84–85.

[56]See *New York Times* (March 20, 1978), p. D1.

[57]*Chicago Sun-Times* (September 29, 1977), p. 40.

[58]*U.S. News and World Report* (October 16, 1978), p. 98.

become more responsive and sensitive to total population needs. It would tend to democratize decision-making within the bureaucracy because it would bring the diverse characteristics and views of the bureaucracy's employees—and of the population—into internal competition. It would result in a more efficient use of the total human resources of the country. Finally, by increasing the general feeling that governmental decisions rest on the legitimacy of representation and participation, it would contribute to greater public support of governmental policies.[59]

Americans do not have "a government of laws, rather than of men." The study of bureaucracy makes this quite clear. In the United States, there is no sharp distinction between policy-making by constitutional authorities and policy administration by unelected bureaucrats. Bureaucrats do not just implement policy; they are engaged in making policy in a number of ways. Even implementation is a form of policy-making.

Somehow, government's work—which is actually the people's work—must be done. The bureaucratic form of government organization seems to be here to stay. Some advances have been made and others certainly could be made to make the bureaucracy more humane, responsible, and representative.

ADDITIONAL SOURCES

Davis, James W., Jr. *An Introduction to Public Administration: Politics, Policy, and Bureaucracy*. Free Press, 1974.

Downs, Anthony. *Inside Bureaucracy*. Little, Brown, 1967.*

Freedman, James O. *Crisis and Legitimacy: The Administrative Process and American Government*. Cambridge University Press, 1978.

Fritschler, A. Lee. *Smoking and Politics: Policy Making and the Federal Bureaucracy*, 2nd ed. Prentice-Hall, 1975.*

Hess, Stephen. *Organizing the Presidency*. Brookings, 1976.*

Kelman, Steven. "Regulation that Works." *The New Republic* (November 25, 1978), pp. 16-20.

Koenig, Louis. *The Invisible Presidency*. Holt, Rinehart and Winston, 1960.

Krislov, Samuel. *Representative Bureaucracy*. Prentice-Hall, 1974.*

Nathan, Richard P. *The Plot that Failed: Nixon and the Administrative Presidency*. Harper & Row, 1975.*

Redford, Emmette S. *Democracy in the Administrative State*. Oxford University Press, 1969.*

Rourke, Francis. *Bureaucracy, Politics, and Public Policy*, 2nd ed. Little, Brown, 1976.

*Available in paperback edition.

---

[59]See Kranz, *The Participatory Bureaucracy*, pp. 89–133.

15 Law and the Courts
The Judicial Branch

Medical and law schools in America are unable to accept all students who apply for admission. In order to select the most "qualified" applicants, professional schools have developed certain screening criteria, such as college grade-point averages, entrance examination scores, and interviews. But in recent years, these schools have been under pressure to accept more women and minorities, who have been heavily underrepresented in professional studies. *Affirmative-action programs* were developed for that purpose.

The admissions programs of professional schools came to be aimed at two laudable goals: selecting the most "qualified" students on the basis of the traditional criteria; and giving special attention to groups that had been victims of discrimination. These two goals came into conflict in the case of Allan Bakke.

In 1973 and 1974, Allan Bakke, a white male, applied for admission to the medical school at the University of California at Davis. The medical school had places for only 100 beginning students, but it had two classes of admissions. The regular admissions program accepted students who achieved a certain "benchmark" score based on grades, test results, and interviews. The special admissions program reserved sixteen positions for students who were "economically and/or educationally disadvantaged" or who were members of a "minority group," including "blacks," "Chicanos," "Asians," and "American Indians."

In 1973, Bakke attained a strong benchmark score of 468 out of a

Allan Bakke.

possible 500. But the medical school rejected all applicants in the regular admissions program that year whose benchmark scores were under 470. Being white, Bakke was not eligible for the special admissions program, under which minority applicants who achieved lower benchmark scores than Bakke's were admitted. Bakke applied again in 1974 and, under similar circumstances, was again rejected.[1]

What does this story have to do with "law and the courts"? If it ended here, the answer would be—nothing. But Allan Bakke's attempt to enter the medical school at UC-Davis became a landmark case in the American judicial system. We will follow it throughout this chapter to illustrate the role and the workings of the courts. To begin, however, we need to find out how this case entered the judicial system and became a matter of "law."

WHAT IS "LAW"?

Law is the set of rules of conduct established by custom or laid down and enforced by governing authority. The need for predictability of behavior is the basic reason for law. "To some extent and within certain degrees of freedom, the individual members of a society must be able to demand from others certain regularities of behavior, and they must also accord to others the expectation that they, themselves, will behave predictably."[2]

Law can be classified in two principal ways. First, it can be categorized according to whom it involves and protects. This classification divides law into either civil law or criminal law. Second, it can be categorized by source; these sources are constitutional law, statutory law, administrative law, and judge-made law.

Civil law involves offenses—called *torts*—committed by a private individual or corporation against another. It also deals with the relationships between private individuals or corporations, such as contracts, marriages, or property ownership. In civil law, a private individual or corporation may sue another for an offense, such as negligence in causing an automobile accident. If successful, the person who brought the suit may secure damages (a court award in money) or obtain a court order requiring the person who was sued to do something (e.g., admit a person to a public facility) or refrain from doing something (e.g., stop blocking a driveway).

Criminal law involves an offense serious enough to be against the public interest as defined by the government. This kind of an offense—murder or driving while intoxicated, for example— constitutes a crime. Crimes are punishable by fine or imprisonment or

---

[1]Material on the *Bakke* case is from *The New York Times* (June 29, 1978), p. 1A; *Regents of the University of California* v. *Bakke*, 98 S. Ct. 2733 (1978). See also Allan P. Sindler, *Bakke, De Funis and Minority Admissions* (N.Y.: Longman, 1978).

[2]David W. Rohde and Harold G. Spaeth, *Supreme Court Decision Making* (San Francisco: Freeman, 1976), p. 2.

both. More serious crimes can involve the death penalty. Sometimes, an offense (like reckless driving) which causes injury to another person's automobile or body can constitute *both* a tort and a crime. The person who commits the offense may be sued for damages in a civil case and may also have to stand trial separately for a crime.

If we classify law according to its source, *constitutional law* is based on a constitution or constitutional provision, such as the equal protection clause in the Fourteenth Amendment to the U.S. Constitution. *Statutory law* consists of acts passed by a legislative body. One example is the Civil Rights Act of 1964, passed by the U.S. Congress. The rules and regulations issued by executive departments and agencies comprise *administrative law*. The federal regulations requiring affirmative-action programs are administrative law. *Judge-made law* consists of decisions and opinions by courts and judges. It is based on the doctrine of *stare decisis*, a Latin phrase meaning "the decision should stand." That is, in judge-made law, courts and judges give considerable weight to *precedents*, prior decisions and opinions in similar cases. When no clear constitutional, statutory, treaty, or administrative law provision applies, a court or judge may refer back to common law cases or equity cases in basing decisions on precedents.

Common law is made up of judge-made law in actual cases. Some of them are English cases going back hundreds of years, and others are more recent decisions of U.S. courts. *Equity* developed when English courts found that the common law had become too rigid and legalistic. Equity decisions attempted to make the common law more fair and to provide more flexible remedies. Thus, in equity, a court order can direct a person to do something (*mandamus*) or stop doing something (*injunction*), rather than just awarding damages after the fact for an act or a failure to act. Today, statutory law has codified (spelled out) and replaced most of the early judge-made law of common law and equity cases. But judges still make law today.

CHARACTERISTICS AND FUNCTIONS OF THE JUDICIAL SYSTEM

When Allan Bakke was turned down for the second time by the medical school at UC-Davis, he hired a lawyer and filed a lawsuit against the board of regents of the university. He claimed that the medical school's quota system constituted "reverse discrimination," violating his rights under the equal protection clause of the 14th Amendment and the Civil Rights Act of 1964. He asked the trial court to order the regents to admit him to the school.

In becoming a matter of law, the *Bakke* case illustrated the three main functions of our judicial system. Courts and judges hear and process disputes. They administer the law. And they interpret the law—that is, they make policy.

Suppose a Supreme Court justice was stopped on the way to work one morning by an interested citizen who said, "The Supreme Court ought to do something about a recent anti-abortion law passed by Congress. I believe that it violates the U.S. Constitution." Legislators hear similar citizen suggestions and demands for action almost every day. Would the justice—or *could* the justice—act upon such a citizen's suggestion? Or, suppose a federal district judge reads in a magazine article that several electronics firms have illegally joined together to fix the prices of their products. Can the judge intervene and issue an order to stop the price-fixing?

In each instance, the answer is no, because our judicial system is not self-starting. "When it is called upon to repress a crime, it punishes the criminal; when a wrong is to be redressed, it is ready to redress it; when an act requires interpretation, it is prepared to interpret it; but it does not pursue criminals, hunt out wrongs or examine evidence of its own accord."[3] Courts and judges hear and process the disputes that are brought before them. They legitimize a resolution of those disputes, giving the stamp of legal acceptance to them. But, as in the *Bakke* case, they do so in *adversary proceedings*. Under the adversary system, our judges and courts decide only actual "cases or controversies" between parties who have "standing" to sue or bring an action.[4]

Three basic types of cases or controversies are heard by the courts.[5] First, there are private disputes that involve no public authority as a party. For example, a husband or wife may seek a divorce, or one person may sue another for breach of contract or for personal injury. Second, some disputes are initiated by a public authority to enforce government rules or law. Criminal cases, which are initiated by prosecutors such as a district attorney, are disputes of this kind. Third, a public authority is the defendant in some cases, such as the *Bakke* case. In these situations, some private individual or corporation brings a lawsuit to enforce the law against a government agency. To have "standing" to sue in such a case or in a private dispute, a person must actually be an interested party who has suffered harm, or someone who is likely to suffer harm, or who is otherwise entitled to have his or her own contract or other rights *adjudicated*, or decided.

Judges and courts can exercise considerable power in our system. They can say what the law is, for example. But their power is limited by the constraints of the adversary system. They are required to "speak only when spoken to." The executive and legislative branches of our government may initiate action without waiting to be asked.

---

[3]Alexis de Tocqueville, *Democracy in America*, Vol. 1 (N.Y.: Vintage Books, 1954), pp. 103–4.

[4]See Rohde and Spaeth, *Supreme Court Decision Making*, pp. 9–20.

[5]Sheldon Goldman and Austin Sarat, eds., *American Court Systems* (San Francisco: Freeman, 1978), pp. 4–7.

But courts and judges are reactive, or passive.[6] In civil cases, they must wait until one party sues another; in criminal cases, they cannot act until a prosecutor files a complaint against someone or a police officer makes an arrest.

Administration of the Law

Courts and judges are guardians of our legal system and guarantors of our political structure. They administer the law. As noted earlier, the basis for our legal system is the need for predictability or regularity of behavior. A large portion of these norms, or accepted standards of conduct, have been codified in the form of constitutions, acts of legislative bodies, treaties, and judicial decisions. The *judiciary*—that is, courts and judges—are expected to administer these norms as guardians of our legal system. They mete out punishment, award damages, issue orders, and oversee the machinery necessary to do so.

Courts and judges also act as guarantors of the political structure.[7] They do this in three ways. They may interpret state or federal constitutions in a way that limits the authority of the legislative and executive branches of the government. This power was expressly stated in the famous case of *Marbury* v. *Madison*, decided in 1803.[8] Chief Justice John Marshall's opinion first established the doctrine of *judicial review* (the Supreme Court's authority to say what the Constitution means). It then held that an act passed by Congress, which would have enlarged the original jurisdiction of the Supreme Court, was invalid because it conflicted with Article III of the Constitution. Courts may also decide against legislative and executive excesses. The Supreme Court's decree that Richard Nixon could not withhold certain documents and tape recordings on the grounds of executive privilege is a notable example.[9] As guarantors of the political structure—administrators of the law—courts also decide issues involving civil liberties and civil rights, fundamental concepts in any political system.

Courts and judges are expected to be "above politics" and independent of political or other pressures or public opinion in reaching their decisions.[10] They are expected to be neutral referees, deciding each case upon its facts and according to the law that applies to those facts.

Judges are not only expected to speak only when spoken to; they are also generally supposed to speak only in official communications, such as decisions and opinions. They are expected to exhibit judicial

---

[6]Donald Black, "The Mobilization of Law," *Journal of Legal Studies*, 2 (1973): 128.

[7]Herbert Jacob, *Justice in America*, 3rd ed. (Boston: Little, Brown and Company, 1978), pp. 4–6.

[8]*Marbury* v. *Madison*, 1 Cranch 137 (1803).

[9]*U.S.* v. *Nixon*, 418 U.S. 683 (1974).

[10]See Herbert Wechsler, "Toward Neutral Principles of Constitutional Law," *Harvard Law Review*, 73 (1959): 1–35.

demeanor and temperament and refrain from becoming personally or emotionally involved in a case before them. Their behavior is prescribed by the Canons of Professional and Judicial Ethics of the American Bar Association. Violations of these codes can cause public censure, disbarment, and even removal from office. Thus, while senators who cast unpopular votes may frequently make home-state tours to explain their votes and drum up support for them, such behavior by a judge would be highly irregular and censurable.

Administration of the law, then, is an important function of the judiciary. But courts and judges sometimes make law, too.

Policy-making

Because it requires judicial neutrality and impartiality and restricts judicial decisions to those cases involving actual disputes, America's legal system is sometimes referred to as a "system of laws, rather than of men." The law is often described as "no respecter of persons."

Yet the law applicable to a given situation cannot always be scientifically determined. It is not merely a matter of punching the buttons of a computer, for example. Judges and courts must often exercise discretion in determining how a particular case should be decided.

Although courts and judges only decide actual cases, the decisions and opinions they issue can control or greatly influence the outcome of later similar cases. In the *Bakke* case, the court system ostensibly was asked to only decide the actual controversy between Allan Bakke and the Regents of the University of California, but the decision would also apply in any similar cases which come before the courts in the future.

Thus, judges and courts—the judiciary—are not only involved in resolving conflicts in individual disputes and in administering the law; they are also involved in policy-making, or law-making. Courts not only enforce norms; they actually create or establish norms.[11] For example, it was not a legislative act which declared that during the first six months of pregnancy, a state law could not deny a woman's right to an abortion. The U.S. Supreme Court established that rule.[12] Similarly, no executive order or regulation issued by a federal commission decided that all legislative districts should be approximately equal in population. A Supreme Court decision opened up this legislative subject to judicial review and policy-making.[13]

Some critics argue that it is unfair for unelected judges to make policy. Other critics maintain that policy made by judges and courts is often unjust.[14] But the fact remains that judges and courts *do* make policy and that policy-making is one of their major functions.

[11]Jacob, *Justice in America*, p. 32.
[12]*Roe* v. *Wade*, 410 U.S. 113 (1973).
[13]*Baker* v. *Carr*, 369 U.S. 186 (1962).
[14]Goldman and Sarat, eds., *American Court Systems*, p. 3.

STRUCTURE OF THE JUDICIAL SYSTEM

Although the *Bakke* case was finally settled by the U.S. Supreme Court, it did not begin there. Allan Bakke initially filed his lawsuit against the Board of Regents of UC-Davis in the Superior Court of Yolo County, a California state court. The judge of this trial court determined the facts in the dispute: Bakke's benchmark scores; the existence of the special admissions program for minorities and others; and the admission of students in the special admissions category, even though they had lower benchmark scores than Bakke. Next, the trial judge held that under the equal protection clause of the U.S. Constitution, the medical school's special admissions program amounted to unlawful racial discrimination and was an unconstitutional quota system. The Regents promptly appealed this decision to the Supreme Court of California. Accepting the facts that had been established in the trial court, the appellate court also agreed on how the law should be interpreted. The California Supreme Court held that the medical school had violated Bakke's constitutional rights by denying him admission. The court stated that it was improper under the equal protection clause to give *any* consideration to race in the admissions process. It then ordered the case *remanded*, or sent back, to the trial court with instructions to direct the Board of Regents to grant Bakke admission to the medical school.

The case might have ended at this point except for two things. The regents were dissatisfied with the California Supreme Court ruling and appealed for a hearing before the U.S. Supreme Court, and the Supreme Court granted such a review. (The Supreme Court largely decides which cases it will hear on appeal. More than 5000 such petitions come to the Court every year. When four justices vote in

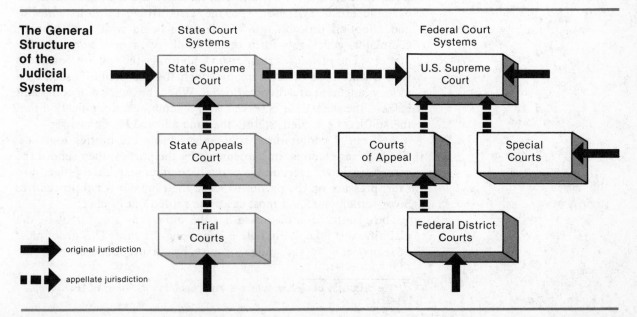

The General Structure of the Judicial System

State Court Systems · Federal Court Systems

State Supreme Court → U.S. Supreme Court

State Appeals Court

Courts of Appeal · Special Courts

Trial Courts

Federal District Courts

→ original jurisdiction

▪▪▪▶ appellate jurisdiction

favor of hearing a case, that is sufficient to put it on the Supreme Court's docket. But most cases are not accepted.) On February 22, 1977, the Supreme Court agreed to accept the *Bakke* case on appeal. The Court issued a *writ of certiorari* to the California Supreme Court, an order directing that all the records of the earlier court proceedings be sent to the U.S. Supreme Court. The Supreme Court also directed both the regents and Bakke to file "briefs" stating their arguments and reasoning concerning the law under which the dispute arose. In addition, the Court permitted briefs to be filed by a number of others, including civil rights groups, the American Civil Liberties Union, and the U.S. solicitor general, the Justice Department official who represents the United States before the Supreme Court. (An interested party who is not an actual party to a lawsuit but is allowed to file a brief is called an *amicus curiae*, or "friend of the court.") The U.S. Supreme Court's eventual decision in the *Bakke* case was the final judicial word on the law applicable to the dispute.

As the *Bakke* case illustrates, our judicial system, like the other branches of government, is decentralized and fragmented. Two factors principally define its structure: jurisdiction and federalism. *Jurisdiction* means the authority to interpret and apply the law. It involves both the kinds of cases a court may hear (civil or ciminal, for example) and at what stage it may hear them (trial or appellate). *Federalism* refers to our dual system of government; thus, the states and the federal government have separate judicial systems.

Civil and Criminal Courts

Civil cases involve private disputes. Controversies stemming from torts, contracts, divorces, antitrust matters, and debt collection, for example, are all civil cases. They may also involve the probate of wills and adoption proceedings.[15] Civil cases begin with a petition or complaint, which sets forth the plaintiff's view of the facts of the matter. (The *plaintiff* is the person who brings the suit.) It concludes with a statement of the remedy sought by the plaintiff, such as a money judgment or a divorce decree. When the petition or complaint is filed, the defendant is served with a summons, a notification that the suit has been filed, stating the time allowed for an answer.

At pretrial conferences, trial judges bring the parties together. Through stipulations, or agreements by the parties, they reduce the controversy over facts and law to a bare minimum. Trial judges also exert pressure on the parties to settle their lawsuit. Civil procedures favor settlements, and most cases *are* settled out of court.

The plaintiff in a civil case has the *burden of proof*; that is, the plaintiff must take the initiative in proving the case. This proof must be convincing to the judge or jury by "a preponderance of the

---

[15]The discussion of civil cases here is based upon Jacob, *Justice in America*, pp. 194–211.

evidence." This standard is less strict than the one required in criminal cases.

Criminal cases may involve *misdemeanors*, which are minor offenses generally punishable by less than one year imprisonment. Or they may involve felonies, more serious offenses that carry possible prison terms of one year or more.[16] Criminal cases begin with an arrest. The accused is *arraigned* (brought before a judge or magistrate), informed of the charge, and asked to enter a plea. Bail is then set (or denied in some serious cases). A grand jury session or preliminary hearing may be held to determine whether there is sufficient evidence to require the accused to stand trial. Plea-bargaining between the accused and the prosecutor may result in a reduction of the charge or punishment in return for a plea of guilty. Prosecutors seek these pleas primarily to reduce the number of cases that have to be tried. If there is no plea of guilty and if the charges are not dismissed, the case will finally go to trial. The burden of proof is much heavier in a criminal case; in our system, a person accused of a crime is presumed innocent until proven guilty. Thus, the accused cannot be convicted unless the prosecutor proves the case "beyond a reasonable doubt."

In the federal system, the district courts, courts of appeal, and the Supreme Court have both civil and criminal jurisdiction. This is usually true of state trial courts, but some states have established separate appellate systems for criminal and civil cases.

Trial and Appellate Courts

In a trial court, the judge determines what law should apply to a particular case. When the trial is conducted without a jury (a fairly common practice, particularly in civil matters), the trial judge also determines the facts of the case.

Federal district courts are the usual trial courts in the federal system, but there are some special federal trial courts. The states have a wide variety of trial courts. Some are established for special kinds of cases. For example, family courts handle divorces and adoptions. Others handle only probate matters (wills and estates). Special state courts often also handle relatively minor civil or criminal matters. Magistrate or municipal courts and justices of the peace are two examples. These minor tribunals, however, are not courts of record. That is, if an appeal is taken from such a minor trial court, the trial may proceed *de novo*, all over again, in a trial court of record. In the states, it is usually a state district court. There can be no trial *de novo* on an appeal from a court of record.

Appellate judges assess the record concerning the facts of a case. They also decide which law should apply to the facts. In determining and assessing the facts and in applying the law, appellate judges

---

[16]Material for this section is taken from James Eisenstein and Herbert Jacob, *Felony Justice* (Boston: Little, Brown and Company, 1977), pp. 192–311.

After the U.S. Supreme Court agreed to hear the *Bakke* case, groups in favor of affirmative action demonstrated in Washington, D.C. They urged the Court to overturn the California court's decision, which held that the program at UC-Davis unconstitutionally discriminated against Bakke.

usually do not hear the testimony of witnesses. Instead, they read the trial record and consider the briefs and arguments of the lawyers.

Nine out of every ten cases are settled by the judgment of trial courts, if they go to trial at all, and they are not appealed. But the federal and state judicial systems do have appellate courts. A case may be appealed from a federal district court to a court of appeal. The eleven federal appeals courts serve judicial districts, which are called circuits. Under certain circumstances, appeals from these courts may be taken to the U.S. Supreme Court, which is the "court of last resort" in the federal judicial system.

The state systems have similar tiers of appellate jurisdiction. There are usually intermediate appellate courts and then a court of last resort, usually a state supreme court. Some states provide separate civil and criminal appellate courts. When a federal question is involved, as in the *Bakke* case, an appeal may be taken from a state's highest court to the Supreme Court of the United States, if it accepts jurisdiction.

Federalism

America has a dual court system based on the principle of federalism. This system means, among other things, that a person may be tried for the same offense in *both* a state court, under state law, and in a federal court, under federal law. For example, a person charged with the possession of heroin could be tried in a state court and in a federal court. Two trials do not in this instance constitute double jeopardy, because there are two separate sovereigns involved.[17] Similarly, an Indian may be tried for the same offense in both an Indian tribal court and in a federal court. In this case, there would also be separate sovereigns. Like states, tribes are not creatures of the federal government but have inherent powers as separate governments.[18]

In civil cases, a plaintiff may often be able to choose whether to bring a lawsuit in a state or federal court. Lawyers have different preferences for these courts, but their choice depends partly upon what kind of cases they have. Federal judges often run their courts with more sternness and authority than do state judges. Too, federal judges may take more of a personal role in bringing pressure on the parties to settle the case. In addition, they may more readily comment to the jury about the veracity of witnesses and the weight that should be given to evidence.

Violations of federal criminal law and federal bankruptcy cases are tried in federal district courts. Whether a federal district court has jurisdiction in a regular civil case depends upon the subject matter of the lawsuit, or who the parties are, or both. A civil case may be filed in the federal district court if it involves more than $10,000 and if the controversy involves the U.S. Constitution or a federal treaty or law, or if it involves admiralty and maritime law, a special body of

---

[17]See *Bartkus* v. *Illinois*, 359 U.S. 121; and *Abbatt* v. *United States*, 359 U.S. 187.
[18]*U.S.* v. *Wheeler*, 98 S. Ct. 1079 (1978).

decisions concerning shipping and the use of the seas. A civil case may also be filed in a federal district court if the parties involved are ambassadors or other foreign diplomats, if the United States is a party, if the parties involve two or more states or two or more citizens of different states.

The Supreme Court's "original jurisdiction"—its power to hear cases directly, which have not gone through the lower federal courts—is limited. According to the Constitution, it is restricted to those cases involving "Ambassadors, other public ministers and Consuls, and those in which a State shall be a Party."

The U.S. Constitution created the Supreme Court but left the establishment of the other federal courts to Congress. Congress has established eleven courts of appeal as well as at least one district court in each of the states. (Some states have more than one district court, depending upon population and caseload.) Congress has also created a number of special federal tribunals, such as the Court of Claims, the Customs Court, the U.S. Court of Customs and Patent Appeals, and the Court of Military Appeals.

THE U.S. SUPREME COURT

Very few cases before the Supreme Court are set for oral arguments. Only the ones that the Court feels are most important are given this kind of attention. The Court decides most cases on the basis of the record in the lower court and the written briefs filed by the lawyers. In the *Bakke* case, however, the Supreme Court decided that the issues were sufficiently important to require oral arguments.

On October 12, 1977, the day the Court was to hear oral arguments in the case, the lawyers, other interested parties, and a limited number of spectators who had been able to gain admission gathered in the awesome marble chamber of the U.S. Supreme Court in Washington, D.C. They sat quietly or spoke to each other in hushed tones as they waited for the members of the Supreme Court to enter and take their places at the high bench in front. The atmosphere was almost as reverent as for the coronation of a pope. Suddenly, the marshal rapped his gavel. Everyone stood as the marshal intoned the traditional words,

The Burger Court: (standing, left to right) William Rehnquist, Harry Blackmun, Lewis Powell, and John Paul Stevens; (seated, left to right) Byron White, William Brennan, Warren Burger, Potter Stewart, and Thurgood Marshall.

"The Honorable, the Chief Justice and the Associate Justices of the Supreme Court of the United States! Oyez, oyez! All persons having business before the Honorable, the Supreme Court of the United States are admonished to draw near and give their attention, for the Court is now sitting. God save the United States and this Honorable Court."

Through the parted red velvet curtains behind the bench, the members of the Supreme Court emerged, solemn and black-robed, and took their places. White-haired Warren Burger, the chief justice who had been appointed by President Nixon in 1969, sat down at his place in the middle of the bench facing the audience. The other justices arranged themselves by seniority on either side of the chief justice: William Brennan and Potter Stewart, both appointed by President Eisenhower; Byron White, named by President Kennedy; Thurgood Marshall, the black former NAACP attorney, appointed by President Johnson; Harry Blackmun, William Rehnquist (the youngest member of the Court), and Lewis Powell, all appointed by President Nixon; John Paul Stevens, named by President Ford.

When the justices and the audience were seated, the chief justice called for the oral arguments. All of the participating lawyers, except the U.S. solicitor general, were dressed in conservative, dark business suits. The solicitor general wore a traditional "morning suit," a charcoal black, swallow-tailed coat and striped trousers. The lawyers made their arguments within strict time limits set by the Court, but they were frequently interrupted by individual justices, who asked pointed questions about specific aspects of their reasoning. Then the marshal rapped his gavel again, the audience stood up, and the justices retired to their offices. Five days later the Court asked Bakke's lawyer, the counsel for the regents, and the U.S. solicitor general to file additional briefs explaining the relevance of the Civil Rights Act of 1964 to their arguments. An important case like *Bakke* is ready for decision after the case record and the lawyers' briefs are before the Court and after the Court has heard the oral arguments. The Supreme Court members then meet in secret conference, presided over by the chief justice. If the chief justice is in the majority on the question of how the case should be decided, he may write the majority opinion of the Court, or he may assign a particular justice who represents the majority to write the opinion. But other justices may also write their own separate opinions. These may be *concurring*—in agreement with the majority opinion—or *dissenting*—disagreeing with the majority opinion. These separate opinions may be circulated among the other members of the Court for their approval. Before the Court makes a final decision, it is possible that what was at first a dissenting opinion may have gained sufficient support to become the majority opinion. Although only the majority opinion has the force of law, lawyers study dissenting and concurring opinions to gain insights into possible arguments that might cause the Court to change its majority opinion in a future case.

No one knew how the Supreme Court would decide the *Bakke* case. As usual, there were no press releases and no "leaks" telling what was going on behind the Court's closed doors. (There have been two rare news leaks concerning Supreme Court proceedings since the *Bakke* case.) No justice gave an interview about the case. No reporter was allowed to cover the conferences where the justices discussed the case. Throughout the country, people speculated about what the Court might say, but none of this speculation purported to be based upon inside information. Universities, students, civil rights activists, members of minority groups, and others knew that what the Court decided in the *Bakke* case would not just affect Allan Bakke and the University of California at Davis. It would also affect all other institutions and students faced with the same question in the future. Moreover, it might affect other kinds of affirmative-action programs, too.

While the Court was considering the merits of the *Bakke* case, it continued to hear other cases and to issue other opinions. The *Bakke* case, in fact, proved to be a difficult one for the justices to decide; eight and a half months had passed after the oral arguments were heard before the Court announced its decision. Even then, the Court's decision was the result of a precarious and disjointed agreement.

On June 28, 1978, the members of the Court formally entered the Supreme Court chamber once more. The marshal repeated the traditional words. This time the Court would announce their decision in the *Bakke* case. The chief justice deferred to Justice Powell, who spoke for a five-member majority of the Court's nine members. But it turned out, in this instance, that there were two majorities. The first majority, made up of Justices Powell, Stewart, Rehnquist, and Stevens, and Chief Justice Burger, held that the special admissions program of the medical school at Davis was unlawful under the equal protection clause of the Fourteenth Amendment. They said that the school would have to admit Bakke. Their reasoning was that under the equal protection clause, the special admissions program was "a line drawn on the basis of race and ethnic status," which amounted to unconstitutional "discrimination," even though the discrimination was against a white person and in favor of minorities. (This first majority opinion went on to say in *dicta*—statements not essential to the ruling and, therefore, not necessarily binding as law—that an admissions program at Harvard College, which provided for no "fixed number of places" for minorities was an "illuminating example" that was not defective on its face. In the Harvard program, the Court said, race or ethnic background was "simply one element—to be weighed fairly against other elements—in the selection process." The Harvard College admissions plan was made an appendix to the majority opinion.)

The second majority opinion, approved by Justice Powell again and by Justices Brennan, White, Marshall, and Blackmun, held that the California Supreme Court had been wrong in attempting to prevent the medical school from giving *any* consideration to race in its admissions process. This majority opinion held that under the Civil Rights Act of 1964, race could be one element in admissions criteria. The opinion stated that the Act permitted "race-conscious remedial action." It said that past discrimination cannot be redressed merely by the actions of a public body "ending its unlawful acts and adopting a neutral stance." Thus, the U.S. Supreme Court affirmed, or approved, the decision of the California Supreme Court in one respect and reversed it in another. The Court said in effect that race could be taken into account as *one* factor in college admissions decisions but that rigid quotas were prohibited. It took two different groups of justices to arrive at these two positions.

"The Winner!"

Justice Powell, who wrote the Court's majority opinions, was the deciding vote in each instance, shifting between the two groups of four justices in order to make a majority for each of the two holdings.

Several dissenting opinions were also written. Justice White (who had joined the second majority) issued a separate *dissenting opinion* in opposition to a fairly technical legal position on which all the other justices were apparently united. He argued that the Civil Rights Act of 1964 did not give an *individual* a right to sue for the Act's enforcement. Instead, he said, only federal agencies could enforce the Act by withholding federal funds, for example, from noncomplying institutions. Justice Marshall (also part of the second majority) wrote a separate *dissenting opinion* addressing the substantive issues of the case. Marshall argued that the special admissions program at the medical school was both necessary and constitutional. Justice Marshall also pointed out that the two majority decisions of the Court would affect far more people than just the regents of the University of California and Allan Bakke, the actual legal parties in the case. He doubted "that there is a computer capable of determining the number of persons and institutions that may be affected by the decision in this case."

Justice Blackmun (another member of the second majority) also addressed the substantive issues in another *dissenting opinion*. Blackmun cited veterans' preferences, aid to the handicapped, the progressive income tax, and various American Indian programs as examples of "reverse discrimination" that have been upheld. Since "geography, athletic ability, anticipated financial largess, alumni pressure, and other factors of that kind have been used to prefer certain college applicants over others," Blackmun argued, why not race? "And in order to treat some persons equally, we must treat them differently," he added. Justice Blackmun also took issue with the *dicta* in the first majority opinion concerning the Harvard College admissions plan. "The cynical, of course," he stated, "may say that under a program such as Harvard's one may accomplish covertly what Davis concedes it did openly."

Justice Stevens wrote another opinion that Chief Justice Burger and Justices Stewart and Rehnquist (all members of the first majority) concurred with. It was partly a *concurring opinion* and partly a *dissenting opinion*. It concurred with the first majority opinion, which declared the special admissions program at Davis unlawful. It dissented from the second majority opinion, which reversed the California Supreme Court's decision preventing the medical school from giving *any* consideration to race in its admissions plan. The Stevens opinion also disagreed with Justice Marshall's reference to the broad impact of the majority opinion, stating, "This is not a class action. The controversy is between specific litigants." The Stevens opinion also took issue with Justice White's opinion, which asserted that private litigants had no standing to enforce the Civil Rights Act of 1964.

Confusing or not, the Supreme Court decision was the final legal episode in the *Bakke* case. The Supreme Court of the United States is the highest court in the land, the court of *very* last resort.[19] Allan Bakke was admitted to the medical school. The Court once again exercised its power to declare what the U.S. Constitution means. It directed a state institution, the regents of the University of California, to act in accordance with the Court's interpretation of the law. The *Bakke* case illustrates the Supreme Court's position in our judicial system—a position that is a product of the U.S. Constitution and the Court's evolving history.

Development of the Supreme Court

Article III, Section 1, of the U.S. Constitution states: "The judicial power of the United States, shall be vested in one Supreme Court, and in such other inferior Courts as the Congress may from time to time ordain and establish." Almost from the beginning, the Supreme Court's exercise of this judicial power has helped to make America's national government strong, and it has made the Supreme Court a powerful branch of that government.

Charles Evans Hughes, who served as chief justice from 1930 to 1941, once said, "We are under the Constitution, but the Constitution

---

[19]Material in this section is taken from Rohde and Spaeth, *Supreme Court Decision Making*.

is what the judges say it is."[20] The Supreme Court's power to say what the Constitution means—the power of judicial review—is based upon Chief Justice John Marshall's landmark opinion in the case of *Marbury* v. *Madison* (1803).[21] Marshall, the country's third chief justice, had been appointed by John Adams in 1801; he served for more than thirty years (1801–1835).

The case arose when Thomas Jefferson, newly elected President, became angered that the Federalist-controlled Congress had created a large number of new judgeships and that out-going President John Adams had hurriedly filled them before Jefferson and the Democratic-Republicans took office. Jefferson discovered that William Marbury had been appointed and confirmed to fill a new justice of the peace position in the District of Columbia—but had never received his commission from the secretary of state. Jefferson directed James Madison, the new secretary of state, to withhold the commission. Marbury then sued Madison under an earlier congressional act that had enlarged the original jurisdiction of the Supreme Court and allowed it to hear such suits. He sought a court order forcing Madison to issue the commission. The case raised serious questions: Would the Court order the secretary of state to obey the law as the Court interpreted it? If such an order was issued, would the President and the secretary of state ignore it? If they did ignore it, what would happen then?

Marshall's majority opinion in the case was an adroit meshing of politics and law. It sidestepped the question of whether the commission should be issued, and instead held that Marbury had no right to sue. Why? Marshall's opinion said that the act that had authorized such suits violated the Constitution and was therefore invalid. The case was thus settled on a technicality, and a confrontation between the President and the Court was averted. Jefferson got what he wanted: Marbury did not take office. But the power of the Supreme Court was enhanced by its assumption of the power to interpret and apply the U.S. Constitution and to determine the constitutionality of congressional acts.

Thirteen years later,[22] the Marshall Court held that U.S. Supreme Court decisions could overrule decisions of state courts in cases involving federal questions (as in the *Bakke* case). Then, in the landmark case of *McCulloch* v. *Maryland* (1819),[23] Chief Justice Marshall's majority opinion declared that a conflicting state legislative act must give way to an act of Congress that is in accord with the Constitution. It held that Congress not only possesses the powers expressly stated in the Constitution but also has such implied powers as are "necessary and proper" to carry them out. Five years later,

---

[20]Quoted in Alpheus T. Mason, *The Supreme Court: Palladium of Freedom* (Ann Arbor, Mich.: University of Michigan Press, 1962), p. 143.

[21]*Marbury* v. *Madison*, 1 Cranch 137 (1803).

[22]*Martin* v. *Hunter's Lessee*, 1 Wheaton 304 (1816).

[23]*McCulloch* v. *Maryland*, 4 Wheaton 316 (1819).

Marshall wrote an opinion which held that New York's attempt to prevent New Jersey steamboats from using its waterways and ports was an unconstitutional interference with the power of Congress to regulate interstate commerce under Article I, Section 8, of the Constitution.

During Roger Taney's tenure as chief justice (1836–1864), the Supreme Court's decisions moved back in the direction of protecting states' rights. However, the Court did not overturn the most fundamental opinions of the Marshall era. After the Civil War and into the twentieth century, the Court continued to follow a conservative line in civil rights cases and in decisions protecting business and industrial interests. President Franklin D. Roosevelt ran head-on into the conservative legal thinking of the Supreme Court soon after he took office in 1933.

The U.S. Constitution does not specify how many members the Supreme Court should have. The Judiciary Act of 1789 set the total membership of the Supreme Court at six: a chief justice and five associate justices. Today, there are nine members of the Court. Angered by the opposition of the "nine old men" (as he called the members of the Court) to his New Deal programs, Roosevelt sought to "pack" the Court with friendly justices. He attempted to persuade Congress to increase the court's membership to twelve. Backed by strong public opinion on the issue, however, Congress refused to pass the needed legislation, and the idea died. But time—and vacancies on the Court—changed the makeup and philosophy of the Court. Under broad interpretations of the commerce clause and the welfare clause, the Court later upheld Roosevelt's proposals for regulating the activities of business and industry and for dealing with the Great Depression. Thus, it further enhanced the power of the national government.

While Earl Warren was chief justice (1953–1969), the Court expanded the civil rights and civil liberties of Americans. Chief Justice Warren Burger, appointed by President Nixon in 1969, has presided over a somewhat more conservative Court. Their decisions have been particularly conservative in the field of civil liberties, including freedom of the press and the rights of a person accused of a crime. Despite its shifting positions on particular issues through the years, the Supreme Court has helped to bring about the primacy of the national government in our federal system. Its decisions have also established the Supreme Court as a powerful institution, one which has political as well as legal effect.

The justices.   According to Article III, Section 1, of the Constitution, Supreme Court justices who have been nominated by the President and confirmed by the Senate may continue in their offices "during good behavior"—that is, for life. Justices of the Supreme Court hold highly prestigious positions in our system. Except for the remote possibility of impeachment, they are insulated (although not totally isolated) from public opinion and political pressures. A

President may take several factors into account when nominating someone to fill a vacancy on the Supreme Court. (The Senate may consider some or all of these same factors when deciding on confirmation.) They include professional qualifications and political, geographical, representational, and ideological considerations.[24]

Nothing in the law or the Constitution requires members of the Supreme Court to be lawyers, but all of them have been. Court members do not have to first serve in some other judicial position, either. Some of the "great" justices, such as Marshall, Warren, and Louis Brandeis, had no previous judicial experience. Normally, however, Presidents consider public opinion and Senate reaction (the Senate has rejected 20 percent of those nominated for court membership), when making Supreme Court nominations; they usually nominate people who have distinguished themselves in the legal profession or in judicial or other public service.

Political considerations and friendship have played a part in some appointments to the Supreme Court. President Eisenhower appointed Earl Warren to the Court, for example, primarily because his support as governor of California had been heavily influential in securing the Republican presidential nomination for Eisenhower. President Johnson appointed his close friend, political supporter, and personal lawyer and adviser, Abe Fortas, as a member of the Supreme Court. Johnson later nominated Fortas to be chief justice, but the Senate refused to confirm Fortas as chief justice, and he thereafter resigned from the Court, when it became known that he had accepted a retainer from a financier while a Court member. Ninety percent of the Supreme Court justices since 1789 have been members of the same political party as the President who nominated them. But this is partly a result of the fact that people with the same political party affiliation are likely to have similar backgrounds and similar views on important issues.

Geographical considerations have also influenced nominations to the Supreme Court. Presidents have generally felt that all regions of the country should be represented on the Court. When President Nixon nominated Southerners Clement Haynesworth and G. Harrold Carswell (who were both rejected by the Senate) and Lewis Powell (who was confirmed), his actions were construed as a part of the Republican Party's "Southern Strategy" to lure the South away from the Democratic Party permanently.

Some nominations to the Supreme Court have been influenced by representational considerations, particularly ethnicity, race, and religion. Beginning with the appointment of Chief Justice Taney in 1835, there has almost always been at least one Catholic member of the Court. Justice Brandeis, appointed in 1916, was the first Jew. The Court continued to have at least one Jewish member until President Nixon broke precedent by failing to name a Jewish justice to replace

---

[24]See Robert Scigliano, *The Supreme Court and the Presidency* (New York: Free Press, 1971).

Abe Fortas. As noted earlier, President Johnson appointed the first black member of the Court, Thurgood Marshall. Supreme Court justices have come from upper-middle and upper socioeconomic levels, just as most of the appointing authorities—Presidents and senators—have. No woman has ever served as a member of the Court, but it is generally believed that a woman may be appointed to fill one of the next vacancies.

A nominee's ideology or judicial philosophy can be an important factor, particularly since members of the Court have wide discretion in making their decisions. In making some nominations to the Court, President Nixon said, "You will recall, I'm sure, that during my campaign for the presidency, I pledged to nominate to the Supreme Court individuals who shared my judicial philosophy, which is basically a conservative philosophy."[25] By the same token, some U.S. senators voted against some of the Nixon nominees for exactly the same reason. Presidents have sometimes been surprised and disappointed by the votes of the justices they have appointed to the court, as Eisenhower was with Warren and as Nixon was when the Court ordered him to turn over the White House tapes. But they have generally been successful in choosing appointees who vote in accordance with their ideology or philosophy.

Policy-making. Like other political institutions, the Supreme Court makes policy. It may from time to time change its mind—and thus the law—as to what federal policy should be. For example, it decided in 1896 that separate but equal public schools were fully constitutional. In 1954, it reversed that earlier ruling and held that separate but equal public schools are inherently unequal and therefore are an unconstitutional violation of the equal protection clause. In the *Bakke* case, the Supreme Court also made policy, deciding for the first time that a required quota system based upon race for admission to a public institution is unconstitutional.

Some Supreme Court justices have preferred a posture of *judicial restraint*. That is, they have sought to avoid deciding what they felt were political questions, and they have been cautious about injecting the power of the Court into new areas. Other justices have stood for *judicial activism*, believing that the Court should not be timid or unduly passive in its policy-making role. Whether the Supreme Court at any given time is characterized by judicial restraint or judicial activism; whether it exemplifies the doctrine of strict construction or broad construction; and whether its opinions expand or contract the concepts of civil liberties and civil rights depends upon the individual persons who at any given time serve as the chief justice and associate justices of the Supreme Court.

There is a difference between the drift or trend of opinions under the Burger Court, headed by Chief Justice Warren Burger, and the Warren Court, headed by Chief Justice Earl Warren. At first, the

---

[25]*New York Times* (October 22, 1971), p. 24.

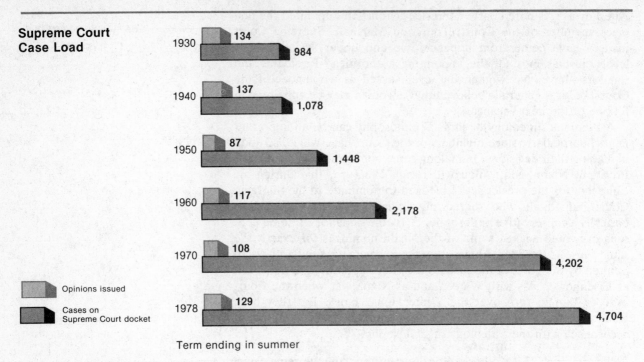

Supreme Court Case Load

1930 134 / 984
1940 137 / 1,078
1950 87 / 1,448
1960 117 / 2,178
1970 108 / 4,202
1978 129 / 4,704

Opinions issued

Cases on Supreme Court docket

Term ending in summer

Note: Some opinions settle more than one case; for example, the 129 opinions in term ending in 1978 covered 161 cases.
SOURCE: Supreme Court of the U.S., Office of the Clerk.

Burger Court usually seemed to follow a policy of judicial restraint. But in its 1978 decisions, the Burger Court became more unpredictable. According to one authority, a majority of the Burger Court has recently exhibited no central philosophy. "The justices take a different approach on each issue, and so you are left with shifting alliances."[26] The *Bakke* case made this abundantly clear. Chief Justice Burger and Justice Rehnquist are the consistent conservatives on the present Court, and Brennan and Marshall are the consistent liberals. The key votes in the middle are cast by the other five justices—Powell, Blackmun, White, Stewart, and Stevens. In 1978, the Court's decisions favored criminal defendants more than half of the time. This contrasted with the Court's decisions in the previous five years, which favored the prosecution in almost two thirds of the cases that the Court decided during that period.

"This zigzag course by the Court shows every sign of continuing next term," one national news magazine reported in 1978. "Legal scholars say they cannot find any simple explanation for the Court's shifting pattern. But some scholars argue that, for whatever reason, the justices increasingly seem to be deciding first the just outcome of a case and then concocting legal arguments to reach that result."[27]

[26]Jesse Choper, professor of constitutional law, University of California at Berkeley, quoted in *U.S. News & World Report* (July 17, 1978), p. 23.
[27]*U.S. News & World Report* (July 17, 1978), p. 24.

Thus, the Court has the discretionary power to make policy and to say what the Constitution, treaties, and federal statutes mean. It can review and overturn the decisions of state courts and the acts of state legislatures when federal questions are involved. The Supreme Court clearly looms large in our system. Yet there are several important limits on the power of the Supreme Court:

1. The Court does not fix its own jurisdiction. Beyond the jurisdiction specifically granted in the Constitution, Congress has this power. Congress can therefore change or reduce the appellate jurisdiction of the Court.

2. The Supreme Court does not choose its own members. That is done by the President, by and with the advice and consent of the Senate.

3. The Court has no militia or army. It must depend upon the executive department (and ultimately, the President), for enforcement of the Court's orders.

4. The members of the Court are subject to impeachment and removal by Congress.

5. Congress decides upon the amount of money that will be allocated for the operation of the Court. For example, it determines whether to grant the Court additional law clerks and other staff members.

6. If Congress does not agree with a Court interpretation of the meaning of a congressional act, it can pass another act. The new act can spell out the intent and meaning of the legislation definitively enough to avoid any adverse interpretation of it.

7. If there is sufficient outcry against a Supreme Court interpretation of the U.S. Constitution, Congress can, by a two-thirds vote, refer a constitutional amendment to the states. If three fourths of the states ratify the proposed amendment, the constitutional change becomes law, and the unpopular Supreme Court holding is avoided.

8. Since the Supreme Court cannot possibly hear and decide every case presented to it on appeal, much of the enforcement of its rulings and much of the federal judicial policy-making occurs in the lower federal courts.

9. Whether a Supreme Court ruling is actually put into effect at the local level depends to some degree upon whether public opinion is in favor of the ruling. Thus, public opinion puts a limit on the powers of the Supreme Court.

The Court and government. Like the other arms of the federal judiciary, the U.S. Supreme Court is the ultimate judicial guarantor of our political structure. In that capacity, the Court has continuously defined and redefined the nature of that structure. From a 1796 decision giving a federal treaty precedence over a conflicting state statute,[28] to the 1976 ruling allowing Congress to apply federal wage

---

[28]*Ware* v. *Hylton*, 3 Dallas 199 (1796).

and hour laws to private employees but not to state government employees,[29] the Court has established and adjusted the boundaries of state and national sovereignty within the federal system.

The Court has also continuously defined and redefined the powers of the other two branches of the national government, Congress and the Presidency. From *Marbury* v. *Madison* (1803)—which declared an act of Congress unconstitutional—to *Buckley* v. *Valeo* (1976)[30]— which invalidated an act of Congress that infringed on the President's power to make appointments—the Court has enforced limits on the powers of Congress. The Court has also held that a President may not seize steel plants by executive order.[31] It has ruled that a President has no inherent power to order surveillance of citizens without first securing court warrants.[32] And it has decided that a President cannot withhold information required by a court in a criminal prosecution.[33]

The Supreme Court, then, serves as a check on Congress and the President. It referees their disputes, and it umpires disputes among the states and between a state and the federal government.

PARTICIPANTS IN THE JUDICIAL SYSTEM

The *Bakke* case was highly unusual because it went all the way to the Supreme Court of the United States. The overwhelming majority of cases does not. Most people experience the judicial system at the "lower reaches." How does it work for them, and who are the participants in the system?

The adversary nature of our judicial system makes it comparable to a boxing match. In a boxing match, there are two fighters in a ring. Each fighter has one or more "seconds," such as advisers and trainers. A neutral referee enforces the rules. Judges award the decision to one of the fighters. These are the *formal* participants in a boxing match. In a lawsuit, the formal participants are similar. *Litigants*, who are the actual parties to the lawsuit, are like the fighters in the ring. The lawyers are similar to the seconds. The judge is comparable to the referee. Lawsuits may also involve a jury, which is similar to the fight judges.

A boxing match also has *informal* participants. Most notably, there is an audience; in lawsuits, public opinion also plays some part. There are reporters at boxing matches; in lawsuits, the media is involved, too. Each fighter has interested backers (financial or otherwise); in lawsuits, interest groups can also play a part.

---

[29]*National League of Cities* v. *Usery*, 426 U.S. 833 (1976).
[30]*Buckley* v. *Valeo*, 96 S. Ct. 612 (1976).
[31]*Youngstown Sheet & Tube Co.* v. *Sawyer*, 343 U.S. 579 (1952).
[32]*United States* v. *United States District Court for the Eastern District of Michigan*, 407 U.S. 297 (1972).
[33]*United States* v. *Nixon*, 418 U.S. 683 (1974).

The litigants are the activators of the system. In a criminal case, the state or federal government may bring a charge against the accused, or *defendant*. In a civil case, the person who brings the action is generally called the *plaintiff*. (The terms *claimant* and *complainant* are also sometimes used.) The person against whom the action is brought is called the *defendant* (or, sometimes, the *respondent*). These are the litigants.

Theoretically, the courts are open to everyone. "If welfare assistance is arbitrarily cut off, if a landlord flagrantly ignores housing codes, if a merchant demands payment under an unfair contract, the poor—like the rich—can go to court," declared the National Commission on the Causes and Prevention of Violence.[34] But in reality, many people cannot gain *access* to our judicial system because they cannot afford it: "The poor are discouraged from initiating civil actions against their exploiters. Litigation is expensive; so are experienced lawyers." Consequently, most Americans do not go into court to settle their disputes or protect their rights.[35]

Some local, state, and federal programs have been established to provide free legal aid or legal services for poor people. Still, the civil law courts are used primarily by middle-class Americans, while criminal law defendants are mostly poor people.[36]

The tendency toward crimes of violence and crimes against property are greatest among young males who are poor or who are members of minority groups. They generally comprise a large percentage of the unemployed in any area; they often live in crowded conditions; and they frequently feel that they are victims of discrimination and relative deprivation. This combination often creates internal tensions and hostilities. Thus, in urban felony courts, most of the defendants are from the lower-income or working classes, while the administrators of the felony justice system are usually white and from the middle class.

This difference between criminal defendants and administrators of the criminal law system usually begins with the arresting police officers. At the local level, they are usually members of the county sheriff's staff or part of the municipal police force. For federal crimes, the arresting officers may be agents of the Federal Bureau of Investigation (FBI). Police officers often feel embattled and unappreciated. They fill dangerous roles, which are frequently not well

[34]"Violence and Law Enforcement," in *To Establish Justice, to Insure Domestic Tranquility*, Final Report of the National Commission on the Causes and Prevention of Violence (Washington, D.C.: U.S. Government Printing Office, December 1969), pp. 143–44.

[35]See Craig Warner, "The Public Ordering of Private Relations," *Law and Society Review*, 8 (1973): 421–40.

[36]See Gerrold S. Auerbach, *Unequal Justice* (New York: Oxford University Press, 1976).

defined.[37] They make policy, because they exercise considerable discretion in deciding whether to make an arrest and on what charge.[38] Black people and other minorities in a local community or neighborhood may feel considerable hostility toward local police officers, particularly if the officers are white, because the police are symbols of the power and discrimination of the dominant segment of society. Efforts have been made in recent years to increase the number of minority members on police forces, but progress has been somewhat slow. One reason is that minority members who can qualify for police work are often able to find other jobs that have much more attractive pay, working conditions, and prestige.

Lawyers

Our judicial system is an expert system. Thus, a litigant must be represented by a licensed lawyer (or attorney) unless, of course, the party chooses to represent himself or herself personally. But that is rather unusual. The process and the substance of the law are complicated, and most people turn to professionals to guide them through it.[39] Except in minor courts, judges are also usually required to be lawyers.

The professional nature of the expert system raises questions about citizen access to it. A person does not need to be a lawyer or to hire a lawyer in order to approach a state governor, say, or a member of Congress. But legal training or the services of a lawyer are nearly always essential if a person wishes to seek the assistance of a court or judge. Further, judicial assistance cannot be sought informally. It can only be secured in the formal forum provided by the law—the courtroom—and in accordance with established legal procedures.

Prior to World War I, a person usually became a lawyer by studying or interning in a law office. Today, a person becomes a lawyer by completing a three-year program at a law school and by passing a licensing examination.

Practicing lawyers in America are called *the bar* because they are admitted within the low rail, or "bar," in a courtroom, while the general public must remain outside. In most states, bar associations are "integrated." That is, a lawyer must belong to a state bar association in order to be admitted to practice in the state courts. Lawyers are bound by professional codes, which bar associations have developed. They are required to observe the confidentiality of the "lawyer-client relationship"; they cannot reveal what their clients say to them. They are expected to avoid conflicts of interest; they

---

[37]James F. Campbell, Joseph R. Sahid, and David P. Stang, *Law and Order Reconsidered*, Report of the Task Force on Law and Law Enforcement to The National Commission on the Causes and Prevention of Violence (Washington, D.C.: U.S. Government Printing Office, 1969).

[38]See James Q. Wilson, *Varieties of Police Behavior* (Cambridge, Mass.: Harvard University Press, 1968).

[39]See Jacob, *Justice in America*, pp. 43–93.

must not represent one party in a lawsuit when they have a conflicting tie to an opposing party. And they must not solicit law business. In recent years, however, a certain amount of professional advertising has been allowed, and the American Civil Liberties Union and similar groups may encourage someone to take a case to court. Lawyers who violate the professional code are subject to disciplinary action by their state bar association. They can be "disbarred," which means that they can no longer practice law. Bar associations not only police their membership; they also intervene as interest groups in governmental decision-making. They lobby state and local governments for laws that they feel are favorable to lawyers and for an improved system of justice.

What do lawyers do? They may, of course, appear in a trial court—in civil or criminal cases—to represent their client's interests. In an appellate case, they may file legal briefs and make oral arguments on behalf of a client. But most lawyers do not practice criminal law,[40] and most of a civil lawyer's work does not involve the drama of court proceedings. Lawyers draft contracts and wills. They advise their clients on tax matters. And they appear before local, state, and federal boards, commissions, and other agencies.

Lawyers' fees are set by agreement with the client or based upon the time involved. (The amount of money or the seriousness of the question is sometimes taken into account, too.) Personal injury cases are frequently taken by plaintiffs' lawyers on a contingency basis; that is, a fee will be collected only if the case is won. The fee is a percentage of the plaintiff's award, usually one fourth of any amount received before trial and one third of any amount received after trial.

Many states allow no-fault divorces on grounds such as "incompatibility," the inability to live together satisfactorily as husband and wife. Some states have instituted no-fault insurance. According to this system, an insurance company must pay damages in a personal injury case, for example, regardless of who may have been at fault in the matter. These reforms have reduced the time-consuming complications of trials in such cases and have therefore reduced attorneys' fees for handling them.

There are several types of lawyers. "In-house" lawyers work full-time for business corporations or other organizations. They generally work for regular salaries. Most large corporations, such as General Motors and Exxon, have their own legal departments. These departments are maintained on a permanent basis to provide routine advisory, drafting, and negotiating services for the company. In-house lawyers usually do not handle lawsuits or make appearances in trial or appellate courts, except in minor cases. For major legal services, corporations and organizations usually use outside attorneys, who may be on a monthly retainer, or set fee.

Attorneys in private practice work for themselves or for private law

---

[40]See Jacob, *Justice in America*, pp. 71–78.

firms. They make up about 70 percent of the practicing lawyers in America. Most private lawyers do not practice alone; they are either partners in a law firm or employees of such a firm. These firms can be very large. Some big-city firms have more than one hundred lawyers, including partners and employees. Law firms generally divide their work into specialties. Lawyers in these firms handle particular kinds of cases like tax or property law matters. Lawyers who are partners in law firms generally make more money than do those who practice alone. In 1976, the median income of all attorneys in the United States was approximately $30,000 (compared with $50,000 for medical doctors). Partners in large law firms usually earn much more. The larger law firms in the big cities choose their new associate lawyers (who may, in time, become partners) from the cream of the best law schools. They often pay them as much as $25,000 per year as a starting salary. The large law firms usually do not handle criminal cases. They do not often produce the politician-lawyers who run for public office, either; these people are likely to be solo practitioners or members of smaller firms.

Government lawyers work for local, state, or federal agencies. The federal government alone employs more than 18,000 lawyers. The Justice Department is the principal federal employer of government lawyers because it is the main law office for the general public in America. The Justice Department, headed by the attorney general, contains the following divisions: Antitrust, which attempts to enforce greater competition in American industry; Civil Rights; Civil; Criminal; Internal Security; Land and Natural Resources; and Tax. Also within the Justice Department is the office of the U.S. solicitor general, who represents the federal government in appellate cases.

At least one U.S. attorney is located in each state; the number depends upon the size of the state. They are responsible for prosecuting federal crimes in their districts. U.S. district attorneys are nominated by the President and confirmed by the Senate. If senators in a state have the same party affiliation as the President, they will usually exercise considerable influence (if not control) over the appointment of a U.S. district attorney. These appointments are sought by lawyers, particularly younger attorneys who may hope to use the high visibility and relatively high prestige of the office to launch political careers or to enhance their legal reputations.

State and local governments also employ full-time or retained lawyers, who fulfill the same duties at their levels as government lawyers do at the federal level.

There are a growing number of public-interest lawyers in America.[41] The idea behind this kind of law practice is that lawyers should not passively wait to be hired by a paying client before tackling a

---

[41]Robert Borosage, Barbara Brown, Paul Friedman, Paul Gewritz, William Jeffress, and William Kelly, "The New Public Interest Lawyers," in Goldman and Sarat, eds., *American Court Systems*, pp. 231–38.

particular legal problem. Some public-interest lawyers specialize in the problems of poor people, handling either civil or criminal cases. The U.S. Supreme Court has held that in both state and federal courts, a person who is charged with a crime that may result in a jail sentence is entitled to have free legal counsel if the person cannot afford to hire a lawyer.[42] Most large cities have "public defender" offices, which are paid for with public funds. In rural areas, private lawyers are frequently assigned to represent particular criminal defendants. In civil cases, poor people may obtain advice and representation from legal aid offices, which are privately funded on a charity basis in a number of cities. In addition, the federal government provides funds through the Legal Services Corporation for free legal services in civil matters. Nevertheless, in civil cases, less than half of the people who need legal assistance actually get it. In criminal cases, the representation that defendants get is often considerably less effective than it would be if they were able to hire their own private lawyer.[43]

Clarence Gideon had been arrested, tried, and convicted of breaking and entering a pool hall and stealing coins from a cigarette machine. Gideon studied the law while in jail and eventually won an appeal to the Supreme Court in 1963, arguing that his right to counsel had been violated because he was too poor to hire a lawyer to defend himself. The landmark decision established that the courts have a responsibility to provide free counsel for anyone who cannot afford to hire a lawyer.

A number of public-interest lawyers specialize in civil rights and civil liberties cases. Some are associated with the American Civil Liberties Union (ACLU), which seeks to preserve and expand civil liberties in America. Typically, the ACLU raises funds through private contributions and dues from its members. But many lawyers handle ACLU cases without being paid a legal fee. Some lawyers for dissidents, such as William Kuntsler, who has represented controversial defendants like the Black Panthers and the Chicago 7, are financed by public fund-raising drives for particular, widely publicized cases. Some organizations—like the Legal Defense Fund of the NAACP and the Native American Rights Fund—are financed by foundations and other private contributors. These public-interest law groups have been highly important in expanding the civil rights of their clients and protecting their interests.

Public-interest lawyers who specialize in consumer problems and environmental protection—like Ralph Nader—perform a variety of functions. Some focus on making governmental commissions and agencies perform their jobs more responsibly. They often use legal

---

[42]See *Gideon* v. *Wainwright*, 372 U.S. 335 (1963); and *Argersinger* v. *Hamlin*, 407 U.S. 25 (1972).

[43]Jacob, *Justice in America*, pp. 70–71.

actions not only to settle the particular disputes involved, but also to mobilize public opinion to affect government policy-making outside the courts.

Even if people with legal problems can afford to hire lawyers, most of them do not, because they are not informed about legal services, do not know how to choose the appropriate lawyer, or are afraid that legal fees will be too high. Despite the growing number of public-interest lawyers, poor people are still at a disadvantage in our judicial system. Law schools now take a much more aggressive interest in opening their admissions to women and minorities—although the *Bakke* case might prove to be a setback for affirmative action—but bar associations in America are still made up largely of white, middle-class males.[44] Progress is being made, but there is still much to be done before ordinary citizens will have full access to the judicial system in America through lawyers.

Judges

Judges exercise considerable discretion in determining the facts (when there is no jury), in assessing the facts, and in applying the law. Thus, the judicial selection and removal processes, as well as who judges are, constitute very important matters.

All federal judges are nominated by the President and confirmed by the U.S. Senate. Before a judicial appointment is sent to the Senate, the nomination goes through several steps. If a district judgeship is to be filled, and the senator or senators in the state of the appointment have the same party affiliation as the President, "senatorial courtesy" plays an important part in the selection. As a rule, the U.S. Senate will not approve a nomination unless the relevant senator or senators actively support it. A federal district judgeship is considered to be a highly prestigious position. Like other federal judicial appointments, it is for life. Appointments to these positions are greatly prized and much sought after by lawyers. Most senators take an active part in recommending judicial appointments to Presidents of their own party. They often use this influence over judicial appointments as a means of rewarding important friends and supporters. Some senators, however, have set up local commissions to handle these recommendations. President Carter has attempted to establish a system for choosing federal judges based on merit. This system, however, has worked far better at the appellate level than at the district court level, where the traditional senatorial patronage system continues to have strong influence.[45]

After the local recommendation is determined, the names of the people being considered for a federal judicial appointment are subjected to two screening processes—one public and one private.

---

[44]See G.S. Auerbach, *Unequal Justice* (New York: Oxford University Press, 1976).

[45]Norman C. Miller, "The Merit System, or Patronage," *The Wall Street Journal* (February 28, 1977), p. 12.

Public screening of each prospective nominee is performed by the Federal Bureau of Investigation. The FBI makes a written report, which later becomes available to the President and to the Senate Judiciary Committee, regarding the nominee's background, reputation, and other related matters. This screening process is intended to eliminate people with questionable habits, morals, or associations.

The Committee on the Federal Judiciary of the American Bar Association conducts the private screening of each judicial nominee. This committee looks into the qualifications of prospective nominees. Its recommendations are also submitted in writing to the President and the Senate Judiciary Committee. A finding by the ABA committee that a nominee is not qualified will nearly always block the nomination. This screening power of the American Bar Association, a private organization, has been criticized on the grounds that the ABA is a conservative and unrepresentative group. One authority has stated:

The twelve members of the ABA Committee on the Federal Judiciary—a chairman and one from each of the eleven federal circuits, chosen by the ABA president—are a cadre of well-established, generally conservative old boys who patrol the summit of their profession. There has never been a black, Spanish-speaking, or female member. Most committee men are in their fifties or sixties.[46]

After the recommendation and screening stages, the attorney general and the President become involved in the final selection of the nominee. They consult with the senators involved and perhaps with other advisers as well.

The same factors that influence the appointment of Supreme Court justices—especially professional qualifications, and political, representational, and ideological considerations—also have an impact on the nomination and confirmation of other federal judges. Congress can change the number of federal judgeships and can create new federal courts. When the President and a majority of the Senate are of the same party affiliation, a special pressure exists for creating new positions; the filling of these positions can be influenced by political and partisan considerations.[47] In 1978, for example, with a Democrat in the White House and a Democratic majority in the Senate, Congress passed an act creating 152 new federal judgeships, the largest one-time increase in history.[48]

At the state level, judges are usually elected by the people, but most elections of this kind are on a "nonpartisan" basis. In a few states, the legislature selects judges. In some states, the governor makes such appointments. Even in those states where judges are

---

[46]Donald Dale Jackson, "Federal Roulette," in Goldman and Sarat, eds., *American Court Systems*, p. 265.
[47]Richard J. Richardson and Kenneth N. Vines, *The Politics of Federal Courts* (Little, Brown, and Company, 1976), p. 17.
[48]*Time* (December 11, 1978), p. 67.

elected, governors may play a dominant role by being able to make interim appointments to fill vacancies.[49] But a growing number of states use a system of merit selection. The selection process usually involves a nominating commission of lawyers, who recommend a list from which the state governor may choose. Under the "Missouri Plan," judges who are appointed—and in some other states, those who are elected, too—do not run for reelection against an opponent. Instead, they are simply required to submit themselves to the electorate for a "vote of confidence" or "no confidence"; a no-confidence vote results in removal from office.[50]

Most federal judges come from middle-class backgrounds.[51] Although women and minorities have been seriously underrepresented in past appointments, the percentages have improved under President Carter.[52] Most federal judges are white males who have had some connection with a political party and usually with political activism, too. Most of them are relatively old; they are usually in their fifties when appointed and, with life tenure, they frequently serve until their death or retirement at age seventy or older.[53]

Federal judges may be removed through the impeachment process in Congress. But this procedure is more of a threat than a reality, since it has rarely been used.[54] This weakness has given rise to a proposal for the creation of a special federal commission to handle questions concerning the removal of federal judges.

Elected state judges are subject to *recall*, or removal by vote of the people. State judges may also be impeached by state legislatures, and in most states a special panel made up of other judges may remove an incompetent judge or one guilty of misbehavior. Regardless of the judicial selection and removal processes, it is clear that judges are never as subject to the will of the momentary popular majority as other public officials are.

Juries

Our judicial system is dominated by professionals—lawyers and judges—but the jury system allows a way for ordinary citizens to take part in the process without being litigants. However, as we indicated earlier, most lawsuits and criminal prosecutions do not actually go to trial; they are settled beforehand. Those that do go to trial,

---

[49]For judicial selection methods in the states, see The Council of State Governments, *The Book of the States 1976–1977* (Lexington, Kentucky: The Council of State Governments, 1976).

[50]See James Herndon, "Appointment as a Means of Initial Accession to State Courts of Last Resort," *North Dakota Law Review*, 38 (1962): 60–73.

[51]Sheldon Goldman, "Judicial Backgrounds, Recruitment, and the Party Variable: The Case of the Johnson and Nixon Appointees to the United States District and Appeals Courts," *Arizona State Law Journal* (1974): 221–22.

[52]See Goldman and Sarat, eds., *American Court Systems*, pp. 257–60.

[53]Jacob, *Justice in America*, p. 110.

[54]See Karl D. McMurray, *The Impeachment of Circuit Judge Kelly* (Tallahassee: Florida State University Institute of Governmental Research, 1964).

particularly civil cases, are often tried by a judge, without a jury. Further, most Americans have never served on a jury, and those who have are not representative of the total population.[55]

Still, juries are an important symbol of democratic participation in our country. Their existence encourages the American people to accept the way our judicial system works and to believe in its fairness. For those who are actually called to serve on juries, their experience as jurors provides an opportunity to learn more about how the American governmental system works. As one early observer of the American scene suggested, such service may also encourage greater citizen participation and greater respect for law.[56]

There are two kinds of juries, the *grand jury* and the *trial jury* (also called *petit jury*). The Fifth Amendment to the U.S. Constitution states, "No person shall be held to answer for a capital, or other infamous crime, unless on a presentment or indictment of a Grand Jury"—except in certain military cases. State constitutions usually contain similar provisions, although most also allow prosecutions on "information" after a preliminary hearing. Grand juries, usually composed of twenty-three people, decide on the basis of the evidence presented to them in secret whether an *indictment*, a statement of criminal charges, should be handed down against an accused person. Critics of the grand jury system say that its secrecy and the fact that the accused is not allowed to have a lawyer present during the proceedings can lead to harassment by prosecutors.

A trial jury is usually composed of twelve people, but juries of six people are sometimes used in minor or special state and federal cases. A trial jury is responsible for determining what the facts are in a civil or criminal case and how the law should be applied. The Sixth Amendment to the Constitution states, "In all criminal prosecutions, the accused shall enjoy the right to a speedy and public trial, by an impartial jury of the State and district wherein the crime shall have been committed. . . ." And the Seventh Amendment says in part that "in suits at common law [meaning, basically, civil cases], where the value in controversy shall exceed twenty dollars, the right of trial by jury shall be preserved. . . ." Similar provisions are contained in state constitutions. In both federal and state courts, the parties may waive their right to a jury and may have a case tried by a judge alone.

Juries are required to be randomly selected, except in minor cases in some states. But juries are seldom representative of the population as a whole. The lists from which potential jurors' names are taken are usually voter registration lists or telephone directories, which may be biased against people in lower socioeconomic classes. The Supreme Court has held that racial discrimination in jury selection is unconstitutional, but minorities are still often underrepresented on

[55]Except as otherwise indicated, the material in this section is based upon Jacob, *Justice in America*, pp. 124–46.

[56]Alexis de Tocqueville, *Democracy in America*, Vol. 1 (New York: Vintage Books, 1954).

Prospective jurors are sworn in before being questioned by lawyers, who seek to ensure that only "fair and impartial" jurors are empaneled.

juries, particularly because of bias of jury lists.[57] A number of professions and occupations—lawyers, doctors, police officers, and others—are quite regularly excused from serving on juries. Wage earners often ask to be excused because the jury fee is seldom equal to their regular pay.

At the beginning of a civil or criminal trial, prospective trial jurors are assembled in the courtroom. The court clerk calls out several of their names, and those who are called rise and take their places in the "jury box." In a process called *voir dire*, the lawyers for both sides then take turns questioning the prospective jurors to determine whether they have any biases that would prevent them from serving as "fair and impartial jurors." The attorneys may seek to find out whether a prospective juror is biased against certain types of cases. For example, one of the lawyers might ask, "When one person brings a lawsuit against another for personal injury in an automobile accident, do you have a tendency, even before you hear the facts, to feel that either the plaintiff or the defendant is right?" These questions may also be used to find out whether a prospective juror may already have made a decision in the case. In this instance, the prospective juror might be asked, "Have you been reading in the papers about this case and have you formed an opinion about it?" Depending on the type of case involved, the lawyer might try to elicit additional, presumably relevant information by asking questions like the following: "Have you ever been a law enforcement officer? Do you agree with that law which says that a person who loses an eye because of the negligence of another is entitled to be compensated?"

---

[57]Howard Erlinger, "Jury Research in America," *Law and Society Review*, 4 (1970): 345; and Hayward R. Alker, Jr., Karl Hosticka, and Michael Mitchell, "Jury Selection as a Biased Social Process," *Law and Society Review*, 11 (1976): 9.

The goal here might be to seek a "fair and impartial," but sympathetic, jury.

Each side in a case has a small number of peremptory challenges, which allows them to have a few prospective jurors excused from a jury without stating any reason whatsoever. Each side also has an unlimited number of challenges for "cause," and the judge can direct that a prospective juror not serve in the case if the judge feels (for any of several reasons) that the person is unlikely to be able to render a fair verdict.

Upon application of one of the parties, the judge can grant a *change of venue*, or move the case to some other town or county. This is done when it is shown that it will be impossible to find a sufficient number of impartial jurors in the original jurisdiction, perhaps because of widespread publicity about the case.

During the trial, jurors serve in a passive role. They simply sit and listen. Any questions that they have for witnesses in the case must usually be submitted in writing to the trial judge. Lawyers' arguments concerning the admissibility of evidence are made outside the hearing of the jurors—in quiet tones at the bench, in the courtroom after the jury has retired, or in the judge's chambers.

At the conclusion of the trial, and before both sides make their final oral arguments in the case, the trial judge "instructs" the jury about the law that governs the case. The judge normally reads these instructions aloud, but they are also handed to the jury in writing so that they can be taken to the jury room when the jurors retire to make their decision.

Federal courts require unanimous verdicts in criminal cases. In federal courts and most state courts, civil verdicts can be reached by majority vote. In criminal cases, state courts require either unanimous verdicts or at least something more than just a majority verdict. The Supreme Court has upheld state laws requiring less than unanimous verdicts in criminal cases that do not involve the possibility of capital punishment.[58] When a jury is "hung"—unable to arrive at a verdict by the required vote—the judge may first send the jury back to try again. If they remain deadlocked, however, the judge must eventually declare a mistrial. The case can be retried, but a new jury must be selected.

Critics of the trial jury system have focused on the problem of using ordinary citizens to decide technical cases. But one study showed that the judges involved agreed with the jury verdicts in 81 percent of the cases.[59] Juries may be more likely to use their own "common sense" notions of fairness in deciding a case, but judges often do the same. In any event, most Americans do not want to eliminate the possibility

---

[58]*Johnson* v. *Louisiana*, 406 U.S. 356 (1972).
[59]D. W. Broeder, "University of Chicago Jury Project," *Nebraska Law Review*, 38 (1959): 746–47.

of having a jury decide their own case. They feel that a jury may be fairer, that "twelve heads are better than one," and that juries may be less harsh and less prejudiced or corrupt than some judges.

Informal Participants

Interest groups may be formal litigants. They may also participate informally in the judicial process in a number of ways. They may finance a "test case"—an action brought by an individual litigant to test the legality of a statute or of a public official's acts.[60] Our discussion of the civil rights struggles in Chapter 4 showed that the NAACP used this tactic to great advantage during the 1950s and the 1960s. This kind of activity of interest groups can lessen the passive, reactive nature of the courts by stirring up cases that the courts are forced to decide. Interest groups also frequently file *amicus curiae* briefs, as we saw in the *Bakke* case, arguing the group's point of view in cases on appeal.[61] Finally, interest groups often publish articles in legal periodicals.[62] By so publicizing legal positions favored by the group, they hope to affect "professional opinion" and thus gain acceptance for their views among lawyers and judges.

Judges sometimes refer to public opinion on an issue in a case before them. In abortion and death penalty cases, the U.S. Supreme Court has taken notice of public opinion, but the justices made it clear that public opinion was not a controlling factor in their decisions.[63] The Supreme Court opinions in the *Bakke* case also referred to public opinion.

It is unusual for public opinion to have a direct effect upon judicial decisions, and this relationship cannot usually be proved. But public opinion can certainly affect judicial decision-making indirectly. Members of the executive and legislative branches are directly affected by public opinion, especially through elections. When these elected officials are involved in the selection of judges, their choices may reflect public attitudes and pressures. Consequently, the decisions of the judges they select may indirectly reflect public opinion. Further, courts and judges have few if any means of enforcing their decisions in the face of strongly opposing public opinion. In one study, political scientists observed the results of the Supreme Court's decision prohibiting reading of the Bible and recitation of the Lord's

---

[60]See Clement E. Vose, "Litigation as a Form of Pressure Group Activity," *Annals of the American Academy of Political and Social Science*, 319 (1958): 20–31.

[61]See Samuel Krislov, "The Amicus Curiae Brief: From Friendship to Advocacy," *Yale Law Journal*, 72 (1963): 694–721.

[62]See Chester A. Newland, "Legal Periodicals and the United States Supreme Court," *Midwest Journal of Political Science*, 3 (1959): pp. 58–74.

[63]In regard to abortion, see *Roe* v. *Wade*, 410 U.S. 113 (1973). For capital punishment cases, see for example, *Furman* v. *Georgia*, 408 U.S. 208 (1972); and *Gregg* v. *Georgia*, 428 U.S. 153 (1976).

Prayer in the public schools.[64] They concluded that the general public is less likely to comply with a Supreme Court decision if it requires a great deal of change in public behavior, if it affects a great number of ordinary citizens, and if the enforcement of the ruling depends largely upon local officials and courts.[65]

The media can also influence the judicial process. Inflammatory news reports about a criminal case may influence jurors toward conviction.[66] A biased or incomplete report of a decision can also affect public opinion and, thus, the degree to which people may comply with the decision.

CONCLUSION

America's judicial system has come under increasing attack in recent years from both the left and the right. Conservatives maintain that the system is too easy on criminals. This criticism raises a fundamental question about the tension in our system between law and order, on one hand, and individual liberty, on the other. Our system makes a great effort to protect the liberty, reputation, and money or property of a criminal defendant. Yet we all are aware that individual liberty would mean nothing and that human life would be "solitary, poore, nasty, brutish, and short," as Thomas Hobbes put it, if there were no government to maintain law and order.[67]

Americans believe in the rule of law; that is, they think that the law should be impartially administered. They would not want judges to show favoritism or partisanship or to be swayed by public opinion or political influence. Still, many of us would want to be treated with a little more mercy than justice if we were involved in a legal dispute. Daniel Boorstin, an American historian, has observed that Americans have ambivalent expectations of courts and judges: "We wish to believe that our laws are both changeless and changeable, divine and secular, permanent and temporary, transcendental and pragmatic."[68]

A democracy must ensure that a neutral judiciary is representative and allows citizen participation. The American judicial system is rightly criticized because it is not accessible to all—rich and poor, minority and majority—alike. A majority of the American people feels that the judicial system presently serves the rich and powerful

---

[64]*School District of Abington Township, Pennsylvania* v. *Shempp*, 374 U.S. 203 (1963).

[65]See Kenneth N. Dolbeare and Phillip E. Hamond, "Local Elites, The Impact of Judicial Decisions, and the Process of Change" (paper prepared for the annual meeting of the American Political Science Association, Washington, D.C., 1969).

[66]See Alice M. Padawer-Singer and Alan H. Barton, "The Impact of Pretrial Publicity on Jurors' Verdicts," in Rita James Simon, ed., *The Jury System in America* (Beverly Hills: Sage Publications, 1975), pp. 125–39.

[67]Thomas Hobbes, *Leviathan* (Oxford: Clarendon Press, 1958), p. 97.

[68]Daniel J. Boorstin, "The Perils of Indwelling Law," in Robert P. Wolff, ed., *The Rule of Law* (New York: Simon and Schuster, 1971), p. 76.

best.[69] There is too much of a differential in the way people are treated in regard to arrests, bail, conviction, and sentencing. The overcrowded dockets in American courts create too much delay in securing justice. Still, as Herbert Jacob says:

> . . . the courts in the United States provide relief to millions of persons seeking redress of grievances that they cannot obtain elsewhere. While far from perfect, courts in the United States provide more equal treatment to American citizens than do most social and governmental institutions. The quest for more perfect justice must continue, but it must not blind us to the considerable achievements that American courts have already obtained.[70]

ADDITIONAL SOURCES

Abraham, Henry J. *The Judicial Process*, 2nd ed. Oxford University Press, 1968.*

Hamilton, Charles V. *The Bench and the Ballot: Southern Federal Judges and Black Voters*. Oxford University Press, 1973.*

Horowitz, Donald L. *Courts and Social Policy*. Brookings, 1977.*

Jacob, Herbert. *Justice in America: Courts, Lawyers, and the Judicial Process*, 2nd ed. Little, Brown, 1972.*

Kratcoski, Peter C., and Donald B. Walker. *Criminal Justice in America: Process and Issues*. Scott, Foresman, 1978.

Rogers, Harrell R., Jr., and Charles S. Bullock, III. *Law and Social Change: Civil Rights Laws and Their Consequences*. McGraw-Hill, 1972.*

Rohde, David W., and Harold J. Spaeth. *Supreme Court Decision Making*. Freeman, 1975.*

Schwartz, Bernard. *Law in America*. McGraw-Hill, 1974.

Shapiro, Martin, and Rocco J. Tresolini. *American Constitutional Law*, 4th ed. Macmillan, 1975.

Silberman, Charles E. *Criminal Violence, Criminal Justice*. Random House, 1978.

Smith, Page. *The Constitution: A Documentary and Narrative History*. Morrow, 1978.

Wasby, Stephen L. *The Supreme Court in the Federal Judicial System*. Holt, Rinehart & Winston, 1978.

*Available in paperback edition.

---

[69]See Barbara Curran and Francis O. Spalding, *The Legal Needs of the Public* (Chicago: American Bar Foundation, 1974), p. 95.

[70]Jacob, *Justice in America*, p. 240.

16 State and Local Governments
Federalism and the Grass Roots

If you wanted to get a job teaching American history in a public high school in Cleveland, San Diego, Boston, Lukenbach, Texas, or anywhere else in the country, you would first have to enter into a contract with a local school board. The board would set your salary and authorize the issuance of your paycheck. Local school boards make the basic decisions concerning the day-to-day operations of a public school system. Local taxes levied on the value of property in the school district are usually the basic source of public school funds.

It would be incorrect to assume from these statements that public education in America is the sole province of local government, however. The federal and state governments also play important roles in public education.

State governments provide a substantial portion of the funds for local education. These funds, which are derived from state taxes, are partly supplied to school districts according to their financial need. This distribution equalizes local revenues from local property valuations, which vary widely in different school districts. In addition, state governments typically control teacher certification, set educational standards for public schools, and prescribe the textbooks and other materials that must be used in them. The states also have inspection and enforcement systems to maintain educational standards.

The Bay Area Rapid Transit system (BART), a mass transportation network in the San Francisco area, operates through a combination of federal, state, and local funding.

The federal government is also very involved in public education. Federal aid programs in education help to equalize state funding, which varies from state to state, just as state funds are used to reduce the differences in educational spending among local school districts. Some "strings" are attached to these federal funds. For example, no school district that receives federal funds may discriminate on the basis of race in hiring teachers and other personnel. The same kind of overlap in governmental powers and responsibilities that exists in American public education is also found throughout a wide spectrum of governmental activity in the United States, including pollution control, public health, the welfare system, and the construction and maintenance of public roads and highways.

STATE AND LOCAL GOVERNMENTS IN THE FEDERAL SYSTEM

The governmental system embodied in the U.S. Constitution is a compromise between the idea of national consolidation, with a supreme national government, and the idea of confederation, with supreme state governments. Today, we are the inheritors of this kind of government, which is called *federalism*—a system of dual state and federal sovereignty, or power. States have authorized and created many local jurisdictions within the states: municipal and county governments, school boards, water districts, and others.

Our federal system is not neatly and separately layered. It is not correct, for example, to visualize the federal system as a three-layered cake, with the national, or federal, government as the top layer, resting on the state government layer in the middle, which rests upon the local government layer on the bottom. Instead, as one authority has pointed out, the American federal system is more like a rainbow or marble cake "characterized by an inseparable mingling of differently colored ingredients, the colors appearing in vertical and diagonal strands and unexpected whirls. As colors are mixed in the marble cake, so functions are mixed in the American federal system."[1]

The whirls in the federalism cake do not just represent the local, state, and federal governments. They also stand for the less conspicuous Indian tribal governments, which are neither creatures of state governments nor of the federal government. Tribal governments predated both, but they *are* subject to the plenary, or supreme, power of the federal government under the doctrine of discovery and conquest.[2]

---

[1] Morton Grodzins, "The Federal System," in Irwin N. Gertzog, ed., *Readings on State and Local Government* (Englewood Cliffs, N.J.: Prentice-Hall, 1970), p. 4.

[2] See, *United States* v. *Kagama*, 118 U.S. 375 (1886); *Lone Wolf* v. *Hitchcock*, 187 U.S. 553 (1903); and *United States* v. *Sandoval*, 231 U.S. 28 (1913).

Why do we continue to have a federal system today? For one thing, it is a strongly ingrained tradition. The early church congregations in New England cherished and jealously guarded the autonomy of their local congregations against central church authority. In the colonies, towns and villages exercised considerable governmental authority on their own, separate from the central power of the colonial governments. Like tribal governments, many local and state governments were already in existence when the U.S. Constitution was written. A tradition of decentralization, then, nurtured by a distrust of concentrated central power, has always been an important factor in American politics. It continues today as a strong current in American thought and is one important reason why our federal system has endured and is likely to continue for the foreseeable future.

Another reason why America continues to have a federal system is the U.S. Constitution. The framers of the Constitution at first called the federal system that they had created a "compound republic." They wrote:

In the compound republic of America, the power surrendered by the people is first divided between two distinct governments, and then a portion allotted to each subdivided among distinct and separate departments. Hence, a double security arises to the rights of the people. The different governments will control each other, at the same time that each will be controlled by itself.[3]

Thus, within the federal government and each of the state governments, the framers of the U.S. Constitution intended that each of the three branches would play its powers against the others. The framers also expected a similar playing off of power between the federal government and each of the state governments.

The U.S. Constitution is not a *compact*, or agreement, among states. It is more properly understood as an agreement among the "people" of the United States. Thus, the first words of the Preamble of the Constitution are: "We, the people of the United States . . . ." The framers of the Constitution specified that it should go into effect when it was ratified, not by state legislatures, but by delegates selected by the people and assembled in state conventions. Nevertheless, under the federal system created by the Constitution, a system of dual sovereignty was created. The federal government is supreme in regard to certain matters, the state governments are supreme on others, and the states and the federal government have concurrent, overlapping powers on still other matters. Thus, the federal government has the exclusive and supreme power to coin money and issue currency, make war, deal with foreign governments, raise and finance armies, and to regulate commerce with foreign nations, with Indian tribes, and among the states. The states are prohibited from engaging in these activities and also from impairing private contracts,

---

[3] *Federalist*, No. 51.

taxing exports or imports, or from entering into compacts with each other without the approval of Congress.

The Constitution requires the federal government to guarantee to each of the states a *republican*, or nonmonarchal, form of government, equal representation in the U.S. Senate, and protection and defense in time of war or domestic violence. No new state can be carved out of the territory of an existing state unless the state agrees.

Each state has an inherent *police power* to deal with the health, safety, and morals of its own citizens. Each state also has the authority to regulate commerce within its own borders. The federal government and the state governments have concurrent powers in certain fields, such as the power to tax, to spend, and to enact and enforce criminal laws.

Finally, our federal system continues to exist because each state has a cultural identity of its own. This identity is based upon its own peculiar history and development, its own politics, and, to some degree, upon its own peculiar mix of dominant interests. Citizens within a state tend to identify with their own state, even though the state border may be nearby and the state capital may be far away. One study of the neighboring cities of Angola, Indiana, Reading, Michigan, and Montpelier, Ohio, found that their residents were oriented toward the elections and politics, radio stations and newspapers, and jobs and employment in their own state, despite the fact that they lived closer to the other cities, across state borders, than to their own state capitals.[4]

A number of factors have increased federal powers over the years. These include Supreme Court rulings; federal action and state inaction during the Great Depression; the emergence of the United States as a world power following World War II; and expanded federal activity in the civil rights field.

Consider how the Supreme Court has handled the question of states' rights. The Tenth Amendment to the U.S. Constitution, adopted as a part of the original Bill of Rights in 1791, provides: "The powers not delegated to the United States by the Constitution, or prohibited by it to the States, are reserved to the States respectively, or to the people." As early as 1819, however, the U.S. Supreme Court held that the federal government not only possesses the express, or stated, powers set forth in the Constitution, but that it also has such other "implied" powers as are necessary to carry out the stated powers. Contrary state laws, it ruled, must give way to federal action exercising those implied powers.[5] In modern times, the U.S. Supreme Court has taken the view that "the Tenth Amendment states but a truism that all is retained which has not been surren-

---

[4] See a study by Arthur R. Stevens, "Political Culture in the Tri-State Area of Michigan, Indiana, and Ohio," (term paper, Michigan State University, 1965), cited in Charles R. Adrian, *State and Local Governments* (New York: McGraw-Hill, 1976), pp. 7–8.

[5] *McCulloch* v. *Maryland*, 17 U.S. 316 (1819).

dered."[6] The Court has pointed out that the Tenth Amendment does not declare that the powers that are not *expressly* delegated to the federal government are reserved to the states or the people; the word "expressly" is not used in the Amendment. Thus, the Court has held that the Tenth Amendment does not add or take anything away from the other provisions of the U.S. Constitution; therefore, it is no basis for states' rights claims. The Supreme Court has also ruled that, under the Fourteenth Amendment (1869), the federal government can act to protect the civil rights of all Americans, whether a particular state approves or not.[7]

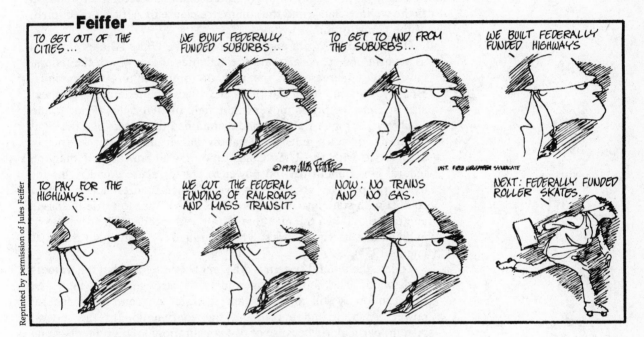

Reprinted by permission of Jules Feiffer

The balance of power between the states and the federal government was further tipped in favor of the federal government during the Great Depression, when the federal government became the prime mover in regard to the health and welfare of Americans, the regulation of business and industry, and the economic policy of the nation. Writing at that time, one observer set forth what happened:

Where were the states when the banks went under? Powerless Maryland, hysterical Michigan, safety-first New York! Where were the states when all the railroads were on the verge of passing into the hands of the bondholders and suspending operation? Where were the states in regulation of power and the control of utilities? Where are the states now in regulating insurance companies, with their fake balance sheets and high salaries? Where were the states in controlling blue sky

---

[6] *United States* v. *Darby*, 312 U.S. 100 (1941).

[7] See, for example, *Brown* v. *Board of Education of Topeka*, 347 U.S. 483 (1954).

securities? Where were the states in preventing destructive business competition and in protecting labor and the public? Where were the states in the development of security through social insurance? In none of these fields affecting economic life was it possible for any state to do anything decisive without driving business out of its jurisdiction into areas where there was no regulation and no control.[8]

The expansion of federal power during the Great Depression was due to President Franklin Roosevelt's aggressiveness in a time of great national trouble. The Supreme Court eventually backed him by reversing earlier rulings and giving a broad and liberal interpretation to the welfare clause and the commerce clause of Article I, Section 8, of the Constitution.

During World War II and its aftermath the United States emerged as a world power. As a result, the activities and power of the federal government increased in the area of foreign affairs and national security. Particularly in the 1950s and 1960s, the federal government also became the prime mover in the field of civil rights. Prior to the Civil War, John C. Calhoun had maintained that states had the right to nullify, or veto, federal legislation that, in their view, was not in accordance with the U.S. Constitution.[9] Calhoun argued that the federal government had no power to act to secure equal rights for black people—to abolish slavery—if such federal action would conflict with state law. It took a terrible Civil War to settle this issue and to strike down the idea that a state can secede. (The doctrine of nullification, however, was still being argued seriously in the South as late as 1957).[10]

Today, the federal system is different from the one that the framers envisioned. The federal government is stronger. Yet the U.S. Constitution is still an important restraint on centralized federal power. Also, it still encourages the continuation of the federal system, particularly because of two constitutional requirements—one guarantees two U.S. senators for every state, large or small, and the other relies on the states as the basic units for elections, even national elections. Further, since political parties in America are fragmented—reflecting both the principle of federalism and the principle of separation of powers—there are no unitary, national political parties as such, which would enable the American people to express their opinions and power as a single "national will" through national elections only. Instead, in elections, American public opinion must be expressed in fragmented state, or local, units.

Thus, our federal system is not so much a system of competition between the states, on the one hand, and the federal government, on

---

[8] Luther Gulick, "Reorganization of the State," *Civil Engineering*, 3 (August 1933): 421.

[9] *See* John C. Calhoun, *Disquisition on Government* (New York: Liberal Arts Press, 1953).

[10] See J.J. Kilpatrick, *The Sovereign States: Notes of a Citizen of the State of Virginia* (Chicago: Henry Regnery Company, 1957).

the other, as it is a system of cooperation. Indeed, government in the United States could be called a system of *cooperative federalism*. Like the sprockets in a watch, the activities of state governments mesh with those of the federal government. Further, there are both formal and informal relations between the states; and within each state, state-and-local relations are those of a creator to its creature.[11]

Thus, the interwoven whirls in the "marble cake" of federalism cannot be easily separated. But to make these whirls—federal, state, local, and Indian tribal governments—easier to understand, they will be dealt with separately in the remainder of this chapter.

THE STATES

States are the original governmental building blocks of our federal union, and there is a richness and strength in their diverse characteristics. One champion of state governments has argued that the cultural, economic, and political diversity among states is an important justification for the federal system and an explanation for its continued vitality.[12] This state admirer writes:

> For an observer who is sensitive to regional patterns, Massachusetts means political clambakes; Italian, Irish, and Yankee names balancing one another on the state ballot; intense Catholic versus Protestant feelings about public schools and birth control; and frequent exposés of public corruption. Georgia's politicians make their public appeals with barbecue and sweetened iced tea or Coca-Cola; their names are as uniformly Anglo-Saxon as the characters in Dick and Jane; and their campaigns center on roads, school teachers' salaries, the assorted economic woes of the little man, and the eternal verities of Old and New Testaments. While Georgia's politicians abstain in public, Wisconsin's slosh beer with the voters. German bratwurst takes the place of barbecue or clambake. Issues and sometimes sophisticated ideology dominate Wisconsin's campaign, taking the place of the scandals that appear in other states. Wisconsin elections deal with dairy farming and whatever else troubles serious people in the country: war, crime, or rebellious youth. A vestigial tax on oleomargarine and a low tax on beer are as typical of Wisconsin politics as the ubiquitous peanut sellers who prowl the Georgia capitol when the legislature is in session and the job-seekers and arrangers who hang onto the State House in Boston.[13]

Despite their differences in size, populations, per capita income, and other characteristics, states share a number of common problems. In particular, they have transportation, welfare, law enforcement,

---

[11] *Hunter* v. *City of Pittsburgh*, 207 U.S. 161 (1907).

[12] Ira Sharkansky, *The Maligned States: Policy Accomplishments, Problems, and Opportunities* (New York: McGraw-Hill, 1972).

[13] Sharkansky, *The Maligned States*, pp. 20, 21.

education, and environmental pollution problems. The nature of these common problems has changed greatly because of the urbanization that has occurred in all of the states, although more in some than in others. But people have not just moved from the rural areas into the cities. Instead, America has experienced a process of "suburbanization." Central cities are economically depressed, and there has been a large growth in the suburbs.[14]

State officials are often like the exasperated guitar player who said, "If I ever get this thing tuned again, I'm going to weld it." But Americans cannot be welded to one locality. They move. Problems cannot be welded, either. They change. To meet these new problems, there were 410 increases in state taxes in the major states in the eleven years preceding 1970. Some state taxes, however, have been reduced more recently, particularly in the West, in the face of taxpayer revolts.[15]

The Structure of State Governments

After the Revolution, each of the newly created American states established a system of government in which governmental powers were divided among the executive, legislative, and judicial branches. This separation of powers was later carried over into the national government, and it is a chief characteristic of all of the present state governments. The pattern for the government of each state is contained in its constitution.

State constitutions.   Just as the U.S. Constitution is the fundamental law at the national level, state constitutions are the basic law at the state level. The U.S. Constitution, of course, governs on matters that fall within its written provisions and on Supreme Court interpretations of them.[16] The constitutions of the various states enumerate protected individual rights that are similar to the U.S. Bill of Rights. Some states have special protections in their constitutions, such as a state version of the Equal Rights Amendment.

Unlike the U.S. Constitution, state constitutions typically fragment authority within the executive department. The governor has only limited power to appoint various officials; usually, the attorney general, the secretary of state, the state superintendent of public instruction, the state treasurer, and others are separately and independently elected by the people.

Except in Delaware, state constitutions can be amended by a vote of the people after a referral by the state legislature. In a number of states, constitutional amendments may be placed on the ballot for

---

[14] See Daniel R. Grant and H.C. Nixon, *State and Local Government in America*, 3rd ed. (Boston: Allyn and Bacon, 1975), pp. 9–15.
[15] Ira Sharkansky, *The Maligned States*, p. 153.
[16] Material for this section is taken from Grant and Nixon, *State and Local Government in America*, pp. 107–38.

popular vote by initiative petition. Constitutional conventions may be called by state legislatures, subject to popular vote ratification of any proposed changes recommended by the convention. Some states provide for constitutional commissions, which are established by state legislatures, to propose wholesale constitutional changes.

State constitutions are generally much longer than the U.S. Constitution. They include many details that might well have been left to legislation rather than to constitutional provision. This detail, which usually sets limits on what the governor or a state legislature can do, tends to make state constitutions inflexible, difficult to apply to changed conditions. The work of interest groups can usually be plainly seen in the provisions of state constitutions.

Taxpayers' groups and property interests have been able to secure strict and detailed limits on state legislatures' taxing, borrowing, and spending powers. The strength of veterans' groups and their lobbyists is revealed in constitutional guarantees of veterans' preference in public employment and even constitutional provisions for bonuses, pensions, tax exemptions, and other privileges. The influence of church groups, sometimes opposed to other church groups, may be measured in constitutional contests. A case in point is the conflict over outlawing bingo as a form of gambling, as Protestant groups have urged, or making it legal, as urged by Catholic groups. The influence of farm interests is reflected in a variety of special privileges . . . .[17]

Because of their detailed and rather inflexible provisions, many state constitutions have undergone serious changes over the years, either through numerous amendments or through outright replacement with new constitutions. There are frequent state votes on constitutional changes. For example, in 1978, the voters of New Mexico rejected a proposed constitutional amendment that would have provided a $3,600 annual salary for state legislators, who are now restricted to expenses and a daily allowance when the legislature is in session. The voters of Mississippi repealed a constitutional requirement that the state librarian be a woman.

But the U.S. Constitution, because of its brief statement of fairly general principles, which are subject to interpretation by the U.S. Supreme Court, has proved to be much more flexible. As a result, it has been amended only twenty-six times in nearly two hundred years.

State executive branches.   In some ways, the functions of state governors are the same as those of U.S. Presidents; in other ways, they are different.[18] Governors do not, for example, serve as the chief diplomats of their states; that is, they are not expected to carry on negotiations with foreign governments. As a matter of fact, foreign relations and matters of war and peace are subjects which, according

---

[17] Grant and Nixon, *State and Local Government in America*, pp. 108–9.
[18] See Grant and Nixon, *State and Local Government in America*, pp. 272–329.

Connecticut Governor Ella Grasso. Within their own states, governors perform many of the same functions that U.S. Presidents do; they act as chief of state, chief executive, commander in chief, party leader, and policy-maker.

to the U.S. Constitution, are exclusively the province of the federal government. A governor is not considered the "symbolic" leader of the state to the same degree that the President is thought of as the symbolic leader of the nation.

A governor is the *chief of state* in his or her state, the ceremonial official of the state. Presidents have the same role in the national government. Of course, state citizens do not tend to identify as closely with their governor as they do with a President. But they usually want to be represented by a person who will reflect well on their state when dealing with the media or making national appearances.

A state governor is the *chief executive* of the state. Usually, however, this does not mean the same thing at the state level as it does at the federal level. The constitutions of many states provide for a "long ballot," as noted earlier. Thus, in half the states, ten or more officials in the executive department are separately elected, not appointed by the governor. Most states, for example, have an elected lieutenant governor, secretary of state, attorney general, and state treasurer.[19] The office of lieutenant governor is typically a weak one. The attorney general's office, which is generally responsible for advising state officials and agencies on the law, conducting investigations, and representing the state in court and often in utility and other regulatory commissions hearings, is usually second in power only to the office of governor. The secretary of state's office has been called the "wastebasket of state government" because it is responsible for a wide variety of ministerial functions, such as keeping the state's official records and seal, issuing charters for business corporations, and supervising state elections. In recent years, several states have attempted to reduce the number of state officials who are elected and to increase the appointive powers of the governors. Other reforms in some states have reduced the number of state departments, grouping them together like federal cabinet departments.[20]

Governors preside over their state bureaucracies. In this respect, they have many of the problems a President has. States have "merit systems" which, like the federal civil service, insulate a large percentage of state jobs from political appointment or dismissal. Today, states are required to avoid racial discrimination in state employment, but minorities are underrepresented in the better state jobs.[21]

In recent years, the unionization of state and local employees has greatly increased. Most states have passed laws that allow collective bargaining for public employees but make strikes by them illegal. Still, as inflation has increased the cost of living for state and local employees, the same as it has for everyone, devices such as "sick

[19] See Russell W. Maddox and Robert F. Fuquay, *State and Local Government*, 3rd ed. (New York: D. Van Nostrand Company, 1975), pp. 82–87.

[20] David R. Berman, *State and Local Politics*, pp. 137–40.

[21] See Adam W. Herbert, "The Minority Administrator: Problems, Prospects, and Challenges," *Public Administration Review* (November/December, 1974), pp. 556–63.

outs" have accomplished the same purpose as strikes. Therefore, some people have suggested that state laws should be revised to provide some regular way for state employees to put legal teeth into their collective bargaining power.[22]

State governors also play a kind of *commander in chief* role. They are able to call out and direct the state militia, or National Guard. But the National Guard today is largely financed by federal funds and can be "nationalized" at a moment's notice by presidential order. In 1957 Governor Orval Faubus of Arkansas called out the state's National Guard to prevent black students from attending Little Rock High School as a court had ordered. He said that this action was necessary to prevent violence. But President Eisenhower "nationalized" the Arkansas National Guard and ordered it to enforce desegregation, instead of blocking it. When a state's National Guard is nationalized, the governor is no longer its commander in chief; the President is. In other times, governors may use the state's National Guard to quell disorders, to police and assist with disasters, and for other similar purposes.

Like Presidents, governors are *party leaders*, dominating their state party organization and usually preventing it from taking part in any political activities or taking stands on any issues that are not to their liking. Governors regularly name the state chairpersons of their parties. They typically lead their party delegations to the national conventions, where they are among the more influential figures.

A state governor also has an important role as a *policy-maker*, just as a President does. Governors exercise discretion in issuing executive orders, and agencies and departments under their control issue rules and regulations to implement the laws. Governors initiate policy through their influence on legislation. Governors may not be able to mobilize public opinion as forcefully as a President—and thus affect legislation—because governors cannot preempt network and other television programs virtually at will, as a President can. But governors do affect legislation in a number of ways. They give a state of the state message at the beginning session of each legislature; assume responsibility to propose a state budget and particular legislative measures; exercise the power to veto legislation (except in North Carolina); and influence legislators through patronage and preferments. In forty-three states, governors have an *item veto*; that is, they can veto a particular item in an appropriations bill without having to veto the whole bill, a power that the President of the United States does not have. This item veto power affords a state governor considerable extra power over the appropriations process. State governors usually have more political patronage at their

[22] In regard to collective bargaining for state and local employees, see, Advisory Commission on Intergovernmental Relations, *Labor-Management Policies for State and Local Government* (Washington, D.C.: U.S. Government Printing Office, 1969); and Sterling D. Speror and John N. Capozzola, *The Urban Community and its Unionized Bureaucracies: Pressure Politics in Government Labor Relations* (New York: Deunellen, 1973).

disposal than a President does. They can also sometimes use state construction projects as a way of influencing members of the state legislature. For example, they can agree to the building of a highway in a particular district in exchange for support on other issues.

Who are the governors? Most of them are men, although there were two women governors, in Connecticut and Washington, in 1978.[23] Governors are usually native sons, college graduates, and middle aged. A majority are attorneys, and most have had prior experience in state government—as legislators, lieutenant governors, or attorney generals, for example. Many state governors go on to become U.S. senators. Since Franklin D. Roosevelt, however, no governor except Jimmy Carter has been elected President.

Most state constitutions provide for a four-year gubernatorial term of office, although some still provide for a two-year term. State constitutions typically limit governors to one or two terms. In all but one of the fifty states, governors may be removed through impeachment. Oregon provides for removal through popular recall.

State legislatures. The U.S. constitutional guarantee of a republican form of government for each state theoretically allows a wide latitude as to the type of government each state might adopt as long as it is not a monarchy or a dictatorship. But all the states have governments that parallel the federal pattern. All have separated the legislative functions from the judicial and executive functions. All except Nebraska have two-house legislatures. Most states call their upper house the senate; lower houses are typically called a house of representatives, an assembly, or a house of delegates.[24]

State legislatures do most of their work in committees, as the national Congress does. The legislative route followed by a bill is much the same, too: introduction, referral to committee, committee hearings and report, floor action, and if there is a disagreement between the two houses, resolution by a conference committee.

There is a speaker and a majority and minority leader in the lower house of each of the state legislatures, and these officers have much the same powers as they do in the U.S. House of Representatives. A majority of the state constitutions provide that the state's lieutenant governor will preside over the state senate, but usually without real power. As in the U.S. Senate, each state senate elects a president pro tempore and a majority and minority leader. Unlike the U.S. Senate, however, the office of president pro tempore in state senates is usually not just an honorary office but one that has actual power and influence. Typically, the president pro tempore and the majority leader work together as the most influential leaders in a state senate.

State legislatures are different from the U.S. Congress, too, in

---

[23] See Samuel R. Solomon, "Governors: 1960–1970," *National Civic Review* (March 1971), pp. 126–46.

[24] See Grant and Nixon, *State and Local Government in America*, pp. 205–71; and Berman, *State and Local Politics*, pp. 98–126.

A public hearing in the Massachusetts state legislature.

that, while most of their important work is done in committees, seniority is usually of much less importance in determining committee assignments and chairpersons. Often, those running for leadership positions in a state legislative body—for president pro tempore of the state senate, for example—may make commitments concerning appointments to chair committees, or assignments to committees, in return for promises of support. There is greater turnover in leadership positions in state legislatures than in the U.S. Congress.

Membership on state legislative committees is less constant and permanent than on congressional committees. State legislators are usually not careerists and do not serve in the state legislature for as long a period as the average member of Congress does. Because of these facts, a few senior members of a state legislature tend to acquire considerable power and influence.

State legislative bodies and committees—with, again, the exception of Nebraska—are organized along party lines. Just as in the national Congress, the two major parties in each house caucus separately at the beginning of each legislature and agree upon nominations for legislative offices. Then all of the members of a particular party caucus are expected to vote unanimously for the party choices. Thus, the majority party elects the principal officers. In 1978, when one lower house seat in Pennsylvania was tied up for some time in an election dispute, the house was deadlocked—101 Democrats to 101 Republicans—and could not choose a speaker. No Republican member was willing to vote for the Democratic candidate for speaker, and no Democrat was willing to vote for the Republican candidate. Just when the issue was about to be decided by a flip of a coin, the one remaining election dispute was settled in favor of the Democrat. But, before a vote could be taken in the speaker's race, a Democratic member died, and the coin had to be brought out again.[25]

Members of both houses of the state legislatures are usually elected from single-member districts, generally for a two-year term for the lower house and a four-year term for the upper house. A majority of state legislators come from the legal profession, from farming, or from businesses—such as the insurance or real estate business—that allow them to take time off for legislative duties. Most state legislatures meet only for a fraction of each year, and, therefore, a legislator's job is not thought to be a full-time job in most states. However, legislators are expected to attend committee meetings during the interim (between legislative sessions), to consult with constituents, and act upon their problems and requests year-round.

In the larger, urbanized states—particularly California, Massachusetts, Michigan, and New Jersey—there is a greater degree of legislative professionalism than in some of the smaller, less populated states, such as South Dakota, New Mexico, and Vermont. In the larger states like California, there are more nearly full-time legislative salaries and adequate staffing for the legislature and its members. Sessions tend to be longer in these states, also. States that pay small salaries, or monthly salaries only when the legislature is in session, have legislatures that are less likely to be fully representative of all the diverse elements of the state's population—wage-earners, women, minorities, and others—who cannot afford to leave home or take off from work to serve.

In 1959, James David Barber studied one legislature and classified its members into four categories: the Spectator; the Advertiser; the Reluctant; and the Lawmaker.

> *The passive Spectators who enjoy watching the legislative show and want to continue on appear to have been attracted by the prestige of legislative office, thus compensating for feelings of social inferiority. The Advertisers, active but unwilling to return, are out to become known, usually for business purposes, and show occupational insecurity and marked inner conflicts. The Reluctants are legislators under protest, performing a civic duty for their small-town neighbors, but experiencing difficulty in adapting to a strange, fast-moving situation. The Lawmakers, active and tentatively committed to extended legislative service, concentrate on the substantive issues, being freed for this by personal strength and powerful adjustive techniques.*[26]

State legislatures are usually much smaller than the national Congress. New Hampshire's lower house is the largest, with 400 members. Four other state lower houses have around 200 members, but the rest have 125 or fewer members. All of the state senates are small. Minnesota's is the largest, with 67 members. Only four state senates have over 50 members. Most are in the 30 to 40 range.

After World War II, America experienced a rapid process of urbanization and suburbanization. But, with the exception of Wisconsin and Massachusetts, state legislatures steadfastly refused to reapportion themselves. They refused to change legislative district

---

[26] James David Barber, *The Lawmakers: Recruitment and Adaptation to Legislative Life* (New Haven: Yale University Press, 1965), p. 163.

lines to reflect the rearrangement of state population, even though their state constitutions required them to do so. The result was that state legislatures were almost uniformly dominated by rural areas and small towns until 1964; cities were uniformly underrepresented. In those days, even in states where the membership in one house was fairly well apportioned on the basis of population, the other house was malapportioned. Thus, in 1960, three fourths of the total population of the state of Maryland, for example, lived in the state's four largest counties plus the city of Baltimore, but these areas were represented in Maryland's upper house by only one third of that body's members.[27]

Then came the landmark U.S. Supreme Court decision of *Reynolds* v. *Sims* in 1964.[28] Two years earlier, in *Baker* v. *Carr*[29] (which we discussed in Chapter 12), the Court had ruled that malapportionment of a state legislature was a justiciable issue and violated the Fourteenth Amendment. Still, many people did not realize that the Court would go all the way and order "one person-one vote"—equal population districts—in *both* houses of a state legislature, thus rejecting the "federal analogy." But that is exactly what the Supreme Court did in *Reynolds* v. *Sims*. Chief Justice Warren stated that "legislators represent people, not trees or acres."

Enforcement of the *Reynolds* decision brought dramatic changes in the makeup of state legislatures. Old combinations of power were broken up. Many familiar rural faces disappeared from legislative halls. But the suburbs probably gained more than the central cities did, because, as it turned out, the suburbs had been most underrepresented all along.[30] One authority has stated, "The United States is an urban nation but not a big-city nation. The suburbs own the future."[31] One mayor has complained that legislative representatives from the suburbs are as hostile to the problems of the central cities as were the old rural representatives.[32]

Has legislative reapportionment improved the quality of legislative policy-making? There is not enough evidence yet to give a definitive answer, but one study shows that fairly apportioned legislatures have discriminated less against metropolitan areas.[33] In the 1970s, state legislatures generally moved toward greater modernization, improved decorum, and more openness—whether or not this was attributable to reapportionment.

---

[27] Grant and Nixon, *State and Local Government in America*, p. 250.

[28] *Reynolds* v. *Sims*, 377 U.S. 533 (1964).

[29] *Baker* v. *Carr*, 369 U.S. 186 (1962).

[30] See Paul T. David and Ralph Eisenberg, *Devaluation of the Urban and Suburban Vote* (Charlottesville, Va.: Bureau of Public Administration, University of Virginia, 1961).

[31] William J.D. Boyd, "Suburbia Takes Over," *National Civic Review*, 54 (June 1965): 294–98.

[32] Mayor Wes Uhlman of Seattle, quoted in Jack Rosenthal, "The Year of the Suburbs: More People, More Power," *New York Times* (June 21, 1970), p. 54.

[33] H. George Frederickson and Yong Hyo Cho, "Sixties' Reapportionment: Is It Victory or Illusion?" *National Civic Review* (February 1971), pp. 73–78, 85.

State courts and judges. American citizens are far more likely to appear in a state court than in a federal court. State courts handle many times more cases than federal courts do.[34]

Like federal judges, state judges are involved in conflict resolution, administration of laws, and policy-making. State courts interpret laws passed by the state legislatures, and they interpret the state constitutions, too, exercising a state "judicial review" power.

State court rulings and judgments must conform to the U.S. Constitution, as interpreted by the U.S. Supreme Court. When a "substantial federal question" is involved in a case in a state court, a decision by the state's highest court may be appealed to the U.S. Supreme Court, if the U.S. Supreme Court thinks the matter serious enough to warrant acceptance of the appeal.

Most state court decisions are not appealed to the U.S. Supreme Court. In those that are, state courts thereafter have some discretion in the final interpretation and implementation of the Supreme Court's decision in the case. One authority who studied the way state judges enforced the 1954 U.S. Supreme Court decision in *Brown* v. *Board of Education*,[35] which outlawed segregation in the public schools, classified the judges as "Federalists," who saw it as their duty to implement the Supreme Court decision as fully as possible; as "Compromisers," who gave greater weight to local needs and problems; and as "States' Righters," who considered local conditions and state judicial independence to be superior to their duty to implement the desegregation policy.[36]

Whether appointed or elected, state judges usually come from backgrounds of party or political participation and activism. Many have served in a state legislature or in some other public office prior to becoming a judge. In some states, particularly New York, young lawyers become active in political parties and in politics in order to be able to eventually secure a judicial appointment. Once they take office, state judges usually feel bound by the norm of judicial independence from political pressure and public opinion.

Financing State Government

Where state governments get their revenues and how they spend them are among the essential elements of state politics. Education, highways, welfare, law enforcement and prisons, public health, and environment are all special concerns of state governments and of state budgets. Three fourths of the state budgets are spent on education, highways, and welfare.[37] Since the end of World War II,

---

[34] Material in this section is based primarily on Herbert Jacob, *Justice in America*, 3rd ed. (Boston: Little, Brown and Company, 1978).

[35] *Brown* v. *Board of Education of Topeka*, 347 U.S. 483 (1954).

[36] Kenneth N. Vines, "Southern Supreme Courts and Race Relations," *Western Political Science Quarterly*, 18 (March 1965): 5–18.

[37] Advisory Commission on Intergovernmental Relations, *State-Local Finances: Significant Features and Suggested Legislation* (Washington, D.C.: U.S. Government Printing Office, 1972), p. 121.

state and local expenditures have risen at a faster rate than spending by the federal government.[38] Today, considering domestic expenditures only, state and local governments spend more than the federal government each year.[39]

Taxes. As a general rule, state and local taxes are not nearly as "progressive" (based upon the ability to pay) as federal taxes. Forty-five states collect a sales tax, a "regressive" tax which falls heaviest on poor people. All the states depend on motor fuels taxes, particularly taxes on gasoline. Four-fifths of the states have income taxes, and the trend in recent years has been toward increased reliance on the income tax. However, this tax still accounts for only about eleven percent of total state and local taxation.

Local governments are more dependent on property taxes than on any other kind of tax. However, the California Supreme Court ruled in 1971 that public schools' reliance on property taxes as a major source of school financing in that state was unconstitutional.[40] There have been several other state rulings of similar impact. In 1978, the people of California adopted Proposition 13, which drastically curtailed property taxes for all purposes. For a time, some observers thought that this kind of "taxpayer revolt" would spread throughout the country, bringing similar "meat-axe" property tax cuts in other states. But in 1978, voters in several states rejected the drastic approach of Proposition 13, although they did adopt a number of more moderate measures to hold property taxes down.[41]

Liberal tax reform groups advocate steps to make property assessments more equal and fair and to eliminate present property tax breaks for business. For example, the Chrysler Building in New York City pays no tax because it is owned by an engineering art college, and the city of Cleveland recently granted property tax breaks to Standard Oil of Ohio as well as to the National City Bank, one of the fifty most profitable banks in America. Tax reform groups also argue that "intangible" property—stocks and bonds, which are now largely exempt from local property taxes—should be taxed. They also say that sales taxes should be made less regressive by eliminating the sales tax on food, clothing, and medicine.[42]

Because of growing taxpayer opposition to property taxes, and in some instances because of court rulings against heavy reliance on property taxes to finance the public schools, a greater burden for financing public education has been placed on the revenues of some

Copyright 1980 by Sidney Harris

". . . plus Federal Tax, State Tax, City Sales Tax and a special tax we have here on 34th Street."

---

[38] Alan K. Campbell and Donna E. Shalala, "Problems Unsolved, Solutions Untried: The Urban Crisis," in Alan K. Campbell, ed., *The States and the Urban Crisis*, p. 25.

[39] For this and related information contained in this section, unless otherwise indicated, see, Berman, *State and Local Politics*, pp. 246-263.

[40] *Serrano* v. *Priest*, 487 P.2d 1241 (1971).

[41] *U.S. News & World Report* (November 20, 1978), p. 103.

[42] See Public Citizen's Tax Reform Research Group, *People and Taxes* (September 1978); and Movement for Economic Justice, *Just Economics* (August 1978).

states in recent years. All states have increasingly been called upon to help meet urban problems, and they have shown varying degrees of responsiveness.

Federal funds. Primarily through federal grants-in-aid, block grants, and revenue sharing, state (and local and tribal) governments get substantial funding from the federal government. Under federal grants-in-aid, the federal government sets the basic policy, or framework of action, and sometimes spells out many of the details of a program, but leaves the actual management and administration of the program to state or local governments. The initial impetus for such grant-in-aid programs has sometimes come from state and local governments. Many, on the other hand, have been initiated at the federal level. Most federal expenditures are direct payments, not shared with state or local governments. For example, federal spending for defense and national security, foreign aid, social security, and veterans assistance is done this way. But when federal policy-makers inaugurate a new program—as, for example, with the unemployment compensation program—they have frequently elected to have it administered at the local or state levels. To give another example, the federal government may say to the states, in effect, "If you will administer a new Federal Interstate Highway program and put up 10 percent of the construction costs, the federal government will pay 90 percent of such costs." The Interstate Highway Program, enacted under President Eisenhower, provided just such an attractive carrot for state participation in a mammoth, nationwide highway-building project.

Federal grants-in-aid may go from the federal government to a state government, as they did under the Federal Highway Program. Grants may also sometimes bypass states and go directly to local governments, such as the federal-local program for hospital construction and the federal-local program which provides federal matching funds for construction of sewage disposal systems. Frequently, federal grants-in-aid may go to both state and local governments. For example, this occurs under the Law Enforcement Assistance Administration, which provides federal funds for state and local governments to improve their law enforcement systems. Federal grants are also available to Indian tribes, as units of government.

The availability of federal grants-in-aid has been seen as both a blessing and a curse for state and local governments. These grants have created in state and local governments a tendency to apply for whatever programs are available—"whatever Washington is calling money this year"—whether or not this distorts the priorities that local and state governments might otherwise set on their own. But federal grants-in-aid have also greatly increased the ability of state and local governments to meet local problems and needs, while allowing state and local officials to avoid raising taxes to pay for new programs.

**Sources
of Revenue
for the Federal
Government
and for State
and Local
Governments:
1975-1976**

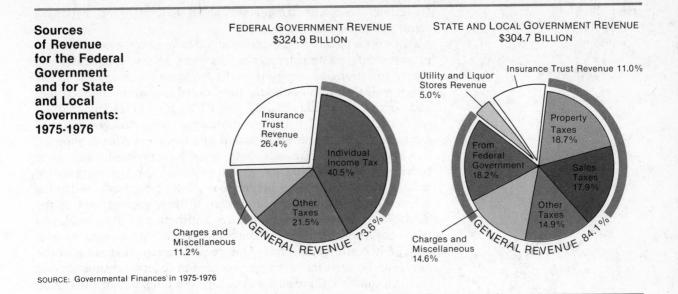

FEDERAL GOVERNMENT REVENUE
$324.9 BILLION

Insurance
Trust
Revenue
26.4%

Individual
Income Tax
40.5%

Other
Taxes
21.5%

GENERAL REVENUE 73.6%

Charges and
Miscellaneous
11.2%

STATE AND LOCAL GOVERNMENT REVENUE
$304.7 BILLION

Utility and Liquor
Stores Revenue
5.0%

Insurance Trust Revenue 11.0%

Property
Taxes
18.7%

From
Federal
Government
18.2%

Sales
Taxes
17.9%

Other
Taxes
14.9%

GENERAL REVENUE 84.1%

Charges and
Miscellaneous
14.6%

SOURCE: Governmental Finances in 1975-1976

Still, state and local officials regularly complain about the "strings" attached to federal grants-in-aid. Members of Congress, on the other hand, often feel that they will not be doing their duty to the federal taxpayers if they do not set standards under which these federal funds will be spent. So, a state which receives grants-in-aid for welfare or for unemployment compensation, for example, must set up a state merit system acceptable to the relevant federal agency for the hiring, promotion, and dismissal of the state employees who will administer such programs. This is done to assure that the goals of the programs will not be undermined through the incompetence or partiality of state employees who might otherwise be chosen through political patronage.

These *categorical grants-in-aid* have been criticized because they bypass elected officials in favor of unelected bureaucrats or technocrats. Governors, mayors, and some tribal officials have complained about this:

Practically all of the new grant programs were functionally oriented, with power, money, and decisions flowing from program administrators in Washington, to program specialists in regional offices, to functional department heads in State and local governments—leaving Cabinet officers, governors, county commissioners, and mayors less and less informed as to what was actually taking place . . . .[43]

[43] U.S. Advisory Commission on Intergovernmental Relations, "Federalism in the Sixties: A Ten-Year Review," *Eleventh Annual Report* (Washington, D.C.: Government Printing Office, 1970), p. 2.

Governors have also complained about federal grants bypassing states and going directly to cities.

Objections to categorical grants-in-aid from governors and mayors in particular, as well as suggestions from liberal economists and others for strengthening state and local governments,[44] led to the enactment, first, of block grants (also called special revenue sharing) and, second, of revenue sharing (also called general revenue sharing) for state, local, and tribal governments. These changes occurred during the Nixon administration and with President Nixon's support. *Block grants*, which include both some new programs and some conversion of certain old categorical grant-in-aid programs, provide federal funds for broad functions but allow state, local, and tribal officials to exercise greater discretion in their specific uses of the funds. *Revenue sharing* is a system of distributing to state, local, and tribal governments a set percentage of federal tax collections with only limited strings attached. One requirement is that none of the funds can be used for lobbying in regard to federal revenue sharing itself. In addition, there must not be any discrimination of any kind in the expenditure of such funds; and local and state governments receiving revenue-sharing funds must hold public hearings to allow local citizens to say how they think the money should be spent.

Today, $6 billion in federal funds are being sent back to state, tribal, and local governments under the revenue-sharing system. Two thirds of these funds are going directly to local and tribal governments; one third is going to states.

Criticisms of the revenue-sharing system include the objection by political scientists that the accountability of public officials is lessened when the taxing responsibility is separated from the spending responsibility. "Don't jump on me about how high taxes are," a local or state official might say, "because it's the Congress that has raised your taxes." On the other hand, if a citizen criticizes the way local or state officials spend revenue-sharing funds, a member of Congress might respond, "Don't blame me. We just raise the money; they decide how to spend it."

Many mayors and governors criticized the Nixon administration for reducing categorical grants-in-aid when revenue sharing was enacted, thus not actually increasing overall funds. Liberals have also criticized revenue sharing, arguing that state governments are not as interested in the problems of central cities and minorities as the federal government is.[45]

But, criticized or not, federal categorical grants-in-aid, block grants, and revenue sharing are politically palatable ways for the

[44] See Walter W. Heller, *New Dimensions of Political Economy* (Cambridge, Mass.: Harvard University Press, 1966); and Melvin R. Laird, "Strengthening the Federal System—the Case for Revenue Sharing," *Congressional Record* (February 15, 1967).

[45] Reagan, *The New Federalism*, p.111; and Vernon E. Jordan, Jr., "Local Control Hurts Blacks," *The Wall Street Journal* (September 19, 1973), p. 13.

federal government to assure state, local, and tribal cooperation in the implementation of federal policies. From the state, local, and tribal viewpoint, they are seen as politically palatable ways of increasing funds for their needs.

There are so many different kinds of federal programs, administered by so many different federal agencies, that the state and local governments that are most successful in securing these funds have had to hire people who do nothing else but handle such grants. The federal government has divided the nation into ten standard federal regions, with regional offices, to reduce red tape in the programs. Some local and state officials—and many conservative citizens— continue to be worried about the addictive effect of federal grants. But most state and local officials feel the same way about federal grants as an old-time state tax collector did, who once attempted to justify a tax on illegal liquor. "It's tainted money, but tain't enough," the tax collector declared. Today, one fourth of state and local budgets throughout the country are financed by federal funds. This represents one sixth of all the money spent by the federal government.

Borrowing.   In addition to operating revenues raised through taxation and funds received from the federal government, states may also borrow money. They may borrow by issuing general obligation bonds, which pledge the "faith and credit" of the state. Thus, they must be paid through increased taxation, if necessary. States also issue revenue bonds, which pledge, or mortgage, only the revenues from a particular project to be financed, such as a turnpike. Under federal law, both kinds of state bonds (and similar local bonds, as well) are called "municipal bonds" and are exempt from federal taxation. This federal tax exemption is intended to make it possible for state and local governments to borrow money at low interest rates, because investors are attracted to bonds in which they can invest without having to pay federal income taxes on the bond income. Of course, the present federal tax exemption on municipal bond income gives a special tax break to wealthy people who can afford to invest in such bonds. They are generally in $5,000 denominations. As an alternative to this system of tax-exempt state and local financing, a number of national leaders have suggested that the federal government should establish an urban bank, which would make loans directly to state and local governments or would guarantee such loans. Such a system would thus provide low-interest financing without special tax breaks for a small number of wealthy Americans in the process.

State Politics

The opportunities for effective political participation by Americans would be greatly reduced if we had only a centralized national government. It is true that our federal system of shared sovereignty fragments power and limits immediate popular control of overall government policies. But, at the same time, the federal system also increases the number of entry points for popular participation and brings these entry points closer to home. An active Democrat or Republican, for example, has a much better chance of making his or her influence felt at a state party convention than at a national convention because it is easier to become a state party delegate and because state party conventions usually have a smaller number of delegates than national party conventions do.

Political issues at the state level may often have just as serious an impact on the everyday lives of citizens as those at the national level. The same may be said of state elections, as compared with national elections. Yet more Americans get involved in, and feel more intensely about national politics than about state politics. Local elections usually produce even smaller turnouts than state elections. Because of the drama and excitement of politics at the national level, the average citizen probably knows more about the President's last summit meeting with international leaders than about last week's session of the state legislature. Whether lower public interest in state and local politics is the cause or result of media attention to national politics, or a mixture of both cause and result, we have a troublesome political paradox: political participation is least prevalent where it might prove most effective.

While there is less participation in party activities, campaigns, interest group activities, and elections at the state and local levels, in several states and localities citizens can engage in direct democracy through the initiative and referendum and through the device of the recall. As noted in Chapter 11, the *initiative*—primarily used in the western states of California, Washington, Colorado, Oregon, North Dakota, Oklahoma, and Arizona—allows voters to propose a law by securing a sufficient number of signatures on a petition. In the indirect initiative, the measure first goes to the legislature, and then to the voters if the legislature fails to act. A direct initiative brings the matter at issue to a vote of the people directly.[46] In the 1978 election, for example, the voters of California defeated a direct initiative that would have prevented homosexuals from teaching in public schools.

A *referendum* may come up for a vote of the people in three ways.[47] In a protest referendum, the people petition for a popular vote on whether a measure passed by the state legislature should be approved or repealed. A compulsory referendum, usually involving a proposed constitutional amendment, *must* be referred to a popular vote by the legislature. In a voluntary referendum, the legislature may decide to refer a legislative proposal to the people, rather than

---

[46] See Karl E. Lutrin and Allen K. Settle, "The Public and Ecology: The Role of Initiatives in California's Environmental Politics," (paper presented at the annual meeting of the American Political Science Association, New Orleans, September 4–8, 1973).

[47] Berman, *State and Local Politics*, pp. 86–91.

take action on the measure itself.[48] In 1978, the voters of New Jersey, for example, rejected a voluntary legislative referendum that would have permitted gambling on the game of jai alai.

The *recall*, which is a kind of "reverse election," is a way by which the people may remove public officials before the end of their term by petition and popular vote.[49] Only thirteen states permit the recall of state officials, but it is much more widely available at the local level. The use of the recall is restricted by the rather large number of signatures required on a recall petition (commonly 25 percent of the eligible voters) and the usual limit of one recall vote during a single term of office.

Proponents of the recall say that it is an important threat that helps keep public officials on their toes and accountable to the people. Opponents argue, on the other hand, that it is used mostly as a selfish and partisan harassment of officeholders. There has not been sufficient research to determine who is right about the value of the recall, but it has only been successful once at the state level (the governor, attorney general, and secretary of state of North Dakota were recalled in 1921). The recall has been used more frequently and more successfully at the local level. In 1977, for example, voters in Madison, Wisconsin, recalled a trial judge who had acquitted a man charged with rape. The judge had said that the dress of today's women is a provocation for such assaults, touching off a storm of outrage among the city's voters. On the other hand, voters in Cleveland narrowly rejected a recall of Mayor Dennis Kucinich in 1979; the recall campaign had been led by groups that opposed the mayor's fiscal and other policies.

INDIAN TRIBES

As we mentioned in Chapters 3 and 4, American Indians today are different from other American ethnic groups in that their tribal organizations are recognized units of government. From earliest times, the U.S. government dealt with most tribes through treaties, as it did with foreign nations. These treaties were grants of rights *from* Indian tribes, not grants of rights *to* them. Thus, tribes possess reserved, or retained powers; they include all the powers that the tribes have not given up or that have not been taken away by federal action.[50]

---

[48] See Raymond E. Wolfinger and Fred I. Greenstein, "The Repeal of Fair Housing in California: An Analysis of Referendum Voting," *American Political Science Review*, 62 (September 1968): 753–69.

[49] For discussions of the recall, see Maddox and Fuquay, *State and Local Government*, pp. 287–89; and Alan Shank and Ralph W. Conant, *Urban Perspectives* (Boston: Holbrook Press, 1975), pp. 60–61.

[50] See Charles F. Wilkinson and John M. Volkman, "Judicial Review of Indian Treaty Abrogation: 'As Long As Water Flows or Grass Grows Upon the Earth'— How Long a Time Is That?" *California Law Review*, 63 (1975):601.

American Indians are U.S. citizens. This was specifically stated in the 1924 Indian Citizenship Act. Thus, tribal members have a kind of dual citizenship: U.S. citizenship, from which state citizenship flows, as well; and citizenship in their own tribes.

A tribal meeting of the Sandoval Pueblo Indians. Indian tribes constitute a separate level of government in America; they are not considered parts of state or local governments.

Some federal officials, particularly those in the U.S. Bureau of Indian Affairs, continue to think of Indian reservations as federal colonies, which are subject to federal rule rather than self-government. In 1975, Congress passed the Indian Self-Determination Act to force an end to this federal colonial policy. The Act seeks to strengthen tribal governments; it turns over to them many of the educational, transportation, welfare, environmental, and other programs previously administered by the federal government but provides continued federal funding of these programs. This transition from federal to tribal control is moving slowly, however, and the tribes suspect that some Bureau of Indian Affairs officials, fearing a loss of power, are dragging their feet.

Indian tribes are not foreign, state, or local governments. They are tribal governments, and they are unique in our federal system. States do not have jurisdiction over them, unless such power has been specifically delegated to the states by the federal government, which has usually not been done. While the U.S. Congress can abrogate Indian treaties—paying just compensation for any property rights thus taken—it has not chosen to do so in most instances. The treaties that have not been abrogated are upheld as binding by the courts. Although the federal government's taxing and regulatory power extends to reservations, states generally have no such taxing and regulatory power on reservations, particularly if state action would conflict with federal action or infringe upon governmental powers already being exercised by a tribal government.

Indian reservations and tribal populations range from the small to the large. One half of all Indians are members of one of nine tribes: Navajo, the largest tribe; Chippewa; Choctaw; Cherokee; Pueblo; Apache; Sioux; Lumbee; and Iroquois. The history, language, customs, traditions, and present tribal governments of these and other tribes vary greatly. A majority of the Pueblos of New Mexico continues to be governed by traditional officials. The principal official is the "Cacique," a theocratic (religious) leader, who, with other tribal elders, chooses the tribal governor and other governmental officials each year. Most tribes, however, have an elected tribal council, or business committee. Usually, this tribal council elects the chairperson of the tribe. A number of such chairpersons today and the chairperson of the National Congress of American Indians, a national Indian organization, are women.

In most tribes, the legislative and executive functions are performed by some of the same people, much as they are in a parliamentary system; the executive officials are selected by and from the tribal council. Tribal constitutions differ, however. Later constitutions tend to separate more sharply the executive, legislative, and judicial functions of the tribal government. The Navajo tribe has a tribal council, with members elected by districts, and an executive tribal chairperson, elected by popular vote of the tribe. Local government is provided in the Navajo system by "Chapters." Aside from those of the Navajo tribe, most tribal executives are not full-time, paid officials, and most tribal governments face considerable funding problems.

Indian tribes have been moving very rapidly to enact taxing, zoning, environmental, and other law codes, and to set up law enforcement systems, tribal courts, and other governmental agencies. Under the federal Major Crimes Act, crimes such as murder and rape committed by an Indian person on a reservation, must be tried in the federal courts. Under tribal codes, crimes which involve the possibility of punishment of no more than a $500 fine or six months in jail are tried in tribal courts. Non-Indians who commit crimes on reservations are tried in either state or federal courts, depending on the offense.

Despite their differences in history, culture, language, and other backgrounds, American Indians have been able to forge a pan-Indian movement. They have joined together on important issues, such as tribal sovereignty and jurisdiction, education, health, economic development, and pollution. The Northern Cheyenne tribe of Montana has adopted the strictest air pollution standards of any governmental unit in America, thus stopping, at least temporarily, a huge electricity-generating project just north (upwind) of their reservation.

American Indian tribes are attempting to improve their tribal economy. Today, tribes own a large portion of America's coal, oil and gas, uranium, and other energy resources. The Council of Energy Resource Tribes has been formed to allow tribes to share information concerning energy development. Tribes also own large tracts of land, much timber, copper, and other natural resources. Many tribes are involved in fishing and "aquaculture." And the Indian tribes' control of up to one half of the water in Western streams and rivers is becoming increasingly important.

Americans for Indian Opportunity, a national Indian organization, pioneered the idea that Indian tribes are very much like emerging foreign nations in that they can never achieve real self-government until they wrest back control over their natural resources from non-Indian corporations and individuals who lease them for small money payments alone. Some tribes are now demanding joint ventures and other arrangements to give them a share of the profits, risks, jobs, and control. Thus, economic development on these reservations will proceed, if at all, in ways that the tribes themselves find to be economically, culturally, and environmentally sound.

LOCAL GOVERNMENTS

For most Americans, the governmental units which are closest to them are counties, special districts, and cities or towns. And at this grass roots level, governmental functions often overlap.

**Types
of Local
Governments:
1977**

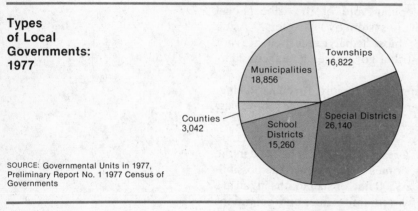

SOURCE: Governmental Units in 1977, Preliminary Report No. 1 1977 Census of Governments

Counties

The most universal type of government in America is county government.[51] All but three states—Connecticut, Rhode Island, and Alaska—are divided into counties. (Louisiana calls its counties "parishes"). There are more than 3,000 such local subdivisions throughout the United States.

The courthouse in each county is at a town designated as the "county seat." In the early days, the idea behind county government and the location of county seats was that citizens should be able to go by horse and buggy from their homes to the courthouse and back on the same day. Today, because of automobiles and highways, many people have suggested that there should be a consolidation of counties within each state; they argue that it is too expensive to have so many separate governments for relatively small geographic areas. But the people in all the states have tenaciously held on to their county governments, and the consolidation movement has not progressed very far.

Counties are generally governed by a board of commissioners, board of supervisors, or some similar board, which are elected by the people. Other, separately elected county officials usually include a county treasurer, a county assessor, a county clerk, and a county sheriff. This is called a "plural executive" form of county government. Some of the more populous counties have adopted a "county manager" form of government. In this system, the voters elect the county board, which then chooses a county manager. The county manager is responsible for choosing and supervising the other appointed officials of the county. Some counties elect a county executive who performs a similar function. But most county governments have changed very little over the years. They are criticized for this lack of modernization.

---

[51] See Grant and Nixon, *State and Local Government in America*, pp. 375–89.

The functions of a county that contains within its boundaries all or a part of a large city often overlap and conflict with those performed by the city government. In some instances, the city and county governments have merged, or some specific common function, such as law enforcement, has been combined.

Towns and villages within a county may achieve a measure of local rule by incorporating. When this is done, they may collect certain local taxes and provide basic services for their citizens which otherwise would be performed exclusively, if at all, by the county government. In New England's traditional *town meetings*, which are still held in some towns, all of the qualified voters of the town elect the town officials and adopt positions in regard to taxes and policy. In many New England towns today, the traditional town meeting has been revised into a representative town meeting of elected delegates.

Special Districts

Within each state and county, there are numerous special districts. A water, irrigation, or conservancy district, for example, is supported by local taxes or fees and is governed by a board chosen by the district's voters. The most important local district government is the school district. It is responsible for the local schools, is basically financed by a property tax, and is governed by an elected school board. City and county governments usually have little, if any, control over school and other district boards. This fragmentation of authority means that voters must have a relatively high level of understanding of how the various units of local government work and a relatively high level of persistent political participation, if they are to affect local policy. School and other district elections are nearly always on a nonpartisan basis, and voter turnout is typically very low. The result is that political power and control at the school and other district level of government is usually concentrated in a relatively small number of activists or interest groups.

Cities

The people of ancient Greece thought of themselves, first, as citizens of a city-state like Athens or Sparta. Each Greek citizen was proud of his or her city-state, which was called a *metropolis*, meaning "mother city." Today, central cities in America do not engender as much local pride, and a metropolitan area is not usually subject to one government only. Metropolitan areas—or urban areas, as they are also called—are made up of a central city and surrounding suburbs, which are often separately governed.[52]

A town meeting in Victory, Vermont. In a traditional town meeting, a form of direct democracy, there are no representatives; the voters themselves are the legislators.

[52] See Charles R. Adrian and Charles Press, *Governing Urban America* (New York: McGraw-Hill, 1977).

"Urban problems" are among the most difficult to solve of any domestic problems in America. (Sometimes they are only local manifestations of larger national problems.) The development of these problems centers around four major urban characteristics and developments. First, there was rapid growth of the cities. Second, a "flight" to the suburbs followed, leaving behind decay and rising poverty in the central cities. Third, the cities, which were financially weak to begin with, found their costs going up while their tax base was shrinking. Finally, politics in the central cities has generally been characterized by apathy, which stems primarily from citizens' sense of futility.

Two thirds of Americans live in metropolitan areas—cities and suburbs—which constitute only about 10 percent of the total land area in America. From 1860 until 1900, the population of cities doubled. Then it doubled again during the next twenty-five years, jumped up after World War I, and surged upward again dramatically after World War II. People moved from rural areas and small towns into the cities for a number of reasons, but mostly because they were poor and needed jobs. This was particularly true of poor blacks, most of whom came from the South and moved to northern cities, or in many instances, into southern cities.

For many white immigrants from rural areas and small towns—and later, for their children—the city never became "home." Seeking a "nice neighborhood" to raise their children, they moved out to the suburbs as soon as they could afford it. Real estate developers encouraged and catered to them. The automobile, and federal urban highways, made their move practical; they could still drive back and forth to work. Often, they formed their own town and village governments and school districts. Lured by lower taxes, industries soon began to move to these suburbs. Frequently, local town and village governments then adopted ordinances which sought to raise barriers against poor people moving into the neighborhoods. For example, some ordinances specified that no house could be built on less than one half acre. The poorest people in the cities, mostly black people and other minorities, were left behind because they could not afford to move.

The central cities began to decay. The jobs, especially those with lower educational and skill requirements, were increasingly in the suburbs, while the poorest people who most needed those jobs were in the central cities. They were usually without automobiles or adequate public transportation to take them from their central city homes to the jobs in the suburbs each morning and back again at night. The jobs that were left in the central cities were increasingly in the banks and other offices in high-rise, metal-and-glass buildings that sprang up downtown in the midst of residential squalor and abandoned retail establishments. But these jobs usually required a higher level of skills and education than most poor city residents possessed.

The central cities became increasingly black, while the suburbs were mostly white. However, as more blacks have moved into the economic middle class in recent years, blacks have been moving to the suburbs, also.

Poverty is the hallmark of the modern American central city. Poverty primarily means a lack of money. And in this regard, the problems of the central cities can be seen as local concentrations of wider, national problems: lack of jobs for people who can work, and lack of income for those who cannot work or who cannot find work. People with low incomes cannot afford good housing or good health care.

In 1978, the national unemployment rate stood at about seven percent, but it was much greater than that in the central cities, particularly among young black people and other minorities. Lack of income in the central cities manifests itself in a number of distressing symptoms. A high crime rate seems to go hand-in-hand with a high poverty rate. In 1977, during a city-wide blackout because of a power failure, there was a great amount of looting in New York City. But, as an editorial in the *New York Times* later pointed out, the looting occurred only in the poor sections of the city, and only people from those parts of the city seemed to take part in it. The *Times* suggested that the connection between "civic virtue" and "prosperity" seemed too obvious to ignore.[53]

THE GEOGRAPHY OF CIVILITY

The lights are on and the heat is gone, but the anger still burns in New York, and even far from New York. Our desks are piled high with letters that not only condemn the looting during the blackout but also compete in expressions of hate for the looters. Those of us who perceived a social overload alongside the electrical one are accused of sponsoring permissiveness. We are reprimanded for seeking economic, sociological and pathological explanations. We are rebuked for undermining the discipline of the poor. The looters have merged in many minds with the muggers and the addicts and even with blacks and Hispanics in general. Fear has fused with rage.

To further address this passion, we suspect, may be to inflame it. But we remain haunted by a question that will not go away. So the looters were animals and psychotics and welfare cheats, seeking something for nothing, seizing targets of opportunity. Denounce them, jail them, hate them. Still the question lingers. The looters appeared that dark night in dozens of spontaneous formations on many separate places—but not everywhere. Not on Staten Island, not on Central Park South, not in Riverdale, or Yonkers, or Rockaway, or Jackson Heights. They appeared only in the poorest sections of town and drew recruits only from the poorest population groups, albeit only a tiny fraction of them. The question is, why there, and only there? Why, bluntly, were there no white looters in white neighborhoods?

Unless you believe that race and ethnic origins define or explain civic virtue, that question must be faced. Not all, not even many, in the slums became looters. But all the looters appeared in slums. No single explanation may be valid—not poverty, not unemployment, not discrimination, not deprivation—but whatever the right combination of reasons, there was a geography to this pathology. Could it be that the civility we prize is related unavoidably to prosperity?

If even the prosperous cannot remember to ask that question, more than we think was lost that night.

SOURCE: *New York Times* (July 29, 1977).

High crime rates in the central cities have been a major cause of the flight to the suburbs. Suburban flight has left a higher incidence of poverty among central city residents. The higher incidence of poverty has increased the tendency toward higher crime.

The cities have historically been dependent upon a relatively weak financial base—consisting primarily of property taxes and water, sewer, and garbage fees—both for operating funds and for bond issues. After World War II, state legislatures began to allow cities to

---

[53] *New York Times* (July 29, 1977).

levy other taxes. These were principally sales taxes, although some cities have also been permitted to enact income taxes. Most people who live in the suburbs have been reluctant to allow themselves to be taxed to meet the problems of central cities, even though many of them make their living from jobs in the central cities and regularly go into the central cities to take advantage of entertainment and other attractions there.

Cities have found themselves with declining tax bases at a time when the demands for governmental expenditures—for law enforcement, housing, health, transportation, water and sewer, and other needs—have been escalating. A portion of the increased city expenditures—for urban highways and streets, for example—are actually needed to serve suburbanites. Many cities have not given sufficient attention to maintenance and repair of water and sewer systems. As one newspaper headline has put it, "Beneath the Streets, Old Cities Crumble and Decay."[54] Cities have increasingly gone to the federal government for help, bypassing the state governments, which have not been as responsive to the plight of the central cities as they have been to the demands of the suburbs, the small towns, and the rural areas.

Politics in the central cities has been characterized by low voter participation. This low rate of participation has resulted partly from the urban dwellers' lack of a sense of community and the lack of opportunity to participate in community and other organizations because they have moved often or recently. It has also resulted from city residents' sense of futility in dealing with large political organizations and bureaucracies. Some people have simply said, "You can't fight city hall." Others have felt that city government is run by machines and bosses and is characterized by corruption and favoritism. While this may once have been true, we see today a decline in the power of political bosses and machines. This decline has resulted from the adoption of merit systems to remove city jobs from political patronage; from the advent of welfare systems based upon need rather than political influence (partly because of federal requirements); and from the rise in importance of the mass media, particularly television, which allows candidates to go over the heads of political bosses and machines, directly to the people. Local political parties have declined in importance for some of the same reasons. The result is that candidates run primarily as "personalities"; issues have become less important. The number of "reform" mayors who have been elected in recent years has increased.

Most of the large cities in America are governed by a "strong mayor-council" form of government. Under this system, members of the city council and the mayor are separately elected. The mayor has a great deal of executive authority, in addition to presiding at meetings of the city council. Some large cities still have a "weak mayor-council" form of government. In this system, the mayor is

Jane Byrne successfully opposed the machine candidate in the primary and handily won a general election to become mayor of Chicago in 1979. Both elections were characterized by a high voter turnout.

---

[54] *New York Times* (April 9, 1978).

more of a figurehead. In some cities, the people elect "commissioners," who choose one of their number from time to time as the commission chairperson. The number of cities using the commission system is declining. Some cities have adopted the "council-manager" form of government, under which a professional, "nonpolitical" administrator is hired as the city executive. This system today is mainly used by middle-sized and smaller cities.

Certain "reforms" of the 1950s—the council-manager form of government, election of members of the city council at large, rather than by districts, and nonpartisan elections—have lost much of their support in liberal quarters in recent years as it has become increasingly apparent that these devices have resulted in reduced control and participation by average city citizens. In nonpartisan elections in a large city, many citizens simply do not have sufficient information to cast a vote, and they are deprived of a party cue, which might give them a better idea of which candidate is more like them in outlook and ideology.

More recent local government reforms have involved city-county consolidation, annexation, and the formation of regional councils of government (COGs).[55] All are aimed at reducing the number of overlapping local governments or providing more coordination of their activities. The enactment of such reforms has been limited by the degree to which the local citizens have accepted them. Attempts to form "metro" governments by consolidating cities and counties have met with the greatest voter opposition. This resistance is partly attributable to the differences between the cities (which are likely to have greater percentages of poor and minority people) and the suburbs (which are likely to have greater percentages of wealthier white people). Annexations by cities that are not already hemmed in by incorporated towns or villages have offered a way to broaden their tax bases and to standardize the services offered within those areas. A large number of COGs have been formed throughout the country to coordinate the activities of various governmental units within particular regions. They have met with little citizen opposition because their functions are ministerial and because they do not make policy or attempt to redistribute tax burdens or revenues among the cooperating governments.

City officials must deal with and, to some degree, accommodate the demands of the city power structure and interest groups. These include the local banks and other businesses, utilities, contractors and developers, real estate interests, taxi owners, liquor interests, newspapers, and organized labor. There is some indication that local power structures are also related to power elites at the national level.[56]

---

[55] See Vincent L. Marando, "The Politics of Metropolitan Reform," in Alan K. Campbell and Roy W. Bahl, eds., *State and Local Government; The Political Economy of Reform* (New York: The Free Press, 1976), pp. 24–49.

[56] See G. William Domhoff, *Who Really Rules?* (Santa Monica, California: Goodyear Publishing Company, 1978).

VIEWPOINT

The Cities: "We must be about the business of decentralizing, de-institutionalizing, and deregulating"

Professor Louis Masotti is Director of the Center for Urban Affairs at Northwestern University. The following is excerpted from a paper presented at the 1978 American Political Science Association Convention, which will be included in "Urban Policies in a Period of Retrenchment," a collection of articles to be published by Sage Publications.

Rhetoric to the contrary, urban policy in the United States, by and large, has been designed to be therapeutic: to treat the symptoms of urban malaise rather than to uncover its causes and prevent their spread. Our approach has been to develop more programs, create more bureaucracy and spend more money to stem the tide of urban decay.

The result has been bureaucratic, institutionalized policy failures that have tended to produce dependence: for people in relation to their governments, for cities in relation to federal agencies. This dependency reduces the chances for the emergence of effective, self-sustaining citizens—and of viable cities.

More important, it does not seem likely that an approach focused on increases in budgets, personnel and institutions can function effectively as we become increasingly a "society of limits."

Clearly, more of what we have done in the past is an inadequate way to approach the future. It becomes necessary to explore options and alternatives in policy and procedure. The necessity for asking some tough questions and finding appropriate answers is obvious. It's imperative that we begin to think about policies that are both different and more effective. The real contemporary challenge to the cities, and especially to their leaders, both public and private, and indeed to their citizens, is to design imaginative policies that use scarce resources more creatively to pursue policies that do as much or more with less.

This requires significant adjustments and alterations in the allocation of authority and accountability. The centralization of government and the concentration of corporate economic power have resulted more often than not in the stifling of imagination, the rigidity of policy and the growth of institutional dependency and counterproductive bureaucratization. We must be about the business of decentralizing, de-institutionalizing and deregulating where and when it can be demonstrated that this will benefit citizens as well as their cities.

In a society of limits we must begin the process of enabling and empowering individuals, neighborhoods, communities and organizations to help themselves by facilitating the flow of private capital, public funds and professional/technical assistance where these resources will improve the quality of life through the active participation of those affected. There is some evidence to indicate that such programs already in force are not only more effective but also more efficient in using scarce resources.

These are some of the new directions being discussed by social scientists as ways to achieve that grass-roots "enablement" and "empowerment":

• Use "mediating structures"—neighborhoods, family, church and voluntary organizations—as bridges between individuals and society's megastructures. Some argue forcefully that these "mediators" should be protected and fostered by public policy as essential ingredients for building individual capacity and, thus, improving democracy. Also, they believe that policymakers can use these mediators to realize their social goals.

• Redesign technology on a smaller scale for more effective use at the community and family level—the so-called "appropriate technology" (or "small is beautiful") approach. In Chicago, the new Center for Neighborhood Technology is helping 14 community organizations use technology to enhance family, neighborhood and community well-being. Its projects include household solar energy and solar rooftop greenhouses that help supply inexpensive fresh vegetables in low-income neighborhoods and, at the same time, create neighborhood jobs.

• Upgrade neighborhoods through newly available mortgage money resulting from anti-redlining legislation and by rehabilitation brought on by new interest of the affluent in older neighborhoods.

• Reduce dependency on professionals and bureaucrats through the self-help phenomenon, another low-cost, high-effectiveness movement that has grown simultaneously with the disaffection with human-service bureaucracies. By banding together in groups whose members share similar problems, the self-help groups have achieved considerable success—from the venerable Alcoholics Anonymous to organizations for child-beating parents, the overweight, the divorced, parents of twins, cancer patients and an endless variety of physical, mental and emotionally distressed persons. It is estimated there are more than a half million self-help groups in the United States comprising more than 15 million members. Self-help is for the most part a nonprofessional, nonbureaucratic, grass-roots response to the increasing inefficiency of our complex society.

All of these constitute a sort of "service populism." The critical question may be whether these small-scale, cost-efficient, high-efficacy efforts at providing advice, aid and service to millions of people can be and should be a substitute for, or a complement to, existing large-scale bureaucratic programs. It is tempting to suggest that, since such programs seem to have real potential for effectiveness, they be substituted for existing, inefficient programs in the public sector. But they work because they are not bureaucratic; institutionalizing them would thus undermine them.

What is possible, however, is careful reconsideration of how private interests and purposes can be "leveraged" in the public interest. Governments will have to begin to think more seriously about using their authority to regulate and to use tax expenditures (subsidies, loans, credits) rather than spending reduced public dollars on maintenance and income services and on incentive reducing grants. Governments must increasingly use their authority to provide incentives for the private sector, including groups and individuals, to do things in their own best interest—and in the public interest.

SOURCE: Reprinted from the *Chicago Sun-Times*, March 6, 1979.

Atlanta Mayor Maynard Jackson (top) and Newark Mayor Kenneth Gibson. Despite the efforts of these and other reform-minded mayors, urban problems remain, and cities continue to need large amounts of federal funding.

Even the new crop of modern, reform-oriented mayors—such as black mayors Young in Detroit, Gibson in Newark, Bradley in Los Angeles, Hatcher in Gary, and Jackson in Atlanta—have experienced extreme difficulty in alleviating the problems of their core cities. They have had to bypass unresponsive state governments more and more, going to Washington for financial assistance. In 1978, direct federal aid to cities made up more than 50 percent of the revenues raised and spent in ten of America's largest cities. During the same year, big-city mayors asked for an increase of eleven billion dollars annually in federal aid.[57]

President Carter named a black woman, Patricia Roberts Harris, to head the Department of Housing and Urban Development. Despite her advocacy of increased federal attention to urban problems, President Carter's 1980 budget put "severe limits" on federal programs for the cities as he launched an all-out effort to reduce the federal budget deficit.[58] At the same time that President Carter was attempting to reduce his domestic budget by approximately eighteen billion dollars, he recommended an increase in the military budget by approximately that same amount. This domestic budget cut came at a time when rising inflation and rising unemployment were sure to hit poorest people—and thus the central cities—hardest.

In the past, federal-city urban renewal efforts and urban highway programs often made the problems of poor people living in the central cities even worse. They destroyed neighborhood communities, tearing down housing and replacing it with business buildings. Suburbanites have steadfastly resisted building public housing for low-income people in their communities. Thus, poor people have been squeezed into more and more densely populated poverty areas. The renovation of old downtown houses by members of the middle class who have begun to move back into central cities has often been done only at the cost of pushing out poor people.[59]

The reform movement to create metropolitan governments, which would enclose cities and suburbs, has not been widely supported. Liberals have opposed such efforts because, they feel, they would increase the power of the white middle class and dilute the power of poor people and minorities in a much larger unit of government. Some liberals have suggested that the taxing area of cities should be increased, but the actual governing units should be made smaller, conforming to smaller communities and neighborhoods. Suburbanites do not look kindly upon the idea of increasing their tax burden in this fashion.

Some progress, however, has been made toward greater neighbor-

[57] Neal Peirce, "A New Approach to Urban Woes," *Chicago Sun-Times* (March 26, 1978), p. 64.
[58] United Press International (November 28, 1978).
[59] See Jerome Watson, "Co-ordinated Urban Effort Tough Task For New Panel," *Chicago Sun-Times* (June 20, 1977), p. 8.

hood control of city services.[60] The greatest impetus for increased neighborhood participation and greater community control of essential services came in the War on Poverty during President Lyndon B. Johnson's administration. President Carter recommended reducing the federal revenue-sharing funds given to states more and increasing the portion of these funds that are allocated to the cities. To make this suggestion more palatable to the states, he has sought to provide federal incentives and extra assistance to states that increase their efforts to solve city problems. By reducing revenue-sharing funds for the states but attempting to increase their involvement in city affairs, however, he has antagonized both mayors and governors.[61] Some mayors also resent being bypassed by direct federal grants to neighborhood groups. Mayor Richard Hatcher of Gary has declared that "the cities are under assault from two sides—the states and the neighborhoods."

Something has to give. Cities cannot meet their problems alone. More money is needed from the federal and state levels. More federal action is needed to meet nationwide unemployment and poverty and other problems that hit the central cities hardest. But these improvements must be made in a way that allows and encourages greater participation and control by central city residents—not an easy set of goals to accomplish simultaneously.

CONCLUSION

Is government best if it is closest to the people? How you answer that question depends in part upon how satisfied you are with the *status quo*, the way things are. Conservatives, who are not in favor of great change or increased governmental action to meet social and economic problems, have generally favored keeping as much governmental control as possible in the states. They do not want to see this controlling power shift to the federal government.[62] Indeed, one of the main reasons why federal power has grown so much in recent decades may be because of the states' slowness in meeting new problems, such as urban decay, lack of adequate housing, and environmental pollution. Former North Carolina Governor Terry Sanford has said of the states, "Because of their timidity and lack of initiative, it has become the pattern to turn to the federal government for the solutions of problems."[63]

Some states have been willing to experiment, and their activities have served as laboratories for producing new solutions that other states and the federal government have adopted. But innovation has

---

[60] See Milton Kotler, *Neighborhood Government: The Local Foundations of Political Life* (Indianapolis and New York: Bobbs-Merrill, 1969).

[61] See Robert Reinhold, "Carter Weighs Pushing States to Assist Cities," *New York Times* (February 12, 1978), pp. 1, 16.

[62] See Robert J. Harris, "States' Rights and Vested Interest," *Journal of Politics*, 15 (November, 1954): 457–71.

[63] Quoted in Adrian, *State and Local Governments*, p. 53.

generally not been a characteristic of most state governments. New York and Massachusetts are the most innovative states, and Nevada and Mississippi are the least innovative.[64]

The federal government's power has also increased because certain matters *must* be handled at the national level. For example, some business corporations and some unions are so large, and their operations stretch across so many states—or so many nations, with multinational business corporations—that states simply cannot adequately regulate them. Only the national government can. In addition, most people have come to agree that issues like racial discrimination and whether a child will have real opportunity for an adequate education should not be matters left to individual states, but should be decided by nationwide policy.

What do American citizens think about the various levels of American government? Most Americans seem to be better informed about national politics than they are about state and local politics. They tend to give greater priority to national politics.[65] Not surprisingly, then, national elections usually draw 20 to 30 percent more voters than do state and local elections.[66] One reason for this lower percentage of participation and information at state and local levels is that people feel that they get more for their money from the national government than they do from state and local governments.[67] Another reason is that people tend to identify much more strongly with the American nation than they do with the state or locality where they live, partly because forty million people move every year, many of them from one state to another, severing old ties.[68] According to one authority, "The most attentive and supportive of state governments are those raised in small towns or rural areas, who currently live outside metropolitan areas, who have lived in a state for the longest periods, and who are from the southern part of the country."[69] One study has found that public officials are more likely to respond to the problems of citizens who are more active political participants.[70] The federal government has been more active in meeting new problems precisely because more Americans are informed about national politics and are more likely to participate in national politics than in state and local politics.

[64] Jack L. Walker, "The Diffusion of Innovations Among the American States," *American Political Science Review*, 63 (September 1969): 883.

[65] M. Kent Jennings and Harmon Ziegler, "The Salience of American State Politics," *American Political Science Review*, 64 (June 1970): 525.

[66] See Howard D. Hamilton, "The Municipal Voter: Voting and Non-Voting in City Elections," *American Political Science Review*, 65 (December 1971): 1135–40.

[67] See Advisory Commission on Intergovernmental Relations, *Public Opinion and Taxes* (Washington, D.C.: U.S. Government Printing Office, 1972, 1973, 1974, 1975).

[68] See Norton Long, "The City as Underdeveloped Country," *Public Administration Review*, 32 (January/February 1972): 57–62.

[69] Berman, *State and Local Politics*, p. 11.

[70] Sidney Verba and Norman H. Nie, *Participation in America: Political Democracy and Social Equality* (New York: Harper and Row, 1972), pp. 332–333.

Still, many Americans feel that the federal system has merit. They believe that it represents a protection against concentrated governmental power at the federal level. The concern about centralized federal power was one of the main reasons for the adoption of federal revenue sharing. "Federal revenue sharing is needed to check the steady centralization of power in Washington, an imbalance situation that can be traced to the growing revenue superiority and increasing Federal control over State and local expenditure decisions," the Advisory Commission on Intergovernmental Relations stated in 1970.[71]

Through revenue sharing and other federal grants-in-aid programs, the federal government has been able to use its tax system to collect and shift back to state and local governments large amounts of money. This sum was about 56 billion in 1976. With this shift in money has come increased local and state power over policy-making and policy implementation. How that power is exercised—how responsive local and state governments are to citizen needs—may largely depend upon citizens' willingness to participate increasingly in politics at the state and local levels. One authority says, "In the last analysis, it is up to the people. They will get what they fight for." He adds that the ultimate strength of state government (and this also applies to local and tribal government) is that "there is no place to hide."[72]

ADDITIONAL SOURCES

Adrian, Charles R. *State and Local Politics*, 4th ed. McGraw-Hill, 1979.

Banfield, Edward C. *The Unheavenly City Revisited*. Little, Brown, 1974.*

Jacobs, Jane. *The Death and Life of Great American Cities*. Random, 1961.*

———. *The Economics of Cities*. Random, 1970.*

Leach, Richard H., and Richard D. Lambert, eds. *Intergovernmental Relations in America Today*, new ed. American Academy of Political Science, 1974.*

Lineberry, Robert. *Equality and Urban Policy: The Distribution of Municipal Public Services*. Sage, 1977.*

———, and Ira Sharkansky. *Urban Politics and Public Policy*, 3rd ed. Harper & Row, 1978.*

Nathan, Richard P. *Revenue Sharing: The Second Round*. Brookings, 1977.*

Sharkansky, Ira. *The Maligned States: Policy Accomplishments, Problems, and Opportunities*. McGraw-Hill, 1972.*

Yates, Douglas T., Jr. *Neighborhood Democracy: The Politics and Impacts of Decentralization*. Lexington, 1973.

*Available in paperback edition.

---

[71] Advisory Commission on Intergovernmental Relations, *Revenue Sharing—An Idea Whose Time Has Come* (Washington, D.C.: U.S. Government Printing Office, 1970), p. 3.

[72] Dan Lufkin, *Many Sovereign States* (N.Y.: David McKay, 1975), p. 68.

PART 5

The People and Public Policy

America's government was established to "insure domestic Tranquility, provide for the common defence, promote the general Welfare, and secure the blessings of Liberty . . . ." How it carries out those broad responsibilities—the goals and assumptions underlying the laws it passes, the programs it establishes, and the other actions it takes—are called *public policy*. In the following chapters we will examine how public policy is made in America, taking a serious look at governmental policy-making in four areas.

Chapter 17 pulls together our earlier discussions of political actors and governmental institutions; it describes how they interact to determine what the government's policies in various areas will be. We take a general view of the policy-making process here as a prelude to our discussion of specific policies in the chapters that follow.

The related problems of the environment and energy, and the governmental policies intended to deal with them, are the subjects of Chapter 18. Both of these policy areas in turn affect and are affected by government's involvement in the economy, especially its taxation and spending policies and its attempts at economic management; these are the subjects of Chapter 19. In Chapter 20, we turn to foreign policy; here again the complex, interrelated nature of the issues facing America in the 1980s will be apparent. Other policy areas could have been chosen for examination; these areas were chosen because they involve vital, current, and continuing issues. Indeed, some observers have argued that the effectiveness of America's democracy can be measured by how well it deals with these issues.

17 Public Policy
Process and Participants

After deciding to formally recognize the People's Republic of China, President Carter hosted Chinese Vice-Premier Deng Xiaoping at a White House state dinner in 1979.

"Make policy, not coffee!" was a slogan frequently heard from activist women throughout America during the 1970s, as the women's movement gained national attention. But what is policy?

Public policy consists of the goals and assumptions that underlie what government does. It is a kind of guide for government action.[1] Like individuals, governments are limited by scarce resources and by the inability to do everything at once.[2] So policy-making means that governments must make choices—to do one thing rather than another or to do a little of this and a lot of that.

Policy analysis—the study of public policy—does not just examine what politicians *say* and analyze how political institutions are *supposed* to work; it attempts to describe and explain the causes and consequences of governmental activity. "Policy analysis is finding out what governments do in education, health, welfare, housing, civil rights, environmental protection, natural resources, defense, and foreign policy; why they do it; and whether it really makes any difference in the lives of their citizens."[3]

Policy-making is complicated—and policy analysis is made more difficult—by the fragmentation of the American political system: the separation of powers, checks and balances, and federalism. In the federal government, as we have seen, policy is made in all three branches of the government: legislative, judicial, and executive (including the bureaucracy). Thus, Congress was engaged in policy-making in 1978 when it decided to pass a law lifting price levels of, and then gradually deregulating, natural gas. The U.S. Supreme

---

[1]Grover Starling, *The Politics and Economics of Public Policy: An Introductory Analysis with Cases* (Homewood, Ill.: The Dorsey Press, 1979), p. 4.

[2]Robert L. Lineberry, *American Public Policy* (New York: Harper and Row, 1977), p. 3.

[3]Thomas R. Dye, *Policy Analysis* (University of Ala.: The University of Alabama Press, 1976), pp. 2–3.

Court made policy with its 1978 *Bakke* decision. It prohibited the use of quota systems in admissions to professional schools but allowed race to be taken into account as one element in admissions. President Carter engaged in policy-making in 1978 when he decided to formally recognize the People's Republic of China and withdraw formal recognition from Taiwan. Within the federal bureaucracy, the Internal Revenue Service made policy in 1978 when it decided that private schools that are exempted from federal income taxes must take affirmative action to end racial discrimination. In addition to the federal government, fifty state governments and more than 77,000 local governments make public policy. A resident of Park Forest, Illinois, for example, pays taxes to the following policy entities: the United States of America; the state of Illinois; Cook County; Cook County Forest Preserve District; Suburban Tuberculosis Sanitary District; Rich Township; Bloom Township Sanitary District; Non-High School District 215; Rich Township High School District; Elementary School District 163; Regional Transportation Authority; and South Cook County Mosquito Abatement District.[4]

Each of these governmental bodies is responsible for developing and carrying out public policy. How is public policy made and carried out? Who is involved; what is the role of the *public* in the making of public policy? To answer these questions, it is useful to look at the five principal steps involved in the policy-making process: agenda-building; policy formulation; policy adoption; policy implementation; and policy evaluation.[5]

AGENDA-BUILDING

When you go to a restaurant for breakfast, you are usually asked to order from a prepared menu. The menu may list hotcakes but not "menudos," a favorite of many Chicanos in the Southwest. Or the menu may list bagels and lox but not fried ham. Or the menu may be a relatively long and eclectic one, offering all of these choices. In policy-making, the *agenda*, the list of things to be done or considered, is like a restaurant menu. The items on the public policy agenda—the *issues* that are subject to governmental policy-making—are like the items on the restaurant menu.

What is an issue? First, we have to know what a problem is, because issues develop from problems, and it is with problems that the policy-making process begins. A problem is a situation that annoys, hinders, or injures a particular group.[6] Not all problems

---

[4]Morton Grodzins, *The American System* (Chicago: Rand McNally, 1966), pp. 3–4.

[5]This breakdown of the policy process follows the analysis framework used in James E. Anderson, ed., *Cases in Public Policy-Making* (New York: Praeger Publishers, 1976).

[6]Robert Eyestone, *From Social Issues to Public Policy* (New York: John Wiley and Sons, 1978), p. 5.

become issues, just as all conceivable food dishes are not included as items on a restaurant menu. A problem develops into an issue when a group demands government action; when there is a disagreement about solutions; and when the choices among alternatives involve the conflicting interests of groups.

Just because a problem has developed into an issue, however, does not necessarily mean it will get on the agenda for governmental policy-making. The importance of the agenda in government policy-making is that only those issues on it are available for decision, just as a restaurant customer may choose only from items on the menu.

How does an issue get on the agenda, then? There are two kinds of agendas. The *public agenda* exists in the minds of a sizable portion of the general public. It consists of all the issues that a large segment of the population believes should be considered and acted upon by government decision-makers. Thus, the public agenda is like an unwritten menu; it is customer demand, which a restaurant owner ignores at the risk of business failure. The *official agenda* is the set of issues that are formally before government decision-makers for active and serious consideration. It is the written menu.[7] Both agendas are important. But until an issue is put on the official agenda, it is not subject to official policy-making.

Just because a bill has been introduced or a speech has been made in Congress, however, does not necessarily mean that the issue involved is on Congress' official agenda. Thousands of bills are introduced and thousands of speeches are made without causing the issues they are concerned with to be seriously and actively considered by Congress. Some interplay must usually occur between the public agenda—public demand—and the official agenda of government decision-makers before congressional leaders reach a consensus that an issue warrants active consideration.[8]

Every item on an official agenda is not necessarily on the public agenda. This is especially true in the judicial system, where an individual may sometimes bring before courts and judges issues that do not have any substantial public support or interest. In addition, the day-to-day policy decisions in Congress, the executive department, and the bureaucracy are often made on issues that the public, or a substantial segment of it, may hardly be aware of.

Similarly, issues on the public agenda may not necessarily get on the official agenda. Governmental decision-makers may refuse jurisdiction. The Supreme Court, for example, may decide that a case does not involve a serious enough question to warrant the Court's accepting an appeal. Or the courts may say that the issue in a

---

[7]See Eyestone, *From Social Issues to Public Policy*, pp. 78–87. The two types of agendas are sometimes called "systemic" and "formal" agendas, as in Roger W. Cobb and Charles D. Elder, "Issue Creation and Agenda-Building," in Anderson, ed., *Cases in Public Policy-Making*, pp. 13–17.

[8]See John W. Kingdon, "Dynamics of Agenda Formation in Congress," in Anderson, ed., *Cases in Public Policy-Making*, pp. 35–49.

particular case involves a "political," not a "justiciable," question, as the Supreme Court did for a long time on the legislative reapportionment question. Congress may decide that an issue should be decided at the state rather than the federal level, as it did for a long time on civil rights issues. Governmental decision-makers may also fail or refuse to address an issue on the public agenda because they feel that government should not act upon it. Until the Civil Rights Act of 1964 was adopted, Congress took this position on the issue of access to privately owned restaurants and other accommodations. In addition, governmental decision-makers may not act upon an issue on the public agenda because they feel that it would be too risky to do so. For this reason, policy-makers did not confront certain issues with religious overtones, such as abortion and contraception, for years. These issues were eventually taken into the courts.

Access to the public and official agendas depends upon the type of issue involved, the actors, and sometimes upon events. Frequently, it is contingent upon an interplay among all three factors.

The type of issue involved may have an impact upon agenda-building. Some issues automatically get on the official agenda, such as proposed budgets, which come up regularly. An issue has a far better chance of gaining access to the official agenda if it is acceptable, as measured by traditional American beliefs and current public opinion. Thus, although most current social welfare programs, such as the Social Security system, were controversial when first enacted, today they are largely outside the bounds of political debate, even by conservatives, except for tinkering with details. And government policy-makers do not actively and seriously consider proposals to end, or substantially modify, America's "free enterprise" system of private ownership of property.

Issues that are "out of bounds" for political discussion in America, however, can sometimes rapidly become "in bounds" because of events and actors. Such events might include natural catastrophes, such as a mine explosion or a flood; human acts, like a riot or political assassination; technological changes, such as the growth in air travel; ecological changes, like the rural-to-urban shift in America's population; and external events, such as wars or other foreign developments.[9]

Events do not put issues on agendas by themselves; actors are also involved. Citizens may put issues on agendas. People with higher socioeconomic status have a better chance of doing so than those with lower socioeconomic status do, because they are more likely to have access to information, to know how the political system works, and to have been socialized toward political participation. Governmental decision-makers are more likely to consider issues raised by these citizens because such officials tend to have similar backgrounds to

---

[9]For a discussion of the role of events, see Cobb and Elder, "Issue Creation and Agenda-Building," pp. 11–13.

begin with; but, more important, they hear more about issues raised by active citizens and are likely to respond more to those views.

Interest groups may be important actors in the agenda-building process. For example, militant farmers blocking traffic with their tractors or striking truckers virtually force consideration of their concerns and demands. Issue activists can also be important actors. Environmentalists who devote themselves to publicizing an issue such as the dangers of nuclear waste disposal, consumer activists like Ralph Nader, and civil rights leaders such as the late Dr. Martin Luther King, Jr., would all be considered issue activists.

Politicians and public officials are also important actors in putting issues on agendas. Once agendas have been drawn up, they can become policy-makers as well. They may have strong personal feelings about an issue, or they may think there is political capital to be made out of a particular issue, or both. As one writer has put it, "Gaining . . . sympathizers or members rarely occurs through a mere combination of a pre-established appeal and a pre-established individual psychological bent on which it is brought to bear. Instead the prospective sympathizer has to be aroused, nurtured, and directed."[10]

As we know, the President, members of Congress, and other politicians and public officials help to create, as well as respond to, public opinion. "Congress is not a passive body, registering already-existent public views forced on its attention by public pressures," observers have pointed out. "Congress, second only to the president, is rather the major institution for initiating and creating political issues and projecting them into a national civic debate."[11]

The media—and particular reporters and columnists within the media—can be important actors in agenda-building. Like politicians and public officials, they may uncover and publicize scandals and governmental wrongdoing, such as the Watergate scandal or the personal financial manipulations which caused Bert Lance to resign as President Carter's Director of the Office of Management and

Interest groups like the truckers are influential actors in the agenda-building process. Truckers blockaded the Ohio Turnpike in December 1973 to protest the quadrupling of gasoline prices and the lowering of the speed limit to 55 miles per hour.

---

[10]Herbert Blumer, "Collective Behavior," in J.B. Gittler, ed., *Review of Sociology* (New York: John Wiley and Sons, 1957), p. 148.

[11]Raymond Bauer, Ithiel Pool, and Lewis Dexter, *American Business and Public Policy* (New York: Atherton Press, 1963), p. 478.

Budget. They may also editorialize on public issues. In these ways, they may bring matters to the attention of government policy-makers and of the general public, which may then pressure government policy-makers. An important interaction sometimes occurs between public officials and the media in this process. For example, here is the way one member of Congress was able to get a matter that was important to him on the official agenda of Congress.

> *He had been making speeches on the floor and writing the committee chairman for months, to no avail. Then an editor for a minor magazine noticed it and asked him to write an article. When the article, drawn from his speeches, appeared, the editor of an important newspaper in the district of a senior committee member picked it up and wrote a prominent editorial. That committee member, in turn, inquired of this congressman and became a leading advocate of hearings. Then the editor of another newspaper, this time in the district of another committee member, also picked it up and wrote a prominent story. That committee member called the congressman, asking for a copy of his bill, and eventually introduced it. Finally, after the chairman's initial reluctance, hearings were scheduled.[12]*

Agenda-building, then, consists of bringing an issue "to the attention of large numbers of people, who are already conscious of a shared interest, or who discover a shared interest as a result of becoming aware of the potential issue at about the same time."[13]

We have discussed restaurants and menus, but what about a concrete example of agenda-building? The issues raised by the women's movement are a good example. There was little public interest in these issues, and even less governmental attention, between the adoption of the Nineteenth Amendment (1920), which gave women the right to vote, and the beginning of renewed feminist activism in the 1960s. The problems were there, of course, but they did not become issues. Events—including the civil rights movement, which caused the basic idea of equality to spread; the antiwar movement; and the rise in female employment outside the home—brought an increasing awareness of discrimination against women.

Actors played important roles in the feminist movement; author Betty Friedan, for example, was very active in the movement. Interest groups, such as the National Organization for Women (NOW), were formed. Speeches, writings, and demonstrations caught the attention of the media, which reported them to the public, building greater public awareness and activism. Politicians and public officials, like Presidents John F. Kennedy and Lyndon Johnson, began to take an interest in the issues involved, and the media carried their statements. By the late 1960s, the status of women in America was an issue on America's public and official agendas.

---

[12]Kingdon, "Dyamics of Agenda Formation in Congress," p. 36.
[13]Eyestone, *From Social Issues to Public Policy*, p. 89.

POLICY FORMULATION

Once an issue gets on the official agenda, the next step is the *formulation* of policy. This simply means that a proposal, or proposals, must be developed for remedying the problem embodied in the issue. What shall we do about environmental pollution? How shall we reduce the waste of energy in America? The formulation process seeks to provide answers to questions like these.

Policy formulation occurs in two stages. First, decisions must be made concerning the type of action that is needed. Second, the action must be converted into a particular form, such as legislation, administrative rules, or court opinions. All the actors involved in agenda-building can also be involved in policy formulation; therefore, formulation involves much bargaining and compromising.

At the national level, the President, as a policy initiator or "chief legislator," is an important actor in policy formulation. The Office of Management and Budget (OMB), which is part of the Executive Office of the President, is an especially important institution in terms of policy formulation by the President. OMB is the final clearinghouse for the federal budget before it is approved by the President and submitted to the Congress. Today, Presidents also use this agency as a clearinghouse for *all* executive proposals—not just budget proposals—that will be submitted to Congress, and for specific testimony that executive department officials may give before congressional committees.[14]

Presidents have been prone to use presidential task forces, or advisory commissions, to assist them in policy formulation. These task forces or commissions are usually created to handle specific issues like pornography, urban disorders, violence, or population growth.[15] Presidents sometimes appoint task forces to indicate "symbolic action." By giving the appearance of action through the inauguration of a study, they attempt to placate disgruntled groups or to allay public fears.

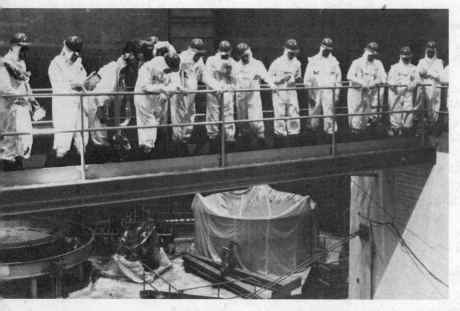

After the Three Mile Island nuclear power plant overheated and leaked radiation into the air in 1979, President Carter appointed a commission to investigate the causes of the accident. Here, commission members inspect the inside of the plant.

[14]See Robert Gilmour, "Policy Formulation in the Executive Branch: Central Legislative Clearance," in Anderson, ed., *Cases in Public Policy-Making*, pp. 80–96.

[15]See Norman C. Thomas and Harold L. Wolman, "The Presidency and Policy Formulation: The Use of Task Forces," in Anderson, ed., *Cases in Public Policy-Making*, pp. 97–118.

Congress also formulates policy. It has especially been the source of policy in such fields as environmental pollution.[16] The creation of House and Senate budget committees in 1974 and establishment of a joint procedure for making comprehensive decisions about the federal budget sought to overcome the fragmentation of policy-making within Congress.

The ideal policy formulation process would involve considering every possible solution of a problem and then choosing the best solution. This process might be called the "comprehensive" method of policy formulation. In the real world, however, it does not happen quite like that. Since policy-makers cannot always control all elements of a problem, they may not be able to offer a complete solution to it. For example, when President Johnson appointed the National Advisory Commission on Civil Disorders (the Kerner Commission) to investigate urban disorders in the black sections of many American cities in the summer of 1967, he asked them to make a comprehensive report that would recommend ways to prevent such disorders from ever happening again. The trouble was that when the Kerner Commission went to work, it found that the frustrations felt by so many black people in America's central cities were not a product of racial discrimination alone. They also resulted from economic powerlessness, which was caused by a lack of jobs and adequate income. Further, the Commission found that with poor people moving into the central cities and with middle-class people moving out of them and into the suburbs, the tax-bases of the central cities were lowered, reducing their ability to take care of their mounting problems. So, the Kerner Commission soon realized that it could not treat the problem of racial discrimination in isolation. The Commission decided that it also had to make recommendations about economic-class problems and the decay of America's central cities.

The Commission was then faced with the question of how its detailed recommendations—for employment programs, for example—should be financed. This brought the Commission to take a sweeping look at all of the federal government's activities and expenditures. One Commission member passionately and logically argued that the Commission could not make a comprehensive report about urban disorders unless it also recommended an end to the Vietnam War. The war, he said, was wasting funds that could be used to solve domestic problems. The Kerner Commission stopped short of accepting this suggestion, but its report was still so comprehensive that it covered virtually every other conceivable aspect of urban disorders and was seven hundred fifty pages long.

The comprehensive method of policy formulation is also difficult to use because it is not always possible to know all the facts, to have all the information needed to consider all possible choices and suggest

---

[16]See Charles O. Jones, "Speculative Augmentation in Federal Air Pollution Policy-Making," in Anderson, ed., *Cases in Public Policy-Making*, pp. 54–79.

the best solution. In addition, the ability of government policy-makers to formulate a comprehensive policy is limited by the risks involved, such as the political repercussions from interest groups with a vested interest in existing programs.

Unintended results are another barrier to the comprehensive approach to policy formulation. Taking aspirin, we now know, causes some people to have stomach bleeding. Unintended results also came from the federal government's good intentions in regard to housing and urban renewal. As one authority has written:

> *Since the creation in 1934 of the Federal Housing Authority (FHA), the government has subsidized home-building on a vast scale by insuring mortgages that are written on easy terms and, in the case of the Veterans Administration (VA), by guaranteeing mortgages. Most of the mortgages have been for the purchase of new homes. (This was partly because FHA wanted gilt-edged collateral behind the mortgages that it insured, but it was also because it shared the American predeliction for new-ness.) It was cheaper to build on vacant land, but there was little such land left in the central cities and in their larger, older suburbs. These were almost always zoned so as to exclude the relatively few Negroes and other "undesir-ables" who could afford to build new houses. In effect, then, the FHA and VA programs have subsidized the movement of the white middle class out of the central cities and older suburbs, while at the same time penalizing investment in the rehabilitation of the run-down neighborhoods of these older cities. The poor—especially the Negro poor—have not received any direct benefit from these programs.*[17]

TYPES OF POLICIES

Theodore Lowi has classified government policies according to their effect on society ("American Business, Public Policy Case Studies, and Political Theory," *World Politics*, July 1964, pp. 677–715): *Distributive* policies are government actions that provide tangible benefits for certain individuals, corporations, or groups; examples include special government services or subsidies for farmers and government contracts for particular businesses. *Regulatory* policies involve granting or withholding benefits for various interests; one corporation rather than another, for example, may be granted a federal license to operate a radio station. *Redistributive* policies involve granting benefits to one group at the expense of another group, changing the wealth, property, or income balance between the "haves" and the "have-nots." The progressive income tax system and social welfare programs are obvious examples.

The comprehensive approach to policy formulation is further hampered by the fact that it is not always possible to make an accurate cost-benefit analysis of solutions. How shall we quantify the value of a human life, for example? Is a program that costs $50 million justified on a cost-benefit basis if it will save one hundred lives? One thousand? One hundred thousand? How does one make a cost-benefit analysis when the goal of a program is to produce more artists or musicians? What is the value of art or music? How does a

---

[17]Edward C. Banfield, *The Unheavenly City Revisited: A Revision of the Unheavenly City* (Boston: Little, Brown and Co., 1974), pp. 15–16.

government policy-maker weigh relative values in setting priorities? Which is more important or valuable if you cannot do both: cleaning up the air or providing more jobs?

Presidents have attempted to establish systems for cost-benefit analysis of government policy and with them, a comprehensive approach to policy formulation, particularly in regard to the federal budget. President Carter favors a "zero-based" budget system. According to this plan, each federal agency is supposed to completely justify its budget each year, starting from zero. President Johnson instituted the Planning Programming Budget System (PPBS), which had been developed in the Defense Department by Johnson's Secretary of Defense, Robert McNamara. President Johnson's declaration of the purposes of PPBS is a textbook approach to comprehensive policy formulation:

1. Identify our national goals with precision and on a continuing basis;

2. Choose among those goals the ones that are most urgent;

3. Search for alternative means of reaching those goals most effectively at the least cost;

4. Inform ourselves not merely on next year's costs but on the second, third, and subsequent year's costs of our programs;

5. Measure the performance of our programs to insure a dollar's worth of service for each dollar spent.[18]

One problem with this system was that it produced what has been called "policy politics." Those who could come up with the best quantification—or the best justification for their programs in mathematical, cost-benefit terms—could prevail over those who could not do so. For example, the budget of the Department of Defense went up, while little was done about environmental pollution.

Another problem with the PPBS system—and with comprehensive policy formulation in general—was that it presumed that "goals" could be scientifically determined, separate from politics, and could be clearly defined and stated in advance. "It is impermissible to treat goals as if they were known in advance. 'Goals' may well be the product of interaction among key participants rather than . . . some 'spook' that posits values in advance of our knowledge of them."[19]

President Johnson launched the "War on Poverty" in 1964, stating the national objective as "total victory." Studies were undertaken, programs were devised, legislation was passed. But the legislation left much discretion to the administrators of the new programs. Why? Because no one had a clear idea of what the administrators were supposed to do. The goals of the "War on Poverty" were never

---

[18]Quoted in Charles O. Jones, *An Introduction to the Study of Public Policy* (Belmont, Ca.: Wadsworth Publishing Company, 1970), p. 55.

[19]Aaron Wildavsky, "The Political Economy of Efficiency," in Austin Ranney, ed., *Political Science and Public Policy* (Chicago: Markham, 1968), p. 80.

clearly defined, primarily because no one was quite sure what poverty was. Was poverty just a lack of money, or was it also a state of mind? If it was just a lack of money, would giving poor people money reduce their incentive to work and to take care of themselves? If poverty involved some psychological cause, how could rehabilitation be made most effective? These are hard questions to answer fully even now.

But government policy-makers cannot be paralyzed because they cannot formulate policy in a comprehensive way. Inflation, unemployment, energy waste, and environmental pollution are real problems in America. Just because there may not be a comprehensive, perfect method of policy formulation for these issues does not mean that government policy-makers can ignore them. So, they do the best they can. Three basic approaches have been used: incremental; branching; and inventive.[20]

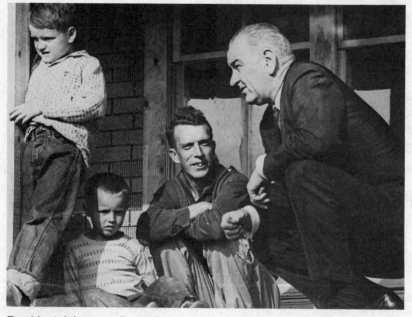

President Johnson talks to the father of a family living in Appalachia—one of the most economically depressed regions of the country—after declaring his "unconditional war on poverty" in 1964. Johnson's policy-making initiative resulted in legislation that provided funds for vocational training and community antipoverty programs.

The *incremental* method of policy formulation involves considering relatively small changes in existing policy, such as extending, updating, strengthening, or cutting back. State and federal budgetary processes are prime examples of this method. One authority has written that the best way to predict what government policy, as embodied in a state budget, will be *next* year is to look at what it was *last* year.[21] The incremental method is the most popular approach in government, largely because it stirs up the least opposition and is the easiest way to build majority coalitions for action. But although the incremental method requires no jarring change at any one time, the cumulative impact of incremental decisions can be enormous. Thus, America became involved in the Vietnam War incrementally: first, through material and financial aid; then, by sending military advisers; next, by sending combat troops; and finally, by heavily increasing combat troops. President Johnson eventually "became the victim of his earlier neglect to consider fully the implications and costs of an indeterminate and deepening American involvement" and decided not to seek reelection.[22]

[20]See Starling, *The Politics and Economics of Public Policy,* pp. 206–48.
[21]See Ira Sharkansky, *Spending in the American States* (Chicago: Rand McNally, 1968).
[22]Eugene Eidenberg, "The Presidency: Americanizing the War in Vietnam," in Allen P. Sindler, ed., *American Political Institutions and Public Policy* (Boston: Little, Brown, and Company, 1969), pp. 68–126, quotation, pp. 119–20.

The *branching* method of policy formulation uses variations of a previously established policy to meet new situations. The Rail Passenger Act of 1970, which set up a government-sponsored private corporation to meet railroad problems, was a branching (like a tree branch) from the theme (or tree trunk) that had previously been established in the Communications Satellite Corporation, created in 1962.

Invention, which might also be called innovation, involves the use of new ideas. The amount of invention in government policy is very small. One reason for this is the U.S. Constitution itself, which balances conflicting powers against one another, making it more difficult for new ideas to run the gauntlet of approval and gain acceptance. Another reason is that many people have some aversion to taking risks or trying something new. This may be especially true of politicians, who have to get elected. But invention does occur when an issue on the public and official agendas is widely recognized as a serious one that requires action but when much of the public is undecided about what the policy should be. New ideas put forward by leaders are most likely to be considered and accepted at such times. Within the federal government, 62 percent of the inventive policies have come from executive departments or agencies and presidential commissions and task forces; 33 percent have come from congressional committees or commissions. Some examples of inventive policies are the Social Security Act, the Marshall Plan, the interstate highway program, the Economic Opportunity Act of 1964 (War on Poverty), Medicare, and revenue sharing.[23]

Another example of inventive policy formulation was the National Environmental Policy Act of 1969. It requires agencies to prepare a detailed statement about the environmental impact of any new federal programs before they can be put into effect. This requirement has given rise to some new jokes. For example, a former head of the Council of Environmental Quality once began a speech with a statement about how the Lord reportedly gave Moses both good news and bad. The good news was that the Egyptians were going to be smitten with plagues of frogs, locusts, gnats, flies, cattle deaths, and hail and darkness, while the children of Israel would be able to escape Egypt through the parted Red Sea, eating manna strewn on the desert. The bad news that the Lord reportedly gave to Moses was, "It will be up to you, Moses, to write the environmental impact statement."[24]

The law requiring environmental impact statements prior to the implementation of new federal policies could serve as a branching model for making similar advance assessments of the impacts of other federal programs before they are put into effect.

Consider a concrete example of policy formulation—feminist

---

[23]See Starling, *The Politics and Economics of Public Policy*, pp. 219–20; and James E. Anderson, *Public Policy-Making* (New York: Praeger, 1975), p. 94.

[24]Quoted in Starling, *The Politics and Economics of Public Policy*, p. 333.

Left to right: First Ladies Lady Bird Johnson, Rosalynn Carter, and Betty Ford, along with Presiding Officer Bella Abzug at the National Women's Conference in 1977. The Conference approved the National Plan for Action, a twenty-six point agenda of feminist goals.

issues. President Kennedy created a Commission on the Status of Women in 1961. After the Commission made its report, similar commissions were set up at the state level, and a National Advisory Council was created. Congress held hearings on sex discrimination. President Nixon set up a Presidential Task Force on the Status of Women in 1969. Congress then held hearings on the proposed Equal Rights Amendment. Presidents Ford and Carter appointed members to a U.S. Commission on the Observance of the International Women's Year. In 1977, during President Carter's administration, this Commission sponsored a nationwide Women's Conference in Houston. From these policy formulation processes came proposals that presented choices to government policy-makers on feminist issues.

POLICY ADOPTION

The people who formulate policy must look both backward and forward—backward to problems and issues, forward to policy adoption. Policy formulation and adoption cannot be neatly separated from each other. Like the other steps in the process, they are interactive. In the policy formulation step, government decision-makers usually show concern for the political realities of the alternatives under consideration.

Many people may be involved in the adoption process, but the actual decisions are made by public officials, such as legislators and executives. (As the term is used here, adoption may also include rejection of alternatives.) Regarding the congressional adoption of policy, one writer says:

When the debate ends, the main point of congressional decision, the calling of the roll, is reached. . . . Here on the floor, the ultimate

Senate Foreign Relations Committee members (left to right) Javits (R., N.Y.), Baker (R., Tenn.), Chairman Church (D., Idaho), Sarbanes (D., Md.), and Pell (D., R.I.). The Committee began hearings in July 1979 on the SALT II agreement signed by President Carter and Leonid Brezhnev. The Senate must confirm all treaties before they can take effect.

policy choice is made; here the bill is accepted or rejected; here the nature of the system's output is specified. Put another way, when the roll is called, the coalitions for and against the bill are identified.[25]

Policy adoption requires policy-makers to make judgments about the facts, the alternatives, the risks, and the probable consequences of their decisions.[26] It is usually the result of a certain amount of bargaining and compromise and coalition-building. The coalitions are presumably *traceable* to majorities, or majority opinion, in the general public because they are made by public officials who are elected by the voters or by officers who were chosen by elected officials.

Government policy-making does not just involve decisions to do something. It can also involve inaction, a decision, in effect, not to do something. A lack of action implies a policy in favor of the *status quo*, the way things are.

Concrete examples of policy adoption may again be found in the history of government action on feminist issues. For example, in 1963 Congress passed a law requiring equal pay for women and amended the 1964 Civil Rights Act to prohibit sex discrimination in employment. In 1967, President Johnson issued an executive order prohibiting sex discrimination in federal employment and in corporations doing business with the federal government. Two years later, President Nixon issued an executive order extending this policy to the military services. Congress passed a resolution proposing the Equal Rights Amendment to the U.S. Constitution in 1972. Thereafter, a number of states took action, either ratifying or rejecting this proposed amendment.

[25]Leroy N. Rieselbach, "Congressional Voting Decisions," in Anderson, ed., *Cases in Public Policy-Making*, pp. 122–23.

[26]See Robert A. Dahl, *Modern Political Analysis* (Englewood Cliffs, N.J.: Prentice-Hall, 1970), pp. 100–12.

POLICY IMPLEMENTATION

Adopted public policies are "outputs" of America's political system. They are like the automobiles produced by Detroit's assembly lines. But they are not just end products or results of the political system. Once adopted, policies are also stimulators; they are causes as well as effects.

Policy implementation means putting the goals and objectives set forth in policy decisions into practice.[27] Therefore, policies have impact. Assessing that impact is one of the goals of policy analysis: What happens—or does not happen—once a government policy is adopted?

Policy is generally not self-executing, that is, it does not implement itself. Policies usually consist of instructions to administrators and others who will carry out the law, rather than of commands to citizens.[28] Since the details of any new policy are often left to the discretion of those who will administer or apply it, implementation is not only a *result* of policy; it also involves *making* policy. As Robert Lineberry has written, implementation is "a continuation of policy-making by other means."[29]

There are three elements in the implementation of policy. First, a decision must be made concerning the organizational structure that will be used to put the program into effect.[30] This structure may take the form of an old agency that shifts its mission to accept incremental changes in policy, or it may be a new agency, either created separately or within an existing department.[31] Second, policy goals must be translated into specific rules and guidelines. Third, resources must be allocated, and the rules must be applied to the specific problem addressed by the policy. At the second and third stages, considerable discretion may be exercised.

A basic goal of public policy is to secure compliance, "to cause those affected to behave in desired ways and not to behave in undesired ways."[32] Public reaction to a new policy has an important impact on the administrators' ability to implement it. "If a law is deemed to benefit all, compliance will probably be the rule. If it is considered to benefit none, it will probably not be obeyed." What about the typical situation in which a new policy benefits some people but is a burden to others? "If the individual determines that he stands to suffer a greater loss from obedience, than disobedience, he will break the law. If he judges that he will suffer the greater loss by

---

[27]Donald S. Van Meter and Carl E. Van Horn, "The Policy Implementation Process: A Conceptual Framework," *Administration and Society* 6 (February 1975): 447.

[28]Theodore Lowi, *The End of Liberalism: Ideology, Policy, and the Crisis of Public Authority* (New York: Norton, 1969), p. 144.

[29]Lineberry, *American Public Policy*, p. 71.

[30]See Starling, *The Politics and Economics of Public Policy*, pp. 430–37.

[31]Jones, *An Introduction to the Study of Public Policy*, pp. 93–94.

[32]Anderson, ed., *Cases in Public Policy-Making*, p. 195.

disobedience, he will comply."[33] To bring about compliance in this kind of situation, administrators use education, persuasion, and sanctions (punishments and rewards).

Political power may be brought to bear in the policy implementation stage, just as in the formulation and adoption stages. Antitrust laws, for example, have been a part of the federal statutes for many years. But because of International Telephone and Telegraph Company's political influence within the Nixon administration in 1972, for example, the company was able to achieve a favorable out-of-court settlement of a government antitrust action against it.[34]

The actors in policy formulation and adoption are also usually involved in implementation. They include citizens, interest groups, the media, and politicians and public officials. The public officials who are involved in policy implementation come not just from the executive department and the bureaucracy, but also from the legislature and the courts.

Legislators can influence implementation by exercising their oversight powers—through hearings, investigations, required reports—and by doing "casework."[35] When handling casework, legislators intervene with administrators on behalf of constituents who have particular complaints about a government program or service, such as Social Security benefits. This type of legislative intervention in specific cases, or even the possibility of it, can sometimes affect the way administrators implement policies. Often, administrators also consult legislators about how to carry out policies. This is particularly true for those legislators who serve on the committees that helped to formulate the policy in the first place.

Judges are also involved in policy implementation. In handling individual cases, they must interpret laws and administrative regulations. They are also administrators of the law in naturalization proceedings, bankruptcies, paroles, and passport applications.[36]

The bureaucracy is, of course, an important actor in policy implementation. As a matter of fact, bureaucrats sometimes come up with many of the ideas that become policy. They also help to sell these ideas to the executive and legislative branches of government.[37] In the implementation of policy, bureaucrats are often allowed to exercise discretion in interpreting the laws, filling in the details through rules and guidelines, and deciding on applications of laws and rules in particular cases.

---

[33]Charles S. Bullock, III, and Harrell R. Rodgers, Jr., "Civil Rights and the Matter of Compliance," in Anderson, ed., *Cases in Public Policy-Making*, p. 237.

[34]See Harlan M. Blake, "Beyond the ITT Case: the Politics of Anti-Trust Enforcement," in Anderson, ed., *Cases in Public Policy-Making*, pp. 196–207.

[35]See Morris S. Ogul, *Congress Oversees the Bureaucracy* (Pittsburgh: University of Pittsburgh Press, 1976).

[36]In regard to legislators and judges as actors in policy implementation, see Jones, *An Introduction to the Study of Public Policy*, pp. 91–92.

[37]See Alan Altshuler, ed., *The Politics of the Federal Bureaucracy* (New York: Dodd, Mead, 1968), p. 412.

There is an old saying that goes: "There is many a slip 'twixt the cup and lip." Similarly, just because a policy has been adopted does not necessarily mean that it will be carried out in full or in the way the policy-makers envisioned. We have already noted that the lack of public acceptance of a policy or the application of political power to prevent its implementation can thwart the intentions of government policy-makers.

There are other reasons why policies may not be fully implemented by government bureaucrats.[38] Administrators may be uncertain about orders. They may ask, "What exactly are we supposed to do?" The policy may be too difficult to implement. Administrators may wonder, "I was told what to do, but how am I supposed to do it?" Bureaucrats may simply resist implementing a policy. President Harry Truman once said, "The difficulty with many career officials in the government is that they regard themselves as the men who really make policy and run the government. They look upon the elected officials as just temporary occupants."[39] Thus, bureaucrats may delay or postpone; obey the letter but not the spirit of orders; ask for a hearing and suggest changes in the orders before carrying them out; go over the heads of their executive superiors to the legislative branch; and "go public" with their complaints, particularly through information "leaked" to the press.

As we noted in Chapter 14, there are remedies for bureaucratic resistance to policy implementation. For example, the policy may be spelled out in more detail. Further, policy-makers and the public can pay more attention to its implementation. Currently, most citizens tend to think that a problem has been solved, an issue fully met, once a policy has been adopted. The fanfare ends. The television crews turn off their lights and leave. Reporters give their attention to other matters. The excitement of debate no longer engages public attention. But if the decisions made when policies are adopted are to be carried out, more attention must be given to implementation, not just to the steps of policy formulation and adoption.

POLICY EVALUATION

Policy evaluation involves the assessment or appraisal of the effects of policy. *Outside* the government, the media may play an important role in policy evaluation. Interest groups, which are never hesitant in pointing out alleged policy defects, particularly when they affect them, and individual citizens, such as academic researchers, may also be important outside actors during the evaluation stage.

Inside the federal government, Congress—and various congres-

---

[38]This material is taken from Morton H. Halperin, "Implementing Presidential Foreign Policy Decisions: Limitations and Resistance," in Anderson, ed., *Cases in Public Policy-Making*, pp. 208–36.

[39]Harry S. Truman, *Memoirs, Vol. II: Years of Trial and Hope* (New York: Doubleday, 1956), p. 165.

sional committees—exercise oversight over policy implementation, providing continuous surveillance as policy is formulated, adopted, implemented, evaluated, and adjusted.[40] Presidents maintain a system of evaluating policy implementation, too. Many have found it advantageous to set up commissions or task forces for this purpose.[41]

The aim of evaluation is to provide "feedback" for the policy-makers, which assists them in adjusting the policy or its implementation, or both. The impressionistic or "seat-of-the-pants" kind of evaluation is the least useful. It is based upon fragmentary evidence ("Somebody told me that people drive up in Cadillacs to get food stamps") or bias ("Republican policies always help big business").[42]

"Operation-centered" policy evaluation focuses only on questions concerning the honesty and efficiency of policies or programs: "Is the program honestly run? What are its financial costs? Who receives benefits (payments or services) and in what amounts? Is there unnecessary overlap or duplication with other programs? Were legal standards and procedures followed?"[43]

"Systematic" evaluation is the most useful to policy-makers. It is more scientific than impressionistic evaluation is, and its purposes are much broader than, but include those of, operation-centered evaluation. Systematic evaluation seeks to measure the extent to which policy objectives are actually achieved and what effect they have on society. Evaluation of a policy may reveal that administrative resistance to its implementation is thwarting the achievement of its goals. Or, the policy itself may be at fault because its goals are undesirable, too vague, or based upon erroneous information or a mistaken interpretation of the problem. Evaluation may also reveal undesirable side effects, or unintended results of policy. New and related problems may also be discovered through evaluation.

Policy implementation and evaluation may affect public opinion, institutions (and how they are organized and behave), and policy-makers. There is, in effect, a kind of "policy cycle."

CONCLUSION

Government policy-making can have serious consequences. It can result from, and bring about, serious conflicts. Some people say that policy-making should be taken "out of politics," or removed from the contentiousness and conflict of partisan politics. But this is both impossible and undesirable. Government policy-making necessarily involves exercising great political discretion when making choices.

---

[40]See John Bibby, "Committee Characteristics and Legislative Oversights of Administration," *Midwest Journal of Political Science*, 10 (February 1966): 78–98; and Seymour Sher, "Conditions for Legislative Control," *Journal of Politics*, 25 (August 1963): 526–51.

[41]Jones, *An Introduction to the Study of Public Policy*, pp. 116–18.

[42]For types of policy evaluation, see Anderson, *Public Policy-Making*, pp. 132–60.

[43]Anderson, *Public Policy-Making*, p. 133.

And, therefore, to paraphrase Clemenceau's famous statement about war and generals, policy-making is too important to be left to the "experts." The people should be allowed to participate.

Governments are human institutions; they are as complex as human nature. Thus, policy-making is a complicated process. The relatively new field of policy analysis, within the discipline of political science, attempts to break this process into its various interactive steps.[44] Citizens and policy-makers who understand those steps have a better chance of improving and participating in the process.

Policy-making begins with a problem, which grows to become an issue. Some issues get on the public agenda and then on the official agenda. They are, therefore, available for decision.

Policy-making involves making choices, choosing among alternatives. At the policy formulation stage, the available choices are spelled out and considered. During the adoption stage, a set of goals or assumptions is legitimated in the political process, or approved by government officials. But the process does not end there; policy implementation is the next step. Policy is not an end in itself; it is also a beginning. Because it often involves using considerable discretion, policy implementation may also be policy-making. At the evaluation stage, the results, the effects, and the impact of policy are judged. This assessment may then be fed back into the policy-making process.

Policy-making is not a neat system or an easy process to understand. But by examining its component parts, we can improve our ability to understand the process and therefore to participate in it.

ADDITIONAL SOURCES

Baybrooke, David, and Charles E. Lindblom. *A Strategy of Decision*. Free Press, 1963.

Cobb, Roger W., and Charles D. Elder. *Participation in American Politics: The Dynamics of Agenda-Building*. Johns Hopkins, 1975.*

Dolbeare, Kenneth, ed. *Public Policy Evaluation*. Sage, 1975.*

Dye, Thomas R. *Understanding Public Policy*, 3rd ed. Prentice-Hall, 1978.

———. *Policy Analysis: What Governments Do, Why They Do It, and What Difference It Makes*. University of Alabama Press, 1976.*

Edwards, George C., and Ira Sharkansky. *The Policy Predicament: Making and Implementing Public Policy*. Freeman, 1978.

Lindblom, Charles E. *The Policy-Making Process*. Prentice-Hall, 1968.

Lineberry, Robert L. *American Public Policy: What Government Does and What Difference It Makes*. Harper & Row, 1977.

Murphy, Irene L. *Public Policy on the Status of Women*. Heath, 1973.

Pressman, Jeffrey L., and Aaron Wildavsky. *Implementation: How Great Expectations in Washington Are Dashed in Oakland, or, Why It's Amazing That Federal Programs Work at All*. University of California Press, 1973.*

*Available in paperback edition.

---

[44]For a discussion of political science appoaches to the subject, see Jones, *An Introduction to the Study of Public Policy*, pp. 5–7; and Dye, *Policy Analysis*, pp. 1–5.

18 Energy and the Environment

On March 28, 1979, a Pennsylvania dairy farmer awoke as usual before dawn and prepared to go about another routine day. But in the dial-packed control room of the nearby nuclear generating plant of Metropolitan Edison Company, things were far from routine. At 4:00 A.M., the early-hour calm had been shattered by the jarring blare of a warning siren and the pulsing flash of red lights.[1]

At first, technicians assumed that the problem was merely a replay of one of a number of troubles that had plagued the nuclear plant since its cooling towers had first risen five years earlier over Three Mile Island in the middle of the Susquehanna River near Harrisburg. This time, however, the trouble was much more serious. A water pump had malfunctioned, and the system for cooling the radioactive rods of the nuclear core had ceased to work. Thousands of gallons of extremely toxic water gushed out on the floor of the reactor building. Almost instantly the nuclear core began to heat up ominously. A dangerously explosive bubble of hydrogen gas was reported to be forming within the reactor. Radioactive gas was released into the Pennsylvania air. Scientists and politicians began to contemplate the possibility of a meltdown—of the kind depicted in a recently released movie starring Jane Fonda, "The China Syndrome"—which could contaminate a whole area the size of a state for years.

The days and weeks that followed the nuclear accident at Three Mile Island were not good ones for the nuclear industry or for federal officials. Industry spokespersons seemed more interested in issuing reassuring statements than in explaining what had really happened. Officials of the federal Nuclear Regulatory Commission seemed to

---

[1]On the Three Mile Island nuclear accident, see Congressional Quarterly, *Weekly Report* (April 7, 1979), pp. 621–30; *Time* (April 9, 1979), pp. 8–20; *Newsweek* (April 9, 1979), pp. 24–39; and Barry Commoner, "Reflections: The Solar Transition—1," *New Yorker* (April 23, 1979), pp. 53–98.

Above left: The cooling towers of the Three Mile Island nuclear generating plant. For many people, the seriousness of the near-accident at Three Mile Island raised grave concerns about the safety of nuclear power. Above right: In May 1979, a huge crowd—reminiscent of the mass demonstrations during the Vietnam War—gathered in Washington, D.C., to express their opposition to nuclear power.

bumble around in confusion, tinkering with the words of press releases and wondering aloud what to do next.

Overnight the American antinuclear movement gained great masses of new adherents. Thousands of them swarmed into Washington, D.C., for a huge rally. The size and intensity of the rally had not been seen in the capital since the days of the movement to end the war in Vietnam.

Five months later, scientists and engineers had still not been able to decide what to do with the truckloads of highly radioactive water inside the reactor building. It was clear that it would be years, if ever, before the plant could be put into use again. It was also clear that millions of Americans had become seriously worried about the use of nuclear power for the generation of electricity, and the industry had suffered a serious setback.

The accident at Three Mile Island (and the related threat to the surrounding community) was a dramatic example of some of the problems confronting policy-makers today in the intertwined fields of energy and the environment. "Environment" simply means "surroundings." Environmentalists are people who are concerned about their surroundings, or environment. The suddenness with which environmental issues first seemed to burst upon the American scene in the late 1960s can be illustrated by paraphrasing an old joke in which a character says, "Last week, I couldn't even spell 'environmentalist,' and now I are one!"

By 1970 large numbers of Americans called themselves environmentalists. On "Earth Day"—April 22 of that year—public rallies, teach-ins, seminars, and other demonstrations were held simultaneously throughout the country to show concern about environmental issues.

Were there no pollution problems in America prior to 1970? Of course there were! By and large, however, pollution had been a "quiet crisis," in the words of President Kennedy's Secretary of the Interior, Stewart Udall. A small number of naturalists, conservationists, and politicians were concerned. But environmental issues were not on the nation's agenda because not enough people had discovered a shared interest in a need for action on environmental problems.

Why *then*? Why, in 1970 and the years immediately following, did environmental issues suddenly get on the political agenda? We saw in Chapter 17 that agenda-making involves both events and actors. So it was with issues concerning the environment. But before considering those events and actors, we should first examine some fundamental principles in nature.

THE ENVIRONMENT: BASIC CONCEPTS

The ecosphere is the thin skin of air, water, and soil that envelops the earth. Within it, living things interact with each other and with the elements of the ecosphere as a unit. We call this interactive unit the *ecosystem*. The study of the way the ecosystem works, or concern about it, is called *ecology*.

Long before words like "ecosystem" were coined, though, the Sioux—and many other American Indian tribes—had already sensed the interactive character of the ecosphere and living things within it. For them, the "sacred circle" illustrated the interdependence of the "two-leggeds," "the four-leggeds," the trees, the grass, the waters, the air, the rocks, the mountains—and above all these, the sun.

Today many other Americans have become increasingly aware of the environmental circles, or cycles, of interdependence on the earth. One such cycle is the soil system.[2] Grass grows on the soil. Cattle eat the grass. Their bodies convert the grass into organic matter, which the cattle then deposit on the soil as waste. Microorganisms break the waste down into nutrients, which are taken up again by the grass. There are thousands of such cycles in our ecosystem. For the most part, what is naturally produced in the ecosystem can be naturally degraded, or deteriorated, renewed, and reused.

---

[2]See Barry Commoner, "Energy, Environment, and Economics," in Gary D. Eppen, ed., *Energy: The Policy Issues* (Chicago: University of Chicago Press, 1975), pp. 25–26.

But humans can alter the natural cycles, and therein lie our environmental problems. Biological cycles, such as the grass-cattle cycle of the soil system, have a "carrying capacity," or maximum sustainable yield, based upon the size of the cycle and its regenerative powers. In nature, biological cycles are self-regulating. Predators like wolves help to keep the number of deer from increasing excessively and overgrazing the available grass. But humans have the ability to thwart such self-regulating mechanisms. They can change the rules—and they have.

Conscientious stewards of the soil—environmentalist ranchers or farmers, for example—are careful to rotate crops, terrace the land against water erosion, plow under organic crop residues, and avoid overgrazing. In other words, they work with, rather than against, the self-regulating tendencies of the natural biological cycle. But when natural resources which are held in common are subject to unrestrained individual use for personal gain, the rules of the biological cycle can be drastically affected.

English villages once had village greens—called "the commons"—on which any villager could graze his or her cattle. An 1883 English pamphlet pointed out that individual owners of cattle, seeking to maximize their own interests, would overgraze the commons unless they were restrained. Individual cattle owners, the pamphlet said, would each know that they were exceeding the carrying capacity of the commons, but there would be no incentive for each to remove his or her cattle or to reduce their number.[3]

Today, those concerned about the environment have pointed out that our commons includes the whole earth: its atmosphere and outer space, its water, its oceans, and its biological cycles. Involved in the modern "Tragedy of the Commons" are overfishing of the oceans, deforestation, overgrazing, and overplowing.[4]

Pollution is the process or result of making the environment impure, as with human wastes. It, too, is an alarming part of our modern tragedy of the commons:

In a reverse way, the tragedy of the commons reappears in problems of pollution. Here it is not a question of taking something out of the commons, but of putting something in—sewage, or chemical, radioactive, and heat wastes into water; noxious and dangerous fumes into the air; . . . The rational man finds that his share of the cost of the wastes he discharges into the commons is less than the cost of purifying his water before releasing them. Since this is true for everyone, we are locked into a system of 'fouling our own nest,' so long as we behave only as independent, rational, free-enterprisers.[5]

---

[3]W. F. Lloyd, *Two Lectures on the Checks to Population* (Oxford, England, 1883).

[4]See Garrett Hardin, "The Tragedy of the Commons," *Science* (December 13, 1968); and Williams Ophuls, *Ecology and the Politics of Scarcity* (San Francisco: W.H. Freeman and Co., 1977).

[5]Hardin, "The Tragedy of the Commons."

The "Law of Materials Balance" says, in effect, that "everything has to be somewhere," that the total weight of materials taken from their natural state and converted to forms more readily available for human use must be discharged back into our environment, unless they are recycled. Today, these discharges amount to 400 million tons of solid wastes a year and untold amounts of nonsolid wastes.[6]

Why has the tragedy of the commons come to the attention of the public so recently? To put it another way, how did environmental issues come to be on the political agenda?

THE ENVIRONMENT AND THE POLITICAL AGENDA

As we noted earlier, agenda-making is a result of both events and actors. In regard to environmental issues, powerful new events came into play following World War II: population growth; growth in production; and the development of new technologies.

Population Growth

It has only been since World War II that human numbers have grown by 2 to 3 percent per year.[7] A population growth of 3 percent per year means that the number of people will multiply nineteenfold within only one century. It took two million years for the human population on earth to reach one billion. The second billion took only one hundred years. After that, the rate accelerated. At the present rate of population growth, the sixth billion in human population will come in only one decade. A rising standard of living in many parts of the world, coupled with available birth control methods, has helped to significantly reduce the population growth rate. But population growth is still a threat, and it has already greatly stretched the carrying capacity of our ecosystem. For example, during the twenty years between 1950 and 1970, the ocean fish catch—which is such an important part of the human food supply—tripled, but since then, obvious symptoms of overfishing have occurred, and catches have begun to decline.[8] There has also been dangerous deforestation throughout the world, overplowing, and overgrazing (reducing the production of oxygen). And the ecosystem has been overloaded with wastes.

---

[6]See Allen V. Kneese, Robert O. Ayers, and Ralph C. d'Arge, *Economics and the Environment: A Materials Balance Approach* (Baltimore: Johns Hopkins University Press, 1971); and Robert L. Lineberry, *American Public Policy* (New York: Harper and Row, 1977), pp. 269–70.

[7]See Lester R. Brown, *The Twenty-Ninth Day* (New York: W.W. Norton, 1978), pp. 71–96.

[8]See Brown, *The Twenty-Ninth Day*, pp. 17–23.

Production Growth

Not only has America's population grown since World War II; Americans' consumption of goods has grown dramatically, too. This has resulted in a sharp rise in production, an event that has also made environmental issues more acute. During the 1960s, the United States represented 6 percent of the world's population, but used 30 percent of the world's output of natural resources.

Growth in production, coupled with population growth, has, for example, produced a huge expansion in the number of electricity generating plants—with their familiar smokestacks—and in the number of automobiles—with their internal combustion exhausts. The air we breathe is part of our commons, too, and its pollution is a part of our modern tragedy.

But population and production growth cannot by themselves explain the environmental crisis. Since World War II, population has increased by 50 percent and Gross National Product (GNP)—total goods and services produced—has increased by 250 percent. During the same period, however, pollution levels have increased ten to twenty times![9] Thus, we must consider the intervention of other events: new technological developments.

Technological Developments

Environmentalist Barry Commoner has pointed out that in agriculture, for example, the development of new technologies has greatly increased environmental pollution. Cattle are fattened in huge feedlots, chickens and eggs are produced in long buildings with rows of cages, and crop rotation has been abandoned for intensive one-crop farming. "Where once the animal's manure made the fields fertile, now it has become feed-lot waste. Instead, the crops are nourished by purchased chemicals. Other chemicals are used to kill weeds and insect pests, no longer kept in check by shifting crops from field to field."[10] In other words, organic wastes have become a problem rather than a solution. To take their place, new chemicals have been developed and introduced. These chemicals are a result of human changes in the ecosystem rules, and they are thus not biodegradable, renewable, and reusable. We will return to this subject later in this chapter.

Environmental Actors and Action

Events alone do not put issues on the political agenda; actors are also involved. With environmental issues, these actors included activist citizens, interest groups, the media, and politicians and public officials. Rachel Carson's *Silent Spring* (1962)[11] was a fundamentally

---

[9]Commoner, "Energy, Environment, and Economics," p. 27.
[10]Commoner, *The Poverty of Power* (New York: Knopf, 1976), p. 160.
[11]Rachel Carson, *Silent Spring* (Houghton, Mifflin, 1962).

"Earth Day"—April 22, 1970—marked a new stage in concern about the environment. Environmental activists led teach-ins, seminars, and public rallies to increase ecological awareness among the general public.

important element in the development of environmental issues. In it she described the harmful effects of the "grim specter" of pesticide use. There was a rising tide of citizen concern about pollution. Congress passed the Clean Air Act in 1963. The Water Quality Act and the Clean Water Restoration Act were passed in 1965 and 1966. On April 22, 1970—"Earth Day"—Congress adjourned for the day so that members could address environmentalist rallies throughout the nation.[12] Politicians and public officials were responding to, and in some cases leading, activist citizens and interest groups as their views and activities were increasingly reported in the media. "Tons of popular literature" concerning environmental issues were published in the media in 1970.[13] Many older groups experienced an enormous jump in membership. For example, the Sierra Club, founded in 1892, increased its membership from 15,000 to 85,000 during the 1960s; by 1977 membership had grown to 180,000. New environmental groups, including Friends of the Earth and Environmental Action, sprang up everywhere. The Oil, Chemical and Atomic Workers Union became increasingly active on pollution issues, which had such a direct effect on their members in their places of work. A political leader in the environmental movement was U.S. Senator Edmund S. Muskie of Maine. He and others led successful efforts to pass the Clean Air Act in 1970, which was aimed particularly at reducing the noxious emissions of automobile exhausts. In 1970, too, the U.S. Environmental Protection Agency (EPA) was created, and the Water Quality Improvement Act, aimed at establishing liability for cleanup of oil spills, was passed. In announcing the creation of a new Council on Environmental Quality, President Nixon said that the 1970s "absolutely must be the years when America pays its debt to the past by

Senator Edmund S. Muskie (D., Maine) was among the first political figures to press for legislation to protect the environment.

---

[12]For a discussion of the history of the environmental movement in America, see Norman J. Ornstein and Shirley Elder, *Interest Groups, Lobbying and Policymaking* (Washington, D.C.: Congressional Quarterly Press, 1978), pp. 155–85.

[13]Edwin S. Mills, *The Economics of Environmental Quality* (New York: W.W. Norton, 1978), p. 184.

reclaiming the purity of its air, its water and our living environment. It is literally now or never."

The issues, then, were defined in terms of the environment, not in terms of energy use, for example, or the state of America's national economy. Environmental policy was formulated and adopted on the basis of that narrow definition of the issues. Implementation of the new policy began.

Backlash

By the mid-1970s, however, a backlash had begun to set in. The automobile and oil industries, interest groups representing business and industry generally, such as the U.S. Chamber of Commerce and the National Association of Manufacturers, the major electric power companies and some unions, like the United Auto Workers, had begun to demand a relaxation of government regulations on pollution. They maintained, in effect, that the formulation of environmental issues had been too narrowly focused; they argued that policy should be based on a broader definition, which would also include the issues of jobs and energy shortages.[14]

Two important events helped to put energy issues on America's agenda—the 1973 oil embargo by nations belonging to the Organization of Petroleum Exporting Countries (OPEC), and a dramatic increase in oil prices. Instead of an "environmental crisis," many Americans began to think in terms of an "energy crisis," particularly after sitting in gasoline lines at filling stations and having to pay larger bills for ever-increasing heating and other fuel costs.

THE ENERGY CRISIS: BACKGROUND

As a matter of fact, the environmental crisis and the energy crisis were intertwined all along. Each was, in a sense, a different aspect of the same problem.

Consider beer bottles, for example.[15] The per capita consumption of *beer* in the United States has stayed about the same since 1946, but during the same period, the production of beer *bottles* has increased tenfold—a result of the new technology, which has developed throwaway bottles to replace returnable bottles. This development has resulted in both greater environmental problems and greater energy problems. The increased numbers of bottles pose a new environmental problem: what to do with these additional solid wastes, which are not biodegradable. Making new glass to replace throwaway bottles, rather than reusing the old ones, also requires the burning of extra amounts of nonrenewable energy fuels. This, incidentally, produces additional air pollution.

---

[14]See Ornstein and Elder, *Interest Groups, Lobbying and Policymaking*, p. 163.
[15]See Commoner, "Energy, Environment, and Economics," pp. 27–29.

Like environmental issues, energy issues got onto the American political agenda through the effects of both events and actors. The oil embargo by the OPEC nations and the fourfold increase in world crude prices were highly significant events that first brought the "energy crisis" to the attention of most Americans. Interest groups played their part. Population and production growth were important causative events, as they were with environmental issues. And so were new technological developments—many of the same new developments that had also helped cause the environmental crisis.

Is There Really an Energy Crisis?

The answer to that question is yes and no. First, consider oil. Oil is a fossil fuel like natural gas and coal. They are called fossil fuels because they are the fossil residues of ancient plants. All three of these fossil fuels, as well as uranium, are nonrenewable. No more of these fuels are being made on the earth. Thus, as they are used, they are used up permanently. In the United States, oil production peaked in 1970 and has steadily declined since then. One reason for this was that the major oil companies found it more profitable to produce oil in foreign countries. With some increase in price to make domestic production more lucrative, the United States probably has enough oil to take care of its national demand (unless there is a great increase in demand) for fifty to sixty years, but the price rise involved will cause considerable economic problems.[16]

At any rate, whether we are talking about oil produced in this country or abroad, sometime during our lifetimes we will see a shift from petroleum to other energy sources because oil is a nonrenewable resource that is being steadily depleted. Some even argue that this shortage of oil may come sooner than thirty years from now.[17]

But the problems in regard to oil involve more than just the shortage issue. There are political problems, too. U.S. dependence on foreign oil has been steadily increasing. In 1977, 40 percent of our oil needs came from imports, and this figure is expected to increase to 50 percent by 1985.[18] Most of this foreign oil is controlled by Saudi Arabia, Iran, the United Arab Emirates, Kuwait, Iraq, Libya, Algeria, Nigeria, Venezuela, and Indonesia. The political problems inherent in the control of the oil by a few foreign countries was made dramatically clear when the Shah of Iran was deposed in 1979. The flow of Iranian oil was shut off for a time, causing economic dislocations in the U.S. and elsewhere. The importance of oil in world politics was also dramatized in 1978 and 1979 by the intensified American interest in improving relations with Mexico, after the announcement of their vast new oil discoveries. In February 1979, President Carter visited Mexico City for important talks with

---

[16]See Commoner, *The Poverty of Power*, p. 57.
[17]See Brown, *The Twenty-Ninth Day*, pp. 102–7.
[18]Brown, *The Twenty-Ninth Day*, p. 101.

President Lopez Portillo concerning how much oil and natural gas the United States could expect to import from Mexico—and at what price. These negotiations are likely to continue for some time, and they are not likely to be easy. Mexico considers its oil to be a national treasure, one which it hopes can help solve its own internal problems. It is not likely to be very moved by the problems of the "the giant to the North," which has often treated its Southern neighbor with disdain.

Representatives of the thirteen OPEC nations, including Saudi Arabia's Oil Minister Sheikh Yamani (middle), met in Geneva, Switzerland, in 1979 and agreed to increase the price of oil. The ministers also decided to meet again before the end of the year to decide upon a further increase.

Dependence on foreign oil—for the United States and for most countries—also poses serious economic problems. The fourfold increase in oil prices by the OPEC nations helped to cause a serious global economic recession in 1974 and 1975, with a reduction in total goods and services produced in the world.[19] In the United States, our balance of payments—the money we pay for imports compared to the money we receive for our exports—continued to show a serious deficit through 1979, partly because of the increasing amount of oil we imported.

But the energy problem is not just one of shortages, the precarious nature of international politics, or economic stresses. It is also an environmental problem. Oil's energy is released by burning, which produces air pollutants that are hazardous to the health of human beings. Why not switch from oil to coal? The world's coal resources are much greater than its oil resources. In the United States alone, there is probably enough coal—which can be turned into both gaseous and liquid fuels through new processes—to last three hundred years.[20] But gasification, liquification, and the burning of coal produce more pollution problems than does the burning of oil.

So, is there an energy shortage? Whether or not there is an *immediate* shortage, it is clear that there is an energy crisis. By the end of most college students' lifetimes, the world probably will have been required to switch from oil to other energy sources. Before that time, the United States will have become increasingly dependent upon foreign sources of oil. For a number of generations thereafter, there will be plenty of coal in the United States but we will have to become increasingly concerned about the pollution problems inher-

[19]Brown, *The Twenty-Ninth Day*, p. 102.

[20]See John M. Fowler, "Energy and the Environment," in Lon C. Ruedisili and Morris W. Firebaugh, eds., *Perspectives on Energy* (New York: Oxford University Press, 1975), p. 81.

ent in the use of coal. What shall we do? Before we get to that question, we must first understand the causes of the energy crisis and that means we must again consider some basic principles in nature.

The Laws of Thermodynamics

Thermodynamics is a field of physics that concerns itself with heat and its characteristics. Like the "Law of Materials Balance," the "First Law of Thermodynamics" holds that the energy of the universe is constant. It can neither be created nor destroyed.[21]

The "Second Law of Thermodynamics" has greater implications for our present environmental and energy problems. It teaches us that in the conversion of energy sources for useful work—such as burning oil to turn electricity generating turbines or to run an internal combustion engine in a city bus—a certain amount of heat is produced and lost. The amount of this lost energy in the form of heat is constantly increasing in the universe and cannot be recovered. This means that thermal pollution is an increasing problem which results from energy conversion; it raises the heat of the globe and, more particularly, raises the temperature in streams or lakes, which can endanger the life cycles in them. But the "Second Law of Thermodynamics" also means that we should examine all types of energy conversion processes to determine which are most efficient—produce the least amount of wasted, nonusable heat—for doing useful work.[22]

Technological Developments

What does thermodynamics have to do with the energy crisis? Consider petrochemical products—the modern-day unnatural "wonders" derived, through chemistry, from the natural components of petroleum and natural gas. These products include detergents, fertilizers, synthetic fibers, plastics, and pesticides.[23]

Detergents replace soap, which is made from natural fats. Chemical fertilizers replace organic wastes. Synthetic fibers replace wool and cotton. Plastics replace leather and wood. Crop rotation (planting one crop one year and a different one the next) was once used to prevent the build-up of one particular kind of pest. Now pesticides are used instead of crop rotation and as a replacement for helpful insects and birds, many of which have been increasingly destroyed by the pesticides, making even more pesticides necessary.

The production of petrochemical products to replace similar products found in nature involves an enormous and extremely inefficient use of energy. Indeed, one of the principal reasons why we have an energy crisis is that our energy sources are being inefficiently

---

[21]See Commoner, *The Poverty of Power*, pp. 12–28.
[22]See Commoner, *The Poverty of Power*, pp. 15–32.
[23]Commoner, *The Poverty of Power*, pp. 155–210.

used to produce petrochemical products. The Second Law of Thermodynamics teaches us that in converting energy sources to useful work there is inevitably some waste of energy in the form of nonusable heat. When we use petroleum and natural gas to produce modern-day petrochemical products, instead of converting such energy sources directly into work as an electricity generating turbine does, we get the lowest level of efficient use of energy sources. Much of the energy potential is lost, wasted.

For example, six times as much petroleum is necessary to produce the same kind of product out of plastic as is needed to produce the product from leather or lumber—natural products.[24] The same is true in regard to fertilizers:

> *Because of the shift from manure, legumes, and other organic fertilizers, the crop's nutrition is no longer provided by biological cycle, driven by renewable, freely available solar energy; instead, by using inorganic fertilizer, it has become dependent on non-renewable, increasingly expensive fossil fuels.*[25]

These new petrochemical products, which were developed to replace old, natural products, do not just pose energy problems for us, however. Again, we see that the energy and the environmental crisis are two faces of the same problem. Not only do these new petrochemical products use energy in a highly inefficient manner, but they also produce enormous pollution problems. In 1972 alone, seven billion pounds of synthetic fibers were produced, eight and a half billion pounds of synthetic detergents, twenty-two and a half billion pounds of plastics, and over one billion pounds of synthetic pesticides. One hundred and thirty times more synthetic organic chemicals were produced in 1974 than were produced in 1946. The production of plastics presents enormous problems of what to do with these solid wastes, which are not biodegradable. In addition, one common plastic gives off vinyl chloride, a compound which has been found to cause cancer. The use of petrochemical fertilizers has resulted in enormous runoffs of nitrates into our surface waters, and these nitrates can cause cancer.[26]

If we broadened the policy formulation focus in regard to petrochemicals from "environment" to "environment and energy use" and then to "environment, energy use, and jobs," we would still come up with essentially the same policy formulation to meet the issues involved. The fact is that the problems of more energy use, more environmental pollution, and fewer human jobs are all involved in the production of detergents instead of soap; of chemical fertilizers instead of organic fertilizers; of synthetic fibers instead of cotton and wool; of plastics instead of leather or wood; and of pesticides instead

---

[24]Commoner, "Energy, Environment, and Economics," p. 35.
[25]Commoner, *The Poverty of Power*, p. 165.
[26]Commoner, "Energy, Environment, and Economics," pp. 32–34.

of organic methods for controlling insects and other crop pests. Thus, a return to organic products instead of petrochemical products would usually involve less energy use, less environmental pollution, and more jobs.

Why, then, do we produce petrochemical products in place of natural ones? Is it because there is a shortage of the natural products? No, the fats necessary for soap can be produced in great abundance. The source for these fats is a renewable, inexhaustible one. Similarly, leather, wool, and cotton can be produced abundantly.

Do we produce petrochemical products in place of the natural ones because it is more "efficient" to do so? Not if we consider the "hidden" costs of such petrochemical products. Plastics manufacturers, for example, make good profits. There is no question about that. But suppose these manufacturers had to bear all the *real* costs of disposing of the solid wastes they produce? The price of their products would not then be nearly as attractive. Today, solid waste disposal costs are not charged, by and large, to the producer of them but are borne separately by the taxpay-

By the mid-1970s, many communities had established "recycling centers" where residents could bring bottles, paper, and tin cans to be recycled. To accomplish the same goal, several states passed laws requiring large deposits on bottled and canned products, thus discouraging littering and encouraging recycling.

ers. Suppose petrochemical fertilizer manufacturers had to bear the costs of removing runoff nitrates from surface waters. The price of such products would, of course, be much higher. But these costs are now hidden; they are borne by the public, which makes the price of the petrochemical products actually *artificially* low. The difference between the costs they pay to produce their products and the real costs, including the hidden costs, are charged to the public.

But pollution costs amount to far more than just the price of clean-ups. For example, the EPA has found that the costs of air pollution damage to human health, crops, and property values in America is $16 billion annually, an "extra-hidden" cost of over $80 for every man, woman, and child in America.[27]

If we moved back to natural products instead of relying increasingly on petrochemical products, would the quality of human life decline? Not necessarily. Who would not prefer a leather belt to a plastic one, for example? Experiments indicate that organic farming can produce yields and profits comparable to those produced with petrochemical fertilizers and pesticides.[28]

---

[27]Commoner, *The Poverty of Power*, pp. 173–75.
[28]See Council on Environmental Quality, *Environmental Quality* (Washington, D.C.: U.S. Government Printing Office, August, 1971), p. 107.

Why, then, has the use of petrochemicals proliferated so much since World War II? Because petrochemicals have produced greater profits for the corporations involved. But these increased profits have usually been obtained at the cost of greater energy use, greater capital investment, and a reduction in the number of jobs available for people.

The same is true in other aspects of American economic life. Two minor, but revealing, examples immediately come to mind. Petrochemical developments made possible the production of "Astroturf" for the indoor Houston Astrodome, where grass could not readily be grown. But Astroturf has now replaced grass on many *outdoor* football fields, too. Astroturf production requires the inefficient use of energy sources, greater capital investment, and reduced amounts of human labor. Grass, on the other hand, gets its production energy from the sun. Growing it requires greater human labor and reduced amounts of capital investment. Grass is renewable. It does not pollute the environment. Instead, it takes carbon dioxide from our atmosphere, where industrialization has produced too much of it, and converts it to oxygen, which humans need.

Somehow we have been taught to believe that the production of such unnatural products as "Astroturf" is "progress." Another example of that kind of "progress" is the plan for "automatic check-out" at supermarket counters. According to this plan, computer-sensitive designs are printed on supermarket products; when they are rubbed across an electric eye at check-out time, the cash register automatically records the price and totals the bill accurately and rapidly. "Progress" in this instance, as in so many like it, means fewer human jobs, more capital investment, and greater use of energy.

ENERGY AND THE ENVIRONMENT: PUBLIC POLICY

Something has to give. We cannot go on forever using up nonrenewable energy sources at an accelerating rate and continuing to pollute our common environment at the same time. According to Barry Commoner, the big problem is that the natural cycles of the ecosystem are being subverted by our privately owned economic and production systems. His solution is government ownership of the production system in America—socialism—rather than a continuation of private ownership of the means of production.[29]

Complete public ownership of the means of production may be a fairly impractical solution. It is not necessarily a guarantee against wasteful use of energy or environmental pollution, either. Any traveler to a socialist country rapidly becomes aware of this fact. In the United States, the federally owned Tennessee Valley Authority

---

[29]See Commoner, *The Poverty of Power*, pp. 235–64.

(TVA), which is governed by a three-member board appointed by the President and confirmed by the Senate, was organized to generate electricity from hydroelectric power and provide other economic benefits for the region it served. But the TVA is not really subject to the control of people who live in the area where it operates. Partly because of this, it has been strongly attacked in recent years by environmentalists and others for its increasing reliance on nuclear power and on strip-mining to provide fuel for its coal-fired generator plants.

Whether or not one agrees with government ownership as a solution, it is clear that the modern "tragedy of the commons" cannot be corrected without government intervention. One authority has written:

Given the cornucopia of the frontier, an unpolluted environment and a rapidly developing technology, American politics could afford to be a more or less amicable division of the spoils with the government stepping in only when the free-for-all pursuit of wealth got out of hand. In the new era of scarcity, laissez-faire and the inalienable right of the individual to get as much as he can are prescriptions for disaster.[30]

How much government intervention—and what kind—is necessary? What can be done about the twin problems of energy and the environment? The answers to these questions are more difficult to discover because of the fragmentation of the federal system. Congress has enacted certain national environmental standards, for example, particularly in regard to air pollution. But even in this field, cities, states, and Indian tribes are accorded considerable autonomy in deciding upon the strictness of the air quality standards they adopt. Incidentally, the Northern Cheyenne Tribe in Montana has adopted the toughest air pollution standards of any governmental entity in the United States. These standards have halted the intensive developments of electricity-generating plants, based upon coal strip-mining, just north and upwind from the tribe's reservation. In other aspects of environmental pollution, particularly in regard to water pollution, the federal government has provided incentives—in the form of grants-in-aid—to encourage the states, cities, and tribes to clean up their surface waters. Federal laws and laws in a number of states and

Although stricter federal laws have helped to improve America's air and water quality, environmental pollution continues to be a major problem.

---

[30]William Ophuls, "The Scarcity Society," *Harper's* (April 1974).

local communities now require that no new projects can be started until an environmental impact statement has been prepared to evaluate their environmental effect.

The fragmentation inherent in the federal system is a problem in the formulation of energy policy. New England states favor cheap, foreign sources of oil. Producer states like Texas have traditionally sought import and pricing policies that protected against cheap foreign oil.[31] The interest of Indian tribes and their authority as governmental units must also be taken into account in the formulation of federal energy policy. Indian tribes are thought to own a third of all low-sulphur coal in the United States and over one half of the nation's uranium.[32] They have increasingly asserted their right to develop these resources (or not develop them) in ways which seem most economically, culturally, and environmentally sound to them.

Another problem for energy and environmental policy-makers is that policy has been made on an incremental basis. Despite studies calling for "comprehensive" planning, policy-makers have not found it possible thus far to start afresh in regard to energy and the environment. President Carter's energy plan of 1977, which he called the "moral equivalent of war," was in fact an incremental plan; it built upon earlier government policies, rather than replacing them with a comprehensive one.

Corporate power—especially the economic and political power of the energy companies—poses an additional problem in regard to the formulation of energy and environmental policy. One expert, the late John M. Blair, formerly the chief economist of the U.S. Senate Subcommittee on Anti-Trust and Monopoly, pointed out that the government has almost always had to depend upon the oil companies for information concerning the amount of oil available. Blair also documented how supply and price in the energy field have largely been subject to energy company manipulation and control, rather than competition.[33] Among the solutions that he and others have suggested for reducing the power of the energy companies—and thereby increasing the federal government's ability to formulate and implement energy and environmental policy—are new federal laws which would require horizontal and vertical divestiture. (The horizontal divestiture law would force the oil companies to sell their coal and uranium operations to competing companies; the vertical divestiture measure would split up companies that engage in production, refining, and marketing into separate, competing corporations.) U.S. Senator Edward M. Kennedy of Massachusetts heads Senate forces seeking the increased competition that these forms of divesti-

---

[31]See Alfred R. Light, "The Carter Administration's National Energy Plan: Pressure Groups, and Organizational Politics in the Congress," *Policy Studies Journal*, 7, no. 1 (Autumn, 1978): 72.

[32]See David A. Schaller, "An Energy Policy for Indian Lands: Problems of Issue and Perception," *Policy Studies Journal*, 7, no. 1 (Autumn 1978): 40.

[33]John B. Blair, *The Control of Oil* (New York: Pantheon Books, 1976).

ture would bring to the energy industry. So far, they have been unsuccessful.

Blair and others have also suggested the possibility of creating a public energy corporation, similar to TVA or the Corporation for Public Broadcasting, to produce the vast energy resources on federal land. It would furnish produced resources, such as crude oil, to independent refiners, thereby again introducing greater competition into the energy industry. This proposal was introduced in the U.S. Senate by Senator Adlai E. Stevenson III of Illinois, and it has been endorsed by the Consumer Federation of America. So far, this proposal, too, has not garnered sufficient Senate support to gain passage.

Policy-makers in the environmental field have been under considerable pressure in recent years to relax environmental standards in order to increase economic growth and reduce the problems of the energy crisis. Intense lobbying efforts partially succeeded in 1977 in amending the Clean Air Act to relax existing standards for automobile emissions, to extend deadlines for cities to meet National Air Quality Standards, and to give more time to industrial polluters.[34] But by and large, the foes of stricter environmental standards have not been successful in turning back the clock. They have only been successful in securing delays in the implementation or enforcement of stricter environmental standards.

Mike Peters with permission by Dayton Daily News.

Although the stricter standards of the 1970s have measurably improved the nation's air quality, carbon monoxide and photochemical oxidants continue to be a serious air pollution problem in most U.S. cities. The amount of carbon dioxide in our atmosphere also continues to rise, which threatens to increase the average temperature. This continues to be a major global environmental problem.

The 1970s have seen an improvement in water quality in America. Several varieties of fish have returned to certain U.S. rivers and lakes, for example. But toxic, or poisonous, pollutants—from pesticides and from industrial metal and chemical wastes—continue to constitute important water pollution problems in America.[35]

---

[34]Ornstein and Elder, *Interest Groups, Lobbying and Policymaking*, pp. 155–85.

[35]See *Environmental Quality—1977: The Eighth Annual Report of the Council on Environmental Quality* (Washington, D.C.: U.S. Government Printing Office, 1977), pp. 151, 152, 190, 200, 227.

THE ENERGY CRISIS: ALTERNATIVE SOLUTIONS

Proposals for new energy policies in the United States fall into three principal categories: increase supply; decrease demand; and develop alternative sources.

Increase Supply

President Carter's national energy plan, first proposed in 1977, was largely based upon the assumption that if the price of energy derived from oil and natural gas was raised, supply would increase because of the incentives of the higher price. It was also intended to curtail demand because of the higher prices that consumers would have to pay. But studies indicate that energy supplies do not usually increase with an increase in price and that demand does not significantly decrease.[36] One reason for this is that in regard to natural gas, for example, all available drilling rigs are in operation now, and an increase in the price of natural gas will not soon cause a significant increase in drilling. Another reason is that many people must drive to work in automobiles (since there is no mass transit for them) regardless of what the cost of gasoline is. Thus, even though there was a decline for a short while in gasoline consumption in the United States after the fourfold increase in the cost of petroleum in 1974 and 1975, consumption thereafter assumed its regular rate of increase.

Despite this, President Carter recommended an increase in energy prices. He suggested a boost in gasoline taxes, for example, but this proposal was rejected in both the Senate and the House.[37] The President also recommended raising the price of energy by an increased tax on crude oil. This proposal was approved in the House of Representatives but was rejected by the Senate. President Carter suggested that the price of natural gas should continue to be regulated by the federal government but that the price ceiling should be raised considerably. The House approved this idea. The Senate rejected it, approving instead a phased end to federal regulation of the price of new natural gas. This "deregulation" of natural gas prices was the proposal finally enacted into law by Congress in the last hours of the 1978 session. Senators Howard Metzenbaum of Ohio and James Abourezk of South Dakota, now retired, tried every maneuver to defeat deregulation, including two filibusters, but they were unsuccessful. They and others felt that increased prices would not greatly curtail demand and that energy price increases would create the greatest burden for working-class and low-income people.

---

[36]See Blair, *The Control of Oil*, pp. 323–24.
[37]For a report on the President's 1977 proposals and their outcome in the U.S. Congress, see *Congressional Quarterly Weekly Report* 36, no. 41 (October 14, 1978): 2925.

Instead, Metzenbaum and Abourezk proposed greater competition in the energy field—through horizontal and vertical divestiture—to loosen the giant oil companies' control over oil production, intending thereby to increase the supply. During the 1979 congressional session, President Carter changed his position on the deregulation of natural gas. In order to secure passage of *some* "energy plan," Carter agreed to deregulation and ordered his subordinates, particularly Secretary of Energy James Schlesinger, to lobby on the same side as the oil and gas companies. This side won.

Decrease Demand

In addition to a price rise, four methods have been suggested for reducing energy demand in America: mandatory restrictions; incentives for conservation; penalties for excessive energy use; and removal of artificial encouragements for greater energy use. Conserving energy in America—or, to put it another way, decreasing the demand for energy—is especially important because the United States is responsible for about one third of world energy consumption, although we represent only about 6 percent of the world's population.[38] A reduction in America's energy use would reduce its political dependence upon foreign governments. It would also improve the U.S. balance-of-payments problem, which results from Americans' buying of more things abroad than they sell in foreign countries. Decreasing energy demand in the United States would also reduce its pollution problems. One expert has said,

> *As best as I can tell, abating pollution by 50% throughout the nation would add three to five years to the life expectancy of a child born in 1970. Abating pollution would be worth about $2 billion a year in terms of the economic benefits of (a) increased work days and (b) decreased direct health expenditures.*[39]

Certain mandatory controls on energy use could be enacted. For example, the federal government could ban nonreturnable cans and bottles, as some states have done. This would conserve energy and reduce solid-waste litter. Thus far, the federal government has not decided upon this strategy. Federal laws have, however, set highway speed limits at fifty-five miles per hour, an energy conservation measure that also saves lives. In 1977, the Senate approved a ban on the production of "gas guzzling" cars, but the House of Representa-

---

[38]See Ford Foundation Energy Policy Project, *A Time to Choose* (Cambridge, Mass.: Ballinger, 1974); David H. Davis, *Energy Politics* (New York: St. Martin's Press, 1974); and Gerald Garvey, *Energy, Ecology, Economy* (New York: Norton, 1972).

[39]See "Air Pollution Damage: Some Difficulties in Estimating the Value of Abatement," in Allen Z. Kneese and Blair T. Bower, eds., *Environmental Quality Analysis: Theory and Method in the Social Sciences* (Baltimore: John Hopkins University Press, 1972), p. 240.

tives did not agree to this proposal. Congress did agree to mandatory energy efficiency standards for home appliances. President Carter asked for the authority to force utilities and industrial companies to convert from oil and gas to coal, but Congress would only agree to a very weak version of this proposal. President Carter also recommended a tax on utilities and other industrial users of oil and natural gas, but this proposal was killed by Congress.

President Carter's national energy plan contemplated certain incentives for energy conservation. The President recommended giving homeowners a tax credit for installing energy-conserving home insulation. This proposal was approved by Congress. Coupling the idea of incentives with the idea of penalties, President Carter recommended a tax on "gas-guzzling" cars, with a tax rebate for buyers of gas-saving cars. Congress agreed to the penalty idea—the tax on "gas-guzzling" cars—but rejected the incentive idea—the tax rebate to buyers of gas-saving cars.

Proposals have been made for removing present artificial incentives for greater energy use. Consider the use of energy resources for generating electricity, for example. Today the generation of electric power depends almost entirely on fossil fuels, with the resultant pollution of the environment. And there has been a rapid increase in electrical energy production and consumption in America.[40] But the incentives for this increasing use of electrical energy have not all been natural ones. Instead, the electricity companies, seeking to increase their sales, have granted special low rates for the use of power during off-peak periods. At first, off-peak promotion was done to increase power consumption during the summer months, to use idle generating capacity and balance the peak-time use during the winter months, when nights were longer and more lighting and heating were needed. This promotion was so effective that summer soon came to be the peak time. The power companies then turned back to promoting greater power use in the winter. President Carter recommended a reform of electric utility rates to require utilities to provide lower rates for customers who use power in off-peak times. This proposal was watered down considerably by Congress.

Utility companies have also promoted greater use of electricity by granting declining rates for increased use. This policy discriminates against residential users, who are charged flat rates, and gives an incentive to large industrial customers to use greater amounts of electricity. Proposals have been made for making this system of declining rates illegal under federal law, but they have not gained acceptance in Congress. This is partly due to the federalism argument—the idea that such utility rate regulations should be left to the individual states. All states today allow such "promotional" declining rates for large users, thus encouraging greater use of a scarce commodity.

---

[40]See Ruedisili and Firebaugh, *Perspectives on Energy*, pp. 72–75.

The use of electricity for heating is most inefficient because it wastes a great deal of heat. No federal efforts have been undertaken to prevent utility companies from promoting the use of electricity for home heating.

Transportation accounts for 26 percent of all energy consumed in the United States.[41] Railroads are far more efficient energy users than are trucks or buses. Electrified trains are more efficient than diesel-fueled trains. But government efforts have not been very successful in promoting trains over trucks, especially because—through publicly built highways—trucks and buses receive a kind of public subsidy—publicly built highways—that is not available to trains. Most *city* transportation systems are now publicly owned. It has been suggested that the federal government should move toward public ownership of the railroads to increase the efficiency of energy use in transportation and to reduce pollution from internal combustion engines.[42] Instead, railroads continue to receive increasing amounts of federal subsidies themselves and are allowed frequently to relinquish additional routes to trucks and buses.

Alternative Energy Sources

Our energy and environmental problems suggest the necessity of switching to greater reliance on alternative energy sources. Since the United States has greater domestic reserves of coal than of oil and natural gas, President Carter and others have recommended that a short-term part of our energy strategy should include greater coal use. In its natural state, of course, coal cannot be used economically to run automobiles. It can be converted into liquid and gas, but, today, the costs of this conversion are so high that the resulting synthetic fuels are noncompetitive.[43]

Coal can best be used to power electric generators for electrified trains. But mining it underground presents a number of serious health hazards for miners, notably "black lung" from breathing coal dust. Both underground and strip-mining of coal can cause serious water pollution. The costs of reclaiming strip-mined land are great. And the burning of coal for fuel produces greater air pollution problems than those resulting from oil. The worst pollutant from certain types of coal comes from burning the sulphur associated with them.

What about nuclear power? This is the power that can be generated from the energy produced from the splitting, or fission, of certain types of heavy atoms, notably Uranium-235. United States government policy places extremely heavy emphasis upon this type of

---

[41]Grover Starling, *The Politics and Economics of Public Policy: An Introductory Analysis with Cases* (Homewood, Ill.: Dorsey Press, 1979), p. 576.

[42]Commoner, *The Poverty of Power*, pp. 180, 194.

[43]See Commoner, *The Poverty of Power*, pp. 66–81.

In the following excerpt, Barry Commoner argues that we can solve the energy crisis by using a variety of renewable energy sources—the "solar transition," as he calls it, which is technologically feasible today. But to do so means that we must debate the issue of "social" versus "private governance."

. . . If the energy crisis is due to the nonrenewability of our present fuels, why has the government done so little to encourage the production of renewable fuels? If a major solar technology, such as the photovoltaic cell, is now technologically feasible and, with a relatively small expenditure of public funds, could be broadly commercialized, why did President Carter specifically refuse to permit this expenditure, despite congressional authorization? If one of the most effective single steps that could be taken to conserve fuel would be the vast expansion and electrification of the railroads and urban mass-transit systems, why has the government done so little to implement these options, and, instead, proposed to cut Amtrak trackage almost in half?

The answer to each of these questions is the same: the specific problem cannot be solved without violating the taboo that has thus far protected the private interests of the energy industries from the encroachment of the social interest. If the nation undertook to develop renewable solar fuels, and fuel prices became stabilized, the oil industry would lose the huge profits it is certain to gain if prices continue to escalate. If photovoltaic cells became commercial, the private electric utilities would not long survive the competition. If the railroads were to expand and carry more passengers, they could not operate as private, profitable enterprises and would need to be nationalized. (Most of the railroads in the rest of the world carry many passengers and operate, at a loss, as nationalized systems.) Each of these energy problems depends on the solution to a single, much larger one: social governance. This is the problem that seems to be "too big" not only for the President but for Congress as well. There, apart from a few voices calling for the creation of a federal energy corporation, nothing was heard about this crucial issue during the debate on the energy plan.

VIEWPOINT
Solving the Energy Crisis

Now, having failed to produce an energy policy capable of combatting inflation rather than abetting it, the Carter Administration has prescribed a regimen of austerity for the country. The energy crisis, we are told, symbolizes a new limit to the nation's capacities, which we must acknowledge by lowering expectations. . . . No one, it seems, is ready to ask why the richest nation in human history must act as though it were poor, or why its citizens must fight over who will suffer least from this counterfeit poverty. This is the most dangerous result of the nation's failure to understand, let alone resolve, the energy crisis. Once we do understand that crisis, it becomes clear that energy is wasted carelessly, not by design; that the energy we need is not running out but is replenished with every dawn; that the nation is not poor but mismanaged.

The resolution of the energy crisis—the solar transition—is an opportunity to turn this knowledge into action, to embark on a historic new passage. But to find our way we will need to be guided by social rather than private interests. There are many known ways—and many yet to be invented—of introducing social governance into production: national planning; local or regional planning; public utilities; co-operatives; and, if need be, public ownership on a national or local level. These measures will, of course, clash with the notion that every productive decision must be privately governed, for private profit, in order to insure economic efficiency. But we now know from the energy crisis that these inefficiencies are outside the realm of private governance, and are accessible only to social decisions.

It will be difficult—some say impossible—to learn how to merge economic justice with economic progress, and personal freedom with social governance. If we allow the fear of failing in this effort to forestall the effort to make it, then failure is certain. But if we firmly embrace economic democracy as a national goal, as a new standard for political policy, or even only as a vision of the nation's future it can guide us through the passage that is mandated by the energy crisis, and restore to the nation the vitality inherent in the richness of its resources and the wisdom of its people.

SOURCE: Barry Commoner, "The Solar Transition—II," *The New Yorker*, April 30, 1979, pp. 91–93.

alternative energy source. Like coal, uranium is a nonrenewable resource.[44] Today, privately owned electricity generating plants in America that use uranium are the beneficiaries of huge expenditures by the federal government. Mined uranium is "enriched" to make it most efficiently fissionable in government-built plants. In recent years, the price of the original uranium ore in semi-processed form, before it is enriched—called "yellow cake"—has increased almost as much as the price of oil. This has occurred partly because the same energy companies that are involved in the oil business are also involved in the uranium business, and they do not want to compete with themselves. Because of the increased cost of yellow cake and because of rising construction costs, nuclear generating plants have in recent years become less financially attractive to the utility companies and their investors. The rate of construction of such plants has slackened.

The mining of uranium poses health hazards for miners. The leftover ore, or "tailings," present radiation dangers. The federal government has recently provided some funding for removing tailings from New Mexico sites. The possibilities of an accident at a nuclear power plant are always present, and their consequences would be far more damaging, potentially, than any conceivable accident at a coal-fired plant, for example. The problems of nuclear power do not end with the production and delivery of the electricity that it produces. There is the enormous and growing problem of what to do with nuclear wastes.

The life of the wastes which result from using uranium to produce energy extend into many thousands of years. They must be stored somewhere where they will be safe for many, many times longer than our government, or any other government on earth, has lasted. The federal government, which takes care of the nuclear waste disposal problem for private utility companies with nuclear plants, is finding it increasingly difficult to persuade states to accept nuclear wastes for storage within their borders. If the "hidden" costs of producing electric power from nuclear reactors were added to present costs, the total would be prohibitive. In addition, nuclear reactors generate an enormous amount of lost heat and thermal pollution. Nuclear power involves a nonrenewable energy resource and seriously damaging side effects—considerably more damaging than coal, in fact. It involves great financial costs, too, whether they are borne by the private companies or by the taxpayers.

What about the breeder reactor, which uses Uranium-235 and turns it into *more* useable fuel, in the form of Plutonium-239, than it starts out with? President Carter has halted the breeder reactor program because of the overwhelming problems involved. Plutonium-239 can rather readily be turned into a devastating bomb, and the dangers of terrorists getting their hands on this dangerous

---

[44]See Commoner, *The Poverty of Power*, pp. 80–120.

raw material in a breeder reactor society would grow increasingly great. Breeder reactors would have to operate at such great heat levels that the dangers of terrible explosions would be very high. The Soviets suffered such an explosion in 1974. For the foreseeable future, the costs involved with breeder reactors will be prohibitive when compared to the useful value of the energy they might produce.

Environmentalists have suggested using a number of "clean" and renewable alternative energy sources. Burning organic wastes from garbage to produce energy in the form of heat is now being tried in a number of places. This is an especially attractive idea because it would "kill two birds with one stone": get rid of some solid wastes while producing needed energy.

In June 1979 President Carter presided as the newly installed solar panels on the West Wing of the White House were put into operation. The panels will use the sun's energy to heat water for the building. Though Carter expressed the hope that solar energy will provide 20% of the nation's energy needs by the year 2000, critics argue that it could provide much more, much sooner, if the proper incentives were available from the federal government.

Harnessing the power of the tides and the wind is the object of new federal interest. Tidal power would provide only a fraction of our power needs, but in particular locations it could be developed in relatively large units.[45] Significant amounts of electricity could be generated by wind power in many areas of the United States.[46] Geothermal power—power produced from natural underground steam or from water pumped down into "hot rock" formations—is not likely to produce more than 10 percent of our energy needs. In selected parts of the country and the world, however, it could be of major importance.[47]

Solar power has the greatest potential of all the renewable energy fuels. More than 20 percent of the energy use in America is for residential and commercial heating and cooling of space.[48] This could largely be done by the solar technology we already have for individual-unit use. Sometime in the future, the use of solar power for the central power station production of electricity could

[45]M. King Hubbert, "Tidal Power," in Ruedisili and Firebaugh, eds., *Perspectives on Energy*, p. 363.

[46]William E. Hieronemus, "Wind Power: A Near-Term Partial Solution to the Energy Crisis," in Ruedisili and Firebaugh, ed., *Perspectives on Energy*, p. 376.

[47]L. J. P. Muffler and D. E. White, "Geothermal Power," in Ruedisili and Firebaugh, eds., *Perspectives on Energy*, p. 358.

[48]Robert G. Sachs, "Our Energy Options—So What Else Is New?" in Eppen, ed., *Energy: The Policy Issues*, p. 10.

become commercially feasible. Barry Commoner thinks we have time before our oil runs out to develop this technology, and he criticizes present federal policy for putting more research money into nuclear power than into solar power.[49] Solar power is, of course, nonpolluting and renewable (at least for billions of years). Its use does not raise the heat on our globe. In recent years, home use of solar power has been increasing, and some government incentives have been provided. Environmentalists have faulted federal subsidization of solar research, however, for favoring large corporations, such as General Electric, rather than smaller, independent organizations.

CONCLUSION

Energy and environmental issues illustrate once again that political problems and the formulation and implementation of policy cannot exist in a separate, pure state, independent of politics. Governments and the political process are not neutral. Public participation at each stage in the policy process—or the lack of public participation, leaving the field to the special interests—can have important repercussions on the way that political agendas are made up, issues are defined, and policies are formulated and implemented. The policy process in regard to environmental and energy issues, as well as other issues, is a continuing one in America.

ADDITIONAL SOURCES

Blair, John. *The Control of Oil.* Pantheon, 1977.
Carson, Rachel. *Silent Spring.* Houghton, Mifflin, 1962.*
Commoner, Barry. *Closing Circle.* Bantam, 1972.*
_____. *The Politics of Energy.* Knopf, 1979.
_____. *The Poverty of Power.* Knopf, 1976.*
Harrington, Michael. *The Twilight of Capitalism* (esp. Chapter 10: "The Common Good as Private Property"). Simon and Schuster, 1976.*
Meadows, Donna, et al. *Limits to Growth: A Report for the Club of Rome's Project on the Predicament of Mankind.* Universe, 1974.*
Schneider, Stephen A. "Common Sense About Energy, Part I—Where Has All the Oil Gone?"; Part II—Less Is More: Conservation and Renewable Energy." *Working Papers for a New Society,* January/February 1978 and March/April 1978.
Stobaugh, Robert, and Daniel Yergin, eds. *Energy Future: Managing and Mismanaging the Transition.* Random House/Harvard Business School, 1979.
Udall, Stuart. *The Quiet Crisis.* Avon, 1964.*
*Available in paperback.

---

[49]See Commoner, *The Poverty of Power,* pp. 121–54.

19 Taxation, Spending, and Economic Policies

In February 1979, when state governors met in Washington, D.C., for one of their regular conferences, the main topic of conversation was a proposal by California's Governor Jerry Brown. He urged the governors' conference to go on record in favor of calling a national constitutional convention to propose an amendment requiring a balanced federal budget. Some observers said that Brown had become a "born-again" fiscal conservative only after the voters of his state had adopted Proposition 13, which reduced property taxes in California. It was also widely believed that Brown had seized upon the idea of a budget-balancing amendment as a way of gaining support for his candidacy against President Carter in 1980.

California Governor Jerry Brown at a news conference with Howard Jarvis, leader of the Proposition 13 campaign to cut the state's property tax rates. Following the success of Proposition 13, Brown and others began promoting the idea of a constitutional amendment to require a balanced federal budget.

Just prior to the 1979 Governor's Conference, Iowa had become the twenty-eighth state (of a required thirty-four) to pass a legislative resolution calling for such a constitutional convention. Yet Iowa's Governor Robert Ray stated that he had misgivings about the idea. Governor James Hunt of North Carolina also expressed reservations about calling a constitutional convention. The two governors reflected the views of a number of political figures, including President Carter, who felt that a convention called by Congress at the request of two thirds of the states—a procedure that had never been used for amending America's Constitution—might refuse to limit itself to the topic stated in the call. Instead, they feared, it might propose amendments to other parts of the Constitution or might even attempt to revise the entire Constitution.

Both Governor Ray, a Republican, and Governor Hunt, a Democrat, did call for a reduction in federal spending. They stated that Congress should bring the federal budget into balance, eliminating deficit financing—that is, the borrowing required to finance federal budgets when expenditures exceed revenues. But when Governors Ray and Hunt were asked by a CBS-TV interviewer whether they thought it would be appropriate for Congress to eliminate federal revenue-sharing—a program under which state governments receive federal funds—they both expressed opposition to this particular method of balancing the federal budget.[1] And therein lies one of the great problems that face those who would reduce federal spending. Many people are for a reduction in government spending—and the elimination of federal deficits—as long as the cuts will not affect them.

One objection to a *constitutional* amendment requiring the federal government's budget to always be balanced is that so many broad exceptions would have to be written into the proposed amendment that it would be virtually meaningless. When national security required deficit financing, for example, or when a balanced budget would cause too much of a national economic slowdown and too much unemployment, exceptions would have to be made. Another objection is that a balanced budget requirement would put a straitjacket on federal economic policy-makers, denying them the flexibility necessary to treat national economic problems in whatever way circumstances require at a given time.

Regardless of the merits or demerits of the constitutional amendment approach, Governors Brown, Ray, and Hunt were not alone in advocating a reduced federal budget. In 1979, President Carter himself recommended what he called a "lean and austere" federal budget, requiring fiscal belt tightening.[2] Many liberals opposed this emphasis on federal austerity in 1979. Many others questioned the President's priorities; they wondered how he could recommend an increase in federal defense spending, for example, while attempting to put a lid on spending for so-called human needs, such as health, housing, and employment. But few people questioned the vital importance of the federal government's regulation of the national economy and the effect of federal action on the country's inflation and unemployment rates. This central economic federal role is a far cry from what was expected of the national government during the first decades of the Republic.

---

[1] Interview on "Monday Morning," CBS-TV (February 26, 1979).
[2] *Time* (January 29, 1979), p. 30.

THE GOVERNMENT'S ROLE IN THE ECONOMY

America's economic system has always been based upon *capitalism*. In this system, the means of production are privately owned by individuals and corporations, rather than publicly owned by the government or some governmental unit. Thus, in both the Fifth Amendment, which is a part of the Bill of Rights, and the Fourteenth Amendment, the Constitution speaks of the right to life, liberty, and *property*. Individuals and privately owned corporations in America may own land and other natural resources, factories, and businesses.

In addition to the capitalist idea of private ownership of the means of production, America's beginning economic system was based upon the concept of *free enterprise*, or competitive capitalism—that is, the right of people to start or invest in whatever business or other enterprise they please, and the right of workers to move from job to job as they please (with the glaring exception of slaves and indentured servants, of course), without government interference.

"Laissez-faire," a French phrase meaning roughly, "leave things alone," characterized our early government's economic policy. The bible of this free-enterprise philosophy was the *Wealth of Nations*, written in 1776 by a Scot, Adam Smith.[3] Smith declared that if left alone, the "invisible hand" of competitive self-interest—the "uniform, constant, and uninterrupted effort of every man to better his own condition"—would improve society in general and the lives of each individual in particular.[4] This philosophy was so heretical that it represented economic sacrilege in eighteenth-century England, where business people and industrialists were accustomed to the government's *protection* of their enterprises from competition.[5] Even today, some business people in America profess to believe in the type of free competition espoused by Adam Smith, while demanding government subsidies and protection against the competitive pressures of free enterprise.

The classic laissez-faire period in American economic history ended in 1887, when Congress passed an act establishing the Interstate Commerce Commission (ICC). The ICC was created to regulate the railroads, which at that time had a virtual monopoly in transportation. This new law and the Sherman Antitrust Act of 1890 were based upon the realization that not only could government *action* preserve monopolies, but government *inaction* could, too. These and other federal laws passed in the early years of the twentieth century, particularly during President Theodore Roosevelt's administration, launched the federal government upon an

---

[3] Adam Smith, *The Wealth of Nations* (New York: Random House, Modern Library, 1937).

[4] Smith, *The Wealth of Nations*, p. 326.

[5] See Robert Lekachman, *Economists at Bay* (New York: McGraw-Hill, 1976), pp. 209–15.

effort to prevent the abuses that resulted from the unrestricted power of American business and industry in a wholly free-enterprise economy.

Then came the Great Depression of the 1930s. It produced unprecedented economic problems in America: intolerably high unemployment, increased millions of extremely poor people, idle businesses and factories, surplus productive capacity in farming, failing banks, and stagnated foreign trade. During his famous first "hundred days," in office in 1933, President Franklin Roosevelt recommended a rush of federal legislation and other action to meet these problems and also to protect working people from exploitation.

Roosevelt's policies did not, of course, go so far as to embrace the socialism that Karl Marx, a German, had advocated in his book, *Das Kapital* (1867), and in other writings.[6] Like Adam Smith, Marx was a humanist, but his idea about how to improve the human condition was radically different from Smith's. Marx advocated the abolition of private property and the establishment of an economic system based upon public ownership of the means of production. He believed that capitalism led naturally to monopolies in industries and had within itself the seeds of its own destruction. Capitalist abuses, he wrote, would make it a virtual "scientific" inevitability that revolution would eventually destroy capitalism and replace it with socialism:

Along with the constantly diminishing number of the magnates of capital . . . grows the mass of misery, oppression, slavery, degradation, exploitation; but with this too grows the revolt of the working class always increasing in number, and disciplined, united, organized by the very mechanism of the process of capitalist production itself. The monopoly of capital becomes a fetter upon the mode of production, which has sprung up and flourished along with it and under it. Centralisation of the means of production and socialisation of labour at last reach a point where they become incompatible with their capitalist integument. This integument is burst asunder. The knell of capitalist private property sounds. The expropriators are expropriated.[7]

Although President Franklin Roosevelt did not believe that the means of production should be socialized in America, he did support the creation of the Tennessee Valley Authority (TVA), a federal enterprise (still in existence today) established to generate and transmit electricity and improve living conditions in its service area. Today, the publicly owned Corporation for Public Broadcasting, like TVA, competes with private enterprises and furnishes a "yardstick" to measure the performance of the private broadcasting companies. In North Dakota, there is a state-owned bank. The electricity distribution systems in some American cities are owned by city

---

[6]See Karl Marx, *Capital* (New York: Random House/Modern Library).
[7]Marx, *Capital*, pp. 836–37.

governments. There are also a number of electricity, food, and other kinds of cooperatives throughout the country that are owned by the people they serve. But the Marxist idea of public ownership of the means of production has not proved to be an inevitable and widespread force in America.

America, however, does not have a wholly free-enterprise economy, either. It is, instead, a *mixed economy*. Although most property and the means of production are owned by individuals and private corporations, the government is deeply involved in controlling and regulating how private property may be used and how private enterprises may be allowed to function.

Franklin Roosevelt, then, did not seek to replace capitalism. He sought to reform and regulate it. Especially since Roosevelt's time, the federal government has assumed an accepted role as a regulatory police officer, protecting consumers and workers against the abuses of business and industry. The 1970s saw additional governmental regulation of business and industry to protect the environmental rights of citizens.

Franklin Roosevelt's administration also recognized the federal government's responsibility to find jobs for idle workers, even if it meant putting them to work in government jobs, providing federal funds to pay workers to build community buildings and other public improvements and to replant forests. It was not until 1946, however, that this responsibility was specifically stated in legislation. In that year, Congress passed the Employment Act,[8] committing the federal government to three basic goals: promoting maximum employment, maximum production, and economic stability. The Act also established the President's Council of Economic Advisers, required a regular economic report from the President, and established the Joint Economic Committee in Congress to receive and study the President's economic report. Since 1946, both liberals and conservatives in America have more or less agreed that the federal government cannot ignore unemployment. In addition, they recognize that the government must act to hold down the rate of inflation—that is, the rate of increase in the price of goods and services in the country.

The Employment Act of 1946 and related government actions since then are largely based upon the earlier writings of an Englishman, John Maynard Keynes. In *The General Theory of Employment, Interest, and Money* (1936),[9] Keynes argued that unemployment resulted from inadequate spending by consumers, investors, and government. His remedy, then, for unemployment was greater spending; if necessary, he declared, in effect, government should tax the rich in order to provide jobs for the poor. Since 1946, the federal government has continued to practice some version of Keynesian

---

[8]See Stephen K. Bailey, *Congress Makes a Law* (New York: Columbia University Press, 1950).

[9]John Maynard Keynes, *The General Theory of Employment, Interest and Money* (New York: Harcourt Brace Jovanovich, 1936).

economics. This calls for greater consumer, investor, and government spending during periods when some factories and workers are idle. The government itself may spend more money in such times. It may also cut taxes, leaving more money in the hands of taxpayers and thus increasing their spending for consumer goods and investment purposes. Or, it may do both.

As practiced in the United States since 1946, Keynesian economics also means that government should act in times of excessive spending, especially when too much consumer money is chasing too few goods, producing "demand-pull" inflation. Keynesians maintain that in such times governments should act to reduce total spending. This can be done by raising taxes, thus taking money out of the hands of consumers and investors, or by reducing government spending, or both.

This use of governmental taxing and spending powers is called *fiscal policy*. It may involve taxing less or spending more, or both, to stimulate the economy and decrease unemployment. It may also mean taxing more or spending less, or both, to dampen the economy and hold down the rate of inflation. The government's fiscal policy is contained in the federal budget.

THE BUDGETARY PROCESS

Some issues get on the official agenda automatically. Issues that revolve around the federal budget are a good example. Every year, the President of the United States must propose a federal budget for the next "fiscal year," which begins on October 1 and ends on September 30 of the following year.

The President's responsibility for proposing the federal budget stems from the Budget and Accounting Act, passed by Congress in 1921. Surprisingly, the President played no direct role in the preparation of the budget before the law was passed. Instead, the Secretary of the Treasury prepared it. A further increase in the President's role in the budgetary process occurred in 1939 with passage of the Executive Reorganization Act. It created the Executive Office of the President and transferred the Bureau of the Budget from the Treasury Department to this new office. As a result of a Nixon reorganization plan in 1970, the duties of the budget bureau were expanded and its name was changed to the Office of Management and Budget (OMB). The President appoints the director of OMB (by and with the advice and consent of the Senate).

Preparation of the proposed budget begins more than a year before it is presented to Congress. The Council of Economic Advisers provides the President (and OMB) with estimates of national income and productivity and projections concerning unemployment and inflation. With these estimates and projections as background, OMB considers budget requests from the various federal agencies and

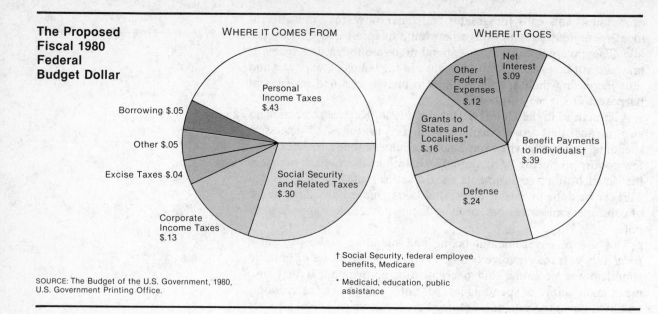

The Proposed Fiscal 1980 Federal Budget Dollar

WHERE IT COMES FROM

Personal Income Taxes $.43

Social Security and Related Taxes $.30

Corporate Income Taxes $.13

Excise Taxes $.04

Other $.05

Borrowing $.05

WHERE IT GOES

Other Federal Expenses $.12

Net Interest $.09

Grants to States and Localities* $.16

Benefit Payments to Individuals† $.39

Defense $.24

† Social Security, federal employee benefits, Medicare

* Medicaid, education, public assistance

SOURCE: The Budget of the U.S. Government, 1980, U.S. Government Printing Office.

departments. The President then approves the finished product. The entire process is incremental; budget-makers use the preceding year's budget as a base of reference, rather than beginning from the ground up each year.[10]

When the President approves the final budget proposals, he presents them to Congress. In January 1979, for example, President Carter presented his budget for Fiscal 1980, with proposed spending of $531.6 billion. The budget projected a deficit of $29 billion for the fiscal year.

The President's proposals not only recommend overall federal spending expenditures; they also propose total taxes and thus the overall deficit or surplus. The bare dollar figures in the proposed federal budget represent fundamental and highly important national policy decisions. The expenditure side of the budget tells "who gets what"; it may recommend increased expenditures for some government programs or services and, possibly, reductions for others. The tax side of the budget tells "who pays the costs." The President's budget proposal also represents an assessment of the budget's impact on the national economy, especially on the unemployment and inflation rates.

All of these priorities and assessments are highly political in nature. So it should not be surprising to learn that the budgetary process does not end with the President's presentation of his

---

[10]Except as otherwise indicated, material in regard to the federal budget is taken from Thomas R. Dye, *Understanding Public Policy*, 2nd ed. (Englewood Cliffs, N.J.: Prentice-Hall, 1975), pp. 217–41.

proposed budget to Congress. An old saying in Washington—"The President proposes, but the Congress disposes"—is as true for the budget as it is for other legislative proposals made by the chief executive.

However, the President has an advantage over Congress in putting together the overall federal budget. Through OMB, the President is able to make more *comprehensive* decisions about total federal revenues, expenditures, borrowing, expenditure priorities, and the impact of the proposed budget on the national economy. The President has the advantage of being able to speak with one voice for the entire executive department. Congress, on the other hand, speaks with many voices because its budgetary authority is so fragmented.

The most obvious fragmentation of authority in Congress is the division of power between its two chambers: the House of Representatives and the Senate. But there is additional fragmentation, too. Within each house, much of the decision-making power in regard to the federal budget, as with other congressional decisions, is exercised by numerous standing committees. Committees with jurisdiction over taxes—the Finance Committee in the Senate and the Ways and Means Committee in the House—are separate from the appropriation committees in each body. Appropriations committees are themselves fragmented into subcommittees, which deal with separate federal agencies and programs.

No appropriation bill may be passed in either the House or the Senate until a separate "authorization bill" has been voted through. Substantive standing committees, not appropriations committees or subcommittees, have jurisdiction over these authorization bills. For example, before Congress can pass an appropriation bill to provide money for the U.S. Corps of Engineers to build new dams, it must first pass an authorization bill, based upon a report by the committee in each house that has jurisdiction over such public works. An authorization bill sets the upward limits for expenditures and the terms governing them. Thereafter, appropriations bills must conform to these limits, and the money appropriated must not be more (but may be less) than the amount authorized.

With the passage of the Congressional Budget Act of 1974, Congress sought to pull together the various elements of its fragmented budget power. The Act created new budget committees in both the House and Senate. It also set up the Congressional Budget Office, which seeks to unify the congressional budget effort and to assess the President's recommended budget with some semblance of the more comprehensive approach used by the Office of Management and Budget.

Under the Budget Act, Congress adopts a *tentative* federal budget in May of each year through votes in both houses. It sets forth projections for total revenues, expenditures, and for the federal surplus or deficit. Then, in September of each year, Congress adopts the *final* budget. Tax measures and appropriations bills that are

The Congressional Budget Timetable

On or Before:	Action to be completed:
15th day after Congress convenes	President transmits his budget proposals to Congress
March 15	Committees submit budget-estimate reports to Budget Committees
April 1	Congressional Budget Office submits its fiscal policy report to Budget Committees
April 15	Budget Committees report first concurrent resolution, setting budget targets, to their Houses
May 15	Committees report bills providing new budget authority
	Congress completes action on first concurrent resolution, setting budget targets
7th day after Labor Day	Congress completes action on bills providing budget authority
September 15	Congress completes action on second concurrent resolution, setting budget ceilings
September 25	Congress completes action on reconciliation bill or resolution, or both, implementing second concurrent resolution
October 1	New fiscal year begins

thereafter agreed to by Congress must conform to this final budget. Thus, the Congressional Budget Act of 1974 has given Congress its first opportunity to take an overall look at federal taxes and spending and their effect on the economy. (As noted in an earlier chapter, the act also limits the President's power to "impound"—that is, to refuse to spend—appropriations approved by Congress.)

After appropriations are made, the various committees of Congress exercise "oversight" on federal spending. Congressional committees call federal agencies and departments to account. In addition, the General Accounting Office, an arm of Congress, audits executive agencies and departments to attempt to ensure that money appropriated by Congress is spent wisely and in accordance with the law.

THE FEDERAL BUDGET AND FISCAL POLICY

The lines, ". . . late and soon/Getting and spending," from one of Wordsworth's well-known poems could very well apply to the federal government or any unit of government. Who the government takes money from and who it gives money (or benefits) back to, and for what purpose, could almost be said to describe the very essence of government.

Spending

Federal spending has a threefold effect on Americans and the national economy. First, the *fiscal effect* causes unemployment and inflationary pressures on prices to rise or decline as a result of more or less federal spending. Second, there is the *regulatory effect* of spending. For example, the federal government grants subsidies to local and regional airlines for beginning and continuing service to cities that might not otherwise be served. And the Department of Agriculture has long granted various cash and loan subsidies to farmers who comply with governmental regulations aimed at holding down agricultural production of certain items such as cotton. Third, there is the *distributional effect*; that is, spending can redistribute wealth from one group to another. Most of us tend to think that this distribution is from the more wealthy to the poor. Indeed, that is the object of such social welfare programs as Medicaid, welfare assistance, the food stamp program, and public housing. But an enormous amount of redistribution also goes from the working class in America to the more wealthy by means of federal subsidies. For example, a minute percentage of Americans own their own airplanes; yet the small number who do receive the benefit of hundreds of millions of dollars in federal subsidies in the form of free traffic control, weather reporting systems, and airport construction, instead of having to pay the full costs of these special benefits. In addition, more than three fourths of the costs of flights by privately owned airplanes are deducted as business expenses for tax purposes.

In 1972, the Joint Economic Committee of Congress, under the direction of U.S. Senator William Proxmire of Wisconsin, began the first study *ever* done on federal subsidies. This study showed that federal subsidies amounted to $63 billion—not counting welfare, Social Security, or even the subsidizing effect for industry of "protective" federal regulation, licensing, and import quotas.[11]

How the government spends our money may have great impact on the economy, and spending may also produce dramatic results regarding the distribution of wealth and income in America.

Taxes

Taxes, like spending, can have three important effects. The *fiscal effect* may increase or decrease unemployment or inflation as money is taken out of the hands of consumers and investors, or left in their hands for consumption and investment. The *distributional effect* results from tax decisions about "who will pay the costs."[12] The *regulatory effect* of taxes may either seek to discourage or promote certain activity. A new tax on "gas-guzzling" automobiles, for example, seeks to discourage consumers from purchasing them in order to hold down gasoline use. On the other hand, special tax incentives, such as the one to encourage better home insulation, have

---

[11]Joint Economic Committee of the Congress, *Economics of Federal Subsidy Programs*, Parts 1–6 (Washington, D.C.: Government Printing Office, 1972).

[12]Except as otherwise indicated, material in regard to federal tax policy is taken from Joseph A. Pechman, "Federal Tax Policy," in John E. Elliott and Arthur Grey, *Economic Issues and Policies*, 3rd ed. (Boston: Houghton Mifflin Company, 1975), pp. 290–95.

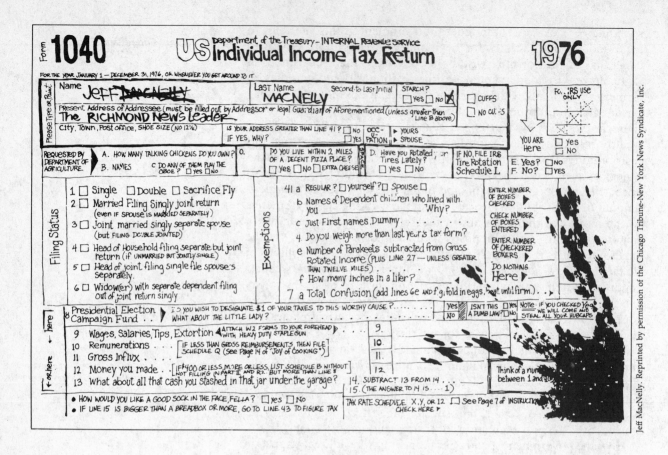

also been enacted. So, while taxes have the primary purpose of raising money to finance the operations, programs, and services of government, they are also sometimes used for other purposes as well.

How high are federal taxes? Not as high as taxes in many foreign countries. Among countries comparable to the United States, only the citizens of Switzerland and Japan pay lower taxes than American citizens pay to their federal government. Citizens of Holland, Sweden, France, Great Britain, West Germany, Canada, and Italy all pay more.[13] And taxes in America are not as high as they once were. Federal income taxes were lowered in 1961, 1964, 1969, 1971, and 1975. These tax cuts reduced annual federal income tax collections by $70 billion.[14]

Despite the favorable comparison of American's tax burden with those of most comparable foreign countries, and despite recent federal income tax reductions, America has experienced a near

---

[13]Robert Lekachman, "Distribution Wars," *The New Republic* (July 29, 1978), pp. 15–18.

[14]Lekachman, *Economists at Bay*, p. 90.

"taxpayers' revolt" in recent years. Aside from the fact that hardly any American citizen derives pleasure from paying any taxes, there are three main reasons for the growing dissatisfaction of American citizens with our tax system.

First, economic growth in the United States has slowed in recent years, while inflation has increased and oil-producing foreign countries have skimmed off much of America's economic growth potential through higher crude oil prices. Thus, after taking inflation into account, the real income of most Americans outside the South has remained stagnant for almost all of the last ten years.[15]

A second principal reason for dissatisfaction with government taxes is that the total tax bite in America involves considerable recent increases in social insurance, local, and state taxes. These taxes are largely "regressive"; they take a larger share of the income of low-income groups than they do from high-income groups. A "progressive" tax, on the other hand, takes a larger percentage of the income of high-income groups than it does from low-income groups. A progressive tax, in other words, is supposed to be based upon the ability to pay. Whether a tax is progressive or regressive, then, depends upon what *percentage* of income the tax takes from various income groups.

The federal income tax was designed to be a progressive tax, with higher rates for those in higher income brackets. That is generally not true of federal *excise taxes*—on liquor, tobacco, gasoline, telephones, and air travel—which account for about 5 percent of federal tax collections.

Of much greater regressive impact are *social insurance taxes*, which fund Social Security and Medicare, because they take such a large bite out of the paychecks of most Americans. These taxes are regressive because they are not based upon the ability to pay. Yet, they constitute 28 percent of all federal tax collections. In 1980, employee paychecks were subject to a 6.13 percent deduction for social insurance purposes. This flat rate was the same for all income brackets, regardless of how much money an employee made, because Social Security (or, more accurately, social insurance) taxes are not graduated like federal income taxes, which levy higher rates on higher earnings. As a matter of fact, maximum earnings subject to Social Security taxes in 1980 were $25,000. If a person made more than that amount in wages or salary, the extra earnings were not taxable for this purpose. The maximum taxable earnings figure was to increase to $29,700 in 1981; the rate of the tax on employee earnings was scheduled to increase in the same year to 6.65 percent. The rate is scheduled to rise in stages until it reaches a level of 7.65 percent in 1990. So, while federal income taxes have actually declined in recent years, the regressive Social Security taxes have been steadily increasing, and these increases have been especially felt by working-

---

[15]Lekachman, "Distribution Wars," p. 16.

class Americans. "These ducks (deducts) are nibbling us to death!" one worker was quoted as saying in a humorous story.

The portion of the federal budget dollar that comes from individual income taxes has dropped from 41 percent in 1964 to 38 percent in 1979. More dramatically, the percentage of the federal budget that comes from corporate income taxes decreased from 20 percent in 1964 to 13 percent in 1979. On the other hand, during this same period, there was a dramatic increase in the percentage of the federal budget that comes from social insurance taxes: it rose sharply from 18 percent in 1964 to 28 percent in 1979.[16] The original idea of Social Security was that it was an insurance system. Through deductions from their checks, wage earners pay into the system, much as they might purchase an annuity insurance policy to provide for their old-age retirement. They then collect a pension when they reach age sixty-five or become disabled. While an equal contribution is collected from employees and employers to fund this system, most economists believe that both the employee's and the employer's contributions are actually paid, directly or indirectly, by the employee, since the employer's contribution is taken into account in decisions about wage increases.

In a sense, then, this system pits wage earners against old people. It was originally sold to wage earners as a way to provide for their old-age days and also relieve them from financial responsibility for their parents, at a time when they were struggling to pay their own living expenses and those of their families. As the life expectancy of Americans has increased over the years, the cost of providing benefits for retirees has also risen. In addition, Congress has steadily increased Social Security benefits in an attempt to keep up with rising costs of living for retirees. Congress has also added benefits such as Medicare, a system of health insurance for older Americans, which is paid from social insurance taxes and from direct contributions by the beneficiaries. For all of these reasons, social insurance taxes have increased sharply in recent years, giving rise to demands for reform in the way Social Security and related programs are financed. The most widely supported reform calls for the federal government to pay the increased portion of Social Security and related benefits from its general revenues, which are largely collected from the more progressive federal income tax. To date, however, Congress has clung to the notion that the Social Security system ought to be funded from insurance-like payments alone, and the idea of funding a portion of social insurance benefits from general revenue has been rejected.

Regressive state and local taxes have also taken a large bite out of the incomes of most Americans. While two thirds of the states have some kind of state income tax, most states rely heavily on *sales taxes*, which are not based upon the ability to pay. Some states exclude certain necessities, such as food and medicine, from the sales tax, but

---

[16]See Congressional Quarterly, *Weekly Report* (January 28, 1978), p. 158.

in most states, the sales tax still takes a larger percentage of the incomes of working-class and low-income citizens than it does from high-income citizens.

Most Americans are hit particularly hard by local *property taxes*, which are also regressive. Even renters are affected by the property tax, since landlords may pass these taxes on in the form of higher rents. Proposition 13 in California was the result of a revolt against higher property taxes. Its adoption by a vote of the people required a property tax reduction throughout the state.

A third reason for taxpayer dissatisfaction in America is that most Americans are aware of "loopholes" in the federal income tax system, which give special breaks to people and corporations in high-income brackets.

The federal government levies a number of different taxes. In addition to excise, social insurance, and corporate and individual taxes, the federal government also collects estate and gift taxes, customs duties, and tariffs. The theory behind *estate and gift taxes* is that they should reduce

California homeowners carry signs indicating the large increases in property taxes that contributed to the overwhelming response by voters to the Proposition 13 initiative.

the unequal distribution of wealth by collecting a percentage of estates or gifts. But there are a number of ways to avoid these taxes, and they have had very little effect on the distribution of wealth.

Tariffs and customs duties were responsible for a large portion of federal tax collections during the early years of the U.S. government. Today, this is no longer true, but they have been used from time to time for regulatory effect. That is, they have been employed to increase the cost of imported goods, thus making them less competitive with goods manufactured in the United States.

Corporate and individual income taxes are today the most important sources of federal revenue. To pay for the high costs of the Civil War, Congress first enacted a federal income tax in 1861.[17] The tax was not questioned in the courts before it expired in 1873. Congress next enacted an income tax in 1894, but the Supreme Court declared this tax unconstitutional. The Court held that the income tax was a direct tax and therefore could not be levied unless it was apportioned

---

[17]See Joseph J. Klein, *Federal Income Taxation* (N.Y.: Wiley).

*"Other folks have to pay taxes, too, Mr. Herndon,
so would you please spare us the dramatics!"*

among the states on the basis of their population.[18] In 1913, the states ratified the Sixteenth Amendment to the U.S. Constitution. It gave the federal government the power, through Congress, "to lay and collect taxes on income, from whatever source derived, without apportionment among the several states, and without regard to any census or enumeration." The modern income tax was born.

Almost from the beginning, loopholes existed in the federal income tax. Consider the special tax treatment of "capital gains," for example. A capital gain is the difference between the purchase price and the sale price of property, if the sale price is higher. The property involved may be real estate, corporate stock, a horse or other animal, or other personal property, such as a truck. This type of income, when the property has been held a year or more, is taxed at only 40 percent of the rate that applies to ordinary earned income. Suppose one person makes a living by working on an automobile assembly line in Detroit, making Ford cars, and another makes a living by buying Ford Motor Company stock at a lower price and selling it at a higher price. If both make $20,000 a year, the person who makes Ford cars will pay a considerably higher federal income tax than the person who buys and sells Ford stock. Many people find it objectionable, particularly in a "work ethic" society, that "money earned from work" is taxed more than "money earned from money."

Consider another example: "municipal bonds." State governments and agencies and local governments, such as cities and school boards, issue municipal bonds when they borrow money. These bonds are usually sold to finance capital improvements, such as buildings or water and sewer systems. Individual and corporate investors, such as

---

[18]*Pollack* v. *Farmers' Loan and Trust Company*, 158 U.S. 601 (1895).

banks, buy municipal bonds in order to earn the interest income that is paid on these bonds by the issuing authority. Investors are particularly attracted to municipal bonds because the interest income on them is *totally* exempt from federal income taxes. The idea behind this exemption is to help create a stable and low-interest market for municipal bonds, assisting state and local governments and their agencies to finance their capital needs. For those individuals and corporations with the necessary money to invest (and most bonds cost $5,000 or more), it is possible to receive a considerable amount of income and pay *no* federal income tax on it whatsoever.

From these two examples—the special treatment of capital gains and the tax exemption for municipal bonds—two main points will probably occur to you. First, if you have money, the tax laws help you to make more money. These special tax provisions, or loopholes, are not available to those who do not have money to invest. Second, and not so apparent, is the fact that these special tax provisions are actually "tax expenditures." That is, they have the same effect on the federal treasury as if the taxes were first collected and then paid back to particular citizens, depending upon their behavior (whether they invest in property or in municipal bonds, for example).

When Jimmy Carter was a candidate for President in 1976, he called the federal income tax system and its loopholes "a disgrace to the human race," and he promised to recommend a fundamental reform. He particularly criticized the loophole which allows a deduction for business entertainment, saying that it was especially unfair. He pointed out that it permitted a business executive to deduct the cost of a "three-martini lunch" but did not allow any deduction for a blue-collar worker's bologna sandwich.

Once in office, President Carter apparently yielded to advice and pressure that favored business people and others in higher-income brackets. The tax "reform" package he recommended to Congress was considerably less fundamental and sweeping than his campaign speeches had proposed. And he did not put nearly as much pressure on Congress to pass even these limited reforms as the White House had done for passage of the President's "energy package" or for ratification of the Panama Canal Treaty, for example.

In Congress, tax legislation falls within the jurisdiction of the House Ways and Means Committee and the Senate Finance Committee. Until recently, the committee "mark-up" sessions—when members actually decide upon the finished version of the tax bill, which is recommended to the full body—were held behind closed doors. The public and the press were excluded. The wave of reforms that brought about open meetings throughout the federal government produced open mark-up sessions in these tax-writing committees as well. However, the members of these committees have still shown a considerable degree of favoritism for special-interest groups. And since tax bills, like income tax reforms, are highly complicated, special-interest lobbyists and friendly members of Congress generally know more about them than do the taxpayers, who often do not learn what new tax laws have been passed until well after the fact. So, each new tax "reform" bill frequently has new loopholes for the special interests. For example, the 1978 "tax-reform" bill passed by Congress *lowered* the federal income tax on capital gains. New tax breaks for business and for higher-income taxpayers in 1978 caused U.S. Senator Edward M. Kennedy of Massachusetts to call that tax bill the worst example of special-interest legislation that Congress had passed since President Calvin Coolidge's administration.

Thus, what is sometimes called "tax reform" may turn out to be "tax relief" for those who need it least. California's Proposition 13, for example, did not only lower property taxes for California homeowners, but also greatly reduced taxes for the more well-to-do owners of apartments and commercial real estate. The political process and government are not neutral. They are especially not neutral about "who pays the costs," or federal tax policy.

Borrowing

When federal expenditures exceed revenues, the federal government must borrow money and pay interest on it like any other borrower. Since 1968, there has been only one year—1969—when the federal government had a balanced budget and did not have to borrow additional money. By 1979, the national debt was more than $785 billion. The greatest amount of borrowing—and the biggest increases in the national debt—came during World War II, when the national debt rose by more than $200 billion. The federal government had borrowed $23 billion during World War I and about $13 billion during the depression years of the 1930s. The Vietnam War required borrowing, too, but not nearly as much as the slow-growth years between 1975 and 1980. During this last period, high inflation increased the costs of government, and slowed growth idled workers and plants, reducing the government's tax collections.

How worried should we be about the national debt? We should be concerned but not hysterical. Interest on the national debt was 7 percent of all federal expenditures in 1964; it had only increased to 8 percent in 1979.[19] Further, the national debt as a percentage of Gross National Product (GNP)—total goods and services produced in the country—has declined sharply since World War II. This is a point of fundamental importance in understanding the impact of the national debt.

The national debt limit is set by law, and Congress periodically raises it. If the limit were not raised, the federal government would not be able to pay its bills because it would be prohibited from borrowing money after it had been spent. So, in 1979, Congress raised the debt limit again. A few days later, a television critic went

---

[19]See Congressional Quarterly, *Weekly Report* (January 28, 1978), p. 158.

out on the streets of one American city and asked people what they thought about this action. The responses were predictable. "How can they keep on increasing the national debt all the time? It's got to stop somewhere, and we've got to settle up and get even with the board." Another person said, "My wife and I have to live within our means; we can't spend more than we take in, and the government should have to do so also." Someone else asked, "Why don't they run the government like a business and balance out expenses with income?"

As a matter of fact, the government *is* operated, in some ways, very much like a family or a business. Few families, and virtually no businesses, could get along without incurring debt. Rather than pay cash, a family with an income of $25,000 will borrow money to buy a car, a house, or a refrigerator. The basic question for the family is: Will our future income be sufficient to make the payments? That is the basic question for a government also.

When a family or an individual goes to the bank to borrow money to buy a car, the bank will require a "financial statement" setting forth what the borrower owns, the "assets," and what the borrower owes, the "liabilities." The bank will also want to know the borrower's regular income and expenses in order to assess the borrower's "ability to repay" the loan with interest.

Unlike a private borrower, though, the federal government usually lists only its liabilities—the national debt and interest—and not its assets. For example, no attempt is made to put a value on national parks and forests, military reservations, or government cars and limousines. And listing these assets is really not that important because the real security for loans to the federal government is the government's "ability to repay" the loan with interest. The government's ability to repay depends upon a sufficient amount of expected income, and this in turn depends upon tax collections resulting from the strength of the national economy and the goods and services turned out by the economy.

But should we not settle up sometime, get even with the board? We probably never will. But this is also true for most families and most American businesses. A family or an individual borrows money for thirty-six months to buy a new car, and at the end of that period or before, trades that car in and borrows money again for a new car. People also borrow money for twenty-five years to buy a house, and in ten years, say, they sell that house and take on a new mortgage for another twenty-five or thirty years in order to buy a new house, never getting out of debt. Similarly, American business corporations, such as American Telephone and Telegraph Company, have the same kind of rising debt as the federal government does; fortunately, it is matched by rising corporate revenues, its ability to repay.

Citizens should be concerned to see that borrowing does not outpace our economy's ability to grow enough to finance the debt. They should also be concerned to see that federal policies ensure economic health, with low percentages of idle workers and idle plants, so that earnings will stay high enough to ensure adequate federal tax collections. And citizens should be concerned to see that federal policies ensure tolerable rates of inflation, including reasonable increases in the interest rate that must be paid on the national debt.

In addition to fiscal policy—spending and tax policies, and borrowing—the federal government affects the national economy through its influence on the money supply, its *monetary policy*.

MONETARY POLICY

The amount of money in circulation at any time has much to do with the rate of interest that will be charged for lending money and with the amount of money it takes to buy things. What is money? *Money* is, first of all, coins and paper currency. This is called "fiat" money because it is based upon faith. This kind of U.S. money today is not redeemable in silver or gold but can only be exchanged for other coins and currency. Thus, the value of this money depends upon faith in the economic strength of the government, which backs it. The value of money also depends to some degree upon how much of it exists. Money is *somewhat*, but not altogether, like a commodity such as wheat. If there is a huge surplus of wheat one year, wheat will not "buy" as much money per bushel. If there is a great shortage of wheat in another year, a bushel of wheat will "buy" more money than in the year of the surplus. There is no such ratio that links the supply of money so directly with its value. No one doubts, however, that if money were in unlimited supply, it would have little value. Thus, governments—ours included—control the creation of money by law.

But money does not just consist of coins and currency. It also consists of demand deposits, or checking accounts, which can be withdrawn from banks by depositors at will. Coins, currency, and *demand* deposits together are called "M_1" by economists. Today, economists also increasingly consider *time* deposits in banks and savings and loan institutions, called "M_2," to be money. When we speak of "money," then, we must consider coins and currency, demand deposits, and time deposits, all of which serve to carry out the most important function of money: to serve as a medium of exchange, more convenient and reliable than trading or bartering goods.

The banking system and savings and loan institutions are allowed by law to create money as a result of what they do with the deposits they hold. If you save $500 from summer work and put it in a checking account in a local bank, the bank does not hold that same $500 until you ask for it in person or by checks drawn on the account. Instead, the bank is required only to keep about one-sixth or one-seventh of the amount of your deposit as "reserves"—in the form of till cash, deposits in other banks or with a Federal Reserve

Bank, or in government bonds. What does the bank do with the rest of your checking account money? It loans it out, charging interest. Banks, then, make a profit in two ways: by charging for checking services; and most important, by loaning money at interest. Checks drawn by you are deposited by their payees in other banks, which use the several deposit accounts to loan to borrowers, who make demand deposits in other banks. By the time your $500 has gone through the banking system, it has swelled to something like $3000 to $3500 in total money in circulation.

Since banks (and savings and loan institutions) never have enough money on hand to pay off all depositors at once, state and federal governments have passed laws to protect depositors. The banks must be chartered before they can go into operation—state banks by state authorities, federal banks by the Comptroller of the Currency. Their operations are continuously and closely audited and regulated by the chartering authorities. In addition, almost all state and federal banks have their deposits insured by the Federal Deposit Insurance Corporation for up to $40,000 per account. The Federal Savings and Loan Insurance Corporation performs the same function for savings and loan institutions. These insuring federal agencies also audit and regulate the insured banks and institutions.

To further protect the public interest in the way banks operate and to regulate the amount of money in circulation in the country at any one time, the U.S. Congress created the *Federal Reserve System* in 1913.[20] The Federal Reserve System—or the "Fed," as it is called—is run by a seven-member Board of Governors appointed by the President and subject to confirmation by the U.S. Senate. They serve for fixed, staggered terms of fourteen years. The President also names the chairperson of the Board of Governors, with Senate confirmation, for a term of four years. Because of their fixed terms and because they can only be removed for cause, neither the chairperson nor the members of the Board of Governors are subject to direct control by the President.

The Federal Reserve System operates through twelve regional Federal Reserve Banks (with branches), which are owned by the member commercial banks. All national banks must belong to the Federal Reserve System. A substantial percentage of state banks also voluntarily belong to it; since these federal and state member banks are among the largest in the country, together they account for more than three fourths of all bank deposits in the United States.

All countries have "central banks," which have regulatory power over the money supply in the country. But our central bank—the Fed—is unique because it is both privately owned and operates almost independently of immediate, day-to-day government control. By contrast, the Bank of England—that country's central bank—is

---

[20]See Michael D. Reagen, "The Political Structure of the Federal Reserve System," *American Political Science Review* (March 1961), pp. 64–76.

President Carter's major economic advisers: (top) Alfred Kahn, chairman of the Council on Wage and Price Stability (left), and George Schultze, chairman of the Council of Economic Advisers, enjoy a break from testifying before the House Ways and Means Committee; (bottom) Paul Volcker, chairman of the Federal Reserve Board (left), ponders a question during his confirmation hearings before the Senate Banking Committee; and Treasury Secretary G. William Miller.

government owned, and it must follow the monetary policy set by the British cabinet.

How does the Fed regulate the money supply? How does it make the money supply grow at a faster rate or more moderately? And what difference does it make? To answer the last question first, when there is faster growth in the total amount of money in circulation, consumers tend to buy more and businesses invest more, because interest rates are lower and credit is easier to get. This tends to stimulate spending, increasing the production of goods and services and reducing unemployment. Conversely, when growth in the money supply is slowed, consumers tend to spend less and businesses tend to invest less because interest rates are higher and credit is harder to get. Thus, tightening the money supply tends to slow down spending and reduce the rate of inflation—often at the expense of slowed production and higher unemployment. Looser monetary policy may stimulate spending, decreasing unemployment—often at the price of higher inflation.

The Fed affects growth in the money supply in three major ways. First, and most important, the Fed (through its "open market committee," made up of the seven-member Board of Governors and five representatives from district banks) may buy or sell the government bonds it owns and holds in its investment portfolio. Since these and other kinds of decisions by the Fed are made in secret, observers, economists, banks, and investors can only discern after the fact what the Fed has been doing.

When the Fed sells government bonds (mostly to dealers in bonds, who ultimately sell mostly to banks, insurance companies, and large business corporations), the purchasers pay by writing checks on their demand deposit accounts in their various banks, thereby reducing the amount of such deposits against which these banks may loan money. When the Fed sells government bonds on the open market, then, it contracts the total money supply.

On the other hand, when the Fed buys government bonds on the open market, the people who sell such bonds deposit the sale proceeds in their bank accounts, thereby increasing the amount of total deposits against which banks can make loans. This, in turn, expands the total money supply. The Fed's "open market" operation is its most important monetary tool.

Second, and next in importance, the Fed can expand the total money supply by raising or lowering the "discount rate" it charges member banks to borrow from it. Banks have to borrow money. One place they borrow money is from the Fed. If you, as a private citizen, went to a bank to borrow $100, you would agree to pay that amount back to the bank, with interest. Rather than keeping your note until it is due, the bank might decide to use it to borrow more money from the Fed—money which the bank could then loan out again. The Fed would not, of course, loan one hundred cents on the dollar for your note. Instead, it would require the note to be "discounted." That is, the Fed might only loan ninety or ninety-five cents on the dollar, say, to your bank on your note.

By raising or lowering this discount rate, the Fed can encourage or discourage borrowing by member banks, making such borrowing more or less attractive. When member banks are encouraged to borrow from the Fed, they will have more loan proceeds to loan out again, thus increasing the money supply. When they are discouraged from borrowing from the Fed, they will have less loan proceeds to loan out again—thereby restricting the total money supply.

The third and least used of the Fed's major monetary tools for affecting growth in the money supply is its power to change the "reserve requirements" for member banks. Banks are required to keep a certain amount of reserves on hand (through till cash, deposits in other banks, including the Fed, and government bonds) to back up their liability to pay demand deposits. In other words, by changing reserve requirements for member banks, the Fed may determine what portion of demand deposits a member bank can loan out. When the Fed raises reserve requirements, member banks can loan less. When the Fed lowers reserve requirements, member banks can loan more. More loans mean greater growth in the money supply. Fewer loans mean less growth in the money supply.

When the Federal Reserve System is moving to expand the money supply more rapidly, the interest rates that borrowers have to pay banks inch downward. When the Fed acts to slow growth in the money supply, interest rates tend to inch upward. The first signal of what is happening to interest rates generally comes when some of the largest banks in the country—such as Chase Manhattan or First National City, both in New York—announce an increase or decrease in their "prime rate." This is the rate of interest that banks charge their biggest and best borrowers. Ordinary borrowers usually pay 1½ percent more.

"Monetarists" believe that monetary policy is the only proper way to manage the economy. (The "Chicago school" of economics, led

Economists John Kenneth Galbraith (left) and Milton Friedman.

by Milton Friedman, is made up of monetarists who believe that the Fed should be held to a prescribed annual and automatic growth rate—about 4½ percent—in the money supply.)[21] Other economists, principally John Kenneth Galbraith, take the opposite view. He would put more emphasis on fiscal policy and on wage and price controls. He argues against reliance on monetary policy because he says that "tight money"—restricted monetary growth—and high interest rates do not have a predictable effect on the whole economy but do have a predictably discriminatory effect on the weakest borrowers:

Any active monetary policy operates by recurrent and discriminatory reduction in investment in the weakest part of the economic system. (The case of housing is especially dramatic.) It thus contributes directly to inequality in income and inequality in development. It thus intensifies the central and most painful faults of the modern economy. And, all but sadistically, it puts the pain on those least able to bear it.[22]

[21]See Milton Friedman, "The Role of Monetary Policy," *American Economic Review* (March 1968), pp. 12–17; and Milton Friedman and Anna J. Schwartz, *A Monetary History of the United States, 1867–1960* (Princeton, N.J.: Princeton University Press, 1963).

[22]John Kenneth Galbraith, *Economics and the Public Purpose* (Boston: Houghton Mifflin Company, 1973), p. 310.

Thus, Galbraith argues that restrictive monetary policy does not limit borrowing by the best and biggest borrowers but only affects the weakest.

Most American economists agree with economist Paul A. Samuelson, who believes that monetary policy matters a great deal. If the federal government is to manage the economy effectively and in the public interest, he says, it must use *both* monetary and fiscal policy.[23] But many liberals who acknowledge the importance of monetary policy criticize the way the largely independent Federal Reserve System is allowed to use it. While the Fed usually follows the monetary policy recommended by the President, it does not always do so. Congress sets the limits within which the Fed must operate, but, within these limits, the Fed has rather wide discretion. Thus, it is quite possible that while the President and the Congress were using fiscal policy to increase spending and decrease unemployment, the Fed might be using monetary policy to slow growth in the money supply and to bring down inflation and increase unemployment. Some suggested reforms in the Federal Reserve System include making the term of the chairperson of the Fed the same as the President's. Every President would then be able to appoint the person who would head the system during his term, thus increasing executive control over the Fed and bringing about greater coordination between fiscal and monetary policy. More fundamentally, the original Humphrey-Hawkins bill, introduced in the U.S. Congress by Representative Gus Hawkins of California and the late Senator Hubert Humphrey of Minnesota, provided for much more open and public decisions by the Fed. It also would have made the Fed more subservient to the monetary policy recommended by the President and enacted by Congress. This provision for greater executive and legislative control over monetary policy was stricken from the Humphrey-Hawkins bill before it was passed, in largely emasculated form, in 1978.

OTHER FEDERAL ECONOMIC MANAGEMENT TOOLS

In addition to fiscal and monetary policy, there are several ways that the federal government affects—or might affect—the national economy and therefore the inflation and unemployment rates. Economist John Kenneth Galbraith makes a strong case for greater planning and greater federal regulation of the economy, particularly through wage and price controls. He aruges that in strong unions and strong corporations, particularly in industries dominated by a few firms, wages and prices are set by "planning" rather than by the market. He

---

[23]See Paul A. Samuelson, *Readings in Economics,* 7th ed. (New York: McGraw-Hill, 1973).

goes on to state that this planning is private rather than public, leaving ordinary consumers unable to participate in the economic decisions that have great impact on their lives. In effect, he says, we cannot vote with our dollars in these "organized" segments of our economy because prices and wages are a result of private decisions. Therefore, Galbraith states, we should be able to vote, at least indirectly, with our *actual* votes by making these wage and price decisions public ones. Galbraith is for *permanent* wage and price controls, but only in situations where wages are set by collective bargaining and prices are set by noncompetitive companies.

> *This means that the decision no longer lies with the market and thus with the public, it lies with the planning system. Intervention by the government is not in a public process. Intervention is in a private decision that is in a pursuit of private goals. Government intervention, if it reflects the public cognizance, means public government instead of private government.*[24]

The federal government already attempts to regulate some prices. It does this through price supports for certain agricultural products, through price limits on such items as gasoline, through purchases and sales of government stockpiles such as metals needed for defense, and through regulatory bodies such as the Interstate Commerce Commission. Congress enacted wage and price controls during World War II and again during the Korean War. Most recently, President Nixon was also given the authority to invoke such controls, but his exercise of this power gave rise to widespread complaints. Business thought it represented unnecessary government interference, and labor complained of unfair enforcement. Since then, Congress has been reluctant to give the President the power to institute federal wage and price controls, and Jimmy Carter announced early in his administration that he would not ask for such authority.

Enforcement of greater competition in business and industry is another way to hold down prices. This would require more aggressive action by the Justice Department and the Federal Trade Commission, both in court suits to break up noncompetitive companies into smaller, more competitive firms, and through government blockage of mergers that reduce competition. U.S. Senator Edward M. Kennedy of Massachusetts has advocated legislation that would require a breakup of "vertically integrated" energy companies—those engaged in buying and selling to themselves through their involvement in all three phases of the energy industry: production, marketing, and refining. He and others would also like to see the adoption of a new law mandating the breakup of energy companies that are "horizontally integrated," as most of them are. These companies are involved in what would otherwise be competitive

---

[24]Galbraith, *Economics and the Public Purpose*, p. 315.

energy sources, such as coal, oil and gas, and uranium. So far, such legislation has not been agreed to by the Congress.

U.S. Senator Adlai E. Stevenson of Illinois has advocated bringing greater competition to the energy industry by establishing a *public* oil and gas corporation to compete with private companies, both at home and in the purchase and importation of foreign oil. This proposal, too, has thus far been rejected by the Congress.

THE RESULTS OF FEDERAL ECONOMIC MANAGEMENT

How successful has the federal government been in managing the economy? How well has it been able to keep most American people employed while maintaining stable prices? The answer is that the government has not done very well, especially during the last several years.[25] The U.S. has not been able to hold down inflation and unemployment to the low levels that Japan and western European countries have consistently achieved over the years.

When President Kennedy came into office in 1960, the economy was stagnant, with idle plant capacity and unacceptable unemployment. In line with Keynesian economics, President Kennedy took the then novel step of recommending a large tax *reduction* in order to "get the economy moving again." There was considerable opposition to this idea, which would increase the federal deficit, at least for the shortrun. But Kennedy and his advisers argued that the tax cut, which would leave more money in the hands of consumers and investors, would stimulate private spending (he also recommended increased federal *spending*) and that this would eventually result in increased federal collections. This proved to be true.

At the time Kennedy took this step, and until today, many people believed that the so-called Phillips Curve meant that if the government moved to decrease inflation, its actions would necessarily increase unemployment, and that if the government moved to decrease unemployment, on the other hand, its actions would necessarily increase inflation. This widespread belief in the almost automatic "trade-off" between inflation and unemployment was based upon the research of an English economist, A. W. Phillips. However, Phillips had *not* said that there was a trade-off between inflation and *unemployment*. He had found in the British economy that as unemployment diminishes, *wage rates* tend to increase.

In any event, believers in the popular version of the Phillips Curve trade-off between inflation and unemployment were confounded by what happened during the Kennedy administration. The application of Keynesian economic policy did indeed reduce unemployment; yet

---

[25]Except as otherwise indicated, material for this section is based upon Lekachman, *Economists at Bay.*

VIEWPOINT

The Causes of Inflation

According to traditional textbook theory, inflation occurs when costs (particularly labor costs) rise, or when overall demand for goods and services is greater than the economy's capacity to produce them. The proper prescription is to tighten up the money supply, reduce government spending (thereby reducing overall demand), or put a lid on wage increases. All three measures are ordinarily popular with conservatives.

Understanding Inflation, a booklet issued . . . by the Washington-based Exploratory Project for Economic Alternatives, looks at the problem somewhat differently and suggests quite different solutions. Most of the last decade's inflation, the booklet says, centered on price hikes in four necessities—food, energy, housing, and health care—that together account for about 70 percent of an average household's budget. Prices in these areas went up between 1970 and 1976 at a rate of 44 percent greater than the inflation rate for other goods and services (7.5 percent vs. 5.2 percent annually). If the inflation rate for the four necessities had been held to 5 percent a year during that period, the Consumer Price Index would have risen only 34.6 percent instead of the 47 percent it actually did rise.

When prices go up, the textbook says, people purchase less, and inflation then levels off. Precisely because these four items are necessary to most consumers, however, demand is not likely to fall just because prices have risen. Whatever the price, most people won't stop going to the doctor when they are sick, and once they are there the decision to "purchase" more health care is ordinarily made by the doctor and paid for by insurance. Consumers may make some adjustments in energy or housing consumption, but changes in both areas involve major shifts in living patterns that require a long time to effect. As a result, overall demand stays just about where it was before prices began to go up.

Wage controls will not keep prices down either. Wage increases in these industries simply do not account for much of the price increases. In health care, for example, a study for the Council on Wage and Price Stability found that hospital spending for items other than labor went up faster than spending on labor; labor costs "have actually been a declining fraction of total costs per patient day." The same is true of housing: labor costs went from 17.3 percent of total construction costs in 1970 to 15.6 percent in 1974.

Another major reexamination of inflation is a study prepared by Howard M. Wachtel and Peter D. Adelsheim for the Joint Economic Committee and reported in the September-October [1977] issue of the economics magazine *Challenge*. Wachtel and Adelsheim divide the economy up into sectors that range from "high concentration" (a few large firms) to "low concentration" (many small firms). If the firms operate according to conventional theory, inflation ought to occur in all these sectors only when the economy is operating near full employment; during a recession, demand drops and prices fall.

In fact, precisely the opposite often happens, especially in parts of the economy (like steel and auto) that are highly concentrated. A big firm that dominates much of its industry can set its prices (within certain limits) to realize a target profit rate. If demand for the product drops off, the authors explain, these big firms can raise the prices in order to maintain their profit rates. The bigger a firm is, the more it can get away with such behavior. So inflation is likely to *increase* during recessions, at least in highly concentrated sectors of the economy.

Evidence gathered for five different recession periods during the last 30 years supports this hypothesis. Firms in highly concentrated industries, the authors found, were much more likely than smaller firms to raise prices during a recession, to raise prices more than those smaller firms that did raise prices, and even to raise prices more in a recession than in a boom period. The difference between small and large firms cannot be explained by differences in labor costs; wage fluctuations were distributed randomly across the various sectors.

Policy that attacks inflation by inducing recession—tight money or spending cuts, for example—may thus achieve precisely the opposite of what is intended, particularly as the economy grows more concentrated. A similar conclusion flows from the Exploratory Project's study. Since expenditures in the four necessary areas are such a big part of the economy and are so hard to cut, reducing overall demand will affect prices only in marginal economic sectors. Both studies suggest that a better anti-inflation policy would be to challenge phenomena like economic concentration, the health-care system, and the high cost of housing finance directly. Without institutional changes in these areas, conventional fiscal and monetary policies won't work.

SOURCE: *Working Papers for a New Society*, January-February 1978, p.3.

prices remained relatively stable. The same was true during most of the Johnson administration until costs of the Vietnam War skyrocketed. For a time, Johnson maintained that the country could have both "guns and butter" without having to increase taxes; that is, the government could continue high expenditures for war without reducing domestic spending.

Johnson had pushed through Congress many new "Great Society" social programs, but as the Vietnam War expanded in intensity and scope, spending for this purpose rose to approximately $30 billion annually. For political reasons, President Johnson did not ask Congress for a tax increase to finance the Vietnam War until a year after he was advised to do so. Even then, Congress was slow to accept this dampening—and politically unpopular—proposal. The result was a kind of classic "demand-pull" inflation; too much money—too much spending—was chasing too few goods. Prices began to go up.

Despite the "guns and butter" philosophy of the Johnson administration, the rate of inflation was still only 4.8 percent, and unemployment was only 3.5 percent in 1969, when Richard Nixon took office. During the Nixon administration, both these figures more than doubled. At first, Nixon tightened fiscal policy by impounding funds and cutting down expenditures. At the same time, the Fed restricted the growth in the money supply under the stern hand of Arthur Burns, whom Nixon appointed to head the Federal Reserve System. The result was that unemployment began to shoot upward, and so did prices. Then, as the 1972 election approached, Burns loosened up on the money supply—some people said too much—and Nixon began to release impounded funds and increase federal spending. As a result, things did get better around election time. Some observers say that this kind of politically motivated manipulation of economic conditions around election time is a predictable and regular cycle in our economy.[26]

Under Nixon, the U.S. economy experienced what observers call "stagflation." High unemployment, as a result of a stagnant economy, and high inflation occurred at the same time. After having said over and over again that he would never do so, President Nixon invoked wage and price controls, under legislation that Congress had previously passed. Then he began to relax these controls in phases and finally ended them altogether. The rate of inflation shot upward again with no compensating trade-off reduction in unemployment. Even conservative economists such as Arthur Burns began to say that the old rules of economics were not working and that the main reason why a deliberate government policy of dampening the economy and increasing unemployment did not bring down prices was that there was insufficient competition in too many of America's industries. This situation enabled companies to administer prices, regardless of

---

[26]See Edward R. Tufte, *Political Control of the Economy* (Princeton, N.J.: Princeton University Press, 1978).

market pressures. Thus, in the face of declining demand for automobiles, automobile companies were able to make up for decreased sales volume by increasing unit costs—by more than $1000 per car on the average.

President Nixon's successor, Gerald Ford, had to contend with an event of enormous political and economic importance. That was the decision of oil-producing countries (OPEC) to embargo oil going to the United States for a time and to engineer a quadrupled price in crude oil. The OPEC action meant that Americans, in effect, paid increased taxes to foreign powers amounting to something like $25 billion. These increased energy costs had the same kind of dampening effect on the economy that a government tax increase would, except that these taxes did not stay in the United States but went to foreign countries and to multinational oil companies.

Annual Inflation Rate, 1978–79 (By Quarters)

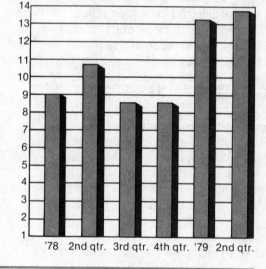

'78   2nd qtr.   3rd qtr.   4th qtr.   '79   2nd qtr.

SOURCE: Economic Report of the President

The economy continued to perform at less than optimum levels during the Ford administration and throughout the 1976 presidential campaign. In debates, President Ford took the view that the most important economic problem was bringing down the rate of inflation. The Democratic candidate, Jimmy Carter, said that the most important economic problem was bringing down the rate of unemployment. Carter won the election, promising tax reform and support for the Humphrey-Hawkins bill, which proposed to make a job a civil right for every American.

Carter's policies did help bring down the rate of unemployment; during the first three years of his term, it hovered around 6 percent. But the rate of inflation began to climb, and halfway through his term Carter came to believe that inflation, not unemployment, was the "number one" problem in the country. Accordingly, he recommended changing the proposed Humphrey-Hawkins bill so that it would not require the government to actually do anything to ensure full employment and would instead make it a nonbinding goal. A provision stating that the rate of inflation must also be brought down was added to the bill. In that relatively weak form the bill was passed by Congress and signed by President Carter.

Carter also agreed with the "tight money" policy instituted by the Federal Reserve System under the leadership of G. William Miller, whom Carter appointed to replace Arthur Burns (and later appointed

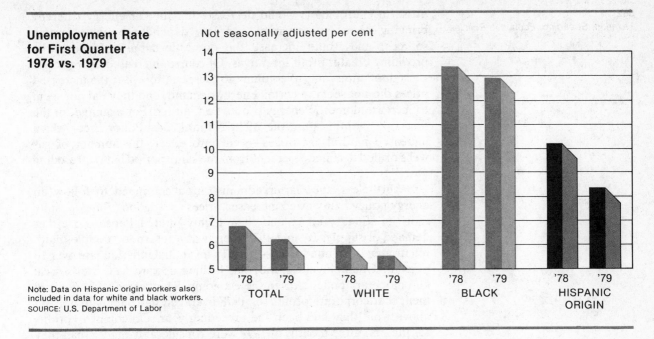

Unemployment Rate for First Quarter 1978 vs. 1979

Not seasonally adjusted per cent

Note: Data on Hispanic origin workers also included in data for white and black workers.
SOURCE: U.S. Department of Labor

secretary of the treasury). But Carter's major anti-inflation policy was a voluntary program of wage and price guidelines. He urged workers and employers to limit wage and price increases to 7 percent. These guidelines were not totally voluntary because the President threatened to cut off federal contracts for companies that violated them.

Carter's proposed budget for fiscal 1980 sought to limit increases in expenditures for social programs, while increasing spending for the Defense Department. It projected a reduced deficit, and Carter expressed the hope that a balanced budget could be achieved by 1981. The Carter administration expected that its fight against inflation would cause unemployment to inch upwards, and, indeed, it began to do so during the third year of his term.

As we saw in the last chapter, energy continued to be a major concern during the Carter administration, and Carter's economic policies were complicated by the energy problems. At first, Carter seemed to vacillate about what should be done. Eventually, however, the administration adopted a policy based on the belief that

Jim Borgman © 1978 The Cincinnati Enquirer.

a rise in energy costs would decrease demand for energy (thereby bringing about conservation and less dependence upon foreign sources) and would increase the domestic supply of energy by providing greater profit incentives. Of course, increased energy costs caused inflation rates to continue to increase, too. But the increased prices did not seem to curtail energy demand, and they did not seem to increase domestic energy production, either. For example, in the first two months after the 1978 Natural Gas Policy Act—which increased natural gas prices—went into effect, the number of gas wells drilled declined 7 percent from the same period in the preceding year.[27]

Nevertheless, the Carter administration continued to follow an energy policy that viewed increased prices as a "good" thing, despite their inflationary effect and their highly limited impact on either demand or supply. By mid-1979 there was a return to "double-digit" inflation in the United States—that is, an annual inflation rate over 10 percent. Unemployment, too, was inching upward as Carter's fiscal and monetary policy slowed the economy. Then came an announcement that corporate profits for 1978 averaged more than 26 percent above what they had been the preceding year. Oil company profits for the first three months of 1979 were considerably higher than they had been during the same period in 1978, as much as 100 percent more in some cases. Wage demands and settlements could not be held within Carter's 7 percent guideline. The nation's economic problems mounted as gasoline shortages and lines at filling stations developed. To make matters worse, OPEC announced yet another hike in crude oil prices, and Carter said that this would mean both greater inflation and greater unemployment. A little over six months before the first presidential primary was to be held in New Hampshire in February 1980, the polls showed that more than 70 percent of Americans disapproved of the job President Carter was doing, primarily because of his handling of energy and economic issues.

CONCLUSION

Economics is not an exact science; even economists disagree among themselves as to what policies should be adopted to solve the nation's economic problems. Still, making economic policy is a vital function of the federal government—a function that has political repercussions. Thus, what the government decides about levels of taxation and spending; what happens in regard to growth in the money supply; whether government intervenes to enforce greater competition in noncompetitive industries (allowing the market to exert regulatory pressure on prices); and whether the government intervenes directly in wage and price decisions by establishing some general system of

---

[27]*Time* (March 19, 1979), p. 74.

controls—all become highly charged political decisions that affect every citizen. The people's ability to participate in these important decisions depends upon the degree to which economic policy-making is subject to more open and public processes. This is clearly a fundamental measure of the extent of Americans' participation in the major decisions that affect their lives.

ADDITIONAL SOURCES

Fisher, Louis. *Presidential Spending Power*. Princeton University Press, 1975.*

Galbraith, John Kenneth. *Economics and the Public Purpose*. Houghton-Mifflin, 1974.*

———, and Nicole Salinger. *Almost Everyone's Guide to Economics*. Houghton-Mifflin, 1978.

Hapgood, David. "Progress and Poverty Continued." *The New Republic* (May 12, 1979), pp. 21–23.

Pechman, Joseph, and Benjamin A. Okner. *Who Bears the Tax Burden?* Brookings, 1974.*

Raskin, Marcus, ed. *The Federal Budget and Social Reconstruction: The People and the State*. Transaction Books, 1978.*

Roberts, Paul Craig. "The Breakdown of the Keynesian Model." *The Public Interest* (Summer 1978), pp. 20–33.

Sharkansky, Ira. *The Politics of Taxing and Spending*. Bobbs-Merrill, 1969.

Shultz, George P., and Kenneth W. Dam. *Economic Policy Behind the Headlines*. Norton, 1977.*

Silk, Leonard. *Economics in Plain English*. Simon and Schuster, 1978.

Walton, Clarence C., ed. *Inflation and National Survival: Proceedings of the Academy of Political Science*, vol. 33, no. 3. The Academy of Political Science, 1979.*

Ward, Benjamin. *The Ideal Worlds of Economics: Liberal, Radical, and Conservative Economic Worldviews*. Basic Books, 1979.

Wildavsky, Aaron. *The Politics of the Budgetary Process*, 2nd ed. Little, Brown, 1974.*

*Available in paperback edition.

20 Foreign Policy and National Security

Early in 1979, Iranian demonstrators held many rallies like this one to pledge support for an Islamic republic led by the Ayatollah Khomeini.

Americans watched with mixed fascination and dread when, early in 1979, the Shah of Iran was forced to flee his country.[1] Through the Central Intelligence Agency (CIA), the United States had originally helped to put the Shah in power in 1953, assisting in the overthrow of an elected government. Thereafter, America had sold great amounts of highly sophisticated armaments to the Shah and had trained his armed forces, making Iran one of the important military powers in the world and the major military power in the Persian Gulf region. The United States had also assisted the Shah in developing a highly effective secret police and intelligence organization, SAVAK.

Why had we done all this for a regime that was recognized to be dictatorial and heavily repressive of freedom of speech, freedom of the press, and other forms of democratic dissent? How did we square our support for the Shah with President Carter's outspoken proclamations of our dedication to "human rights" around the world? The answer is that our support for human rights did *not* square very well at all with our support for the Shah's government and practices. But the makers of America's foreign policy thought that, in this instance at least, pragmatic considerations required us to support the Shah, irrespective of our human rights ideals. Why? Primarily because our nation had become increasingly dependent on foreign oil: 40 percent of our oil supplies came from foreign sources in 1979. Iran not only supplied 5 percent of America's oil needs in 1979, but our leaders thought that its military might was vital to the stability of the Middle East region, from which a large percentage of America's oil and virtually all of Western Europe's and Japan's oil comes.

---

[1]For reports concerning 1979 developments in Iran and the resultant importance of Saudi Arabia to the U.S., see *U.S. News & World Report* (January 15, 1979), pp. 24–28; *New York Times*, Sunday, January 28, 1979, section 4, p. 1; *Time* (January 15, 1979), pp. 18–28; and *U. S. News & World Report,* (April 2, 1979), pp. 10, 23–29.

Catering to the Shah prior to his fall, the U.S. government had agreed to the unprecedented step of severing all ties and contacts with opposition organizations and leaders within Iran. In a very real sense, the United States had put all of its Iranian eggs in the Shah's basket. Then these eggs were severely jostled and broken as the Shah was toppled from his so-called Peacock Throne. Americans and U.S. officials were startled to find that popular opposition to the Shah in Iran was overwhelming and ran deeply throughout all levels of Iranian society. This finding was contrary to earlier reports in the American press, which had indicated that the Shah's opposition came only from extremists on the left, who did not think the Shah was moving rapidly enough toward economic and political reforms, and from extremists on the right, so-called Islamic fanatics.

Neither American public opinion nor American officials were prepared, then, for the major popular upheaval that forced the Shah's removal. Not only had the United States been officially allied exclusively with the Shah, but President Carter and other U.S. officials had continued to express public support for him until the very last, even after it no longer seemed possible that his reign could survive. Millions of demonstrating Iranians, who called for "death to the Shah," were almost equally vocal against the United States. Having stayed with the Shah too long, the U.S. government then moved too quickly to endorse the government of Shahpour Bakhtiar, whom the Shah designated as premier when he left Iran. But the cry of "death to the Shah" gave way almost immediately to "down with Bakhtiar," and he, also, was linked to the United States in the minds of most Iranians. Before long, Bakhtiar was out of office and in hiding.

Millions of ecstatic Iranians welcomed back an Islamic religious leader, the Ayatollah Khomeini, who had earlier been forced into exile in Paris by the Shah. The Ayatollah proclaimed Iran an Islamic republic—which proved easier to proclaim than to establish. Unrest continued. Iran's oil wells, which had been shut down for months as part of a general strike to show opposition to the Shah's regime, began to pump again, but at a slower rate and at a much higher price than before.

As a result of the governmental turnover in Iran and the consequent instability that U.S. leaders saw developing in the Middle East, the United States began to focus on Saudi Arabia. In 1979, some officials even said that for the next few years, Saudi Arabia would be the most important country in the world for the United States.

Saudi Arabia is an oil-rich country, ruled by a kind of medieval, feudal family of five thousand princes and headed by King Khalid and his son, Crown Prince Fahd. Saudi Arabia's rulers have long been both anticommunist and anti-Zionist (that is, anti-Israel). The Saudis were alarmed by the popular overthrow of the Shah of Iran and the ineffectiveness of the Shah's military might and antidisorder methods against widespread popular discontent. Saudi rulers were said to be dismayed that the United States could not somehow have acted to keep the Shah in power. After the Shah's fall, they were worried that similar disorders within their own country might threaten their own rule.

The rapid sequence of events in the Middle East illustrated several important points about U.S. foreign policy. First, it showed that American foreign policy cannot be neatly separated from domestic policy. America's domestic energy needs, for example, led the U.S. government to unquestioningly support the Shah, and the overthrow of the Shah, in turn, affected U.S. domestic policies.[2] A second point illustrated by the changes in Iran was that America's power to influence events in foreign countries is limited—a point that had also been demonstrated earlier in Vietnam. Despite its great missile and nuclear strength and its great numbers of airplanes and naval vessels, the United States was unable to prevent the Shah's overthrow. The Shah's own counterinsurgency, or anti-riot, forces, which we had helped to train, were also unable to do so.

Third, the Iranian situation indicated that our foreign policy cannot focus only on narrow East-West issues—that is, the differences and the competition, military and otherwise, between the United States and the Soviet Union. The upheaval in Iran did not seem to be Soviet-inspired, however much Soviet leaders might have been pleased by its anti-American tone. Instead, it appeared to be the result of popular dissatisfaction within the country, strong feelings of Iranian nationalism (devotion and loyalty to country), and resurgent religious fervor.

Finally, the Iranian uprising illustrated the potential conflict between a foreign policy based on support of human rights around the world and a "pragmatic" foreign policy which supports regimes that are "on our side," no matter what their domestic policies are.

THE HISTORY OF AMERICAN FOREIGN POLICY

Foreign policy consists of what a government says and does in regard to other nations, along with the goals and assumptions that underlie those official statements and actions. The basic purpose of any country's foreign policy, of course, is to preserve its existence and security as a nation. Thus, foreign policy involves matters of both peace and war, as well as economic matters.

Historically, there have been three major themes in America's foreign policy.[3] In 1801, President Thomas Jefferson warned Ameri-

---

[2]The interdependence of international and domestic affairs has been called "intermestic." See Bayless Manning, "The Congress, the Executive and Inter-mestic Affairs: Three Proposals," *Foreign Affairs* (January 1977), pp. 306–24.

[3]For a more detailed history of American foreign policy, see James Lee Ray, *Global Politics* (Boston: Houghton Mifflin Company, 1979), pp. 1–45.

ca against "permanent alliances" with other countries. That spirit of *isolationism* has always been a strong strain in American public opinion and foreign policy. Isolationism was strongest in America during the period preceding World War I, although even then isolationism applied more to our desire for noninvolvement outside our hemisphere than within it. European countries were engaged at that time in various efforts to maintain a "balance of power" in the world; each acted, negotiated, and intrigued to prevent some other nation, or combination of nations, from becoming too powerful. These balance-of-power efforts arose from their concerns for national security, nationalism, and economic interests. Until World War I, the United States was able to remain relatively aloof from European foreign policy maneuvers. Then in August 1914 Europe was engulfed in war. Economic and political tensions that had been building up for years were ignited by the assassination of Austria's Archduke Franz Ferdinand by a Serbian nationalist. Austria declared war on Serbia. Interests and alliances caused Germany and later Bulgaria and Turkey to join Austria, while France, Great Britain, and Russia lined up with Serbia. Eventually, President Wilson came to feel that the war affected America's interests and we, too, declared war on Germany, Austria, and their allies.

Patriotism and nationalism swept the U.S. As is usual in wartime, Americans were led to believe that they were engaged in a kind of holy war—a war "to end all wars," as President Wilson put it.

Of course, World War I did not end all wars. After the war, the United States Senate rejected the League of Nations, which President Wilson had negotiated with France, England, and other nations. The League, which was to be a kind of world peace-keeping organization, was established, but without United States membership. The United States went back to its historical isolation from world affairs outside the western hemisphere. The peace imposed on Germany—including a considerable loss of territory and a heavy burden of reparations, or war costs—helped to sow the seeds of a new world explosion that would come twenty years later.

Within our own hemisphere, especially in Latin America, American foreign policy has been characterized, at least until recently, by *interventionism*. During the Revolution, Americans looked forward to a Canadian revolt against Britain, similar to their own. Periodically thereafter, some American leaders (notably Theodore Roosevelt) talked about making Canada a part of the Union, but Canada did not share that sentiment. In recent years, Canada has tightened its protections against economic domination by American companies.

Historically, U.S. foreign policy has treated Latin America as our special province. This policy dates back to the *Monroe Doctrine*, the 1823 declaration by President James Monroe that warned European nations to stay out of the affairs of nations in this hemisphere. But the Monroe Doctrine did not limit our involvements there. A war with Mexico, settled in 1846, brought the independent Republic of Texas into the Union as a state and enabled the U.S. to acquire the territory that later became the states of New Mexico and Arizona. After the Spanish-American War in 1898, the U.S. seized Puerto Rico (as well as the Pacific islands of Guam and the Philippines).

From 1904 to 1934, the United States intervened militarily eight times in various Latin American countries. In that region, American foreign policy largely paralleled the interests of American business corporations that operated there. In 1938, when all private oil holdings and operations in Mexico were expropriated—converted to government ownership—America's foreign policy supported the private oil companies, which were mostly American, and sought to punish Mexico for this act.

Even as late as the 1960s, the United States was actively involved in the violent overthrow of the elected leftist government of Guatemala; it intervened militarily in the Dominican Republic; and it moved immediately to recognize and support a military government in Brazil that had overthrown an elected leftist government there. In the 1970s, the United States—through the CIA—joined with a private American company, International Telephone and Telegraph Company (ITT), to help bring down the elected leftist government of Salvador Allende in Chile.

In recent years, the United States has begun to move toward a foreign policy that treats Latin American nations more nearly as the independent countries that they are and have a right to be.

With the United States entrance into World War II, America's foreign policy entered a new period of *internationalism*, which continues to this day. Adolf Hitler had come to power in Germany at a time of great economic problems and dislocations. He had taken advantage of a furnace of nationalism fueled by Germany's supposed humiliation by the Allies at the end of World War I and by his fanning of anti-Semitic attacks against Germany's Jews (which later sent millions to death in the "Holocaust"). Germany, Japan, and Italy began a period of violent expansionism: Japan invaded China, asserting that Asia was its special sphere of influence; Italy invaded Ethiopia; Germany invaded Czechoslovakia, Poland, and Austria.

Great Britain declared war against Germany, as did France, which was rapidly overrun and occupied by German forces. Although Hitler and Russia's authoritarian leader, Joseph Stalin, at first agreed to a nonaggression pact, Russia and Germany eventually became war adversaries, too.

In the United States, President Franklin D. Roosevelt, who had been engaged in intensive efforts to bring America out of the Great Depression, watched the developing conflagration with much sympathy for Britain, France, and China. But American public opinion was at first strongly opposed to American involvement. Still, though constrained by American public opinion and by laws passed by Congress, Roosevelt sought to aid Great Britain. When the Japanese attacked Pearl Harbor, President Roosevelt went before Congress, calling December 7, 1941, "a day which will live in infamy" and asked for a declaration of war against Japan. Congress rapidly complied. Following the Japanese attack on Pearl Harbor, Germany joined Japan by declaring war on the United States.

America's productive capacity became a crucial element in the eventual victory of the "Allies" over the "Axis" powers of Germany, Japan, and Italy. American troops and armaments were heavily engaged in the Pacific, in Africa, Italy, and eventually Europe. Before World War II had ended, President Roosevelt began to talk with Prime Minister Churchill, Premier Stalin, and others about the formation of an international organization to keep the eventual peace and resolve disputes between nations. These plans culminated in the establishment of the United Nations, but only after Roosevelt's death.

With most of the developed countries devastated by World War II, America was clearly the most powerful nation on earth. Our own country had not been touched directly by war and our factories and farms had retained their full productive capacity. In addition, during the war our scientists had produced an atomic bomb, a horrible new and almost unbelievable force that resulted from splitting the components of a special kind of uranium atom. We had used this new bomb to level Japan's great cities of Hiroshima and Nagasaki. Our exclusive possession of this secret weapon for a number of years after the war added to our influence in world affairs.

In the postwar period, the American foreign policy of internationalism was characterized by the goals of *recovery* and *containment*—economic recovery for Western Europe and Japan, and containment of communism. Under the leadership of President Harry S. Truman and George C. Marshall, the noted Army general whom Truman had appointed as secretary of state, the United States launched the "Marshall Plan" to provide massive aid and loans to help Western Europe recover economically. With General Douglas MacArthur acting as military governor, Japan also set upon the road to economic recovery. At the same time, America and its former ally, Russia, increasingly came to view each other as adversaries. The United States saw Russia's assumption of control over Eastern European nations as evidence of its intent to spread communism throughout the world.

Events in China increased that fear. A corrupt and undemocratic regime headed by our wartime ally, Generalissimo Chiang Kai-shek, had fallen to disciplined Marxist forces led by Mao Tse-tung. Many Americans, particularly through Christian missionary contacts, had felt a special tie with China and with Chiang Kai-shek. Bitter arguments over "who lost China" erupted in the United States. Chiang Kai-shek's forces took over the independent island of Taiwan, where they set up the separate government of Nationalist China. America broke off relations with mainland China and refused to recognize Mao's government there. These ties were not to be renewed until the 1970s, when President Nixon visited China; President Carter later established full diplomatic relations with the People's Republic of China in 1979.

Meeting with Mao Tse-tung (above) and other Chinese leaders, President Nixon renewed American ties with mainland China during his visit there in 1972.

During the late 1940s and 1950s, Senator Joseph McCarthy of Wisconsin made political capital out of a vigorous anticommunist campaign in the United States. His "red-baiting"—making untrue and undocumented charges that communist subversion was rampant within the official circles of the U.S. government—launched America upon a period of fearful anticommunism at home and vigorous "Cold War" abroad, against the Soviet Union and other communist countries. President Truman's second Secretary of State, Dean Acheson, and President Eisenhower's Secretary of State, John Foster Dulles, viewed communism as a monolithic force ruled from Moscow that threatened to spread throughout the world; both pursued a hardline policy of containment.

In the midst of this frigid atmosphere, both at home and abroad, the communist regime in North Korea invaded South Korea. President Truman secured the approval of the United Nations Security Council for military action against the invasion. This Security Council action was possible because the Soviets at that time were boycotting the Security Council and thus were not present to exercise their veto. In order to reestablish the status quo and the recognition of the border between South Korea and North Korea, the United States plunged into a war that resulted in the deaths of approximately 35,000 American soldiers.

The Cold War was still a very strong factor in American domestic and foreign policy when President John F. Kennedy came into office. He created a new counterinsurgency force called the "Green Berets," which was intended to put out "brush fires" that might be started by the communists anywhere in the world. He approved an invasion of Cuba (which had been planned under Eisenhower) that ended in disaster; American-trained forces were soundly defeated at the "Bay of Pigs." He supported a secret army in Laos. He threatened war with Russia during the "Cuban missile crisis," when it was discovered that the Soviet Union had placed offensive missiles on the island, only 90 miles from the United States.

President Kennedy also sent 16,000 American military "advisers" to Vietnam. American involvement in that country had begun in the mid-1950s, after the French had been defeated at Dien Bien Phu by Ho Chi Minh's forces, who were fighting for independence and unification of South Vietnam and North Vietnam. Though the Geneva Accords, which had attempted to settle the conflict, had guaranteed the Vietnamese free elections to choose their own government, President Eisenhower feared that the communists would win; he sent military aid and advisers to help the South Vietnamese government.

American involvement in Vietnam escalated rapidly when Lyndon Johnson took office after President Kennedy's assassination in 1963. By 1967, more than 500,000 Americans were fighting in Vietnam. As casualties mounted, public opinion began to turn against Johnson. Antiwar sentiment, at first restricted to a relatively small number of liberals and college students, soon spread throughout the country. In March 1968, Johnson ordered a partial bombing halt to encourage negotiations, and he shocked the nation by announcing he would not be a candidate for reelection.

After campaigning on a platform that included a "secret plan" to end the war, President Nixon and his major foreign policy adviser, Henry Kissinger, followed a twofold policy in Vietnam. While pursuing harsh military action, including massive bombing attacks on the North, they also vigorously negotiated with representatives of North Vietnam. Finally, in January 1973, a Vietnam truce was signed. American troops were withdrawn. The government we had supported soon collapsed, and the Marxist government of North Vietnam was able to exercise control throughout the country.

The post-Vietnam period in America was an unsettled one in a number of ways. The world was changing. Marxism was no longer a monolithic force in the world, if it had ever been. China and the Soviet Union had become bitter enemies. Americans became increasingly distrustful of foreign involvements, especially if they could lead to war. More and more, it became clear that America's military might was of limited use in small "brush fires," or civil wars, as in Vietnam. More and more, too, America began to see that its security did not depend solely upon military might, alliances, or containment of communism—that it was also vulnerable, for example, to economic pressures, particularly those involving energy. The Middle East, therefore, became a vital focus of American foreign policy because so much of the world's oil—and America's—came from this region.

The United States has had close ties with Israel ever since it was created as an independent nation following World War II. As more and more Jews throughout the world immigrated to their "historic homeland"—carved out of what had been Arab Palestine—Israel was almost continuously embroiled in bitter and sometimes violent conflict with its Arab neighbors.

With the increased importance of Arab oil to America's economy,

Nixon and Kissinger began a major effort to seek a stable peace in the Middle East. After 31 years of hostility and war, Egypt and Israel finally negotiated a bilateral peace in 1979, with active involvement by President Carter. But at about this time, the Shah of Iran was overthrown. Some Arab leaders in other nations became more antagonistic toward the United States and Israel. The ruling family in Saudi Arabia began to be increasingly concerned about its own future and its ties with the United States.

Thus, American foreign policy in the 1970s was less concerned with a direct confrontation between the two great powers, the Soviet Union and the United States. The People's Republic of China—neither in the American nor the Russian "camp"—was a separate power that had to be reckoned with. Japan, with a resurgent economy, had become an important power. Europe, too, had grown economically strong. Economic power had become as important as political power, particularly in regard to energy. The oil-producing countries had formed a cartel (monopolistic arrangement) that enabled them to control the production and the price of world oil.

U.S. foreign policy concerns were not easy to deal with. They were not just simple matters of what to do about containing communism anymore. One of the basic foreign policy questions was: What shall the United States do about finding a more stable supply of foreign oil? This question was tied up with the domestic issue of how to cut down America's reliance on foreign oil sources. There was the question of what to do in regard to the "Third World"—the less developed or developing nations of the world, most of which had gained their independence following World War II. Despite progress toward détente with the Soviet Union, American leaders felt that the United States was still faced with a need to spend more to maintain military equality with them. With President Carter's recognition of the People's Republic of China, America played what was called the "China card." Although it was clear that China was a long way from becoming a modern, industrialized nation, the United States hoped that China's power might become a balance against the Soviet Union's.

In short, by the late 1970s, the world had become a much more complicated place. But it was not necessarily more dangerous than during the tension-filled and easily understood, though certainly oversimplified days of the Soviet–U.S. Cold War period.

WHO MAKES AMERICA'S FOREIGN POLICY?

Like other policy matters, our foreign policy issues get on our official agenda primarily because of the influence of events and actors, both foreign and domestic. The overthrow of the Shah of Iran was a dramatic foreign event that greatly influenced our foreign policy agenda-making, formulation, adoption, and implementation. An example of a related domestic event that has considerably influenced our foreign policy is our increased dependence upon foreign oil sources. But, like other policy issues, events alone do not dominate the making of foreign policy. Actors are centrally important, too.

The actions and statements of foreign politicians and public officials can dramatically affect American foreign policy. The unprecedented decision of Egypt's President Anwar Sadat to visit Jerusalem in 1978 was an important influence on America's foreign policy in the Middle East. Similarly, the decision of Deng Xiaoping, the Vice-Premier of the People's Republic of China, to visit the United States made it easier for President Carter to win support for his recognition of that country and for the United States to exchange ambassadors with them.

Groups of nations can have impact on American foreign policy. The less developed, or developing nations of the world (sometimes called the southern nations because most of them are in the south half of the globe) have increasingly attempted to work and act together to affect the foreign policies of the more developed nations, including the United States. The developing nations particularly want freer access to the markets of the developed nations and better prices for their products.

Of vital significance in recent years has been the formation and actions of the Organization of Petroleum Exporting Countries (OPEC). OPEC nations have been able to stick together as a unit to hold down the world production of oil and to increase world oil prices. They have sometimes used their group power for political purposes, too; in 1973 they used an oil embargo to punish nations which supported Israel. Following the Shah's fall in 1979, the OPEC countries met and agreed upon a 9 percent *minimum* price hike. Thus, the actions of this cartel greatly influenced the making of foreign policy in the United States. For other products, such as rubber, copper, coffee, and bauxite, producer nations have made attempts to form similar cartels.[4]

Individual nations themselves can be actors with an influence on America's foreign policy. When Vietnam invaded Cambodia and when China later invaded Vietnam, foreign policy decisionmakers in the United States had to take these actions into account in planning America's statements and possible actions in response to them.

Who are America's foreign policy actors and decision-makers? Who influences foreign policy-making? As with domestic policy issues, politicians and public officials, interest groups, the media, and the public are all involved in making America's foreign policy.

The President

The U.S. Constitution makes the President America's principal actor in the field of foreign policy. The President has the power to appoint U.S. ambassadors and cabinet officials, such as the secretary of state

---

[4]See "Creeping Cartelization," *Business Week* (May 9, 1977), pp. 64–83.

and the secretary of defense. All of them, of course, are subject to confirmation by the U.S. Senate. The Constitution gives the President the authority to act as commander in chief of the armed services. Further, the Constitution states that the President has the power to receive ambassadors from other nations, and thus to extend diplomatic recognition to other nations, as President Carter did with the People's Republic of China in 1979. The President also has the authority to negotiate treaties, although a treaty must be ratified by a two-thirds vote in the Senate before it can go into effect. These constitutional powers give the President great control over both the initiation and implementation of foreign policy. As a result of these formal constitutional powers, the President has three primary political resources in the field of foreign policy: information control; personal diplomacy; and crisis management.[5]

President Carter meeting with Western European leaders at a 1979 summit conference. Left to right: French President Giscard d'Estaing; James Callaghan, then the British prime minister; Jimmy Carter; and West German Chancellor Helmut Schmidt. The leaders exchanged views and information on common problems, such as inflation and energy.

Information control. With the consent of the Senate, the President names the heads of the principal foreign policy bureaucracies, such as the secretary of state, the secretary of defense, and the director of the Central Intelligence Agency. Although these officials cannot take office except with the Senate's approval, they are still primarily loyal and responsible to the President. As part of the executive establishment, they report directly and regularly to the President but only irregularly to relevant congressional committees.

Even closer to the President is the national security adviser, who heads the staff of the National Security Council. The Council was established in 1947 to coordinate the nation's foreign policy. Indeed, President Nixon's national security adviser, Henry Kissinger (who later served simultaneously in both that position and as secretary of state), once argued, with Nixon's approval, that because of the President's "executive privilege," he (Kissinger) could not be required to go before the Senate Foreign Relations Committee and divulge how the preceding year's foreign military aid funds had been divided among the various recipient nations. The Senate committee stopped short of forcing a showdown on this issue.

President Carter appointed Zbigniew Brzezinski as his national security adviser. Brzezinski, a professor at Columbia University, had

---

[5]Howard Bliss and M. Glen Johnson, *Beyond the Water's Edge: America's Foreign Policies* (Philadelphia: J.B. Lippincott Company, 1975), pp. 145–54.

been executive director of the Trilaterall Commission, established by Chase Manhattan Bank President David Rockefeller to promote the concept that America's foreign policy should be primarily based upon the common interests of the United States, Western Europe, and Japan.

The President is the head of the executive department, with the power to name its chief officials, direct them, and receive their reports. Thus, the chief executive usually has far better and more complete information upon which to base foreign policy decisions than Congress or the general public does.

Personal diplomacy. The U.S. Supreme Court has held that the President is the "sole organ" of the federal government that can deal with other nations.[6] Neither the Congress nor any other official of the United States may conduct unauthorized negotiations on behalf of the United States. That is prohibited by law. Usually, such negotiations are carried on by members of the executive branch under the President's authority and ultimate control. In recent years, however, Presidents have often engaged in "personal diplomacy." Thus, President Carter—without the involvement of senators or representatives—took a major role in the 1978 Camp David summit negotiations between Egypt's President Sadat and Israel's Prime Minister Begin. In 1979, he conducted what had come to be called "shuttle diplomacy" during the time of Henry Kissinger, flying to Egypt and Israel to help complete a peace treaty between those two countries. President Carter negotiated the final details of the Panama Canal Treaty; only after the Treaty had been agreed upon did he report the details to Congress and the public. Similarly, President Carter moved to extend diplomatic relations to the People's Republic of China, with little prior consultation with Congress.

If diplomacy results in treaties, they must be submitted to the Senate for ratification. But nothing requires the President to involve the Senate in any negotiations preceding an actual treaty signing. Further, modern Presidents have sometimes entered into "executive agreements"—accords between the President and the head of a foreign government—without submitting them for ratification as treaties. Such executive agreements have been used in recent years to station American troops and to establish military bases and other installations in foreign countries. Theoretically, succeeding Presidents are not bound by the executive agreements of their predecessors, but in practice the earlier commitments have been honored.[7]

Crisis management. As commander in chief, the President is expected to act to resist military attacks on our country, without waiting for a formal declaration of war. Presidents have also frequently moved to assist nations that were thought to be important to our

---

[6]See *United States* v. *Curtiss-Wright Export Corp.*, 299 U.S. 304 (1936).

[7]Henry T. Nash, *American Foreign Policy,* rev. ed. (Homewood, Ill.: The Dorsey Press, 1978), pp. 151–52.

national security, when these countries have come under external or internal attack. For example, President Carter sent arms and other assistance to North Yemen when it was attacked by South Yemen in 1979.

The President of the United States clearly plays a very important role in the adoption and implementation of American foreign policy. But the President's power is not unlimited. Foreign events and actors cannot always be predicted. America cannot always impose its will in foreign situations or sometimes can do so only at too great a cost. The President's power in foreign policy is also limited by public opinion. In the past, the general public and most members of Congress tended to support the idea that the "President knows best" in regard to foreign policy. But, today, there is far less willingness to blindly support the President's foreign policy initiatives, especially after the Vietnam War and the Watergate affair.[8] According to one authority, "In today's complex world, the President must take into account more than his own judgment and the advice of a few chosen advisers."[9] Still, although subject to certain limits, the President stands astride the making of foreign policy in America as the Jolly Green Giant towers over his fields of green beans.

The Foreign Policy Bureaucracy

The President of the United States—America's chief diplomat and commander in chief—has a wide range of federal bureaucracies and many federal officials available for assistance and advice. Indeed, this assistance is necessary: in regard to foreign policy (not counting the attention which must be given to purely domestic matters) the President must be like a busy juggler, keeping several balls in the air at once. Issues in one part of the world do not subside in importance just because other issues somewhere else in the world become more pressing. In 1978, for example, President Carter was simultaneously concerned with continued East-West problems between the United States and the Soviet Union; with America's relations with Western Europe; with developments in Asia, particularly new diplomatic relations with the People's Republic of China; with the Middle East negotiations between Egypt and Israel; with North-South world problems and America's responsibilities to developing nations in Latin America and Africa. Cutting across these more or less regional foreign policy problems, President Carter also continued his efforts to improve the recognition of human rights around the world. In addition, he and his administration were deeply enmeshed in serious international economic problems, partly caused by our own domestic economic troubles, notably inflation.[10]

---

[8]See Daniel Yankelovich, "Farewell to 'President Knows Best,'" *Foreign Affairs*, 57, no. 3 (1978): 670–93.

[9]Yankelovich, "Farewell to 'President Knows Best,'" p. 693.

[10]See Headley Bull, "A View from Abroad: Consistency Under Pressure," *Foreign Affairs*, 57, no. 3 (1978): 441–62.

Some people feel that President Carter's foreign policies have been inconsistent and even "incoherent" because he has not been able to satisfactorily resolve the conflicting advice he has received from U.S. foreign policy bureaucracies and officials.[11] Who advises the President on foreign policy? One answer might be: everybody who gets a chance to do so. But in our system of government, there are certain *formal* offices and bureaucracies established for that purpose.

Clyde Wells. Courtesy Augusta (Ga.) Chronicle.

The State Department. There was a secretary of state before there was a President of the United States. Robert R. Livingston served in that capacity under the Articles of Confederation, which predated the Constitution.[12] The U.S. secretary of state is today the second-ranking official in the executive department next to the President. The official seal of the United States is kept by the secretary of state, and it was a secretary of state—Henry Kissinger—who received and accepted President Nixon's resignation.

Aside from rank and ritual functions, the secretary of state is the

[11]See Stanley Hoffmann, "A View from at Home: The Perils of Incoherence," *Foreign Affairs*, 57, no. 3 (1978): 463–91.

[12]See Marian Irish and Elke Frank, *U.S. Foreign Policy* (New York: Harcourt Brace Jovanovich, 1975), pp. 226–27.

head of the State Department and as such is formally designated as the principal foreign policy adviser to the President. The secretary of state presides over the sprawling State Department, which has its principal offices in Washington D.C. The Department also maintains embassies and other offices in all the countries of the world.

The State Department is involved in the formulation, adoption, and implementation of foreign policy. To assist with the formulation and adoption of foreign policy, it engages in gathering and interpreting foreign "intelligence" (facts and information). As one of the implementers of foreign policy, the State Department handles negotiations with foreign countries and international organizations, coordinates the various activities of the United States government overseas, and represents U.S. interests—including the protection and promotion of U.S. citizen and business interests—in foreign countries.

The top positions in the State Department are filled by a number of political appointees, including twenty-one assistant secretaries. Under them are members of the "foreign service," specially trained nonclerical career people who serve in key positions in the Washington offices of the State Department and in our various embassies throughout the world. A majority of the State Department officials and employees are members of the U.S. Civil Service.

Whether a President *really* relies upon the secretary of state and the State Department for advice on foreign policy matters varies greatly from Presidency to Presidency and depends upon the kind of personal relationship that exists between the President and the secretary of state. Under President Truman, for example, the secretary of state (first George C. Marshall, and later Dean Acheson) was a major foreign policy figure. So was John Foster Dulles, who served in the Eisenhower administration. On the other hand, Dean Rusk, who served as secretary of state under Presidents Kennedy and Johnson, was much less influential. William Rogers, secretary of state under President Nixon, was weakest of all among modern holders of that office. President Nixon preferred to rely on his national security adviser, Henry Kissinger, for foreign policy advice and action. As noted earlier, President Nixon eventually appointed Henry Kissinger to hold both offices at once—secretary of state *and* national security adviser, a very unusual arrangement (which President Ford ended by making Kissinger secretary of state only). Under President Carter, Secretary of State Cyrus Vance has had considerable influence on foreign policy, but he is not without competitors in the executive department.

Most modern Presidents have complained about the State Department. President Kennedy said that trying to get it to act was like "punching a bowl of jelly."[13] The State Department is said to be slow to make decisions, slow to initiate new ideas, and bureaucratically self-protective, in that its advice is often hedged and not clear-cut.

Henry Kissinger served simultaneously as secretary of state and national security adviser during the Nixon administration.

[13]See Arthur Schlesinger, Jr., *A Thousand Days* (Boston: Houghton, Mifflin, 1965).

These problems lessen the State Department's influence in foreign policy matters. They are partly the result of serious organizational problems within the Department, both at the top and in the field. At the top, in its Washington headquarters, the State Department is organized in two *overlapping* ways. It is organized by world regions; there are separate bureaus within the Department for Europe, Latin America, Africa, East Asia and the Pacific, and the Middle East and South Asia. The State Department is also organized by functions; there are separate bureaus within the Department for administration, congressional relations, international organizations (including the United Nations), consular affairs, and intelligence and research. Carrying out a traditional "clearance" procedure, the State Department checks with all officials and bureaus that might conceivably have an interest in any new issue or development before taking an official stance on it. This procedure takes time and sometimes produces a bland "committee" decision.

Like any large bureaucracy staffed by career employees, the State Department's influence is limited because its foreign service members feel some pressure to conform to the norms of the offices they work in and to avoid controversy. This restrictive system discourages some would-be careerists from staying in the service. Other people in the foreign service are discouraged because the top positions—the assistant secretary jobs and those above them in Washington, as well as ambassadorships abroad—are often filled by the President's appointment of people outside the career service. This gives foreign service careerists a feeling of limited possibilities for advancement.

Another reason for the State Department's limited influence in foreign policy decisions is that it is difficult to make the "country team" concept really work; it is not easy to funnel and focus all of the government's representation and intelligence-gathering activities in any one country through the U.S. ambassador there. In foreign countries, representatives of the U.S. Defense Department and the Central Intelligence Agency, in particular, often continue to operate with some independence from the U.S. ambassador; their primary loyalty is to their own departments in Washington.[14]

Lastly, the State Department's influence on foreign policy is limited by the way the general public and members of Congress and other officials perceive the Department. It is sometimes seen as representing foreign interests—that is, being too willing to agree with foreign countries for diplomatic reasons—rather than being "tough" and standing up for America's national security interests and the economic interests of American business and industry.[15]

---

[14]For a survey of views concerning the State Department and how it operates, see John Franklin Campbell, *The Foreign Affairs Fudge Factory* (New York: Basic Books, 1971); Morton Halperin, *Bureaucratic Politics and Foreign Policy* (Washington, D.C., The Brookings Institution, 1974); and Graham Allison and Peter Szanton, *Remaking Foreign Policy* (New York: Basic Books, 1976).

[15]See John Spanier and Eric M. Uslaner, *How American Foreign Policy Is Made*, 2nd ed. (New York: Holt, Rinehart and Winston/Praeger, 1978), p. 63.

The Defense Department.   People often speak of the "Pentagon" when they refer to the Defense Department. This is because the Department's headquarters is housed in a massive five-sided building on the Virginia shores of the Potomac River, just across from the Capitol. The Pentagon is almost big enough to sink through the ground. A visitor searching for a particular office inside wishes for a golfcart to negotiate the wide and seemingly endless halls. If the State Department is an elephantine bureaucracy, the Defense Department is a woolly mammoth. It has many of the same organizational and chain-of-command problems, too.

The Department of Defense was organized in 1947 with passage of the Unification Act. The Act had been recommended by President Truman in order to integrate and put under one secretary of defense the three military services: Army, Navy, and Air Force. Until that time they had been operating relatively separately, reporting directly to the President. Today, under the secretary of defense, a number of assistant secretaries preside over such functional areas as installations and logistics, manpower and reserve affairs, financial management, intelligence, systems analysis, telecommunications, public affairs, congressional affairs, and international security affairs.[16] Also within the Department are the separate and relatively autonomous departments of the Army, Navy, and Air Force, which are headed by civilian secretaries, who report to the secretary of defense.

Within the Department, too, and operating with even more autonomy are the Joint Chiefs of Staff—the military commanders of the Army, Navy, Air Force, and Marine Corps. The specific mission of the secretary of defense is to coordinate national security policy with foreign policy, while that of the Joint Chiefs of Staff is to decide upon strategies and tactics to put the military aspects of this policy into effect. Although the Joint Chiefs report to and advise the secretary of defense, they also report directly to the President. In addition, they enjoy both formal and informal relationships with members of Congress and with the congressional committees that have jurisdiction over military affairs and national security. The Joint Chiefs also have considerable contact with newspaper columnists, with a network of civilian organizations (such as the Association of the U.S. Army, which promotes the interests of that branch of the armed services), and with private research and development organizations and business and industrial corporations engaged in contract defense work. Thus, while our traditional idea of civilian control of the military is technically preserved, the military establishment is very involved in influencing the formulation and adoption of policy; it is not just engaged in the implementation of policy.

The secretary of defense's influence, like that of the secretary of state, may depend upon the person who holds the office and on what kind of relationship that person has with the President. But Defense

---

[16]See Irish and Frank, *U.S. Foreign Policy*, pp. 234–41.

has some advantages over State in influencing policy, regardless of who the particular head of the Defense Department is.

First, in this age of missiles and nuclear weapons, the Defense Department deals with awesome concepts: "first strike capability," the ability to completely disable an opponent before the opponent can attack; "second strike capability," the ability to inflict unacceptable damage on an enemy after having suffered a first attack; and "mutually assured destruction," the idea that the ability to destroy each other ensures no attack will occur.

Second, the Defense Department is especially influential in foreign policy matters because of the huge sums of money it spends—more than $1 trillion since the end of World War II. Upon leaving office, President Eisenhower warned about the worrisome and growing strength of what he called the "military-industrial complex." This term refers primarily to private organizations and corporations that work closely with the Defense Department and whose economic interests are strongly supported by influential lobbyists, campaign activity, and grass-roots propagandizing.

Third, military matters seem to be more quantifiable (expressible in numbers) than most of the foreign policy matters with which the State Department deals. These hard numbers, unlike the "soft" State Department policy alternatives, often give military recommendations greater standing in the policy-making process. As one authority has put it, "Perhaps defense decisions—so heavily involved with troop commitments, weapons procurements, and resource allocation—lend themselves more easily to the appearance of order, rationality and cost-benefit analysis than do the less quantifiable and more subtle means of diplomatic discourse." Thus, the Defense Department's ability to provide numbers has been ". . . one more stepping stone to increase its importance in foreign policy."[17]

Finally, the Defense Department's "symbolic appeal" for the general public and, to some degree, for members of Congress and other officials gives it a certain advantage in influencing foreign policy. "The identification of the military with national pride and achievement—in a word, with patriotism—is a quite extraordinary bureaucratic resource—setting the Defense Department apart from all other executive agencies in the country."[18]

The intelligence establishment. During World War II, the Office of Strategic Services (OSS), headed by William "Wild Bill" Donovan, performed almost legendary clandestine (secret) spying, sabotage, and military functions for the United States. After the war, the OSS was replaced by a permanent intelligence organization, the Central Intelligence Agency (CIA). The National Security Act of 1947 gave

---

[17]Bliss and Johnson, *Beyond the Water's Edge*, pp. 165–66.

[18]Francis E. Rourke, *Bureaucracy and Foreign Policy* (Baltimore: Johns Hopkins University Press, 1973), P. 30. See also Dean Acheson, "The Eclipse of the State Department," *Foreign Affairs* (July 1971), pp. 593–606.

the CIA the function of both gathering and interpreting intelligence. A large portion of CIA employees are engaged in research and assessing and analyzing "overt" intelligence—information gained from *public* sources. The CIA also uses sophisticated electronic equipment to gather intelligence information. This overt part of the CIA's work has generally been noncontroversial. By contrast, the "covert" or secret operations of the CIA have been criticized considerably in recent years. These operations involve spying and secretly gathering intelligence, as well as so-called "dirty tricks." Without specific authorization by law, the CIA has in the past engaged in efforts to overthrow governments, subvert free elections in other countries, bribe officials, and attempt assassinations. It has also illegally involved itself in domestic surveillance of American citizens and private organizations.[19] Congress and Presidents Ford and Carter have taken steps to end the illegal activities of the Central Intelligence Agency, to severely curtail its covert operations in foreign countries, and to bring it under tighter executive and congressional control. Both houses of Congress have established special committees to oversee CIA activities.

No one doubts that our government must have reliable information on which to base its foreign policy and national security decisions. Nearly all modern Presidents have complained at one time or another about their inability to get enough information of this kind. President Kennedy, for example, blamed the CIA for the Bay of Pigs invasion of Cuba, which our government organized and financed under the mistaken assumption that it would result in a general uprising in Cuba—a major miscalculation. President Carter has been critical of the quality of American intelligence. For example, he was reported to be very upset that the CIA was not able to predict the fall of the Shah of Iran.

Most Americans now agree that the CIA should be subject to strict political control. But some supporters of the CIA fear that as more officials—particularly congressional members—are kept advised of what the CIA does, there may be a damaging loss of the advantages of secrecy. Some CIA critics have suggested that it should not be engaged in covert operations at all, that it should be involved only in gathering and analyzing intelligence and not in such actions as "dirty tricks." CIA defenders say that recent investigations and disclosures about the agency have hampered its activities too severely. Others are deeply concerned about the fundamental paradox of secrecy in a democracy: how representative are the public officials who make fundamental foreign policy decisions, and how can the public hold

---

[19]See *Commission on CIA Activities Within the United States*, Report to the President (Washington, D.C.: U.S. Government Printing Office, 1975). See also U.S. Senate Select Committee to Study Governmental Operations with Respect to Intelligence Activities, *Alleged Assassination Plots Involving Foreign Leaders: Interim Report* (1975); *Foreign and Military Intelligence*, Final Report (Washington, D.C.: U.S. Government Printing Office, 1976).

them accountable for such decisions when much of the information on which these decisions are made is secret?[20]

The CIA is not the only intelligence organization in the federal government.[21] Both the Defense and State Departments have their own intelligence bureaus, as does each branch of the armed services within the Defense Department. Also in the Defense Department is the National Security Agency, which was established to gather intelligence by using highly sophisticated, modern technology, including missiles, satellites, and electronic surveillance and code-breaking devices.

After President Carter took office, he felt that intelligence gathering and analysis needed to be centralized—much the same need which had brought about the creation of the Central Intelligence Agency in the first place. He gave the CIA overview and coordinating powers in the intelligence field, and he named an old Naval Academy classmate, Admiral Stansfield Turner, to be CIA director.

The National Security Council. Any survey of the various bureaucracies and officials involved in making America's foreign policy makes it clear that one of the major problems any President faces in this field is organizing and making sense of the bureaucracies and administering them in a way as to make them most useful.

. . . any bureaucracy is a double-edged sword; it provides the essential assistance to an overworked chief executive, but it also creates and embodies a whole series of problems—management, discipline, loyalty, communication—which must be dealt with if it is to aid rather than hinder, to dispatch rather than delay, to process rather than impede. In reality, such problems are never wholly resolved and much of any president's time is spent in organizing and reorganizing—in managing—his foreign affairs bureaucracy. Every president has chafed under the limitations and restraints imposed upon him by the machinery of foreign policy-making.[22]

The President's ability to maintain control over all the federal foreign policy bureaucracies and to organize them in an optimum way is limited in at least two major respects.[23] First, as we have seen, great and growing numbers of participants in the policy-making process limit the President's control. So many people are involved and there is such an overwhelming flow of information that it is increasingly difficult to stay on top of it all. Second, the executive bureaucracies involved in foreign policy have their own different constituencies and interests to which they are somewhat loyal.

---

[20]See Y.H. Kim, ed., *The Central Intelligence Agency: Problems of Secrecy in a Democracy* (Lexington, Mass.: D.C. Heath, 1968).

[21]Henry T. Nash, *American Foreign Policy: Changing Perspectives on National Security* (Homewood, Ill: Dorsey Press, 1978), pp. 207–12.

[22]Bliss and Johnson, *Beyond the Water's Edge*, p. 159.

[23]Bliss and Johnson, *Beyond the Water's Edge*, pp. 170–73.

To improve the President's ability to coordinate the advice and reports from various officials and bureaucracies and to integrate "domestic, foreign, and military policies relating to the national security," the National Security Act of 1947 created the National Security Council (NSC). As we noted earlier, the President's national security adviser heads the NSC staff. Inevitably, some rivalry develops between the President's national security adviser and the other foreign policy bureaucracies. Under President Carter, there were numerous reports that Secretary of State Cyrus Vance and Brzezinski were competing bitterly for the President's mind; Brzezinski seemed to favor a tougher line toward the Soviet Union than did Vance.

President Carter talks with two of his primary foreign policy-makers, National Security Adviser Zbigniew Brzezinski (center) and Secretary of State Cyrus Vance (right).

Presidents generally have liked their ability to use their own White House staff to make speedy foreign policy decisions and to quickly implement them. Before he took office in the Nixon administration, Henry Kissinger wrote about the flexibility and freedom of action that a President could gain in foreign policy matters by not involving all the foreign policy bureaucracies. "One reason for keeping the decisions to small groups," he wrote, "is that when bureaucracies are so unwieldy and when their internal morale becomes a serious problem, an unpopular decision may be fought by brutal means, such as leaks to the press or to Congressional committees."[24]

Other foreign policy bureaucracies. The Agency for International Development (AID) is attached to the State Department but operates with a great deal of independence. Its job is to supervise America's foreign aid and much of the military assistance America gives to other countries.[25] Foreign aid has never been popular with the general public in this country. Policy-makers support it on the grounds that, in addition to America's moral obligation to help people who are less fortunate than ourselves, assisting people of other nations to get on their feet economically will help to produce a more stable world and thus a more secure one for America. Some advocates of foreign aid to developing nations have suggested that all

[24]Henry A. Kissinger, "Bureaucracy and Policy-Making: The Effects of Insiders and Outsiders on the Policy Process," in Morton H. Halperin and Arnold Kanter, eds., *Readings in American Foreign Policy* (Boston: Little Brown, 1973), p. 89.

[25]In regard to the other bureaucracies involved in foreign policy today, see Bliss and Johnson, *Beyond the Water's Edge*, pp. 168–69.

industrial nations should allocate at least 1 percent of their gross national products for this purpose, partly through private donations and partly through governmental appropriations. The United States and most industrial countries have not come near this level of assistance.

Since the Vietnam War, foreign military assistance has declined somewhat. It was expected to increase, however, as a result of President Carter's commitments to President Sadat and Prime Minister Begin as a part of the 1979 Egyptian-Israeli peace settlement. Israel has always been a major recipient of American military assistance.

Recipient nations use a great part of foreign aid for purchases from American suppliers. Foreign arms sales, which are handled through the Pentagon, have also resulted in huge purchases from American suppliers. America has been one of the great arms sellers of the world, despite President Carter's declarations in favor of reducing these sales.

The United States Arms Control and Disarmament Agency is housed in the State Department. Its director's job is to advise the secretary of state and the President on agreements concerning armament control. But the Defense Department, the Joint Chiefs of Staff, and key members of Congress, such as Senator Henry M. Jackson of Washington, have probably had more impact on U.S. arms control policy than has the agency which is nominally charged with this responsibility. Many military people and some members of the Congress view the Arms Control and Disarmament Agency as being "soft" on the Soviet Union—too willing to agree to too great a limit on U.S. arms. Thus, Paul Warnke, who was appointed by President Carter to head this agency, came under fire in Congress for not being "tough" enough with the Russians during 1978 and 1979 arms control negotiations. Significantly, as the Strategic Arms Limitation Talks neared agreement and the treaty-signing stage with the Russians in 1979 (SALT II), Paul Warnke stepped down from his post as director of the U.S. Arms Control and Disarmament Agency. President Carter appointed in his place a former military man who was thought to have a better chance to "sell" the agreement to Congress and the country.

The United States Information Agency, attached to the State Department, has the responsibility for disseminating information abroad that is favorable to the image and policies of the United States government. It also administers the international radio system, "Voice of America."

Particularly with the rise in importance of trade and economic matters, the federal bureaucracies involved in making foreign policy are not just the ones whose missions *obviously* concern foreign policy and national security matters. Aside from its major domestic responsibilities, the Department of the Treasury is also involved in foreign policy matters relating to America's balance of payments and to international monetary negotiations. The Department of Commerce is deeply involved in international trade, promoting the sale of American products. Likewise, the Department of Agriculture is concerned with agricultural sales abroad. The Department of Justice supervises immigration and naturalization matters and attempts to control traffic in illegal drugs.

In the Executive Office of the President, a trade negotiator with "ambassador" status aids the President on trade matters. President Carter named Robert Strauss, a former chairman of the Democratic National Committee, as his first trade negotiator.

The Congress

The formal foreign policy powers of Congress are plainly stated in the Constitution: Congress alone has the power to declare war and to raise and support armies; it has the "power of the purse" through its control over federal expenditures; it has investigative and oversight powers to call executive officials to account; it has the law-making power; and the Senate has the power to ratify treaties and confirm appointments. Clearly, the framers of the Constitution intended the control of foreign policy to be shared between the President and the Congress. As John Jay wrote in *Federalist* 64, "The Constitution provides that our negotiations for treaties shall have every advantage that can be derived from talent, information, integrity, and deliberate investigations, on the one hand, and from secrecy and dispatch, on the other."

There is a considerable difference, however, between the *formal* powers of Congress in the field of foreign policy and its *actual* influence in that area.[26] Congress is at a disadvantage in dealing with the President as a foreign policy-making equal for four principal reasons. First, Congress is often hampered by a lack of unbiased information. Congress has no intelligence-gathering apparatus of its own. It must depend largely upon executive sources for its information. Much of this comes to the Congress in filtered, neatly packaged form, put together in a way that supports a single policy alternative.

Second, Congress does not have the organizational capability to prepare a set of carefully thought-out policy alternatives on a given foreign policy issue because its work is done by a number of different committees. Individual members of the Senate and House may be brought in by the President and the executive department for consultation at the foreign policy formulation stage, but this is an informal and irregular process. As an institution, Congress usually comes into the foreign policy picture *after* the various alternatives have been considered, privately and internally, by the executive department. Congress, then, is typically asked to react to a course of

---

[26]For discussions on the role of Congress in foreign policy, see Spanier and Uslaner, *How American Foreign Policy Is Made*, pp. 66–76; and Bliss and Johnson, *Beyond the Water's Edge*, pp. 181–204.

action that has already been decided upon by the executive department; rarely does it have the benefit of being able to look carefully at all the policy alternatives that might be considered.

Third, unlike the President, Congress usually cannot act quickly. It is indeed a "deliberative" institution—and a very deliberate one at that. Each house is coequal. Within each house, the authorization committees—the Senate Foreign Relations Committee and the House International Relations Committee—are separate from the appropriations committees. And the appropriations committees themselves have numerous semi-autonomous subcommittees. In addition, a number of other committees, such as the armed services committees, the commerce committees, the Senate Finance Committee, and the House Ways and Means Committee, sometimes have partial jurisdiction over issues involving foreign policy matters.

Fourth, Congress is at a disadvantage in that it is made up of 435 representatives and 100 senators who are expected to speak, to some degree, for local rather than national interests if they hope to be reelected. The President, on the other hand, is expected to be a spokesperson for the entire nation.

There is also some pressure on members of Congress to show national unity, especially in crisis situations, by supporting the President as the nation's leader in foreign affairs. Though they have sometimes been overstated by observers, similar pressures call for "politics to end at the water's edge," with both Republicans and Democrats standing together—in bipartisan support—when serious national interests are at stake.

The more urgent a foreign policy issue is—that is, the degree to which it arises in a crisis atmosphere—the more influence a President has and the less influence Congress has. Congress has not taken the initiative in foreign policy very often, but it has had increased influence when it has done so. Congress is better at helping to end a policy, such as our involvement in the Vietnam War, than it is at helping to originate a policy. And Congress is more influential on foreign policy when the decisions concerning an issue stretch out over a period of time.

During the Johnson and Nixon administrations, rising public dissatisfaction with America's involvement in the Vietnam War was reflected in congressional actions to redress the imbalance of power in the foreign policy field between Congress and the President. President Johnson had secured a virtual "blank check" for his escalation of America's involvement in the war when he was able to get both houses of Congress (88 to 2 in the Senate, and 416 to 0 in the House) to pass the Gulf of Tonkin Resolution in 1964. The Resolution, while not a formal declaration of war, expressed congressional support for almost anything the President wanted to do in Vietnam, "including the use of armed force." Johnson had presented the Resolution to Congress as a crisis response to what he said had been a North Vietnamese attack on two American destroyers in the Tonkin Gulf. As Congress learned much later, the supposed incident had been greatly exaggerated and had been exploited by President Johnson to secure congressional approval for what he had already wanted to do.

From Roosevelt to Nixon, the pendulum of foreign policy power swung widely toward the President and away from the Congress. But during President Nixon's administration, the pendulum began to be pulled back the other way. At that time, the Senate passed a nonbinding but important resolution stating that no executive agreement entered into by the President with a foreign country should be allowed to go into effect until it had been approved by Congress. The Case Act, which required the President to report the details of any international agreement to Congress, even if it did not have the formal status of a treaty, was also adopted. The War Powers Act, passed over President Nixon's veto, limited the President's power to involve America in military hostilities for more than sixty days without formal congressional approval.

Interest Groups

As with domestic policy, foreign policy is not neutral, and it is not decided upon in a neutral way. The results of foreign policy often hurt some groups and help others. Thus, it is not surprising that interest groups attempt to influence foreign policy decisions. While foreign citizens and even foreign governments sometimes seek to influence America's foreign policy, domestic interest groups are more vigorous and persistent in their day-to-day efforts to do so.

One authority has written that the domestic interest groups that are active in the foreign policy field fall into seven major categories.[27] First, there is organized labor. The AFL-CIO, for example, has been militantly opposed to foreign imports because it feels that such imports compete with American industry and reduce the number of available domestic jobs.

Second, business organizations are active in attempting to influence American foreign policy. As a matter of fact, business interest groups, including the U.S. Chamber of Commerce and the National Association of Manufacturers, probably have more influence on American foreign policy than any other domestic interest groups. U.S. multinational corporations have important impact on American foreign policy, too. Some American multinational corporations, such as Exxon, are bigger and more powerful than most of the nations of the world.[28] They attempt to influence foreign governments—even through bribery and, in the case of ITT in Chile, through efforts to

---

[27]See Gabriel A. Almond, *The American People and Foreign Policy* (New York: Praeger, 1960).

[28]Richard J. Barnet and Ronald E. Muller, *Global Reach—The Power of the Multinational Corporations* (New York: Simon and Schuster, 1974).

overthrow a government[29]—and they attempt to influence America's own government as well.

Business interest groups are increasingly powerful in influencing foreign policy because of the growing prominence of economic issues in international affairs.[30] Among the business groups influencing foreign policy are those that fall within the definition of the "military-industrial complex" and that have a vested interest in selling arms and military research and development to our own government and to the governments of foreign countries.[31]

Third, agricultural groups, such as the Farm Bureau and the Farmers Union, are interested in foreign policy. Usually, these groups support free-trade concepts, opposing tariff and other restrictions on imports. They feel that if America's agricultural products are to be sold abroad, which is necessary if the United States is to dispose of its abundant agricultural products, it must buy things from other countries.

Fourth, verterans' groups like the American Legion and the Veterans of Foreign Wars are active in the foreign policy field. They usually support a strong American military capability and a confrontationist American military stance, especially as it relates to the Soviet Union.

Fifth, women's groups—such as the American Association of University Women and the League of Women Voters—operate in the foreign policy field. They have particularly taken an interest in foreign aid and in the problems of developing countries.

Sixth, religious groups are also involved in seeking to influence America's foreign policy. These include organizations like the National Council of Churches and the Society of Friends (Quakers). They are generally internationalist in their viewpoints.

Finally, ethnic groups influence America's foreign policy. In Greek-Turkish disputes, for example, a number of members of Congress are likely to support the Greeks, responding to the persuasion and lobbying of Greek American groups. In the Middle East, America's policy has been consistently and heavily influenced by the activity and lobbying of America's Jews, a large percentage of whom identify with Israel.

The Mass Media

The media—television, radio, newspapers, and magazines—are important actors in the foreign policy process. They report what the government is doing, and from time to time they engage in criticism and advocacy.[32] The media's influence is limited by the fact that, even more than in domestic policy, the government is anxious to keep much of its foreign policy activity secret. Some of this government

---

[29]See A. Sampson, *The Sovereign State of ITT* (New York: Stein and Day, 1973).
[30]Bliss and Johnson, *Beyond the Water's Edge,* p. 223.
[31]See Seymour Melman, *Pentagon Capitalism* (New York: McGraw Hill, 1970).
[32]See Irish and Frank, *U.S. Foreign Policy*, pp. 119–33.

The media influence the foreign policy process by bringing information to the American public. During the Vietnam War, television cameras carried images of the conflict into Americans' living rooms.

secrecy may be justified. For example, highly difficult negotiations could be made more difficult, or even impossible, if there were day-to-day reports in the press on the negotiations. But in the past, secrecy was often used to keep the American people in the dark for fear of adverse public opinion, as when President Nixon ordered an invasion of Cambodia. In such instances and in reporting on foreign policy matters generally, the media help to call policy-makers to account. It should be noted, though, that Presidents have the advantage in their dealings with the media.[33] Presidents can produce or withhold information or preempt television time for major statements. They can call press conferences whenever they want to. They can favor some journalists with interviews and "leaks" and punish others, depending to some degree upon their willingness to be helpful to the President's personal and national goals. The President can float "trial balloons" to gauge the reaction to various policy alternatives under consideration.

The President has the upper hand in dealing with the media. But the media in America operate as an important restraint on foreign policy; most importantly, they bring information to the general public, which can result in public pressure on the formulation and adoption of foreign policy.

Public Opinion and Participation

For a long time, the most active foreign policy-makers and the people who influence such decisions have felt that the general public in America should not be involved as much in making foreign policy as they are in domestic policy. For example, Theodore Sorenson, who served on President Kennedy's staff, has said that the public is often

[33]See Bliss and Johnson, *Beyond the Water's Edge*, pp. 215–21.

ill-informed and mercurial, or changeable, and therefore should not be depended upon for great participation in foreign policy-making.[34]

Political scientists have also written about the "unreliability" of the general public on foreign policy. Again, they have said that the general public is not very well informed about foreign policy and that its moods are too changeable.[35] Professor Samuel P. Huntington has said that in regard to foreign policy, ". . . there could be problems in having too much participatory democracy," primarily because of "shifts in public opinion."[36] Those who worry about public participation in foreign policy-making were generally pleased when Seymour Lipset wrote in 1966, "The President makes public opinion, he does not follow it."[37]

But American public opinion cannot be ignored by those who make America's foreign policy. Seymour Lipset's disdainful view of the effect of public opinion on American foreign policy was expressed on the very eve of the enormous upheaval in American public opinion resulting from the Vietnam War—an upheaval that forced President Johnson to decide not to run for reelection and that eventually forced a deescalation and then an end to the war.

Public opinion in the foreign policy field, as in other policy matters, may be expressed through opinion polls, lobbying—either individually or through interest groups—and elections. One historian has said, "Looking back through history, one can almost count on one's fingers the numbers of occasions when American statesmen made major decisions that they thought contrary to the public will."[38] Another authority has written that peace and war issues have been decisive political issues in a number of presidential elections through the years: "Those who doubt the importance of foreign affairs in presidential elections should be aware of how consistently the party which the general public has considered best able to end war or maintain peace has won the next election."[39]

It is true, of course, that some portions of the public are more interested in foreign policy than others. About 30 percent of the American public might be called the "mass public," a group that is sporadically interested in foreign policy issues. Another 45 percent might be called the "attentive public," because they are aware of major foreign policy issues and developments. The remaining 25 percent of the American public might be called "opinion-makers,"

---

[34]See Theodore Sorenson, "Statement on the Impact of Public Opinion on Foreign Policy," a National Public Radio *Options* Program (January 31, 1978), cited in Daniel Yankelovich, "Farewell to 'President Knows Best,'" pp. 672–73.

[35]Almond, *The American People and Foreign Policy*, p. 53.

[36]Interview with Samuel P. Huntington, *U.S. News & World Report* (November 27, 1978), p. 65.

[37]Quoted in Ralph B. Levering, *The Public and American Foreign Policy, 1918–1978* (New York: William Morrow and Company, 1978), p. 152.

[38]Ernest R. May, "An American Tradition in Foreign Policy: The Role of Public Opinion" in William H. Nelson, ed., *Theory and Practice in American Politics* (Chicago: University of Chicago Press, 1966), p. 117.

[39]Levering, *The Public and American Foreign Policy, 1918–1978*, p. 153.

since they are generally knowledgeable about foreign affairs and communicate their opinions to others.[40]

Foremost among the opinion-makers, as well as among the smaller group of policy-makers, is the President of the United States. What is the relationship between the President and public opinion in foreign policy matters? One view is that public opinion serves as a "dictator" of foreign policy. It is true that when the public is well informed and extremely upset, as it was when President Nixon ordered the invasion of Cambodia in 1970, it can act as a powerful critic and can even dictate policy. But it is probably more accurate to think of public opinion as an "accomplice" to the President in foreign policy matters, so that the President and public opinion influence each other.[41]

The public is much more reliable than some of the critics of public participation in foreign policy have indicated. A recent study has shown that the old idea about an unstable and fickle public on foreign policy issues is not supported by the facts. Instead, public opinion is characterized "by a *strong* and *stable* 'permissive mood' toward international involvement."[42] It is true that the general public in America is not as supportive of foreign aid and military involvements as some of the foreign policy elites are. Usually, the general public is more interested in domestic problems and priorities than in foreign issues. But that is also increasingly true of the attentive public and the opinion-makers. Since the Vietnam War, these better-informed and more active members of the American public have become increasingly aware of the limits on America's ability, right, or need to reshape the world; and they have become more and more convinced that we should place greater emphasis on domestic problems.[43]

Those who criticize the idea of greater public participation in making American foreign policy—on the grounds that the general public is not well informed on foreign policy matters—are often the same people who feel that "national security" dictates that foreign policy matters should be carried on largely in secret. Elites who disdain the public's ability to deal with foreign policy matters feel that vital information should be withheld from the general public. This, in turn, further supports the idea that the general public is ill informed. Thus, this philosophy, in a very real sense, blames the victim—the general public—for being poorly informed, when it is the elites or leaders themselves who withhold information from the public. These leaders

. . . harbor the assumption that the public is simpleminded, capable of holding only one extreme alternative in mind at a time—black or white, for or against, friend or foe. As policy needs dictate, the appropriate

[40]Barry B. Hughes, *The Domestic Context of American Foreign Policy* (San Francisco: W.H. Freeman and Company, 1978), pp. 23–25.
[41]Bliss and Johnson, *Beyond the Water's Edge*, pp. 206–15.
[42]William Caspary, "The 'Mood Theory': A Study of Public Opinion and Foreign Policy," *American Political Science Review* (June 1970), p. 546.
[43]Hughes, *The Domestic Context of American Foreign Policy*, pp. 56–57.

Goals of U.S. Foreign Policy

Question: I am going to read you a list of possible foreign policy goals that the United States might have. For each one please say whether you think that should be a very important foreign policy goal, a somewhat important foreign policy goal, or not an important goal at all (read list).

	Very important	Somewhat important	Not important
Keeping up the value of the dollar	90%	8%	2%
Securing adequate supplies of energy	82%	16%	2%
Protecting jobs of American workers	81%	16%	3%
Worldwide arms control	70%	25%	5%
Containing communism	64%	26%	11%
Combating world hunger	62%	33%	5%
Defending our allies security	54%	38%	8%
Strengthening the United Nations	51%	35%	14%
Protecting interest of American business abroad	48%	43%	10%
Promoting and defending human rights in other countries	42%	43%	15%
Helping to improve the standard of living in less developed countries	37%	50%	13%
Protecting weaker nations against foreign aggression	37%	52%	11%
Helping to bring democratic forms of government to other nations	29%	48%	23%

SOURCE: Survey by the American Institute of Public Opinion (Gallup) for the Chicago Council on Foreign Relations, November 17-26, 1978.

---

switch is thrown in an attempt to elicit the appropriate single-dimensioned response . . . the public mind is [not] one-dimensional, but . . . to the extent foreign policy leaders act on this assumption, they risk creating the ogre they fear: a public intolerant of ambiguities in a world filled with ambiguities.[44]

Those who favor greater control of foreign policy by the elites, with less public participation, probably place too much faith in the elites. Thus, it was not the general public, but foreign policy leaders who got America involved in the disastrous Vietnam War. But there are other reasons why the public should be involved in foreign policy decisions. Our system of government is based upon the "consent of the governed"; and foreign policy matters, particularly with their current inter-relationship with economic matters, involve the vital interests of all American citizens. Such decisions should not be made without concern for what American citizens want and believe. Why? First of all, how will "truth" be arrived at in foreign policy—or in other policy

---

[44]Daniel Yankelovich, "Farewell to 'President Knows Best,'" *Foreign Affairs*, 57, no. 3 (1978): 687–88.

matters—unless there is a competitive market of ideas? How better can competing ideas come to the surface than through the general involvement of the public? As one authority has stated, ". . . political truths are different from technical truths, and in a democracy, can only be arrived at through the ego-bruising process of political debate." This is particularly necessary today because Presidents tend to be isolated from unpleasant or conflicting views.[45]

Second, we should desire a well-informed public that cannot be stampeded because of fear or prejudices to accept a foreign policy that is not in the national interest:

In a democracy armed to the teeth with nuclear weapons, public noninvolvement is a terrifying danger and not a desirable goal. An 'irresponsible public' is one that is kept in the dark most of the time, leaving it to the 'experts' to run the show. Such a public is manipulable, apathetic, and panic-prone, in sharp contrast to an informed public that feels it must share responsibility for its own future with its leaders.[46]

Third, the general public should be involved in foreign policy for self-protection. There are no "neutral" or "pure" decisions in foreign policy matters, just as there are none in domestic policy matters. When the elites run things in foreign policy, they tend to favor policies that take care of their own interests. These may be the concerns of banks, oil companies, or other special interests. Securing the support of average citizens for America's foreign policy decisions today requires policy-makers to take into account the interests of the general public, not just those of the elites and the special interests. For example, some foreign policy elitists fault the general public for not being willing to pay for greater amounts of foreign aid to other countries. But America's tax system, which finances foreign aid, places a disproportionately high burden on wage earners, compared to the rich. According to one authority,

If, on the basis of concrete evidence, the people decide that the government is treating everyone alike and fairly—that the costs of public policy choices on both foreign and domestic issues are more equitably shared—our leaders may stand some hope of regaining the public trust they once had.[47] . . . these people have so much less to give away. Logically, they should be more concerned than higher income people about the financial consequences of a decision to increase, say, the foreign aid budget, or, for that matter, any public policy budget that does not directly benefit them.[48]

[45]Yankelovich, "Farewell to 'President Knows Best,'" pp. 692–93.
[46]Yankelovich, "Farewell to 'President Knows Best,'" p. 692.
[47]Charles W. Maynes, Jr., "Who Pays for Foreign Policy," *Foreign Policy*, 15 (1974): 168.
[48]Charles W. Maynes, Jr., "Can We Afford Not to Have It?" *Foreign Policy*, 18 (1975) 117.

Thus, whether the general public will approve America's foreign policy may depend upon the degree to which the public's opinion is taken into account, the degree to which the costs are fairly shared, and the degree to which their interests are served—and why not?

Contrary to the views of some foreign policy elites, the general public has shown increased sophistication on foreign policy issues:

Perhaps the most hopeful development during the past sixty years has been the increased sophistication of large portions of the public in regard to foreign affairs. This has resulted from greater educational opportunities, more contacts with other peoples both directly and through media such as television, broader participation in foreign policy organizations, and experiences such as Vietnam. The declining belief in American superiority has been accompanied by the realization that other cultures are different and that they should not necessarily adopt American institutions and values.[49]

When policy-makers have shared information with the public, trusted them with the facts, the American public has been able to sort out the facts and find their own self-interest, as they did in late 1978 in approving the new Panama Canal Treaty.

Another important reason for trusting the public is that American public opinion has a very strong moral component.[50] Some foreign policy elites support a foreign policy "pragmatism," which has no moral consistency to it; it exemplifies no particular and continuing American principles. The American public is more idealistic than that; for example, it has generally approved President Carter's advocacy of human rights around the world.

THE U.S. AND INTERNATIONAL ORGANIZATIONS

In addition to its domestic institutions, the United States carries out its foreign policy through a number of international organizations. It belongs to more than two hundred of them. The most important are the Organization of American States; the World Bank and similar financial institutions; the North Atlantic Treaty Organization; and the United Nations.

The Organization of American States (OAS) is a regional organization made up of the United States and Latin American nations. The United States has dominated the organization and has used it in recent years to strengthen the present governments of Latin American countries against *internal* enemies. The United States has also used the OAS to provide concerted sanctions, such as the boycott of

---

[49]Levering, *The Public and American Foreign Policy, 1918–1978*, p. 169.
[50]Yankelovich, "Farewell to 'President Knows Best,'" p. 674.

Cuba, against nations that do not follow policies in accord with our international desires.[51]

Policy-makers have always disputed as to whether the United States should "tie" more of its foreign aid to recipient-country conformity to American policy. Barbara Ward has written that "the political slant of communist economic policies—whether of loans or technical assistance or barter or ordinary trade—is a great strength. Equally, the lack of any political or ideological framework is the greatest single source of weakness in the aid program undertaken by the West."[52] But more and more, those involved in American foreign policy-making have come to believe that America cannot "buy friends," though it has an interest in promoting security and stability in the world by helping developing nations become more economically self-sufficient.

Much of the world is very poor.[53] Recipient countries have resented heavy-handed attempts to buy their cooperation and approval through foreign aid. There is an instructive Chinese proverb question that says: "Why do you hate me? I never did anything for you." Similarly, George F. Kennan has written, "To those who come to us with a request for aid one would like to say: 'You tell us first how you propose to assure that if we give you this aid it will not be interpreted among your people as a sign of weakness or fear on our part, or of a desire to dominate you.'"[54] Thus, the United States has increasingly oriented its foreign aid policy toward financial support through international financial organizations such as the World Bank and the InterAmerican Development Bank (for Latin America).

The North Atlantic Treaty Organization (NATO) links the United States and Western European countries in a military alliance. NATO has been used primarily as a military counter to the Warsaw Pact, which is made up of the Soviet Union and the countries of Eastern Europe. These two military alliances are the most important of the two superpowers, the United States and the Soviet Union.[55] NATO attempts to integrate the military operations of its member nations and to provide a joint deterrent to Soviet aggression in Europe. In recent years, Americans have increasingly taken the view that European nations—some of which, like West Germany, are economically stronger than America—should take on more responsibility for the costs of NATO.[56] In 1979, as a result of an agreement he made with NATO nations, President Carter recommended an increased

---

[51]In regard to the OAS see Ray, *Global Politics*, p. 181.
[52]Barbara Ward, "For a New Foreign Aid Concept," in Robert A. Goldwin and Harry M. Clor, eds., *Readings in American Foreign Policy* (New York: Oxford University Press, 1971).
[53]See Robert L. Heilbroner, *The Great Ascent* (New York: Harper & Row, 1963).
[54]George Kennan, "Limitations of Economic Aid," in Goldwin and Clor, eds., *Readings in American Foreign Policy*.
[55]Ray, *Global Politics*, pp. 177–80.
[56]*Business Week* (August 8, 1977), pp. 78–79.

U.S. contribution to NATO, despite the fact that some authorities have stated that the "Soviet scare" of an attack on Western Europe has been greatly exaggerated. These observers point out that, among other things, more than half of Soviet military forces are engaged in activities that are unrelated to NATO security (such as Soviet-China border protection) and that Soviet allies in Eastern Europe, such as Poland, do not in any way match the reliability of NATO allies.[57]

The United Nations (UN) is a universal peace-keeping organization, much as the League of Nations was intended to be following World War I. As World War II began to move toward an allied victory, there was strong feeling that the failure of the United States to become a member of the League of Nations after World War I had contributed to the outbreak of World War II. Whether or not this was true—and there is reason to doubt it—Franklin Roosevelt and his successor, Harry S. Truman, took the position that some universal peace-keeping organization should be established as soon as World War II was over. The United Nations was the result.[58] It elects the fifteen justices of the International Court of Justice, which has as its mission the settlement of disputes between nations. Court decisions are not binding, and no nation can be brought before the Court without its consent, but the establishment of the Court is a step toward increasing the power of international law.

The United Nations operates through a General Assembly and a Security Council. The Security Council seeks primarily to provide representation for the big powers; each member has a veto on Council matters. The General Assembly in recent years has been greatly expanded to include membership for the developing nations, which have won their independence from former colonial powers. The United Nations maintains no regular peace-keeping force; this function is irregularly performed by volunteer forces furnished from time to time by member countries. The UN is unable to collect mandatory dues from its members. Its financial base depends upon voluntary contributions. The United States provides considerably more funds to the UN than any other nation. In recent years, the United Nations has increasingly become a sounding board for the developing countries, which make up a majority of the General Assembly. When the great powers disagree, the UN has had limited effect in international conflicts or disputes. Nevertheless, it has been an important forum for talking rather than fighting, and it has provided a mechanism for countries to work together on such problems as environmental pollution, nuclear proliferation, monetary fluctuations, and public health.

The United Nations has not enjoyed strong popular support in America in recent years, particularly because of the emerging aggressiveness of developing countries.

---

[57]Fred Kaplan, "NATO and the Soviet Scare," *Inquiry* (June 12, 1978), pp. 16–20.
[58]In regard to the United Nations, see Ray, *Global Politics,* pp. 208–19.

As U.S. ambassador to the United Nations, Daniel Patrick Moynihan was able to parlay his role as a militant spokesperson for American interests and against what he and others thought were "pushy" developing nations into his 1978 election to the U.S. Senate from New York.

FOREIGN POLICY AND THE FUTURE

America's foreign policy concerns continue to be both regional and issue-oriented. Such issues as energy shortages and inflation cut across regional lines. Regional concerns involving the Soviet Union, Western Europe, the Middle East, and the developing nations cut across economic and energy issues.

President Carter's initiative in helping to bring about an Egyptian-Israeli peace treaty in 1979 heightened tensions in the Middle East in some ways; Syria, Jordan, and Iraq, with the somewhat reluctant support of Saudi Arabia and others, moved to interrupt their diplomatic and economic relations with Egypt. The Soviet Union continued its attempts to increase its influence in Africa and in the Middle East, while also negotiating with the U.S. for arms limitations. The 1979 debate in the U.S. Senate on the second Strategic Arms Limitation Treaty (SALT II) produced charges that the Soviet Union was becoming stronger militarily than the U.S. But, as proponents of SALT II pointed out:

The United States possesses 9,000 nuclear warheads, twice as many as the Soviet Union. These are hydrogen bombs, each having from four to 450 times the explosive power of the weapons that devastated Hiroshima. In a war, only about 400 warheads would be needed to wipe out half the Soviet Union's urban population and two-thirds of its industrial capacity. The Soviet Union has more and bigger land-based inter-continental ballistic missiles than the U.S. does, and more submarine-launched missiles, but the United States leads in bombers and in technology. Our missiles are vastly more accurate. Our submarines are quieter, therefore less vulnerable to attack, and more of them are at sea at any one time than the Soviets'. Two-thirds of the Soviet bomber force is still propeller-driven, while our planes have long been jet-powered and we are far ahead in the development of super-accurate cruise missiles.[59]

There are great social costs for the arms race, but Americans who support increased expenditures for health, welfare, education, housing, and other social needs do not always have the most influence in the American political arena.[60]

President Carter and Soviet Premier Leonid Brezhnev signed the SALT II agreement in Vienna on June 18, 1979.

---

[59]Morton Kondracke, "Carter's Nuclear Confidence Gap," *The New Republic* (April 15, 1978), pp. 15–17.

[60]See Ruth Leger Sivard, "Social Costs and the Arms Race," *The Nation* (June 17, 1978), pp. 730–32.

Americans who favor increased military expenditures—and President Carter sided with them when he proposed his 1980 budget—make much of the military strength and successes of the Soviet Union. But the Soviets have many weaknesses, too. They could actually be said to have lost overall strength in the world since the 1950s. China is now independent of them. The Russians must be worried about the growing independence in Poland, Czechoslovakia, and Eastern Europe generally. Their client nations, such as Afghanistan, Angola, Cuba, and Ethiopia, are among the most impoverished countries in the world, draining Soviet resources. In Africa, the Soviet Union has lost more footholds (Egypt, Guinea, Somalia, and Sudan) than it has maintained (Angola and Ethiopia). The Communist parties of Western Europe have increasingly expressed their autonomy from the Kremlin. Internally, the Soviet Union has very serious economic and political problems.

Thus, one authority has written that, while we should not ignore the problems that the Soviet Union poses for our security, neither should we overestimate their strengths:

In the competition for influence in other countries, primarily in the Third World, Americans have potent advantages. Our ability to help raise living standards still serves as a magnet to the less-developed nations. The example of our free society still pulls people to our shores from every continent. The fundamental beliefs of our Founding Fathers managed to find their way onto wall posters in Peking. Many in the world still aspire to what we take for granted.[61]

ADDITIONAL SOURCES

Almond, Gabriel. *The American People and Foreign Policy*, 2nd ed. Greenwood, 1977.

Barnet, Richard J. *The Giants: Russia and America*. Simon and Schuster, 1977.

FitzGerald, Frances. *Fire in the Lake: The Vietnamese and the Americans in Vietnam*. Little, Brown, 1972.*

Halberstam, David. *The Best and the Brightest*. Random House, 1972.*

Halperin, Morton H., ed. *Bureaucratic Politics and Foreign Policy*. Brookings, 1974.*

Hilsman, Roger. *The Politics of Policy Making in Defense and Foreign Affairs*. Harper and Row, 1971.*

Kirk, Grayson, and Nils H. Wessell, eds. *The Soviet Threat: Myths and Realities, Proceedings of the Academy of Political Science*, vol. 33, no. 1. The Academy of Political Science, 1978.*

Melman, Seymour. *The Permanent War Economy*. Simon and Schuster, 1974.*

Mueller, John E. *War, Presidents, and Public Opinion*. Wiley, 1973.*

*Available in paperback.

---

[61]Sanford Gottlieb, "Russia's Weaknesses," *Newsweek* (March 26, 1979), p. 19.

America's Democracy:

The Future

We began this book by noting that the reality of America's democracy is not always the same as the ideal. In succeeding chapters we examined the realities of the American political system to see how closely our system approaches the ideals on which it is founded.

In these two concluding chapters, we summarize and evaluate the continuing tensions between our founding principles and our institutions and practices, and we look briefly toward the future of America's democracy. In Chapter 21, we ask whether more widespread and effective political participation is in fact a desirable goal in a modern political system. Contemporary democratic theorists have given conflicting answers. Some argue that America's democracy "works," even if it is different from classical democracy; others maintain that the ideals of Jeffersonian democracy are still valuable, relevant, and worth striving for. The approach we adopt as a nation—indeed, the future of America's democracy—ultimately depends on the people. Chapter 22 deals with suggestions that have been made for increasing political participation in America, for moving toward the ideal.

21 Modern Democratic Theory

How Much Participation Is Desirable?

As we saw in Chapter 1, America is a kind of "democratic republic." Jefferson declared that in such a democracy the people should elect public officials, and government policy should reflect the popular will (while, of course, protecting the rights of the minority).

A central characteristic of America's democracy, then, is political participation; that is, citizens should be able to take part in political decision-making. Throughout this book, we have analyzed America's democracy on the basis of this standard; now it seems appropriate to summarize what we have found. But determining how well America's democracy measures up to the standard only raises another crucial question: Does it *matter* how well America measures up? Should we be satisfied with the level and effectiveness of political participation, or should we be concerned about it? We will conclude this chapter by looking at two major answers to these questions, provided by contemporary theories of democracy.

AMERICA'S DEMOCRACY TODAY: A REVIEW

In the Jeffersonian sense, political participation is both a *process* (political activity to elect and influence public officials) and a *result* (government policy that reflects the popular will). The process we are considering here does not include political violence, which is clearly outside the realm of legitimate political activity. Nor does it include mere "expressions of support" for the government, such as putting out the flag or attending parades. We are concerned with affirmative and legitimate political activity such as voting, campaigning, attending a party meeting, lobbying, or running for public office.

What is the level of political activity in America? Our political system appears to be extremely participatory. We elect vast numbers of public officials—local, state, and federal. Over the years, we have expanded the suffrage in America to include all citizens over the age of 18. Yet only 53.3 percent of the eligible voters voted in the 1976 presidential election. Voter turnout is even smaller in elections involving less prestigious and local offices.

If a relatively small number of Americans vote, even fewer—about 15 percent—could be called "party or campaign activists." They help nominate candidates, get involved in campaigns, and assist in developing party platforms. Few Americans contribute to campaigns. Few lobby or otherwise attempt to influence public officials once they are in office. Still fewer actually run for public office; those who do typically share common characteristics: a majority of them are white, male, and relatively comfortable financially.

We have seen that political socialization—how people learn about the system and their part in it—is an important factor in determining whether people are politically active. Political socialization in favor of participation is greater for those of higher socioeconomic status; and there is a wide disparity in the distribution of wealth and income in America. People are more likely to be politically active if they belong to an organization and feel politically competent, able to understand how the system works. Yet industrialization and urbanization have caused many Americans to move from one place to another, making it more difficult for them to register to vote or to become part of a local group or organization. Many Americans feel alienated or disconnected from both their work and their community. Finally, the level of political activity is higher for those who have a greater feeling of political efficacy, a sense that they can make the system respond; many Americans feel that political activity makes little or no difference. Thus, democratic process and result (or the level and effectiveness of political participation) are intertwined in America. And both are subject to certain additional impediments.

The framers of the U.S. Constitution intentionally shielded American government from immediate popular control. This was accomplished through a number of insulating devices, including federalism; the separation of powers; a bicameral Congress; long, staggered terms for members of the U.S. Senate, with each state having an equal number of senators; an Electoral College for electing the President, with a tradition of unit-rule voting by each state's set of electors; and a Supreme Court, with members appointed for life.

Ours is not a direct democracy; we elect public officials to "represent" us. They serve for specified terms. We cannot recall members of the U.S. House and Senate. In our system there is no way to force new nationwide elections through a vote of "no confidence." Our elected representatives exercise considerable discretion on specific policies, and the decline in the influence of political party organizations has increased the amount of this discretion. The size and power of unelected governmental bureaucracy have greatly increased. Both elected and appointed officials hold hearings and otherwise provide opportunities for public input in making and implementing policy, but few citizens participate in this way. Organized special-interest groups have the advantage.

This is not to say that the people have no way to influence governmental policy-makers: they can do so by writing letters; participating in public opinion polls; joining interest groups; campaigning; talking with representatives; and lobbying. But "money talks," and it says, "Give me access to political power." In addition to the wide disparity in the distribution of individual wealth and income in America, the number of huge business corporations has grown enormously. Through campaign financing, advertising on public questions, lobbying, and in other ways, economic power translates into political power.

Does government policy reflect the popular will in America? A study by Warren E. Miller and Donald Stokes showed that members of Congress very frequently do not even know what a majority of their constituents thinks or wants.[1]

Using polls taken by the Survey Research Center over a period of a dozen years, Professor Richard F. Hamilton has shown that—to take two examples—a majority of Americans favors a federal government role in assuring low-cost medical care for all citizens and a federal government guarantee of a job for all citizens.[2] Yet, despite the fact that national health insurance has been widely discussed since President Harry S. Truman proposed it in 1947 and (more recently) a similar proposal authored by Senator Edward Kennedy has been pending in the United States Senate for a number of years, such a system is still not law. Similarly, full employment legislation was originally proposed by President Truman in 1945. Although many of the provisions of the Humphrey-Hawkins bill introduced in Congress in 1976 by the late Senator Hubert H. Humphrey and Representative Gus Hawkins, were similar to those in Truman's bill, the version of the Humphrey-Hawkins bill that passed in 1978 had no real teeth in it.

Politically, some Americans are "more equal" than others. Some are more active political participants. Some are more likely to have their way—to have more influence on government policy—than others. In general, however, most Americans continue to support their government and the political system, even though they may disagree with its policies on specific issues. This raises a crucial question, mentioned at the beginning of this chapter: Does it *matter* if

---

[1] Warren E. Miller and Donald Stokes, "Constituency Influences in Congress," *American Political Science Review* (March 1963), pp. 45–47.

[2] Richard F. Hamilton, *Class and Politics in the United States* (New York: John Wiley and Sons, 1972), pp. 89, 93.

America's democracy measures up to the Jeffersonian standard? Different answers to that question, provided by contemporary democratic theorists, will be described in the remainder of this chapter. Which answer America subscribes to as a nation will have profound implications for the future of America's democracy.

IS WIDESPREAD POLITICAL PARTICIPATION DESIRABLE?

As an American election nears, particularly a presidential one, patriotic appeals are quite regularly broadcast and printed, exhorting all citizens to vote: "Tuesday is election day; be sure to do your duty as a free American and vote." Civic organizations regularly organize "get out the vote" drives, which are usually not tied to any particular candidate or issue: "Vote as you please, but vote!"

Such efforts seldom if ever say why it is important to vote. It is just assumed to be somehow good for people and good for society, too. Some people have even advocated making voting compulsory for all eligible voters in the United States, as it is in a few democracies such as Australia, Belgium, the Netherlands, and parts of Switzerland. However, it is questionable whether this would be constitutional in America. In any event, most Americans would probably find the idea of being "forced to act as free people" offensive and unacceptable.[3]

Still, as we have seen with "noncompulsory voting," the number of Americans who "act as free people" is discouragingly low. The number who participate in other ways is even lower. Should we be concerned about the level of political participation in America today? Or should we perhaps decide that America's democracy "works" well enough?

Participation and its role in modern democracies are subjects of controversy among modern democratic theorists.[4] (Indeed, even the definition of what a "democracy" is today, when a modern system may be called "democratic," is debated.) Modern theories tend to fall into two general categories, which are distinguished by their approaches to the concept of "democracy" and the role of participation. For the sake of our discussion, we will refer to one category of democratic theories as *realism*, and to the other as *idealism*. (The theorists we will be discussing would not necessarily identify their theories with these labels, but it is a useful way to distinguish between the two approaches.)

---

[3]See generally, Alan Wertheimer, "In Defense of Compulsory Voting," in J. Roland Pennock and John W. Chapman, eds., *Participation in Politics* (New York: Lieber-Atherton, 1975), p. 276.

[4]See Charles F. Cnudde and Deane E. Neubauer, eds., *Empirical Democratic Theory* (Chicago: Markham Publishing Company, 1969).

Realism

Modern *realist* political theorists largely maintain that their research and writing are *empirical*, that their conclusions can be verified by observation or experiment. These theorists say, in effect: "We don't say how things *should be*; we say how things *are*. Our work, in other words, is not prescriptive, but descriptive."

Realism in democratic theory began to gain acceptance after World War II and blossomed during the 1950s and 1960s. It is important to note what was happening during this period. Supporters of democracy were still trying to understand how and why Germany's democratic Wiemar Republic could have been toppled and an antidemocratic Nazi leader, Adolf Hitler, could have come to power with the support of so many of the German people.[5] Similarly, in the 1950s in the United States, Senator Joseph McCarthy was able to build a substantial political following through a demagogic assault on the basic American freedoms of speech, thought, and association. McCarthy irresponsibly attacked Americans who had ever had any association with the Communist party or had been, even in thought alone, what McCarthy called "fellow travelers" of the Communist party on a particular issue or issues.[6] During the 1950s, too, many leaders and writers believed that America was becoming a classless "affluent society" and that democracy could safely emphasize democratic processes more than results. (This euphoria was shattered in the 1960s with the "rediscovery" of abject poverty in the midst of plenty in America and with the terrible explosions of violence that afflicted the black sections of so many of America's major cities.)[7] In the 1960s, one of the realists' special concerns was to account for the considerable appeal of the presidential campaigns of Alabama Governor George C. Wallace among the lower socioeconomic classes. His core support was apparently based on white fears and hostilities resulting from black people's efforts to achieve equality.[8] Throughout this period, the relatively low level of American political participation continued to worry the supporters of democracy.

Realists ask: How does democracy survive when so many of the masses do not appear to support its basic concepts or do not take part in its processes?

Pluralism, elites, and the masses. One theory that seeks to explain how democracy works even though a large number of Americans are not politically active is called *pluralism*.[9] Pluralist theory holds that

---

[5]For a general treatment of Hitler and fascism, see Seymour M. Lipset, *Political Man* (Garden City, N.Y.: Doubleday/Anchor Books, 1963), pp. 127–179.

[6]For a treatment of McCarthyism, see Seymour M. Lipset, *The Politics of Unreason* (New York: Harper and Row/Torchbook, 1973), pp. 209–47.

[7]See Lipset, *Political Man*, pp. 439–56.

[8]See Thomas R. Dye and L. Harmon Zeigler, *The Irony of Democracy* (North Scituate, Mass.: Duxbury Press, 1975), pp. 165–89.

[9]See David B. Truman, *The Governmental Process* (New York: Knopf, 1951); and Robert Dahl, *Who Governs* (New Haven: Yale University Press, 1961).

political power is fragmented among various competing groups, such as veterans', farmers', labor, business, and professional organizations. According to the theory, people in a democracy may not only participate in politics directly but may also do so through their membership in groups. Pluralists say that government policy does not result from imposed "public" decisions but from compromises worked out by the competing groups in a kind of bargaining process; government acts as a kind of referee and enforces the compromises. Competition among the groups is said to be kept from becoming too sharp because group memberships overlap. For example, a person may belong to a veterans' group, a school teachers' group, and a property taxpayers' group—each of which has a different focus.

There are two principal criticisms of the pluralist explanation.[10] First, most people do not think of organizations as agencies for realizing their political aims; only about one of every three people belongs to any organization that seeks to exert political influence. People with low incomes, who are least likely to vote, generally do not participate in groups or organizations, either. As E. E. Schattschneider has put it, "The flaw in the pluralist heaven is that the heavenly chorus sings with a strong upperclass accent. Probably about 90 percent of the people cannot get into the pressure system. . . . The system is skewed, loaded and unbalanced in favor of a fraction of minority."[11] Second, critics maintain that there is probably a tendency for organizations to be dominated, not by their members, but by a small number of leaders and activists. Indeed, E. H. Carr writes that "mass democracy has, through its very nature, thrown up on all sides specialized groups of leaders—what are sometimes called elites. Everywhere, in government, in political parties, in trade unions, in cooperatives, these indispensable elites have taken shape with startling rapidity."[12] This finding has given rise to the *elite theory* of democracy. According to Harold Lasswell, the "division into elite and mass is universal,"[13] and "government is always government by the few."[14]

Do the elites compete among themselves, or are they in agreement on the basic issues? C. Wright Mills and more recently William Domhoff, both sociologists, have asserted that there is a "unified" elite in America, a group with common interests that are mutually protected.[15] Mills said that the top men in the military, in the

---

[10]Hamilton, *Class and Politics in the United States*, pp. 34–36.

[11]E. E. Schattschneider, *The Semisovereign People* (New York: Holt, Rinehart and Winston, 1960), p. 35.

[12]E. H. Carr, *New Society* (Boston: Beacon Press, 1951), p. 72.

[13]Harold Lasswell and Abraham Kaplan, *Power and Society* (New Haven: Yale University, 1960), p. 219.

[14]Harold Lasswell and Daniel Lerner et al., *The Comparative Study of Elites* (Stanford, Calif.: Stanford University Press, 1952), p. 7.

[15]C. Wright Mills, *The Power Elite* (New York: Oxford University Press, 1956); G. William Domhoff, *Who Rules America?* (Englewood Cliffs, New Jersey: Prentice-Hall, 1967).

corporations, and in political affairs, and the "considerable traffic of personnel within and between these three, as well as . . . the rise of specialized go-betweens as in the new style high-level lobbying," have created an "elite whose power probably exceeds that of any small group of men in world history."[16] According to Mills and Domhoff, then, there is one powerful elite separate from the masses.

Other theorists argue that the elites are divided and competing among themselves.[17] This amounts to a melding of the elite and pluralist theories into a theory of plural elites. Some of the elites or groups, according to these theorists, are more open to new members than others, and some are more responsive to the public interest than others.[18] It is said that because elites in America are varied in composition, recruitment, and perspectives, they tend to serve as a check on the actions and decisions of each other. That is the way democracy works in America, these theorists believe, as long as the elites present a "united moral front" or consensus on fundamental democratic beliefs and ideals.[19]

What about the rest of the people? Schattschneider has written that the great majority of people are politically unorganized, fragmented, and passive.[20] Bernard Berelson reported that his "empirical" study of Elmira, New York, showed that the "average citizen" does not have enough sustained interest in political affairs to participate sufficiently to make democracy work in the "classical" sense.[21]

Emphasis on stability.   The realists believe that the lower socioeconomic classes, who are less likely to participate politically, often possess antidemocratic, authoritarian attitudes. In *Political Man*, Seymour Lipset wrote:

The poorer strata everywhere are more liberal or leftist on economic issues; they favor welfare measures, higher wages, graduated income taxes, support of trade unions, and so forth. But when liberalism is defined in noneconomic terms—as support of civil liberties, internationalism, and so forth—the correlation is reversed. The well-to-do are more liberal; the poorer are more intolerant.[22]

---

[16]See Irving Louis Horowitz, ed., *Power, Politics and People: The Collected Essays of C. Wright Mills* (N.Y.: Oxford University Press, 1956); Peter Bachrach, *The Theory of Democratic Elitism, A Critique* (Boston: Little Brown, 1967), pp. 55–58. Bachrach points out that Mills disliked the characteristics of the "power elite" and hoped they could be held accountable by an intellectual elite.

[17]Raymond Aron, "Social Structure and the Ruling Class," *The British Journal of Sociology*, 1 (March 1950): 10.

[18]See generally, Robert A. Dahl, *Pluralist Democracy in the United States* (Chicago: Rand McNally and Company, 1967); and Robert A. Dahl, *Who Governs?*

[19]Susanne Keller, *Beyond the Ruling Class* (New York: Random House, 1963), pp. 273–74, 126–27.

[20]Schattschneider, *The Semisovereign People*, pp. 20–42.

[21]Bernard R. Berelson, Paul R. Lazarsfeld, and William N. McPhee, *Voting* (Chicago: Chicago University Press, 1954).

[22]Lipset, *Political Man*, p. 92.

The "empirical" question of the realist, then, is: "How does it happen that on matters of free speech, for example, some norms that seem to be weakly held or even opposed by a majority of citizens are nonetheless applied vigorously by the Supreme Court, enforced by the executive branch, and at least tolerated by the Congress?"[23]

One answer is that the elites, not the masses, are the guardians of democracy and human rights. As V. O. Key, Jr., has written, "The critical element for the health of a democratic order consists in the beliefs, standards, and competence of those who constitute the influentials, the opinion-leaders, the political activists in the order."[24] According to Key, this consensus among the "upper activist stratum" must encompass the "technical rules of the game by which the system operates."[25] Thus, it is asserted that a crucial function of a democracy, if it is to continue in existence, is the "training" of those who will, with each succeeding generation, become the elites.[26]

Another answer given to the empirical question is that the lack of participation by many people in the lower socioeconomic classes may perform a positive service for the continuity of the system. Berelson has written that "the voters least admirable when measured against individual requirements contribute most when measured against the aggregate requirement for flexibility . . . they may be the least partisan and the least interested voters, but they perform a valuable function for the entire system."[27] That is, the system can compromise and accommodate flexibly to change without being torn apart. The trick in a democracy, then, is "to combine a substantial degree of popular participation with a system of power capable of governing *effectively* and *coherently*."[28]

Although he is a realist in his research and writing, Robert Dahl has expressed a desire to see more political participation, particularly among those segments of society whose participation has been lowest. But Dahl has written that an increase in political activity by people in lower socioeconomic classes *could* mean a decline in the "consensus" or agreement on democratic ideals, which he feels is necessary to democracy, or "polyarchy."[29]

In his book, *Democratic Theory*, Giovanni Sartori argued that a democratic society has no obligation to increase participation greatly. Once democracy is established, he said, the threat to it is not from a

---

[23]Robert Dahl, "Further Reflections on 'The Elitist Theory of Democracy'" in Peter Bachrach, ed., *Political Elites in a Democracy* (New York: Atherton Press, 1971), p. 93.

[24]V. O. Key, Jr., *Public Opinion and American Democracy* (New York: Alfred A. Knopf, 1961), p. 558.

[25]Key, *Public Opinion and American Democracy*, p. 155.

[26]Robert Dahl, *A Preface to Democratic Theory* (Chicago: University of Chicago Press, 1967), p. 77.

[27]Berelson, Lazarsfeld, and McPhee, *Voting*, p. 316.

[28]Louis Hartz and Samuel Beer, "New Structures of Democracy: Britain and America," in W.N. Chambers and R.H. Salisbury, eds., *Democracy in the Mid-20th Century* (St. Louis: Washington University Press, 1960), p. 46.

[29]Dahl, *A Preface to Democratic Theory*, pp. 89, 103.

powerful few, but from the masses. "What we have to fear . . . is that democracy—as in the myth of Saturn—may destroy its own leaders, thereby creating the conditions for their replacement by undemocratic counter-elites,"[30] or *demagogues*, who appeal to the emotions or prejudices of the masses to further their own personal ends.

In the 1970s, realist theory in the Sartori mold has been taken to a near-advocacy extreme by Harvard University Professor Samuel P. Huntington. Huntington's analysis was expressed in the unsigned introduction to *The Crisis of Democracy: Report on the Governability of Democracies to the Trilateral Commission*. The Commission, a group of prominent corporate executives, academics, and government and political leaders (including President-to-be Jimmy Carter and many of the people he would later appoint to the highest positions in the government), was founded by Chase Manhattan Bank President David Rockefeller. Its stated goal was to foster strong, stable, cooperating governments and economies in the United States, Western Europe, and Japan (hence, "Trilateral" Commission).

The predominant trend in the 1960s, Huntington writes in the Report's introduction, was "a dramatic renewal of the democratic spirit in America." It consisted of challenges to the authority of political, social, and economic institutions; renewed commitment to the idea of equality by intellectuals and other elites; the emergence of "public interest" lobbying groups; increased concern for the rights and opportunities of minorities and women, "and a pervasive criticism of those who possessed or were even thought to possess excessive power or wealth."[31]

Huntington does not find this "increase in the vitality of democracy" a cause for celebration, but a reason for grave concern. It *necessarily* meant, he says, a decrease in the "governability" of democracy. Indeed, he states that the "challenge to democracy" posed by the growth in advanced industrial societies of a "stratum of value-oriented intellectuals who often devote themselves to the derogation of leadership, the challenging of authority, and the unmasking and delegitimation of established institutions" (contrasted with the more praiseworthy and also increasing numbers of "technocratic and policy-oriented intellectuals") is potentially as serious as the threat posed to democracy in the past by "aristocratic cliques, fascist movements, and communist parties."[32]

Echoing Sartori, Huntington states that the vulnerability of

---

[30]Giovanni Sartori, *Democratic Theory* (Detroit: Wayne State University Press, 1962), p. 119.

[31]Michael J. Crozier, Samuel P. Huntington, and Joji Watanuki, *The Crisis of Democracy: Report on the Governability of Democracies to the Trilateral Commission* (New York: New York University Press, 1975), pp. 59–60.

[32]Introduction to *The Crisis of Democracy: Report on the Governability of Democracies to the Trilateral Commission*.

democracy comes from the "internal dynamics of democracy itself in a highly educated, mobilized and participant society." He adds that "a value which is normally good in itself is not necessarily optimized when it is maximized. We have come to recognize that there are potentially desirable limits to economic growth. There are also potentially desirable limits to the indefinite extension of political democracy."[33]

Other writers also envision an increasingly authoritarian rule by experts as a likely consequence of moving into "an age of scarcity." Robert Heilbroner suggests that "passage through the gauntlet ahead may be possible only under governments capable of rallying obedience far more effectively than would be possible in a democratic setting."[34] Others, including Thomas R. Dye, acknowledge that elites themselves have at times posed serious threats to democracy. Offering no clear course for checking this tendency, Dye concludes that "in a world where only the most careful planning can prevent rapid deterioration of the quality of life, social control, drastic restrictions in individual freedom, and rule by 'experts' are inevitable." Even "bargaining among competing elites, much less mass participation, could not be tolerated."[35] In other words, a "unified" rather than a "divided" elite may become necessary.

Redefining "democracy."   There is a tendency among realist democratic theorists to define "democracy" in terms of means, not ends—to explain not what it does (results), but how it does it (process). In this regard, Joseph Schumpeter's *Capitalism, Socialism and Democracy* (1942), written largely before the advent of modern studies of citizen behavior and attitudes, has had dramatic impact on modern theory. In defining democracy, he said, we are to think of it in terms of "method," rather than ideals or goals; it is "an institutional arrangement for arriving at political decisions in which individuals acquire power to decide by means of a competitive struggle for the people's vote."[36]

According to Schumpeter's definition, a government could still be correctly called a democracy even if it did not grant its citizens a universal right to vote and even if it is discriminated against people on the basis of race, religion, sex, or property. The main requirement for a democracy, Schumpeter said, is that "the people have the opportunity of accepting or refusing the men who are to rule them." Between elections, he wrote, it is better for the system if the people do not attempt to pressure their elected officials on particular issues.

According to Harold Lasswell, a system can be termed a democra-

---

[33]Crozier, Huntington, and Watanuki, *The Crisis of Democracy: Report on the Governability of Democracies to the Trilateral Commission*, pp. 64, 114, 115.

[34]Robert L. Heilbroner, *An Inquiry into the Human Prospect* (New York: W.W. Norton and Co., 1974), p. 110.

[35]Dye and Zeigler, *The Irony of Democracy*, p. 458.

[36]Joseph Schumpeter, *Capitalism, Socialism and Democracy* (New York: Harper and Brothers, 1960), p. 269.

cy, even if power is exercised by a small number of leaders, as long as there is "accountability."[37] Robert Dahl expands this to say that in a democracy the exercise of power need not be equal. He sees that as being a vain hope which would only breed cynicism if espoused as an ideal—but that equal *access* to power, or the opportunity to exercise power, is sufficient.[38]

What is democracy, then, to the realists? There are democratic theories, not *one* theory.[39] However, the emphasis is primarily on process. Austin Ranney and Wilmore Kendall have said that the *minimum characteristics* of a democracy are:

1. *popular sovereignty*; that is, "those who hold office . . . must stand ready, *in some sense*, to do whatever the people want them to do, and to refrain from doing anything the people oppose . . .";

2. *political equality*; that is, "each member of the 'community' . . . should have, *in some sense*, as good a chance as his fellows to participate in the community's decision-making—no better and no worse . . . ";

3. *popular consultation and majority rule*; that is, there must be "an understanding that when the enfranchised members of the community disagree as to what ought to be done, the last word lies, *in some sense*, with the larger number and never the smaller—i.e., the majority of the electorate and not the minority should carry the day."[40]

Similarly, E. E. Schattschneider writes that "democracy is a competitive political system in which competing leaders and organizations define the alternatives of public policy in such a way that the public can participate in the decision-making process." The essential element of the democratic process is "socialization of the conflict," that is, *in some way* involving the widest number of people in the decision.[41]

It can be seen that these definitions amount to something different from Jefferson's idea of an "equal voice" for all citizens and his notion of decisions which "embody the will" of the people—not government *by* the people, but government *approved* by the people. In effect, realists have said that since the facts of participation do not fit the democratic theory, we must change the theory.[42]

---

[37]Lerner, Lasswell et al., *The Comparative Study of Elites*, p. 7.

[38]Robert Dahl, "Power, Pluralism and Democracy: A Modest Proposal," (Paper delivered to American Political Science Association, Chicago, September 9–12, 1964).

[39]Charles F. Cnudde and Deane E. Neubauer, "New Trends in Democratic Theory," in Cnudde and Neubauer, eds., *Empirical Democratic Theory*, pp. 511–23.

[40]Austin Ranney and Wilmore Kendall, "Basic Principles for a Model of Democracy" in Cnudde and Neubauer, eds., *Empirical Democratic Theory*, pp. 41–63.

[41]Schattschneider, *The Semisovereign People*, pp. 141–42.

[42]"What we need is a modern definition of democracy explaining the facts of life of the operating political system," Schattschneider, *The Semisovereign People*, p. 130.

Idealism

While realists claim their theories are empirical (based on observation and subject to verification by experiment), *idealists* frankly state that their research and writing on democratic theory is *normative*, that is, relating to or prescribing desirable standards. They ask, in effect, "How can you sensibly measure the way things *are* without starting with some notion about how they *should be*?" While realists argue that "democracy" should be redefined to fit the "facts," idealists assert that "if classical or Jeffersonian democratic theory does not fit the facts of modern practice—change the practice."

Idealists make four principal arguments against realist democratic theory. They say that realist theory is actually normative; that there is value in the democratic ideal; that there is value in participation; and that realist theory "blames the victim." We will now consider each of these arguments.

Realist theory is actually normative. Idealists argue that realists are not as objective as they purport to be. When realists say they "just want the facts, ma'am," and that the appropriate theory will "emerge" from the facts, it is obvious that every single "fact" is not considered, the idealists say. They point out that the realists select what facts to take into account and which to ignore; therefore, whether they admit it or not, normative decisions *are* being made and desirable standards *are* being set.[43]

For example, suppose (as the realists state) the "facts" are that people from lower socioeconomic classes are more liberal on "economic" issues (such as jobs and health care) than people from the upper class and that the upper class is more liberal on "libertarian" issues (such as freedom of speech). Is not the decision that libertarian liberalism is essential to the stability of democracy—and therefore that the continuation of democracy depends upon the upper class—a "normative" rather than an "empirical" choice? If, by comparison, economic liberalism were considered vital to democracy, then it could be argued that "empirical" evidence supports a finding that political participation by the *upper* class poses a threat and that the stability and continuity of democracy depends upon widespread participation by the masses. Thus, realist theory "purports to be above ideology but is actually deeply rooted in an ideology. This ideology is grounded upon a profound distrust of the majority of ordinary men and women and a reliance upon the established elites to maintain the values of civility and the 'rules of the game' of democracy."[44] Idealists

---

[43]C. Taylor, "Neutrality in Political Science," in P. Laslet and G. Runciman, eds., *Philosophy, Politics and Society* (Oxford: Blackwell Publishing Co., 1967).

[44]Peter Bachrach, *The Theory of Democratic Elitism,* pp. 93–94. See also Carole Pateman, *Participation and Democratic Theory* (London: Cambridge University Press, 1970), pp. 15–16; and Jack L. Walker, "A Critique of the Elitist Theory of Democracy," in Peter Bachrach, ed., *Political Elites in a Democracy* (New York: Atherton Press, 1971), p. 71.

argue further that realism is normative because it inevitably tends to support the *status quo* and is biased toward social conservatism, allowing only modest, incremental change to protect the stability of the existing system. Idealists also claim that realists essentially take as a "given" that the present system is functioning satisfactorily and go on from there.[45]

Value of the ideal. Idealists ask whether a doctor can diagnose an ailing heart if the doctor does not know how a well heart should function. As Peter Bachrach has asked, should we reject the "brotherhood of man" as a sound principle by which to appraise human relations, just because it may be unattainable in pure and unblemished form? The answer is clearly "no," he says.[46] He quotes Max Weber to support his position: "Certainly all historical experience confirms the truth that man would not have attained the possible unless time and again he had reached out for the impossible."[47] Thus, according to the idealists, without an ideal of democracy there is no inspiration toward which we can strive, no standard by which our society can be judged. Therefore, in the absence of a clear showing that the ideal of democracy actually contributes to a cynical attitude, the idealists say that the democratic ideal should be retained.

Value of participation. As we have seen, realists tend to focus on the democratic processes or methods. Idealists say that this does not give sufficient weight to the results of participation for the participants and for society.[48] They say that when the realists do consider the results of political participation, they are almost exclusively content with examining the *instrumental*, or "self-protective," effect of participation[49]—an old person writing letters to get social security benefits increased or a householder going to the polls and voting against a county assessor who has raised assessments for property taxes, for example.

Idealists see participation as having positive results for individuals and society that go beyond instrumental effects. Yet even in this instrumental effect alone, idealists see considerable value in more widespread participation. It is obvious that no one knows the best interests of a particular person better than that person.[50] Verba and Nie have found that participation does indeed make a difference: leaders are more likely to concur with the problem priorities of

[45]For a discussion of this, see David Easton, "The New Revolution in Political Science," *American Political Science Review*, 63 (1969): 1051–61.

[46]Bachrach, *The Theory of Democratic Elitism*, p. 6.

[47]Bachrach, *The Theory of Democratic Elitism*, pp. 86–87.

[48]Bachrach, *The Theory of Democratic Elitism*, p. 94.

[49]Bachrach, *The Theory of Democratic Elitism*, pp. 98–99. See also J. Roland Pennock, in J.R. Pennock and J.W. Chapman, eds., *Participation in Politics* (New York: Lieber-Atherton, 1975), p. 7.

[50]Geraint Parry, "The Idea of Participation," in Geraint Parry, ed., *Participation in Politics* (Manchester, England: Manchester University Press, 1972), p. 19.

participants than with those of nonparticipants. (They say that this is not because leaders and participants come from the same backgrounds, but appears to be an independent result of participation itself.)[51]

What would happen if more Americans with low incomes were to become active political participants for instrumental, or self-protective, reasons—to get jobs or better health care, for example? According to the Verba and Nie study, there would be increased likelihood that decision-makers would concur in and respond to the priorities of the new participants. If their socioeconomic status and the quality of their lives were thereby improved, the new participants would further gain by becoming more aware of their own problems and becoming more skillful in articulating them.[52]

The idealists argue that society would also gain. Governments would be better informed about the conditions and feelings in the country.[53] More important, the idealists turn the realists' own "stability" argument back against them. They say that a society with fewer deep economic cleavages among its people is more stable than one with such cleavages. A recent study by Harry Brenner shows that there are indeed clearly discernible correlations between increased unemployment and increases in physical and mental illness, suicides, murder, and admissions to mental institutions and prisons.[54] The evidence is that a participant citizen is more loyal to the political system, while "the frequent outbursts of violence in the American student movement and Black politics (of the 1960s) also seem traceable to an alienation from the 'bias' of the political, social and economic system."[55]

Idealists cite Rousseau's assertion that a society is held together by a kind of social contract; they claim that the social contract will break down if it is made to serve "individuals or groups that have gained special privilege through power or wealth."[56] A commune might experience the same thing if there were a grossly uneven distribution of duties and privileges. The idea of the underlying social contract as the basis for government is well expressed by Ernst Cassirer in *The Myth of the State*: "Written constitutional or legal charters have no real binding force, if they are not the expression of a constitution that is written in the citizens' minds. Without this moral support, the very

---

[51]Sidney Verba and Norman H. Nie, *Participation in America: Political Democracy and Social Equality* (New York: Harper and Row, 1972), pp. 332–33.

[52]Donald Keim, "Participation in Contemporary Democratic Theories" in Pennock and Chapman, eds., *Participation in Politics*, p. 44.

[53]Parry, "The Idea of Political Participation," p. 20.

[54]Study by Professor Harvey Brenner, School of Hygiene and Public Health, Johns Hopkins University; quoted by Senator Hubert H. Humphrey in *Congressional Record* (October 28, 1977), p. 518093. Similarly, see Ramsey Clark, *Crime in America* (London: Casell and Company, 1970), pp. 56–84.

[55]Dennis Kavanaugh, "Political Behavior and Participation" in Parry, ed., *Participation in Politics*, pp. 118–19.

[56]Kalman H. Silvert, *The Reason for Democracy* (New York: Viking Press, 1977), p. 9.

strength of a state becomes its inherent danger."[57] In other words, the people have to see the law as *their* law, as "fair" law that they have helped to make.

According to Dennis Kavanaugh, the kind of "stability" in government that the realists prize can only be purchased at the cost of the relatively unorganized and inarticulate. "When the sense of injustice among the 'outs' is allied to a sense of confidence that change can be brought about—perhaps by extra-constitutional means—then the stability may prove short-lived."[58]

DEBATE ON DEMOCRACY

The time has arrived in the United States for a grand debate over whether we wish to reconstitute democracy or continue our submersion in elitist authoritarianism. Let us debate honestly, with crystalline frankness, putting aside lies and euphemisms. If the new authoritarians believe the 'masses' are fatally and permanently flawed, untrustworthy, and unworthy of effective or positive political activity in an increasingly specialized and scientific world, then they should say so. Let them put aside the word 'democracy' entirely, and explain how they propose to establish sensible governance. If democrats are to make their case, . . . they must face up to democratic imperatives: Equality must be the precondition for full human attainment however unequal; the link must be broken between inherited private privilege and public advantage; intellectualism must be understood as a skill all may learn, not just a small intelligentsia; and reason and power must flow together to create democratic efficacy.

SOURCE: Kalman H. Silvert, *The Reason for Democracy* (New York: Viking Press, 1977), p. 105.

The idealists also believe that another aspect of participation, the *developmental* effect, is important. They claim that a person gains a sense of "self-rule" and "self-realization"—becomes a more developed, more human person—from the act of participating itself.[59]

They often quote the early writings of Karl Marx concerning participation's educative effect and the increase in freedom that comes from control of one's own life.[60] And Peter Bachrach has written that because an autocratic regime would not provide sufficient opportunities for participatory self-development for most citizens, "benevolent despotism thus becomes a contradiction in terms. . . ."[61]

"The objective of equality (of power) is not merely the recognition of a certain dignity of the human being as such," writes J. Roland Pennock, "but it is also to provide him with the opportunity—equal to that guaranteed to others—for protecting and advancing his interests and developing his powers and personality."[62] In other words, the idealists say, in a society of widespread participation, all citizens would have a chance to live among a "better class of people" because of the developmental effect, since participation improves people, makes them "better."

In short, idealists agree with New York's Governor Al Smith, who once declared that the cure for the ills of democracy is a little more

---

[57]Ernst Cassirer, *The Myth of the State* (Yale University Press, 1946), p. 76.

[58]Kavanaugh, "Political Behavior and Participation," p. 120.

[59]Parry, in Parry, ed., *Participation in Politics*, pp. 26–38.

[60]Michael Evans, "Karl Marx and Political Participation," in Parry, ed., *Participation in Politics*, p. 128.

[61]Bachrach, *The Theory of Democratic Elitism: A Critique*, p. 4.

[62]J. Roland Pennock, "Democracy and Leadership," in William Chambers and Robert Salisbury, eds., *Democracy Today* (New York: Collier Books, 1962), pp. 126–27.

democracy. Many years earlier, Alexis de Tocqueville wrote in much the same vein: "When I am told that the laws are weak and the population is wild, that passions are excited and virtue is paralyzed, and that in this situation it would be madness to think of increasing the rights of people, I reply that it is for these very reasons that they should be increased."

"Blaming the victim." In *The Reason for Democracy*, Kalman H. Silvert wrote that modern criticism of demands for more democracy is like saying, "If the road is bumpy, it is because of all those misguided people who are throwing themselves down in front of the wheels."[63] Studies attempting to show more "authoritarian" or antidemocratic attitudes among manual workers and people with low incomes have been the basis for much of the realists' concerns about mass participation. But they have recently come under severe attack, both for their methodology and their substance. For example, in *Class and Politics in the United States*, Richard F. Hamilton cites a Michigan Survey Research Center study, which shows that outside the South, there is no significant difference between workers and middle-class people on civil rights attitudes, except for a slightly more progressive attitude on the part of *workers*. Another study of people with low incomes in six southern cities found that they tended to be more progressive on racial issues than those of higher socioeconomic standing.[64] Still, belief in a "low-income/antidemocratic" link is strong; Hamilton cites one analysis that dismissed two earlier studies showing correlation between racial prejudice and high economic status. The analysis concluded, "This curiosity has no obvious explanation and makes us suspicious of these data. . . . There is just too much independent evidence that prejudice is inversely associated with current occupational status . . . ."[65]

Hamilton has pointed out that the assumption that the general population is "ignorant" on issues is misleading, because it does not take into account the use by the "higher circles" of frivolous and distractive themes in campaigns or the often careful and deliberate avoidance of serious issues by candidates and parties.[66] For example, each party's candidate in a particular election might avoid making a clear statement on abortion; then after the election, a poll of citizen attitudes might pronounce the citizens "uninformed" on how the candidates stood on this issue. Hamilton sees issue avoidance by candidates and parties as part of the "incomplete competition" problem in American politics. He asserts that this is another instance of attributing blame to "low status" when, in fact, the sources of the presumed disability are higher up. This in turn produces a democratic theory that is biased against people of lower socioeconomic status:

---

[63]Silvert, *The Reason for Democracy*, p. 97.
[64]Hamilton, *Class and Politics in the United States*, p. 135.
[65]Hamilton, pp. 456–57.
[66]Hamilton, pp.59–60.

"In addition to the original misreading, ironically, in this case, we also have a 'theory of democracy' developed that entails further penalities for the disadvantaged groups."

What about the findings of mass support for the red-baiting tactics of Senator Joseph McCarthy of Wisconsin? Bachrach points out that the elites—including newspaper editors and U.S. senators—did not speak out against McCarthy until he began to challenge the Army and the Republican administration of President Dwight D. Eisenhower.[67] Hamilton argues that while Seymour Lipset focuses on "intolerance" within the lower socioeconomic class, this intolerance has its roots outside the class, partly in the "initiatives of upper class influentials who have sponsored 'red scares' and supported rightist demagogues, and who themselves redefine the 'rules of the game' in order to justify guilt by association."[68] Most people seem to be most interested in and to best understand the economic or "bread and butter" issues that affect them. In a 1952 Wisconsin campaign between Senator Joseph McCarthy and a candidate who was both more "responsible" on libertarian issues and more "progressive" on economic issues, working-class and "ethnic" wards in Milwaukee voted for McCarthy's opponent by a two-to-one margin. At the same time, McCarthy was winning in upper-middle-class districts and piling up a three-to-one margin in the area where the city's richest and most influential citizens lived.[69]

The danger in considering only "libertarian" and not "economic" issues in attempting to assess the attitudes and behavior of different citizen groups is shown by the finding that Alabama Governor George Wallace had more than just a racist appeal to Americans.[70] His support did not correlate with class outside the South.[71] Similarly, Max Lerner has maintained that Hitler was able to topple the Wiemar Republic in prewar Germany, not because the masses were authoritarian, but because the former government had failed or refused to act on the serious economic problems faced by a majority of its citizens.[72] Similar views prompted idealist democrat Carl Becker to write that the survival of democracy depends upon correcting the "flagrant inequality of possessions and of opportunity now existing in democratic societies."[73]

Thus, the idealists say that the alienation of a large percentage of citizens from the political system is not a failure of the citizens, but a failure of the system. "What is sometimes taken as a *cause* of the

---

[67]Bachrach, *The Theory of Democratic Elitism,* pp. 50–55. See also Hamilton, *Class and Politics in the United States*, pp. 447–51.

[68]Hamilton, *Class and Politics in the United States*, p. 460.

[69]Hamilton, p. 450.

[70]Andrew Levison, *The Working Class Majority* (New York: Coward, McCann, and Geoghegan, 1974), pp. 163–69.

[71]Hamilton, *Class and Politics in the United States*, pp. 460–67.

[72]Max Lerner, *It Is Later Than You Think* (New York: Viking Press, 1943). See also Alan Bullock, *Hitler: A Study in Tyranny* (London: Harper and Row, 1954), pp.253–55.

[73]Carl Becker, *Modern Democracy* (New Haven: Yale University Press, 1941), p. 67.

politics of power, the unpolitical nature of ordinary citizens, turns out to be an effect of the politics of power. . . ."[74] In fact, a 1976 study found no justification for the charge that nonparticipants are more negative and antidemocratic than the total population; the fundamental reason why these people participate less is that they do not think it will really make any difference.[75]

Two important and inherent tensions in American democracy are the tension between liberty (human rights) and democracy (majority rule); and the tension between the haves and the have-nots. The idealists say that *each* is at least as vital as the other for the stability and continuity of democracy; they argue that the freedom-democracy tension and the have–have-not tension can best be managed by relying on the masses rather than the elites.

Can the elites—and those in the upper-middle and upper classes— be counted upon to be more moderate, responsible, and beneficent? Do their actions and attitudes on issues evidence statesmanship or self-interest? Hamilton's answers to both questions are unfavorable to the elites.[76] The governing elites, not the masses, got America into Vietnam, concealed information concerning America's invasion of Cambodia and involvement in the overthrow of the elected Allende government in Chile, and directed or condoned the excesses of the U.S. Central Intelligence Agency. On the other hand, "popular movements," not the governing elites, marshaled public opinion against the Vietnam War and pressed for advances in minority and women's rights.[77]

"Do extraordinarily low voter turnouts signal satisfaction with the system or, instead, a belief that our political parties and their nominees are empty of significance for what bothers us?" asks Kalman H. Silvert. He leaves no doubt about which answer he would give.[78] He and other idealists would say that "training" for the masses (part of it from participation itself) is as important as "training" for the elites, if democracy is to be preserved and expanded.

CONCLUSION

America stands for the ideals of human rights and political participation, as expressed in the Declaration of Independence. Our written Constitution was the result of a pragmatic attempt to organize a government that would accomplish these twin and sometimes conflicting goals: protecting minority rights while assuring at least ultimate majority rule through a representative system.

---

[74]Robert Pranger, *The Eclipse of Citizenship* (New York: Holt Rinehart and Winston, 1968), p. 52.

[75]James D. Wright, "Alienation and Political Negativism: New Evidence from National Survey," in *Sociology and Social Research*, 60, no. 2 (January 1976): 111.

[76]Hamilton, *Class and Politics in the United States*, pp. 27–34.

[77] See Silvert, *The Reason for Democracy;* and Hamilton, *Class and Politics in the United States.*

[78]Silvert, p. 44.

Our Constitution is a "living" document, changing with the times. Our political system has also changed with the times, sometimes limiting but more often expanding the protection of human rights. But we have seen that a gap between the ideal and the reality of participation still exists. "Realists" develop theories that attempt to describe and explain how democratic reality works. "Idealists" say that the ideal of participation is valuable and important for society as a whole and for each participating individual. And they point out that the best way to protect human rights for all citizens is through expanded participation.

Given the realities of America's democracy today, *can* political participation be expanded? Idealists maintain that it can be. We will discuss a variety of ways for doing so in the following chapter.

ADDITIONAL SOURCES

Bachrach, Peter. *The Theory of Democratic Elitism: A Critique*. Little, Brown, 1967.*

Bezold, Clement, ed. *Anticipatory Democracy: People in the Politics of the Future*. Random House, 1978.*

Cnudde, Charles F., and Deane Neubauer, eds. *Empirical Democratic Theory*. Markham, 1969.

Crozier, Michael J., Samuel P. Huntington, and Joji Watanuki. *The Crisis of Democracy: Report on the Governability of Democracies to the Trilateral Commission*. New York University Press, 1975.*

Dahl, Robert. *Pluralist Democracy in the United States*. Rand McNally, 1967.*

———. *Who Governs?* Yale University Press, 1961.*

———. *A Preface to Democratic Theory*. University of Chicago Press, 1967.*

G. William Domhoff, *Who Rules America?* Prentice-Hall, 1967.*

———. *Who Really Rules?* Transaction Books, 1978.

Hamilton, Richard F. *Class and Politics in the United States*. John Wiley and Sons, 1972.*

Heilbroner, Robert L. *An Inquiry into the Human Prospect*. Norton, 1974.*

Key, V. O., Jr. *Public Opinion and American Democracy*. Knopf, 1961.

Lasswell, Harold, and Abraham Kaplan. *Power and Society*. Yale University Press, 1960.

Mills, C. Wright. *The Power Elite*. Oxford University Press, 1956.*

Pateman, Carole. *Participation and Democratic Theory*. Cambridge University Press, 1970.*

Schattschneider, E. E. *The Semisovereign People*. Holt, Rinehart and Winston, 1960.*

Schumpeter, Joseph. *Capitalism, Socialism, and Democracy*. Harper, 1960.*

Silvert, Kalman. *The Reason for Democracy*. Viking Press, 1977.

Walker, Jack. "A Critique of the Elitist Theory of Democracy." *The American Political Science Review* 60 (1966): 285–95.

*Available in paperback.

22 Toward the Ideal

Throughout this book, we have considered both the ideal and the reality of America's democracy. At the beginning, we compared the *ideal* of political participation to the attractive picture of marigolds or green beans on the front of a seed packet. *Reality*, we said, is like the plants that actually sprout and grow. When the actual plants do not match up to the picture, should we change the picture or try to improve the plants? That was the basic question we considered in Chapter 21. Idealists, we found, answer that there is great value in keeping the ideal and trying to move reality closer to it. They say that this is not only important for the individuals involved but for the nation itself. According to Kalman Silvert, America's national interest "lies in a responsible community of universal membership, with equal obligations and equal rights to protection and adjudication of interests. Any other politics is one of special interest, not of national interest."[1]

We also saw in Chapter 21 that the ideal of participation involves both process and results. That is, it includes both the level and the effectiveness of participation.[2] Further, the level and effectiveness of participation are interactive: a person is more likely to take part in political activity if participation proves effective; and a person who participates more is likely to be more effective. The effectiveness of participation depends upon the degree to which the system responds; it involves not only a particular participant's influence, but also the relative influence of other competing participants.

Is it possible to increase the level and effectiveness of participation

---

[1]Kalman H. Silvert, *The Reason for Democracy* (New York: The Viking Press, 1977), p. 42.

[2]Some political scientists study political participation in terms of its *mode*, or method such as voting or campaigning; its *intensity*, the degree of frequency and the amount of fervor a person has; and its *quality*, or effectiveness.

in America? Throughout this book, we have considered various suggestions for doing so. In this final chapter, we will review those suggestions briefly.[3] It is useful to consider them under three principal headings: complete and public competition; equal access to power; and equal exercise of power. These groupings of the possibilities for increased participation are partly based upon a synthesis of the formulations of E. E. Schattschneider and J. Roland Pennock. As noted in Chapter 21, Schattschneider has written that "democracy is a competitive political system in which competing leaders and organizations define the alternatives of public policy in such a way that the public can participate in the decision-making process"; he says that it is essential to "socialize," rather than "privatize," conflict by involving the widest number of people in decisions.[4] Pennock has said that the democratic ideal has been useful in "pushing democratic reality in the direction of equality not only of *access* to power but also equality in the *exercise* of power."[5]

The suggestions we will consider have been made in the context of the American system. They do not include constitutional changes that would make ours a parliamentary system or establish a popularly elected one-house Congress. Nor are these suggestions intended to be a final or complete list. They are offered as a review and as a springboard for further discussion.

COMPLETE AND PUBLIC COMPETITION

In a representative democracy, not everyone can participate personally in every decision. Many decisions are made by leaders (elites), subject to later *ratification* by the citizenry. Or the citizenry may replace the leaders. Between elections, citizens may let decision-makers know their wishes, either personally or through their associations and groups. They may be directly involved in decisions in either an advisory or decisive role. In any event, to facilitate the widest possible citizen participation in decision-making—whether directly or indirectly—it is necessary to encourage public and germane debate and discussion of issues. This involves two requirements: party and candidate responsibility; and openness in decision-making.

---

[3]These suggestions for increasing participation are based on Peter Bachrach, *The Theory of Democratic Elitism; A Critique* (Boston: Little, Brown and Company, 1967); Carol Pateman, *Participation and Democratic Theory* (London: Cambridge University Press, 1970); and Robert A. Dahl, "On Removing Certain Impediments to Democracy in the United States," *Political Science Quarterly*, 92, no. 12 (Spring 1977): 1–8.

[4]E.E. Schattschneider, *The Semisovereign People* (New York: Holt, Rinehart and Winston, 1960), pp. 141–42. See also Richard F. Hamilton, *Class and Politics in the United States* (New York: John Wiley and Sons, 1972), pp. 59–60.

[5]J. Roland Pennock, "Democracy and Leadership" in William Chambers and Robert Salisbury, eds., *Democracy Today* (New York: Colliers Books, 1962), p. 127.

Historian Howard Zinn has proposed the following series of criteria as a measure of how democratic a society is. The criteria, Zinn says, go "beyond formal political institutions, to the quality of life in the society (economic, social, psychological), beyond majority rule to concern for minorities, and beyond national boundaries to a global view of what is meant by 'the people' in that rough but essentially correct view of democracy as 'government of, by, and for the people.'"

VIEWPOINT

How Democratic Is America?

1. To what extent can various people in the society participate in those decisions which affect their lives: decisions in the political process and decisions in the economic structure?

2. As a corollary of the above: do people have equal access to the information which they need to make important decisions?

3. Are the members of the society equally protected on matters of life and death—in the most literal sense of that phrase?

4. Is there equality before the law: police, courts, the judicial process—as well as equality *with* the law-enforcing institutions, so as to safeguard equally everyone's persona and his freedom from interference by others, and by the government?

5. Is there equality in the distribution of available resources: those economic goods necessary for health, life, recreation, leisure, growth?

6. Is there equal access to education, to knowledge and training, so as to enable persons in the society to live their lives as fully as possible, to enlarge their range of possibilities?

7. Is there freedom of expression on all matters, and equally for all, to communicate with other members of the society?

8. Is there freedom for individuality in private life, in sexual relations, family relations, the right of privacy?

9. To minimize regulation: do education and the culture in general foster a spirit of cooperation and amity to sustain the above conditions?

10. As a final safety feature: is there opportunity to protest, to disobey the laws, when the foregoing objectives are being lost—as a way of restoring them?

SOURCE: Howard Zinn, "How Democratic Is America?" in Robert A. Goldwin, ed., *How Democratic Is America?* (Chicago: Rand McNally, 1969, 1971).

Party and Candidate Responsibility

Political party organizations (such as a county central committee), parties-in-government (such as the Democratic Caucus in the U.S. Senate), and political candidates could take positions and campaign for election on issues. Voters have become more issue-oriented in their national voting decisions. Party activists are increasingly motivated by ideology. Parties and candidates (and the media) could do much to reinforce these trends.

Openness in Decision-Making

How can people participate in decision-making unless they know what the issues are? How can they participate unless they know when important decisions will be made? Improved federal and state laws require governmental agency meetings to be open to the public. Congressional committees now hold most of their important meetings in public. The extension of such practices will permit greater political participation. But too much federal information is still unjustifiably classified as secret because of "national security." And the rules governing participation in political and governmental meetings at all levels need to be standardized and published.

EQUAL ACCESS TO POWER

Like the door to a storehouse, the door to participation is frequently locked. But we can provide a "key" to open the door and allow access for the people (adult members of the community, say, who helped stock the storehouse or who, together with their families, have a call on its provisions). We can make sure that the "key" can be more easily reached and that people are adequately informed about how to use it. This involves removing voting barriers; localizing decision-making; improving education for participation; reducing wealth and income disparities; and politicizing "private" decisions.

Remove Voting Barriers

President Carter proposed that Congress enact a law which would allow people to vote without prior registration, simply by showing adequate identification. Congress has not acted on this proposal. In states that have abolished registration, there has been an increase in voting.

Localize Decision-Making

In some places, at-large school and city elections have been replaced by district elections. This gives voters more direct influence on individual district candidates and officials. Decision-making could be further segmented and decentralized by establishing schools and police departments in big cities by neighborhood districts.

Education for Participation

In the family, in the schools, and among associates, people could be better educated and socialized (both formally and informally) concerning the workings of the participatory system and its rewards. Variations in school teachings and materials which are related to the socioeconomic status of students could be eliminated. As Thomas Jefferson put it, "If a nation expects to be ignorant and free, in a state of civilization, it expects what never was and what never will be."

Reduce Wealth and Income Disparities

People's socioeconomic status is very much related to their knowledge of how to participate and their ability to do so. To reduce the disparities of wealth and income in America, it would not be necessary—and not necessarily possible or desirable—to make everyone's wealth and income the same. But in the Rousseauian sense, people cannot be fully free if they are so poor that they have to sell their "consent," or if others are so rich that they can buy "consent." There are implications here for government policies related to taxes, jobs, welfare, and so on.

Politicize "Private" Decisions

In the workplace, at school, and in their apartment buildings and housing projects, citizens could easily have more involvement in what are usually thought of as "private" decisions. Workers could have more say about safety and working conditions and practices. Students and faculty could have more voice in education. Tenants could be more involved in how their housing projects are run. This would require that such decisions be politicized, or made "public," by law or agreement. Allowing such private decisions to "spill over" into the political arena would open up to public participation some of the most important decisions that affect people's lives.

EQUAL EXERCISE OF POWER

It would be of little use for a person to participate fully in America's political system if some other participants had such inordinate power that they could cancel out and "trump" the ordinary person's influence. There are ways to move America toward greater equality in the exercise of power and increase the effectiveness of participation.

Restrain Corporate Power

A person's right to vote for or against a member of Congress may pale in significance compared to that person's inability, say, to afford skyrocketing bread or gasoline prices; and many prices are set by private corporations without regard for market pressures, consumer wishes, or the public interest. Such concentrated economic power that blocks participation in economic decisions can have just as serious an effect on people (and sometimes more serious) as barriers to political participation. There does not have to be a single, uniform solution to the problem of restraining corporate power. As Robert Dahl has written, the question of how a corporation should be organized, controlled, or owned—how citizens may be able to participate in corporate decisions which affect them—is open to different technical, ideological, and philosophical answers. But it is clear that unrestrained corporate power presents a threat to the ideal of participation.

Reduce the Political Power of Money

In a number of ways, such as through lobbying and campaign contributions, economic power can be translated into political power. To reduce this power—toward the goal of "one person, one vote," rather than "one dollar, one vote"—changes must be made in the various ways that economic power can be translated into political power. Stricter laws have been proposed to control congressional lobbying. Public financing of presidential campaigns could be extended to congressional and state races. The great increase in recent years in the amount of special-interest contributions to state and congressional campaigns poses an alarming problem for America's democracy.

CONCLUSION

In the end, how participatory our political system is or will be—that is, how closely we approach the democratic ideal of "government by the people"—depends upon *you* and upon all of *us*. An ideal, by definition, may never be wholly achievable. But perhaps nowhere else is the opportunity to create a truly participatory society so great as it is in America. The truth of the matter is, however (though this may sound like a repetition of the same thought), that to achieve a participatory society we must participate in its creation. That is our challenge for the present and for the future.

The unanimous Declaration
of the thirteen united States of America,

When in the Course of human events, it becomes necessary for one people to dissolve the political bands which have connected them with another, and to assume among the Powers of the earth, the separate and equal station to which the Laws of Nature and of Nature's God entitle them, a decent respect to the opinions of mankind requires that they should declare the causes which impel them to the separation.

We hold these truths to be self-evident, that all men are created equal, that they are endowed by their Creator with certain unalienable Rights, that among these are Life, Liberty and the pursuit of Happiness. That to secure these rights, Governments are instituted among Men, deriving their just powers from the consent of the governed. That whenever any Form of Government becomes destructive of these ends, it is the Right of the People to alter or to abolish it, and to institute new Government, laying its foundation on such principles and organizing its powers in such form, as to them shall seem most likely to effect their Safety and Happiness. Prudence, indeed, will dictate that Governments long established should not be changed for light and transient causes; and accordingly all experience hath shown, that mankind are more disposed to suffer, while evils are sufferable, than to right themselves by abolishing the forms to which they are accustomed. But when a long train of abuses and usurpations, pursuing invariably the same Object evinces a design to reduce them under absolute Despotism, it is their right, it is their duty, to throw off such Government, and to provide new Guards for their future security.—Such has been the patient sufferance of these Colonies; and such is now the necessity which constrains them to alter their former Systems of Government. The history of the present King of Great Britain is a history of repeated injuries and usurpations, all having in direct object the establishment of an absolute Tyranny over these States. To prove this, let Facts be submitted to a candid world.

He has refused his Assent to Laws, the most wholesome and necessary for the public good.

He has forbidden his Governors to pass Laws of immediate and pressing importance, unless suspended in their operation till his Assent should be obtained; and when so suspended, he has utterly neglected to attend to them.

He has refused to pass other Laws for the accommodation of large districts of people, unless those people would relinquish the right of Representation in the Legislature, a right inestimable to them and formidable to tyrants only.

He has called together legislative bodies at places unusual, uncomfortable, and distant from the depository of their Public Records, for the sole purpose of fatiguing them into compliance with his measures.

He has dissolved Representative Houses repeatedly, for opposing with manly firmness his invasions on the rights of the people.

He has refused for a long time, after such dissolutions, to cause others to be elected; whereby the Legislative Powers, incapable of Annihilation, have returned to the People at large for their exercise; the State remaining in the mean time exposed to all the dangers of invasion from without, and convulsions within.

He has endeavoured to prevent the population of these States; for that purpose obstructing the Laws for Naturalization of Foreigners; refusing to pass others to encourage their migrations hither, and raising the conditions of new Appropriations of Lands.

He has obstructed the Administration of Justice, by refusing his Assent to Laws for establishing Judiciary Powers.

He has made Judges dependent on his Will alone, for the tenure of their offices, and the amount and payment of their salaries.

He has erected a multitude of New Offices, and sent hither swarms of Officers to harass our people, and eat out their substance.

He has kept among us, in times of peace, Standing Armies without the Consent of our legislatures.

He has affected to render the Military independent of and superior to the Civil Power.

He has combined with others to subject us to a jurisdiction foreign to our constitution, and unacknowledged by our laws; giving his Assent to their acts of pretended Legislation:

For quartering large bodies of armed troops among us:

For protecting them, by a mock Trial, from Punishment for any Murders which they should commit on the inhabitants of these States:

For cutting off our Trade with all parts of the world:

For imposing taxes on us without our Consent:

For depriving us in many cases, of the benefits of Trial by Jury:

For transporting us beyond Seas to be tried for pretended offences:

For abolishing the free System of English Laws in a neighbouring Province, establishing therein an Arbitrary government, and enlarging its Boundaries so as to render it at once an example and fit instrument for introducing the same absolute rule into these Colonies:

For taking away our Charters, abolishing our most valuable Laws, and altering fundamentally the Forms of our Governments:

For suspending our own Legislatures, and declaring themselves invested with Power to legislate for us in all cases whatsoever.

He has abdicated Government here, by declaring us out of his Protection and waging War against us.

He has plundered our seas, ravaged our Coasts, burnt our towns, and destroyed the lives of our people.

He is at this time transporting large armies of foreign mercenaries to compleat the works of death, desolation and tyranny, already begun with circumstances of Cruelty & perfidy scarcely paralleled in the most barbarous ages, and totally unworthy the Head of a civilized nation.

He has constrained our fellow Citizens taken Captive on the high Seas to bear Arms against their Country, to become the executioners of their friends and Brethren, or to fall themselves by their Hands.

He has excited domestic insurrections amongst us, and has endeavoured to bring on the inhabitants of our frontiers, the merciless Indian Savages, whose known rule of warfare, is an undistinguished destruction of all ages, sexes and conditions.

In every stage of these Oppressions We have Petitioned for Redress in the most humble terms: Our repeated Petitions have been answered only by repeated injury. A Prince, whose character is thus marked by every act which may define a Tyrant, is unfit to be the ruler of a free people.

Nor have We been wanting in attentions to our British brethren. We have warned them from time to time of attempts by their legislature to extend an unwarrantable jurisdiction over us. We have reminded them of the circumstances of our emigration and settlement here. We have appealed to their native justice and magnanimity, and we have conjured them by the ties of our common kindred to disavow these usurpations which, would inevitably interrupt our connections and correspondence. They too have been deaf to the voice of justice and of consanguinity. We must, therefore, acquiesce in the necessity, which denounces our Separation, and hold them, as we hold the rest of mankind, Enemies in War, in Peace Friends.

We, therefore, the Representatives of the united States of America, in General Congress, Assembled, appealing to the Supreme Judge of the world for the rectitude of our intentions, do, in the Name, and by authority of the good People of these Colonies, solemnly publish and declare, That these United Colonies are, and of Right ought to be Free and Independent States; that they are Absolved from all Allegiance to the British Crown, and that all political connection between them and the State of Great Britain, is and ought to be totally dissolved; and that as Free and Independent States, they have full power to levy War, conclude Peace, contract Alliances, establish Commerce, and to do all other Acts and Things which Independent States may of right do. And for the support of this Declaration, with a firm reliance on the Protection of Divine Providence, we mutually pledge to each other our Lives, our Fortunes and our sacred Honor.

THE CONSTITUTION OF
THE UNITED STATES OF AMERICA

We the People of the United States, in Order to form a more perfect Union, establish justice, insure domestic Tranquility, provide for the common defence, promote the general Welfare, and secure the Blessings of Liberty to ourselves and our Posterity, do ordain and establish this Constitution for the United States of America.

ARTICLE 1

Section 1.

All legislative Powers herein granted shall be vested in a Congress of the United States, which shall consist of a Senate and House of Representatives.

Section 2.

The House of Representatives shall be composed of Members chosen every second Year by the People of the several States, and the Electors in each State shall have the Qualifications requisite for Electors of the most numerous Branch of the State Legislature.

No Person shall be a Representative who shall not have attained to the Age of twenty five Years, and been seven Years a Citizen of the United States, and who shall not, when elected, be an Inhabitant of that State in which he shall be chosen.

Representatives and direct Taxes shall be apportioned among the several States which may be included within this Union, according to their respective Numbers, which shall be determined by adding to the whole Number of free Persons, including those bound to Service for a Term of Years, and excluding Indians not taxed, three fifths of all other Persons.[1] The actual Enumeration shall be made within three years after the first Meeting of the Congress of the United States, and within every subsequent Term of ten Years, in such Manner as they shall by Law direct. The Number of Representatives shall not exceed one for every thirty Thousand, but each State shall have at Least one Representative; and until such enumeration shall be made, the State of New Hampshire shall be entitled to chuse three, Massachusetts eight, Rhode-Island and Providence Plantations one, Connecticut five, New-York six, New Jersey four, Pennsylvania eight, Delaware one, Maryland six, Virginia ten, North Carolina five, South Carolina five, and Georgia three.

When vacancies happen in the Representation from any State, the Executive Authority thereof shall issue Writs of Election to fill such Vacancies.

The House of Representatives shall chuse their Speaker and other Officers; and shall have the sole Power of Impeachment.

Section 3.

The Senate of the United States shall be composed of two Senators from each State, chosen by the Legislature thereof, for six Years; and each Senator shall have one Vote.

Immediately after they shall be assembled in Consequence of the first Election, they shall be divided as equally as may be into three Classes. The Seats of the Senators of the first Class shall be vacated at the Expiration of the second Year, of the second Class at the Expiration of the fourth Year, and of the third Class at the Expiration of the Sixth Year, so that one third may be chosen every second Year; and if Vacancies happen by Resignation, or otherwise, during the Recess of the Legislature of any State, the Executive thereof may make temporary Appointments until the next Meeting of the Legislature, which shall then fill such Vacancies.[2]

No Person shall be a Senator who shall not have attained to the Age of thirty Years, and been nine Years a Citizen of the United States, and who shall not, when elected, be an Inhabitant of that State for which he shall be chosen.

The Vice President of the United States shall be President of the Senate, but shall have no Vote, unless they be equally divided.

The Senate shall chuse their other Officers, and also a President pro tempore, in the Absence of the Vice President, or when he shall exercise the Office of President of the United States.

The Senate shall have the sole Power to try all impeachments. When sitting for that Purpose, they shall be on Oath or Affirmation. When the President of the United States is tried the Chief Justice shall preside: And no Person shall be convicted without the Concurrence of two thirds of the Members present.

Judgment in Cases of Impeachment shall not extend further than to removal from Office, and disqualification to hold and enjoy any Office of honor, Trust or Profit under the United States: but the Party convicted shall nevertheless be liable and subject to Indictment, Trial, Judgment and Punishment, according to Law.

Section 4.

The Times, Places and Manner of holding Elections for Senators and Representatives, shall be prescribed in each State by the Legislature thereof; but the Congress may at any time by Law make or alter such Regulations, except as to the Places of chusing Senators.

The Congress shall assemble at least once in every Year, and such Meeting shall be on the first Monday in December, unless they shall by Law appoint a different Day.[3]

Section 5

Each House shall be the Judge of the Elections, Returns and Qualifications of its own Members, and a Majority of each shall constitute a Quorum to do Business; but a smaller Number may adjourn from day to day, and may be authorized to compel the Attendance of absent Members, in such Manner, and under such Penalties as each House may provide.

Each House may determine the Rules of its Proceedings, punish its Members for disorderly Behaviour, and, with the Concurrence of two thirds, expel a Member.

Each House shall keep a Journal of its Proceedings, and from time to time publish the same, excepting such Parts as may in their Judgment require Secrecy; and the Yeas and Nays of the Members of either House on any question shall, at the Desire of one fifth of those Present, be entered on the Journal.

Neither House, during the Session of Congress, shall, without the Consent of the other, adjourn for more than three days, nor to any other Place than that in which the two Houses shall be sitting.

Section 6.

The Senators and Representatives shall receive a Compensation for their Services, to be ascertained by Law, and paid out of the Treasury of the United States. They shall in all Cases, except Treason, Felony and Breach of the Peace, be privileged from Arrest during their Attendance at the Session of their respective Houses, and in going to and returning from the same; and for any Speech or Debate in either House, they shall not be questioned in any other Place.

No Senator or Representative shall, during the Time for which he was elected, be appointed to any civil Office under the Authority of the United States, which shall have been created, or the Emoluments whereof shall have been encreased during such time; and no Person holding any Office under the United States, shall be a Member of either House during his Continuance in Office.

Section 7.

All Bills for raising Revenue shall originate in the House of Representatives; but the Senate may propose or concur with Amendments as on other Bills.

Every Bill which shall have passed the House of Representatives and

---

[1] "Other Persons" being black slaves. Modified by Amendment XIV, Section 2.
[2] Provisions changed by Amendment XVII.

[3] Provision changed by Amendment XX, Section 2.

the Senate, shall, before it become a Law, be presented to the President of the United States; If he approve he shall sign it, but if not he shall return it, with his Objections to that House in which it shall have originated, who shall enter the Objections at large on their Journal, and proceed to reconsider it. If after such Reconsideration two thirds of that House shall agree to pass the Bill, it shall be sent, together with the Objections, to the other House, by which it shall likewise to be reconsidered, and if approved by two thirds of that House, it shall become a Law. But in all such Cases the Votes of both Houses shall be determined by yeas and Nays, and the Names of the Persons voting for and against the Bill shall be entered on the Journal of each House respectively. If any Bill shall not be returned by the President within ten Days (Sundays excepted) after it shall have been presented to him, the Same shall be a Law, in like Manner as if he had signed it, unless the Congress by their Adjournment prevent its Return, in which Case it shall not be a Law.

Every Order, Resolution, or Vote to which the Concurrence of the Senate and House of Representatives may be necessary (except on a question of Adjournment) shall be presented to the President of the United States; and before the Same shall take Effect, shall be approved by him, or being disapproved by him, shall be repassed by two thirds of the Senate and House of Representatives, according to the Rules and Limitations prescribed in the Case of a Bill.

Section 8.

The Congress shall have Power To lay and collect Taxes, Duties, Imposts and Excises, to pay the Debts and provide for the common Defence and general Welfare of the United States; but all Duties, Imposts and Excises shall be uniform throughout the United States;

To borrow Money on the credit of the United States;

To regulate Commerce with foreign Nations, and among the several States, and with the Indian Tribes;

To establish an uniform Rule of Naturalization, and uniform Laws on the subject of Bankruptcies throughout the United States;

To coin Money, regulate the Value thereof, and of foreign Coin, and fix the Standard of Weights and Measures;

To provide for the Punishment of counterfeiting the Securities and current Coin of the United States;

To establish Post Offices and post Roads;

To promote the Progress of Science and useful Arts, by securing for limited Times to Authors and Inventors the exclusive Right to their respective Writings and Discoveries;

To constitute Tribunals inferior to the supreme Court;

To define and punish Piracies and Felonies committed on the high Seas, and Offences against the Law of Nations;

To declare War, grant Letters of Marque and Reprisal, and make Rules concerning Captures on Land and Water;

To raise and support Armies, but no Appropriation of Money to that Use shall be for a longer Term than two Years;

To provide and maintain a Navy;

To make Rules for the Government and Regulation of the land and naval Forces;

To provide for calling forth the Militia to execute the Laws of the Union, suppress Insurrections and repel Invasions;

To provide for organizing, arming, and disciplining, the Militia, and for governing such Part of them as may be employed in the Service of the United States, reserving to the States respectively, the Appointment of the Officers, and the Authority of training the Militia according to the discipline prescribed by Congress;

To exercise exclusive Legislation in all Cases whatsoever, over such District (not exceeding ten Miles square) as may, by Cession of particular States, and the Acceptance of Congress, become the Seat of the Government of the United States, and to exercise like Authority over all Places purchased by the Consent of the Legislature of the State in which the Same shall be, for the Erection of Forts, Magazines, Arsenals, dock-Yards, and other needful Buildings;—And

To make all Laws which shall be necessary and proper for carrying into Execution the foregoing Powers, and all other Powers vested by this Constitution in the Government of the United States, or in any Department or Officer thereof.

Section 9.

The Migration or Importation of such Persons as any of the States now existing shall think proper to admit, shall not be prohibited by the Congress prior to the Year one thousand eight hundred and eight, but a Tax, or duty may be imposed on such Importation, not exceeding ten dollars for each Person.

The Privilege of the Writ of Habeas Corpus shall not be suspended, unless when in Cases of Rebellion or Invasion the public Safety may require it.

No Bill of Attainder or ex post facto Law shall be passed.

No Capitation, or other direct, Tax shall be laid, unless in Proportion to the Census or Enumeration herein before directed to be taken.

No Tax or Duty shall be laid on Articles exported from any State.

No Preference shall be given by any Regulation of Commerce or Revenue to the Ports of one State over those of another; nor shall Vessels bound to, or from, one State, be obliged to enter, clear, or pay Duties in another.

No Money shall be drawn from the Treasury, but in Consequence of Appropriations made by Law; and a regular Statement and Account of the Receipts and Expenditures of all public Money shall be published from time to time.

No Title of Nobility shall be granted by the United States: And no Person holding any Office of Profit or Trust under them, shall, without the Consent of the Congress, accept of any present, Emolument, Office, or Title, of any kind whatever, from any King, Prince, or foreign State.

Section 10.

No State shall enter into any Treaty, Alliance, or Confederation; grant Letters of Marque and Reprisal; coin Money; emit Bills of Credit; make any Thing but gold and silver Coin a Tender in Payment of Debts; pass any Bill of Attainder, ex post facto Law, or Law impairing the Obligation of Contracts, or grant any Title of Nobility.

No State shall, without the Consent of the Congress, lay any Imposts or Duties on Imports or Exports, except what may be absolutely necessary for executing its inspection Laws: and the net Produce of all Duties and Imposts, laid by any State on Imports or Exports, shall be for the Use of the Treasury of the United States; and all such Laws shall be subject to the Revision and Controul of the Congress.

No State shall, without the Consent of Congress, lay any Duty of Tonnage, keep Troops, or Ships of War in time of Peace, enter into any Agreement or Compact with another State, or with a foreign Power, or engage in War, unless actually invaded, or in such imminent Danger as will not admit of delay.

ARTICLE II

Section 1.

The executive Power shall be vested in a President of the United States of America. He shall hold his Office during the Term of four Years, and, together with the Vice President, chosen for the same Term, be elected, as follows:

Each State shall appoint, in such Manner as the Legislature thereof may direct, a Number of Electors, equal to the whole Number of Senators and Representatives to which the State may be entitled in Congress: but no Senator or Representative, or Person holding an Office of Trust or Profit under the United States, shall be appointed an Elector.

The Electors shall meet in their respective States, and vote by Ballot for two Persons, of whom one at least shall not be an Inhabitant of the same State with themselves. And they shall make a List of all the Persons voted for, and of the Number of Votes for each; which List they shall sign and certify, and transmit sealed to the Seat of the

Government of the United States, directed to the President of the Senate. The President of the Senate shall, in the Presence of the Senate and House of Representatives, open all the Certificates, and the Votes shall then be counted. The Person having the greatest Number of Votes shall be the President, if such Number be a Majority of the whole Number of Electors appointed; and if there be more than one who have such Majority, and have an equal Number of Votes, then the House of Representatives shall immediately chuse by Ballot one of them for President; and if no Person have a Majority, then from the five highest on the List the said House shall in like Manner chuse the President. But in chusing the President, the Votes shall be taken by States, the Representation from each State having one Vote; A quorum for this Purpose shall consist of a Member or Members from two thirds of the States, and a Majority of all the States shall be necessary to a Choice. In every Case, after the Choice of the President, the Person having the greatest Number of Votes of the Electors shall be the Vice President. But if there should remain two or more who have equal Votes, the Senate shall chuse from them by Ballot the Vice President.[4]

The Congress may determine the Time of chusing the Electors, and the Day on which they shall give their Votes; which Day shall be the same throughout the United States.

No Person except a natural born Citizen, or a Citizen of the United States, at the time of the Adoption of this Constitution, shall be eligible to the Office of President; neither shall any Person be eligible to that Office who shall not have attained to the Age of thirty five Years, and been fourteen Years a Resident within the United States.

In Case of the Removal of the President from Office, or of his Death, Resignation, or Inability to discharge the Powers and Duties of the said Office, the Same shall devolve on the Vice President, and the Congress may by Law provide for the Case of Removal, Death, Resignation or Inability, both of the President and Vice President, declaring what Officer shall then act as President, and such Officer shall act according-ly, until the Disability be removed, or a President shall be elected.

The President shall, at stated Times, receive for his Services, a Compensation, which shall neither be encreased nor diminished during the Period for which he shall have been elected, and he shall not receive within that Period any other Emolument from the United States, or any of them.

Before he enter on the Execution of his Office, he shall take the following Oath or Affirmation:—"I do solemnly swear (or affirm) that I will faithfully execute the Office of President of the United States, and will to the best of my Ability, preserve, protect and defend the Constitution of the United States."

Section 2.

The President shall be Commander in Chief of the Army and Navy of the United States, and of the Militia of the several States, when called into the actual Service of the United States; he may require the Opinion, in writing, of the principal Officer in each of the executive Departments, upon any Subject relating to the Duties of their respective Offices, and he shall have Power to grant Reprieves and Pardons for Offences against the United States, except in Cases of Impeachment.

He shall have Power, by and with the Advice and Consent of the Senate, to make Treaties, provided two thirds of the Senators present concur; and he shall nominate, and by and with the Advice and Consent of the Senate, shall appoint Ambassadors, other public Ministers and Consuls, Judges of the supreme Court, and all other Officers of the United States, whose Appointments are not herein otherwise provided for, and which shall be established by Law: but the Congress may by Law vest the Appointment of such inferior Officers, as they think proper, in the President alone, in the Courts of Law, or in the Heads of Departments.

The President shall have Power to fill up all Vacancies that may happen during the Recess of the Senate, by granting Commissions which shall expire at the end of their next Session.

Section 3.

He shall from time to time give to the Congress Information of the State of the Union, and recommend to their Consideration such Measures as he shall judge necessary and expedient; he may, on extraordinary Occasions, convene both Houses, or either of them, and in Case of Disagreement between them, with Respect to the Time of Adjournment, he may adjourn them to such Time as he shall think proper; he shall receive Ambassadors and other public Ministers; he shall take Care that Laws be faithfully executed, and shall Commission all the Officers of the United States.

Section 4.

The President, Vice President and all civil Officers of the United States, shall be removed from Office on Impeachment for, and Conviction of, Treason, Bribery, or other high Crimes and Misdemean-ors.

ARTICLE III

Section 1.

The judicial Power of the United States, shall be vested in one supreme Court, and in such inferior Courts as the Congress may from time to time ordain and establish. The Judges, both of the supreme and inferior Courts, shall hold their Offices during good Behaviour, and shall, at stated Times, receive for their Services, a Compensation, which shall not be diminished during their Continuance in Office.

Section 2.

The judicial Power shall extend to all Cases in Law and Equity, arising under this Constitution, the Laws of the United States, and Treaties made, or which shall be made, under their Authority;—to all Cases affecting Ambassadors, other public Ministers and Consuls;—to all Cases of admiralty and maritime Jurisdiction;—to Controversies to which the United States shall be a Party;—to Controversies between two or more states;—between a State and Citizens of another State;—between Citizens of different States;—between Citizens of the same State claiming Lands under Grants of different States, and between a State, or the Citizens thereof, and foreign States, Citizens or Subjects.[5]

In all Cases affecting Ambassadors, other public Ministers and Consuls, and those in which a State shall be Party, the supreme Court shall have original Jurisdiction. In all the other Cases before mentioned, the supreme Court shall have appellate Jurisdiction, both as to Law and Fact, with such Exceptions, and under such Regulations as the Congress shall make.

The Trial of all Crimes, except in Cases of Impeachment, shall be by Jury; and such Trial shall be held in the State where the said Crimes shall have been committed, but when not committed within any State, the Trial shall be at such Place or Places as the Congress may by Law have directed.

Section 3.

Treason against the United States, shall consist only in levying War against them, or in adhering to their Enemies, giving them Aid and Comfort. No person shall be convicted of Treason unless on the Testimony of two Witnesses to the same overt Act, or on Confession in open Court.

The Congress shall have Power to declare the Punishment of Treason, but no Attainder of Treason shall work Corruption of Blood, or Forfeiture except during the Life of the Person attainted.

ARTICLE IV

Section 1.

Full Faith and Credit shall be given in each State to the public Acts, Records, and judicial Proceedings of every other State. And the Congress may by general Laws prescribe the Manner in which such Acts, Records and Proceedings shall be proved, and the Effect thereof.

---

[4]Provisions superseded by Amendment XII.

[5]Clause changed by Amendment XI.

Section 2.

The Citizens of each State shall be entitled to all Privileges and Immunities of Citizens in the several States.

A Person charged in any State with Treason, Felony, or other Crime, who shall flee from Justice, and be found in another State, shall on Demand of the executive Authority of the State from which he fled, be delivered up, to be removed to the State having Jurisdiction of the Crime.

No Person held to Service or Labour in one State, under the Laws thereof, escaping into another, shall, in Consequence of any Law or Regulation therein, be discharged from such Service or Labour, but shall be delivered up on Claim of the Party to whom such Service or Labour may be due.

Section 3.

New States may be admitted by the Congress into this Union; but no new State shall be formed or erected within the jurisdiction of any other State; nor any State be formed by the Junction of two or more States, or Parts of States, without the Consent of the Legislatures of the States concerned as well as of the Congress.

The Congress shall have Power to dispose of and make all needful Rules and Regulations respecting the Territory or other Property belonging to the United States; and nothing in this Constitution shall be so construed as to Prejudice any Claims of the United States, or of any particular State.

Section 4.

The United States shall guarantee to every State in this Union a Republican Form of Government, and shall protect each of them against Invasion; and on Application of the Legislature, or of the Executive (when the Legislature cannot be convened) against domestic Violence.

ARTICLE V

The Congress, whenever two thirds of both Houses shall deem it necessary, shall propose Amendments to this Constitution, or, on the Application of the Legislatures of two thirds of the several States, shall call a Convention for proposing Amendments, which, in either Case, shall be valid to all Intents and Purposes, as Part of this Constitution, when ratified by the Legislatures of three fourths of the several States,

or by Conventions in three fourths thereof, as the one or the other Mode of Ratification may be proposed by the Congress; Provided that no Amendment which may be made prior to the Year One thousand eight hundred and eight shall in any Manner affect the first and fourth Clauses in the Ninth Section of the first Article; and that no State, without its Consent, shall be deprived of its equal Suffrage in the Senate.

ARTICLE VI

All Debts contracted and Engagements entered into, before the Adoption of this Constitution, shall be as valid against the United States under this Constitution, as under the Confederation.

This Constitution, and the Laws of the United States which shall be made in Pursuance thereof; and all Treaties made, or which shall be made, under the Authority of the United States, shall be the supreme Law of the Land; and the Judges in every State shall be bound thereby, any Thing in the Constitution or Laws of any State to the Contrary notwithstanding.

The Senators and Representatives before mentioned, and the Members of the several State Legislatures, and all executive and judicial Officers, both of the United States and of the several States, shall be bound by Oath or Affirmation, to support this Constitution; but no religious Test shall ever be required as a Qualification to any Office or public Trust under the United States.

ARTICLE VII

The Ratification of the Conventions of nine States shall be sufficient for the Establishment of this Constitution between the States so ratifying the Same.

done in Convention by the Unanimous Consent of the States present the Seventeenth Day of September in the Year of our Lord one thousand seven hundred and Eighty seven and of the Independence of the United States of America and the Twelfth[6] IN WITNESS whereof We have here unto subscribed our Names.

---

[6]The Constitution was submitted on September 17, 1787, by the Constitutional Convention, was ratified by the conventions of several states at various dates up to May 29, 1790, and became effective on March 4, 1789.

AMENDMENTS TO THE CONSTITUTION

[AMENDMENT I]

Congress shall make no law respecting an establishment of religion, or prohibiting the free exercise thereof; or abridging the freedom of speech, or of the press, or the right of the people peaceably to assemble, and to petition the Government for a redress of grievances.

[AMENDMENT II]

A well regulated Militia being necessary to the security of a free State, the right of the people to keep and bear Arms, shall not be infringed.

[AMENDMENT III]

No Soldier shall, in time of peace be quartered in any house, without the consent of the Owner, nor in time of war, but in a manner to be prescribed by law.

[AMENDMENT IV]

The right of the people to be secure in their persons, houses, papers, and effects, against unreasonable searches and seizures, shall not be violated, and no Warrants shall issue, but upon probable cause, supported by Oath or affirmation, and particularly describing the place to be searched, and the persons or things to be seized.

[AMENDMENT V]

No person shall be held to answer for a capital, or otherwise infamous crime, unless on a presentment or indictment of a Grand Jury, except in cases arising in the land or naval forces, or in the Militia, when in actual service in time of War or public danger; nor shall any person be subject for the same offense to be twice put in jeopardy of life or limb; nor shall be compelled in any criminal case to be a witness against himself, nor be deprived of life, liberty, or property, without due process of law; nor shall private property be taken for public use, without just compensation.

[AMENDMENT VI]

In all criminal prosecutions, the accused shall enjoy the right to a speedy and public trial, by an impartial jury of the State and district wherein the crime shall have been committed, which district shall have been previously ascertained by law, and to be informed of the nature and cause of the accusation; to be confronted with the witnesses against him; to have compulsory process for obtaining witnesses in his favor, and to have the Assistance of Counsel for his defence.

[AMENDMENT VII]

In Suits at common law, where the value in controversy shall exceed twenty dollars, the right of trial by jury shall be preserved, and no fact tried by a jury, shall be otherwise re-examined in any court of the United States, than according to the rules of the common law.

[AMENDMENT VIII]

Excessive bail shall not be required, nor excessive fines imposed, nor cruel and unusual punishments inflicted.

[AMENDMENT IX]

The enumeration in the Constitution, of certain rights, shall not be construed to deny or disparage others retained by the people.

[AMENDMENT X]

The powers not delegated to the United States by the Constitution, nor prohibited by it to the States, are reserved to the States respectively, or to the people.[7]

[AMENDMENT XI]

The Judicial power of the United States shall not be construed to extend to any suit in law or equity, commenced or prosecuted against one of the United States by Citizens of another State, or by Citizens or Subjects of any Foreign State.[8]

[AMENDMENT XII]

The Electors shall meet in their respective states, and vote by ballot for President and Vice-President, one of whom, at least, shall not be an inhabitant of the same state with themselves; they shall name in their ballots the person voted for as President, and in distinct ballots the person voted for as Vice-President, and they shall make distinct lists of all persons voted for as President, and of all persons voted for as Vice-President, and of the number of votes for each, which lists they shall sign and certify, and transmit sealed to the seat of the government of the United States, directed to the President of the Senate;—The President of the Senate shall, in the presence of the Senate and House of Representatives, open all the certificates and the votes shall then be counted;—The person having the greatest number of votes for President, shall be the President, if such number be a majority of the whole number of Electors appointed; and if no person have such majority, then from the persons having the highest numbers not exceeding three on the list of those voted for as President, the House of Representatives shall choose immediately, by ballot, the President. But in choosing the President, the votes shall be taken by states, the representation from each state having one vote; a quorum for this purpose shall consist of a member or members from two-thirds of the states, and a majority of all the states shall be necessary to a choice. And if the House of Representatives shall not choose a President whenever the right of choice shall devolve upon them, before the fourth day of March next following, then the Vice-President shall act as President, as in the case of the death or other constitutional disability of the President.—The person having the greatest number of votes as Vice-President, shall be the Vice-President, if such number be a majority of the whole number of Electors appointed, and if no person have a majority, then from the two highest numbers on the list, the Senate shall choose the Vice-President; a quorum for the purpose shall consist of two-thirds of the whole number of Senators, and a majority of the whole number shall be necessary to a choice. But no person constitutionally ineligible to the office of President shall be eligible to that of Vice-President of the United States.[9]

[AMENDMENT XIII]

Section 1.

Neither slavery nor involuntary servitude, except as a punishment for crime whereof the party shall have been duly convicted, shall exist within the United States, or any place subject to their jurisdiction.

Section 2.

Congress shall have power to enforce this article by appropriate legislation.[10]

[AMENDMENT XIV]

Section 1.

All persons born or naturalized in the United States and subject to the jurisdiction thereof, are citizens of the United States and the State wherein they reside. No State shall make or enforce any law which shall abridge the privileges or immunities of citizens of the United States; nor shall any State deprive any person of life, liberty, or property, without due process of law; nor deny to any person within its jurisdiction the equal protection of the laws.

Section 2.

Representatives shall be apportioned among the several States according to their respective numbers counting the whole number of

---

[7]The first ten amendments were all proposed by Congress on September 25, 1789, and were ratified and adoption certified on December 15, 1791.

[8]Proposed by Congress on March 4, 1794, and declared ratified on January 8, 1798.
[9]Proposed by Congress on December 9, 1803; declared ratified on September 25, 1804; supplemented by Amendments XX and XXIII.
[10]Proposed by Congress on January 31, 1865; declared ratified on December 18, 1865.

persons in each State, excluding Indians not taxed. But when the right to vote at any election for the choice of electors for President and Vice-President of the United States, Representatives in Congress, the Executive and Judicial officers of a State, or the members of the Legislature thereof, is denied to any of the male inhabitants of such State being twenty-one years of age and citizens of the United States, or in any way abridged, except for participation in rebellion or other crime, the basis of representation therein shall be reduced in the proportion which the number of such male citizens shall bear to the whole number of male citizens twenty-one years of age in such State.

Section 3.

No person shall be a Senator or Representative in Congress, or elector of President and Vice President or hold any office, civil or military, under the United States or under any State, who, having previously taken an oath, as a member of Congress, or as an officer of the United States, or as a member of any State legislature or as an executive or judicial officer of any State to support the Constitution of the United States, shall have engaged in insurrection or rebellion against the same, or given aid or comfort to the enemies thereof. But Congress may by a vote of two-thirds of each House, remove such disability.

Section 4.

The validity of the public debt of the United States authorized by law, including debts incurred for payment of pensions and bounties for services in suppressing insurrection or rebellion, shall not be questioned. But neither the United States nor any State shall assume or pay any debt or obligation incurred in aid of insurrection or rebellion against the United States, or any claim for the loss or emancipation of any slave; but all such debts, obligations and claims shall be held illegal and void.

Section 5.

The Congress shall have power to enforce, by appropriate legislation, the provisions of this article.[11]

[AMENDMENT XV]

Section 1.

The right of citizens of the United States to vote shall not be denied or abridged by the United States or by any State on account of race, color, or previous condition of servitude.

Section.

The Congress shall have power to enforce this article by appropriate legislation.[12]

[AMENDMENT XVI]

The Congress shall have power to lay and collect taxes on incomes, from whatever source derived, without apportionment among the several States, and without regard to any census or enumeration.[13]

[AMENDMENT XVII]

The Senate of the United States shall be composed of two Senators from each State, elected by the people thereof, for six years; and each Senator shall have one vote. The electors in each State shall have the qualifications requisite for electors of the most numerous branch of the State legislatures.

When vacancies happen in the representation of any State in the Senate, the executive authority of such State shall issue writs of election to fill such vacancies: *Provided*, That the legislature of any State may empower the executive thereof to make temporary appointments until the people fill the vacancies by election as the legislature may direct.

This amendment shall not be so construed as to affect the election or term of any Senator chosen before it becomes valid as part of the Constitution.[14]

[AMENDMENT XVIII]

Section 1.

After one year from the ratification of this article the manufacture, sale, or transportation of intoxicating liquors within, the importation thereof into, or the exportation thereof from the United States and all territory subject to the jurisdiction thereof for beverage purposes is hereby prohibited.

Section 2.

The Congress and the several States shall have concurrent power to enforce this article by appropriate legislation.

Section 3.

This article shall be inoperative unless it shall have been ratified as an amendment to the Constitution by the legislatures of the several States, as provided in the Constitution, within seven years from the date of the submission hereof to the States by the Congress.[15]

[AMENDMENT XIX]

The right of citizens of the United States to vote shall not be denied or abridged by the United States or by any State on account of sex.

Congress shall have power to enforce this article by appropriate legislation.[16]

[AMENDMENT XX]

Section 1.

The terms of the President and Vice President shall end at noon on the 20th day of January, and the terms of Senators and Representatives at noon on the 3d day of January, of the years in which such terms would have ended if this article had not been ratified; and the terms of their successors shall then begin.

Section 2.

The Congress shall assemble at least once in every year, and such meeting shall begin at noon on the 3d day of January, unless they shall by law appoint a different day.

Section 3.

If, at the time fixed for the beginning of the term of the President, the President elect shall have died, the Vice President elect shall become President. If a President shall not have been chosen before the time fixed for the beginning of his term, or if the President elect shall have failed to qualify, then the Vice President elect shall act as President until a President shall have qualified; and the Congress may by law provide for the case wherein neither a President elect nor a Vice President elect shall have qualified, declaring who shall then act as President, or the manner in which one who is to act shall be selected, and such person shall act accordingly until a President or Vice President shall have qualified.

Section 4.

The Congress may by law provide for the case of the death of any of the persons from whom the House of Representatives may choose a President whenever the right of choice shall have devolved upon them, and for the case of the death of any of the persons from whom the Senate may choose a Vice President whenever the right of choice shall have devolved upon them.

Section 5.

Sections 1 and 2 shall take effect on the 15th day of October following the ratification of this article.

---

[11]Proposed by Congress on June 13, 1866; declared ratified on July 28, 1868.
[12]Proposed by Congress on February 26, 1869; declared ratified on March 30, 1870.
[13]Proposed by Congress on July 12, 1909; declared ratified on February 25, 1913.

[14]Proposed by Congress on May 13, 1912; declared ratified on May 31, 1913.
[15]Proposed by Congress on December 18, 1917; declared ratified on January 29, 1919; repealed by Amendment XXI.
[16]Proposed by Congress on June 4, 1919; declared ratified on August 26, 1920.

Section 6.

This article shall be inoperative unless it shall have been ratified as an amendment to the Constitution by the legislatures of three-fourths of the several States within seven years from the date of its submission.[17]

[AMENDMENT XXI]

Section 1.

The eighteenth article of amendment to the Constitution of the United States is hereby repealed.

Section 2.

The transportation or importation into any States, Territory, or possession of the United States for delivery or use therein of intoxicating liquors, in violation of the laws thereof, is hereby prohibited.

Section 3.

This article shall be inoperative unless it shall have been ratified as an amendment to the Constitution by conventions in the several States, as provided in the Constitution, within seven years from the date of the submission hereof to the States by the Congress.[18]

[AMENDMENT XXII]

Section 1.

No person shall be elected to the office of the President more than twice, and no person who has held the office of President, or acted as President, for more than two years of a term to which some other person was elected President shall be elected to the office of the President more than once. But this Article shall not apply to any person holding the office of President when the Article was proposed by the Congress, and shall not prevent any person who may be holding the office of President, or acting as President, during the term within which this Article becomes operative from holding the office of President or acting as President during the remainder of such term.

Section 2.

This article shall be inoperative unless it shall have been ratified as an amendment to the Constitution by the legislatures of three-fourths of the several States within seven years from the date of its submission to the States by the Congress.[19]

[AMENDMENT XXIII]

Section 1.

The District constituting the seat of Government of the United States shall appoint in such manner as the Congress shall direct:

A number of electors of President and Vice President equal to the whole number of Senators and Representatives in Congress to which the District would be entitled if it were a State, but in no event more than the least populous State; they shall be in addition to those appointed by the States, but they shall be considered, for the purposes of the election of President and Vice President, to be electors appointed by a State; and they shall meet in the District and perform such duties as provided by the twelfth article of amendment.

Section 2.

The Congress shall have power to enforce this article by appropriate legislation.[20]

[AMENDMENT XXIV]

Section 1.

The right of citizens of the United States to vote in any primary or other election for President or Vice President, for electors for President or Vice President, or for Senator or Representative in Congress, shall not be denied or abridged by the United States or any state by reason of failure to pay any poll tax or other tax.

Section 2.

The Congress shall have the power to enforce this article by appropriate legislation.[21]

[AMENDMENT XXV]

Section 1.

In case of the removal of the President from office or his death or resignation, the Vice President shall become President.

Section 2.

Whenever there is a vacancy in the office of the Vice President, the President shall nominate a Vice President who shall take the office upon confirmation by a majority vote of both houses of Congress.

Section 3.

Whenever the President transmits to the President pro tempore of the Senate and the Speaker of the House of Representatives his written declaration that he is unable to discharge the powers and duties of his office, and until he transmits to them a written declaration to the contrary, such powers and duties shall be discharged by the Vice President as Acting President.

Section 4.

Whenever the Vice President and a majority of either the principal officers of the executive departments or of such other body as Congress may by law provide, transmit to the President pro tempore of the Senate and the Speaker of the House of Representatives their written declaration that the President is unable to discharge the powers and duties of his office, the Vice President shall immediately assume the powers and duties of the office as Acting President.

Thereafter, when the President transmits to the President pro tempore of the Senate and the Speaker of the House of Representatives his written declaration that no inability exists, he shall resume the powers and duties of his office unless the Vice President and a majority of either the principal officers of the executive department or of such other body as Congress may by law provide, transmit within four days to the President pro tempore of the Senate and the Speaker of the House of Representatives their written delcaration that the President is unable to discharge the powers and duties of his office. Thereupon Congress shall decide the issue, assembling within 48 hours for that purpose if not in session. If the Congress, within 21 days after receipt of the latter written declaration, or, if Congress is not in session, within 21 days after Congress is required to assemble, determines by two-thirds vote of both houses that the President is unable to discharge the powers and duties of his office, the Vice President shall continue to discharge the same as Acting President; otherwise, the President shall resume the powers and duties of his office.[22]

[AMENDMENT XXVI]

Section 1.

The right of citizens of the United States, who are 18 years of age or older, to vote shall not be denied or abridged by the United States or any state on account of age.

Section 2.

The Congress shall have the power to enforce this article by appropriate legislation.[23]

---

[17]Proposed by Congress on March 2, 1932; declared ratified on February 6, 1933.
[18]Proposed by Congress on February 20, 1933; declared ratified on December 5, 1933.
[19]Proposed by Congress on March 24, 1947; declared ratified on March 1, 1951.
[20]Proposed by Congress on June 16, 1960; declared ratified on April 3, 1961.

[21]Proposed by Congress on August 27, 1962; declared ratified on January 23, 1963.
[22]Proposed by Congress on July 6, 1965; declared ratified on February 10, 1967.
[23]Proposed by Congress on March 23, 1971; declared ratified on June 30, 1971.

Glossary

Administrative law: The rules and regulations issued by administrative agencies and other executive departments.

Adversary proceedings: The system of law requiring each side to present its best arguments with a judge or a jury deciding the issue.

Advice and consent: Provision of the Constitution (Article II, Section 2) granting the Senate the authority to approve or reject treaties and certain presidential appointments.

Affirmative action: The federal policy of favoring the employment of minorities and females to help overcome the effects of past discrimination.

Amicus curiae: A brief submitted by a "friend of the court" recommending a particular decision and showing that the decision will apply beyond the case under contest.

Antitrust: Laws regulating cartels, trusts, pools, monopolies, interlocking directorates, and other restraints to trade.

Articles of Confederation: The first constitution of the United States, drafted by the Second Continental Congress in 1776, approved by Congress in 1777, and ratified by all the states by 1781; replaced by the Constitution in 1789.

Assimilation: The process of absorbing a minority group into a nation by introducing them to the political culture of that nation.

Authority: The recognized, legitimate, and accepted power of an organization to act for its members or citizens.

***Baker v. Carr*:** Supreme Court case setting the precedent for court intervention in legislative apportionment in states; established "one person, one vote" principle.

Bakke: See *Regents of the University of California* v. *Bakke*.

Bandwagon effect: The tendency of voters to vote for the candidate who seems to be leading.

Bicameral: A legislature made up of two chambers or houses; the form of the United States Congress and every state legislature except Nebraska.

Bill of attainder: A law declaring a person or group guilty of a crime and providing punishment for that crime.

Bill of Rights: The first ten amendments to the Constitution containing certain fundamental rights and privileges shared by all citizens.

Black cases: Supreme Court cases testing the constitutionality of state laws regulating the activities of the NAACP.

Black codes: Laws passed by southern states following the Civil War and preceding the Fourteenth Amendment that were designed to restrict the rights and activities of blacks.

Block grants: Federal grants that are given to states and localities for specific program areas but allow the state and local administering agencies to decide on specific uses.

Broad construction: An interpretation of the Constitution which expands powers specifically granted to the separate branches of government.

***Brown v. Board of Education*:** 1954 Supreme Court case reversing *Plessy* v. *Ferguson* and prohibiting segregated public schools.

Bureaucracy: A formally established organization characterized by job specialization, hierarchy of authority, a system of rules, and impersonality.

Bureaucrat: Someone who works within a bureaucracy, especially within the federal bureaucracy.

Cabinet: The combined heads of the executive departments.

Capitalism: An economic system in which the means of production are privately owned and operated for profit.

Cartel: An organization of countries for the purpose of regulating supplies and prices of products, goods, or resources they control.

Casework: The work done by members of Congress in helping constituents with problems, complaints, or claims—especially with the federal bureaucracy.

Caseworkers: Members of congressional staffs who handle constituent services.

Categorical grants-in-aid: Federal grants provided for specific purposes and requiring specific standards of administration on the part of the states or localities receiving the grants.

Caucus: A meeting of a political group, such as elected members of a party, to decide its position on an issue, to elect leaders, to vote on a bill, or to decide other matters within its interests.

Certiorari, writ of: An order from an appeals court to a lower court demanding all records of earlier proceedings in a particular case.

Checks and balances: The system of the separation and overlapping of powers by which the branches of government limit and protect the powers of each.

Civil disobedience: Purposefully breaking a law to bring attention to its alleged injustice (or to some other injustice) and accepting punishment for the offense.

Civil law: Law concerning offenses committed by private individuals, groups, or organizations against other private parties.

Civil War amendments: The Thirteenth, Fourteenth, and Fifteenth Amendments to the Constitution.

Clear and present danger doctrine: Judicial rule established in a decision written by Justice Oliver Wendell Holmes and stating that the right of freedom of speech can only be restricted if the words spoken and the circumstances in which they are spoken will obviously and quickly lead to substantive evil.

Closed primary: A primary election in which party members choose only among the candidates of their own party.

Cloture: Means by which the Senate shuts off a filibuster.

Coattail effect: The tendency of voters selecting a popular candidate to vote for other candidates on the same party ticket.

Cold War: The post-1945 political and ideological conflict between the Western democracies and the Communist countries.

Commerce clause: A statement in Article I, Section 8 of the Constitution giving Congress the exclusive power to regulate interstate commerce.

Committee of the States: A delegation (established under the Articles of Confederation and made up of one member from each state) that acted for Congress when Congress was out of session.

Common law: Judge-made law based on court decisions and customs; the basic law of England and the United States, excepting Louisiana.

Concurring opinion: A written explanation by a judge or judges voting with the majority but disagreeing with the grounds for the decision.

Confederation: A union of states in which sovereignty is retained by the separate states.

Conglomerate: A corporation owning or controlling companies in many unrelated industries.

Connecticut Compromise: A plan that resolved the consolidation/confederation conflict within the Constitutional Convention by making state delegations equal in the Senate and based on population in the House of Representatives.

Consolidation: A union of states in which sovereignty is given to the central government.

Constitution: The basic principles of a state or political body that embody its fundamental and supreme law; a written document embodying the rules of a governing body.

Constitutional law: Law based on the Constitution or a constitutional provision.

Constitutionally suspect classification: Applying extra scrutiny and skepticism in Supreme Court cases involving laws that treat people on the basis of sex, race, or national origin in order to ensure that the laws are indeed constitutional.

Criminal law: Law concerning offenses committed against the public interest as defined by government.

Dangerous tendency doctrine: A doctrine stating that freedom of speech may be restricted if the words or expressions tend to bring about substantive evil; more restrictive than the clear and present danger doctrine.

Delegate role: Concept of representatives who believe their votes should agree with the majority opinion in their districts.

Demagogue: A leader who gains and maintains power by appealing to the emotions and prejudices of the people.

Democracy: Rule of the people and of the majority either directly or through representatives.

Deregulation: The removal of government controls from a particular industry.

Detente: A lessening of tensions between nations.

Direct action: Self-help efforts by citizens to influence policies of government, corporations, and public utilities; may or may not be political.

Direction: An individual's opinion concerning a particular political issue or question.

Dissenting opinion: A written explanation by a judge or judges disagreeing with the majority decision in a court case.

Double jeopardy: A person's being tried twice for the same offense.

Dual citizenship: The status of being a citizen of two or more nations; possessed by some American Indians who are citizens both of their tribes and of the United States.

Due process: Administering the law fairly and following established procedures, rules, and principles.

Elector: A member of the Electoral College.

Electoral College: A body of electors, popularly chosen in the separate states in presidential elections, who meet in December and theoretically cast their votes for the candidates who received a plurality in their respective states; each state has one elector for each senator and representative.

Elite theory: The concept that a relatively small group of people who dominate the major institutions of government, politics, education, the media, unions, industry, etc., hold and share actual power in democracies.

Eminent domain: The power of governments to take private property for public use upon paying just compensation to the owners.

Enumerated powers: Those powers explicitly granted by the Constitution.

Equal Rights Amendment (ERA): A proposed constitutional amendment stating that "Equality of rights under the law shall not be denied or abridged by the United States or by any state on account of sex."

Exchange: Trade for mutually satisfying benefits.

Executive agreement: A presidential agreement with a foreign power which does not require Senate approval.

Executive Office of the President: The White House staff and the heads of the Office of Management and Budget, the National Security Council, the Council of Economic Advisers, and other special offices.

Executive privilege: Presidential claims that information and details of private presidential conversations may be withheld from the public, Congress, and the courts in order to protect national security.

Ex post facto law: A retroactive law.

Fairness doctrine: Federal Communications Commission requirement that broadcasters and telecasters present differing points of view on public issues.

Federalism: A system of government in which authority is divided between central and regional governments; in the United States a division of powers between the federal and state governments.

Federalist Papers, The: A series of newspaper articles written by James Madison, Alexander Hamilton, and John Jay supporting the Constitution, calling for its ratification, and emphasizing the need for a strong government.

Federalists: Proponents calling for the ratification of the Constitution and a strong central government.

Filibuster: A tactic whereby a senator or a small number of senators can kill a bill by holding the floor and preventing the bill from coming to a vote.

Fiscal power: The authority of Congress to control revenues, taxes, and appropriations.

Foreign policy: The statements, actions, goals, and assumptions expressed by the government of one nation in its relationships with other nations.

Free market: The economic system generally allowing economic priorities to be established by the law of supply and demand.

Gerrymandering: The practice of dividing territory into election districts so that one party will have a majority in as many districts as possible and the other party will have a majority in as few as possible.

Government: The people, institutions, and processes through which a political unit exercises authority.

Grand jury: A group of people who hear the preliminary evidence in a case and decide whether an indictment should be issued.

Grants-in-aid program: A program in which the federal government provides grants to states and local governments for specific purposes determined by the federal government.

Grass-roots opinion: The attitudes of leaders in localities.

Great Compromise: *See* Connecticut Compromise.

Gross national product: The total value of goods and services produced and sold in a nation in a fiscal year.

Habeas corpus: A writ issued to bring a prisoner before a court to determine the legality of his or her confinement.

Hatch Act: A 1939 law controlling the political activities of federal employees.

Hegemonic theory: The belief that political socialization results from the contact between dominant and dominated groups.

Human rights: Basic social and economic rights.

Illegal direct action: Direct action using violence or civil disobedience in violation of standing law.

Impeachment: A formal charge by the House of Representatives delivered to the Senate accusing a civil officer of treason, bribery, or other high crimes and misdemeanors.

Implied powers doctrine: The doctrine that powers not specifically enumerated in the Constitution are constitutional if they are necessary and proper for executing powers that are expressly granted by the Constitution.

Impoundment: The refusal by a President to spend all the money appropriated by Congress.

Incrementalism: The tendency of government programs and services to grow gradually while their budgets gradually increase.

Incumbent: The person holding an elective political office.

Independent agency: A regulatory commission or a government corporation in the executive department that reports directly to the President.

Indocumentados: Illegal Mexican immigrants.

Inherent powers: Powers presumed to belong to the federal government even though they are not expressly stated in the Constitution.

Initiative petition: A petition asking for the signatures of citizens to support putting a proposed new law to the vote of the people of a state.

Injunction: A court order preventing a person or a group from doing something specific.

Interest group: An organized body of people who have shared attitudes on one or more issues and who work to influence government policy.

Item veto: The authority possessed by some state governors to veto a part of a bill without vetoing the entire bill.

Jim Crow: Segregation laws passed in the southern and border states.

Joint committees: Committees made up of members of both houses of Congress and used to speed legislation or increase efficiency.

Judicial review: The doctrine that the courts shall decide if acts of Congress, states, or localities are in accord with the provisions of the Constitution.

Judiciary: The Supreme Court and all other courts.

Justiciable question: A contested issue that falls within the jurisdiction of courts to decide.

Keynesian economics: Practices based on the theory of John Maynard Keynes that government should intervene in the economy whenever intervention will be beneficial; government should spend more in periods of high unemployment to create jobs.

Laissez-faire: The policy of nonintervention in the economy by the government.

Legal direct action: Direct action supported by the constitutional guarantees of freedom of speech, freedom of the press, freedom of assembly, and freedom of association.

Libel: The publication of false and injurious statements about another person.

Libertarian: A person who places high value on human rights and freedoms.

Litigation: Using due process to pursue a case or a claim.

Lobbies: Interest groups that attempt to influence government policy.

McCulloch v. Maryland: An 1819 Supreme Court case establishing the doctrines of implied powers and of national supremacy.

Machine: A political organization, usually aligned with a major party and headed by a boss or a small group of leaders, which controls nominees, patronage, party activities, and government services within its area of de facto jurisdiction for the benefit of its members.

Majority: One-half plus one.

Majority leader: The leader of the majority party in the Senate.

Majority opinion: A written explanation by one or more of the judges voting for the majority in a court case; usually associated with the Supreme Court.

Majority whip: The second-ranking senator in the majority party and the leader responsible for gathering support from other members of the majority party for programs advanced by the majority leadership.

Mandamus, writ of: Court order directing a private individual, a government official or agency, or another court to do something specific.

Marbury v. Madison: An 1803 Supreme Court case establishing the doctrine of judicial review.

Marshall Plan: The United States program to assist European economic recovery following World War II.

Media: Mass communication techniques and systems; radio, television, newspapers, periodicals.

Merit system: Civil service system of choosing federal employees on the basis of competitive testing.

Military-industrial complex: President Dwight Eisenhower's term for the mutually beneficial relationship between the military and the defense industries.

Minority leader: Principal leader of the minority party in the House of Representatives and in the Senate.

Misdemeanor: Minor offense punishable by a fine or imprisonment of generally less than one year.

Monroe Doctrine: A warning to European nations not to interfere with nations in the Western Hemisphere; delivered by President James Monroe in 1823.

National Security Council: A council established in 1947 to plan and coordinate foreign policy; the President, Vice-President, secretary of state, secretary of defense, and the chairman of the joint chiefs of staff are permanent members.

Natural rights: The inalienable rights (including life, liberty, and the pursuit of happiness) which every person has at birth.

Necessary and proper clause: Statement in Article I, Section 8 of the Constitution, which grants Congress power "to make all laws which shall be necessary and proper" to carry out its stated powers.

New Jersey Plan: An alternative to the Virginia Plan; a plan of union submitted to the Constitutional Convention by William Paterson, attorney general of New Jersey, which called for revising the Articles of Confederation and strengthening the United States Congress, but preserving the individual states as the most significant units of government.

Oligarchy: Rule by the wealthy or powerful.

Oligopoly: A few firms monopolizing an industry.

Open primary: A primary election in which voters may choose candidates from any party; allows crossover voting.

Opinion leaders: Persons well-informed on issues and politics who tend to influence others.

Organization of Petroleum Exporting Countries (OPEC): A cartel of nations which control the world supply of oil.

Oversight: The responsibility of Congress to act as a "watchdog" primarily over the executive and to a lesser degree over the judiciary.

Party-unity voting: Members of Congress voting with the majority of their own party and against the majority of the opposing party.

Patronage: Government jobs used as a reward for political supporters of incumbents.

Perquisites: The privileges of office over and above fixed salary and income.

Petit jury: The jury that decides on the evidence presented in an individual case.

Platform: A statement of the philosophy and positions held by a political party or by a candidate for political office.

Plessy v. Ferguson: An 1896 Supreme Court case establishing the "separate but equal" doctrine in regard to facilities for blacks and whites.

Plural executive: In county government, the system in which both the county governing board and the other officials are elected (as opposed to the county manager system in which only the governing board is elected, while other officials are appointed).

Pluralism: The theory that government policy results from competition and compromise among different interest groups.

Plurality: In an election, at least one vote more than the number of votes received by any other candidate, but less than a majority.

Pocket veto: Indirect veto; occurs when Congress adjourns during the ten days allowed for the President to sign a bill and the President does not sign it.

Policy power: The authority of each state to pass laws concerning the health, safety, and morals of its citizens.

Political action committees (PACs): Organizations formed by corporations and large unions to influence elections and government.

Political party: A body of voters organized for the purpose of running candidates in elections in order to control policies and conduct the business of government.

Political question: A case that the courts consider to be within their jurisdiction but prefer not to accept at a particular time; a case that involves questions dealing with the powers of the executive and the legislative branches.

Political socialization: The process of learning political ideas, systems, and roles from a person's family, environment, and peers.

Politicization: The process of an individual's becoming aware of authority outside the family.

Politics: The process used by individuals and groups to secure and preserve authority; the rules that evolve in a government.

Precedent: Prior judicial decisions and opinions in a particular area of law.

Preferred position doctrine: A judicial concept that the First Amendment takes precedent over other constitutional provisions because of its location.

President pro tempore: A senator from the majority party chosen to preside over the Senate in the absence of the Vice-President; largely an honorary office.

Pressure group: An interest group that attempts to influence government policy.

Primary: An election that allows voters to choose party candidates for the general election.

Prior restraint: Laws or court decisions attempting to restrict expression in advance; censorship.

Progressive tax: A tax system that applies progressively higher tax percentages to those with greater resources.

Proposition 13: Successful 1978 California initiative cutting property taxes and limiting possible increases in property tax rates.

Protectionism: Establishing high tariffs and/or low import quotas in order to protect domestic production from foreign competition.

Public-interest group: Interest group that represents broad, diffuse, noncommercial interests or the interests of the general public.

Public opinion: Beliefs and attitudes spoken or written by individuals and groups on public issues.

Publicus: The name under which *The Federalist Papers* were published.

Quasi-judicial function: The authority possessed by executive department regulatory agencies to render decisions that have the force and status of judicial decisions and to settle disputes.

Quasi-legislative function: The authority possessed by executive department regulatory agencies to establish rules which have the force of legislated law for the organizations and activities they regulate.

Quorum: The number of members of an organized group who must be present for business to be transacted.

Quota method: In scientific polling, selecting a certain number of interviewees from each demographic subgroup of the population being measured.

Random sampling: In scientific polling, randomly selecting interviewees in an attempt to give each member of the universe or population being measured an equal chance of being chosen.

Recall: The removal of a public official from office by a vote of the people; the right of the people to remove public officials.

Red cases: 1940s and 1950s Supreme Court cases testing the constitutionality of federal and state anticommunist laws and orders.

Red tape: The formal and mechanical adherence to rules, regulations, and forms used in government functions.

Referendum: A voting process in which the people accept or reject a law or resolution proposed by a legislature.

Regents of the University of California v. Bakke: A 1978 Supreme Court case prohibiting the University of California from establishing an entrance quota system based on race.

Regressive tax: A tax system which places the greater burden on the poor.

Regulatory bodies: Largely autonomous federal agencies governed by boards and commissions that issue rules governing the activities under their jurisdiction, such as transportation, mass communications, the stock market, labor and management, and so on.

Representative sample: In scientific polling, a selected group of people assumed to represent the thinking of the universe or population being measured.

Republic: A form of government in which authority lies in that body of citizens entitled to vote and in which authority is exercised by elected representatives.

Revenue sharing: A program under which federal taxes are shared with state and local governments for uses determined by these state and local governments.

Reverse discrimination: Giving preference to minorities to help overcome the effects of past racial and ethnic discrimination.

Reynolds v. Sims: Supreme Court case which applied the principle of "one person, one vote" to both houses of state legislatures and required that both houses be based on equally populated districts.

Safe seat: Offices representing districts that tend to vote overwhelmingly in favor of the party of the representative in office.

Scientific polling: Measuring public opinion by surveying randomly selected groups.

Sedition: Advocating the use of force to bring about public disorder or rebellion against a standing government.

Self-Determination Act: A 1975 law allowing Indian tribal governments the authority to administer their own federally supported programs.

Senatorial courtesy: Custom that the Senate will approve federal judge appointments only if the senators from the appointee's state approve, especially if one or more of the senators from that state are of the President's party.

Seniority system: A system in which the senior member of a committee becomes the chairperson; recently weakened in Congress.

Separation of powers: The division of duties and authority among the executive, legislative, and judicial branches of the United States government.

Shays' Rebellion: 1786–87 rebellion in western Massachusetts led by Daniel Shays and protesting mortgage foreclosures; the debtors' revolt increased support for a stronger national government.

Social contract: The idea that government is based upon agreements among individuals—or between the rulers and the ruled—that define the rights and duties of each.

Sovereign: The person or political body holding authority over citizens.

Speaker of the House: The principal leader of the majority party in the House of Representatives.

Special-interest group: An interest group that represents economic, professional, ethnic, or other narrow interests.

Special public: People intensely interested in a specific issue or holding a specific opinion.

Split ticket: A ballot on which a voter chooses candidates from more than one party.

Spoils system: The use of political patronage by the victorious official or party to reward supporters; greatly expanded by President Andrew Jackson.

Stagflation: Simultaneous high inflation and high unemployment.

Standing committees: Permanent congressional committees.

Stare decisis: The principle of allowing precedent to determine decisions until the precedent is overturned and replaced by another decision.

Statutory law: Law enacted by a legislative body.

Straight ticket: A ballot on which a voter chooses candidates from only one party.

Strategic Arms Limitation Talks (SALT): Negotiations between the United States and the U.S.S.R. aimed at limiting offensive and defensive weapons systems.

Straw poll: A poll used to measure public opinion by unscientific methods.

Strict construction: A literal interpretation of the Constitution.

Sunset laws: Laws requiring government programs to be periodically reviewed for effectiveness and then either renewed or terminated.

Sunshine laws: State laws requiring public agencies to hold their business meetings in public.

Systems theory: The concept that political socialization results from political knowledge being passed from one generation to the next.

Test cases: Court actions used to challenge the constitutionality of selected laws.

Trustee role: Concept of representatives who believe they should vote on the basis of their own judgment and conscience.

Unalienable rights: Those rights so basic that they cannot be relinquished nor justly taken away—among them being life, liberty, and the pursuit of happiness.

Underdog effect: The tendency of voters to vote for the candidate who is behind.

Unicameral: A one-house legislature; the form of the legislature of Nebraska.

Universe: The population being measured in a scientific poll.

Veto: Power granted the President to refuse to approve a bill passed by Congress; Congress may override a veto by a two-thirds majority vote for the bill in both houses.

Virginia Plan: A plan of union, submitted by Governor Edmond Randolph of Virginia to the Constitutional Convention in 1787, calling for the popular election of the lower house of Congress, for the election of the upper house by the lower house, and for Congress to have veto power over state laws.

Whip: The member of a legislative body responsible for party-unity voting within his or her party.

Zero-based budgeting: A system requiring that each government program be justified during each annual budgeting process.

Index

Please participate!

Your reactions and ideas can help me make *America's Democracy* serve students better. What did you like best and least? What would you like to see more or less of? How could it be presented better? Please note your evaluations and suggestions, cut out this page, fold and seal it, and mail it to me; no postage is necessary.

Thanks,
Fred Harris

Please check your evaluation of each chapter that you read. (It would be a good idea to do this as soon as you finish reading each chapter.)

Chapter	Information Value				Interest		
	Much	Some	Little		Much	Some	Little
1							
2							
3							
4							
5							
6							
7							
8							
9							
10							
11							
12							
13							
14							
15							
16							
17							
18							
19							
20							
21							
22							

CUT HERE

What did you like best about *America's Democracy?*

How could *America's Democracy* be improved?

Did the book seem useful in terms of your political activities?

Besides the text, did you use *Studying America's Democracy?*

Was it helpful in preparing for class and for tests?

FOLD HERE

Your probable major (or career goal): _____

Will you take more political science courses? _____

Overall evaluation of *America's Democracy*

All things considered, how does *America's Democracy* compare to introductory
texts you have used in other courses?

| much better | better | about average | worse | much worse |

Would you recommend continued use of *America's Democracy* at your school?

____ definitely yes ____ yes ____ uncertain ____ no ____ definitely no

FOLD HERE

BUSINESS REPLY MAIL

FIRST CLASS   PERMIT NO. 282   GLENVIEW, IL.

POSTAGE WILL BE PAID BY ADDRESSEE

Scott, Foresman and Company
College Division

Attn: Fred R. Harris
1900 East Lake Avenue
Glenview, Illinois 60025

NO POSTAGE
NECESSARY
IF MAILED
IN THE
UNITED STATES

CUT HERE